Strategic
Retail
Management

Strategic Retail Management

Danny R. Arnold
Louis M. Capella
Garry D. Smith

All of the College of Business and Industry
Mississippi State University

ADDISON-WESLEY PUBLISHING COMPANY

Reading, Massachusetts · Menlo Park, California · London
Amsterdam · Don Mills, Ontario · Sydney

To our wives —
Peggy, Micki, and Charlotte —
and children —
Wade, Daryl, Michael, Matthew,
Michele, Brad, and Ryan

Library of Congress Cataloging in Publication Data

Arnold, Danny R., 1948–
   Strategic retail management.

   Bibliography: p.
   Includes index.
   1. Retail trade—Management.   I. Capella, Louis M., 1943–   . II. Smith, Garry D., 1948–
III. Title.
HF5429.A737 1983   658.8'7   82–8852
ISBN 0–201–10085–1   AACR2

ISBN 0–201–10085–1
ABCDEFGHIJ–HA–89876543

Preface

The focus of this text is on retail decision making. Our approach and method of organization depart somewhat from academic tradition, for we employ a *strategic retail management* framework that is used to integrate traditional retailing topics with strategic planning. The content, however, is traditional and includes such concepts as buyer behavior, location analysis, merchandise and inventory planning, and atmosphere.

Why is the strategic retail management approach appropriate for a retailing text? Our students have found this approach easier to understand, digest, integrate, and implement. We feel that it is not enough for students simply to memorize retailing concepts; they should also be able to use these concepts to formulate strategies and make decisions. To this end, the results of using the strategic retail management approach in the classroom have been excellent.

Another important feature of the strategic retail management approach is its appropriateness for students from a relatively wide range of educational backgrounds. Our experience has been that students with an adequate but limited business and marketing background have found the approach beneficial, particularly as a framework for new retailing concepts. Students with more extensive marketing educations or experience have found it particularly useful for organizing and integrating previously acquired knowledge. All types of students have found it useful for improving their planning and decision-making abilities.

One of the major benefits of the approach is that it helps the retailer formulate effective strategies for adapting to constantly changing retailing environments. The small retailers of years ago, for instance, have become today's giants, while many of the older large retailers such as W. T. Grant no longer exist. Changes have occurred in both merchandising and operations: computer software can now be purchased in retail stores, shopping can be done by cable television, and checks can be verified electronically. Computerized inventory mechanisms allow retailers to obtain up-to-the-minute inventory and sales information via UPC scanners and OCR-A "wand" readers. Shopping centers now offer acres of merchandise, while some once-proud downtown merchants are undergoing extensive renovation or moving to the suburbs. In summary, retailing epitomizes the old adage that "the only thing constant is change."

FEATURES

The approach that we take in this text is embodied in the *strategic retail management model,* which is used to open each chapter. Beginning with Chapter 3, each chapter is designed to develop and explain a specific part of the model. Thus the model serves as the integrating framework for the entire textbook.

Just as the strategic retail management model provides the structure for the entire text, most chapters are also built around a *decision model* such as the location decision model and pricing decision model. These decision models flow from the strategic retail management model and serve to extend it into each conceptual and functional area. Each decision model is translated into a corresponding planning framework that forms the basic outline of the chapter.

To further the student's understanding of and interest in retailing and retail decision making, other features are included in this text. Strategy in Action inserts in each chapter are designed to acquaint the student with solutions employed by retailers in developing strategies. Retailers from such trades as department store retailing, discount retailing, franchising, supermarket retailing, and specialty store retailing have been included. These inserts should help the student relate current retail strategies to the basic concepts of retailing management. Note that these inserts are intended only as real-world examples of strategies, not as examples of correct or proper strategies.

Appendixes are included at the ends of Chapters 1, 2, 10, 14, and 20. The appendixes provide additional in-depth treatment of specialized topics, which include service retailing, portfolio analysis, mathematical location models, markup calculations, and the retail audit.

Decision Situations are included at the end of each chapter. Each situation is a short "mini-case" and provides a means by which the student can apply the chapter material to strategic decision making. Nine Comprehensive Cases are positioned at the end of the text material. The student must "bring together" all of the material in the book to arrive at solutions for these cases. The nine cases present situations faced by actual retailers (some of whom are disguised). By combining the Decision Situations with the Comprehensive Cases, the student becomes involved with both specific and integrative applications of chapter material.

Learning Exercises are placed at the ends of most chapters. These exercises focus on local retailers and present the student and instructor with optional activities that can inject more realism into the classroom.

The Key Concepts and Review Questions following each chapter provide the student with a method for reviewing the major topics covered in the chapter. Questions are designed not only to assist the student's review process but also to require the student to integrate and apply chapter material.

ORGANIZATION

The text is organized so as to enhance strategic retail decision making. Beginning with Chapter 3, each chapter is devoted to a specific part of the strategic retail management model. The overall strategic model is extended in each chapter to form an individual decision model in order to create a consistent, logical flow of material. In essence, the text attempts to take the student through the entire strategic planning sequence from identifying a retail mission to completing and controlling the finalized retailing mix.

In Chapter 1 an appreciation for retailing is developed by discussing the background of retailing, some of its historical aspects, and various types of retailing institutions. An appendix to Chapter 1 discusses service retailing and compares it to merchandise retailing. Retailing strategy and planning are discussed in Chapter 2. Basic philosophical and strategy-formulation concepts establish the structure for the remainder of the text. The strategic retail management model is explained and presented in this chapter. An appendix to Chapter 2 provides additional discussion of portfolio analysis techniques. Chapter 3 explains the financial aspects of retailing and relates them to the retailing strategy.

Beginning with Chapter 4, the specifics of retail strategy formulation are discussed. Analyzing and forecasting the macroenvironment are the earliest stages of strategy formulation. Chapter 5 continues the environmental analysis by structuring and examining the competitive and channel environments. In order for the strategy to be successful, the consumer must be considered and subsequently influenced. The consumer's behavior and the retailing implications are discussed in Chapter 6. Segmenting consumer markets and developing a retailing mix strategy are presented in Chapter 7.

Information must be gathered, processed, and organized at all stages of strategy formulation. Chapter 8 discusses how a retailer can manage information for maximum benefit in retail decision making.

One of the most important aspects of operating a retail outlet is to acquire, train, motivate, and maintain good personnel. Chapter 9 systematically develops the subject of human resources decisions and how to effectively manage personnel matters.

The material in Chapters 10 through 19 is concerned with developing specific strategy decisions to enable the retailer to compete with other retailers. The location decision is paramount in determining retail success. Chapter 10 analyzes this decision and discusses the broader implications of location. An appendix to this chapter presents mathematical models for selecting a retail site.

Chapters 11 through 13 provide a strategic perspective to merchandise planning, selection, and control. Each phase is interactive and serves as a base for other retail decisions.

Pricing relates merchandise value to the entire retailing strategy. Chapter 14 discusses the process a retailer should use in making this decision. An appendix to Chapter 14 provides detailed coverage of the mechanics of markup and markdown calculations.

Being able to communicate the retailing strategy to consumers is a requirement for success. Chapters 15 through 19 explain the uses of the communication tools of advertising, personal selling, sales promotion, atmospherics, and customer services in strategic retail planning.

In order to determine whether the retailer's strategy was and is successful, control is necessary. Chapter 20 presents methods for evaluating the success of an ongoing strategy and for judging a strategy at the completion of a planning period. Appendixes to Chapter 20 present control measures that can be used to implement the control function.

ACKNOWLEDGMENTS

We wish to thank the following individuals for their assistance in reviewing and providing insight and comments on our manuscript:

Ronald J. Dornoff, University of Cincinnati
Marsha L. Richins, Portland State University
Dale D. Achabal, University of Santa Clara
B. J. Dunlap, Appalachian State University
Dorothy S. Rogers, New Hampshire College
Gordon L. Wise, Wright State University
William B. Locander, University of Houston
Elizabeth Hirshman, New York University
William A. Staples, University of Houston at Clear Lake City
Bert McCammon, University of Oklahoma

We would also like to acknowledge the contributions by many other sources of information used in the preparation of this manuscript. Especially useful were *Chain Store Age Executive*, *Stores*, *Journal of Retailing*, *Retail Week*, *Progressive Grocer*, and *Business Week*.

Mississippi State, Mississippi   D.R.A.
December 1982   L.M.C.
                                                                      G.D.S.

Contents

Chapter 2
Retailing Strategy

Chapter 3
Financial Planning, Control, and Analysis

PART II
THE RETAILING ENVIRONMENTS

Chapter 4
The Retailing Macroenvironment

Chapter 5
The Task Environment:
Competition and Marketing Intermediaries

Chapter 6
Buyer Behavior

Chapter 7
Market Segmentation

Chapter 8
Information Management

Chapter 9
Human Resource Decisions

PART III
THE RETAILING MIX

Chapter 10
Store Location Decisions

Chapter 11
Merchandise Planning and Budgeting Decisions

Chapter 12
Merchandise Buying Decisions

Chapter 13
Merchandise Control

Chapter 14
Pricing Decisions

Chapter 15
Communications and Promotion Decisions

Chapter 16
Advertising Decisions

Chapter 17
Personal Selling and Sales Promotion Decisions

Chapter 18
Atmosphere and Layout Decisions

Chapter 19
Customer Service Decisions

PART IV
RETAILING CONTROL

Chapter 20
The Retail Control Process

Comprehensive Cases

Index

PART I

INTRODUCTION TO STRATEGIC RETAIL MANAGEMENT

STRATEGIC RETAIL MANAGEMENT MODEL

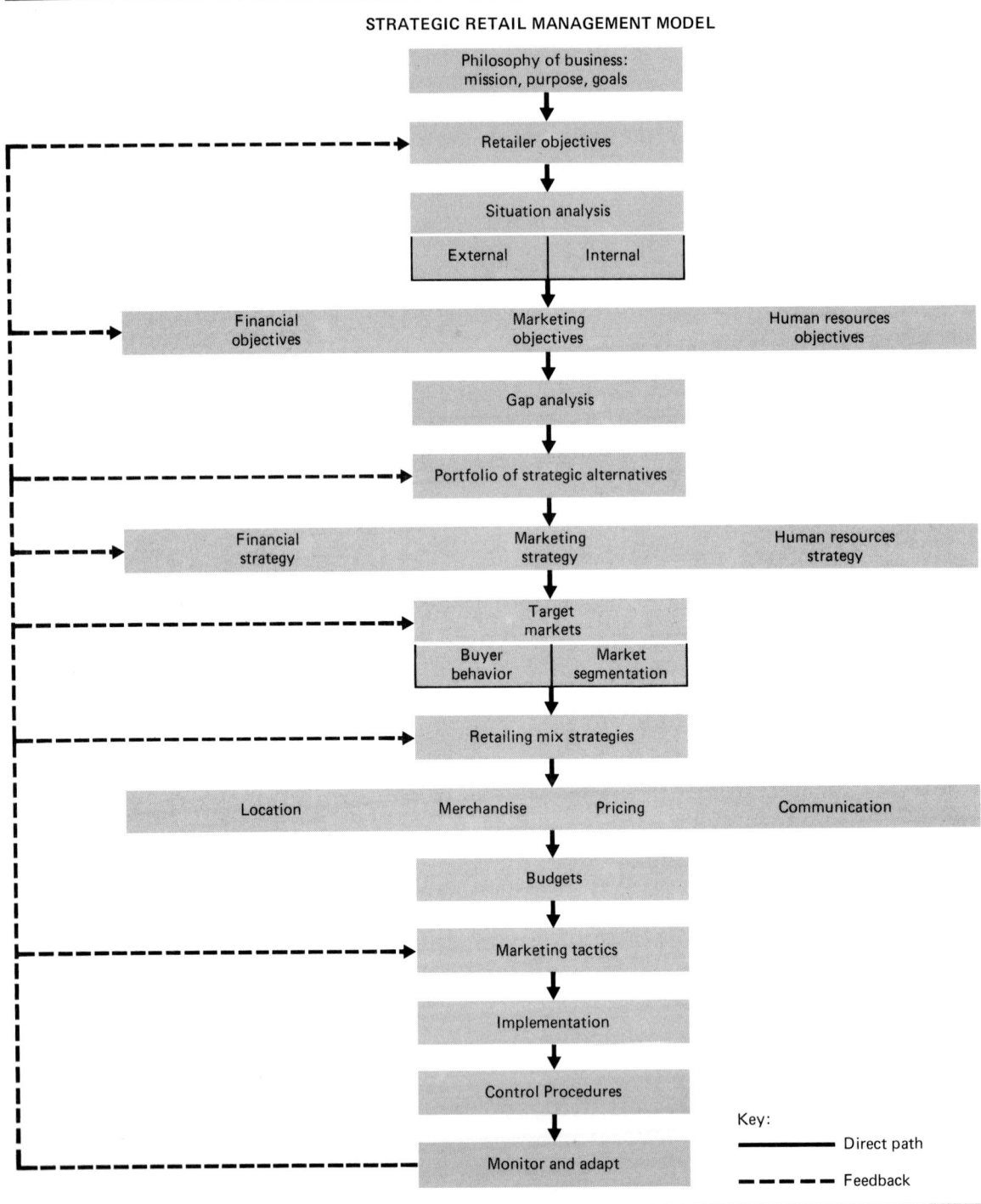

Chapter 1
An Introduction to Retailing

LEARNING OBJECTIVES

1. To understand the basic definition of retailing.
2. To understand the diverse perspectives and role of retailing in our society and economy.

INTRODUCTION

The influence of retailing in our daily lives is so pervasive that retailing and retailers are often taken for granted. The average person seldom goes more than a few days without visiting at least one retail store. Consider the following events for a hypothetical family consisting of working parents and one daughter. On Saturday morning, Mom starts a shopping trip by dropping off some clothes at a *dry cleaner's*, stops at a *boutique* that is having a sale, picks up some items at a *hardware store*, fills a prescription at a *pharmacy*, and buys food at the *grocery store* and *bakery*. Meanwhile, Dad visits an *auto parts store*, a *barber shop*, a *shoe store*, a *produce stand*, and a *sporting goods store*. Bored with Saturday television fare, the daughter walks to a nearby *convenience store* for gum, to the *discount store* for some school supplies, and then on to a *record shop*. Since everyone is by now too tired to cook, the consensus is to splurge on dinner at a local *restaurant*.

This series of events portrays our reliance on retailers for basic goods and services. The retail stores visited by the hypothetical family represent a cross section of the types of American retail stores, which we will discuss throughout this text.

Most people would understand that the firms mentioned above are retail firms, or retailers. But what is retailing?

WHAT IS RETAILING?

Retailing has historically been viewed as simply the "final link" or "point of contact" between producers and consumers.[1] The current view of retailing is somewhat broader: *Retailing includes all business activities that involve the sale of goods and services to the ultimate consumer for personal, family, or household use.*

Several key aspects of the definition deserve elaboration. First, retailing involves more than just selling. Retailers may perform any combination of the functions of marketing: buying, selling, transportation, storage, standardization and grading, financing, risk taking, and providing market information. Further, successful retailing operations require attention to business disciplines in addition to marketing, such as accounting, finance, management, and data processing.

Second, retailing involves more than tangible products; it also encompasses the sale of services. The consumer may desire a service as part of a purchase (alterations and delivery, for example) or the service alone (haircuts and insurance).

Third, an "ultimate consumer" must be involved for a transaction to be called retailing. Purchases for business or industrial uses are not retail transactions. Perhaps the key factor that distinguishes retailing from other business forms is the consumer's *motive* for the purchase. The sale of a typewriter to a student is a retail transaction; the sale of an identical typewriter to a business for office use is not a retail transaction. Therefore, firms we normally think of as "retailers" may also participate in transactions other than retail transactions.

Fourth, a retailer does not necessarily have to be involved in every retail transaction. Manufacturers, importers, and wholesalers who sell directly to ultimate consumers participate in retail transactions.

PERSPECTIVES OF RETAILING

Retailing can be viewed and studied from a variety of perspectives. Bert Rosenbloom observed four basic ways in which retailing can be considered:

1. As a *social institution*, focusing on the role of retailing in our society.

2. As a *subset of the economic system*, focusing on the role of retailing in our economy.

3. As a *member of distribution channels*, focusing on the role of retailing in . . . [serving manufacturers' distribution needs].

4. As an *entity to be managed*, focusing on the management of the firm.[2]

Many readers will recognize the first three perspectives as "macro" approaches to studying retailing. The managerial perspective is a "micro" approach in that it focuses on the individual firm; this is the perspective we use in this text.

REASONS FOR STUDYING RETAILING

The four perspectives of retailing can be used to develop the major reasons for our study of retailing. First, as a social institution, *retailing provides benefits to consumers.* Second, as a subset of the economic system, *retailing has a major impact on the economy.* Third, as a member of distribution channels, *retailing is critically important to manufacturers.* Fourth, as an entity to be managed, *retailing offers a broad range of career opportunities.*

Consumer Benefits   Viewed as a social institution, retailing benefits consumers by providing them with an assortment and variety of offerings to choose from. Retailers also provide consumers with certain basic utilities, such as a place, a time, and a form in which to purchase goods and services. Without retailing, consumers could obtain goods and services only with a great deal of effort and inconvenience. Consider what you would have to do to gather a simple wardrobe if there were no retailers. You would probably have to visit different factories to buy your clothing: a separate factory (maybe different states) for each type of shirt or blouse (knit, cotton, polyester), different places for each type of pants or dress (suit pants, blue jeans, work dress, party dress), and so on. Clothes buying could be a full-time activity. Food buying would also be a problem; few consumers even know where to find the valley of the Jolly Green Giant!

Economic Impact

Viewed as a subset of the economic system, retailing has a significant impact on our economy. Total retail sales in 1979 were 886.0 *billion* dollars, a per capita average of $4,025.[3] Retailing also accounts for a significant portion of employment — 15,989,000 people, or about 16.4 percent of the labor force, in 1979.[4] Table 1.1 shows 1979 sales for various retail trades.

The twenty-five largest American retailers are shown in Table 1.2. These retailers had combined sales of over $162 billion in 1980 and accounted for over 2½ million workers or 15.7 percent of all retail employees.

Role in Distribution

Retailing makes several important contributions to distribution channels. One major contribution, especially to manufacturers, is that retailing makes mass production possible. Because retailing reaches mass markets, the output of mass production can be distributed all over the country, not just in the immediate vicinity of factories and plants.

Retailing also helps eliminate quantity and assortment discrepancies between producers' supply and consumers' demand. Depending on the situation, retailers often provide one or more marketing functions (such as buying, selling, transportation), which allows the manufacturers to concentrate on manufacturing rather than on eliminating discrepancies. Consider a pecan farm and a peanut farm. Each can produce more than any consumer would demand (a quantity discrepancy) and neither can satisfy the average consumer's overall demand for nuts (an assortment discrepancy). The retailer's role is to collect the assortments desired by consumers and provide them in appropriate quantities.

A third contribution is that retailers serve as a two-way communication link in the distribution channel. Information is transmitted to consumers concerning product availability and characteristics (such as price), store location and hours, and so on. Manufacturers receive information from retailers about sales expectations and results, customer complaints, inventories, turnover, and the like.

Retailing Careers

The fourth perspective of retailing focuses on the management of retail firms. The managerial positions available in retail firms can provide an attractive career path for college graduates from a variety of disciplines. There are two basic types of management opportunities: as a retail business owner and as an employee. Approximately 82 percent of all retail firms are either sole proprietorships or partnerships; these businesses are privately owned and account for about 20 percent of retail sales.[5] The

Table 1.1
Retail store sales by kind of business, 1979

KIND OF BUSINESS	1979 SALES[a]
Durable goods stores	
Automotive dealers	
Motor vehicle, miscellaneous automotive dealer	$ 161.3
Auto and home supply stores	16.4
Furniture, home furnishings, equipment	
Furniture, home furnishings stores	26.7
Household appliances, radio, TV stores	12.1
Others	
Building materials, hardware, garden supply, mobile-home dealers	
Building materials, supply stores	35.1
Hardware stores	9.0
Others	8.1
Total durable goods stores	308.2[b]
Nondurable goods stores	
Apparel and accessory stores	
Men's, boys' clothing, furnishings	8.8
Women's clothing, specialty stores, furriers	15.8
Shoe stores	7.1
Others	12.7
Drug stores and proprietary stores	27.2
Eating and drinking places	75.1
Grocery stores	177.1
Other food stores	13.6
Gasoline service stations	71.9
Department stores	89.1
Variety stores	7.9
Other general merchandise stores	13.2
Liquor stores	15.6
Mail-order house (department store merchandise)	5.3
Total nondurable goods stores	312.8[b]
Retail trade, total	886.0

[a]In billions of dollars.

[b]Includes kinds of business not shown separately.

Source: Adapted from *Statistical Abstract of the United States,* 101st ed. (Washington, D.C.: Bureau of the Census, 1980), p. 840.

Table 1.2
Twenty-five largest retailers in the United States (1980)

RANK 1980	COMPANY	SALES ($000)	NET INCOME ($000)	NUMBER OF EMPLOYEES
1	Sears Roebuck (Chicago)	25,194,900	606,000	390,000
2	Safeway Stores (Oakland, Calif.)	15,102,673	119,368	150,013
3	K mart (Troy, Mich.)	14,204,381	260,527	256,000
4	J. C. Penney (New York)	11,353,000	233,000	194,000
5	Kroger (Cincinnati)	10,316,741	94,386	124,642
6	F. W. Woolworth (New York)	7,218,176	160,915	196,527
7	Great Atlantic & Pacific Tea (Montvale, N.J.)	6,684,179	(3,807)	58,000
8	Lucky Stores (Dublin, Calif.)	6,468,682	90,458	65,000
9	American Stores (Salt Lake City)	6,419,884	51,553	63,000
10	Federated Department Stores (Cincinnati)	6,300,686	277,727	116,600
11	Montgomery Ward (Chicago)	5,496,907	(137,122)	131,994
12	Winn-Dixie Stores (Jacksonville, Fla.)	4,388,979	91,950	60,700
13	Southland (Dallas)	4,758,656	77,672	44,600
14	City Products (Des Plaines, Ill.)	4,462,378	43,015	58,000
15	Jewel Companies (Chicago)	4,267,922	55,893	55,000
16	Dayton Hudson (Minneapolis)	5,033,536	146,719	70,000
17	May Department Stores (St. Louis)	3,172,976	116,915	66,000
18	Grand Union (Elmwood Park, N.J.)	3,137,612	30,669	33,000
19	Albertson's (Boise)	3,039,129	41,621	28,000
20	Wickes Companies (San Diego)	2,876,973	8,276	43,219
21	ARA Services (Philadelphia)	2,806,020	42,582	120,000
22	Carter Hawley Hale Stores (Los Angeles)	2,632,921	58,082	55,000
23	Supermarkets General (Woodbridge, N.J.)	2,628,851	26,067	30,000
24	R. H. Macy (New York)	2,373,531	103,026	45,000
25	Rapid-American (New York)	2,351,591	27,566	46,000

Source: Reprinted by permission from the July 13, 1981, issue of FORTUNE Magazine. © 1981 Time Inc.

STRATEGY IN ACTION 1.1

Franchising: "Sweet Talkers"

An organization of 2000 bakeries is beginning to market seriously a service known as *telecake marketing*. This service is part of the telegift market, which is probably best known for long-distance flower giving. The franchise organization has hopes of enlisting 7000 bakeries nationwide to become part of the cake delivery system.

Franchise bakeries that become members of the organization will contribute $200 monthly plus a percentage of each cake sale to a common advertising fund. Through this organization, independent bakeries may recover from the inroads made into their markets by brand name baked products and frozen baked items sold in supermarkets.

Telecake franchisors envision long-distance "sweet talkers" becoming an increasingly common method of gift giving. Long-distance flower giving was just in its infancy twenty years ago and is now a widely accepted telegift method.

Source: Adapted from "Telecake Cooks Up Franchise." Reprinted with permission from the 10 August 1981 issue *of Advertising Age*. Copyright 1981 by Crain Communications, Inc.

remaining 18 percent of retail businesses are corporations, which hire many college graduates and account for about 80 percent of retail sales.[6]

Owning a Retail Business. Although the prospect of owning a retail business intimidates many people, many others find ownership an attractive career opportunity. In fact, many of the present-day retail giants, including Sears, McDonald's, and J. C. Penney, began as small independent retailers. Opportunities to own a retail business also exist in the franchising area (see Chapter 5).

Small retail stores face an array of opportunities and problems different from those of larger retailers and other businesses. The first advantage is ease of entry, or simply the opportunity to start a business. The initial investment required can be relatively small, sometimes only a few thousand dollars; normally the fledgling retailer can obtain additional start-up capital from other sources, such as banks, the Small Business Administration, and trade credit.

A second key opportunity is that small retailers can often specialize in satisfying a specific (and perhaps narrow) market segment. All of the retailer's attention and resources can be focused on the selected customers and on a narrow range of needs. Consider the target market and specific needs emphasized by bridal shops, western stores, men's, women's, and children's shoe stores, and ethnic food stores.

A third opportunity involves the speed and coordination of decision making. The smaller retailer does not have as many layers of management (often there is one layer--the owner/manager), which normally enables the

smaller retailer to make quicker decisions. The smaller retailer also will
not have managers in each functional area (an advertising manager, a
transportation manager, and so on), which minimizes coordination problems.

Despite the advantages and opportunities available to smaller retailers, there are also some disadvantages and problems. In fact, each of the
opportunities mentioned above can lead to problems. The low initial investment can encourage an entrepreneur to open a retail store without
enough working capital to sustain operations during a downturn or off-
season. Sometimes the market segments or niches left to small retailers
are not profitable because they are too small or elusive. Although the
small number of managers can enhance the speed and coordination of
decision making, it also limits the possibilities for managerial specialization (that is, there is no one to specialize in accounting or advertising).
More specific problems include financial barriers (with television advertising, for instance) and difficulty in competing on a price basis with
larger discount retailers. The potential result of all problems is low profits
and inadequate cash flow, which can lead to bankruptcy. The source of
most of the small retailer's problems can generally be traced to an inadequate quantity or quality of resources such as managerial experience, marketing or purchasing skills, and qualified personnel.

From the standpoint of his or her career, the owner of a smaller retail business also faces an array of personal advantages (or opportunities)
and disadvantages (or problems). Many entrepreneurs see retailing as
an opportunity to earn higher income than is otherwise possible, but their
problems can include working long hours, shouldering responsibility
alone, lack of certain specialized skills, and uncertain flow of personal
income.

Opportunities as an Employee. Although buying and merchandising
usually form the primary career paths for retail employees, opportunities
also exist in many other areas, including advertising, accounting, personnel management, and others.

The average starting salary in retailing for 1980–81 college graduates
was over $1100 per month, with the top 10 percent receiving around
$1400 per month.[7]

College graduates hired by larger retailers (especially department
stores) normally begin as trainees in junior executive or junior management positions. The initial training period usually lasts from three to
twelve months and is often a combination of classroom and on-the-job
training.

After the initial training, the career paths available depend on the
particular store and the individual's preferences. Some retailers provide a
path that alternates between buying positions and merchandising (leading
to store management). Such a path is shown in Fig. 1.1. These retailers

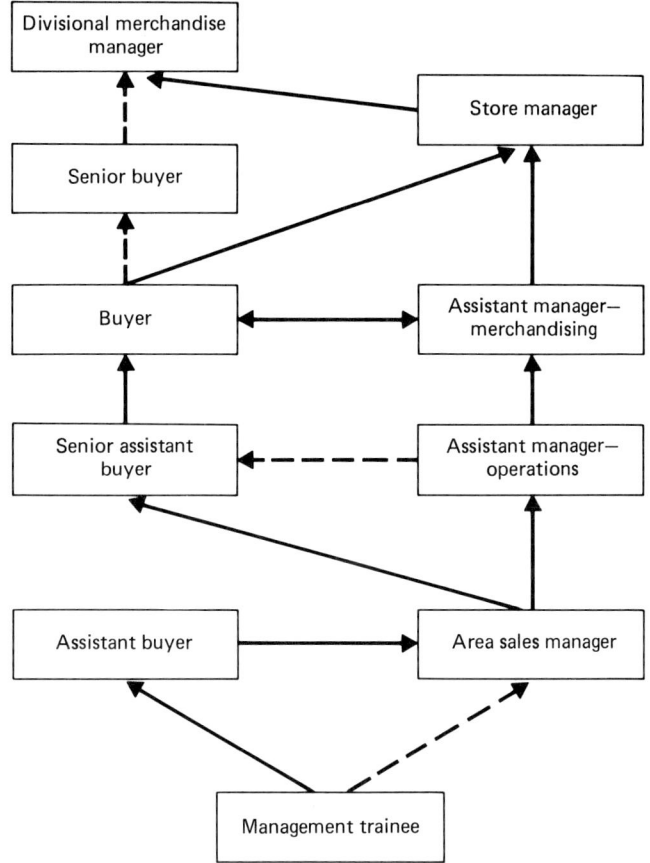

Figure 1.1
Career path at McRae's
Source: McRae's Department Stores (Jackson, Mississippi).

feel that managers who reach the top of the organization should have a broad, solid background in all aspects of retailing. Other retailers maintain more distinct or separate paths for managers after they gain initial experience, as shown in Fig. 1.2.

Consider the buying positions in Fig. 1.1. Although specific job titles vary from one retail organization to another, an individual's progress "up the ladder" generally involves assuming more and broader responsibilities. An assistant buyer for a department store, for example, might be responsible for buying only jewelry boxes. Later, his or her responsibilities might expand to encompass all jewelry, all women's accessories, all women's wear, and eventually all merchandise in the store. In some retail organizations, buyers have a great deal of responsibility and decision-

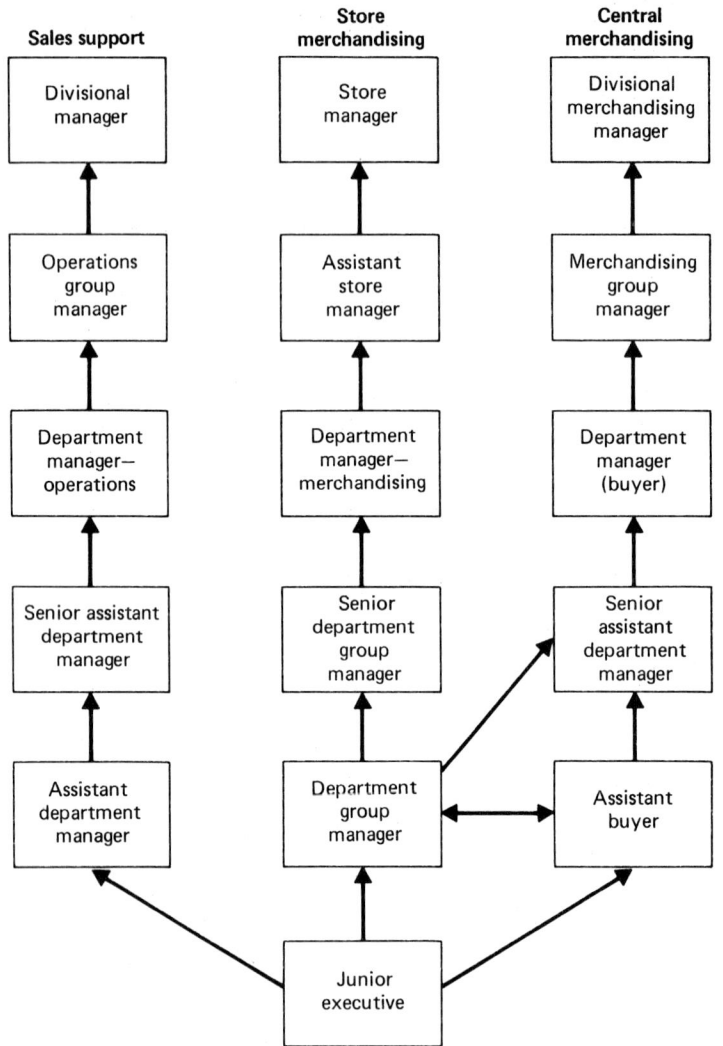

Figure 1.2
Career paths at Sanger Harris
Source: Sanger Harris (Dallas, Fort Worth, Tyler, Tulsa).

making latitude in areas such as merchandise planning and selection, pricing, and inventory levels (see Chapter 12).

Area or department sales managers generally have responsibilities such as supervising clerks, stocking, and maintaining displays. Positions such as assistant manager for operations in Fig. 1.1 usually involve responsibility for the overall functioning of the store, which might include maintenance, cash control, personnel scheduling, and receiving. The assistant manager for merchandising would be involved with activities directly associated with presenting merchandise to the customers; such responsibilities might include planning and implementing special sales events, store themes, and displays.

There are several potential benefits of a career in retailing. Starting salaries and overall management compensation in retailing have become competitive with many other fields, especially for well-qualified people and in certain regions of the United States. Many regional and national retailers have excellent training programs for recent graduates. Retailing generally provides a "fast track" into decision-making positions (many regional chains can promote promising college graduates into store manager positions within two to five years). Many graduates (but obviously not all) find the dynamic nature of the retailing environment both challenging and invigorating, qualities everyone looks for in whatever career they pursue.

CLASSIFICATIONS OF RETAIL FIRMS

Because there are so many different kinds of retail firms a variety of descriptive terminology is necessary. Nine different classifications of retail firms are presented below.

Legal Form of Ownership

The three basic legal forms of ownership are sole proprietorships, partnerships, and corporations. The **sole proprietorship** is the simplest legal form. The firm is not incorporated; the owner/manager goes into business simply by opening the doors. Sole proprietorships are much more numerous than other legal forms, they tend to be small, and they have high failure rates.

Partnerships arise from an agreement of co-ownership between two or more individuals and often from a desire to combine financial resources with technical or business skills. It is critically important that the partners prepare a formal, legal partnership agreement that clearly defines the roles, rights, and responsibilities of each party.

A **corporation** is a legal entity consisting of individuals united for some common purpose who are allowed to use a common name and to change its membership without dissolution. Corporations are usually much larger than the other legal forms. Some of the advantages of corporations include limited liability, perpetual life, and easy transfer of ownership.

Operational Structure

Another common way of classifying retailers is according to the operational structure, which is related to the legal form. The three basic structures are independent retailers, chain stores, and consumer cooperatives.

Independent retailers consist of one retail outlet and are usually sole proprietorships. A **chain store** is a group of retail outlets under common (usually corporate) ownership and management. A **consumer cooperative**

is a retail store owned by a group of consumers (and sometimes managed by a professional retailer).

A related criterion, degree of integration, can also be used to classify retailers. This topic is discussed in Chapter 5.

Size

Size can be viewed from the standpoint of dollar volume and number of outlets. The Small Business Administration classifies a retailer as small if annual sales do not exceed $5 million; the small retailer should also *not* be dominant in the field and should be independently owned and operated. *"Mom' n' pop store"* is an informal term used frequently to describe extremely small independent retailers.

Chain stores vary widely in number of outlets. Some chains have only two or three outlets and are in a sense "independent chains." Others can be called regional chains; these retailers have outlets covering a large part of at least one state. National chains such as Sears and J. C. Penney have outlets all over the United States. Some retailers, such as McDonald's, are even becoming internationalized, with outlets in Europe and Japan.

Types of Merchandise

Retailers can also be classified according to the types of merchandise they offer. The Bureau of the Census uses the classification scheme shown in Table 1.1.

It is also useful to consider a classification scheme based on the breadth and depth of the merchandise offered. **Breadth** refers to the number of generic, noncompeting merchandise lines in a store. **Depth** refers to the number of different brands, sizes, colors, fabrics, etc. of any one product category routinely stocked.

The merchandise offered by a **general merchandise store** might include such diverse products as groceries, hardware, clothing, and tools. Thus these retailers' have wide breadth and, usually, shallow depth in the various product categories. Note that a **department store** is a general merchandise store in which merchandise is grouped into departments. To qualify for the *Stores* annual ranking of department stores, a retailer must carry a full line of general merchandise, including both soft goods and home furnishings (see Table 1.3).

Single-line stores have very narrow merchandise breadth and very deep merchandise depth. They offer an extensive line of products (related in either sale or use) within a single merchandise category. Examples of single-line stores are jewelry stores, furniture stores, and hardware stores.

Specialty stores have even narrower breadth than single-line stores. They usually offer an extremely deep selection in one merchandise line. Examples of specialty stores include plant shops, muffler shops, cutlery stores, and fabric stores (see Strategy in Action 1.2).

Types of Services

Retailers can be classified on the basis of the services they offer. **Full-service retailers** offer many services, such as delivery, credit, gift wrapping, repair, and others. **Limited-service retailers** offer only standard services such as

Table 1.3
Top twenty-five department stores

COMPANY/DIVISION	AFFILIATION	UNITS	SQ. FT. (IN THOUSANDS)	SALES (IN MILLIONS)
1. Macy's/New York	(RHM)	15	5,998	$775
2. Bamberger's/New York	(RHM)	20	5,656	725
3. May Company/California	(May)	31	7,181	650
4. Hudson's/Detroit	(DH)	18	5,832	641.5
5. Broadway/Southern California	(CHH)	40	7,058	625
6. Macy's/California	(RHM)	19	4,221	600
7. Bloomingdale's/New York	(Fed)	15	3,397	566.8
8. Marshall Field/Chicago	(MF)	18	5,764	550
9. Abraham & Straus/Brooklyn	(Fed)	12	4,907	547.6
10. Burdine's/Florida	(Fed)	21	3,980	498.8
11. Dillard's/Little Rock	(Ind)	50	6,342	470.7
12. Lord & Taylor/New York	(ADG)	35	4,902	460
13. Foley's/Houston	(Fed)	10	3,006	453.0
14. Bullock's/Los Angeles	(Fed)	22	4,726	557.4
15. Emporium-Capwell/Northern California	(CHH)	19	4,746	415
16. Dayton's/Minneapolis	(DH)	16	3,149	382.1
17. Hecht's/Baltimore-Washington	(May)	21	4,225	365
18. Jordan Marsh/New England	(All)	14	3,595	360
19. Rich's/Atlanta	(Fed)	17	4,076	351.7
20. Wanamaker's/Philadelphia	(CHH)	16	4,356	335
21. Lazarus/Columbus, Ohio	(Fed)	15	3,607	332.8
22. Joske's/Texas	(All)	27	4,832	315
23. Famous-Barr/St. Louis	(May)	12	3,439	315
24. The Bon/Northwest	(All)	32	3,983	310
25. Woodward & Lothrop/Washington, D.C.	(Ind)	15	2,965	308.4

Note: Figures ending in 5 and 0 are estimates; others are exact sales as reported. Affiliation code: All, Allied; ADG, Associated Dry Goods; CHH, Carter Hawley Hale; DH, Dayton Hudson; Fed, Federated; Ind, Independent; MF, Marshall Field; May, May Co.; RHM, R. H. Macy.

Source: Reprinted from July 1981 STORES Magazine, © National Retail Merchants Association, copyright, 1981.

Retailing Software

The proliferation of personal computers in offices and homes is opening the way for a new breed of retailer: *computer software stores*. In early 1982 at least four companies, including computer-retailing leader ComputerLand Corp., plan to establish franchise chains of stores specializing in computer software. And other retailers are likely to follow.

"Software stores are an idea whose time has come," says Edward Faber, president of ComputerLand, which plans to open its first software store in February. Many computer executives expect personal-computer marketing to follow in the footsteps of the audio industry, with computers and software sold in separate stores, as are stereos and records.

So far, there are only a half-dozen software stores, with most software now sold through mail order or in computer stores. But Future Computing Inc., a Richardson (Tex.) consulting firm, predicts that *1,600 software stores will open by 1986.* "Over the next few years, more software stores will open than computer stores," adds Barry J. Passen, president of Microcon Software Centers Inc. in Watertown, Mass.

Underlying the growing interest in the stores is a surge in the demand for software. Sold on disks or cassettes, software contains the instructions for different computer applications—just as phonograph records contain the information for different songs. More than 5,000 software packages, ranging from inventory control to Space Invaders, are now available. Total sales will top $500 million this year, up from $50 million in 1978, and Future Computing expects sales to grow to $4.6 billion by 1986.

Exceeding Expectations

Software stores hope to win a big fraction of those sales by offering a wide selection and by locating in high-traffic areas, such as malls and downtown shopping districts. Sales at existing software stores have been growing briskly. At the Softwaire Store in Los Angeles, open since June, sales are expected to top $100,000 in December alone. "We've exceeded all expectations," says Charles D. Limmer, store manager.

Wall Street has recognized the potential of software stores. Since Programs Unlimited Inc. went public at $1 per share in September, its price has more than doubled. The Jericho (N.Y.) company currently operates two stores, and it plans to begin selling franchises in mid-January. The Program Store Inc. in Washington and Microcon Software Centers plan to begin selling franchises shortly thereafter.

ComputerLand, which operates a franchise chain of 220 computer stores, probably has the most aggressive plans. The San Leandro (Calif.) company is allowing each of its franchisees to open "satellite" software stores, and Faber expects some franchisees to open four or five of them. By early 1984, he expects that 100 stores will be opened. Although ComputerLand's software stores, at 400 sq. ft. each, will be only 20% the size of its computer stores, they will display nearly four times as much software. "At our main stores, shelf space for software has become a major problem," says Faber.

Many uncertainties still surround software stores. The stores could be plagued by unauthorized copying of software. And customer support remains a dilemma. Some retailers, including Faber, believe that software stores must offer only minimum support, as do book stores and record stores, if they are to be profitable. But others insist that substantial support is required to sell software, particularly in business applications. "Software packages aren't like records. Customers need hand-holding," says Limmer of the Softwaire Store.

credit, check cashing, return privileges, and possibly a few others. **Self-service retailers** offer very few services and arrange their displays so that salespeople are not needed by customers (see Chapter 19).

Service retailers deserve special attention because of their increasing significance in our economy (many claim that services account for almost 50 percent of personal-consumption expenditures in the United States). Service retailers emphasize *primary services,* intangible offerings that are the object of a retail transaction. Examples of service retailers include dry cleaners, barber shops, and photography services. Characteristics of service retailers are discussed in greater detail in the appendix to Chapter 1 and in Chapter 11. Services offered by merchandise retailers are discussed in Chapter 19.

Price Emphasis

Classifying retailers on the basis of their relative emphasis on price is closely related to the service-based classifications. Typically there is a direct relationship between a retailer's initial markup (and, therefore, price) and the quantity and quality of services offered.

Some retailers "price below competition"; these retailers offer few services and employ many cost-cutting practices (see Strategy in Action 1.3). Retailers who "price with competition" do not use price as their main selling point; rather, their sales are made on the basis of service, merchandise selection, or location. Other retailers choose to *price above the competition,* relying on some unique competitive advantage, such as location (7–11 stores) or image (Neiman-Marcus) (see Chapter 14).

Location

Still another way to classify retailers is according to geographic location or neighborhood. Types of sites include central business districts, secondary business districts, regional shopping centers, community shopping centers, neighborhood shopping centers, and free-standing stores (see Chapter 10).

Method of Consumer Contact

The conventional retail store is characterized by customer-initiated, in-store, face-to-face contact. Although this form of retailing accounts for an overwhelming majority of retail sales (and will likely continue to do so), other forms and variations are becoming more significant.

Mail-order retailing has been around since the 1800s and is continuing to grow. The main forms of mail-order retailing involve general merchandise catalogs (such as those of Sears and Montgomery Ward), specialty catalogs (for seeds, hobbies, jewelry, and so on), and direct-mail offers (such as those of gasoline companies and magazine and book clubs).

Telephone selling appears to be growing in popularity. It has been used successfully by retailers such as Sears, J. C. Penney, Montgomery Ward, and even small specialty stores. Customer-initiated telephone transactions are generally based on the retailer's catalog and are an alternative to store visits and catalog orders via mail. Retailer-initiated telephone selling can be focused on building new business, reviving inactive accounts, sim-

STRATEGY IN ACTION 1.3

Off-Price Retailers

A new form of retailer emerged during the 1970s and is expected to grow rapidly during the 1980s—the "off-price" retailers. They differ from the discounter in that off-price retailers sell higher quality merchandise, with an emphasis on brand names.

Discounters have lower price markups and count on high sales volume to make up for lower margins. The off-price retailer has price markups similar to department and specialty stores but cuts costs through buying advantages and minimization of overhead expenses. Purchasing advantages are in the form of buying manufacturers' overruns, end-of-season stocks, large quantity purchases, and perhaps some seconds or irregulars. Overhead expenses are kept to a minimum by avoiding high-rent shopping centers; maintaining a plain store decor; using tables, bins, and pipe racks to display merchandise; and not offering such services as charge accounts, cash refunds, and layaways.

While discounters have traditionally appealed to the lower-middle and lower income consumers, off-price retailers are drawing primarily from middle and upper income consumers. Thus department and specialty store retailers have suffered most from the growth of off-price retailers.

Most of the retailers engaged in off-price retailing are independent companies; however, several of the larger retail chains have entered the area. These include Woolworth (J. Brannam), Zayre (Hit or Miss), and Milville (Marshall's). As off-price retailers increase their market share, more chains will likely enter into this form of retailing. In the past five years the number of off-price stores has grown from 1,000 to approximately 10,000, and their share of the apparel market is expected to reach 15 to 20 percent by 1985.

Some competitive reaction to off-price retailers can be seen in the changing strategies of certain department and specialty stores. Bloomingdale's and Lord and Taylor are emphasizing merchandise carrying their own labels. Several department stores, such as Filene's, have opened "bargain basements." A majority of specialty retailers have attempted to emphasize their "market niche" and sharpen their image in the market. Finally, some retailers believe the off-price retailer is simply a phenomenon of the existing economic conditions and will lose strength when the consumers' economic circumstances improve.

Source: Adapted from Marjorie Leedy, "Price-Cutting Retailers Make Sales Inroads," *The Clarion-Ledger* (Jackson, Mississippi), 10 January 1982, pp. 1–2c.

ply fostering customer relations, or selling complementary goods (Sears, for instance, uses telephone selling for maintenance contracts on durable goods).

Household contact involves selling in the customer's home and takes three basic forms. **Door-to-door selling** has been used successfully for vacuum cleaners, cosmetics, encyclopedias, and other merchandise. Although still important, door-to-door retail sales appear to be diminishing somewhat. **Party selling** involves bringing merchandise into the home to be demonstrated to prospective customers. Firms that have been successful using this approach include Mary Kay, Tupperware, and Stanley Home Products. **Route selling** involves selling to customers along an established delivery route. This approach has been popular for dairy products, dry cleaning, and diaper services.

Vending machines must also be considered a form of retailing. Perhaps the primary advantages of vending machines are that they can be placed in a wide variety of locations and that they can be used by customers any time access is available. Although there have been many problems associated with vending machines (including breakage, theft, and image), increases in machine quality and the range of merchandise offered may open the way to increased vending machine sales.

Nontraditional Classifications

Several nontraditional classifications of retail stores deserve mention because of their increasing significance. In **catalog showrooms** the customer selects merchandise from a display of sample merchandise or from a catalog and often writes up the order and presents it to a clerk. Then the particular merchandise chosen by the customer is brought from storage. Leading catalog showrooms include Service Merchandise, Century House, and Best Products.

Retail warehouses usually use large, low-rent, isolated buildings and offer minimal services. Food warehouses, for example, often have customers perform many services, such as weighing, pricing, bagging and carry-out, in return for lower prices. The warehouse concept is also used by some retailers for furniture, major appliances, auto repair equipment, and floor coverings.

Hypermarkets combine discount store, supermarket, and warehouse operations under one roof. Although first used in Europe, this concept could continue to grow and become very important in the United States.

TRENDS IN RETAILING

Several recognizable trends in the retail field could have a large impact on retailing strategy and on those about to begin careers in retailing. The specific trends include (1) size of retailers, (2) diversification, (3) ownership of stores, (4) channel arrangements, (5) internationalization of products and operations, and (6) nonstore retailing.

Size of Retailers

There appears to be a consensus among knowledgeable observers that the 1980s and 1990s will see a decrease in the number of retailers, along with slowed expansion,[8] which should give those who survive a larger share of the market. This rather general contention, however, does not do justice to the issue of retailer size.

Retail polarization, or the trend toward both larger and smaller retailers, will continue.[9] That is, the giant mass merchandisers will likely continue to prosper, as will the smaller, intensely specialized retailers. Medium-sized retailers will encounter the most trouble because they often have neither the overall power to take market share from the mass merchandisers nor the ability to differentiate their offering enough to tap smaller, specialized market niches.

A related factor involves "normal" store size. Retailers that can truly offer one-stop shopping are likely to have even larger stores. Because of increasing construction costs and interest rates, however, other retailers, such as conventional department stores, are being forced into smaller store sizes. Despite increasing occupancy costs, shopping centers will assume greater importance as conventional and specialized retailers seek to band together to offer one-stop shopping.

Diversification

Sears is the best example of the trend toward diversification of products and services. Sears, the nation's largest retailer, has now purchased (unless the Justice Department intervenes) the nation's largest real-estate broker and the fifth largest securities firm.[10] Thus a customer will be able to shop for clothing, hardware, furniture, appliances, real estate, insurance, stocks, bonds, and other banking services in one stop. Total one-stop shopping may truly be at hand. Other major retailers are also likely to begin offering additional services at their stores.

Ownership of Stores

A third trend is the combining of retail organizations through mergers and acquisitions. This trend is already evident at the department store level; most of the one hundred largest department stores are part of larger businesses (see Table 1.3).[11] Many "small" retailers are also owned by larger organizations but often operate under a separate name to maintain an individual identity. This trend is expected to continue because of the widespread need to achieve improved operating efficiencies.

Channel Arrangements

Retailers are likely to continue acquiring or establishing manufacturing and wholesaling operations, and various producers and suppliers are likely to continue to acquire retail outlets. The basic reasons for these changes in channel arrangements are similar to the reasons for changes in ownership. In addition, many retailers are simply looking for assured supply sources. A related trend involves franchises, which are also expected to continue to grow. The principle advantage to the franchise arrangement is increased efficiency (see Chapter 5). With costs rising and margins being cut, any channel arrangement that yields cost savings through greater efficiency will be utilized in the future. Some changes may involve ownership while others may involve innovative channel arrangements.

Internationalization

As is the case with other industries, retailing will become more internationalized. Three distinct changes are occurring in this area.

Foreign Markets. Large retailers have already moved into foreign countries. Sears has 127 stores in twelve countries other than the United States.[12]

With some U.S. markets slowing in growth or even contracting, expansion into growing foreign markets is likely to continue.

Foreign Products. U.S. consumers' change in attitude toward foreign-made products has been astounding. As recently as the 1960s a product marked "Made in Japan" was generally assumed to be a cheap, low-quality product. By the late 1970s, however, a product so marked was likely to be perceived as an expensive, high-quality one. Conversely, other foreign-made merchandise offers distinct cost advantages owing to lower labor and other production costs. Retailers, consequently, are likely to continue their interest in foreign-made merchandise.

Foreign Retailers. Retail expertise is not confined to the United States. Retailers in many foreign countries are capable of expanding into the United States and are likely to begin doing so. In addition, some innovative foreign ideas and concepts, such as hypermarkets, are beginning to be adopted by U.S. retailers. A related development involves foreign businesspeople investing in U.S. retail companies such as A&P and Albertson's.

Nonstore Retailing   Nonstore retailing encompasses many specific types of selling; as mentioned earlier, these include catalog houses, door-to-door selling, vending, and party selling. These retail forms are likely to continue to grow because of trends such as women in the work force and time poverty (discussed in Chapter 4).

Perhaps the greatest potential change involves **interactive ordering** using cablevision systems. The technology exists for shoppers anywhere in the United States to view a fashion show at Saks Fifth Avenue in New York City and order a dress for immediate delivery. Although only Columbus, Ohio, presently has the technology on-line, any city with cablevision could also have the service now. Although it is not likely in the immediate future, all merchandise could eventually be bought in this manner. If this occurs, retailing as we know it will cease to exist; retailers will simply become large warehouses with a television production studio.

Although the trends discussed to this point represent many major changes, the change with the greatest potential impact involves improved retail management.

CHANGES IN RETAIL MANAGEMENT

As long as there have been retailers there have been problems with retail management. One persistent problem has revolved around a lack of timely and accurate information for decision-making purposes. Most retail managers have had to learn to make decisions with a minimum of good, solid information. Great strides are being made in overcoming this problem; specifically, computer-based information systems are being developed that have the potential to revolutionize retail management.

**The Information
Explosion**

Point-of-sale (POS) equipment linked to computers (replacing outdated cash registers) can provide retailers with much data that have been sorely lacking in the past. Many retailers have to depend on frequent physical counts of merchandise to control their inventories (see Chapter 13). This procedure is generally inefficient and inadequate for managerial purposes. With presently available computer technology, many retailers can use a perpetual inventory control system to keep track of their inventories on a real-time basis.

Other potential computer applications may be even more far-reaching. For instance, it has been almost impossible to effectively utilize economic price theory in retail pricing decisions. Computers can now be used to collect the data necessary to approximate demand curves and calculate the price elasiticity and cross elasticity of demand for specific merchandise items. Computers can also be used to determine optimum selling space and shelf position for specific merchandise items. Research has shown that certain shelf or display spacing and positioning can yield better sales. Since the computer allows accurate checks of exactly what merchandise is selling, a retailer can systematically alter merchandise displays to discover optimum selling space and positions for specific merchandise. Thus accurate experimental results with different store layouts are possible.

Advertising's effect on at least short-term sales can also be checked more closely by computer. Media selection can be improved by using different media to advertise different merchandise and by then monitoring sales of specific merchandise items continually to determine which media yield the best results.

These possibilities do not even begin to touch on the total potential of computer systems. For instance, more accurate consumer records, including credit histories, complaint histories, buying habits and patterns, and maybe even family birthdays, can be kept and accessed by a computer system.

Perhaps the greatest impact of advancing computer technology and applications will be on small retailers. Many small computer systems are now priced within the range of small retailers. Those who are able to take advantage of the computer will have a distinct competitive advantage over those who do not.

**Strategic Planning
and Management**

Most retailers are facing a future of reduced growth and profit opportunities owing to slower growth in consumer spending, continued inflation, scarcity and high cost of capital, and other factors that we will discuss in Chapter 4. Some of the larger companies (mostly nonretailers) have begun to use **strategic management** to help develop appropriate strategies. Although more and more retailers are beginning to become interested in the concept, few are using it, apparently because of lack of understanding and the prevalence of informal, family management arrangements.[13] We hope this text will help alleviate at least the first of these reasons. We feel that strategic management is the key ingredient to retail success during the next decade.

Within the framework of strategic management, several other management concepts are likely to receive increased attention. The strong likelihood of reduced growth and expansion opportunities will put a premium on *market-share management* (also discussed in Chapter 2). Key components of market-share management include (1) identifying the stage of the retail life cycle a store or department is in now and in the relevant planning horizon, (2) identifying the relevant market and market segments, (3) identifying direct and indirect competitors, and (4) developing appropriate strategies for each target market.[14]

Retail productivity will receive increasing attention. This involves the relationship between output and the input required to generate it. Retailers have the opportunity to improve productivity in the personnel, capital and asset, and facilities areas.[15]

Retailers need *high-quality personnel*. The demand for college-educated management personnel will increase because of increased use of the computer, the increasing complexity of retail operations and competition, and the likelihood of more centralized management decisions.

Capital and asset management has probably received inadequate attention from retailers in the past. As management personnel become more professional, emphasis will shift from pure cost control to concepts such as return on investment and portfolio analysis. Cash and other assets must "work harder" for the retailer in the future.

The *productivity of store facilities* will also receive greater emphasis. Store units will be evaluated more heavily on factors such as sales per square foot and gross margin per square, linear, or cubic foot. Improvements might also be available through shifting functions to suppliers (such as price marking and stocking), automation, vertical marketing, and expanded self-service.

ORGANIZATION OF TEXT

This text is organized around the concept of strategic retail management, which will be introduced and discussed in detail in Chapter 2. The remainder of the chapters flow directly from the concept of strategic retail management, which is schematically shown in the strategic retail management model that opens each chapter. Effective financial analysis, planning, and control (Chapter 3) is essential for effective strategic retail management. A critical aspect of strategic planning is that all retail strategy should be predicated on environmental conditions (Chapters 4 and 5) and focused on the customer (Chapters 6 and 7). Obtaining and interpreting information about the environment requires an adequate structure for obtaining information (Chapter 8). Strategic plans must be formulated for human resources and the organization (Chapter 9).

Marketing strategies must be planned for location (Chapter 10), merchandise (Chapters 11–13), pricing (Chapter 13), and communicating with the customer (Chapters 15–19). Control of retail activities is essential to ensure desired performance and efficiency (Chapter 20).

KEY CONCEPTS

Retailing	Self-service retailer
Sole proprietorship	Service retailer
Partnership	Mail-order retailer
Corporation	Telephone selling
Independent retailer	Household contact
Chain store	Door-to-door selling
Consumer cooperative	Party selling
Breadth	Route selling
Depth	Vending machines
General merchandise store	Catalog showroom
Department store	Retail warehouses
Single-line store	Hypermarkets
Specialty store	Retail polarization
Full-service retailer	Interactive ordering
Limited-service retailer	Strategic management

REVIEW QUESTIONS

1. Define retailing.
2. List and briefly describe four perspectives of retailing.
3. Give four reasons for studying retailing.
4. Discuss the role of retailing in distribution.
5. Discuss the advantages and disadvantages of owning a small retail store.
6. Discuss the benefits of a retailing career.
7. List and describe six key retailing trends.
8. Discuss the impact of the potential "information explosion" on retail management.

Appendix
Service Retailing

Service retailers (or retail service establishments) emphasize the delivery of primary services to consumers. A *primary service* is an intangible offering that forms the basis or focal point of the retail transaction. Table A1.1 lists examples of service retailers.

GROWTH OF SERVICE RETAILING

Since World War II, service retailing has become increasingly significant in the United States. Many estimates indicate that close to 50 cents of every dollar is now spent on services. Some service trades have declined in importance (barber shops, for example) while others have grown in importance (travel bureaus, beauty salons, gourmet cooking classes, housesitting, chimney sweeping). Several factors have fueled this growth:

1. More women in the work force.

2. Changing lifestyles, especially regarding a decreased emphasis on material goods and an increased emphasis on intangibles, such as recreational, personal-care, and educational services

3. Increased income levels

4. New service offerings

Table A1.1
Examples of service retailers

Banks	Finance companies
Railroads	Intercity buses
Taxis	Airlines
Intracity buses	Automotive repair shops
Beauty shops	Child care services
Rental services	Hotels
Travel agencies	Country clubs
Dance studios	Barber shops
Shoe repair shops	Movie theaters
Lawn care services	Blood pressure testing units
Specialized schools and classes	Housesitting services
Income-tax preparation services	Storage facilities
Health spas and gyms	Radio, TV, and appliance repair shops
Auto rental agencies	Laundry and dry cleaning shops
Amusement parks	Insurance agencies
Termite control services	Chimney-sweep services
Pet grooming services	Maid services

DISTINCTIVE CHARACTERISTICS

Service retailing possesses a variety of characteristics that distinguish it from merchandise retailing:

1. *Intangible offering.*
   Effects on consumer:
   a) Consumer is not purchasing ownership of a product.
   b) Consumers have difficulty in judging the quality of a service before purchasing it.
   c) Consumers may sometimes engage in a more extensive search process.
   Effects on retailer:
   a) Retailer cannot compile an inventory stock of services.
   b) There may be a greater opportunity for positioning the service offering relative to competition.

2. *Desire for convenience.* Consumers often want *performance convenience* (rather than doing it themselves) and *purchase convenience* (location, time, and payment).

3. *Discretionary expenditure.* Services are generally discretionary expenditures that consumers can postpone or perform themselves.

4. *Labor intensive.* The labor-intensive nature of services puts a great burden on the retailer's human resource strategy and management and limits the potential for improvements in productivity via mechanization or automation.

5. *Small size.* The small size of service businesses usually involves limited financial and human resources.

6. *Ease of entry.* Since service retailing relies heavily on the skill of one or several individuals and the financial outlay to open a service retail establishment is small, it is relatively easy to begin a retail service establishment (except when licensing requirements are applicable).

7. *Ease of exit.* Retail service establishments have a high failure rate primarily because they are based on the specialized skill of the owner (consider barber shops, repair shops, dance studios), which does not necessarily include business skills.

SHORTCOMINGS OF SERVICE RETAILERS

The growth of service retailing in recent years may have occurred despite several general shortcomings. It is possible that the service sector would have grown even more without these shortcomings:

1. *Substandard service performance,* which generally involves the retailer's specialized ability. Even if the retailer is competent, he or she must face the problem of quality control when employees also deliver the specialized service.

2. *Substandard retail management.* As mentioned earlier, service retailers often get into business because of a specialized skill that does not necessarily include business skills. The resulting shortcomings might include

   a) lack of a logical, consistent overall strategy
   b) inadequate profit orientation
   c) inadequate consumer orientation
   d) misinterpretation of the external environment
   e) lack of adequate research
   f) poor personnel management
   g) inadequate promotion

OVERCOMING THE SHORTCOMINGS

If the retailer possesses the basic, specialized skills desired by consumers, eliminating the shortcomings is possible. In general, the retailer must focus more attention on potential shortcomings, which means adopting a logical, consistent overall approach to managing the business. We feel the best approach a service retailer can take is strategic retail management, the subject of this book. Although most of our discussion focuses on merchandise retailers, the concepts of strategic retail management have great potential for service retailers. The primary difference between a service retailer's and a merchandise retailer's strategy and management obviously involves merchandise and, perhaps, pricing. Chapters 11 and 14, which deal with merchandise and pricing, contain sections devoted to service retailing.

Each of the shortcomings previously mentioned can be addressed by the strategic retail management process. Measures for overcoming the shortcomings follow, along with the chapter number in which each issue is covered:

1. Develop a logical, consistent overall strategy (Chapter 2).

2. Emphasize a profit orientation (Chapter 3) *and* a consumer orientation (Chapter 2).

3. Analyze and interpret the relevant environments and their influences on the retail business (Chapters 4 and 5).

4. Analyze consumer's behavior (Chapter 6) and segment markets (Chapter 7).

5. Conduct formal or informal research (Chapter 8).

6. Improve human resource management (Chapter 9).

7. Develop a logical promotion strategy (Chapters 15–19).

In addition to these measures, the service retailer can benefit from a good location (Chapter 10) and from planning a service-offering philosophy (Chapter 11). The reader should keep in mind that most of the material in this text is structured to apply to both service and merchandise retailers; some chapters, however, obviously have limited application to service retailing (such as merchandise control in Chapter 13).

NOTES

1.   Ronald Stampfl and Elizabeth Hirschman, "Retail Research: Problems, Potentials, and Priorities," in *Competitive Structure in Retail Markets: The Department Store Perspective,* ed. Ronald Stampfl and Elizabeth Hirschman (Chicago: American Marketing Association, 1980), p. 69.

2.   Remarks by Bert Rosenbloom at the Conference on Theory in Retailing: Traditional and Nontraditional Sources, New York University, April 25, 1980.

3.   *Statistical Abstract of the United States,* 101st ed. (Washington, D.C.: Bureau of the Census, 1980), p. 840.

4.   *Ibid.,* p. 406.

5.   *Ibid.*, p. 557.

6.   *Ibid.*

7.   *CPC Salary Survey,* Formal Report No. 3 (Bethelehem, Pa.: The College Placement Council, July 1981), p. 6.

8.   See Berry and Wilson, "Retailing: The Next Ten Years"; *Journal of Retailing,* Fall 1977, pp. 5–28; William R. Davidson and Alice L. Rodgers, "Change and Challenges in Retailing," *Business Horizons,* January–February 1981, pp. 82–87; J. Barry Mason and Morris L. Mayer, "Retailing Executive View the 1980s," *Atlantic Economic Review,* May–June 1978, pp. 4–10; and "The Future of Retailing," *Retail Week,* March 1, 1981, pp. 24–27.

9.   Berry and Wilson, *op. cit.,* p. 22.

10. "Where America Will Bank," *Newsweek,* October 19, 1981, p. 80.

11. *Stores,* July 1981, p. 10.

12. *Ibid.*

13. Robert D. Buzzell and Marci K. Dew, "Strategic Management Helps Retailers Plan for the Future," *Marketing News,* March 7, 1981, p. 16.

14. William R. Davidson, "To Understand Retailing in 1980s, Analyze Firms' Responses to Trends," *Marketing News,* March 7, 1981, p. 13.

15. *Ibid.*

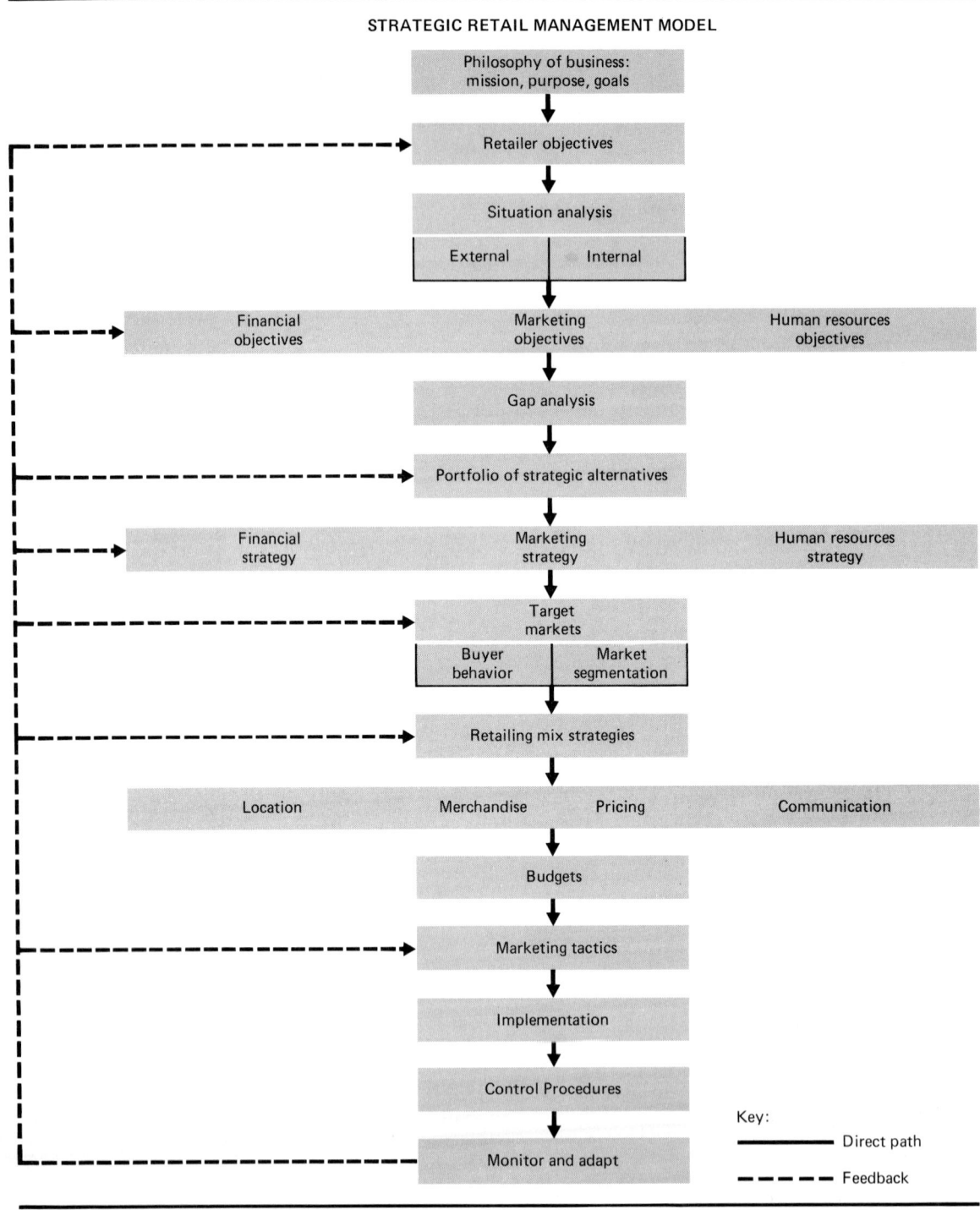

STRATEGIC RETAIL MANAGEMENT MODEL

Philosophy of business: mission, purpose, goals

Retailer objectives

Situation analysis

External | Internal

Financial objectives | Marketing objectives | Human resources objectives

Gap analysis

Portfolio of strategic alternatives

Financial strategy | Marketing strategy | Human resources strategy

Target markets

Buyer behavior | Market segmentation

Retailing mix strategies

Location | Merchandise | Pricing | Communication

Budgets

Marketing tactics

Implementation

Control Procedures

Monitor and adapt

Key:
——— Direct path
– – – Feedback

Chapter 2
Retailing Strategy

LEARNING OBJECTIVES

1. To understand the role and importance of retailing strategy formulation.

2. To understand a logical approach for developing retailing strategy.

INTRODUCTION

Every year thousands of retailers go out of business. For many it simply means finding another job, for some it is the end of a personal dream, and for others failure is the final outcome of many years, possibly a lifetime, of work. While these failures occur, millions of retailers continue to be successful year in and year out. This chapter will discuss and explain how a retailer can increase the chances of success through strategic retail planning. Beginning with some examples of successful strategic planning, we will proceed to the basic concepts of strategy and finally will discuss how a strategy can be developed.

SUCCESSFUL RETAILING STRATEGIES

Some retailers have enjoyed significant growth and success over the past decade. Safeway Stores, Inc., for example, the largest grocery store retailer in the United States, has undertaken several changes in its organization to capitalize on what it sees as growth opportunities. Its management describes the changes this way:

1. We have placed greater emphasis on corporate planning.

2. We have gone outside the Company to supplement our expertise in certain areas.

3. We have consolidated functions that can be performed more effectively or economically on a centralized basis.

4. We have adopted more creative merchandising techniques and have greatly expanded the number of specialty departments in our stores.

5. We have found alternate uses for stores we might otherwise have had to close, and in the process have created new opportunities for internal diversification.

6. We have stepped up our international development program.

7. We have tried to be more accessible to suppliers, the press, and the financial community. At the same time, we have taken a more active role in industry affairs and have worked hard to improve communications with our employees.[1]

Safeway management believes that these changes will allow the organization to continue to grow and remain the number one grocery retailer.

RETAILING PHILOSOPHY

A philosophy of interaction between the retailer and the consumer establishes the base for all retailing decisions. Basically, the retailing philosophy or concept, an adaptation of the marketing concept, rests upon the premise that retailers exist to serve the needs of their customers. The components of this concept imply that the needs of customers are the paramount concern of the retailer and that by satisfying the customer's needs, the retailer can be successful. The **retailing concept** can be organized accordingly:

1. Identify consumer needs.

2. Satisfy customers' needs through an integrated retailing effort.

3. Satisfy customers' needs at a profit.

The retailing concept proposes that the most critical factor contributing to the success of a retail store is the satisfaction of customers' needs. By using this concept, the retailer has a philosophy and understanding on which to base a wide range of retailing decisions. The philosophy can keep the retailer on a successful course by focusing daily decisions on satisfying customers' needs at a profit.

A long-range consumer perspective should be used by the retailer in making retail decisions. Consumers' needs relative to the society's welfare must be part of the basic philosophy of retailing. This *societal retailing concept* adds to the retailing concept a consideration for society's needs in addition to the customers' needs. A restaurant, for example, may serve good-tasting food, but it should also consider the nutritional value of its offerings. Retailers may want to keep their stores cool during the summer months for customers' comfort but must also consider the effect of air conditioning on society's scarce energy resources. Thus, consideration of needs beyond customers' needs is necessary for responsible retailing decision making.

SYSTEMS APPROACH TO DECISION MAKING

A *system* can be defined as a group of units (objects) that combine to operate as a whole, or in unison. The components of a system are defined either by the nature of the system itself or by the organizer of the system. For example, the human body, the ecological system, and the plant system by their nature exist as systems. The components of a system organized by individuals to serve their specific purposes are defined by the human organizers. The interaction of consumers with retailers in the marketplace constitutes a system. A system of retailing (as depicted in Fig. 2.1) has therefore been devised to serve the needs of the consumers in our society. Retailing is a member of the larger distribution system and the consumer is a member of the consumption system. The production system also interacts with the distribution and consumption systems. Of course, our concern is with the retailing system and how retailers can more effectively and efficiently interact with system members.

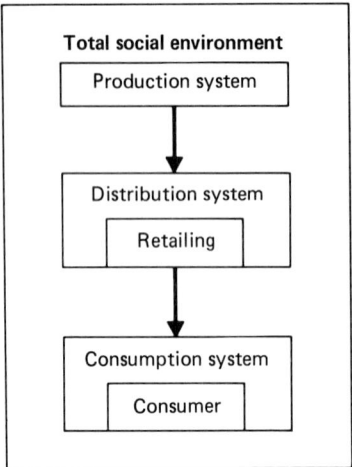

Figure 2.1
Retailing and social needs

Every system, whether it is a **natural system** or a **human-designed system,** has the objective of **optimization,** that is, of obtaining the best possible performance in some respect relative to the environment. In the human-designed system, the designers define the desired optimization level, which becomes the goal for that system. A goal for a retailer may be a desired sales level or profit level. Regardless of how optimization is defined, the system should move in that direction. Optimization is achieved by *adapting to the environment.* In a natural system the movement toward optimization is automatic. The natural system automatically adapts to the changing environment through constant feedback and monitoring. On the other hand, the human-made system does not automatically adapt to the changing environment. For example, the retailer must adapt merchandise offerings to the changing preferences of consumers. Decisions are necessary to do this. The right decisions are required for adaptation and consequently optimization. The retailer desiring a certain level of sales (the goal) must make the correct location, merchandising, pricing, and other retailing decisions.

This suggests that the retailer reaches goals through good decision making based upon adapting to the retail environment. Only an organized decision-making effort on the part of the retailer will accomplish this adaptation. The retailer is involved in continuous attempts to adapt his or her efforts to the constantly changing retail environment. A quote from the G. C. Murphy Company 1980 annual report aptly describes this point: "Only those retailers who can recognize and pursue opportunities brought about by changes in the economy, the industry, and consumer habits will survive and prosper."[2]

RETAILING STRATEGY

To adapt to a constantly changing environment, the retailer must have an indication of what the environment will be in the future. Adaptation to environmental changes may require months or years to complete (as in the case of building a new store). Obviously some type of planning is required to effectively adapt to the environment. R. L. Ackoff defines *planning* as:

> a process that involves making and evaluating each of a set of interrelated decisions before action is required, in a situation in which it is believed that unless action is taken a desired future state is not likely to occur, and that, if appropriate action is taken the likelihood of a favorable outcome can be increased.[3]

As Ackoff's definition suggests, planning can bring about the achievement of a desired goal, which will help the retailer move toward optimization. Without planning, the retailer may reach desired goals, but more likely by chance than through thoughtful decision making. For long-term survival, however, the retailer cannot leave achievement of desired goals to chance. Also note in the definition that appropriate action has some influence on goal achievement. If the outcome of a future event cannot be influenced, then planning is unnecessary. Fortunately for the retailer, most future events can be planned for.

Planning involves taking action in anticipation of future events. A concept known as "strategic windows" suggests that there are certain time periods in which environmental conditions and the retailer's capabilities are at an optimum. The strategic windows are open only at certain points in time. If the retailer has not done any planning, opportunities may be lost and the retailer's capabilities underutilized.

The direction and emphasis a retailer takes are determined by a retailing strategy. More specifically, a **retailing strategy** is the long-term course of action a retailer uses to accomplish future desired goals to effectively compete in the marketplace. This is the *strategic plan* or the specifics of planning.

Formulating a retailing strategy requires four elements: objectives, action, commitment of resources, and controls. Figure 2.2 illustrates the overall process of formulating a retailing strategy. The retailer begins the process by establishing a mission or purpose for being a retailer. Specific objectives flow from the mission. A plan of action is developed to achieve the objectives, and the plan is implemented in the marketplace using appropriate resources. Finally, control mechanisms are established to determine how successful the strategy was in accomplishing the objectives.

Objectives are the quantitative goals a retailer wants to achieve. In effect, objectives give the retailer some direction by stating "where we are going." Objectives should give the retailer a quantitative measure of where the business should be at future points in time. For instance, a grocery store retailer may want to have 5 percent of all grocery store sales in a city by the

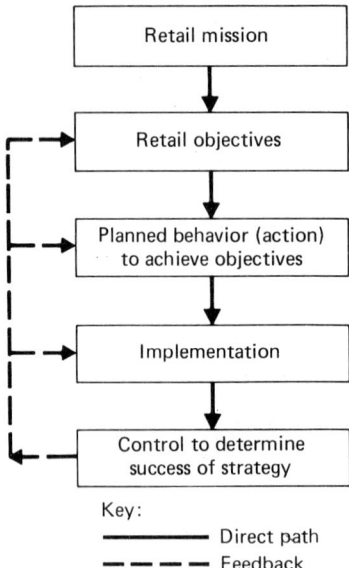

Figure 2.2
Overview of strategy formulation

end of the following year. Quantitative goals normally should be specified for each of the next five years and sketched for 5 years beyond that. Each year the goals should be reevaluated in light of changes that have occurred during the year.

The **action component** of a retailing strategy involves the activities necessary to achieve the stated objectives. This component consists of a *what* element and a *how* element. What is the retailer going to do to accomplish the objectives and how is the retailer going to do this? A major portion of this text relates to the *what* and *how* factors in strategic retailing.

A third element of a good strategy is to have a **commitment of resources** to ensure that the action component is effectively completed. Commitment of resources includes specifying *how much, when, where,* and *who.* Budgeting the action component is necessary, but it is equally important to designate specifically who is responsible for each aspect of the retailing strategy, where it will be completed, and when each of the strategy actions should be completed. Many retailing strategies do not achieve their objectives because specific commitments are not made to the details of implementing the action components.

The final element of retailing strategy is to establish a set of **controls,** methods by which the retailer can determine how well the objectives are being met or have been achieved. A set of controls provides the retailer with feedback that serves as input for future retailing strategy decisions or for adjusting current decisions. The ultimate purpose of controls is to maintain the continuous movement toward the established goals through monitoring performance and indicating what can be done to adjust the retailing effort or the objectives, if the objectives are not being achieved.

All four elements are necessary to develop a retailing strategy. Table 2.1 shows a hypothetical retailer's strategy that uses the four elements. This example indicates the type of detail a retailing strategy should entail. Using this procedure the retailer specifies direction, goals, what must be accomplished to achieve the goals, who is responsible for completing the tasks, when the tasks are to be completed, and how he or she will determine the effectiveness of the strategy.

FORMULATION OF A RETAILING STRATEGY

A retailing strategy provides long-term direction for the retailer and a tactical base for adaptation in the short term. Many firms, including retailers, have experienced difficulty in developing and implementing strategic plans. Some estimates indicate that as many as 80 to 90 percent of all marketing strategies fail to reach their objectives.[4] Certainly the development and implementation of a retailing strategy is a time-consuming, possibly frustrating, and vigorous exercise that influences the future success of the retailer.

The strategy formulation process can be more effectively accomplished if a model is devised for organizing the process. The diagram at the beginning of the chapters presents an outline of a model for retail strategy formulation. The model depicts the process as beginning with a *retailer philosophy* or *mission*. From this mission, *objectives* are established, and the retail *situation* is analyzed both *internally* and *externally*. With a "picture" of the strengths and weaknesses of the business and the problems and opportunities presented by the external environment, the retailer establishes *specific* objectives and develops a *gap analysis*. This leads to a search for *strategic alternatives* and the development of a portfolio of internal, and possibly external, strategic alternatives. At this point, *target markets* are selected as the beginning of a *retailing strategy* and, finally, the specific *retailing mix* is determined for the chosen target markets. The selected strategy or strategies are implemented through the establishment of *budgets* and commitment and deployment of resources. *Feedback* and *control* mechanisms are also established. Finally, *adaptation* and change will occur.

It is essential to the understanding and integration of this chapter and the entire text to periodically review the strategic retail management model to maintain a perspective of the retail management process. (The model is reproduced at the beginning of each chapter.)

Retailer Mission

The **mission** or **purpose** provides the retailer with a general direction for the organization. Essentially, the retailer answers the question "What is my

Table 2.1
Hypothetical retailing strategy

OBJECTIVES

Increase gross profit from 21.5 to 23.0% this year.

ACTION

What   1. Reduce lower-margin, slower-moving merchandise.

2. Increase emphasis on higher-margin merchandise.

How   1.   Analyze margins and sales of merchandise for past 3 years; eliminate products with margins less than 16% and turnover rate less than 3.0.

2.a) Feature higher-margin items in advertisements.

b) Relocate higher-margin items in more desirable areas in store.

c) Add complementary merchandise with margins greater than 30%.

d) Identify and possibly increase the price of selected merchandise.

RESOURCES

Who   1.   Department managers will complete margin analysis and merchandise elimination.

2.a) Advertising and department managers will determine which merchandise to feature in advertising.

b) Department managers will determine location for higher-margin merchandise.

c) Buyers and department managers will determine which merchandise items to add.

d) Department managers and store merchandising managers will determine merchandise for possible price increases.

Where   In-store analysis.

When   1.a) Margin analysis by March 31.

b) Merchandise elimination by June 30.

2.a) Feature items for advertising by January 31.

b) Begin advertising March 1.

c) Location decisions and changes by February 15.

d) Merchandise addition decisions by January 31. Begin ordering February 1.

e) Determine price increases by March 1.

f) Increase prices gradually beginning March 31.

CONTROL

---

1. Determine sales history previous to changes for all action decision areas.

2. Monitor sales and margins; report biweekly.

business?" The retailer must not only establish the basis of the business enterprise but also a connection to the market. The mission should also provide *future* direction.

Certainly the aspects of the retailing concept should be incorporated into the retailer's mission. Various types of missions—economic, social, moral—can be identified. An economic mission may be stated in terms of making money. A moral mission may be to help the poor or the handicapped.

Theodore Levitt states that the mission should be developed at the most meaningful level of generalization. A mission might be to satisfy the clothing needs of male consumers and to attain continued retail growth. To generalize clothing needs beyond this level might broaden the scope of the business into new problem areas focusing on completely different strategic issues and involving completely different merchandise.

Table 2.2 indicates the purposes or mission of Dayton Hudson Corporation. Note that profit is a part of the corporate mission, but it is not the only purpose of existence. Also note that the corporate mission not only provides for the ultimate consumer, but also for other markets with which Dayton Hudson interacts.

Objectives

Objectives provide the retailer with short- and long-term goals within a specified time frame. They act as concrete measures of direction in accomplishing the retailer's purpose or mission. In addition, objectives function as a benchmark for evaluating how well the retailer is attaining the stated mission.

Similar to the retailer's mission, the personal values of the retailer or retailing executives enter into the selection of objectives. An individual that

**Table 2.2
Dayton Hudson's corporate mission**

RETAILING: IT'S A BUSINESS OF PEOPLE

Retailing is a business of people. Nowhere is this more evident than in the strategic mission to which Dayton-Hudson Corporation is committed.

Our mission is to serve people. First and foremost, this means serving the people who are our *customers*—and doing so better than our competition.

It also means serving the people in our *communities* by contributing to the development of a strong and healthy environment in which to live and work.

And it means serving the people who are our *shareholders* by providing them with a superior return on their investment.

There is yet another very important group of people Dayton-Hudson is dedicated to serving. That is its *employees*. It is their effort which makes it possible for the Corporation to fulfill its commitment to its customers, communities, and shareholders.

Source: Dayton Hudson Corporation, *Annual Report* (Minneapolis, Minn., 1980), p. 4.

has strong personal convictions about social values and employee welfare
may set objectives that focus on providing high quality products for a fair
price with emphasis on merchandise innovation, good salaries, and a pleasant working atmosphere. The variety of objectives a retailer seeks to achieve
can vary widely. Marketing objectives may be defined as sales, store image,
or market share; finance objectives as profit or return to stockholders; and
organizational objectives as employee turnover or attracting a certain type of
labor force. Regardless of the level or type of objectives, they should be
specified quantitatively with a time period for accomplishment. Table 2.3
gives some examples of objectives for various aspects of the retail organization.

    As an example of corporate objectives, Hilton Hotels' objectives over
the past ten years are stated as follows:

> Management's objectives during this period were: to produce above average
> growth in earnings per share; to increase the return on stockholders' eq-
> uity; to reduce the Company's vulnerability to the extreme business cycle
> patterns which historically have plagued the lodging industry; to build a

Table 2.3
Sample retail objectives

Marketing Objectives	
Sales	Increase sales from $100,000 to $120,000 in the next year and to $150,000 within two years.
	Maintain unit sales at 20,000 units for the next six months.
Market share	Increase market share of local grocery market from 15 to 18% in the next year, with a five-year goal of 25% market share.
Store	Change store image from lower quality–high volume image to higher-quality image in next two years.
	Maintain prestige store image.
Financial Objectives	
Profit	Increase net profit margin from 2.5 to 3.0% this year with a five-year goal of 4.5%.
	Increase return on net worth from 18 to 20% within two years.
	Maintain a dollar profit of $75,000 next year.
Return to stockholders	Pay a minimum of $2.80-per-share dividends for the next three years.
Organizational Objectives	
Employee Turnover	Reduce employee turnover from 25 to 20% next year with a five-year goal of 10%.
Sales force	Upgrade educational and experience level of employees to a minimum of one year of college and three years' exper-ience over the next eighteen months.

degree of financial stability which would enable the Company to take advantage of exceptional business opportunities and internally finance a substantial portion of expansion and development; and to give stockholders regular and growing dividends and appreciation in the value of their holdings.[5]

Objectives should be realistic in terms of past performance and competitive abilities. Unrealistic objectives do not aid in achieving desirable results and actually may hinder the development of a good strategy. The retailer's objectives are selected in light of the stated mission, but the objectives may be redefined after analyzing the environments in which the retailer must compete.

Situation Analysis

Before a retailer can develop a strategy to adapt to the retail environment, a detailed analysis of the environment must be undertaken. The retailer should be able to identify opportunities and threats in the environment, assess retail capabilities, and evaluate competitive strengths and weaknesses through a situation analysis. The outcome of a **situation analysis** should enable the retailer to better define both the objectives and how they can be attained through a retailing strategy. A situation analysis consists of examining the macroenvironment, task environment, retailer strengths and weaknesses, and the factors necessary for success in the competitive environment.

Macroenvironmental Analysis.   The macroenvironment is the broadest of the environments encountered by the retailer. Within the macroenvironment are the demographic, economic, political and legal, social and cultural, technological, and natural environments. Each has an influence separately and all interact together to affect the success of the retailer's efforts. These environments are essentially out of the control of the retailer, and thus the retailer must adapt to them as they exist. Chapter 4 discusses macroenvironmental analysis and the macroenvironment's influence on retail decisions.

Task Environment Analysis.   The task environment is a subset of the macroenvironment. Consisting of competitors, marketing intermediaries, and consumers, the task environment has day-to-day influence on the retailer's efforts. A thorough analysis of competing retailers, other marketing institutions and consumers is vitally important to the development of a successful retailing strategy. The process for analyzing competition and marketing intermediaries is discussed in Chapter 5, and a discussion of consumer behavior analysis follows in Chapter 6.

The retailer's ability to adapt to the changing macroenvironment and task environment is a function of his or her capabilities. All retailers have different strengths and weaknesses that can affect their ability to succeed.

The retail self-analysis and the analysis of the factors for success provide the retailer with an indication of the opportunities that can most effectively be pursued in the environment.

Retail Self-Analysis.   Before a retailer can realistically plan a course for future behavior, a concise evaluation of his or her ability to compete is necessary. The ideal situation is one in which retailers employ their own retailing strengths against the weaknesses of competing retailers. Although the ideal situation seldom occurs, the retailer should utilize any strengths that may exist and not attempt to compete from a weak position. Table 2.4 presents a self-analysis for a hypothetical retailer.

After establishing strengths and weaknesses, the retailer must determine the impact of these factors on a retailing strategy. A strong location or price advantage can be effectively exploited in the marketplace, while an unclear image can negatively influence the ability to compete against well-positioned retailers. As an example, the Kroger Company perceives its strengths as follows:

1. Retail *stores* that are young in age, modern in design and decor, and contemporary in their appeal to customers;

2. Dedication to *research* in all its forms in order to determine what kind of stores to build and where to build them;

3. Demonstrated excellence in the *merchandising* of the *perishable products* so influential in the customer's choice of where to shop;

4. *Strategically located,* highly efficient manufacturing facilities providing a wide variety of quality label products uniquely available to our customers;

5. *Marketing strategies based on every day low prices* the customer can depend on consistently in the search for values;

Table 2.4
Self-analysis for a hypothetical retailer

STRENGTHS	WEAKNESSES
1. Personal relationships with customers	1. Inadequate definition of customer
2. Dominant market share position	2. Ambiguous service policies
3. Leadership in merchandise innovation	3. Too many levels of reporting in the organization
4. Merchandising efficiency — high turnover of inventories	4. Lack of quantitative goals
5. Effectiveness in sales promotion	
6. Quality sales force	
7. Highly efficient, low-cost facilities	
8. Massive availability of capital	

6. An *executive team* which combines youth and experience in a blend of talents pledged to the attainment of aggressive goals.[6]

Analysis of retail capabilities is discussed in Chapter 20 in relation to the retailing audit.

Factors for Success. Certain minimum performance levels or factors must exist for retailers to be successful. Although these relate to all types of retailers, some success factors are more important for certain types of retailers. Applebee and Nitzberg found six success factors in the operating of department stores.[7]

First, *location* is considered a primary success factor. Most retail stores draw their customers from the local population. Obviously, the more convenience-oriented the consumer and the product, the closer the proximity of the store to its customers. Department stores might be able to attract customers from more than fifteen miles away while the discount retailer may not be able to attract customers from farther away than five miles.

Second, *merchandising decisions* are the key to satisfying customer needs. Having the right merchandise at the right time at the right place is crucial for success, but the exact conditions may vary by type of store. A consumer may be willing to wait for furniture or clothing but want grocery or service items immediately.

Third, attracting and keeping *good personnel* is critical to the success of a retail store. The retail store that relies heavily on personal contact with customers will find this more crucial to its success than a store with limited personal contact. Generally, shopping stores will be required to attract sufficient high-quality personnel to provide information and aid the retail customer.

STRATEGY IN ACTION 2.1

Book Retailing: B. Dalton

One of the major growth areas of retailing during the 1970s was book retailing. B. Dalton, a book retailer that is part of Dayton Hudson, was one of the more successful book retailers. They have "built a reputation for sharp marketing moves based on thorough research." The name itself was based on research that indicated a preference for "B. Dalton" because it was "a little English and a little personal." To increase efficiency, the chain has added an electronic point of sale (POS) inventory system, changed book and magazine assortments to keep up with altered buying patterns, and shifted store personnel to obtain more productive usage of their time, among other strategic moves. One observer of the book retailing trade notes that when the competitive smoke clears, one of the remaining book retailers will be B. Dalton.

Source: Adapted from "Chains Add New Chapter to Book Retailing," pp. 24–34. Reprinted by permission from *Chain Store Age/Executive* © February 1980. Copyright Lebhar-Friedman, Inc. 425 Park Avenue, New York, NY 10022.

Fourth, the *store layout*, the method by which merchandise is organized and presented to the customer, has an impact on the success of a retailer. The combination of merchandise and layout contributes heavily to the store's overall image.

Fifth, *managerial capabilities* are crucial to successful retail operations. Many retailers fail because of insufficient managerial know-how. Having adequate background knowledge of the type of retailing, understanding competition and customers, and being able to make strategic and tactical decisions with this knowledge are necessary for success. General management capabilities are requirements for any successful retailer, but they are especially crucial in highly competitive situations.

Sixth, managing the *financial aspects* of the organization is a key to long-term retail success. The retailer's cash flow is critical to surviving slower periods of retail sales. This problem may be most acute for the small retailer and the new retailer.

After completing a situation analysis, the retailer should be able to determine what business should be continued or undertaken, what merchandise should be carried, what competitors pose the greatest threats, how consumers may respond to retailing efforts, where the greatest opportunities exist, what the environmental and competitive trends are, and what possibilities the retailer possesses for achieving the objectives previously defined.

A complete analysis of opportunities and strengths results in a general forecast of future market conditions and the individual retailer's ability to effectively compete under those conditions. The Levitz Furniture Corporation's perspective or future conditions in 1981 is presented in Table 2.5.

Table 2.5
Levitz perspective of future conditions

Those retailers of home furnishings that have the financial strength to meet consumer demands for quality merchandise, value, convenience, and immediate delivery will prosper significantly and will be far more discriminating in their merchandise purchases. We feel they understand that Levitz offers considerable savings and value and may be the preferred choice when home furnishings purchases are contemplated.

Short term: The outlook for retailers, particularly those of large-ticket merchandise, will continue to be very difficult. High interest rates and recessionary pressures will result in a significant consolidation in our industry. We view this trend as an opportunity to expand market share, and we plan to exploit the situation.

Longer term: We believe the prospects for our industry and Levitz have never looked brighter. The baby-boom generation is now entering the home-buying stage and is forming families. A record number of individuals over the next 15 years will comprise the 30- to 45-year-old age group. Many families will be two income families. They will have greater earning power and discretionary income, and an increased desire to live comfortably.

Source: Levitz Furniture Corporation, *Annual Report* (Miami, Florida, 1981), p. 3.

Gap Analysis

After completing the situation analysis, the retailer forecasts the future performance (in terms of sales, profits, market share, and other aspects) under existing strategies relative to the environment. He or she then compares that forecast with the objectives stated earlier. The gap or difference between the two reflects the degree of change the retailer must undertake to close the gap. A simple illustration is presented in Table 2.6.

The table illustrates the gap between expected and desired performance with no strategic changes. In the sales situation, a small gap appears in two years, which suggests some longer-term strategic changes are necessary, and more drastic measures may have to be planned for the fourth and fifth years. The profit example indicates that both immediate and long-term strategic changes are necessary. A declining profit situation is forecast and the retailer should take steps to reverse this trend.

A gap analysis provides the retailer with a quantitative indication of the extent of change necessary to bring the organization's performance in line with the desired levels of performance. Generally, the greater the gap, the more strategic changes are necessary. The next step is to develop strategies to close the gap.

It is possible that a retailer may alter objectives after analyzing the situational environment. An objective of increasing sales 20 percent may be revised downward after a retailer discovers a slowing economic picture and stronger competition. Thus, the outcome of a situation analysis may also change the gap analysis because of revised objectives.

Selecting Strategic Alternatives

Once it is determined that strategic changes are necessary, a search for strategic alternatives begins, usually with an examination of internal strategic

Table 2.6
A gap analysis

	CURRENT YEAR	YEAR				
		1	2	3	4	5
Current Sales ($000)	160	—	—	—	—	—
Forecast sales ($000)	—	170	180	185	188	190
Sales objective ($000)	—	170	185	195	205	220
Gap		0	5	10	17	30
Current profit (percent of sales)	1.50	—	—	—	—	—
Forecast profit	—	1.50	1.40	1.40	1.35	1.30
Profit objective	—	1.75	1.80	1.90	2.00	2.10
Gap		0.25	0.40	0.50	0.65	0.80

alternatives. If these strategies will not close the gap, it may be necessary to look to external strategies such as acquisition or vertical integration.

Portfolio Analysis.   During the past few years several concepts have been devised to aid the retailer in selecting the appropriate alternative strategy. One of the major conceptual contributions has been portfolio analysis, a method for arriving at a clearer perspective of the retailer's situation. The analysis of the retailer's portfolio or existing situation leads to recommendations for retailing strategies depending upon the location of the retailer in the *portfolio matrix*. A matrix may consist of market growth on one axis (identified as high growth and low growth) and market share (identified as dominant and subordinate share) on the other axis. Within the matrix are four cells, each with certain characteristics. By placing the retail operations or various decision areas of the retail operation, such as merchandise, services, or different locations (chain store), within the portfolio matrix the retailer can establish an improved base from which to select an appropriate strategic alternative.

In selecting a retailing strategy based upon portfolio analysis, the retailer is also linking the retailing strategy to the financial strategy. A retailing strategy identifies the types of efforts with which the financial strategy of the retail operation will interrelate. The Appendix to this chapter presents a more detailed analysis of portfolio management and how it applies to retail strategy selection.

Strategic Alternatives.   After the retailer analyzes the situation, he or she must select the strategy from among a wide range of strategy alternatives. The strategies generally can be grouped in terms of growth, selectivity, and productivity.[8] (See Table 2.7 for a summary outline of alternative strategies.)

Table 2.7
Summary outline of strategic alternatives

Growth Strategies	*Selectivity Strategies*
Penetration	Reduced scope
Market development	Elimination
Product-line development	De-integration
Diversification	
Concentric diversification	*Productivity Strategies*
Conglomerate diversification	Operating efficiencies
External (integration)	Managerial efficiencies
Backward integration	
Forward integration	
Horizontal integration	

STRATEGY IN ACTION 2.2

Dayton Hudson: Strategy for Growth

In the past, Dayton Hudson Corporation concentrated primarily on department stores for growth. Today only 30 percent of its sales are accounted for by department stores. Their three other chains are now looked to for continued growth at the 17 percent annual level enjoyed over the past 5 years through 1980.

Target discount stores, Mervyn's, and B. Dalton, a book retailer, provide most of Dayton Hudson's growth. Over the next five years the company plans to invest $2.7 billion for 750 stores, with 85 percent going to these three chains. The funds for expansion are based upon a "strict profit formula."

Each of the chains is given free rein by Dayton Hudson. Strategy is established by each chain, and the "rewards" for growth are based on the profit the strategy generates. As of early 1982, this strategy has been quite successful in achieving growth for Dayton Hudson Corporation.

Source: Adapted from "In the News," FORTUNE Magazine, January 11, 1982, p. 7.

Growth strategies are based on the premise that growth increases the chances of survival. Theoretically, growth results from adapting to change, which increases the chances of surviving the changing environment. Growth is the goal of most retailers. Either in terms of sales or profits or geographical expansion, growth is a part of the retailer's strategy. The four common internal strategic approaches to achieve growth are penetration, product development, market development, and diversification. A fifth growth strategy, integration, might be classified as an external strategy. Figure 2.3 shows how the four internal growth strategies interrelate.

The strategy of **penetration** to achieve growth relies upon obtaining an increased share of the present competitive market. A penetration strategy might be appropriate when the retailer has a cost advantage. In most situations, the retailer will be growing at the expense of direct competitors. Kroger's increasing its market share at the expense of local grocery retailers would be an example of a penetration strategy.

	Existing offerings	New offerings
Existing markets	Penetration	Product development
New markets	Market development	Diversification

Figure 2.3
Internal growth strategies
Source: Adapted from Roger A. Kerin and Robert A. Peterson, *Strategic Marketing Problems: Cases and Comments,* Second Edition, p. 6. Copyright © 1981 by Allyn and Bacon, Inc. Used with permission.

Market development as a growth strategy is based on expanding into market segments not presently served. This may entail geographic expansion, such as the fast-food retailers that expand into foreign markets or K mart, which now builds in smaller cities. Marshall Field's expansion into the Dallas market with four new stores is a good example of market development. More subtly, market development may involve attracting new target markets in the same geographical area.

Growth through **product development** means adding products or product lines to existing offerings. Convenience stores adding gasoline to their line of merchandise, gas stations adding convenience products, Woolco adding designer names to its merchandise, and grocery stores adding books, lawn products, and many other items are current examples of product development. Montgomery Ward offering dental services is a surprising product development, as is Sears offering financial services.

The most expansive, and probably also the riskiest, internal growth strategy is **diversification.** Along with increased risk is the possibility of higher profits if the strategy is successful: the greatest growth usually is associated with the greatest risk. Diversification is based on adding new products in new markets. It can be accomplished through additional merchandise lines that appeal to new market segments, which can be geographically, demographically, or psychographically new.

Normally a retailer diversifies in a concentric manner. *Concentric diversification* involves moving into closely related areas of current retailing. Adding merchandise lines that relate to existing lines and moving into geographical proximity to existing retail locations is an example. The Carter Hawley Hale Stores' acquisition of the Wanamaker and Thalhimers chains is an example of concentric diversification.

A broader form of diversification is *conglomerate diversification*. This moves the retailer into unrelated lines of retailing. Examples are K mart's purchase of Furr's Cafeteria and Sears' purchase of Dean Witter Reynolds, a financial services firm. The major problem arising from a conglomerate diversification is that the retailer may be moving away from its strengths. Sears, however, believes an innovative method of selling financial services can be developed using Sears' existing merchandising strengths.

Retailing growth can be attained through *external strategies* also. **Integration** brings together two or more separate business units for purposes of growth and/or economies of scale. Essentially, integration involves an upward or downward acquisition or merger within the same channel of distribution (*vertical integration*) or a merger with a competing retailer (*horizontal integration*). Target Stores' purchase of another discount retailer, Ayr-Way Stores, is an excellent example of horizontal integration. One writer commented, "They have a good fit in merchandise and operating philosophies."

Backward integration, or integrating with sources of supply, is done typically to ensure a steady source of merchandise. Sears, for instance, owns a significant interest in serveral of its merchandise suppliers and Holiday

Inns manufactures some of its own motel supplies. Retailers become part of *forward integration* when manufacturers or suppliers merge or acquire them in an attempt to obtain more dependable outlets for their products. The major automobile tire manufacturers, for example, have developed a system of retail outlets, and PepsiCo acquired Pizza Hut several years ago for growth and distribution purposes.

A retailer can also achieve certain objectives by becoming smaller. The three **selectivity strategies** are **reduced scope, elimination,** and **de-integration**. These strategies are largely based on the "80-20" rule," that is, roughly 80 percent of the retailer's profit will result from 20 percent of the merchandise offered. This concept indicates that it is possible to become smaller and more profitable concurrently.

The strategy of *reduced scope* focuses on reducing the geographical scope, the inventory level, or the types of merchandise offered. J. C. Penney eliminated its low-profit departments, added more fashion-related merchandise to their offerings, and also closed its unprofitable chain of Treasury discount stores. A&P has been reducing its geographical scope for several years by closing smaller, unprofitable stores.

Elimination views selectivity from the market perspective. The elimination of certain market segments or customers as a focus is the basis for this strategy. Eliminating special services for elderly customers because they were ineffective is an example. In that case the change in strategy is based on the elimination of the elderly as a special market segment. A home-improvement center that de-emphasizes construction purchases is another example. The removal of special discounts or very early morning hours of operation may result because of the strategic decision to de-emphasize the construction market.

The final method of selective strategic retailing is *de-integration*. Selectivity is much broader with the divestiture of entire segments of the retailing organization. As an example, Fisher Foods sold its California division because of a forecast lack of growth possibilities.

Selectivity strategies are becoming more prevalent in retailing because of the slower growth in population and income in the United States. Pruning back operations, improved use of resources, and making the organization "leaner" may increase the possibility of exploiting future retail opportunities. Many retailers believe, at least during the 1980s, that they no longer can achieve increased profitability through rapid growth. Increased strategic planning and more efficient use of resources are necessary for continued profit growth.

Productivity strategies center on increasing the efficiency of current resources. They fit well into the retailer's perceptions of the current and future environment. Specifically, **operating efficiency** and **managerial efficiency** are the two productivity strategies retailers can employ.

Operating efficiency strategies focus on obtaining more productivity in less space. Improvements in operating efficiency include increasing inventory turnover, lowering operating costs for credit, personnel, energy, security, physical distribution, and other factors, and utilizing retail store space more effectively.

To increase productivity, Woolco is in the process of developing "stores of the future," which will range in size from 70,000 to 90,000 square feet, a substantial reduction from the current 115,000-square-foot average. Woolco claims that through improved store layout, taller and narrower display counters, and improved display techniques the same amount of merchandise can fit into the smaller stores. Sears is starting to carry less inventory, to hire college students part-time to replace more expensive full-time salespeople, and to charge for delivery of durable goods as methods of increasing productivity. Some retailers are spending more of their retail advertising budget on television in an attempt to be more efficient. Increased emphasis on operating efficiency is a key to profitable retailing in the future.

Using managerial talent more effectively can improve retail productivity immensely. Better use of managers' time in the areas of scheduling of activities, preparation for meetings, and allocation of decision-making time between lower-level employees and managers can aid the retail organization. Reducing managerial turnover and dropouts from management training programs can improve the use of managerial training resources. While much of the emphasis in productivity strategies is on operating efficiency, several changes in management techniques can bring about better use of managerial talent. Stasch and Lanktree recommend a training process for managers in developing strategic plans and further suggest that effective use of staff people in the organization enhances the strategic planning process.[9] In addition to getting more and better results from managerial personnel, using personnel for their capabilities can improve a retailer's productivity.

At this point in the strategic management process, the retailer has set general and specific objectives, analyzed the existing environmental situation, and determined the gap between objectives and expected performance. The foregoing analysis should provide the retailer with an improved perspective of the best strategies to implement. Although the growth, selectivity, and productivity strategies were presented independently they are not mutually exclusive. They can be combined in various ways to develop a strategic portfolio for implementation.

Selecting Target Markets

A retailing strategy is usually developed for certain subsets or segments of the market rather than for the entire market. Selecting **target market** segments enables the retailer to employ resources more effectively and efficiently. If properly developed, the segmentation process should also allow the retailer to compete on a favorable basis. The process of selecting the segments that will offer the greatest opportunity is discussed at length in Chapter 7.

Developing Retailing Mix Strategies

The retailer determines functional strategies in light of the environment and the characteristics of each market segment he or she attempts to attract. Several general strategies exist for determining the variation and extent of retailing mixes, which consist of location, merchandise, pricing, and communication decisions. An *undifferentiated strategy* views the market as relatively homogeneous; therefore, one retailing mix suffices for the market. A *differentiated strategy* entails the development of separate retailing mixes for each heterogeneous market segment. A *concentrated strategy* focuses one mix for one, or a separate mix for a few, of the selected market segments. The final strategy of retailing mixes is an *aggregated* or *countersegmentation strategy* in which all segments are grouped by similarities, and separate retailing mixes are developed for each of the segment groups.

Developing Functional Strategies

Decisions about retailing mixes must be made in an integrated framework based on the retailer's environment. Although discussed separately in the text, each of the decisions and functional strategies influence one another. The disastrous effects of the Where Economy Originated (WEO) strategy of A&P, for example, shows how a lack of integration can be damaging. A&P attempted to lower prices and increase volume while changing the merchandise strategy to increase the number of store brands offered. Unfortunately, the decrease in national brands alienated some consumers and the stores were not large enough to handle the additional volume necessary to cover the price reductions. The pricing strategy was not well integrated with the location, the size of stores, and the merchandising strategies. Functional strategies establish the specifics of the *what* and *how* action components of the retailing mix strategies.

Location Strategy.   One of the most critical decisions a retailer makes is where to locate. That decision involves the type of consumers that can be attracted, the relative location of competition and complementary merchandise, and the volume of customer traffic that can be achieved. It is vitally important to integrate all functional strategies, but location and merchandise are particularly interrelated. A certain type of retailer can prosper in one location, while another type of retailer could fail in the same location. The location strategy decision is examined in Chapter 10.

Merchandise Strategy.   The selection of the type of merchandise to offer consumers is the basis for the remaining strategies. Which general merchandise area to enter — sporting goods, groceries, dry-cleaning services, or a variety — is a function of the situation analysis, the particular strengths of the retailer, and the factors for success in the merchandise considered. Specific decisions must then be made on the particular items to carry, the quantity, inventory control, and the combination of suppliers to patronize. These strategy decisions are discussed in Chapters 11, 12, and 13.

Pricing Strategy.   What price to attach to the retail offering is a difficult task. Once the general strategies for retailing and finance are determined, a broad pricing strategy emerges. High margin–low volume or low margin–high volume are the two basic strategies. The target market and the competitive market are of primary importance in the decision about targeting individual items for pricing. Chapter 14 discusses strategies for pricing retail merchandise.

Communication Strategy.   No matter how well the retailer selects a location, merchandise, and prices, if few consumers know of these decisions, the chances of success are minimal. Through advertising, personal selling, sales promotion, atmospherics, and customer services the retailer communicates and establishes a position in the consumer's mind. This position defines the retailer to the consumer in terms of what the retailer is and what the retailer has to offer. Strategic communication decisions are examined in Chapters 15 through 19.

Strategy Implementation

Earlier in this chapter a hypothetical retailing strategy was developed in detail (Table 2.1). For implementation to occur, the resources element must be developed. The first aspect of resources is **budgeting.**

Without financial support even the most effective strategy can falter. The budgeting process determines the amount of financial resources that should be committed to the retailing strategy, how much support should be given to merchandise, promotion, personnel, credit, and so on. In most instances, funds are not available to complete every facet of a strategy and, unfortunately, some areas of the retailing strategy may suffer. A budgeting process should be developed to support the elements and strategies that will be most beneficial to the long-term success of the retailer. These decisions are not easy but they must be made. Chapter 3 deals with budgeting and financial planning.

The other aspects of the resources component concern personnel decisions and scheduling of the strategy implementation. Without adequate personnel it is difficult to enact any retailing strategy effectively. Obtaining, motivating, and retaining quality personnel are crucial to implementing any strategy. These issues are discussed in Chapter 9.

Retailing Tactics

Strategies establish a long-term retail interface with the market but day-to-day decisions are also necessary for the effective operation of a retail store. **Tactics** are short-term marketing decisions that flow from the retailing strategies. Planning for future short-term possibilities, or events, helps prepare the retailer to act quickly in the short term. Functional strategies establish long-term goals that are reflected in day-to-day operating decisions. When to change prices, how often, and how much are tactical decisions influenced by the environment and pricing strategies. Tactical decisions are discussed in each functional area of the text.

Control Procedures

The final element of the retailing strategy is control. **Control procedures** are methods by which the retailer follows up a strategy to determine its impact on performance. The retailer should establish procedures to determine whether the goals he or she set were actually achieved in the time frame desired. Without control procedures the strategic process loses much of its effectiveness. The results of the control component are used as feedback for future strategy decisions. If no control/feedback procedures were established, previous ineffective strategies could be repeated. The control component and strategic control procedures are discussed in Chapter 20.

Monitoring and Adapting

The feedback from the control procedures may indicate that the retailing strategy achieved its purpose or it may indicate varying degrees of unsatisfactory performance. When the results of a retailing strategy indicate a lack of success in achieving goals, some type of adaptation should occur. The degree of change should relate to the level of ineffectiveness. In some instances only slight modifications are required, while other instances may require a completely new strategy. Monitoring and adapting existing strategies and tactics are discussed in each functional chapter and in Chapter 20.

SUMMARY

In a general fashion, the process for developing a strategic retailing plan was presented. The remaining chapters of the text discuss most of these aspects in detail. It might be of value to the reader to periodically return to this chapter to see where each strategic decision fits into the overall process. At this point the reader should have an appreciation for the importance of strategic management in retailing and for how a retailer can go about developing a strategic approach to the marketplace.

KEY CONCEPTS

Retailing concept	Gap analysis
Systems approach	Portfolio analysis
Natural system	Strategic alternatives
Human-designed system	Growth strategies
Optimization	Penetration
Retailing strategy	Market development
Objectives	Product development
Action components	Diversification
Commitment of resources	Integration
Controls	Selectivity strategies
Retailer mission	Reduced scope
Situation analysis	Elimination
Macroenvironmental analysis	De-integration
Task environment analysis	Productivity strategies
Retail self-analysis	Operating efficiency
Factors for success	Managerial efficiency

Target markets   Budgeting
Retailing mix strategies   Retailing tactics
Functional strategies   Control procedures

REVIEW QUESTIONS

1. Explain the retailing concept and how it relates to retail decision making.
2. Why is the systems approach a valuable perspective for retailing?
3. What is a retailing strategy? What should a strategy do for the retailer?
4. Briefly explain each of the four elements of the retailing strategy.
5. How is a statement of mission valuable to the retailer?
6. What is the purpose of a situation analysis?
7. Why does the retailer engage in a retail self-analysis and identify the factors for success before developing a retailing strategy?
8. What is the purpose of the gap analysis?
9. What does portfolio analysis do for the retailer's strategy formulation?
10. Explain the difference in orientation of the five growth strategies.
11. Why have the selectivity strategies become more important recently?
12. What are some methods of increasing productivity through operating efficiency?
13. How do target markets relate to strategy formulation?
14. What are retailing tactics? How do they relate to retailing strategies?
15. Explain the role of control procedures in the strategic retailing process.

LEARNING EXERCISES

1. Interview two local retailers about how they formulate their retailing strategies. How different are their methods from the process discussed in this chapter? Why do these differences exist?
2. Select five retail organizations from the retailing literature and organize, as well as possible, their retailing strategies. Possible sources for information would include company annual reports, *Chain Store Age Executive*, *Retail Week*, *Progressive Grocer*, *Fortune*, *Forbes*, and *Business Week*.

DECISION SITUATION 2.1: **THE GARDEN CENTER**

Joan started the Garden Center fifteen years ago while working full-time at a hospital. She had always enjoyed working with plants in her backyard greenhouse and decided to sell some of the plants she raised. She began by selling mostly vegetable plants and a few houseplants.

Today Joan's operation is much larger; she works full-time at the center and has fifteen other employees. The Garden Center is the largest plant store within one hundred miles. Many new products and services have been added, including wedding services, plant rentals, landscaping services, a "hospital" for sick plants, and a large gift store. With all these additions, the profits for the Garden Center have remained flat for the past five years. It appears that profits for the current year will be lower than last year.

Joan recently had a student group examine her business to determine why her profit performance was not better. Although the students did not give her any specific recommendations, Joan thought that they did find the problem. The students' report indicated that the Garden Center's size is inappropriate. That is, a larger or more specialized store could be more profitable. Joan was trying to offer services that required a bigger operation.

QUESTIONS

1. Would you recommend a growth or specialization strategy to Joan? Why?

2. If Joan chooses a growth strategy, how would you recommend that growth be achieved?

3. If Joan chooses a specialization strategy, how would you recommend that it be achieved?

DECISION SITUATION 2.2: **ABC LUMBER AND HARDWARE**

Jim is a recent marketing graduate of State University. He is now the manager of ABC Lumber and Hardware, which is owned by his father. His father has indicated that he no longer wants to work at the store and intends for Jim to be in complete control.

Jim is trying to determine what changes, if any, he will make in the store. He has identified certain advantages and problem areas.

Advantages include a good relationship with area contractors. In fact, 70 percent of the store's sales are to contractors. The store also has a good reputation in the town of sixty thousand. The store also enjoys good name recognition and a price advantage owing to low overhead.

Disadvantages are in some ways mirror images of the advantages. The boom in do-it-yourself home improvements has almost completely bypassed ABC. The small volume that comes from this segment is usually in standard items such as lumber, but there are very few sales for high-profit items such as fixtures. The price advantage may also be misleading: the low overhead results from its location in an old building in what is now a deteriorating section of the city.

QUESTIONS

1. Would you recommend that Jim try to correct ABC's problems or exploit its advantages?

2. How can ABC get more of the noncontractor business? Will these actions hurt the contractor business? Should ABC try for more of the noncontractor business?

3. How can ABC keep the contractor business and get more of the noncontractor business?

Appendix
Portfolio Analysis

EXPERIENCE CURVES

Much of the recent portfolio analysis conceptualization has resulted from the Profit Impact of Marketing Strategies (PIMS) conducted by the Strategic Planning Institute. The PIMS project is an empirical study of 150 firms with more than 1,000 individual business units. Its major focus is to determine which environmental and company variables influence the company's return on investment (ROI) and cash flow. Return on investment is defined as pretax operating profits divided by the total of equity and long-term debt. The data indicate that seven categories of variables appear to influence ROI: (1) competitive position, (2) industry/market environment, (3) budget allocation, (4) capital structure, (5) production processes, (6) company characteristics, and (7) "change action" factors.[10]

One of the key concepts emerging from these studies is the experience curve, which is an attempt to explain a relationship between relative market share and return on investment. Generally, the larger the relative market share, the greater the return on investment because of the efficiences accruing from the experience gained in obtaining the larger relative market share.

More recently, Michael Porter has offered a revised version of the relationship between market share and return on investment.[11] He proposed a U-shaped relationship rather than a linear relationship. Figure A2.1 depicts Porter's interpretation.

56

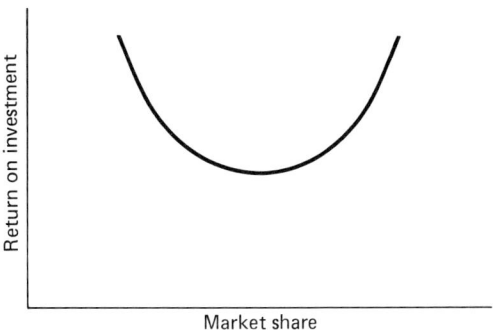

Figure A2.1
Return on investment–market share relationships
After John Haines for FORTUNE Magazine, 5 October 1981,
p. 146.

PORTFOLIO STRATEGIES

The Boston Consulting Group has used the experience curve to develop a portfolio analysis concept. BCG's conceptualization suggests that
analyzing the market situation using a matrix with market growth (a proxy
for product life cycle) on the vertical axis and market share on the horizontal
axis can add precision to the retailer's strategy decisions. The resulting matrix provides the retailer with indications of the best strategies to select.
Figure A2.2 shows the portfolio analysis matrix.

A portfolio of products can be viewed as the retailer's investment in
the market. The strategic focus of portfolio analysis is a balancing of profit,
growth, and risk of investment. By balancing these three factors, the retailer
seeks to maintain growth and profits without extreme risk and to manage
cash flow effectively. (Recall that many retailers fail because of poor cash
flow.) Portfolio analysis provides the retailer with cues for managing cash
flow through various retailing strategies.

Each of the classifications in the portfolio matrix has certain characteristics that indicate specific strategies.

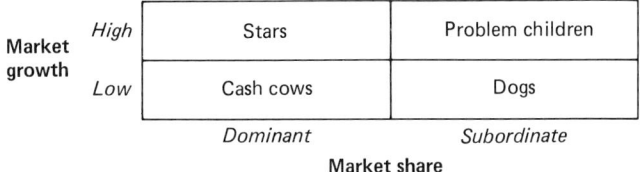

Figure A2.2
Portfolio analysis matrix

Source: Adapted from George S. Day, "Diagnosing the Product Portfolio,"
Journal of Marketing, April 1977, p. 34. Reprinted with permission from the
American Marketing Association.

Cash cows (low growth–dominant share) provide the retailer with excess cash. The cash cow brings large amounts of cash to the retailer, yet it is not costly for the retailer to maintain a dominant share because of the experience curve. The excess cash from the cash cows provides cash for managing the three other classifications.

Stars (high growth–dominant share) are valuable to the retailer because their high growth provides opportunity for future profitability (future cash cows). They provide cash but are costly to maintain because of the strong competition normally encountered in a growth market.

Problem children (high growth–subordinate share) also offer the retailer chances for future success. If the market share is substantial, problem children can be beneficial. However, with small market share, problem children are expensive to maintain relative to the revenue they provide.

Dogs (low growth–subordinate share) constitute the majority of retail offerings. If the market share is fairly large, some excess cash can be generated, but smaller shares normally result in negative cash flow. Each of these classifications suggests some strategic options. The relationships between strategic options and the portfolio matrix appear in Table A2.1.

Porter's reinterpretation of the market share–ROI relationship suggests a different type of portfolio for analyzing the retailer's strategic situation. The retailer (or particular department) can be at any point on the curve (in Figure A2.1), but three conditions or situations are generally identified. The upper left position (small market share, high ROI) is occupied by retailers with a specialized offering who are able to command better-than-average margins. The upper right position in Figure A2.1 (high market share, high ROI) represents the conventional wisdom of the learning curve, which is a reflection of the ability of the retailer to be cost-effective and command a high share because of experience and price. A position in the bottom of the

Table A2.1
Portfolio matrix–strategy relationships

MATRIX CLASSIFICATION	POSSIBLE RETAILING STRATEGY
Cash cows	Maintain leadership through price
Stars	Change to maintain leadership Expand to new markets
Problem children	Segment and specialize Invest heavily or acquire competitor to obtain share
Dogs	Keep costs down Specialize for small segment Harvesting (cut support costs) Possibly withdraw from market

U is the most undesirable position—no clear differentiation or large market share. The retailer in this situation has neither differential (or specialization) advantage nor an experience (or cost) advantage. These disadvantages lead to lower return on investment for the retailer.

Further analysis leads to organizing the strategic environment according to the number of ways competitive advantages can be obtained and the size of the advantages. This perspective of the competitive retail environment is contingent upon the premises that (1) a competitive advantage based on the retailer's ability to differentiate itself from competititon is necessary to be profitable and (2) competitive situations change, which alters the ability to gain an advantage. Figure A2.3 depicts this situation.

Each of the four possible situations is a function of the ability to differentiate the retail offering from competing retailers. The *stalemate situation*, which is illustrated by grocery stores, offers little opportunity for competitive advantages. A *fragmented situation* suggests many ways of differentiating, but none are great advantages and most can easily be duplicated by the competition. Restaurants are an example of a fragmented retailing situation. The *specialization situation* is a positive position in that the retailer is able to differentiate, and this differentiation is substantial and not easily copied. Finally, the *volume situation*, perhaps exemplified by the discount retailers, is a retailing situation in which few methods are available for differentiation but the few that exist offer substantial advantage.

The obvious key to developing a successful retailing strategy is the ability to differentiate and maintain the differential advantage. Retailers attempt to use their unique strengths relative to competitors' weaknesses and to environmental opportunities to achieve differential advantages. The ability to develop a differential advantage is based on retailers' recognizing their own strengths and on a thorough analysis of environmental factors. Long-term success in retailing depends heavily on the retailer's differential advantages. Portfolio analysis provides one perspective for analyzing the environment that enables the retailer to establish a broad base for strategic

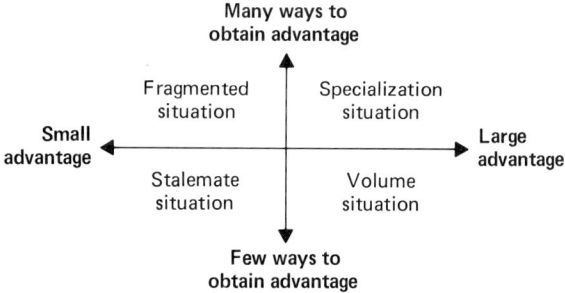

Figure A2.3
Competitive strategic situation matrix

direction concerning differentiation from other retailers. A differential advantage provides the retailer with the ability to request higher prices for the offerings and, consequently, to receive a larger return on investment. As shown in Figure A2.1, the retailers at the bottom of the U-shaped curve have no differential advantage in specialization or cost-volume and thus receive a lower return on investment.

Given the four-cell approach based on differential advantage, certain strategies can be recommended, depending upon the cell in which the retailer is classified. Table A2.2 shows some possible retailing strategies for each situation cell.

It must be remembered, though, that the advantages are only advantages when perceived as such by the consumer. Attempting to compete on advantages not pertinent to the consumer is actually not competing on differential advantages.

Portfolio analysis is a valuable method that can help retailers to improve their understanding of strategy selection. Remember, however, that the PIMS studies and portfolio analysis were developed using data from, and primarily for, manufacturing firms. Thus while portfolio analysis may

Table A2.2
Situation-strategy relationship

STRATEGIC SITUATION	POSSIBLE RETAILING STRATEGIES
Stalemate	Selectively reduce scope
	Reduce expenses
	Search for opportunities
	Exit, if financially possible
Fragmented	Minimize investment
	Strengthen existing position through innovation
	Increase margins, if possible
	Expand cautiously
Specialization	Maintain differential position
	Maintain integrated retailing mix strategy
	Scan and monitor competitors and changing environments closely so as not to lose competitive advantage
Volume	Increase volume through price
	Search for nonprice competitive methods
	If weak, possibly withdraw from market

offer insight into retail strategy development, there may be problems in applying this method directly to retailing. Portfolio analysis should be used cautiously in strategic retail decision making.

NOTES

1. Safeway Stores, Inc., *Annual Report* (Oakland, Calif., 1980), p. 3.

2. G. C. Murphy Company, *Annual Report* (McKeesport, Pa., 1980), p. 3.

3. R. L. Ackoff, *A Concept of Corporate Planning* (New York: Wiley/Intersciences, 1970), p. 4.

4. Louis V. Gerstner, "Can Strategic Planning Pay Off?," *Business Horizons,* December 1972, pp. 5–16.

5. Hilton Hotels Corporations, *Annual Report* (Beverly Hills, Calif., 1980), p. 9.

6. Kroger Company, *Annual Report* (Cincinnati, Ohio, 1980), p. 3.

7. E. Applebee and S. Nitzberg, "Factors Contributing to a Successful Operation of a Retail Department Store" (Research paper, August 16, 1974), reported in G. David Hughes, *Marketing Management* (Reading, Mass: Addison-Wesley, 1978).

8. Thomas J. Cannon, *Business Strategy and Policy* (New York: Harcourt, Brace and World, 1968), pp. 523–530.

9. Stanley F. Stasch and Patricia Lanktree, "Can Your Marketing Planning Procedures Be Improved?" *Journal of Marketing,* Summer 1980, pp. 79–90.

10. Roger A. Kerin and Robert A. Peterson, *Perspectives on Strategic Marketing Management* (Boston: Allyn and Bacon, 1980), pp. 12–13.

11. Walter Kiechel III, "The Decline of the Experience Curve," *Fortune,* 5 October 1981, p. 146.

STRATEGIC RETAIL MANAGEMENT MODEL

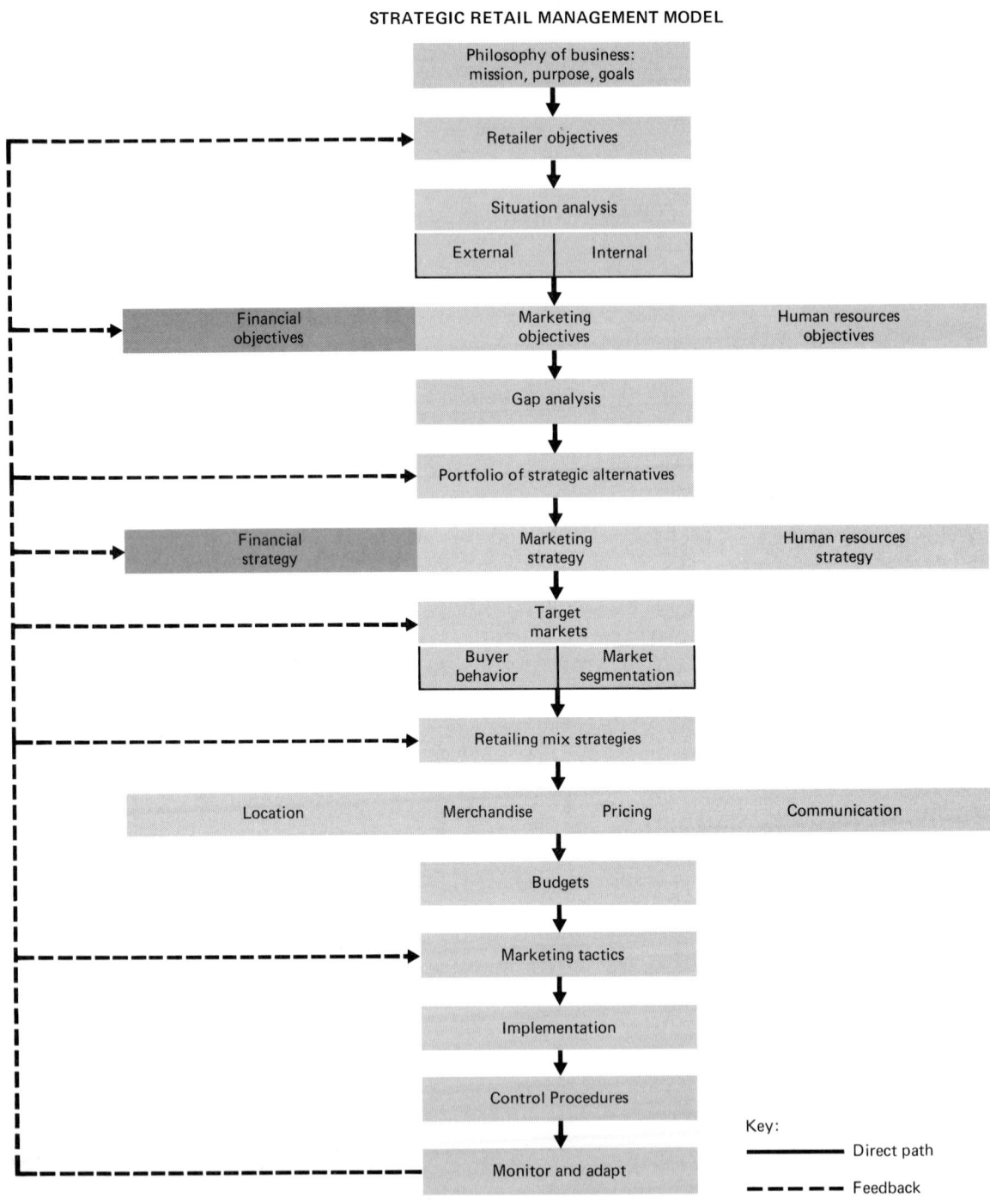

Chapter 3
Financial Planning, Control, and Analysis

LEARNING OBJECTIVES

1. To understand the role and importance of strategic financial decisions.

2. To understand the strategic profit planning process, budgeting, and the fundamentals of analyzing financial performance and position.

INTRODUCTION

Strategic financial decisions are all too frequently left to chance by retailers, but even the smallest retailers can benefit from using sound financial concepts and techniques.

Strategic financial decisions involve both planning and control, which can be divided into three major areas. In effect, retailers should view financial planning and control as a repeating cycle that answers three questions: (1) Where do we want to go? (2) How will we get there? and (3) Did we get there? For a new retailer, the cycle begins with **profit planning,** followed by **budgeting** and **analysis of financial performance and position.** As the cycle repeats for ongoing retail firms, the analysis of financial performance and position actually becomes the basis for subsequent profit planning and budgeting. To facilitate discussion of these three components, the financial cycle is organized into a financial strategy decision model (see Fig. 3.1). The five basic steps are the following:

1. Review all other plans and information

2. Plan for a profit

3. Prepare budgets

4. Analyze financial performance and position

5. Monitor and adapt

REVIEW ALL OTHER PLANS AND INFORMATION

Financial considerations and the retailer's overall strategy are closely intertwined. Profit planning and financial control, for example, should be focused on achieving major retail objectives. Conversely, these objectives should be at least partially based on an analysis of financial performance and position. Thus, the overall retail strategy must be carefully reviewed.

For a new retail establishment, the information available for review is largely *external information,* such as from published trade sources. In addition, the retailer might draw on personal experience or information gathered previously for a feasibility study (if one was performed). The only *internal information* available would be tentative plans for the overall strategy and perhaps general plans for the various functional strategies, such as for location, merchandise, pricing, and advertising.

For an ongoing retail establishment, much more internal information is available in addition to the external information. The results generated by other strategic plans, especially measured from a financial perspective, are extremely important. Consequently, the ongoing retailer should anchor financial planning in the analysis of financial performance and position.

The review should also include an examination of *who* does the financial analysis, planning, and control and *what kind of data* are available. In

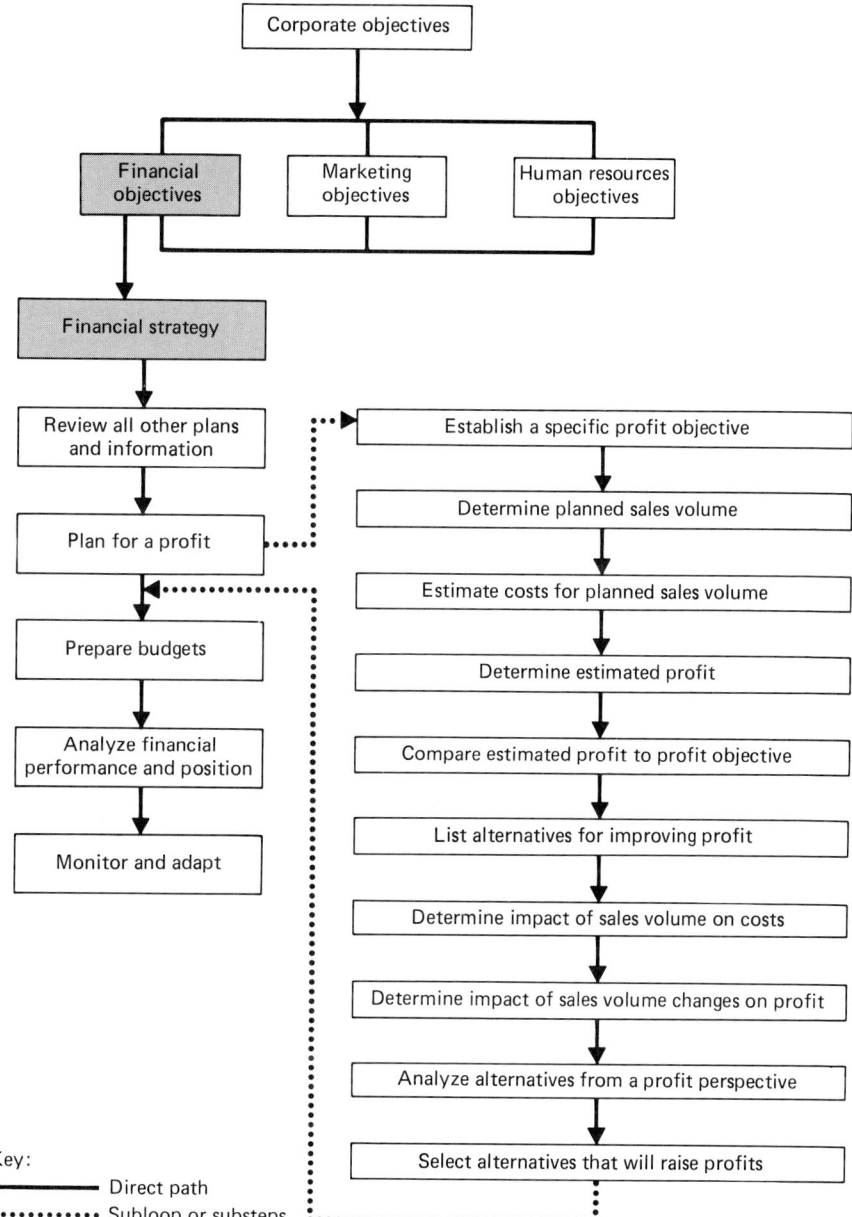

Figure 3.1
Financial strategy decision model

larger retail firms, accounting staffs are normally responsible for providing the data and for the bulk of the analysis. Although the accounting staff may possess the capability for financial analysis, the ultimate responsibility lies with management. There appears to be a trend that retail decision makers are accountable for their financial decisions, and it is quite likely that the financial aspects of retailing will become even more important to those aspiring to retailing careers.

Smaller retailers normally experience a different set of problems in this area. They do not have accounting staffs, and this restricts the quantity and quality of available data and forecasting potential. If the owner/manager does not have time to maintain adequate records and perform the necessary analyses, additional clerical personnel, outside accountants, and/or a small computer should be considered.

PLAN FOR A PROFIT

Retailers must realize profits to stay in business. Unfortunately, few retailers devote the time and effort necessary to plan effectively for a profit; it becomes something that is "left over" after the bills are paid. Healthy profits do not just happen; careful analysis and planning are necessary to establish a reasonable profit plan (consisting of the sales, merchandise, and expense budgets discussed later in this chapter). The profit plan should reflect the overall retail strategy and should serve as a guide for other, more specific strategic plans. This section presents a **strategic profit planning process** designed to help the retailer plan for profits. The ten steps in the process are the following:[1]

1. Establish a specific profit objective.

2. Determine planned sales volume.

3. Estimate costs.

4. Determine estimated profit.

5. Compare estimated profit with profit objective.

6. List alternatives for improving profit.

7. Determine impact of sales volume on costs.

8. Determine impact of sales volume changes on profits.

9. Analyze alternatives from a profit perspective.

10. Select alternatives to improve profit.

Establish a Specific Profit Objective

The retailer's first step is to establish a specific profit objective or target, which can be built up from three separate components. The first component involves the income that could be received if the *original investment* in the firm were invested in stocks, bonds, savings and loan, and so on. Similarly, the second component involves the income that could be received elsewhere on the *previous profits* that have been left in the business. These two components are specific dollar amounts the retailer can identify readily. The third component involves adding a *risk premium* to cover the risk of staying in business.

Smaller retailers should add a fourth component, the *salary* they could earn working for someone else.

Table 3.1 presents an example of profit planning for Michael's Men's Store, an ongoing retail business. The owner, Michael, has established a profit goal of $92,000. Now he is ready to determine the profit potential of forecast sales.

Determine Planned Sales Volume

The details of sales forecasting (Step 2) for an ongoing retailer are discussed in Chapter 11, regarding merchandise planning.

A new retailer faces the problem of not having a historical data base to work with. The next best alternative is to use a "back-door" procedure to estimate *the sales volume required to generate the desired net profit.* The required sales volume can be calculated if the retailer can find reasonable cost of goods sold (CGS) and total expense figures. Suppose (temporarily) that Michael is a new retailer with a desired net profit of $92,000. Further, Michael finds (from trade publications) that similar retailers typically have a CGS of 56.0 percent of sales and total expenses of 34.8 percent of sales. Required sales can be calculated as follows:

Sales − CGS − Expenses = Net profit.

Therefore,

$$\text{Sales} - 0.560\ (\text{Sales}) - 0.348\ (\text{Sales}) = \$92{,}000$$
$$0.092\ (\text{Sales}) = \$92{,}000$$
$$\text{Sales} = \$1{,}000{,}000.$$

Michael as a new retailer would need a sales volume of $1,000,000 to generate a net profit of $92,000, assuming his CGS and expense pattern is similar to the trade average. Michael can now evaluate the overall situation to determine whether $1,000,000 is a reasonable sales estimate, rather than attempting to forecast sales with nonexistent data.

To continue development of the strategic profit planning process for Michael's as an ongoing retailer, let us assume that the $1,000,000 sales figure is a *forecast* figure to be entered on the profit planning worksheet (Table 3.1).

Estimate Costs for Planned Sales Volume

The retailer's third step is to estimate costs for the planned sales volume. The retailer should collect actual cost figures for recent years, if they are available. Michael used the cost data for the previous year and then adjusted them for the planned sales volume. The adjustments are necessary to take into account inflation, specific cost increases, and strategy changes (increased promotion, for example).

Table 3.1
Profit planning for Michael's Men's Store, 19x4

STEP	DESCRIPTION	ANALYSIS	
1.	*Establish specific profit objective*		
	Original investment	$ 100,000	
	Retained earnings	30,000	
	Owner's equity	130,000	
	Desired return % (interest plus risk premium)	20%	
	Desired return $	26,000	
	Salary from alternative employment	20,000	
	Profit desired after taxes	46,000	
	Estimated income tax	46,000	
	Profit needed before taxes	$ 92,000	
2.	*Determine planned sales volume*		
	Owner's sales forecast	$1,000,000	

STEP	DESCRIPTION	ACTUAL: LAST YEAR	ESTIMATE NEXT YEAR
3.	*Estimate costs*		
	Cost of goods sold	$ 536,550	$ 585,200
	Payroll	199,818	176,800
	Advertising	25,455	28,000
	State and local taxes	16,000	16,500
	Supplies	13,364	14,700
	Utilities	9,000	9,500
	Interest	17,000	17,700
	Travel	4,583	5,500
	Communications (telephone, postage)	11,500	12,600
	Insurance	7,300	7,300
	Depreciation	7,900	7,900
	Professional services	6,000	6,900
	Bad debts	3,000	3,200
	Rent	28,500	28,500
	Total costs	$ 885,970	$ 920,300

STEP	DESCRIPTION	ANALYSIS	
4.	*Determine estimated profit*		
	Estimated sales revenue	$1,000,000	
	Estimated costs	920,300	
	Estimated net profit before taxes	$ 79,700	
5.	*Compare estimated profit with profit objective*		
	Estimated net profit before taxes	$ 79,700	
	Desired profit	92,000	
	Difference (shortage)	−$ 12,300	

STEP	DESCRIPTION	ANALYSIS

6. *Some alternatives to improve profit*

Reduce price

Increase advertising

Increase price

Reduce variable costs

Increase sales

Reduce expenses

7. *Determine impact of sales volume on costs*

ITEM	ESTIMATED COSTS	FIXED COSTS	VARIABLE COSTS
Cost of goods sold	$585,200		$585,200
Payroll	176,800	$100,000	176,800
Advertising	28,000		28,000
Taxes	16,500	15,000	1,500
Supplies	14,700	7,000	7,700
Utilities	9,500	6,000	3,500
Interest	17,700	17,700	
Travel	5,500	3,000	2,500
Communications	12,600	6,600	6,000
Insurance	7,300	7,300	
Depreciation	7,900	7,900	
Professional services	6,900	6,900	
Bad debts	3,200		3,200
Rent	28,500	28,500	
	$920,300	$205,900	$714,400

8. *Determine the impact of sales volume changes on profits*

SALES	–	FIXED COSTS	–	VARIABLE COSTS	=	PROFIT
$ 700,000		$205,900		0.7144 × $ 700,000	=	– $ 5,980
720,938		205,900		0.7144 × 720,938	=	0
800,000		205,900		0.7144 × 800,000	=	22,580
900,000		205,900		0.7144 × 900,000	=	51,140
1,000,000		205,900		0.7144 × 1,000,000	=	79,700
1,043,000		205,900		0.7144 × 1,043,000	=	92,000

Note that it is acceptable in some situations to analyze *aggregate cost data* rather than individual items. If Michael's experience had indicated that total expenses have always been 92 percent of sales, he could have estimated expenses at $920,000 for forecast sales of $1 million. Although this procedure can be beneficial, it has several limitations and must be used with care. The limitations are that (1) all costs do not change proportionally with sales (that is, they may be fixed or change proportionally to inflation or local wage rates) and (2) aggregate cost figures provide little guidance for *control* of specific costs. Because of these problems, the retailer is urged to analyze each cost individually, as shown in Table 3.1.

As mentioned earlier, a new retailer faces the problem of not having historical cost data. One useful alternative is to search for published information on costs as a percentage of sales in trade publications and from suppliers. For some expenses, the retailer should investigate the source of the expense. For example, various local taxing authorities could be consulted to determine tax costs. Depreciation can be estimated closely if the retailer can trace the costs of various depreciable assets.

Determine Estimated Profit

Step 4 calls for determining estimated profit by combining Steps 2 and 3. Michael's estimated net profit is $79,700 ($1,000,000 − $920,300).

Compare Estimated Profit with Profit Objective

Step 5 uses Steps 1 and 4 to compare estimated profit with profit objective. Michael finds that desired profit exceeds expected profit by $12,300 ($79,700 − $92,000).

If the comparison is satisfactory, the retailer can stop at this point. Michael, however, would probably not be satisfied and would most likely follow the remaining five steps in order to determine if any improvements can be made.

List Alternatives for Improving Profit

There are many alternatives for improving retail profits. Step 6 calls for the retailer to search for and list these alternatives, which tend to fall into the following four categories:

1. *Increase unit sales volume and/or revenue.* Examples of activities include increasing advertising, improving service, increasing personal selling, and changing prices (either higher or lower).

2. *Decrease planned expenses.* Activities might include better control of cash register, better employee scheduling, reduction of inventory, and service cutbacks.

3. *Add other products and services.*

4. *Add leased departments.*

Several alternatives are listed in Step 6 of Table 3.1. Each of these alternatives must be analyzed and evaluated (Step 9). Before a reasonable analysis can be performed, the retailer must understand the interrelationships among costs, volume, and profit, which is accomplished in Steps 7 and 8, as shown in the table.

Determine Impact of Sales Volume on Costs

Michael recognizes that the overall costs of doing business change as the sales volume changes. Further, each specific cost classification has its own unique response pattern to volume changes. Each cost classification therefore must be analyzed separately.

Michael's cost data for the previous five years were analyzed for each cost classification. The results of this analysis are shown in Step 7 of Table 3.1.

To illustrate the analysis process, the data for three cost classifications are shown in Table 3.2. These particular classifications were chosen to show that costs can be fixed, variable, or semivariable. **Fixed costs** remain constant during the time period, regardless of sales volume. **Variable costs** vary in direct proportion to sales volume. **Semivariable costs** have a portion that does not vary with sales volume and a portion that does vary with sales volume.

To help grasp the overall relationship between cost, volume, and profit, Michael constructed a simple *break-even chart* (see Fig. 3.2). The break-even chart can provide a quick, overall view of the cost, volume, and profit relationships. The retailer must keep two points in mind, however. First, the underlying relationships are likely to exist only within a relatively narrow range of sales volume. In Fig. 3.2, attaining sales volume over $1 million might call for extraordinary promotion expenditures, which would change the cost structure.

Second, the *causes* of the underlying relationships may change, even if sales volume remains in a narrow range. For example, inflation, tax changes, government regulations, and the like can change underlying relationships. The key point is that past relationships may not continue into the future.

Determine Impact of Sales Volume Changes on Profits

Step 8 calls for the retailer to determine the impact on profits of a change in sales volume. Marginal analysis can be quite useful for this task. At the forecast sales volume of $1,000,000, Michael makes a profit of $0.0797 for each dollar of sales [($1,000,00 − $920,300) ÷ $1,000,000] and has a cost of $0.9203 (from Step 3 of Table 3.1).

If sales are increased $1.00 over the forecast, this dollar will not have an associated cost of $0.9203 because fixed costs do not increase with an increase in sales volume. Therefore, this additional dollar in sales will have only variable costs of $0.7144 associated with it ($714,400 ÷ $1,000,000) (from Step 7 in Table 3.1). The increase in profit from the dollar increase in sales (or marginal income) is $0.2856 ($1.00 − $0.7144). Cost and profit are computed for different sales levels in Step 8 of Table 3.1. (Step 8 also includes the numbers from which the break-even chart in Figure 3.2 was constructed.)

Table 3.2
Data collected from Michael's records

YEAR	SALES VOLUME	COST OF GOODS SOLD	INSURANCE	SUPPLIES
1	$800,000	$464,000	$7,300	$13,160
2	$830,000	$489,700	$7,300	$13,391
3	$860,000	$516,000	$7,300	$13,622
4	$850,000	$493,000	$7,300	$13,545
5	$916,866	$536,550	$7,300	$13,364

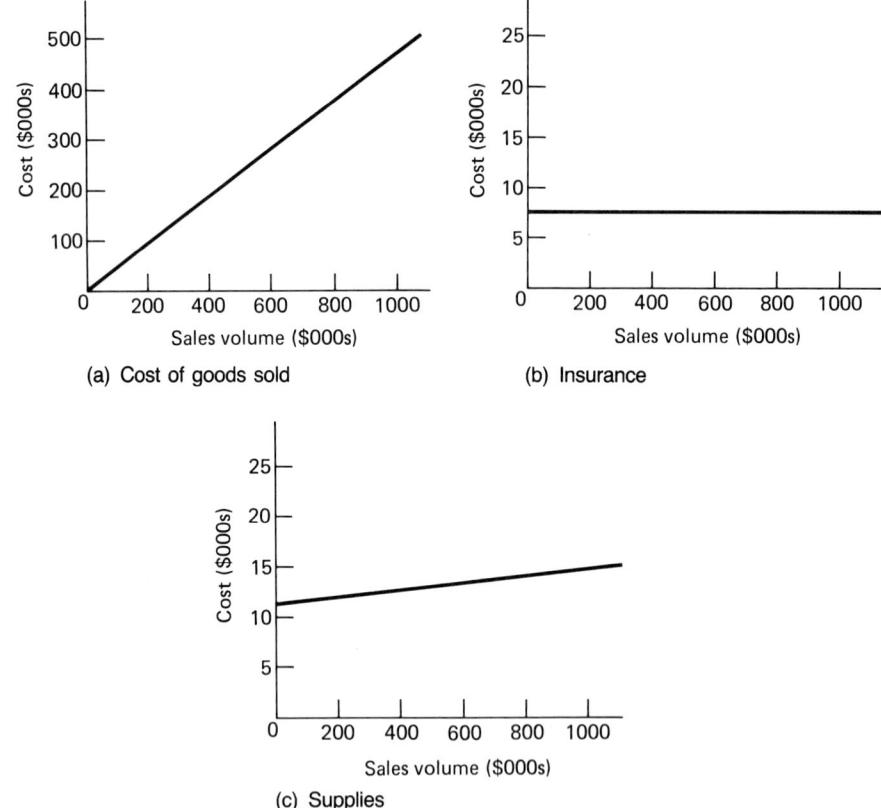

(a) Cost of goods sold

(b) Insurance

(c) Supplies

Cost and volume graphs

Analyze Alternatives from a Profit Perspective

In Step 9 the retailer analyzes the alternatives (listed in Step 6) from a profit perspective. The **marginal analysis** performed in Step 8 can be quite helpful. Consider the following questions related to marginal analysis.

1. *How much can price be reduced for a special sale?* In Step 8, Michael's marginal income from an additional dollar of sales was cal-

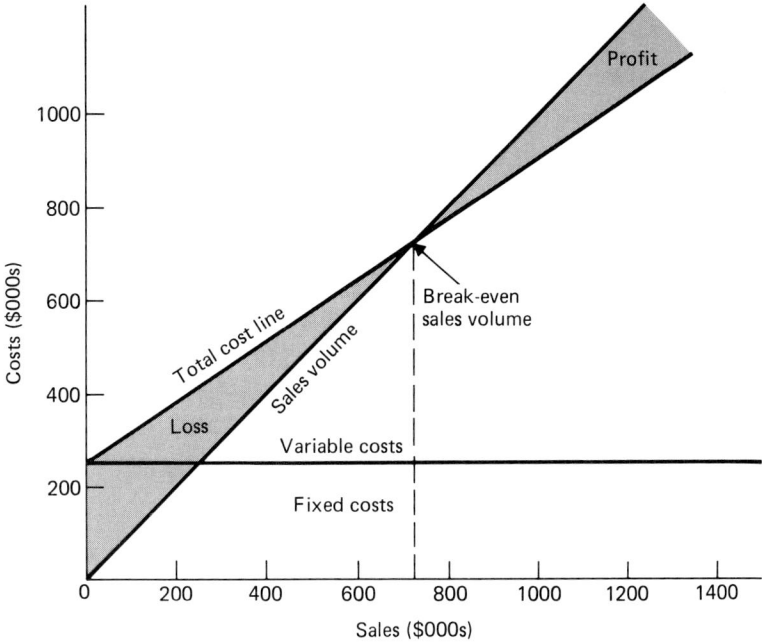

Figure 3.2
Break-even chart for Michael's Men's Store
Note: The break-even sales figure can be calculated with the formula:

$$S = FC + VC(S),$$

where

S = Sales volume
FC = Total fixed costs
VC = Variable cost per sales dollar.

Therefore:

$$S = \$205,900 + .7144(S)$$
$$S - .7144(S) = \$205,900$$
$$.2856(S) = \$205,900$$
$$S = \$740,938.$$

culated as $0.2856 or 28.56 percent. Any price reduction up to 28.56 percent would be break-even or better. Reductions greater than 28.56 percent would result in losses because all of the variable costs ($0.7144) would not be covered.

2. *Would it be profitable for Michael to increase advertising by $5,000 if it increases sales by $20,000?* Marginal income would be $5,712 (0.2856 × $20,000). Therefore, the additional profits would be $712 ($5,712 − $5,000).

3. *Would it be profitable to increase prices 3 percent if sales would drop 6 percent?* Expected profit equals marginal income times sales less fixed costs, or, as shown in Table 3.1, (0.2856 × $1,000,000) −

$205,900 = $79,700. The suggested change would increase marginal income to $0.3156 (0.2856 + 0.03) and reduce total sales to 94 percent of the original forecast. Therefore, (0.3156 × 0.94 × $1,000,000) − $205,900 = $90,764. Since $90,764 is greater than $79,700, the price increase would be profitable.

All of the alternatives listed in Step 6 can be evaluated in a similar manner. When this economic analysis is completed, the retailer is ready to select the alternatives.

Select Alternatives to Improve Profit

Step 10 involves selecting the alternatives for changing current plans and increasing profit. The analyses made in the previous steps should serve as economic inputs. This information should be evaluated along with other objectives. For example, cost reductions might achieve the desired profit but result in employee layoffs, reductions in customer service, or other undesirable situations. Price reductions might result in a less-than-ideal store image, especially in the long run.

A key to this selection process is to understand that a retail business is a system of interrelated flows and components (such as turnover and price). A change in one flow or component will generally have an impact on another flow or component. The retailer therefore must evaluate the long-term ramifications of short-term remedies.

Achieving the desired profit level is a function of generating adequate revenue (via the retailing mix strategies) and controlling costs. Cost control can be greatly enhanced with effective budgeting practices.

PREPARE BUDGETS

Retailers frequently suffer financial crises because of a lack of cost-consciousness and poor cash management practices. Costs and cash should be primary concerns of the retailer. *Budgets* are important tools for managerial control of those areas.

In a sense, budgets are the retailer's *projected operating plans*. Unlike financial statements, which deal with historical data, budgets are concerned with the future. In another sense, budgets are *control devices*. They are formulated before each new accounting period and can then be used to continually monitor performance. Any variations between planned and actual achievements can be analyzed.

Types of Budgets

Three types of budgets are particularly useful for retailers:

1. *Operating budgets.* The general operating budget consists of the sales budget, cost of goods sold budget (merchandise budget), and expense budget.

2. *Cash budget.* The cash budget reflects anticipated cash flow derived from cash receipts and disbursements.

3. *Capital budget.* The capital budget focuses on expected long-range expenditures for specific investments such as equipment and building construction or renovation. (Although the capital budget can be important to retailers, its technical nature places it beyond the scope of this textbook.)

Operating Budget

The overall operating budget is made up of three component budgets: sales, cost of goods sold, and expense. The **sales budget** is a realistic sales forecast for the relevant time periods. The **cost of goods sold** or **merchandise budget** is a realistic forecast of the cost of merchandise for the expected sales volume.

The **expense budget** is a realistic forecast of expenses for the expected sales level. Expense forecasts were discussed earlier in this chapter in terms of profit planning. Several additional points can also be made. Each expense should be analyzed individually and in detail. The retailer might begin by using historical expense data to project a trend to arrive at an initial estimate. Then the retailer must investigate the factors that can alter the estimate. Each expense will not necessarily follow a trend line or changes in inflation rate.

Expenses are generally arranged and divided for accounting purposes, not for the convenience of managerial control. Consequently, the retailer might need to rearrange expenses according to *cost responsibility*; these new groups of expenses are often called *cost centers*. Rather than grouping all payroll expenses together, for example, the expenses could be divided and allocated to the particular cost center (receiving, shipping, sporting goods, jewelry department, and so on) responsible for incurring the expense. The key point here is that somebody must be responsible for each expense. Otherwise control is impossible.

Analysis and control through efficient budgeting practices do not necessarily imply *cost minimization*. Effective control can entail either increased or decreased expenditure. The retailer's goal should be *optimum* rather than *minimum* expenditure.

Expense budgets should not be "written in stone." Budgets should provide for variability and flexibility. **Variability** refers to the concept that many expenses are related to the level of activity or sales volume. Therefore, if sales volume is 10 percent greater than forecast, the retailer should recognize that many expenses will also be greater. Because of the variability of some expenses, the retailer will have to adjust expense forecasts *after* the accounting period to analyze the variation expected and the actual expenses. **Flexibility** refers to the concept of allowing managerial discretion to override budgeted figures. Remember that amounts budgeted prior to an accounting period were devised with less information than a manager will have during the accounting period. As conditions change, budgeted amounts may also have to change.

A crucial part of budgetary control involves analyzing the variations between expected and actual performance, explaining why the variation occurred, and evaluating the desirability of the variation. An unexpected increase in telephone rates is unavoidable; an increase in insurance expense may be desirable because of improved coverage. Variations are not necessarily mistakes.

The use of expense budgets as control tools can be enhanced by the use of several other comparisons. A retailer might perform the following comparisons for labor expense:

1. labor expense as a percent of sales compared with trade's average labor expense as a percent of sales

2. labor expense as a percent of total expenses compared with trade's average labor expense as a percent of total expenses

It is also useful to analyze these percentages and the actual dollar expenses longitudinally simply by plotting the expense figures on a graph over time and analyzing the resulting trend lines.

Cash Budget   For many retailers, a financial crisis is actually a cash crisis. The only effective way to avoid these crises is through good cash management. The **cash budget** is the major tool in this endeavor.

STRATEGY IN ACTION 3.1
New Forms of Financing

The collapse of traditional long-term, fixed-rate private placement financing and the prohibitive cost of money in the public bond market have forced retailers to seek innovative ways of obtaining money. Here are several examples of the new forms of financing being utilized:

Zero Coupon Bond
Originated in 1980 by J. C. Penney under the aegis of senior vp and director of finance Kenneth Axelson, a zero coupon bond does not bear interest. When Penney first issued this debt security, each $1,000 bond was bought by the investor for $332.47. When the bonds mature in 1989, the investor can redeem them for $1,000, which works out to an effective interest rate of 14.25%.

For Penney, the primary advantage includes being able to deduct interest on nonrecurrable expenses (in this case represented by the amount the bond increases in value). The effective interest cost for Penney is 13.6%, as compared with 14.9% Penney would have had to pay on a standard eight-year bond.

Pass-through Mortgage Certificates
K mart was the focus of the first mortgage pass-through certificates issued for retailing real estate. Merrill Lynch marketed $80 million worth of the certificates in November 1981 in a debt security

package involving the sale of a pool of mortgage loans for 25 K mart stores. K mart's leases are the guarantee for the mortgages. For each $1,000 certificate the investor will receive an interest coupon of 15¾%, which is scheduled to be paid by the rent generated from each of the K mart stores over the next 25 years.

The sale of the mortgages, half of which are owned by K mart and half by outside developers, generates badly needed money for development in a market where funds are practically dried up. Also, the money is expected to help K mart compensate for the planned cutback in Industrial Revenue Bonds, a major source of the discounter's expansion financing.

Debt-Equity Swaps
In January, Carter Hawley Hale completed a debt-equity swap through its broker, the investment banking firm of Morgan Stanley. CHH arranged for Morgan Stanley to buy up $11.45 million worth of its outstanding bonds. These bonds were issued years ago at rates ranging from 8.25% to 9.45%, and in January were selling at a deep discount because of the increase in interest rate yields. Morgan Stanley then exchanged the bonds for $564,797 worth of newly issued Carter Hawley Hale common stock. Morgan Stanley, which received a discount on the stock's price, then sold the stock to the public.

The deal is advantageous for CHH because it strengthens its balance sheet by reducing its debt, and it even reports a healthy profit on the difference between the original value of the bond and the amount it paid for it at a discount. What's more, the gain is tax free, because it represents a corporate reorganization, on which the IRS does not impose income tax.

Original Issue Deep Discount Bonds
Similar to zero coupon bonds, OIDS are sold at a deep discount, or a price much below their par, or face value. They carry a relatively low rate of interest, but the investor collects the face value of the bond at maturity, rather than the discounted purchase price.

Issuers of these bonds, including J. C. Penney, receive a tax advantage in that they are allowed to deduct all implicit interest although they actually only pay out the low coupon rate. Also the effective interest cost is lower, because in a period of high rates, the yield to maturity required by investors is lower than a conventional bond.

The major focus of the cash budget is pinpointing the times the retailer will have **cash needs** and **cash excess.** Unfulfilled cash needs cause all sorts of obvious problems, the extreme result of which is *failure.*[2] Cash excesses have an associated opportunity cost (interest that could be earned from investing the excess cash).

Cash budgeting involves projecting **cash inflows** and **cash outflows.** A major concern is the lag between transactions (commitments to receive or pay cash) and the related cash flow. This point can be seen readily in the simple cash-flow diagram in Fig. 3.3.

Cash must be made to "work" for the retailer. This first involves investing the cash to obtain inventory. Inventory is then sold, which either returns cash directly to the retailer or creates accounts receivable, in which

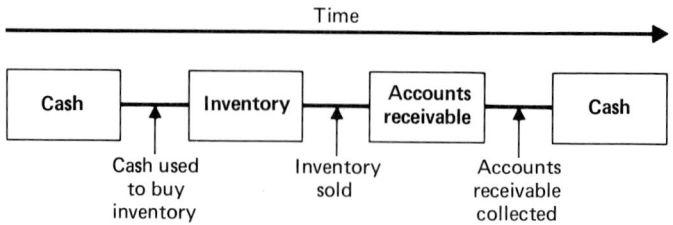

Figure 3.3
Simplified cash-flow diagram

case the accounts receivable collections result in cash for the retailer. This cash flow can be much more complicated when other cash-related factors, such as accounts payable, are incorporated.

Many retailers underestimate the time it takes for cash to return to cash. For a simple illustration, assume a retailer has a merchandise turnover rate of 3 per year and an average collection period for accounts receivable of sixty days. The turnover rate of 3 indicates that goods will be on the retailer's shelves an average of four months (12 months ÷ 3). The inventory–to–accounts receivable segment is therefore four months. Add to this the sixty days for collecting accounts receivable and the cash-to-cash lag is *six months*. Very few creditors are likely to allow a retailer six months to make cash disbursements to them. However, a retailer can influence the timing of cash flows through credit and collection policies and activities, improved inventory turnover, payments on last day of discount periods, discount policies, and so on.

Although the cash budget is closely related to the sales, merchandise, and expense budgets, control of the latter factors does not automatically bring about a desirable cash position. The timing of cash flows often creates situations of cash shortages and excesses. Determining the probable cash position through cash budgeting alerts the retailer to the need for some form of financing to cover projected cash deficits or the need to put excess cash to profitable use.

Constructing a cash budget involves three basic steps: (1) determine format, (2) determine cash inflows, and (3) determine cash outflows.

Format. Determining the cash budget format involves choosing the subperiods and the total time span over which the cash inflows and outflows will be projected. Typical formats for retailers are weekly projections for one month and monthly projections for six months.

Cash Inflows. Once the format is chosen, the retailer is ready to project the cash inflows. The major source of retail cash inflow is operations. The two sources of operations inflow are cash sales and collections from accounts receivable. The nature of the lag between the creation and collection of accounts receivable depends on the retailer's credit policies and the speed with which its customers pay.

Another source of cash inflow is the retailers' financial dealings. Financial inflows include the sale of stock, bond sales, interest and dividend income, receipt of borrowed funds, and the like. Retailers may occasionally have temporary sources of inflow, such as the sale of equipment or land.

Cash Outflows. As with inflows, cash outflows may be due to operating or financial dealings. Typical cash outflows from operations include cash purchases, payment of accounts payable, wages and salaries, and other expenses. Each of these outflows can normally be identified from the appropriate individual budget. Typical outflows from financial dealings include scheduled loan repayment, interest payments, and payment of dividends. Note that depreciation is an expense, but it is not a cash outflow. (The actual cash outflow occurs when the depreciable asset is acquired or when loan repayments occur; the cost of the asset is spread over the years of expected life in the form of depreciation expense.)

Preparation of a cash budget is illustrated in Table 3.3 for Michael's Men's Store. The format chosen is monthly for six months.

Michael's inflows consist of cash sales and accounts receivable collections. For the sake of simplicity, assume that 50 percent of Michael's net

Table 3.3
Cash budget for Michael's Men's Store (monthly for six months)

ITEM	MONTH					
	1	2	3	4	5	6
Inflows						
Cash sales	$ 50,000	$ 55,000	$ 60,000	$ 50,000	$ 55,000	$ 70,000
Accounts receivable collections	48,000	50,000	55,000	60,000	50,000	55,000
Interest	0	0	0	0	0	0
Total inflows	$ 98,000	$105,000	$115,000	$110,000	$105,000	$125,000
Outflows						
Cash purchases	29,460	32,186	35,112	29,460	32,186	40,964
Accounts payable	30,000	29,460	32,186	35,112	29,460	32,186
Expenses	29,420	30,712	32,004	29,420	30,712	34,588
Notes payable						25,000
L.T. debt			50,000			
Total outflows	$ 88,880	$ 92,358	$149,302	$ 93,992	$ 92,358	$132,738
Cash excess or (shortfall)	$ 9,120	$ 12,642	($ 34,302)	$ 16,008	$ 12,642	($ 7,738)

sales are cash sales and 50 percent go into acounts receivable and that all accounts receivable are collected in the month following the sales.

Michael's outflows consist of cash purchases of inventory, payments on accounts payable, expenses, and notes payable. From Table 3.1 we can calculate total expenses by subtracting cost of goods sold from total costs ($335,100 = $920,300 − $585,200). All of these expenses are cash outflows *except* fixed depreciation of $7,900, which is not a cash outflow. Thus, total expenses and the fixed expense component for the year must be reduced by $7,900 before the monthly expenses can be determined. Yearly expenses were calculated by the following formula:

Total expenses = fixed costs + variable costs

Monthly expenses were found as follows:

Monthly expenses = ($205,900 ÷ 12) + (0.1292 × month's sales)

The 0.1292 percentage for variable expenses is derived by subtracting the cost of goods sold percentage from the variable expense percentage in Table 3.1 (71.44 − 58.52). Thus, for month 1 the *cash* expenses (excluding depreciation) can be calculated as follows:

Monthly cash expense = [($205,900 − $7,900) ÷ 12] + (0.1292 × $100,000)

= $16,500 + $12,920
= $29,420.

Cash purchases are 50 percent of total monthly purchases. Thus, for month 1:

Cash purchases = sales × cost of goods sold % × 50%
= $100,000 × .5852 × .50
= $29,260.

Payments on accounts payable equal last month's cash purchases. Notes payable and long-term debt are regularly scheduled repayments.

With the projected cash budget completed, the retailer can now project *cash excess available* or *shortfall financing needed*. This statement (see Table 3.4) helps the retailer know how much and when extra cash will be available or outside financing will be needed.

Summary of Budgeting

Budgeting can benefit the retailer in three ways. First, the planning stage is enhanced because budgeting forces the retailer to think through various ideas, at least to the point where he or she can arrive at a projected dollar figure. Second, budgets provide ongoing guidance for the management staff who are responsible for implementing the strategic plans. Third, budgets provide a means of control during and after a given period.

Table 3.4
Cash excess available or shortfall financing needed for Michael's Men's Store

| | MONTH | | | | | |
ITEM	1	2	3	4	5	6
Cash, beginning of month	$26,991	26,111	28,753	25,000	30,504	33,146
Add: Cash excess during month, or	9,120	12,642	0	16,008	12,642	0
Less: Cash shortfall during month			(34,302)			(7,738)
Cash available:	$36,111	$38,753	($5,549)	$41,008	$33,146	$25,408
Less: Minimum balance	25,000	25,000	25,000	25,000	25,000	25,000
Cash excess available (or short-term financing needed)	$11,111[a]	$13,753[b]	($30,549)[c]	$16,008[d]	$ 8,146	$ 408

[a] Make 30-day short-term investment of $10,000 at 12%.
[b] Make 30-day short-term investment of $10,000 at 12%.
[c] Two 30-day investments mature, providing $20,200. Borrow $10,349 (30,549 − 20,200) for 30 days at 18%.
[d] Pay principal and interest on 30-day note of $10,504.

Systematic budgeting and related cost-control activities are extremely important to retailers, but retailers must guard against budgeting and cost-control systems that are too expensive or cumbersome. The benefits must justify the cost and effort.

ANALYZE FINANCIAL PERFORMANCE AND POSITION

A retailer's financial performance and position are reported on *financial statements.* The three common forms of financial statements are the *balance sheet, income statement,* and *statement of retained earnings.*

Financial Statements[3]

Each of the financial statements provides a unique insight into the retailer's financial performance and position. The reader should note, however, that these statements are based on historical data and do not predict the future.

Balance Sheet. The balance sheet (see Table 3.5) portrays the retailer's financial position or condition on a specific date. The three major portions of the balance sheet are assets, liabilities, and owner's equity.

Assets include all that the retailer owns. It is useful to consider asset liquidity. *Current assets* (or short-term assets) are *liquid* in that they can be converted to cash, consumed, or sold within one year. Current assets that are usually most important to retailers are cash, accounts receivable, and

Table 3.5
Michael's Men's Store balance sheet, December 31, 19x4

ASSETS

			% OF TOTAL ASSETS
Current assets			
Cash	$ 26,991		5.0%
Accounts receivable	231,359		42.9%
Inventories	227,488		42.1%
Total		485,838	90.0%
Long-term assets			
Equipment	75,000		
Less: Accumulated depreciation	− 21,018		
Total		53,982	10.0%
Total assets		$539,820	100.0%

LIABILITIES AND OWNER'S EQUITY

Current liabilities			
Notes payable	$ 50,000		9.3%
Accounts payable	116,861		21.6%
Accruals	20,000		3.7%
Total		186,861	34.6%
Long-term debt		222,959	41.3%
Total liabilities		409,820	75.9%
Owner's equity			
Capital contributed	$100,000		18.5%
Retained earnings	30,000		5.6%
Total owner's equity		130,000	24.1%
Total liabilities and owner's equity		$539,820	100.0%

inventories. *Long-term assets* (or fixed assets) are less liquid and are usually used over a period of several years. Typical examples are land, buildings, and equipment.

  Liabilities are amounts owed to creditors. These debts are categorized in terms of the length of time until payment is due. *Current liabilities* are those due within one year. Examples include accounts payable, notes payable, and accrued expenses (such as salaries and sales taxes that are current but yet to be paid). *Long-term liabilities* are debts due in future years. Installment credit and bond payments not due within the year are examples.

Owner's equity comprises the owner's original investment in the firm (capital or common stock accounts) plus all profits that have been retained in the firm (retained earnings). The original investment in Table 3.5 is in the account Capital Contributed.

Income Statement. The income statement (see Table 3.6) represents the retailer's financial performance over a specific time period by showing income and expenses. The key elements of the retailer's income statement are sales, cost of goods sold, and expenses.

Sales should be reported as net sales, which are gross (or total) sales reduced by sales discounts and sales returns and allowances. These latter figures may or may not be shown on the income statement.

Table 3.6
Michael's Men's Store income statement, for year ended December 31, 19x4

			% OF SALES
Sales		$909,952	100.0%
Less: Cost of goods sold		536,550	59.0
Gross profit		373,402	41.0
Expenses			
Payroll	$169,818		18.7
Advertising	25,455		2.8
Taxes and licenses	16,000		1.8
Supplies	13,364		1.5
Utilities	9,000		1.0
Interest	17,000		1.9
Travel	4,583		.5
Communications	11,500		1.3
Insurance	7,300		.8
Depreciation	7,900		.9
Professional services	6,000		.7
Bad debts	3,000		.3
Rent	28,500		3.1
Total		319,420	35.1*
Net income before taxes		53,982	5.9
Less: Federal income taxes		26,991	3.0
Net income		$26,991	2.9*

*Rounding errors

Cost of goods sold is the computed actual cost of the merchandise sold to customers. It is found as follows: beginning inventory plus purchases minus ending inventory. Subtracting cost of goods sold from net sales leaves *gross profit.*

Expenses are then subtracted from gross profit to leave net income (or profit) before taxes. Federal income taxes are traditionally the final deduction, leaving net income after taxes. Net income after taxes is the proverbial "bottom line."

Statement of Retained Earnings. The statement of retained earnings (see Table 3.7) shows the activity that has occurred in the retained earnings account during the accounting period. It shows the exact breakdown of profit distributed to owners or stockholders and the earnings retained in the business.

Relationship among the Three Statements. You can see that the balance sheet is a statement of the retailer's financial position at a *specific point in time,* analogous to a snapshot. An income statement shows the results of operating *for a specific time interval* or what occurred *between* two points in time.

The statement of retained earnings shows how the retained earnings account is adjusted between two balance sheet dates. The retailer may keep profits in the firm (rather than disbursing to owners) to finance the purchase of assets. However, the retained earnings account shown on the balance sheet *is not cash* and therefore cannot buy anything. The earnings for the current year may be available in the form of cash, but past retained earnings usually have already been converted from cash to assets such as land, building, and inventories.

Common-Size Financial Statements. Analysis of a firm's financial statements is enhanced by comparisons with other firms and over time. To facilitate these comparisons, retailers can use common-size financial statements, which convert each figure on the income statement to a percentage of total sales and each figure on the balance sheet to a percentage of total assets. These conversions are included in Tables 3.5 and 3.6.

Table 3.7
Michael's Men's Store statement of retained earnings,
for year ended December 31, 19x4

Balance of retained earnings, December 31, 19x3	$28,009
Add: Net income, 19x4	26,991
	55,000
Less: Distribution to owner	25,000
Balance of retained earnings, December 31, 19x4	$30,000

Ratio Analysis

Ratio analysis is used to help evaluate a firm's financial performance and conditions. The analysis is based on relationships between two or more financial variables, primarily those reported in the financial statements discussed earlier.

Types of Ratios. The retailer should be familiar with four basic types of ratios[4]:

1. *Profitability ratios*, which measure management's ability to turn each dollar of revenue into profit (operating efficiency) and to produce profits from each invested dollar (financial efficiency)

2. *Liquidity ratios*, which measure the retailer's ability to pay current liabilities (also called short-term solvency)

3. *Leverage ratios*, which measure the retailer's use of debt and ability to meet schedule repayments

4. *Activity ratios*, which measure the retailer's ability to generate sales and profits from assets.

Specific key ratios for each of these ratio types are summarized in Table 3.8.

Using Ratios. Standard or ideal figures for the various ratios cannot be determined and none have been found that will ensure success. However, a reasonable evaluation using these ratios is still necessary. Two types of comparisons are useful: (1) current ratio values with those of similar retailers and (2) current ratio values with previous ratio values.

A primary source of retailers' ratios is the National Retail Merchants Association's *Financial and Operating Results*. Other good sources include Dun & Bradstreet's *Key Business Ratios in 800 Lines* and various trade publications. It is important to understand that these sources usually provide average ratio values and range of ratio values for a particular classification of retailers. The retailer should not view these as ideal ratio values, but simply as indications of other retailers' peformance. Table 3.9 presents Michael's key ratios along with industry averages.

In comparing current ratio values with previous ratios, the retailer should look for trends. A change in the value of various ratios indicates a change in the retailer's financial position or performance. This **trend analysis** can help alert the retailer to potential problems before they get out of hand. Note that this ratio comparison only indicates a change; in-depth analysis is required to determine the cause of the change. Table 3.9 also illustrates ratio trend analysis for selected ratios of Michael's.

The du Pont System of Financial Analysis

The du Pont system of financial analysis has received wide recognition in American industry and can be quite useful to retailers.[5] The system combines **activity ratios** and **profitability ratios** to show how they interact to determine the retailer's **return on investment** (ROI).

Table 3.8
Summary of key financial ratios

RATIO	HOW CALCULATED	WHAT IT SHOWS
Profitability ratios		
1. Gross profit margin	$\dfrac{\text{Sales} - \text{Cost of goods sold}}{\text{Sales}}$	An indication of the total margin available to cover operating expenses and yield a profit.
2. Operating profit margin	$\dfrac{\text{Profits before taxes and before interest}}{\text{Sales}}$	An indication of the firm's profitability from current operations without regard to the interest charges accruing from the capital structure.
3. Net profit margin (or return on sales)	$\dfrac{\text{Profits after taxes}}{\text{Sales}}$	Shows after-tax profits per dollar of sales. Subpar-profit margins indicate that the firm's sales prices are relatively low or that its costs are relatively high or both.
4. Return on total assets	$\dfrac{\text{Profits after taxes}}{\text{Total assets}}$ or $\dfrac{\text{Profits after taxes} + \text{Interest}}{\text{Total assets}}$	A measure of the return on total investment in the enterprise. It is sometimes desirable to add interest to after-tax profits to form the numerator of the ratio since total assets are financed by creditors as well as by stockholders; hence it is accurate to measure the productivity of assets by the returns provided to both classes of investors.
5. Return on stockholders' equity (or return on net worth)	$\dfrac{\text{Profits after taxes}}{\text{Total stockholders' equity}}$	A measure of the rate of return on stockholders' investment in the enterprise.
6. Return on common equity	$\dfrac{\text{Profits after taxes} - \text{Preferred stock dividends}}{\text{Total stockholders' equity} - \text{Par value of preferred stock}}$	A measure of the rate of return on the investment which the owners of common stock have made in the enterprise.
7. Earnings per share	$\dfrac{\text{Profits after taxes} - \text{Preferred stock dividends}}{\text{Number of shares of common stock outstanding}}$	Shows the earnings available to the owners of common stock.
Liquidity ratios		
1. Current ratio	$\dfrac{\text{Current assets}}{\text{Current liabilities}}$	Indicates the extent to which the claims of short-term creditors are covered by assets that are expected to be converted to cash in a period roughly corresponding to the maturity of the liabilities.
2. Quick ratio (or acid-test ratio)	$\dfrac{\text{Current assets} - \text{Inventory}}{\text{Current liabilities}}$	A measure of the firm's ability to pay off short-term obligations without relying upon the sale of its inventories.
3. Inventory to net working capital	$\dfrac{\text{Inventory}}{\text{Current assets} - \text{Current liabilities}}$	A measure of the extent to which the firm's working capital is tied up in inventory.
Leverage ratios		
1. Debt to assets ratio	$\dfrac{\text{Total debt}}{\text{Total assets}}$	Measures the extent to which borrowed funds have been used to finance the firm's operations.
2. Debt to equity ratio	$\dfrac{\text{Total debt}}{\text{Total stockholders' equity}}$	Provides another measure of the funds provided the creditors versus the funds provided by owners.

RATIO	HOW CALCULATED	WHAT IT SHOWS
3. Long-term debt to equity ratio	$\dfrac{\text{Long-term debt}}{\text{Total stockholders' equity}}$	A widely used measure of the balance between debt and equity in the firm's overall capital structure.
4. Times-interest-earned (or coverage ratios)	$\dfrac{\text{Profits before interest and taxes}}{\text{Total interest charges}}$	Measures the extent to which earnings can decline without the firm's becoming unable to meet its annual interest costs.
5. Fixed charge coverage	$\dfrac{\text{Profits before taxes and interest} + \text{Lease obligations}}{\text{Total interest charges} + \text{Lease obligations}}$	A more inclusive indication of the firm's ability to meet all of its fixed-charge obligations.

Activity ratios

1. Inventory turnover	$\dfrac{\text{Sales}}{\text{Inventory}}$	When compared to industry averages, it provides an indication of whether a company has excessive inventory or perhaps inadequate inventory.
2. Fixed assets turnover	$\dfrac{\text{Sales}}{\text{Fixed assets}}$	A measure of the sales productivity and utilization of plant and equipment.
3. Total assets turnover	$\dfrac{\text{Sales}}{\text{Total assets}}$	A measure of the utilization of all the firm's assets; a ratio below the industry average indicates the company is not generating a sufficient volume of business given the size of its asset investment.
4. Accounts receivable turnover	$\dfrac{\text{Annual credit sales}}{\text{Accounts receivable}}$	A measure of the average length of time it takes the firm to collect the sales made on credit.
5. Average collection period	$\dfrac{\text{Accounts receivable}}{\text{Total sales} \div 365}$ or $\dfrac{\text{Accounts receivable}}{\text{Average daily sales}}$	Indicates the average length of time the firm must wait after making a sale before it receives payment.

Other ratios

1. Dividend yield on common stock	$\dfrac{\text{Annual dividends per share}}{\text{Current market price per share}}$	A measure of the return to owners received in the form of dividends.
2. Price-earnings ratio	$\dfrac{\text{Current market price per share}}{\text{After tax earnings per share}}$	Faster growing or less risky firms *tend* to have higher price-earnings ratios than slower growing or more risky firms.
3. Dividend payout ratio	$\dfrac{\text{Annual dividends per share}}{\text{After tax earnings per share}}$	Indicates the percentage of profits paid out as dividends.
4. Cash flow per share	$\dfrac{\text{After tax profits} + \text{depreciation}}{\text{Number of common shares outstanding}}$	A measure of the discretionary funds over and above expenses available for use by the firm.

Source: Arthur A. Thompson, Jr., and A. J. Strickland III, *Strategy and Policy* (Plano, Tex.: Business Publications, 1981), pp. 216–218.
© BUSINESS PUBLICATIONS, INC., 1978 and 1981.

Table 3.9
Michael's ratio trends and comparison with trade values

		19x0	19x1	19x2	19x3	19x4	MICHAEL'S TREND	MICHAEL'S VS. TRADE
Profitability								
Gross profit margin	Michael's	42.00%	41.00%	40.00%	42.00%	41.48%	Good	Good
	Trade average	42.00%	40.50%	40.00%	41.50%	40.98%		
Net profit margin	Michael's	3.5%	3.8%	3.9%	3.9%	3.0%	Poor	Poor
	Trade average	4.4%	4.5%	4.8%	5.0%	5.0%		
Return on total assets	Michael's	5.0%	4.8%	4.9%	4.9%	5.0%	Good	Good
	Trade average	5.6%	5.7%	5.8%	5.9%	6.0%		
Return on equity	Michael's	13.0%	14.0%	15.0%	16.0%	20.8%	Good	Good
	Trade average	9.0%	11.0%	13.0%	14.0%	15.0%		
Liquidity								
Current ratio	Michael's	2.4	2.5	2.6	2.5	2.6	Good	Good, but maybe too high
	Trade average	2.2	2.3	2.1	2.1	2.2		
Quick ratio	Michael's	1.2	1.30	1.40	1.25	1.38	Good	Good, but maybe too high
	Trade average	1.1	.95	1.0	.9	1.0		
Leverage								
Debt to assets	Michael's	75%	76%	75%	75%	76%	Good	Good
	Trade average	60%	60%	60%	60%	60%		
Debt to equity	Michael's	3.1	3.2	3.1	3.1	3.15	Good	Good
	Trade average	3.0	3.1	3.1	3.0	3.0		
Activity								
Inventory turnover	Michael's	4.1	4.0	3.9	4.2	4.0	Good	Poor
	Trade average	5.3	5.2	5.1	5.2	5.0		

As shown in Figure 3.4, a retailer first develops the profit margin on sales and then the asset turnover ratio. Multiplying these two ratios results in return on asset investment according to the following formulas:

$$\frac{\text{Net}}{\text{profit margin}} \times \frac{\text{Asset}}{\text{turnover}} = \text{ROI}.$$

Therefore,

$$\frac{\text{Profit}}{\text{Sales}} \times \frac{\text{Sales}}{\text{Assets}} = \text{ROI}.$$

Michael's net profit margin was 2.97 percent and asset turnover was 1.69 times. These ratios combine to yield an ROI of 5 percent. Since this ROI is

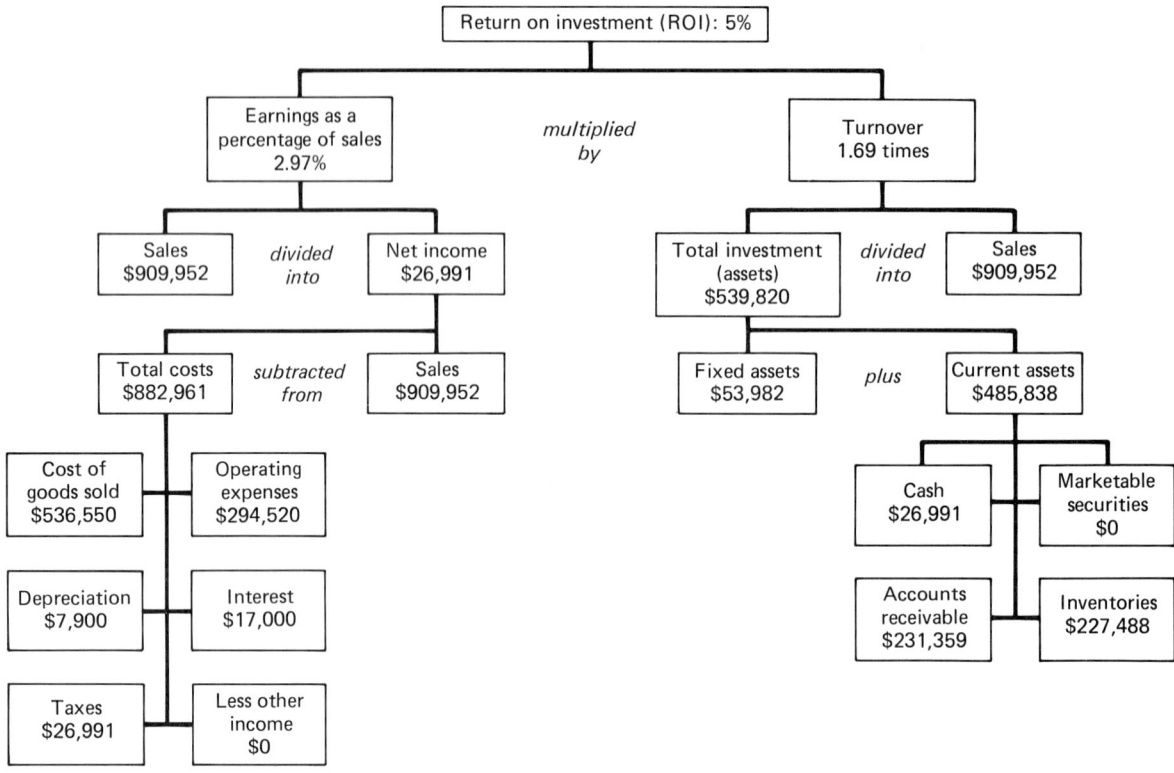

Figure 3.4
Modified du Pont system of financial control applied to Michael's Men's Store

Source: Adapted from Managerial Finance, 7th ed. by J. F. Weston and E. F. Brigham, p. 153. Copyright © 1981 by the Dryden Press, a division of Holt, Rinehart and Winston, © 1962, 1966, 1969, 1977, 1977, 1978. Reprinted by permission of Holt, Rinehart and Winston, CBS College Publishing.

somewhat below the trade average (see Table 3.9), Michael is likely to be interested in improving it.

The usefulness of the du Pont system is in showing the retailer how various changes will eventually impact the ROI. Assume Michael thinks there is an opportunity to reduce cost of goods sold. How much would cost of goods sold have to be for the ROI to become 6 percent? Net profit margin must increase to 3.55% (3.55 × 1.69 = 6). To do so, net income must increase to $32,303 ($32,303 ÷ $909,952 = 3.55%). Therefore, total costs (specifically, cost of goods sold) must decrease by $5,312 ($32,303 − $26,991). Hence, cost of goods sold would have to be $531,238 ($536,550 − $5,312). Michael can trace other alternatives through the du Pont system to gauge their impact on ROI.

It is also useful to consider **leverage.** Michael's 20.8 percent return on equity is substantially greater than the trade's 15.0 percent average (Table 3.9). However, Michael's 5.0 percent return on total assets is *below* the trade average of 6.0 percent. A crucial question is how this can occur. The answer involves Michael's leverage: Michael uses more debt than the average retailer in the trade.

Only 24 percent of Michael's total assets are financed with equity ($130,000 ÷ $539,820); the remaining 76 percent are financed with debt. This extensive use of debt boosts or "levers" the return on owner's equity. To see the effect of this financial leverage, we can arrange the formula for return on equity as follows:

$$\text{Return on equity} = \frac{\text{Return on assets (ROI)}}{\% \text{ of assets financed by equity}}.$$

For Michael:

$$\text{Return on equity} = \frac{5\%}{0.24} = 20.8\%.$$

For the trade:

$$\text{Return on equity} = \frac{6\%}{0.40} = 15.0\%.$$

Therefore, if Michael maintained a 5 percent ROI but reduced debt financing or increased equity (for example, by leaving retained earnings in the firm) to match the trade average, the return on equity would be 12.5 percent (5% ÷ 0.4) or lower than the 15.0 percent trade average.

Michael has used financial leverage to boost return on equity higher than the trade average. Note that there are limitations to this practice. Creditors tend to resist at higher leverage levels and the risk of bankruptcy is greater.

Special Retailing Data

In addition to the conventional ratios and percentages useful to retailers, there are several other types of data that are somewhat unique to retailers and that can also be useful. *Financial and Operating Results* (FOR), published annually by the National Retail Merchants Association, is an excellent source of this information. Table 3.10 shows selected results for 1979. The FOR also includes many expenses expressed as a percentage of sales.

Problems with Using Ratios

Certain problems can arise when retailers use ratio analysis for evaluation and control of financial performance and condition.

1. *Ratios do not provide concrete answers.* Ratios are warning signals. Ratios that seem out of line require further investigation.

2. *Deviation of a single ratio value may be acceptable.* Deviation might be due to some temporary factor. The key point is that the retailer should use a *ratio profile* consisting of many ratios rather than a single ratio.

Table 3.10
Selected results for department stores
with sales between $500,000 and $1 million, 1979

Cash sales, % of total sales	62.58%
Credit sales, % of total sales	33.51%
Third-party credit cards, % of total sales	3.91%
Sales per square foot of selling space	$ 110.75
Sales per square foot of total space	$ 72.29
Selling space, % of total space	68.4%
Average gross sale	$ 20.57
Returns and allowance, % of gross sales	6.49%
Transactions per sq. ft. of selling space	4
Sales per salesperson	$ 55,326
Sales per employee	$ 42,697
Salespeople, % of total employees	77.51%
Percentage of initial markup on purchases	49.41%
Markdowns, % of total sales	13.18%
Total reductions, % of total sales	14.40%
Gross margin, % of total sales	40.98%
Stock turnover	1.97 times
Net operating expense, % of total sales	37.60%
Pretax earning, % of total sales	3.77%

Source: *Financial and Operating Results of Department and Specialty Stores for 1979*, (New York: National Retail Merchants Association, 1980), p. 38.

3.   *Ratios based on interim data may be misleading.* Data for periods of less than one year can be influenced strongly by the normal sensitivity of the retailer's operations.

4.   *Ratios are based on historical data.* Historical data do not necessarily indicate future performance.

5.   *Comparison with trade ratios can be hazardous.* Ratios are constructed from accounting data. Firms in the trade may use a wide variety of accounting methods, such as those for valuing inventory or for depreciation.

MONITOR AND ADAPT

Monitor and adapt, the fifth step of the strategic financial planning and control process, must be discussed from two separate perspectives. First, the process itself must be monitored to ensure effectiveness for both the planning and the control process; inefficiencies should evoke adjustments in the manner in which the process is used for adaptations in the process itself. For example, the authors have observed several situations in which the rudiments of a solid financial analysis were present, but only as a "paper" exercise by the accounting staff; line managers and higher-echelon executives were not exposed to any part of the financial process. These situations represent inefficient utilization of the process.

Adaptations to the process itself should be pursued when the process is not structured to generate appropriate results. As mentioned in the Introduction to this chapter, the financial process can be viewed as a repeating cycle of the key components: planning to control to analysis to planning to control, and so on. Therefore, the process should provide profit planning, serve as a control mechanism, and generate performance and position evaluations.

The second perspective of the strategic financial process actually has broader implications than the first. In effect, *the financial planning, control, and analysis activities are focused on the performance and results generated by all the retailer's strategic decisions.* Let us discuss each of the financial activities in light of this statement.

Profit Planning and Strategic Decisions

We will emphasize throughout this book that the *objectives* stated for each strategic decision area should be anchored in the retailer's overall objectives. Further, the retailer's dominant operating objective should be stated in terms of profits. Therefore, profit planning should actually occur before any of the other functional strategic decisions are completed. For example, merchandise planning, advertising, and the like should all be designed to contribute to achieving the retailer's profit objectives.

Financial Control and Strategic Decisions

We approached financial control as a process of using carefully prepared budgets to monitor performance. The key budgets discussed were operating budgets (consisting of specific budgets for sales, cost of goods sold, and expenses) and cash budgets. In effect, these budgets *control* the implementation of other strategic decisions and *monitor* their performance and results from a financial standpoint. This financial perspective is appropriate and necessary because all the other strategic decisions should have measurable financial outcomes.

Financial Analysis and Strategic Decisions

The primary tools of financial analysis are the retailer's financial statements and ratio analysis. Financial analysis can be viewed as analyzing the bottom-line results of the retailer's strategic decisions. This analysis should help the retailer pinpoint any deviations from desired performance levels. For example, analysis of the *average collection period* for accounts receivable might uncover an undesirable trend toward longer collection periods. Since this trend can lead to cash-flow problems, the retailer should investigate the situation.

SUMMARY

Strategic financial decisions and activities are critical to the retailer's well-being. Interaction between the strategic financial process and other strategic decision areas should occur at the beginning (with profit planning), middle (with budgetary control), and end (with analysis of performance and position) of all strategic planning processes.

The profit planning process is designed to help the retailer analyze sales and costs in order to forecast and improve profit performance. Budgeting is the preparation of operating, cash, and capital budgets; budgets are the retailer's projected operating plans and can be crucial for monitoring and controlling performance. Analysis of financial performance and position helps the retailer evaluate results and serves as input to the strategy and profit planning phases.

KEY CONCEPTS

Profit planning

Budgeting

Analysis of financial performance
  and position

Strategic profit planning process

Fixed costs

Variable costs

Semivariable costs

Marginal analysis

Operating budget

Sales budget

Costs of goods sold budget

Expense budget

Expense variability

Expense flexibility

Cash budget

Cash needs

Cash excess

Cash inflows

Cash outflows

Financial statements

Balance sheet

Assets

Liabilities

Owner's equity

Income statement

Statement of retained earnings

Ratio analysis

Profitability ratios

Liquidity ratios

Leverage ratios

Activity ratios

Trend analysis

du Pont system

Return on investment (ROI)

REVIEW QUESTIONS

1. Outline the strategic financial planning and control process.
2. Outline the strategic profit planning process.
3. Discuss the four components necessary to build a logical profit objective.

4. Discuss the different types of situations that call for "sales forecasting" versus "back-door estimation" of sales volume necessary to achieve a desired profit.

5. Briefly describe the basic alternatives for improving profit.

6. If total costs per dollar are 90 cents for forecasted sales volume, will each additional dollar of sales also have a 90-cent total cost? Why or why not?

7. Distinguish between expenses and cash outflows.

8. Distinguish between sales and cash inflows.

9. Describe each of the four basic types of ratios.

10. Outline the du Pont system of financial analysis.

PROBLEMS

1. Choose a retail trade and obtain average CGS and expenses (as a percent of sales). Calculate the sales level necessary to support various desired profit levels.

2. Using the following information for XYZ Company, determine a specific profit objective:

Original investment	$250,000
Retained earnings	$250,000
Desired return percentage	25%
Salary from alternative employment	$35,000
Assumed tax rate	50%

3. Find the break-even point for XYZ Company if fixed costs are $400,000 and variable costs are 70 percent of sales.

4. Find the break-even point for a retailer if fixed costs are $700,000 and variable costs are 47.5 percent of sales.

5. Would it be profitable to add an employee at a cost of $10,000 if sales would increase by $75,000 and the marginal income rate is 25%.

6. Calculate the cash excess or shortfall, given the following:

Cash sales	$100,000
Accounts receivable collections	100,000
Cash purchases	30,000
Payments on accounts payable	20,000
Notes payable	5,000
Total expenses	50,000
Depreciation expense	15,000

7. Given the following data, construct a du Pont diagram:

Sales	$1,000,000
Cost of goods sold	500,000
Operating expenses	200,000
Depreciation	100,000
Interest	100,000

Taxes	50,000
Fixed assets	100,000
Current assets	450,000
Cash	100,000
Accounts receivable	100,000
Inventories	250,000

8. Using your analysis in Problem 7, determine the impact of the following changes on ROI:

a) 10 percent increase in sales

b) 10 percent decrease in cost of goods sold

c) 10 percent decrease in inventories

d) 10 percent increase in operating expenses

DECISION SITUATION 3.1 **THE NEW STORE**

Dan is contemplating opening a store specializing in woodworking. He is knowledgeable in the field and has sold some products, such as picture frames, breadboxes, and china cabinets at handicraft fairs. To open this business Dan would need to quit his present job, which pays $15,000 a year.

Dan does not know what sales he could expect. He does have a reasonable idea about what the costs would be. The cost of goods sold would be about 60 percent of sales. An available building would cost $200 per month. Other costs would total about $400 per month. Dan has the tools necessary to begin the shop and these were not considered in the costs.

QUESTIONS

1. What is the break-even point for Dan's store?

2. Suppose another cost of $100 per month was incurred because Dan advertised more. What would happen to the break-even point?

3. Should Dan add the cost of tools?

4. Would you recommend that Dan open the store?

DECISION SITUATION 3.2: **KAREN'S FASHIONS**

Karen cannot understand what is happening to her women's clothing store. The store is almost two years old and has been showing a profit for several months, but Karen has had to put additional money into the store each month to pay the bills. She understood this when the store was losing money but not when there were profits.

Karen's bookkeeper assured her that the accounts were correct representations of the data Karen sent him. Karen is sure the answer is more simple than it appears. The income statement was carefully examined and no problems were discovered.

The balance sheet was examined, but Karen did not think the problem could be found there. The following is a condensed version of the last two quarterly balance sheets.

	1/1	4/1
Assets		
Cash	$ 750.00	$ 680.00
Inventory	21,500.00	22,100.00
Accounts receivable	4,650.00	6,250.00
Building and fixtures (less depreciation)	46,780.00	47,000.00
Total	$ 73,680.00	$ 76,030.00
Liabilities and Owner's Equity		
Accounts payable	$ 9,000.00	$ 9,500.00
Notes payable	53,000.00	50,000.00
Other liabilities	3,000.00	3,200.00
Retained earnings	(8,000.00)	(6,000.00)
Owner's investment	16,680.00	19,330.00
Total	$ 73,680.00	$ 76,030.00

QUESTIONS

1. What is Karen's problem? What is the reason for her problem?

2. How can she handle the problem?

3. What would your recommend to Karen?

NOTES

1. This process is adapted from Curtis E. Tate, Jr., Leon C. Megginson, Charles R. Scott, Jr., and Lyle R. Trueblood, *Successful Small Business Management* (Dallas: Business Publications, 1978), pp. 405–406.

2. Subhash Sharma and Vijay Mahajan, "Early Warning Indicators of Business Failure," *Journal of Marketing*, Fall 1980, pp. 80–89.

3. This section draws heavily on Steven E. Bolten and Robert L. Conn, *Essentials of Managerial Finance* (Boston: Houghton Mifflin Company, 1981), pp. 72–78.

4. *Ibid.*, p. 78.

5. This section relies heavily on J. Fred Weston and Eugene F. Brigham, *Managerial Finance* (Hinsdale, Ill.: Dryden Press, 1981), pp. 152–154.

PART II
THE RETAILING ENVIRONMENTS

STRATEGIC RETAIL MANAGEMENT MODEL

Philosophy of business: mission, purpose, goals	

↓

Retailer objectives

↓

Situation analysis

External	Internal

↓

Financial objectives	Marketing objectives	Human resources objectives

↓

Gap analysis

↓

Portfolio of strategic alternatives

Financial strategy	Marketing strategy	Human resources strategy

↓

Target markets

Buyer behavior	Market segmentation

↓

Retailing mix strategies

Location	Merchandise	Pricing	Communication

↓

Budgets

↓

Marketing tactics

↓

Implementation

↓

Control Procedures

↓

Monitor and adapt

Key:

——————— Direct path

– – – – – Feedback

Chapter 4
The Retailing Macroenvironment

LEARNING OBJECTIVES

1. To develop an understanding of the retail macroenvironment and its impact on retailing strategy.

2. To understand the process of macroenvironmental analysis.

INTRODUCTION

As discussed in Chapter 2, a retailing strategy should be designed to utilize the retailer's strengths to achieve the objectives of the organization. Retailing objectives and strategy should also focus on taking advantage of environmental opportunities and minimizing the impact of environmental threats; analyzing and adapting to the environment are the keys to the success of retail organizations.

Retailers are part of the larger environment that affects the functioning of the retail organization. To achieve the desired objectives, the retailer must adapt to the environment, which can offer opportunities or be an impediment. For example, changing age composition in the market, such as an increase in the over-65 age group, can offer opportunities in areas such as medical goods and services or retirement condominiums. Conversely, a decrease in the 14 to 24 age group can threaten the market for pizza restaurants and record stores.

In addition to adapting to and coping with the present environment, retailers must be prepared to cope with the future. Peter Drucker summarizes this concept as follows: "All institutions live and perform in two time periods: today and tomorrow. Tomorrow is being made today—irrevocably in most cases. In turbulent times managers cannot assume that tomorrow will be an extension of today. On the contrary, they must manage for change—change as an opportunity and change as a threat."[1] Strategy in Action 4.1 shows how two retailers adapt to the environment with two different strategies.

STRATEGY IN ACTION 4.1

Adaptations in the Lodging Industry

Holiday Inns, Inc., and Best Western International are the two leading lodging chains in the United States; yet each is developing a separate reaction strategy to the increased price of gasoline. Best Western management believes the rising prices will "drive American travelers off the road." Specifically, their research indicates that when gasoline prices reach $2.00 per gallon, auto driving will fall by 17 percent. Holiday Inns' research, on the other hand, shows that even at $2.00 per gallon, driving habits of Americans will not change measurably. Thus Best Western is embarking on a strategy that will: (1) change the name and symbol of the organization, (2) develop international affiliates, (3) stress the individuality and personality of its lodgings, and (4) make a major effort to attract foreign tourists. Holiday Inns forecasts no major changes in driving behavior patterns because more efficient autos have been developed; and when compared to other methods of traveling, auto travel is relatively inexpensive. Therefore, to Holiday Inns, gasoline prices in the range of $2.00 per gallon are not a significant business problem, and no major strategy changes other than entering into the casino gambling business are planned.

Source: Adapted from "Somebody Must Be Wrong," *Forbes,* 14 April 1980, pp. 82–89.

For our discussion, the total environment can be divided into three levels: the **organization environment,** the **task environment,** and the **macroenvironment.** These three environmental levels are defined and their relationship illustrated graphically in Fig. 4.1.

The retailer must be cognizant of three other factors when determining the environmental influences: environmental complexity, environmental turbulence, and proactive versus reactive decision making.

Environmental Complexity

Environmental complexity is characterized by the number of components influencing the retailing effort.[2] The more complex the environment, the harder it is to make effective retailing decisions. Retailing environments are continually becoming more complex. Increased government involvement in business, increased consumer activity, rapid growth in technology, the fracturing of society, and the increased effect of scarce natural resources are all indications of a very complex environment for the retailing decision maker.

Environmental Turbulence

Environmental turbulence involves the dynamism or rate of change in the retail environment. In a *stable environment,* change can be almost nonexistent. In an *evolving environment,* the degree of change can be relatively slow and predictable. A *turbulent environment* can be characterized by rapid

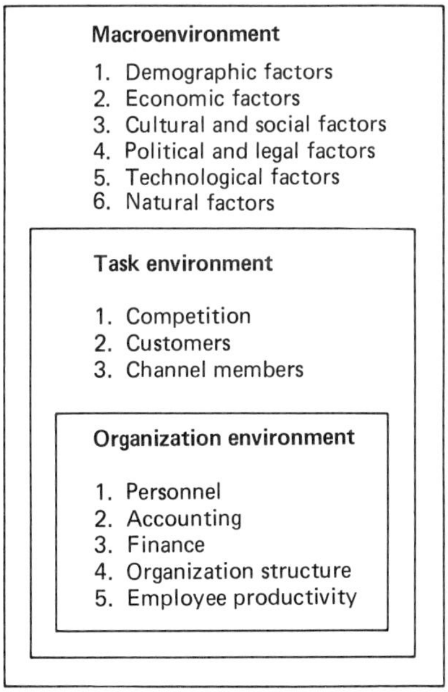

Macroenvironment

1. Demographic factors
2. Economic factors
3. Cultural and social factors
4. Political and legal factors
5. Technological factors
6. Natural factors

Task environment

1. Competition
2. Customers
3. Channel members

Organization environment

1. Personnel
2. Accounting
3. Finance
4. Organization structure
5. Employee productivity

Figure 4.1
Retail environmental definitions and relationships
Organization Environment: consists of forces within the retail organization that are external to the marketing function and that may affect marketing decisions. Task Environment: consists of those forces external to the retail organization with which marketing interacts on a continuous basis and that may affect marketing decisions. Macroenvironment: consists of those forces external to the retail organization that shape and influence the task and organization environment and pose opportunities and threats to the organization's marketing function.

and, in a few instances, unpredictable changes. Most retailers would agree that we are functioning in an increasingly turbulent environment.

Proactive versus Reactive Decision Making

The retailer's ability to influence environmental forces affects the types of decisions that the retailer can make. A **proactive decision** is made with the intention of directly influencing environmental forces. A **reactive decision** is made in response to environmental forces but with no intention of directly influencing the environment.

From the perspective of the three environmental levels, proactive decisions are most effective in the organization environment on factors such as accounting methods and employee morale. Since the retailer has somewhat less influence on the task environment, proactive decisions are less effective there than in the organization environment, and the necessity for reactive decisions is greater. In the macroenvironment, the reactive decisions are critically important while proactive decisions have limited impact on factors such as economic and natural forces.

Although proactive decisions have only limited impact on macroenvironmental forces, retailers should not overlook their potential. Smaller retailers (through local and national trade associations) and larger retailers can sometimes influence areas such as the political and legal forces. Consider a state that proposes to lower the maximum interest rate retailers can charge on open accounts; retailers in that state could probably organize themselves well enough to influence the vote or election on the issue. Similarly, the interests of specific large retailers can influence advances in computer technology.

It is also important to note that reactive decisions regarding the macroenvironment can take two distinct forms. **Passive-reactive decisions** are made *after* the impact of a macroenvironmental force is felt. For example, after the maximum interest rate on open accounts is lowered, the retailer makes a decision to do something. **Aggressive-reactive decisions** are also made in response to macroenvironmental forces, but *before* the impact is felt. A retailer may accept the fact that maximum interest rates on open accounts will be lowered, but he or she makes a decision on how to respond and is ready to implement it when the regulation becomes effective.

The remainder of this chapter focuses on the macroenvironment. The task environment is discussed in Chapter 5, the organization environment in Chapter 9.

As the macroenvironment continues to change and become more complex, the retailer's ability to analyze, understand, and adapt to the environment becomes increasingly important. A five-step **macroenvironmental analysis** model provides the retailer with a planning framework (see Fig. 4.2). The five steps are the following:

1. Determine relevant macroenvironmental influences.

2. Develop a scanning process.

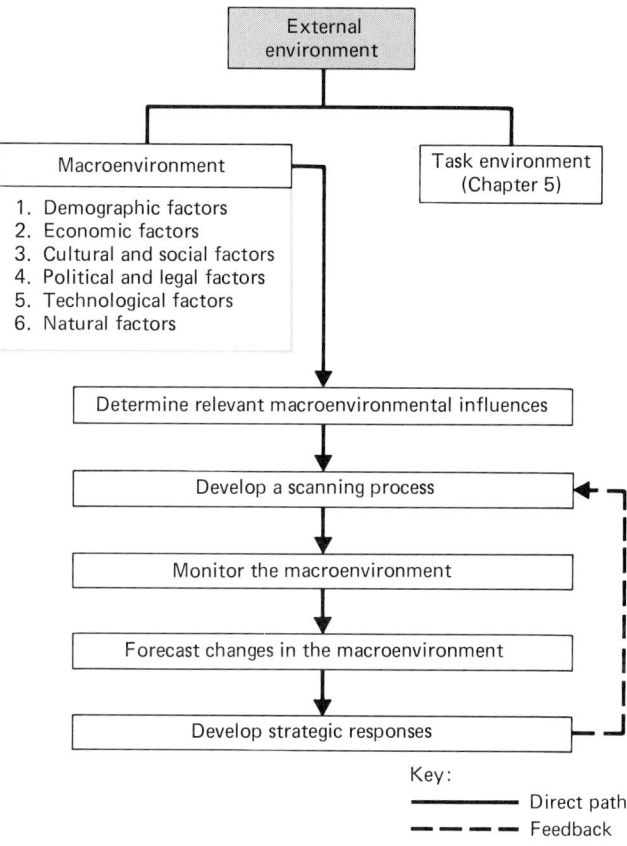

Figure 4.2
Macroenvironmental analysis model

3. Monitor the macroenvironment.

4. Forecast changes in the macroenvironment.

5. Develop strategic responses.

DETERMINE RELEVANT MACROENVIRONMENTAL INFLUENCES

The initial step in analyzing the macroenvironment is to determine which influences are most likely to have an impact on the retailer's decisions. This determination is sometimes called **environmental mapping,** which results in an environmental map.[3] An *environmental map* can be viewed as a "relevance tree" or simply a list of key influences on the retail organization.

Along with the key influencing factors, the map should include information about the relationships among the factors, their *actual* impact on the retailer, and their *potential* impact on the retailer.

Each retailer will have a different set of influences on its environmental map. A small grocery store may have a map primarily concerned with the demographic composition of the local neighborhood (age, income, family size), the local cultural values (subcultures), local competition, and the federal government's policies and attitudes toward small businesses. Conversely, a large retail chain may view *all* of the environmental influences as relevant, with a specific concern for national demographic trends (age, family size), population shifts, lifestyle patterns, government economic policies (interest rates, spending, taxes), economic conditions (income, inflation), and energy costs.

The importance of the environmental map is that its composition determines what macroenvironmental forces are monitored and forecast to determine future strategies. The environmental map sets the stage for the situation analysis.

DEVELOP A SCANNING SYSTEM

Environmental scanning is the process by which the retailer seeks information concerning the macroenvironment. This step involves assigning responsibility and developing an efficient mechanism for information gathering and making decisions for disseminating the information within the retail organization. The importance of this step is highlighted by Kotler's statement: "The more energy a firm devotes to broad environmental scanning, the greater its capacity to survive."[4]

Table 4.1 shows that scanning models can be classified as irregular, regular, and continuous. The *irregular scanning model* can be described as the simplest, least effective, and most widely used scanning model. The *regular scanning model* is more effective than the irregular, but the *continuous scanning model* represents the highest level of sophistication and effectiveness. Unfortunately, although some firms are moving toward use of a continuous model, few, if any, presently have an operating continuous scanning model.

An effective scanning model should focus on the environmental forces defined by environmental mapping to help the retailer pinpoint changes as they occur.

MONITOR THE MACROENVIRONMENT

Once a change in an environmental influence occurs, monitoring begins. The purpose of **environmental monitoring** is to determine *direction, degree, rate,* and *magnitude of change in the macroenvironmental influences.* The

Table 4.1
Scanning model framework

	TYPES OF SCANNING MODELS		
	IRREGULAR	REGULAR	CONTINUOUS
Media for scanning activity	Ad hoc studies	Periodically updated studies	Structured data collection and processing systems
Scope of scanning	Specific events	Selected events	Broad range of environmental systems
Motivation for activity	Crisis initiated	Decision- and issue-oriented	Planning-process-oriented
Temporal nature of activity	Reactive	Proactive	Proactive
Time frame for data	Retrospective	Primarily current and retrospective	Prospective
Time frame for decision impact	Current and near-term future	Near term	Long term
Organizational makeup	Various staff agencies	Various staff agencies	Environment scanning unit

Source: Liam Fahey and William R. King, "Environmental Scanning for Corporate Planning," *Business Horizons,* August 1977, p. 63. Copyright, 1977, by the Foundation for the School of Business at Indiana University. Reprinted by permission.

purpose of identifying these factors is to help establish the probable impact of the changing environment on the retailer and its strategic efforts.[5] Each of the environmental influences will require various monitoring sources. Some of the more common monitoring sources are identified in Table 4.2.

It is first necessary to identify a monitoring approach for the specific environmental influence(s) in question. Once the influencing force in the macroenvironment is being tracked, its behavior patterns can be established

Table 4.2
Sources for monitoring environmental change

DEMOGRAPHIC	ECONOMIC	CULTURAL AND SOCIAL	POLITICAL AND LEGAL	TECHNOLOGICAL	NATURAL
Census data	Economic indicators	Social indicators	Government reports	Identifying "signals" or indicators of change	Government reports
Business publications	Government and association reports	Yankelovich social trends monitor	Trade associations	Government publications	Interest-group reports

Source: Adapted from David W. Cravens, Gerald E. Hills, and Robert B. Woodruff, *Marketing Decision Making* (Homewood, Ill.: Richard D. Irwin, 1980), p. 84. © Richard D. Irwin, Inc., 1976 and 1980.

Table 4.3
The macroenvironment's relationship with retailing decisions

RETAILING DECISION AREAS	MACROENVIRONMENTAL FORCES
Market opportunities	*Demographic:* Changing age group patterns; geographic population shifts; more working women
	Economic: Effects of increased income; economic growth
	Cultural and social: Shifts in values and preferences; socioeconomic trends; lifestyle changes; influence of subcultures
	Political and legal: Effects of federal, state, and local government's actions; opportunities for environmentally safe products (e.g., detergents and foods)
	Technological: Ability to fulfill needs; opportunities for improved cost efficiency
	Natural: Energy efficiencies; substitute products; population shifts to better climates
Information management	*Demographic:* Increased levels of education
	Economic: Effects of increased income; forecasting economic changes
	Cultural and social: Better information to facilitate better serving of needs; social trend prediction; social perspective of research
	Political and legal: Secondary data sources; laws protecting individual privacy
	Technological: Computer usage; improved information gathering, processing, and interpreting; electronic information gathering, cable television
	Natural: Energy costs may limit primary data gathering
Merchandise	*Demographic:* Demand for medical services, books, and convenience items
	Economic: Demand for quality merchandise; inventory costs
	Cultural and social: Fads; core culture values; products for specific lifestyles
	Political and legal: Federal Trade Commission; Product Safety Commission; warranty requirements
	Technological: Increased product complexity (such as electronic games and home computers); better products; more service demanded for complex products
	Natural: Product materials and costs; pollution problems; environmentally safe products

RETAILING DECISION AREAS	MACROENVIRONMENTAL FORCES
Pricing	*Demographic:* Price/value expectations; willingness to pay for quality
	Economic: Impact of inflation and recession; consumer ability to pay; use of credit
	Cultural and social: Perceptions of pricing ethics; behavioral and psychological aspects of pricing; price/value perceptions
	Political and legal: Illegal pricing contraints; pricing regulations; credit legislation
	Technological: Productivity increases leading to lower costs
	Natural: Costs of construction (alternative materials)
Communication	*Demographic:* Provide more information for consumer decision making; need to provide continuous information
	Economic: Costs of communication; economic appeals
	Cultural and social: Changing promotional themes in response to social changes; social responsibility (such as truth in advertising); perceptions of promotion methods
	Political and legal: Legislation (such as Wheeler–Lea Act and "cooling off" laws); Federal Trade Commission; Federal Communications Commission
	Technological: New media techniques (such as cable TV and electronic catalogs); provide more product information; more sophisticated in-store atmospherics
	Natural: Resource usage; environmental concern
Location	*Demographic:* Shift to locations convenient to consumers; present products in more convenient manner
	Economic: Consumer willingness to pay for better locations and facilities; construction costs
	Cultural and social: Location decisions must relate to geographic mobility; distribution efficiency; social decisions (such as ethnic locations)
	Political and legal: Legal constraints; zoning laws
	Technological: Innovative retailing institutions; new physical distribution methods; computer-based location decisions
	Natural: Landscaping; natural disasters, climate

regarding direction, degree, and rate of change. Second, the relationship between the environmental change and the retailer's marketing efforts must be determined. For example, what is the impact of the declining number of young people in the United States on a specific retailer in the toy industry? What is the impact of interest rates on automobile dealers? This relationship must be determined to assess the strategic retailing decisions necessary for adaptation.

Not all retailers will be affected in the same way by their environments. Each retailer must understand how the environment influences its ability to successfully implement marketing strategies and tactics. Table 4.3 on pages 108 and 109 illustrates the interaction of the macroenvironmental forces and strategic retailing decisions. The table is only for explanatory purposes and does not suggest an all-inclusive relationship matrix. The six categories of forces are demographic, economic, cultural and social, political and legal, technological, and natural.

Demographic Environment

The demographics of a society are a statistical representation of its population. In many cases, demographics can help determine types of products and services demanded by the society and can also give the retailer some indication of the ability and location of purchasing power. Our discussion of demographics focuses upon population, geography, income, and family patterns.

Population and Age Distribution. Changes that have taken place and are projected for the next twenty years in the age distribution in the United States are indicated in Fig. 4.3. Population will increase, although no dramatic surges are expected. The age distribution, however, will change enough to alter significantly the retailing environment. During the 1980s, the total U.S. population is expected to grow at the rate of 10 percent, while the 25 to 44 age group will increase 25.5 percent. This increase in this age group is significant because it is the age range in which most families search for their own homes and make numerous home-related purchases such as appliances, furniture, and home accessories. Retailers specializing in these areas will have great opportunities for growth.

Another characteristic of the changing age distribution will be the growth of the over-65 segment. In 1960, this segment constituted 16.7 million people and 9.2 percent of the population, but it is projected to increase to 31.8 million and 12.2 percent of the population by the end of this century. This expected increase suggests a growing demand for retirement homes and communities, medical goods and services, and specialized retail services such as free delivery, larger-print store displays, and special discounts.

Families and Households. The term *households* is defined simply as a dwelling unit that is occupied. *Families,* however, are characterized as two or more persons related by blood or law residing in the same house. The

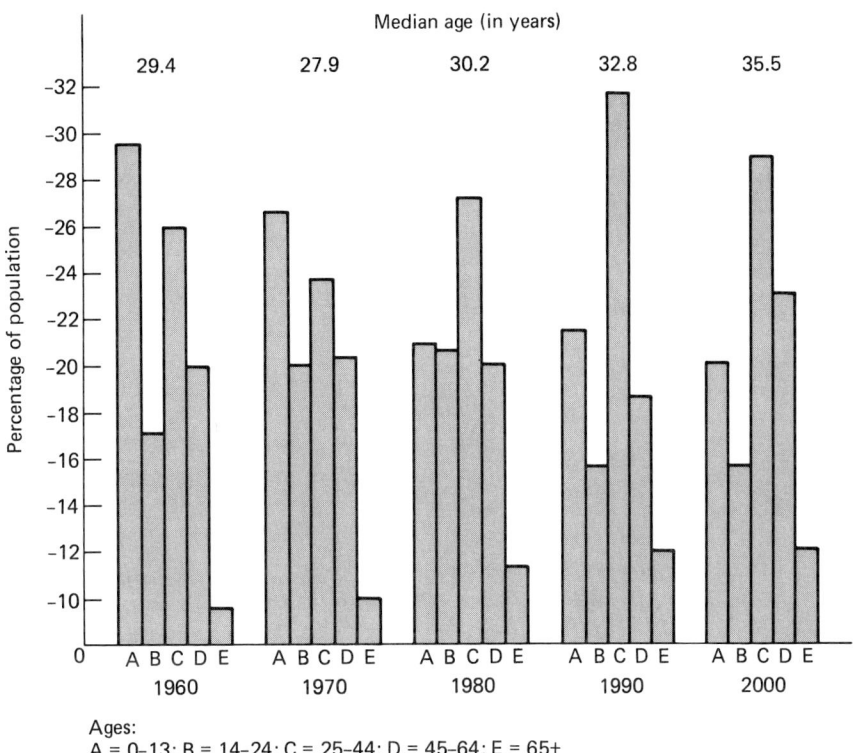

Figure 4.3
Age distribution of U.S. population (1960–2000)
Source: Projections of the Population of the United States: 1977 to 2050, Series P-25, no. 704 (Washington, D.C.: Bureau of the Census, 1977), p. 10.

average size of the U.S. household was 2.8 persons in 1980, and it is forecast to decline in the years ahead, perhaps to 2.4 persons by 1990.[6] At the same time, however, the number of households is expected to increase significantly, perhaps by 21.5 percent in the 1980s. A related demographic trend is the growing number of *primary individual households,* which are individuals not living with family members (they constituted 22 percent of all households in 1980). This type of household occurs as a result of three major factors: the rising divorce rate, the number of young single people living apart from their parents, and the growing number of senior citizens who live by themselves (this category is up 65 percent since 1970). These trends suggest that there will be more households with smaller families in the future and that demand will increase for goods and services oriented toward the home, such as appliances and lawn-care services and products.

In addition, there are at least two specific implications attributable to the primary individual households. First, more individual, as opposed to family, decision making is expected, including more extensive information

STRATEGY IN ACTION 4.2

Marshall Field Moves South

Once the undisputed arbiter of style for Chicago's carriage trade, Marshall Field & Co. has been pummeled by recent demographic and competitive trends in the city even more than its cousin, Carson Pirie Scott & Co. Both department store chains have been hurt by the area's declining population. Yet other retailers based outside Chicago seem undaunted by the demographics, and they have been expanding in the city. Most of the out-of-towners are aiming at Field's market — middle- and upper-income groups. Saks Fifth Avenue, Neiman-Marcus, and I. Magnin — all fashion-oriented — are scheduled to open additional or new Chicago stores this year, and Bloomingdale's is reportedly hunting for space. Unlike Carson, however, Field is determined to fight it out in the business it knows, partly by taking the battle to the doorsteps of some better-heeled competitors in the South and West.

Field's battle began about three years ago, and it has since tripled its number of stores to 93, with most growth in the new markets. In 1978 and 1979, Field acquired John Breuner Co., a big California furniture retailer and renter, and 10 department stores in Oregon and Washington to meld into its Seattle-based Frederick & Nelson unit. In 1980, Field added J. B. Ivey & Co., a 23-unit department store chain in the Carolinas and north Florida, for about $30 million in stock. Field also spent $8 million last year to buy six former Manhattan Industries Inc.'s Union Stores in Columbus, Ohio, to bolster its ailing Halle's chain in Cleveland.

But the pluckiest action to date is Field's recent decision to jump headlong into Neiman-Marcus' turf — Texas. Shunning the local acquisition route, Field plans to build four major-size department stores under its own name in prime Texas locations by the end of 1985 to add to the one huge store it opened in Houston in 1980. Not surprisingly, Field's president and chief executive, Angelo R. Arena, feels at home with this maneuver, since he was Neiman's chairman before coming to Field.

Indeed, Arena sees his entire strategy for the company as the safest route. "Our premise has been to lessen our concentration in the Midwest and expand into our areas where there will be more growth. We could have looked at some nonretail areas, but I felt that first and foremost we were retailers, and that our strategy would be better served expanding in something we already knew," he says. For the same reason, he adds, Field has not followed other department store chains such as Dayton-Hudson Corp. and May Department Stores Co. into discount retailing. Nor is it trying a total change of business, as Carson is doing by moving into airline food service.

Awaiting Results

But after three years of the Sunbelt program, Field has yet to see tangible results. Because its older stores are much bigger than its new ones, the tripling of units has resulted in only a 50% sales increase in the last three years. Profits have stagnated for 10 years, and Field has yet to equal its record earnings of $21.3 million in 1972, even though those profits were culled from roughly half of its current sales volume. In 1979, Field's earnings dropped 9% to $18.9 million on sales of $904.3 million, giving the company returns on sales and on equity that ranked lowest among the nation's top 10 department store chains. In the first nine months of 1980, profits were a tiny $4.6 million on sales of $647 million.

These repeat performances have raised skepticism. At Field, snipes one competitor, "they're doing a lot of changing, but it certainly hasn't shown up on the bottom line." And although Arena began implementing his Sunbelt strategy right after taking the helm in 1977, others see it as a very belated recognition by Field of where the growth markets are in retailing. "I have to commend Mr. Arena for working very hard, but the company should have done this 20 years ago," says Stanley H. Iverson, an analyst at Duff & Phelps Inc., a Chicago investment consultant.

Arena maintains that success is just a matter of time. "Marshall Field is clearly in a transition stage, and I'm enthused about what is happening. But realistically, it's going to be another year or two before we start to feel the compounding effect of our changes," he declares. Arena has succeeded in trimming dependence on the Chicago market to 45% of total sales from 75% three years ago. Still, other aspects of Field's older business are holding the company back.

A Bleeder

The Halle's chain, for example, has been bleeding red ink for almost a decade, primarily because of its big 600,000 sq. ft. store in downtown Cleveland. Arena blames this on the fact that the store "was built when Cleveland was the thriving metropolis that it certainly is not today." He wants to replace the store with another one-third its size, but he cannot find a buyer for the existing property. At home in Chicago, Arena has stemmed some market-share slide in the last two years by replacing most Field store managers with executives who have strong merchandising backgrounds. Field still stresses customer service with in-store shops, but now it is also pushing apparel and accessories aimed at young customers — a traditional weak spot for the company.

But the company is seriously hampered by its prior success in getting customers to use Field credit cards. Once, Field could use its finance charges to make profits on accounts receivable on the cards, and in 1979 an astonishing 66% of Field's total sales were on credit — the highest of the 16 big U.S. department store chains tracked by Harris Trust & Savings Bank. Now, because of growing processing costs and usury laws in some states, Arena says Field must obtain funds at no more than 12% interest to carry these accounts at a profit. Rates of 18% are more common, making profits on the finance charges "just not possible," Arena concedes.

Captial Outlays

Last July, Field executives missed a chance to retire some of their expensive short-term debt. They postponed issuing $30 million to $50 million in long-term bonds at about 11% interest because they expected lower rates by yearend. By late December rates hit 13% instead. Given the substantial financing Field will need to complete its Sunbelt strategy — the Texas stores alone could cost $45 million, observers say — Arena can ill afford similar miscalculations in the future.

Major spending, however, is nearly finished. In fiscal 1979 and 1980 capital expenditures totalled $84 million, more than double the outlay for the prior two years. To maintain such a level would require up to $200 million for store construction and renovation in the next five years — far more than the company could reasonably hope to secure in the debt markets. So Field has little choice but to slow its pace.

Budgeted spending for 1981 already is down to $30 million. Moreover, Arena says his major chain acquisitions are over for now. He plans no new stores for Chicago during the next two years, either. When the Texas stores — including one that is opening in Dallas' posh Galleria shopping center next year — are completed, Arena will have largely restructured Field geographically. His challenge will then become marketing, and outsiders will watch closely for some results — finally — in the profit column.

Source: "Marshall Field: Seeking New Markets in the South and West." Reprinted from the 23 March 1981 issue of *Business Week*, pp. 125, 129, by special permission, © 1981 by McGraw-Hill, Inc., New York NY 10020. All rights reserved.

searches. Second, because of separation from the family, different styles of living are becoming evident, primarily involving more money spent on personal services.

Geographical Distribution.   For the past several decades a sweeping geographical adjustment has been gathering momentum in the United States. The overall movement of population has been from the northeastern and north central states (the *frost belt*) to the southern and western states (the *sun belt*). Linden suggests that these trends will continue because of the rapidly increasing price of heating fuel, which has led to a higher cost of living in the northern regions of the country.[7] Retail growth will follow the population patterns. Strategy in Action 4.2 on pages 112 and 113 shows how one major retailer, Marshall Field, is expanding into the South and West.

One of the most dramatic changes that has taken place over the past thirty-five years is the migration of millions of Americans to the suburbs. The movement to the suburbs continued during the 1970s and it now appears to be slowing down. Presently, 60 percent of the residents living in metropolitan areas live in suburban communities. Rural areas of the United States are also growing faster than urban areas.

The retailing implications of more suburbanites and rural and small-town dwellers include (1) continued location adjustments for retailers, (2) greater demand for house and lawn-care products, (3) increased demand for intracity travel-related services, and (4) possibly increased demand for nonstore retailing.

Income Distribution.   American families have more *real income* (or buying power) than they have had in the past, although the growth in income enjoyed during the 1950s and 1960s slowed during the 1970s. Since 1965, the real standard of living of the average American increased by 50 percent and the number of families with real incomes exceeding $25,000 grew by 80 percent.[8] Much of this growth in family income has come about because of the influx of women into the labor force. This increased income suggests increased demand for better-quality products, more services, and an improved assortment of products. However, the growth of income should be analyzed from a distribution and a geographical perspective.

As Table 4.4 indicates, the number of households with incomes below $15,000 is expected to decline to slightly more than 10 percent of all households by 1990, while the above-$25,000 households will increase to nearly one-third of all U.S. households. By 1990, it is expected that the 32.9 percent of the households with income over $25,000 will have 60.9 percent of the total personal income in the United States at their disposal.

As with population, income is not evenly distributed. Generally, the New England, middle Atlantic, eastern north central, and Pacific states have the highest household incomes. The eastern south central states tend to have the lowest household incomes. However, during the 1970s the states in

Table 4.4
Household income trends (in 1978 dollars)

	1975	1980	1985	1990
Households by income class	100.0%	100.0%	100.0%	100.0%
Under $5,000	15.9	14.1	12.4	10.6
$5,000–$10,000	19.8	18.2	17.2	15.8
$10,000–$15,000	18.1	16.6	15.6	14.4
$15,000–$25,000	27.7	28.1	27.5	26.4
$25,000+	18.5	22.9	27.4	32.9
Income by household income class	100.0%	100.0%	100.0%	100.0%
Under $5,000	3.1	2.5	2.0	1.6
$5,000–$10,000	9.0	7.5	6.5	5.4
$10,000–$15,000	13.7	11.4	10.0	8.2
$15,000–25,000	33.0	30.5	27.7	23.9
$25,000+	41.2	48.1	53.8	60.9

Source: Adapted from Fabian Linden, "Keys to the '80s—Youth and Affluence," *Consumer Markets Indicators,* The Conference Board, December 1979.

the southeastern United States had the fastest-growing household incomes (see Table 4.5). The combined growth in population and income suggests an increasing potential for retailing in the southeastern United States.

Working Women. Probably one of the most significant trends affecting retailing in the United States is the growing number of working women. This trend will continue, with nearly 52 percent of all adult women working by 1990. More than 70 percent of the women in the 25-to-54 age group will be employed by the end of the 1980s.[9] These figures have increased significance when one considers that only 77 percent of all adult males are employed.

The profile of the typical working woman is also changing. Until recently, the majority of working women were employed because they were young, single, or divorced or had a husband who was unable to work. Today the working woman is likely to be married and have children. *U.S. News and World Report* relates that 43.2 percent of all mothers with children under the age of six are working and 59.1 percent of mothers with children between the ages of six and seventeen are in the labor force.

The reasons women work are also changing. The majority of women continue to work for monetary reasons. However, with appreciably better education levels, more women are working for nonmonetary reasons such as career goals or personal satisfaction. Their improved educational level makes available to them more professional jobs with higher pay. This trend

Table 4.5
Forecast rise in per capita income: states with fastest growth, 1978–2000

RANK	STATE	YEAR 2000 INCOME (IN 1978 DOLLARS)	% INCREASE
1.	West Virginia	13,085	97
2.	Kentucky	12,921	96
3.	Mississippi	10,937	96
4.	Alabama	12,216	93
5.	Louisiana	12,801	90
6.	South Carolina	11,796	87
7.	Arkansas	11,415	86
8.	Utah	12,110	84
9.	Montana	12,662	83
10.	Tennessee	12,014	83
	U.S. Average	13,490	72

Source: "States Where Income Will Rise Fastest," *U.S. News and World Report,* 22 December 1980, p. 50.

is also expected to continue, and working women will contribute a larger share of family income in the future. Almost 60 percent of all families now have two or more wage earners, with the wife contributing 40 percent of the income when both husband and wife are employed.

The implications for changes in family life as a result of the increasing numbers of married women in the work force, especially in professional or managerial positions, are immense (see Table 4.6). Some are obvious: less time for shopping during regular daytime store hours, less time to prepare meals, less viewing of daytime television, and more use of labor-saving products. These all suggest more or longer store hours, more dining outside the home, increased patronage of mail-order retailers, more women-oriented television advertising in the evening, more money spent on labor-saving appliances and time-saving foods, and increased one-stop shopping. The expansion of general merchandise lines and longer supermarket hours attest to the impact of working women.

Many other implications are not so obvious. Increased income results in the increased use of services and the possibility of more leisure time. Working women are concerned with quality merchandise and prompt, efficient service that specialty stores and mall boutiques offer. Women's role in the family and society is also being altered. Working women are becoming more independent, more self-confident, and more adept at dealing with their external environment in areas such as financial issues, auto repairs, and insurance purchases. Increasingly, women are demanding a larger role in decision making in the family and society.

Table 4.6
Shopping behavior and meal preparation behavior for working wives (WW) and nonworking wives (NWW)

	% AGREE	
STATEMENT IN SURVEY	WWs	NWWs
Time pressures		
I have more spare time than I need.	11	35
Meal preparation		
Meal preparation should take as little time as possible.	48	38
I always bake from scratch.	39	44
I feel guilty when I serve convenience foods to my family.	39	42
Shopping behavior		
I always check prices even on small items.	78	86
I shop a lot for specials.	79	81

	MEDIAN TIMES	
ACTIVITY	WWs	NWWs
Meal preparation		
How often prepare breakfast per week	4	6
How often prepare lunch per week	3	5
How often prepare dinner per week	7	7
Use frozen TV dinners	less than once a month	
Use frozen pizza	less than once a month	
Use expensive frozen entrées	don't use	
Use regular-priced frozen entrées	don't use	
Preserve by canning	none in the past year	
Shopping behavior		
Use a price-off coupon, per year	18	37
Times went shopping for clothes, per year	10	10
Times purchased from mail-order catalog, per year	3	3
Times went grocery shopping, per month	5.5	5.5

Source: Myra A. Strober and Charles B. Weinberg, "Strategies Used by Working and Nonworking Wives to Reduce Time Pressures," *Journal of Consumer Research,* March 1980, p. 345.

Education.   The number of Americans who have attended or graduated from college continues to grow, and by 1990 it is estimated that almost 35 percent of the adult population will have some exposure to college education. Table 4.7 gives an indication of educational changes between 1975 and 1990. Increased education should create a greater demand for quality products, more printed materials, less television viewing, more travel, and greater acceptance of change. The strategies of increasing product quality in retail offerings, the growth of bookstores, and the broader acceptance of nonstore retailing are some of the likely results increased education will have on retailing.

Hand-in-hand with the increasing levels of educational attainment come higher salaries through white-collar occupations. By 1990, nearly half of all consumer spending will be accounted for by those having some college background. The implications are for a better-educated, higher-income, more leisure-time market for retailers in the future. More demand for quality recreational equipment, facilities, and instruction may be one result of these changes.

All of the foregoing demographic variables are somewhat predictable. In some cases, such as age, the trends have been set in motion. Retailers should be cognizant of these trends and continue to monitor them. There is little reason a retailer should be unaware of demographic changes in the environment.

Table 4.7
Education and employment trends in the United States

	1975	1980	1985	1990
Educational attainment	100.0%	100.0%	100.0%	100.0%
Elementary or less	21.9	18.3	14.4	11.3
Some high school	15.6	16.3	15.4	14.5
High school graduate	36.2	37.9	38.9	39.3
Some college	12.4	12.5	13.7	14.8
College graduate	13.9	15.0	17.5	20.1
	1975	**1980**	**1985**	**1990**
Total employment	100.0%	100.0%	100.0%	100.0%
White-collar workers	49.8	50.3	51.5	52.5
Blue-collar workers	33.0	33.6	32.6	32.0
Service workers	13.7	13.8	14.1	14.3
Other	3.5	2.3	1.8	1.2

Source: Fabian Linden, "Keys to the '80s—Youth and Affluence," *Consumer Markets Indicators,* The Conference Board, December 1979.

**Economic
Environment**

The economic environment also affects the retailer's marketing strategy. The major economic trends affecting retailers are consumers' disposable income and spending patterns, inflation, recession, and cost of credit.

Disposable Income and Expenditures. During the past ten years, inflation has eroded the growth in disposable income to the point of little real growth in consumer spending power (see Table 4.8). With little present growth and only small growth expected in the near future, consumer behavior patterns can be described as cautious. Consumers are becoming more price-sensitive and are considering value more closely. Purchases of private or store brands and, more recently, generic brands has increased. Numerous retailers who have not emphasized price in the past are now emphasizing price and price cutting.

Consumer confidence of future economic expectations has been depressed since the beginning of 1979. This is reflected in decreased purchases of major household goods, automobiles, and houses. To continue, or attempt to continue, major purchases, many families and individuals have extended their credit and/or changed their saving and spending habits.

Inflation. Double-digit inflation became a familiar characteristic of the late 1970s (see Table 4.9). Although some economic forecasters expect inflation to be around 6 to 8 percent during the 1980s, others indicate the probability of higher rates of inflation for the basics—food, energy, housing, and transportation.[10]

Inflation's impact upon the consumer can be identified in a number of ways. Consumers search for methods to stretch their income by purchasing less sweets and snack items, shopping at less expensive retailers, performing their own services and do-it-yourself projects, purchasing generic brands, shopping at distribution centers of national mail-order firms, and using cents-off coupons. Another mechanism for handling inflation is to decrease or delay the purchases of durables, insurance, vacations, and other nonessential products and services.

Recession. Recession (a slowing of growth in an economy) occurs periodically in the United States. During the 1970s we experienced three recessions, the last of which extended into 1980. These downturns in the economy reduce spending power and cause higher unemployment.

The economic growth of an economy affects the money available for spending and, consequently, retail sales. Although the U.S. government has developed economic reinforcement, such as unemployment compensation, for a slowing economy, the retailer must look for declining sales trends and changing behavior patterns during a recession. Especially affected are retailers of major household goods and automobiles. In addition, consumers may be more selective in their purchases by more carefully evaluating their expenditures. The retail emphasis on "value" as projected by Sears and Safeway are indications of these recessionary trends.

Table 4.8
Disposable personal income trends

PERIOD	PERSONAL INCOME	LESS: PERSONAL TAX AND NONTAX PAYMENTS	EQUALS: DISPOSABLE PERSONAL INCOME	LESS: PERSONAL OUTLAYS	EQUALS: PERSONAL SAVING	PER CAPITA DISPOSABLE PERSONAL INCOME		PER CAPITA PERSONAL CONSUMPTION EXPENDITURES		PERCENT CHANGE IN REAL PER CAPITA DISPOSABLE PERSONAL INCOME
	BILLIONS OF DOLLARS					CURRENT DOLLARS	1972 DOLLARS	CURRENT DOLLARS	1972 DOLLARS	
1972	951.4	141.0	810.3	757.7	52.6	3,860	3,860	3,511	3,511	2.9
1973	1,065.2	150.7	914.5	835.5	79.0	4,315	4,083	3,831	3,626	5.8
1974	1,168.6	170.2	998.3	913.2	85.1	4,667	4,013	4,152	3,570	−1.7
1975	1,265.0	168.9	1,096.1	1,001.8	94.3	5,075	4,055	4,521	3,612	1.0
1976	1,391.2	196.8	1,194.4	1,111.9	82.5	5,477	4,161	4,972	3,777	2.6
1977	1,538.0	226.5	1,311.5	1,237.5	74.1	5,954	4,266	5,472	3,922	2.5
1978	1,721.8	258.8	1,462.9	1,386.6	76.3	6,571	4,409	6,058	4,064	3.4
1979	1,943.8	302.0	1,641.7	1,555.5	86.2	7,293	4,493	6,712	4,135	1.9
1980	2,160.2	338.5	1,821.7	1,720.4	101.3	8,002	4,473	7,348	4,108	−.4

[a]Includes personal consumption expenditures, interest paid by consumers to business, and personal transfer payments to foreigners (net).

Source: Department of Commerce, Bureau of Economic Analysis, *Economic Indicators, September 1981* (Washington, D.C.: Government Printing Office, 1981), p. 6.

Table 4.9
Changes in consumer prices, 1971–1980

PERIOD	PERCENT CHANGE FROM PRECEDING PERIOD, SEASONALLY ADJUSTED[a]			
	ALL ITEMS	FOOD	COMMODITIES LESS FOOD	SERVICES
1971	3.4	4.3	2.3	4.1
1972	3.4	4.7	2.5	3.6
1973	8.8	20.1	5.0	6.2
1974	12.2	12.2	13.2	11.3
1975	7.0	6.5	6.2	8.1
1976	4.8	0.6	5.1	7.3
1977	6.8	8.0	4.9	7.9
1978	9.0	11.8	7.7	9.3
1979	13.3	10.2	14.3	13.7
1980	12.4	10.2	11.5	14.2

[a]Annual changes are from December to December (unadjusted).

Source: Department of Labor, Bureau of Labor Statistics, *Economic Indicators, September 1981* (Washington, D.C.: Government Printing Office, 1981), p. 24.

Cost of Credit.   The cost of credit (or interest rates) affects retailers in two ways. First, consumer purchasing patterns and decisions are affected by the availability and cost of credit. With interest rates around 20 percent, consumers do not use credit as freely as they do at lower rates; they also remain cautious in their credit use even when interest rates fall. Second, retailers are directly affected because they also have to *pay* high interest rates. The higher rates are likely to lead to dampened growth and expansion plans, which in turn lead to more repair, refurbishing, or expansion of existing facilities (rather than building new facilities).

Cultural and Social Environment

Culture is the broadest component of social behavior. In a sense, culture is a society's personality. Because of culture's pervasive nature, the beliefs, values, and norms of a culture are almost unconsciously adopted by members of a given society. Their perspective of the world, others in the social system, the institutions with which they interact, the products they purchase, and their perception of time and events are all defined by culture.

American Core Culture.   The culture of a society consists of numerous *values and beliefs*. The *core culture* consists of the values and beliefs that are important and central to the functioning of the society. The core culture is enduring and focuses the overall behavioral patterns of the society. Other values, not as central to the social system's core values may, and frequently do, change over a period of time. The general features of the American core culture and their relevance to consumers' behavior are summarized in Table 4.10.

**Table 4.10
American core culture**

VALUE	GENERAL FEATURES	RELEVANCE TO BEHAVIOR
Achievement and success	Hard work is good; success flows from hard work	Acts as a justification for acquisition of goods ("you deserve it")
Activity	Keeping busy is healthy and natural	Stimulates interest in products that save time and enhance leisure-time activities
Efficiency and practicality	Admiration of things that solve problems (e.g., save time and effort)	Stimulates purchase of products that function well and save time
Progress	People can improve themselves; tomorrow should be better	Stimulates desire for new products that fulfill unsatisfied needs; acceptance of products that claim to be "new" or "improved"
Material comfort	"The good life"	Fosters acceptance of convenience and luxury products that make life more enjoyable
Individualism	Being one's self (e.g., self-reliance, self-interest, and self-esteem)	Stimulates acceptance of customized or unique products that enable a person to "express his [or her] own personality"
Freedom	Freedom of choice	Fosters interest in wide product lines and differentiated products
External conformity	Uniformity of observable behavior; desire to be accepted	Stimulates interest in products that are used or owned by others in the same social group
Humanitarianism	Caring for others, particularly the underdog	Stimulates patronage of firms that compete with market leaders
Youthfulness	A state of mind that stresses being young at heart or appearing young	Stimulates acceptance of products that provide the illusion of maintaining or fostering youth

Source: Leon G. Schiffman, Leslie Lazar Kanuk, *Consumer Behavior,* © 1978, p. 359. Reprinted by permission of Prentice-Hall, Inc., Englewood Cliffs, N.J.

Secondary Cultural Values. A culture's *secondary values* change over time. During the past few decades, the secondary values of the U.S. culture have changed in remarkable ways. Individuals have become more self-centered than in the past, and this has led to an emphasis on "instant satisfaction" among what has been described as the *"me" generation.* Products and services that allow individuals to express themselves and to satisfy short-term goals have grown in importance. Examples of these include self-analysis and self-development techniques, exotic vacations, personal artistic endeavors, designer clothing, and cosmetics.

A concurrent trend is that many people pay more attention to their *quality of life* than to the quantity of life.[11] Retailers will likely feel the impact in the types of merchandise consumers demand and in the way the retailers have to conduct business. Store signs and billboards, for instance, have already been restricted for aesthetic reasons in some cities, and more cities are likely to pass similar ordinances.

Consumer activism, or *consumerism,* has grown out of the widespread attitude that "business is not operating in consumers' best interests." Retailers cannot expect this phenomenon to just go away; rather, the individual retailer must choose a defensive or offensive strategy to cope with consumerism. A defensive strategy involves minimal legal compliance with consumer-oriented government regulations. An offensive strategy, however, appears much more viable in the long run. It is embodied in the retailing concept discussed in Chapter 2 and involves taking advantage of growing consumer concern with value rather than just price, by paying more attention to customer orientation and satisfaction and to providing better-quality merchandise and services.

Lifestyles are patterns of living developed by consumers that largely determine what they purchase. As a result of changing lifestyle patterns, lifestyle marketing is replacing conventional line-of-trade classifications for many retailers (consider the trends in fashion apparel and fashion home furnishings).[12] Great variations in consumer lifestyles exist between geographic locations and the specific target markets of different retailers. The success of smaller retailers will be largely predicated on their personal understanding of the lifestyles of their community or neighborhood and their ability to tailor their offerings to match them. Larger retailers are going to have to rely heavily on research to obtain the understanding they need to become more sophisticated in developing atmospherics, price points, promotion, and operations.

Closely related to changing lifestyles is the increasing time-poverty experienced by many families.[13] Although the widespread assumption is that people have more leisure time, some families (especially two-income families) are experiencing decreasing leisure time. As a result, many retailers may need to think in terms of two types of time markets, one for *time-using* offerings (sports, travel, entertainment) and one for *time-saving* offerings (convenience foods, disposables, microwave ovens). To help

these time-impoverished consumers shop, retailers might consider alternatives such as catalog and telephone ordering, special offers to shift non-
employed consumers' shopping time to off-peak hours, and generally longer
and later hours of opening. Larger retailers might develop extended-hours
"convenience shops" where a limited line of goods is sold in small sections on the perimeter of the building.

A recent study indicated that more than half of the adult population
lacked confidence in most of our major institutions, such as government,
churches, educational institutions, and *business*. This lack of confidence
has developed because of the perceived inability of our major institutions to
solve societal and individual problems. Retailers should be particularly interested in countering such attitudes, first by making a recognizable effort to
be responsible "citizens." Examples of such efforts include hiring minorities, participating in charitable drives, and showing a general concern for
the well-being of the community. Retailers should also demonstrate concern
for individual consumers by providing conveniences such as more information, unit pricing, and a better store atmosphere.

Political and Legal Environment

The relationship between retailers and the legal and political arena is becoming more intertwined. The number of laws and regulations governing
specific business behavior has increased, especially during the past two
decades. In 1979, federal regulations cost the American public and business
$100 billion.[14]

Federal Regulation.   Government regulation aimed at shaping business
behavior is based upon several premises. As business enterprises become
larger relative to consumers, other businesses, and the government (especially local governments), they become a more formidable structure in society. During the period of large-scale growth of manufacturing in the late
nineteenth century, government became an effective part of the business
environment as a "protector" of various public groups. The initial intent of
early legislation was to *protect companies* (retailers) from each other and,
consequently, to ensure consumer choice in the marketplace. In effect, the
rationale was to ensure competition by preventing certain business practices that would be detrimental to other firms. Table 4.11 provides a summary of this early legislation.

During the 1930s legislation was focused on the survival of smaller
firms, especially retailers, rather than on preventing large firms from practicing particular behavior. Since the early 1960s, legislation is oriented more
toward directly *protecting consumers, society, and the environment*. Much
of this legislation is aimed at specific business practices, particularly retailing practices, relating to the consumer. Key laws are explained in Table 4.12.

Regulatory objectives have expanded to include more desirable social
goals such as cleaner air and water, safer working conditions, and equal
employment opportunities. In addition to federal legislation, many state
and local laws pertaining to the locating and managing of a retail establish-

Table 4.11
Major federal laws affecting marketing decisions

LAW	PURPOSES
1890 Sherman Act	Prohibits contracts, combinations, or conspiracies to restrain trade; establishes as a misdemeanor monopolizing or attempts to monopolize
1914 Clayton Act	Prohibits specific practices such as price discriminations and exclusive dealer arrangements in which the effect may substantially lessen competition or tend to create a monopoly
1914 Federal Trade Commission Act	Created the Federal Trade Commission; gives the FTC investigatory powers to be used in preventing unfair methods of competition
1936 Robinson–Patman Act	Prohibits price discrimination that lessens competition among wholesalers or retailers; prohibits producers from giving disproportionate services or facilities to large buyers
1938 Wheeler–Lea Act	Prohibits unfair and deceptive acts and practices regardless of whether competition is injured; places advertising of foods and drugs under the jurisdiction of the FTC
1950 Celler–Kefauver Act; Antimerger Act	Prohibits any corporation engaged in commerce from acquiring the whole or any part of the stock or other share of the capital or assets of another corporation when the effect substantially lessens competition or tends to create a monopoly
1975 Consumer Goods Pricing Act	Prohibits the use of price maintenance agreements among manufacturers and resellers in interstate commerce

Source: William M. Pride and O. C. Ferrell: *Marketing,* 2nd ed. Copyright © 1980 by Houghton Mifflin Company. Used by permission.

ment have emerged. As in the case of the federal laws, the local laws are becoming more practice-specific and many relate to a specific type of retailer. These local laws include zoning regulations, Sunday closing laws, liquor regulations, food-processing laws, door-to-door selling restrictions, and store licensing and permit regulations.

Regulatory Agencies. Regulatory agencies have been established to ensure that various laws are enforced. Beginning with the Food and Drug Administration (1906), the number of federal agencies has increased to more than two thousand as the amount and complexity of business-related legislation has grown. Not only have the regulatory agencies executed the will of the legislature, they have also established a variety of rules, decisions, and standards pertaining to areas such as deceptive advertising, mislabeling products, and product and store safety. Thus, the power of the regulatory agencies has grown over the years through their interpretations and decisions concerning the intent of the federal lawmakers. Table 4.13 gives an indication of the major federal regulatory agencies and their primary responsibilities.

Table 4.12
Selected consumer protection legislation

YEAR	LAW
1906	Pure Food and Drug Act: prohibited the adulteration and misbranding of foods and drugs; set up the Food and Drug Administration (FDA).
1906	Meat Inspection Act: required that meat shipped in interstate commerce be processed under sanitary conditions.
1938	Food, Drug, and Cosmetic Act: expanded the responsibility of the Food and Drug Administration to include cosmetics and therapeutic devices, by amending the 1906 act.
1938	Wheeler–Lea Amendment to FTC Act: expanded the FTC's responsibility to include unfair or deceptive acts or practices and gave it the power to take action whenever it is in the public interest even where there is no proof of competitive injury.
1939	The Wool Products Labeling Act: required that products containing wool carry labels showing the fiber content.
1951	Fur Products Labeling Act: required that all fur products carry labels correctly describing their contents.
1953	Flammable Fabrics Act: prohibited the manufacture or sale of fabrics or wearing apparel that were dangerously flammable.
1958	Textile Fiber Identification Act: required that all clothing and textile products carry proper identification of their fiber content.
1958	Food Additives Amendment (Delaney Act): as an amendment to the Food, Drug, and Cosmetic Act of 1938, required that food additives be limited to those that do not cause cancer in humans or animals.
1958	Automobile Information Disclosure Act: required automobile manufacturers to post suggested retail prices on all new passenger vehicles.
1960	Hazardous Substances Labeling Act: required proper labeling on packages of hazardous household products.
1962	Kefauver–Harris Amendment to Food, Drug, and Cosmetic Act: required that all drugs be tested for safety and efficacy.
1966	Fair Packaging and Labeling Act: permitted the voluntary adoption of industry-accepted uniform packaging standards and required clearer labeling of consumer goods.

The Federal Trade Commission (FTC) has the broadest powers to effect retail decisions. Table 4.14 gives a precise account of the duties and responsibilities of the FTC. The FTC consists of five commissioners appointed by the president with the consent of the U.S. Senate. Each commissioner is appointed for seven years. The powers of the FTC include the ability first to issue a complaint against a company perceived as violating a law under the FTC jurisdiction. If this fails to stop the business behavior, then a cease and desist order is issued to the company. If the cease and desist order is viola-

YEAR	LAW
1966	National Traffic and Motor Vehicle Safety Act: provided for the establishment of compulsory standards for automobiles and new and used tires.
1966	Child Protection Act of 1966: amended the Hazardous Substances Labeling Act to ban all hazardous substances and prohibit sales of potentially harmful toys and other articles used by children.
1966	Cigarette Labeling Act: required health warnings on all cigarette packages.
1967	Wholesome Meat Act: required state meat inspection procedures to meet federal standards.
1968	Consumer Credit Protection Act (Truth in Lending): required full disclosure of the terms and rates charged for loans and credit.
1968	Wholesome Poultry Products Act: required state inspection procedures to meet federal standards.
1969	Child Protection and Toy Safety Act: broadened coverage under the 1966 Child Protection Act to prohibit toys or other articles used by children that involve electrical, mechanical, or thermal hazards.
1969	National Environmental Policy Act: established a national policy on the environment and provided for the establishment of the Council on Environmental Quality.
1970	Fair Credit Reporting Act: regulated the maintenance and distribution of consumer credit records.
1970	Poison Prevention Packaging Act: provided for standards for child-resistant packaging of hazardous substances.
1972	Consumer Product Safety Act: established the Consumer Products Safety Commission and empowered it to set safety standards for a broad range of consumer products and to impose penalties for failure to meet these standards.
1975	Magnuson–Moss Act: established disclosure requirements and minimum federal standards for written warranties.

ted, the FTC may attempt to obtain civil penalties against the company from the courts.

With the increasing number of laws and regulations to shape and guide business behavior, it is not surprising that one of the fastest-growing departments of many organizations is the legal staff. A recent study indicates that the number of practicing lawyers on corporate payrolls has doubled in the past fifteen years. The legal environment will continue to play an increasing role in retail decision making, and retailers must be knowledge-

Table 4.13
Major federal regulatory agencies

AGENCY	MAJOR PURPOSE
Federal Trade Commission (FTC)	Enforces laws and guidelines regarding unfair business practices; takes action to stop false and deceptive advertising and labeling
Food and Drug Administration (FDA)	Protects consumers by enforcing laws and regulations to prevent distribution of adulterated or misbranded foods, drugs, medical devices, cosmetics, veterinary products, and particularly hazardous consumer products
Consumer Products Safety Commission	Ensures compliance with the Consumer Product Safety Act; protects the public from unreasonable risk of injury from any consumer product not covered by other regulatory agencies
Interstate Commerce Commission (ICC)	Regulates franchises, rates, and finances of interstate rail, bus, truck, and water carriers
Federal Communications Commission (FCC)	Regulates communication by wire, radio, and television in interstate and foreign commerce
Civil Aeronautics Board (CAB)	Regulates economic aspects of air transport services and encourages development of an air transportation system that fits the needs of commerce, national defense activities, the postal service, and the general public
Environmental Protection Agency (EPA)	Develops and enforces environmental protection standards and conducts research into the adverse effects of pollution
Office of Consumer Affairs (OCA)	Handles consumers' complaints and conducts investigations, conferences, and surveys regarding problems of consumers with special emphasis on those with limited income, the elderly, the disadvantaged, and other members of minority groups
Federal Power Commission (FPC)	Regulates the following: rates and sales of natural gas producers, thereby affecting the supply and price of gas available to consumers; the rates charged at the wholesale level for electricity and gas; the construction of pipelines; and the imports and exports of natural gas and electricity to and from the United States

Source: William M. Pride and O. C. Ferrell: *Marketing,* 2nd ed. Copyright © 1980 by Houghton Mifflin Company. Used by permission.

able of existing and potentially constraining laws and regulations and be able to support their decision patterns when legal challenges arise.

Political Influences.   The political environment of retailing interacts heavily with the legal environment. Existing *political philosophies* partially dictate the level of government involvement in retailing behavior. A fairly active consumer protection philosophy has existed for the past two decades at the national level. This trend may be slowing in the 1980s as the economic problems of inflation, foreign competition, and unemployment become more prominent. Recent indications of this can be seen in the deregulation of the airline and trucking industries.

Economic policies can also affect retail decisions. The monetary and fiscal policies of the government regarding interest rates, money supply, tax rates, and government spending all directly or indirectly affect retail operations. A small change in interest rates, for instance, may greatly increase the

Table 4.14
What the FTC does

The Federal Trade Commission's job, assigned to it by Congress, is to step into the marketplace when necessary to keep consumers from being cheated. Congress laid the foundation of the FTC's authority in the original Federal Trade Commission Act of 1914, which declared "unfair methods of competition" to be unlawful. To make sure that relief from such methods would extend to consumers and not just injured businesses, the Wheeler–Lea Amendment, passed in 1938, added the words "unfair or deceptive acts or practices in commerce" to the Federal Trade Commission Act.

Building on that mandate, Congress has steadily added to the agency's authority and workload over the years. Here are some things the FTC does to carry out Congressional mandates to aid consumers:

Prevent restraints of trade by business, such as *price-fixing, boycotts,* and *anticompetitive mergers,* all of which may raise prices to consumers.

Prevent *unfair or deceptive advertising* generally.

Specifically prohibit false or deceptive advertising for food, drugs, cosmetics, and medical devices.

Report on *activities of the insurance industry* in such areas as sales techniques, quality of information given to prospects, and value returned for each premium dollar.

Require that *furs and clothing* be accurately *advertised* and *labeled.*

Require *accurate quantitative and descriptive labeling* of packaged items.

Forbid *mail-order firms* to send unordered merchandise, then charge for it.

Require lenders to give borrowers accurate and complete *information about loan terms.*

Give consumers specific rights in correcting erroneous or *disputed credit bills.*

Open up *credit files* to consumers so that misinformation can be challenged.

Compel lessors of *cars and other consumer goods* to disclose *leasing terms* fully and accurately.

Prohibit *debt-collection agencies* from harassing consumers.

Enforce *warranty standards.*

Source: Copyright 1980 by Consumers Union of United States, Inc., Mount Vernon, N.Y. 10550. Reprinted by permission from *Consumer Reports,* March 1980.

cost of maintaining certain levels of inventory. Many retailers felt this during the early 1980s. Tax rates also affect numerous aspects of a retail establishment, including profits, dividends, inventory levels, and location decisions.

Technological Environment

The technological environment probably has the greatest impact of any environment on our future lives and the quality of society. Although it has a major impact, change in the technological environment is highly irregular and, in many areas, grows in a leap-frog pattern. This, of course, makes prediction and adaptation to technological change difficult.

Technological Application. Technology is the application of knowledge. Broadly viewed, it is the means for extending human capability in accomplishing goals and tasks through tools, techniques, products, processes, and methods.[15] Technology has produced innovations ranging from computers, integrated circuits, automobiles, and antibiotics to instant cereal and freeze-dried coffee.

Much of our social and economic welfare results from changing technology. Productivity in manufacturing, wholesaling, and retailing is generally a direct result of improved technology. Better working conditions and improved output have resulted from wise application of our increased knowledge.

A number of technological changes have affected our society, but few have had the impact that electronics has had and will continue to have on our society and its institutions. Drucker speculates that communications through the use of electronics will completely revolutionize our society and the business community.[16] Sharing information almost instantaneously throughout the world, beaming information into consumers' homes, fully automating warehouses, and recording inventory changes immediately are all part of the present and future environment of retailing brought about through electronics.

Many of these changes have already surfaced in retailing. The most important of the electronic changes are computerized checkouts and electronic point-of-sale equipment, electronic funds transfer, and cable television.

Computerized Checkouts. Computerized checkouts offer the retailer the ability to capture all sales data at the time of checkout and to develop and maintain a total inventory control system on a real-time basis. The *universal product code* (UPC), a 12-digit numeric code used in the grocery industry, and the *optical character recognition–font A* (OCR-A), a multifunction alphabetic and numeric code for nonfood retailers, have allowed retailers to implement the computerized checkout. As might be expected, these technological advancements have lowered labor costs, reduced employee errors, and improved inventory control in the retail outlets in which it has been applied.[17] The scanning technology is one of the prime reasons for the anticipated increases in retailing productivity during the 1980s.[18]

Point of Sale (POS) Equipment. Electronic point-of-sale equipment increases the value of the computerized checkout by adding check and charge verification, price verification, real-time sales reports, and the possibility of interstore data communications.[19] Many of the potential problems related to employee error such as pricing errors and many time-consuming activities such as credit card verification can be virtually eliminated by electronic point-of-sale equipment. Jordan Marsh expects to save $60,000 a year from its cash management by using the electronic check remittance processing system. These two technological changes, computerized checkout and POS equipment, are "the most important research tool[s] ever developed" for the grocery industry, according to Ralphs' (a large California grocery chain) president, Patrick Collins.[20]

Electronic Funds Transfer System (EFTS). Another electronics-related change in the retailing environment is electronic funds transfer, by which instantaneous customer-retailer transactions are recorded without the exchange of checks or cash. The amount of the transaction is debited from the customer's bank account and credited to the retailer's bank account. Each consumer has a personalized card to be used for every transaction. Several years ago the electronic funds transfer system was predicted to be widely accepted and implemented by the early 1980s. Of course, this has not occurred. As in the early days of computerized checkouts, there has been some consumer resistance to electronic funds transfer technology. A recent survey of consumers, however, indicated a general and growing acceptance of EFT. The major reason cited for wider consumer acceptance was convenience. Essentially, those more familiar with EFT systems had more favorable responses to the survey. Consumers whose responses were unfavorable generally saw no need for electronic funds transfer. The growth of EFT systems during the late 1970s and early 1980s was impressive and will continue to grow as consumers become more familiar with that particular technology.[21] Although the technology exists for a nationwide electronic funds transfer system, it will be several years before it is implemented on such a broad scale.

Cable Television. Cable television technology will eventually enable many consumers to shop in their own homes. It is estimated that approximately 22 percent of all U.S. homes are hooked up to cable television, that by 1985 it will be 35 percent, and by the early 1990s the figure will be nearly 50 percent.[22] When the cable television in a consumer's home is connected to a computerized ordering network, consumers are able to order products directly via their televisions. Certain channels are designated as marketing information and retailer channels. By turning to these channels consumers can order products by punching in product code numbers on their computer consoles. Consumers are also able to call up certain store information to help their decision making. In addition, the systems should be able to process orders, schedule deliveries, and record all pertinent order information. Some people speculate that the greatest impact of cable television will be in product areas such as food, drugs, and vital necessities. *Teleshopping* probably will not be widespread until the next century, but some systems currently are being employed on an experimental basis.[23]

Natural Environment

The natural environment, almost totally ignored until recently, is of growing concern to retail decision makers. To some extent this concern is a reaction to increased public concern for the quality of the natural environment, but it is also a result of the impact the natural environment has on business decisions. Many environmental groups have brought to the public's and government's attention the environmental problems we face. Pollution, energy shortages, and the wasting of natural resources coupled with increasing demand on our limited resources have motivated the public as well as retailers.

STRATEGY IN ACTION 4.3

Sears' Video Catalog

"America's wish book" is going electronic. Sears, Roebuck & Co. has put its 236-page summer catalog on a video disc to test the future in catalog retailing of this new television-based technology.

The nation's leader in catalog sales scheduled the unveiling of its experimental catalog for May 1, complete with sound and motion, in nine stores and catalog sales offices in the Washington (D.C.) and Cincinnati areas and in 1,000 homes across the country. Customers can browse through the catalog's 5,500 single frames and 17 motion sequences on a television screen, learning how to build a fence or watching Cheryl Tiegs model her line of summer sportswear. They can order from this catalog as they do from its printed counterpart. Eager to determine customer reaction to an electronic presentation of catalog merchandise, the $18.7 billion company will run the test through July 25 and study the results of the experiment.

Sears officials will not disclose the cost of the test. But eventually they hope that by putting some of the company's catalogs on videodisc they can reduce their printing and distribution costs, which last year totaled more than $100 million for 35 books. "More than anything else, we are trying to discover how effective the electronic catalog will be," says Robert E. Wood II, Sears vice-president for advertising sales. He anticipates that customers someday will have even more advanced electronic equipment that will permit direct shopping from home. "We want to gain some experience with the videodisc because we believe it will play some part in that future," says Wood.

Selecting 'Pages'

Although they are not sure whether consumers will eventually shop via cable, satellite, or some other transmission technology, Sears officials think they have found the right electronic storage vehicle for their catalog. Capable of storing up to 54,000 pictures on a side, the videodisc "makes the catalog come alive," says Maynard Kessler of Sears' Catalog Advertising Research Dept.

Sears is using the DiscoVision Associates disc and player, manufactured by Universal Pioneer Corp., a partnership of DiscoVision and U.S. Pioneer Electronics Corp. With this system, the customer can select "pages" of the catalog he wishes to see in any order and freeze still frames to study the product displayed. Consumers who have purchased DiscoVision players will be used in the Sears test.

Ironically, the Sears electronic catalog cannot be played on the Videodisc player Sears plans to sell in its stores this summer through the catalog by Christmas. Manufactured by RCA Corp., that player sells for about $500, $250 less than the Universal Pioneer machine that will be used in the Sears home test and $2,500 less than the industrial model that will be used in the Washington and Cincinnati Sears outlets. The RCA disc and player do not have the random-access or freeze-frame features that Sears considered essential to automate its catalog. Neither Sears nor RCA sees a conflict in the retailer's support of two noncompatible disc systems. Sears wants to keep its options open, and it believes the RCA player is priced for the consumer market. Says an RCA spokesman: "We feel very strongly that they Universal Pioneer player belongs in industrial applications like the Sears catalog. We are aiming at the mass market."

Open Options

Sears has leaped ahead of the rest of the industry. While J. C. Penney Co. has worked with DiscoVision Associates to develop the videodisc to train its employees, it is not ready to announce a project comparable to the Sears test. "When we have something, we'll let the world know," says a Penney spokeswoman. And Montgomery Ward & Co. has no plans to follow in Sears" footsteps.

Source: "At Sears', 'Thumbs Up' to the Video Catalog." Reprinted from the 11 May 1981 issue of *Business Week,* pp. 33–34, by special permission. © 1981 by McGraw-Hill, Inc., New York, NY 10020. All rights reserved.

Retailers may be pressured to handle returnable bottles and other types of environmentally sound products. Because retailers are constantly interacting with the buying public and are highly visible, much of the pressure to conserve will be brought against them.

One of the major concerns of retail executives for the 1980s is the cost of energy. Fuel costs will continue to rise, which means *increased energy costs* for the retailer, which must be absorbed through more efficiency within the retail organization or possibly through increased prices. Obviously, this is an undesirable situation, and the retailer must develop strategies for adaptation. Some retailing forecasters suggest that smaller store size will be one specific result of increased energy costs.

FORECAST CHANGES IN THE MACROENVIRONMENT

The fourth step in the macroenvironmental analysis process is to forecast changes. To develop future strategies for a retailer, it is necessary to predict the type of environment the retailer will be facing in the short and long term. Consequently, the purpose of **environmental forecasting** is to estimate the timing and the likelihood of the impact of environmental influences. In other words, when will the influences occur and what is the probability of their occurrence?

Although environmental forecasting is still in its infancy, significant advances have occurred during the past decade. Nevertheless, environmental forecasting certainly remains an art rather than a science.

A number of methods exist for forecasting environmental change. General Electric begins its forecasting with a **probability/diffusion matrix** for environmental influences, as shown in Fig. 4.4. A number of possible occurrences of events in the macroenvironment are organized and assigned a

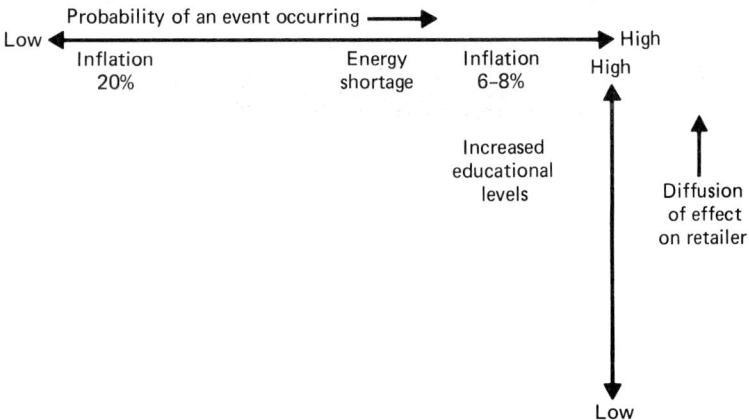

Figure 4.4
Probability/diffusion matrix of the macroenvironment

probability ranging from low to high and a diffusion base ranging from low to high. The *probability level* is the estimate of the likelihood that an event will occur from low to high. The *diffusion base* is the degree of impact the event will have on society. *High diffusion* means widespread impact, while *low diffusion* means a narrowly defined impact. It is possible to adapt the probability/diffusion matrix to a chain of stores or even to one outlet. This method has widespread applicability and is an excellent base for environmental forecasting.

The retailer's strategic responses are developed for future environments that have a high probability of occurrence and a high degree of diffusion. In Figure 4.3, a 6 to 8 percent inflation rate would be viewed as the most probable and most influential macroenvironmental factor, and the retailer should develop a strategy for this environment. An inflation rate of 20 percent, while having a great potential impact, has very little probability of occurring; thus, strategies for such an occurrence need not be developed.

Other methods for environmental forecasting vary in complexity and reliability. Table 4.15 presents short descriptions of the key methods of forecasting.

Once the future environment is forecast, the retailer must then develop marketing strategies to adapt to that environment. The success of the retailer is a function of the ability to forecast correctly and to develop appropriate strategies for the forecast environment.

DEVELOP STRATEGIC RESPONSES

Retailing strategies provide the retailing organization with long-term guidance. Strategies are based on the *forecast environment*, which may not turn out to be the *actual environment* encountered. The basis for prediction is probability, which produces a margin for error. To accomodate this aspect of forecasting, the retailing decision maker should build some flexibility into his or her retailing strategy. A strategy that can be applied to two possible environments or to changes in the highest-probability environment is more desirable than an inflexible strategy designed for only one future environment.

In developing a strategy, the retailer should plan initially for the most probable and far-reaching events. The strategy should adapt to events in decreasing order of probability and diffusion, with the least likely and lowest-impact events being planned for last. Generally, using Fig. 4.4, retailers should develop strategies for events in the upper right side of the matrix. *Contingency strategies* should also be developed for the possibility of a differing environment's occurring.

A retailing strategy should enable the retailer to adapt to the ever-changing but properly forecast macroenvironment. An organized, well-developed strategy should serve as a map for achieving the retailer's purposes relative to an environment that may hinder or advance the retailer's objectives.

Table 4.15
Key methods for environmental forecasting

1. *Expert opinion.* Knowledgeable people are selected and asked to assign importance and probability ratings to various possible future developments. The most refined version, the Delphi method, puts experts through several rounds of event assessment, where they keep refining their assumptions and judgments.

2. *Trend extrapolation.* Researchers fit best-fitting curves (linear, quadratic, or S-shaped growth curves) through past time series to serve as a basis for extrapolation. This method can be very unreliable in that new developments can completely alter the expected direction of movement.

3. *Trend correlation.* Researchers correlate various time series in the hope of identifying leading and lagging relationships that can be used for forecasting.

4. *Dynamic modeling.* Researchers build sets of equations that attempt to describe the underlying system. The coefficients in the equations are fitted through statistical means. Econometric models of more than three hundred equations, for example, are used to forecast changes in the U.S. economy.

5. *Cross-impact analysis.* Researchers identify a set of key trends (those high in importance and/or probability). The question is then put: "If event A occurs, what will be the impact on all other trends?" The results are then used to build sets of "domino chains," with one event triggering others.

6. *Multiple scenarios.* Researchers build pictures of alternative futures, each internally consistent and with a certain probability of happening. The major purpose of the scenarios is to stimulate contingency planning.

7. *Demand/hazard forecasting.* Researchers identify major events that would greatly affect the firm. Each event is rated for its convergence with several major trends taking place in society and for its appeal to each major public group in the society. The higher the event's convergence and appeal, the higher its probability of occurring. The highest-scoring events are then researched further.

Source: James R. Bright and Milton E. F. Schoeman, *A Guide to Practical Technological Forecasting* (Englewood Cliffs, N.J.: Prentice-Hall, 1973). Reprinted by permission of James R. Bright.

SUMMARY

Macroenvironmental analysis is critical to the success of a retail organization because retail objectives are best achieved when there is an appropriate match between retail strategy and the macroenvironment. This chapter was designed to help the retailer analyze the macroenvironment using a logical five-step process.

Step 1 involves determining the relevant macroenvironmental influences. Environmental mapping can be used to determine the key factors most likely to influence the retailer. These factors are categorized into demographic, economic, cultural and social, political and legal, technological, and natural forces.

The second step is to develop a scanning process for the macroenvironment that continually gathers information concerning the key influencing factors determined in Step 1. When a macroenvironmental force shows signs of affecting the retailer, more in-depth analysis is required.

Step 3 involves monitoring the macroenvironmental forces detected in Step 2. The purpose of monitoring is to determine the direction, degree, rate, and magnitude of change in the key influences. (The six categories of macroenvironmental forces are discussed in detail in this section.)

Step 4 involves forecasting changes in the macroenvironment. A probability/diffusion matrix can be used to help analyze the likelihood and potential impact of macroenvironmental events.

Step 5 is the development of strategic responses. Most of this textbook is devoted to helping the retailer complete this step.

Competition and channels of distribution are also key parts of the retailer's external environment; they are covered in the next chapter.

KEY CONCEPTS

Organization environment

Task environment

Macroenvironment

Environmental complexity

Environmental turbulence

Proactive decisions

Reactive decisions

Passive-reactive decisions

Aggressive-reactive decisions

Macroenvironmental analysis

Environmental mapping

Environmental scanning

Environmental monitoring

Demographic environment

Economic environment

Cultural and social environment

Political and legal environment

Technological environment

Natural environment

Environmental forecasting

Probability/diffusion matrix

REVIEW QUESTIONS

1. Why is understanding the macroenvironment of major importance in developing market strategies?

2. Explain the differences between proactive and reactive decisions.

3. What are some of the current trends in age distribution in the United States? Explain the implications of these trends from a retailing perspective.

4. What are the implications for increasing household incomes, especially among the college educated?

5. What type of strategic and tactical changes have retailers made to adapt to the increasing numbers of working women?

6. What impact does inflation have on retailing strategies? What impact does recession have?

7. Identify and explain some of the cultural changes occurring in the United States.

8. How does the Federal Trade Commission affect retail decision making?

9. What is the universal product code (UPC)? Optical character recognition–font A (OCR-A)? How will each affect retailing?

10. What are the implications to retailers of teleshopping via cable television?

LEARNING EXERCISES

1. Determine the satisfaction of several local retailers with computerized checkouts and electronic point-of-sale equipment.

2. Prepare an environmental map for a selected local retailer.

DECISION SITUATION 4.1: **SAVEWAY A**

Saveway is a large, regional grocery chain. Within its region it is on a competitive level with the national chains. In one city of 250,000 where Saveway has nine stores, a large new housing development has been started. Saveway's management is considering building a new store near this development.

Saveway has learned that 1,000 or more homes are planned for the new development. Presently there are almost 150 homes built or under construction. Homes in the area will cost about 30 percent more than the median home in the city. The developer indicated that the average buying family contains two children and the family income is almost $45,000. The area is three miles from the city limit. The closest grocery store is another Saveway, which is almost four miles from the development.

If the area grows as expected, it is likely that other developers will build on farmland adjacent to the area. The area should be able to support a large Saveway shortly. Forty percent of the current residents of this area shop at the Saveway nearest them. The other 60 percent shop at a national chain near the Saveway.

QUESTIONS

1. What other information should Saveway collect now to make the location decision?

2. Would you recommend that Saveway take the opportunity, assuming that the funds are available? Support your answer.

3. If Saveway management decides not to pursue this opportunity at this time, what environmental factors should they continue to monitor?

DECISION SITUATION 4.2: **MIKE'S FURNISHINGS**

Mike's is a successful retailer of modest- to high-priced furniture in the Pacific Northwest. The owner has always made most strategy decisions based on his experience in the furniture business. He realizes, however, that the environment has changed a great deal since he began in the furniture trade. He thinks that to be successful in the future he will need to understand changes in the environment better than he now does.

Mike does not know where or how to begin his analysis of the environment. He has asked you to help him.

QUESTIONS

1. What factors in the external environment should Mike monitor?

2. How can Mike get information on these factors?

3. If Mike finds that most of his customers are two-income families, what type of strategies should he use?

4. Would the factors be different if Mike were a furniture discounter? If Mike were located in a different region of the country?

NOTES

1. Peter F. Drucker, "Managing for Tomorrow," *Industry Week*, 14 April 1980, p. 55.

2. F. John Pessolano, "Futurism: Design for Survival," *Enterprise*, February 1979, pp. 6–11.

3. L. J. Bourgeois III, "Strategy and Environment: A Conceptual Integration," *Academy of Management Review*, vol. 5, no. 1 (1980), pp. 25–39.

4. Philip Kotler, *Marketing Management*, 4th ed. (Englewood Cliffs, N.J.: Prentice-Hall, 1980), p. 98.

5. David W. Cravens, Gerald E. Hills, and Robert B. Woodruff, *Marketing Decision Making* (Homewood, Ill.: Richard D. Irwin, 1976), p. 83.

6. Fabian Linden, "Keys to the '80s—Youth and Affluence," *Consumer Markets*, The Conference Board, December 1979.

7. *Ibid.*

8. *Ibid.*

9. Bob Middendorf, "Your Marketing Plan Cannot Ignore Working Women in the 80s" *Marketing Times*, January–February 1980, pp. 29–31.

10. Leonard L. Berry, and Ian H. Wilson, "Retailing: The Next Ten Years," *Journal of Retailing*, Fall 1977, pp. 5–27.

11. *Ibid.*, p. 10.

12. Roger D. Blackwell, "Successful Retailers of '80s Will Cater to Specific Lifestyle Segments," *Marketing News*, 7 March 1980, p. 3.

13. *Ibid.*

14. Victor E. Millar, and Michael E. Simon, "The Measure of Regulation," *The Chronicle*, vol. 39, no. 1 (1979), pp. 13–16.

15. Donald A. Schon, *Technology and Change* (New York: Delacorte, 1967).

16. Drucker, *op. cit.*, p. 60.

17. Joseph S. Coyle, "Scanning Lights Up a Dark World for Grocers," *Fortune*, 27 March 1978, pp. 76–80.

18. *Ibid.*

19.   Marion B. Rothman, "More Than Merely Cash Registers: Almighty EPOS," *Stores,* October 1977, p. 41.

20.   Coyle, *op. cit.,* p. 80.

21.   Robert E. O'Neill, "Familiarity Breeds Acceptance," *Progressive Grocer,* March 1981, pp. 133–141.

22.   "In Scramble to Bring Cable TV to Your Area," *U.S. News and World Report,* 6 October 1980, pp. 47–48.

23.   Donald G. Sullivan, "How Teleshopping Will Change Marketing," *Marketing Times,* January/February, 1981, pp. 43–44.

STRATEGIC RETAIL MANAGEMENT MODEL

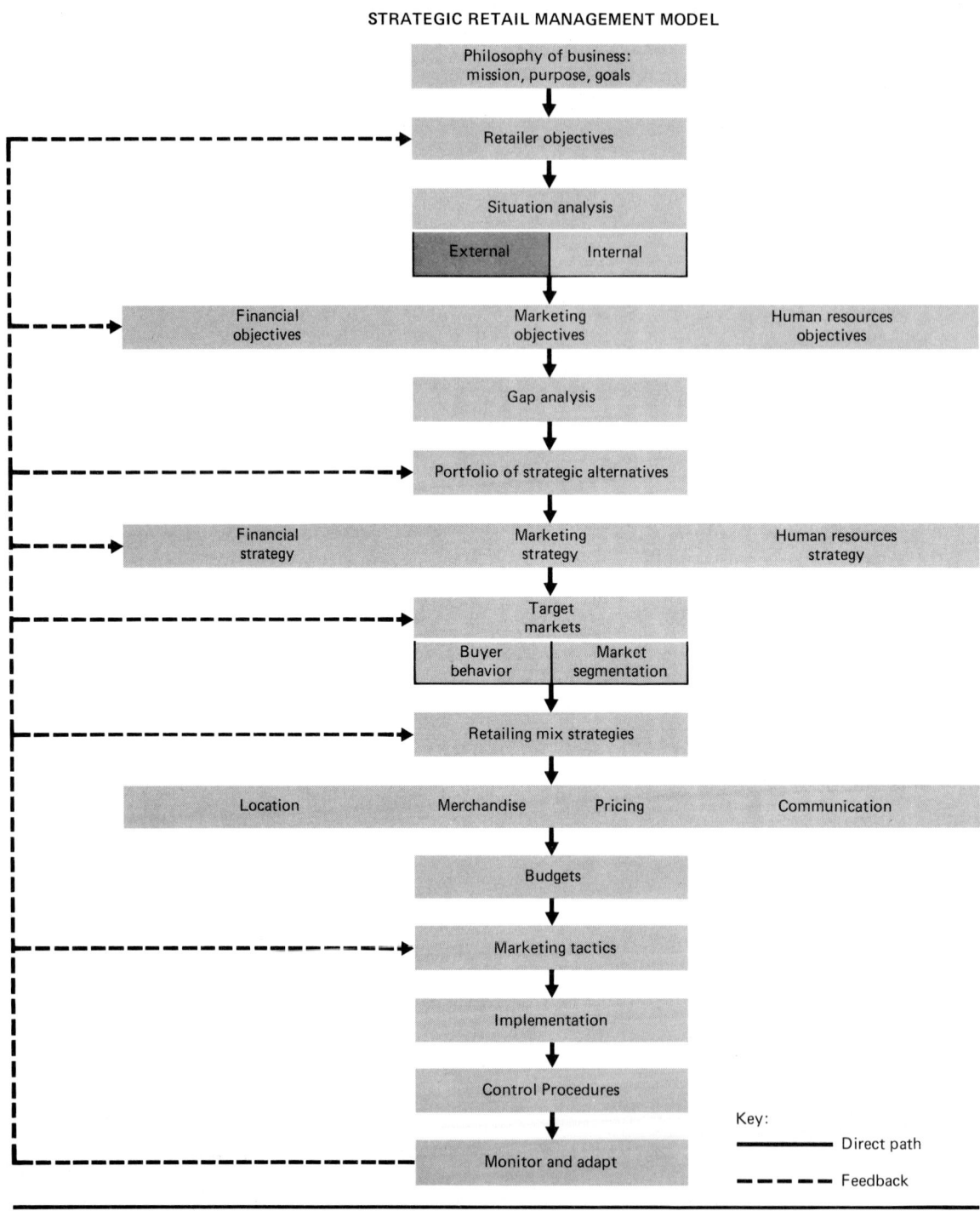

Chapter 5
The Task Environment: Competition and Marketing Intermediaries

1. To understand the impact of competition and the competitive audit process.

2. To understand the nature, importance, and administration of channels of distribution.

INTRODUCTION

In the previous chapter the overall retailing environment was divided into the macroenvironment (which was discussed there), the task environment, and the organization environment. The task environment can be divided into *competition, marketing intermediaries,* and *consumers.* This chapter examines competition and marketing intermediaries; Chapters 6 and 7 focus on consumer analysis and market segmentation, respectively.

The component factors of the task environment (competitors, channel members, and consumers) influence retailers heavily because of direct daily interaction. Consequently, the retailer must understand the impact of the task environment and, further, how the task environment is influenced by macroenvironmental factors.

COMPETITIVE AUDITS

Retailing strategies can be viewed as responses to the total environment, which includes competitors. Since a given retailer's competitors are also continuously developing and implementing their own strategic responses, the retailer must analyze and anticipate competitive marketing efforts. Strategy in Action 5.1 provides an example of competitive strategy maneuvering in the catalog showroom trade.

STRATEGY IN ACTION 5.1

Competitive Behavior among Catalog Showroom Retailers

In the once-booming catalog showroom industry, sales growth has slowed and competition is becoming fierce. Competitive behavior is a major input into strategic decisions. Service Merchandise Company is attempting to customize their own catalog to differentiate themselves from other catalog showroom retailers by creating a distinct identity. Best Products Company, rather than following the same competitive mode, is expanding into secondary markets with smaller stores. W. Bell and Company intends to cater to the higher income market by expanding their offerings of jewelry and fine gifts. While reacting to the total environment, each is reacting to competitive efforts in order to gain a competitive advantage. Interestingly, the Ardan showroom chain has developed the strategy of locating close to Service Merchandise or H. J. Wilson. Thus each firm chooses to react to competition by using differing strategies, some selecting an entirely different emphasis and others selecting to duplicate competitive efforts.

Source: Adapted from "Competition: Catalog Showrooms Now Battle Each Other," pp. 29–31. Reprinted by permission from *Chain Store Age/Executive* © October 1980. Copyright Lebhar-Friedman, Inc. 425 Park Avenue, New York, NY 10022.

Retail marketing strategies are developed to gain a competitive advantage in the market. A competitive advantage can be most effective when a retailer is competing from a position of strength against the weaknesses of competitors. Retailers that can analyze and accurately anticipate competitors' reactions to their retailing efforts and to environmental changes have an invaluable advantage in the marketplace. This analysis of competition can be accomplished by means of a competitive audit.

The **competitive audit** is a formal examination that can help the retailer identify patterns of competitive behavior. Its purpose is to identify strengths and weaknesses in the marketing efforts of competing retailers and to profile and forecast competitive strategies. The competitive audit procedure shown in Fig. 5.1 has six basic steps:

1. Define competition.

2. Determine competitive market shares.

3. Analyze differences in competitive retailing strategies.

4. Establish strategic competitive profiles.

5. Forecast competitors' strategic retailing efforts.

6. Develop strategic responses to competitors.

Table 5.1 on pages 146 and 147 contains a competitive audit checklist that can be used along with the audit procedure.

Define Competition

The first step in a competitive audit is to define competition. J. C. Penney, for example, competes with Sears and Federated Stores and also with K mart, Woolco, and even small independent men's clothing stores. McDonald's competes with Burger Chef and Burger King, as well as with Safeway. Thus the competitors may need to be defined in rather broad terms.

Level of Competition. Retail competition has traditionally been classified according to level of competition. The classifications used are intratype and intertype. **Intratype competition** is competition between retailers of the *same type*. Two grocery stores, such as A&P and Kroger, engage in intratype competition.

Intertype competition occurs between *different types* of retailers selling the *same product*.[1] A&P engages in intertype competition with Super X Drugstores, because each sells health and beauty aids, snack items, paper products, and other similar items. Each competes for similar target markets, although their total product mix is not identical.

Consumer Perspective. Retailers often define their competition as those stores with similar characteristics, such as merchandise, prices, and services. However, competition is more appropriately defined by the consumers

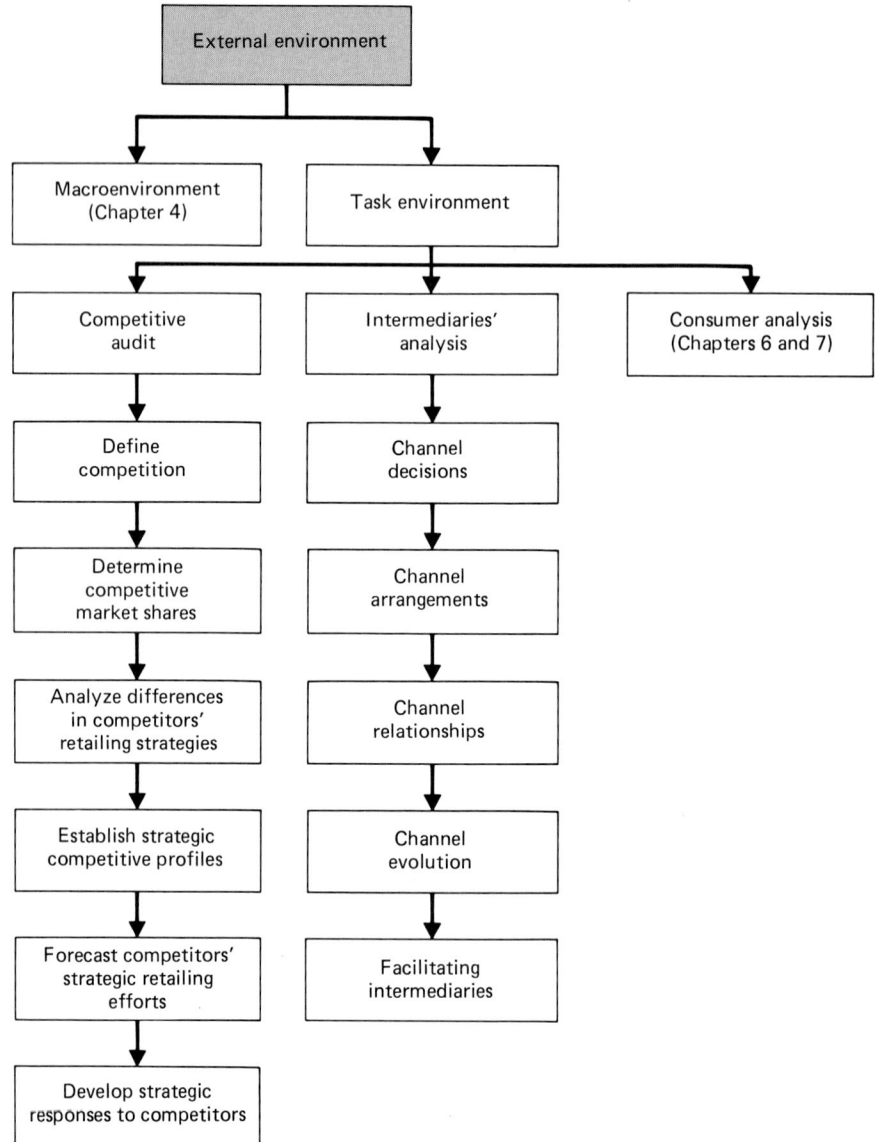

Figure 5.1
Task environment analysis model

in the market. Consumers interpret and organize the retail environment to determine which stores can best satisfy their needs. This process truly determines which retailers are actual competitors.

Philip Kotler notes that many consumers use a **three-subset approach** in viewing the retail environment.[2] Each subset consists of a group of retail stores, with each succeeding subset being more narrowly defined. The *awareness set* consists of all the known retail stores that carry a particular product category. The *consideration set*, a subset of the awareness set, consists of those retail stores that are seriously considered as a source for purchasing. Only a few stores remain in the final subset, the *choice set*, which can truly be identified as competitors.

Positioning, which is based on the key competitive dimensions used by consumers to organize retailers relative to one another, is often used to identify competition. Each retailer can be placed on a *perceptual map*. The position stores occupy on this perceptual map indicates which stores the consumer perceives as competing. Note that it is possible that intratype and intertype competition may be intermingled in the positioning space. Figure 5.2 shows a positioning map for men's fashion apparel.

The key competitive dimensions in Fig. 5.2 are "value for the money" and "store fashionability." Each of the numbers on the graph represents a specific retail establishment. Note that certain stores of different classifications are perceived by consumers as competing with one another, such as mid-range fashion stores (2) with department stores (3). In the situation depicted, a given department store would be able to determine which other department stores are considered close competition *and* which mid-range fashion specialty chains have similar positions. It is also important to note that different market segments may have differing perceptual maps of the retail environment. Certainly, the perceptual map of the retailer's target market is of primary importance.

Since a retailing position is a time-related concept, retailers must reanalyze their competitive position periodically. Consumers' perceptual maps change over time because of retailers' marketing efforts and consumers' personal experience. Local retail markets should be researched at least every other year. Highly competitive situations or rapidly changing markets require more frequent analysis.

Determine Competitive Market Shares

To determine the success of competing retailing strategies, it is necessary to establish the effectiveness of those strategies by analyzing relative market share. This step is simplified if actual sales figures are available on the local level. Few retailers enjoy the luxury of this type of data; however, several surrogate indicators of market share can be employed, such as measure of "store last shopped" and "store most often shopped."[3]

If possible, market share information should be gathered and analyzed for specific *product lines* and *market segments*. This detailed analysis can provide greater insight into competitors' strengths and weaknesses.

Analyze Differences in Competitors' Retailing Strategies

At this point, competitors have been identified and their share of the market or relative success has been established. The third step involves analyzing each competitor's retailing strategy to determine *why* the market share performance differs.

Table 5.1
Checklist of questions/issues in performing a competitive audit

A. *Nature and Structure of Competition*

1.   Who are the retailers which compete in the area and what are their respective market shares? How do these retailers compare in terms of breadth of product line, market coverage, and rates of growth?

2.   What are the trends in sales and market shares among the various competing retailers and how do these vary by type of customer, use of merchandise, geographical area, or other relevant market-segment dimensions?

3.   What are the distinguishing features of each major retailer's competitive strategy? What are the strengths and weaknesses inherent in each approach? How well do they appear to be executing their respective strategies? What kind of store image does each retailer have?

4.   Are there identifiable "clusters" of retailers which have common and strategically relevant features? What is the basis of each cluster, especially in terms of the approach to the market?

5.   What are the pivotal store features that prompt a buyer to purchase from one retailer and not another?

B. *Forecast of Future Competitive Trends and Conditions*

1.   What market opportunities/threats appear to be on the horizon for this type of retailing? How will these likely affect competition in this trade?

2.   What sort of customer needs are presently not being met by existing retailers? Why is this?

3.   What demographic and population-based changes can be anticipated and what do these portend for the size of the market and for competition in this trade?

4.   Are there any reasons to expect major changes in costs or in supply?

5.   Is the probable future course of the economy (i.e., rates of inflation, unemployment, economic growth, interest) likely to produce any unusual change in competition or market direction?

Each element of the competitors' retailing mix (location, product, price, and communication) must be examined. Information on these elements can be gathered through direct observation or by use of consumer attitude research techniques (see Chapter 8).

A great deal of competitive information can be gathered, but time and money considerations dictate that the retailer be extremely selective in acquiring the information. Each retailer should establish specific priorities for the type and amount of information desired. These priorities will vary from retailer to retailer based on the current competitive situation. Jerry Wall found that retailers generally thought pricing, expansion plans, promotional strategy, and sales statistics (in that order) were the most useful pieces of competitive information.[4] Smaller retailers were more concerned with pric-

6. What competitive changes are likely to stem from new or existing governmental poli-
    cies on product liability, consumer protection, taxation, energy conservation, and other
    pertinent areas?

7. What uses can be made of such forecasting techniques as the Delphi method (re-
    searching the consensus of views of experts), trend extrapolation, regression and cor-
    relation analysis, econometric models, and dynamic predictive models (i.e., simula-
    tion) to estimate how future events may influence market trends, competitive
    conditions, and strategic opportunities in this trade?

C. *Evaluating a Retailer's Own Competitive Position*

1. What is the retailer's competitive strategy? What is the key competitive advantage?
    What is it based on?

2. What do consumers think of the company? How does this compare with what they
    think of competing retailers? What are the trends for these images?

3. What are the specific consumer benefits from shopping at this retail store? Which re-
    tailer offers the most value for the money? How important is this?

4. How successful has the retailer been at promoting the key competitive features of its
    store(s)?

5. In what market segments is the retailer strongest? Weakest? What segments are
    being missed or overlooked? How well has the retailer done in expanding the cus-
    tomer base? Why?

6. What are the retailer's biggest competitive weaknesses? How important are they?
    What is it doing and what more can it do about them in terms of competitive strat-
    egy?

7. What specific market opportunities/threats can be identified for this retailer? To what
    extent is the retailer's ability to respond to these opportunities/threats conditioned by
    its competitive strengths/weaknesses?

8. Overall, how strong is the retailer's competitive position in the marketplace? What
    would it take to strengthen its position?

Source: A. A. Thompson, Jr., and A. J. Strickland III, *Strategy and Policy: Concepts and Cases* (Plano,
Tex.: Business Publications, 1981), pp. 134–135. © BUSINESS PUBLICATIONS, INC., 1978 and 1981.

ing and promotional strategy, and larger retailers were interested in expansion plans, sales statistics, and promotional strategy.

Although *direct observation* may not be effective for obtaining certain
types of data (such as local radio advertising), most competitive information
can be gathered through monitoring competitive efforts. Comparison shopping of competitive retailers, for example, is a simple, inexpensive method
for identifying the product mix, service mix, pricing, volume of customer
traffic, and other competitive changes. Of course, it is not necessary to identify all competitive changes, but noting a pattern of change makes it less
difficult to forecast future changes.

Constant scanning, monitoring, and organizing of *competitors' newspaper advertising* can be a valuable method of discovering competitive mix

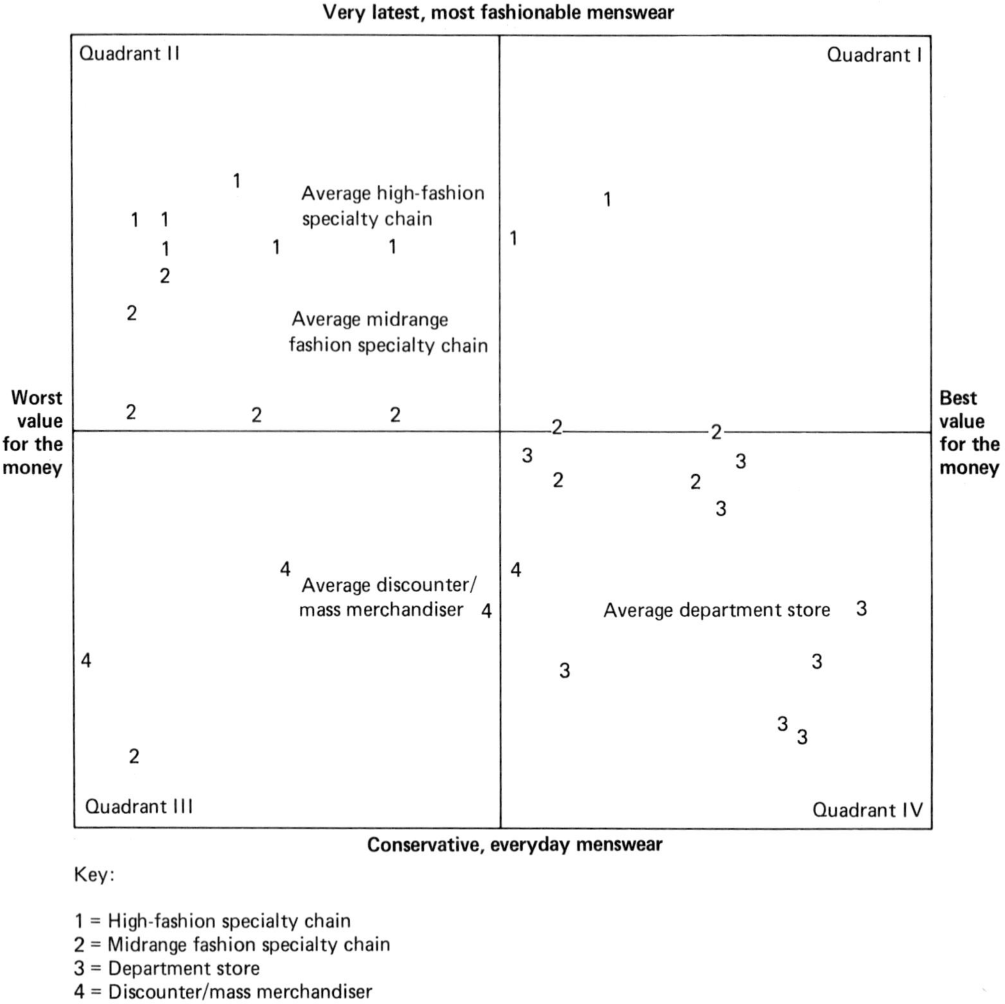

Very latest, most fashionable menswear

Figure 5.2
Two-dimensional perceptual space: store positions on fashionability and value for the money
Source: Charles W. King and Lawrence J. Ring, "Marketing Positioning Across Retail Fashion Institutions: A Comparative Analysis of Store Types." Reprinted with permission from *Journal of Retailing*, Vol. 56, No. 1, Spring 1980, p. 53.

changes and providing an indication of competitors' promotional budgets. For larger retail competitors, *published sources* such as the *Wall Street Journal*, *Business Week*, *Chain Store Age Executive*, *Stores*, and *Progressive Grocer* can provide an excellent means of analyzing competitive retailing efforts. *Financial records* for major competitors, such as annual reports and 10K reports, are also generally available.

Another method of establishing and monitoring competitive retailing efforts is with periodic *consumer attitude research*. Measures pertaining to perceived product mix, services, pricing, promotion, and location can be gathered. Problems with using attitude research as the only method of analyzing competition are estimating competitive budgets and the time delay between strategic competitive changes and the retailer's research study.

Much of the impetus for strategic adaptation comes from within a retail organization. Knowing and understanding the background and philosophies of competing retail managers can be a valuable guide for anticipating competitive strategy changes. Analyzing speeches or public comments and knowing the background (such as merchandising versus finance or progression through the ranks versus moving from a competitor) can give insight into the competing retailer's view of the retailing environment and likely strategic responses.

Establish Strategic Competitive Profiles

The fourth step of the competitive audit involves establishing **strategy profiles** for each competitor. Robert Hershey offers only one universal rule for competitive audits: "Keep permanent files on competitors."[5] Specifically, competitors' retailing mixes must be organized for comparison and analysis.

Table 5.2
Strategy profile for Michelle's Fashions*

MARKETING STRATEGY VARIABLES	INFORMATION SOURCE**	STRATEGY PROFILE	NORMAL RESPONSES TO CHANGING ENVIRONMENT	NORMAL RESPONSES TO OUR STRATEGY CHANGES	FORECAST STRATEGY
Merchandise					
Lines	a, b				
Breadth	a				
Depth	a				
Variety	a				
Turnover	d				
Promotion					
Blend	b, c				
Advertising					
Budget	b				
Media	b, c	Heavy newspaper, TV for sales, radio for reminders	Increase TV when market share declines	Matches increased newspaper advertising	Increase TV and reduce radio

*This table is an *abbreviated* format for a strategy profile. Retailers should also include other promotion variables (sales promotion, sales force, and so on), pricing variables (margins, markdowns), location variables (site factors and the like), service variables, market share, management variables, and any other variables that could affect strategic planning, as discussed in the text.
**a = comparison shopping or observation; b = newspapers; c = business publications; d = financial reports; e = public reports; f = personal contacts; g = marketing research.

Strategy profiles for each competing retailer can help identify strategic changes. Table 5.2 on page 149 presents a strategy profile format. The profile serves as a base for scanning and monitoring competitive efforts.

In addition, a condensed profile should be maintained for competitors on key competitive dimensions. For smaller retailers, a profile containing only promotion and pricing information might be most useful. Larger retailers are probably more interested in sales and promotion information.[6]

Forecast Competitors' Strategic Retailing Efforts

The fifth step involves forecasting competitors' strategic retailing efforts. Competitors change strategies for various reasons, including unsatisfactory performance, environmental trends, and personal reasons. A well-organized and continuously updated profile can be invaluable for forecasting these competitive changes.

Many retailers develop patterns of strategic behavior that can be noted and used to predict future behavior. These patterns might involve responses to new competitors, adaptations of competitive price reductions, or simple patterns of timing for various responses. A competitor might reduce the price of certain merchandise categories at the same time each year. If other competitors can accurately forecast this price reduction and its timing, appropriate strategies (such as increased promotion or earlier markdowns) can be developed.

Retailers must also anticipate how competitors will react to their own strategy. For example, will substantive price increases or decreases be followed by competitors?

Develop Strategic Responses to Competitors

The sixth step in the competitive audit involves developing strategic responses to competitors' strategies. Many markets are large enough to allow retailers to successfully follow different strategies. Thus it is not necessary for a retailer to follow every strategic move by competitors and it is not likely that competitors will follow all of the retailer's competitive moves. It is important, however, that a retailer not allow his or her major strengths to erode through not anticipating competitive behavior.

A good marketing strategy should include *alternative scenarios*, or answers to the "what if" question. It is not possible to forecast correctly or anticipate *all* competitive action. Thus the retailer must have *contingency marketing responses* prepared for any major competitive moves that could severely injure or negate his or her existing strategy. The retailer should simply maintain built-in flexibility for reacting to less damaging competitive activity.

Conclusion

It is important to understand how competition is likely to respond to retailing efforts. The ability and probability of a competitor's neutralizing your strategic efforts are paramount in determining appropriate strategies; obviously, a strategy that can be easily countered is not an effective strategy.

MARKETING INTERMEDIARIES ANALYSIS

The second major component of the task environment concerns those institutions other than competitors that a retailer deals with on a daily basis, specifically **marketing intermediaries.** There are two general categories of marketing intermediaries: *members of the direct channel of distribution* and *facilitating intermediaries,* such as physical distribution specialists and financial institutions.

The retailer's channel decisions must be approached in an organized, systematic manner. The specific channel(s) a retailer aligns with have a great impact on other retailing strategy decisions, such as pricing, type and availability of merchandise, advertising support, and inventory strategy. Channel alignment also influences the functions the retailer performs and the image consumers develop of the retailer.

The channel decision is normally a relatively long-term commitment; these decisions can be altered, but not without some short-term upheaval within the retail organization, such as interruption of merchandise and promotion support. Thus the channel selection decision should be based on careful analysis of alternatives and forecasts of future conditions. As shown in Fig. 5.1, the major considerations in analyzing channels of distribution are channel arrangements, channel relationships, channel evolution, and facilitating intermediaries.

Channel Arrangements

Different types of channel arrangements offer wide latitude to retailers in terms of member interaction and responsibilities for performing channel functions. They range from the loosely organized, conventional marketing channels to the highly interrelated, well-organized, vertical marketing systems.

Conventional Channel Arrangements. The type of arrangement known as the **conventional channel** (which is sometimes identified as the traditional or individualistic channel) is a loosely organized group of autonomous manufacturers, wholesalers, and retailers. Each member of this channel type engages in relatively autonomous decision making concerned largely with the goals of its organization rather than with the entire channel system. This decision-making autonomy often leads to duplication in performing various functions and, consequently, to unnecessary costs. The higher costs associated with conventional channel arrangements make it more difficult for retailers to compete with retailers that are aligned with more efficient channel systems.

Conventional channels still serve the needs of many retailers, especially smaller ones. A small retailer such as a grocery store may have little choice but to align in a conventional arrangement when the only available source of merchandise may be a local wholesaler or a manufacturer willing to sell in small quantities.

Vertical Marketing Systems (VMS) Arrangement.   One of the most significant changes that has taken place recently in retailing is the movement toward **vertical marketing systems.** Bert McCammon defined vertical marketing systems as "professionally managed and centrally programmed networks, pre-engineered to achieve operating economies and maximum market impact."[7]

The systems concept is used to organize and manage a VMS. Functions, such as designing, producing, branding, pricing, promoting, delivery, display, and financing, are performed at the most advantageous level relative to the total channel system. The members' autonomy and functional overlap is greatly decreased in the VMS arrangement. Rather than a competition of "retailer against retailer," the competitive base becomes VMS against VMS. McDonald's competes against Wendy's, and Chevrolet competes against Ford as a system entity, rather than as two independent retailers competing against each other. Thus with the growth of vertical marketing systems, the retail marketplace competes at a more sophisticated, well-organized, stronger financial level than in the past.

Retailers can choose to form or join one of three types of VMS: (1) corporate, with ownership as the basis, (2) administered, with expertise as the basis, or (3) contractual, with legal arrangements as the basis. Figure 5.3 outlines the types of VMS and Table 5.3 identifies their characteristics and provides examples of each type.

In **corporate VMS** arrangements successive stages of manufacturing and distribution are combined under one ownership. To coordinate the efforts of various levels of distribution, ownership can vertically expand to encompass multiple levels, or multiple channel levels can be developed within an existing organization. Examples include Sherwin Williams, a paint manufacturer with more than two thousand retail stores, and Sears, which obtains nearly half of its retail sales through manufacturing organizations in which it has partial ownership.[8] Table 5.4 cites advantages and disadvantages of the corporate arrangement.

Corporate vertical marketing system (Sears, Sherwin Williams)

Administered vertical marketing system (General Electric, Procter and Gamble)

Contractual vertical marketing system ──┬── Retailer sponsored (Certified Grocers)
                                          ├── Wholesaler sponsored (Independent Grocers of America)
                                          └── Manufacturer sponsored ──┬── Wholesaler (Pepsico)
                                                                        ├── Retailer (Chevrolet)
                                                                        └── Service-firm retailer (McDonald's)

Figure 5.3
Types of vertical marketing systems

An **administered VMS** seeks coordination of effort either through the size, power, or expertise of one channel member. Each channel member is independently owned in this arrangement, but each member responds to a dominant member's efforts to control a particular line or classification of products. Manufacturers of a dominant brand, such as General Electric, Procter and Gamble, General Foods, and Nabisco, can normally secure cooperation from wholesalers and retailers because of their size and expertise in the market and their size and power relative to smaller retailers. Despite the potential drawbacks, it may be advantageous for the retailer to become associated with an administered VMS in order to obtain and carry a well-known, strong line of merchandise.

Table 5.3
Characteristics and examples of vertical marketing systems (VMS)

TYPE OF CHANNEL	CHARACTERISTICS	EXAMPLES
Ownership	Ownership may occur at manufacturer, wholesaler, or retailer levels	Evans Products Co. (building products)
	Firms may also utilize contractual systems (e.g., certain franchisers own a portion of retail outlets)	Sears, Roebuck and Co. Singer Co. (retail sewing centers)
	Substantial financial resources and levels of investment required	Sherwin Williams (paint) Genesco, Inc. (shoes, apparel)
Administered	Coordination achieved through power and influence of dominant firm in channel	Magnavox Co. Kraftco Corp. (dairy products)
	Normally involve a line or classification of products	
Contractual	Consist of wholesaler-sponsored voluntary chains, retailer cooperative organizations, and franchise systems	McDonald's Corp. Holiday Inns of America, Inc. Ethan Allen, Inc.
	Normally involve a written agreement in which responsibilities of channel participants are specified	Buick Division of General Motors Corp.
Conventional channel systems	No dominant power in the channel	Channels used by independent supermarkets, shoe stores, and various other retail outlets
	Decision making centered in each firm	
	Channel entry and exit easier to accomplish than in vertically coordinated channels	Use of agent-broker intermediary channels by small manufacturers to access industrial end users
	Lack integrated programmed approach to channel management	

Source: David W. Cravens, G. E. Hills, and R. B. Woodruff, *Marketing Decision Making,* rev. ed. (Homewood, Ill.: Richard D. Irwin, 1980), p. 291. © RICHARD D. IRWIN, INC., 1976 and 1980.

Table 5.4
Retailer advantages and disadvantages of corporate, administered, and contractual vertical marketing systems

TYPE OF VMS	ADVANTAGES	DISADVANTAGES
Corporate	Simplified pricing	Large financial investment
	Simplified product quality	More complex management problems
	Simplified promotion	Inability to pursue other market opportunities
	Simplified location	
	Functional responsibilities	Higher payroll and other costs
		High inventory carrying costs
		Possible diseconomies of scale in larger systems
		Legal restrictions on mergers and acquisitions
Administered	Well-known brand	Remain somewhat loosely aligned (closest to conventional channel)
	Retailer independence	
	System economies	
	Common goals	
	Marketing programs	
Contractual	Increased opportunity for success	Difficult to get out of arrangement
	Increased chances of entering retailing	Loss of some independence and freedom of decision making
	Managerial expertise	Lack of power relative to franchise
	Financial expertise	May compete with franchisor
	Dependable source for merchandise	Start-up problems
		Possible repurchase agreements
	Marketing programs	Shrinking "exclusive territories"
		Centralized decision making

Perhaps the greatest change in vertical marketing systems over the past two decades has been the growth in the **contractual VMS.** This trend has realigned many retailers and has altered growth patterns in retailing. The basis for coordination in the contractual system is *legal*; the responsibilities and functions of each channel member are defined in a written contract. The potential benefit to the retailer is in achieving market economies and impact that cannot be achieved independently.

Contractual systems have developed and grown to serve a variety of purposes. "Defensive systems" have been developed to defend existing markets against aggressive competition. Included in this category are the retailer-sponsored VMS and the wholesaler-sponsored VMS. "Offensive systems" have been developed to take advantage of a market opportunity; the manufacturer-sponsored VMS (or franchise) fit in this category.

A **retailer-sponsored VMS** consists of independent retailers joined in a cooperative arrangement to gain buying economies not available to the independent retailer. Members are required to concentrate their purchases (usually 50 percent or greater) through the VMS, which usually maintains a "wholesale warehouse." Any profits realized by the wholesale warehouse are disbursed to the retail members, usually in the form of *patronage refunds*, credits given for patronage volumes to the cooperative. Associated Grocers and Certified Grocers are probably the best-known retailer-sponsored VMSs.

A **wholesaler-sponsored VMS** is initiated and sponsored by a wholesaler. Independent retailers can voluntarily join this system. The primary benefits to retailer members are volume discounts and managerial assistance from the sponsoring wholesaler. Managerial assistance can be extensive and can include merchandising, advertising, pricing, store layout and organization, data processing, and financial aid. In exchange for the managerial services, retailers are required to purchase a certain percentage of their volume (usually 60 percent) from the sponsoring wholesaler. The advantages are the enhanced chances of success for the independent retailer and the assured retailer loyalty for the wholesaler.

Examples of the better-known wholesaler-sponsored VMSs include Independent Grocers' Alliance (IGA), Western Auto in hardware, and Economist in the drug field. This system has been successful in the grocery field and has grown rapidly in the hardware, drug, and automotive fields during the 1970s. Of the two defensive systems, wholesaler-sponsored systems have enjoyed greater growth, perhaps because of the necessary commitment of members and the concentration of power in one source.

The manufacturer-sponsored VMS is commonly referred to as franchising. **Franchising** as a system of distribution may be defined as "a continuing relationship in which the *franchisor* provides a licensee the privilege to do business, plus assistance in organizing, training, merchandising, and management in return for a consideration from the franchisee." Franchising is the fastest growing area in retailing and accounts for over $300 billion in sales, approximately one-third of all retail sales. In 1978 nearly a half-million retail establishments were classified as members of franchise arrangements.[9]

Much of the growth in franchising has occurred since 1960 in the service firm–sponsored retailing arrangement. The "product" is a service ranging from business services (H&R Block) to hotels and motels (Holiday Inns). This relationship includes as part of the agreement not only a service to sell but also a marketing strategy, operations procedures, quality standards, training, and a communication network. This is sometimes identified as "business-format franchising." The independent retailer in this arrangement pays a franchise fee and a percentage of revenue (normally about 5 percent) to the franchisor (service firm sponsor) in return for the business format offered by the franchisor. A franchisor can expand rapidly under this arrangement while the independent retailer increases its probability of success by becoming part of the complete business program of the franchisor.

Table 5.5 explains some common variations that may take place in the franchise contract agreement. Franchising covers a wide range of diverse business classifications and organizations. Table 5.6 gives some indications of the breadth of franchising.

The presence of several factors can influence the success of the franchising method of distribution. Table 5.7 lists the characteristics that lend themselves to effective franchising. The six factors mentioned in Table 5.7 give some indication of the business or product areas that might be ready for franchising in the future. One writer suggests that specialized retailing such as cookware stores, bath shops, and personal computer franchises could be some of the new franchise areas of the 1980s.[10]

As stated earlier, the initial channel selection decision of the retailer will, to a large extent, determine the success of the retail endeavor. Whether the retailer decides to become part of a traditional channel or a VMS (corporate, administered, or contractual), the decision requires serious thought. Each has its advantages and disadvantages, which should be considered in the decision.

Table 5.5
Variations in franchise agreements

VARIATION IN AGREEMENT		DESCRIPTION OF ARRANGEMENT FRANCHISE AGREEMENT
1.	Distributorship	Franchisee who is the distributor takes title to goods and redistributes goods to subfranchisees who sell goods to consumer.
2.	Leasing	Franchisor leases buildings, equipment, and/or land to franchisee.
3.	Manufacturing	Franchisor gives franchisee the right to manufacture its product via the use of specified process. Franchisee distributes product using franchisor's practices.
4.	Licensing	Franchisor gives franchisee a license to use franchisor's trademarks and business practices. Franchisor may supply product or give franchisee a list of approved suppliers.
5.	Service	Franchisor specifies methods that the franchisee can use to supply the service to consumers.
6.	Co-ownership	Franchisor and franchisee share the investment and profits.
7.	Co-management	Franchisor retains major part of investment and partner-manager share profits on a basis of a predetermined percentage.

Source: From *Retail Management: Satisfaction of Consumer Needs,* 2d ed. by Raymond A. Marquardt, James C. Makens, and Robert G. Roe, p. 107. Copyright © 1979 by the Dryden Press, a division of Holt, Rinehart and Winston. Reprinted by permission of Holt, Rinehart and Winston, CBS College Publishing.

Table 5.6
Types of franchise organizations and selected examples

Automotive services	AAMCO Automatic Transmission, Inc.
Auto/trailer rentals	Budget Rent-A-Car corporation
	Hertz Corporation
Business aids/services	H&R Block, Inc.
	Business Consultants of America, Inc.
Campgrounds	Kampgrounds of America, Inc.
Cosmetics/toiletries	Color Me Beautiful Cosmetics
Drugstores	Rexall Drug Company
Educational products/services	Evelyn Wood Reading Dynamics
Employment services	Dunhill Personnel System, Inc.
Equipment/rentals	United Rent-All, Inc.
Foods—donuts	Dunkin-Donuts of America, Inc.
	Spudnuts, Inc.
Foods—grocery/specialty stores	Hickory Farms of Ohio, Inc.
	Baskin-Robbins, Inc.
Foods—restaurants/drive-ins/ carry-outs	A&W International, Inc.
	Burger King Corporation
	McDonald's Corporation
General merchandise stores	Coast-to-Coast Stores
	Gamble-Skogmo, Inc.
Health aids/services	Health Clubs of America
Lawn and garden supplies/services	Lawn Medic, Inc.
Maintenance/cleaning, sanitation service/supplies	Americlean National Service Corporation
Motels, hotels	Days Inns of America, Inc.
	Holiday Inns of America, Inc.
Printing	Kwik-Kopy Corporation
Real estate	Century 21 Real Estate Corporation
Recreation/entertainment, travel services/supplies	Billie Jean King Tennis Centers, Inc.
Swimming pools	Sylvan Pools
Tools, hardware	Snap-On Tools Corporation
Transit service	Aero Mayflower Transit Company, Inc.
Vending	Ford Gum & Machine Co., Inc.
Water conditioning	Culligan International Company

Source: Selected entries from U.S. Department of Commerce, *Franchise Opportunities Handbook, 1977* (Washington, D.C.: Government Printing Office, 1977), pp. 75–86.

Channel Relationships

In an ongoing channel, the retailer must continuously interact with other members to achieve both channel and independent objectives. Well-organized and cooperative relationships tend to benefit all channel members, including the retailer.

Table 5.7
Trade characteristics that encourage franchising

1. The trade is in a highly fragmented market and independent retailers generally do not have the ability to compete with large retailers.

2. The trade is not offering sufficient service and expertise along with merchandise.

3. The merchandise is sufficiently distinctive and identifiable by brand or trademark, and consumer acceptance has reached a point where customers will search for the merchandise when it is needed or wanted.

4. The offering cannot be provided along with similar offerings and still have public acceptance (i.e., prepared foods, rug and upholstery cleaning services).

5. The offering has unique qualities that require special handling or preparation for proper product consistency and satisfaction when sold to the consumer (i.e., Shakey's Pizza, Coca-Cola).

6. The offering requires installation, periodic service, and a stock of locally available parts (i.e., automobile repair).

Source: From *Retail Management: Satisfaction of Consumer Needs,* 2d ed. by Raymond A. Marquardt, James C. Makens, and Robert G. Roe, p. 111. Copyright © 1979 by the Dryden Press, a division of Holt, Rinehart and Winston. Reprinted by permission of Holt, Rinehart and Winston, CBS College Publishing.

Cooperation, Conflict, and Power.   An effective and efficient channel must have the right mixture of cooperation and conflict. Achieving the right mixture is often predicated on the judicious use of power by a formal or informal channel leader.

Cooperation is the perception by channel members that they are working toward mutually beneficial goals. Increased cooperation leads to more smoothly flowing channel relationships.

Vertical conflict is the perception of one channel member that another is gaining at its expense. A large amount of conflict can hinder the smooth functioning of a channel. If each channel member perceives that it is losing benefits because another channel member is gaining, it will be difficult to maintain cooperation among members. For example, if a franchisee perceives common objectives with the franchisor, the overall functioning of the channel will be enhanced. However, if a franchisee perceives that the franchisor is unfair or is taking advantage of a situation, the franchisee may not follow channel policies or participate in information gathering or other channel-facilitating activities.

Just as high levels of conflict can be detrimental to channel relationships, absence of conflict can also hinder functioning. Conflict is a source of innovative change; without conflict, the channel system could become stagnant and noncompetitive. Thus low levels of constructive conflict are beneficial to the functioning of a channel.

Power is defined as the ability to influence the behavior of another member. The use of power is necessary to *increase cooperation* and *control conflict* in channel relationships. Five types of power (or power bases) are described below:[11]

1. *Reward power* is based on the belief by a channel follower that the channel leader can mediate rewards because the leader has or is believed to have access to some resources that the follower values. Specific rewards that may be used by specific channel members may include granting of wider margins and allocation of promotional allowances.

2. *Coercive power* reflects the expectations of a channel member that he [or she] will be punished for failure to conform to the channel leader's plans. Sanctions may often involve reductions in margins, withdrawals of promotional allowances, denials of exclusive territorial grants, etc.

3. *Expert power* is based on channel members' perception of the leader as having a special knowledge that could help the channel. Thus, manufacturers are often expected to have special knowledge about new products and promotion to assist dealers in that respect.

4. *Referent* or *identification power* is based on the desire of a channel member to join and/or belong to a given organization.

5. *Legitimacy power* stems from recognition of channel members that the channel leader has a "right" to make specific decisions and expect compliance with regard to those decisions.

Robert Lusch analyzed power by separating power into coercive and noncoercive classifications.[12] *Coercive power* is based on a member's begrudgingly acquiescing to the leader or power user, primarily because the member perceives that the leader can punish. *Noncoercive power* is based on the yielding member's willingness to yield to the power user.

In his study of automobile channels, Lusch identified six uses of coercive power: (1) slow delivery of vehicles, (2) slow payment on warranty, (3) unfair distribution of vehicles, (4) turndowns on warranty, (5) threat of termination, and (6) bureaucratic red tape. Sixteen "assistances" were defined as noncoercive uses of power. Included in the list of sixteen assistances were rational advertising, local advertising, executive training, salesperson training, mechanic training, sales promotion kits, salesperson incentive programs, dealer incentive programs, bookkeeping assistance, manufacturer's service representative, manufacturer's sales representative, tools and equipment, product warranty, inventory rebates, floor plan assistance, and service manuals. Lusch concluded that coercive sources of power increase manufacturer-dealer conflict.[13]

Michael Etgar found that conventional and vertical marketing systems contain different methods of bringing about cooperation and controlling conflict. Manufacturers in conventional channel arrangements tend to use product-related support activities such as product development, delivery, and a wide selection of product offerings. Manufacturers in contractual systems tend to use their expertise and their ability to assist dealers in retail management activities.[14] Etgar further proposes that the use of expertise power leads to conflict because the power base erodes over time. The retailer gains expertise over time, thus gaining power relative to the manufacturer.

The Retailer's Perspective.   In general, retailers can be categorized as either leaders or followers in the channels of distribution. Retailers that can assume the role of a channel leader are usually large with a strong consumer following as the source of power. Sears and Safeway are prominent examples. The type of power exercised is usually *reward* or *expert*.

Smaller retailers must normally assume the role of channel follower because they lack an effective power base. Small retailers should seek alignments with channels whose leaders tend to use *reward* power and, perhaps, *expert* power. Although most small retailers are likely to prefer noncoercive power, others will submit to coercive or legitimacy power if adequate economic rewards are provided.

Channel Evolution

Channels of distribution are not static; they change and evolve over time. Understanding channel and institutional evolution can provide the retailer with insight regarding possible future channel arrangements and types of competition. While none of the following explanations of channel and institutional change is complete, each provides a general base for anticipating change and providing a perspective for retailing strategies. As discussed earlier, the major evolutionary trend in recent years has been the growth of vertical marketing systems. As more channel alignments become legitimate vertical marketing systems, retailers can expect the systems themselves to evolve. Further, if a VMS actually behaves as a "total system," the retail institution should evolve and change along with the system.

Joseph Guiltinan has proposed an evolutionary process for changes in vertical marketing systems.[15] The evolutionary process is based upon the VMS's reaction to pressures brought about because of institutional obsolescence, inefficient performance, and/or conflict among channel members. As the marketplace brings about these pressures, VMS objectives change, which results in realignment of channel members and their functions. These structural changes can be explained by an analysis of changes in the strategic distribution objectives of key VMS members. Table 5.8 shows a five-stage sequence of changes of channel objectives and the consequent effects on channel arrangements.

Retail institutions also change, and this can cause the entire channel to change. Five hypotheses of retail institutional change are described below. All of these attempts partially explain certain changes in retail institutions, although no one hypothesis has universal applicability.

Wheel of Retailing.   The basis for retail institutional change according to the **wheel of retailing** hypothesis is the innovative behavior of competitors. An innovative retailer perceives a "void" in the market, primarily at its "low end." These innovative retailers challenge the more mature, established retailers with low margins, low prices, few services, and low expenses. As the innovators grow, they begin to trade up merchandise, add services, move to more expensive locations, improve store appearance, and increase promotional expenses, eventually becoming higher-expense, higher-margin,

Table 5.8
Evolution in channel arrangements

STAGE	PRIMARY SOURCE OF INFLUENCE ON POLICY	ILLUSTRATIVE POLICIES
1. Contractual/ communication	Product characteristics	M-W-R channel Little channel direction
2. Coverage/capacity	Institutional effectiveness in reaching consumers	Intense distribution Multiple brands
3. Control	Channel member relationships and marketing policies	Franchising; administered systems; exclusive distribution
4. Cost	Economic efficiency	Voluntaries, cooperatives
5. Cooperation/ consolidation	Access to capital	Vertical integration

Source: Joseph P. Guiltinan, "Planned and Evolutionary Changes in Distribution Channels," p. 86. Reprinted with permission from *Journal of Retailing,* Vol. 50, No. 2, Summer 1974.

higher-priced retailers. Because of this movement "up the wheel" the innovator eventually evolves into an institution similar to the mature institutions it sought to compete against initially. This leaves the formerly innovative institution vulnerable to new innovators at the low end of the market. The fast-food franchisors are an excellent illustration of this concept, as shown in Strategy in Action 5.2.

The wheel of retailing explanation has been criticized as being too specific to explain everything. Although the evolution of fast-food and discount stores fits the theory, many specialty institutions such as designer boutiques did not enter the market at the low end. The same can be said for department stores, most professional services, convenience stores, and vending-machine selling. Retailers should remain alert, however, for innovations that might cause the "wheel" to "run them over."

Retail Accordion Theory. The **retail accordion theory** involves historical changes in the breadth of product line carried by retailers. This theory describes retailers' product line adjustments as beginning with wide assortments then moving to narrower assortments, and then returning to wide assortments.

The general store of the 1800s maintained an extensive merchandise assortment. During the first half of this century, merchandise assortments became narrower as population became more concentrated and income continued to increase. Beginning in the 1960s, the "accordion" started to move toward broader, more general merchandise lines. Retailers expanded many traditional product assortments. Drugstores began to sell appliances, grocery supermarkets began to sell many nonfood items, and discounters moved into a wide range of product areas they had not sold previously.

STRATEGY IN ACTION 5.2
Look Out McDonald's, the "Wheel" Is Rolling

Innovation

In 1954, a multi-mixer salesman named Ray A. Kroc first "saw" the McDonald concept. Though the McDonald Brothers started some of the chain's technical innovations, it was Kroc who formulated the nationwide operating policies. Maybe this is the innovation spoken of as the wheel hypothesis.

Growth

In 1954, McDonald's menu was featuring hamburgers at 15 cents, cheeseburgers at 19 cents, french fries at 10 cents, and malted milkshakes at 20 cents. This menu was served from red and white (candy-striped) buildings, built between two huge, golden arches. Customers stood outside; their dining rooms were their automobiles.

In 1965, Filet-O-Fish became the first menu addition. In 1967, the price of the McDonald's hamburger increased to 18 cents, and the first McDonald's indoor dining room was introduced. In 1968, the "Big Mac" and "Hot Apple Pie" were added to the menu. In 1970, the price of the McDonald's Hamburger rose to 20 cents. In 1972, the chain included 2000 restaurants and sold its 10 billionth hamburger. The "Quarter Pounder" was added to the menu. Annual sales topped $1 billion. In 1972, McDonald's served more food to more people than any other food operation in the world.

Maturity

In 1974, the "candy-stripe" buildings had reached a point of nostalgia. During that year, McDonald's converted 71 of these models, leaving only 166. In 1974, more than 85 percent of McDonald's restaurants offered the convenience of indoor dining. The average-size restaurant in 1974 was 3700 square feet. Four of the original "candy-stripe" restaurants would fit in the average floor plan of a 1974 model.

Conclusion

The growth of McDonald's adheres well to the wheel of retailing description.

The current status of fast-food hamburger franchisers finds that McDonald's is king. In 1977, McDonald's sales exceeded $3.7 billion. More than $120 million was spent on advertising. Sales per store average $838,000, and company earnings stood at $136.7 million.

The question now is, "Will McDonald's be challenged by some innovative newcomer who will capture the market and cause McDonald's to decline and die?" McDonald's answer is a resounding "No." As innovations appear, they are evaluated, and the operation is altered to capitalize on the better ones. Breakfast is added; a drive-thru window is designed; challenges from innovators are incorporated to help the leader stay in front of the pack.

Source: Condensed from an article by Eugene Teeple, "Look Out McDonald's, The 'Wheel' Is Rolling," in Howard S. Gitlow and Edward W. Wheatley (eds.), *Developments in Marketing Science, Vol. 2, Proceedings of Third Annual Conference of the Academy of Marketing Science, 1979* (Coral Gables, Fla., 1979), p. 379.

This phenomenon probably occurs for several reasons. First, consumer behavior patterns change. One-stop shopping, for example, continues to grow in importance because of limited shopping time and the increased expense of multiple stops. Some grocery stores now have pharmacies, bank machines, post offices, and other conveniences under one roof. This trend is beneficial to stores offering wide assortments of merchandise.

Second, the retailer must overcome increasing costs. Adjusting the merchandise strategy is often a way of decreasing the impact of increasing costs. The retailer can either attempt to decrease costs by eliminating product lines or cover the higher costs by adding higher-margin products. The current situation appears to be one of adding higher-margin products to surmount the growing cost of retailing.

The Dialectic Process. The German philosopher Georg Hegel first developed the **dialectic process:** A concept *(thesis)* inevitably generates its opposite *(antithesis),* and the interaction of the two leads to a new concept *(synthesis).* The new concept becomes the thesis for a new triad.

In terms of retailing institutions, the original retailer (thesis) is challenged by a competitor who offers opposite advantages and characteristics (antithesis). The challenged retailer reacts by adjusting in the direction of the challenge. As time passes, the original challenger upgrades and moves in the direction of the original retailer (thesis), similar to the wheel of retailing concept. The result is a synthesis or blending of the original and innovative retail institutions' marketing offerings. A new dialectic evolution begins when a new antithesis develops to challenge the evolved synthesis. The dialectic process in retailing is illustrated in Figure 5.4. Analyzing the dialectic process will provide the retailer with insight into the type of competition to expect in the future.

Natural Selection Process. In the **natural selection process,** retailing evolution is explained in terms of Charles Darwin's adaptive behavior and survival model. A simplistic "survival of the fittest" description of the theory proposes that members of an environment that best adapt to the changing environment are most likely to survive. As applied to retailing institutions, the retail decision maker who makes the appropriate decisions to adapt the institution's retailing mix to the changing environment will have the best probability of success.

An example of adapting institutions is the discount stores of earlier years that traded up, changed service mix, and selected improved locations

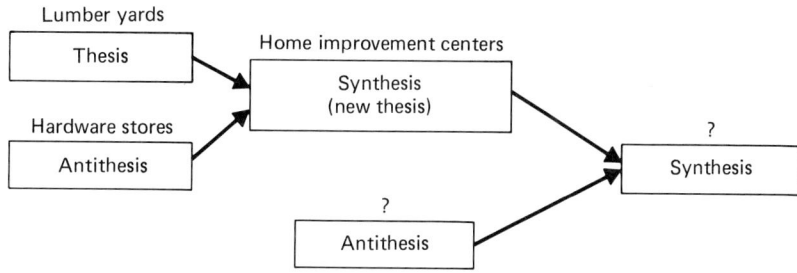

Figure 5.4
The dialectic process

to meet the changing environment. Many single-line institutions, such as small grocery and hardware stores, have not or could not adapt to the changing environment that stresses price, convenience, and one-stop shopping. Although many of these institutions have survived, many have failed. *Retail polarization*, the existence of numerous specialty and general merchandise stores growing on the one hand and single-line stores failing on the other, is a result of this "natural selection" process.

This concept emphasizes the need for retailers to monitor both the macroenvironment and the task environment and to adapt to environmental changes. These monitor-and-adapt activities are key components of the strategic management approach emphasized throughout this text.

Retail Life Cycle. In the **retail life cycle** (RLC), the product life cycle concept is applied to retail institutions. According to the RLC, retail evolution is caused by a combination of the various competitive retailing strategies in the specific retail trade and consumers' reactions to these retailing efforts. The stages through which the institution evolves are innovation, accelerated development, maturity, and decline. Table 5.9 describes the key characteristics and managerial activities appropriate for each stage of the RLC.

Accumulated evidence indicates that retail life cycles are becoming shorter. Table 5.10 illustrates this point. The innovation-to-maturity period of department stores required roughly eighty years, whereas a more current retail innovation, the home improvement center, took only 15 years to reach maturity. Of course, with appropriate retailing strategies these institutions may remain in the maturity stage for decades.

The shorter life cycles demonstrate competing retailers' lower response time to the changing environment or to a more rapidly changing environment. Because competitors react more rapidly to the macroenvironment and task environment, and because consumers react to the changing institutions, the RLC is evolving more rapidly. The implications are rather obvious: (1) the retailer must have a current (and forecast) knowledge of the retailing environment in order to adapt quickly; (2) maximum profit-taking periods are shorter and the retailer must remain flexible to take advantage of opportunities when they arise; (3) consumers will react more rapidly to innovative institutions and the retailer must have some "model" of future expected competitive institutions; and (4) the more effective the retail marketing effort, the quicker the RLC process. The retailer, although successful today, cannot rest on the laurels of the past and present. Long-term strategic plans are mandatory for the turbulent retail environment of tomorrow.

Other Intermediaries

Retailers interact with many other institutions on a daily basis, such as transportation specialists and financial institutions. Transportation specialists influence retailers because of their impact on total channel performance. Transportation rates and possible improvement in transportation performance can alter pricing and merchandise availability for the retailer. Suggestions on route changes, merchandise handling, and order pro-

Table 5.9
Management activities in the retail life cycle

AREA OR SUBJECT OF CONCERN		STAGE OF LIFE CYCLE DEVELOPMENT			
		INNOVATION	ACCELERATED DEVELOPMENT	MATURITY	DECLINE
Market characteristics	Number of competitors	Very few	Moderate	Many direct competitors; moderate indirect competition	Moderate direct competition; many indirect competitors
	Rate of sales growth	Very rapid	Rapid	Moderate to slow	Slow or negative
	Level of profitability	Low to moderate	High	Moderate	Very low
	Duration of new innovations	3 to 5 years	5 to 6 years	Indefinite	Indefinite
Appropriate retailer actions	Investment/ growth/risk decisions	Investment minimization, high risks accepted	High levels of investment to sustain growth	Tightly controlled growth in untapped markets	Minimal capital expenditures and only when essential
	Central management concerns	Concept refinement through adjustment and experimentation	Establishing a preemptive market position	Excess capacity and "overstoring"; prolonging maturity and revising the retail concept	Engaging in a "run-out" strategy
	Use of management control techniques	Minimal	Moderate	Extensive	Moderate
	Most successful management style	Entrepreneurial	Centralized	"Professional"	Caretaker
Appropriate supplier actions	Channel strategy	Develop a preemptive market position	Hold market position	Maintain profitable sales	Avoid excessive costs
	Channel problems	Possible antagonism of other accounts	Possible antagonism of other accounts	Dealing with more scientific retailers	Servicing accounts at a profit
	Channel research	Identification of key innovations	Identification of other retailers adopting the innovation	Initial screening of new innovation opportunities	Active search for new innovation opportunities
	Trade incentives	Direct financial support	Price concessions	New price incentives	None

Table 5.10
Life-cycle characteristics of five retail institutions

INSTITUTION	APPROXIMATE DATE OF INNOVATION	APPROXIMATE DATE OF MAXIMUM MARKET SHARE	APPROXIMATE NUMBER OF YEARS REQUIRED TO REACH MATURITY	ESTIMATED MAXIMUM MARKET SHARE	ESTIMATED 1975 MARKET SHARE
Downtown department store	1860	1940	80	8.5%	1.1%
				of total retail sales	
Variety store	1910	1955	45	16.5%	9.5%
				of general merchandise sales	
Supermarket	1930	1965	35	70.0%	64.5%
				of grocery store sales	
Discount department store	1950	1970	20	6.5%	5.7%
				of total retail sales	
Home improve- ment center	1965	1980 (estimate)	15	35.0%	23.5%
				of hardware and building material sales	

Source: Reprinted by permission of the *Harvard Business Review.* From "The Retail Life Cycle" by Albert D. Bates, William R. Davidson, and Stephen J. Bass (*HBR*, November/December 1976). Copyright © 1976 by the President and Fellows of Harvard College; all rights reserved.

STRATEGY IN ACTION 5.3

Maturity in Retailing

Several of the large mass merchandisers — Sears, Montgomery Ward, J. C. Penney, and K mart — may be experiencing the effects of the maturity stage of the institutional life cycle. All four had slow growth or profitability problems in 1980. Competition from discount stores, "factory outlets," home improvement centers, and "flea markets" have pressed Sears, Wards, and Penney. Regional discounters with newer, more innovative stores and fixtures have hurt K mart's growth. These newer institutions have given the traditional mass merchandisers profitability and growth problems.

As a result, Sears has reorganized into three separate divisions: merchandising, insurance, and financial services. Sears has also developed a strategy of "back to basics." This is an attempt to reaffirm their strong quality image. Penney's is upgrading their fashion image. Ward's is redesigning stores and upscaling their merchandise while eliminating slower selling merchandise. K mart is also redesigning their stores to "feature better merchandise." All four retailers are stressing productivity through the increased use of computers and building smaller stores. These steps are intended to increase growth and reduce expenses in hopes of expanding profit margins. Some retail experts believe these strategies may help alleviate the profit and growth problems but note that greater changes might be necessary to "create some excitement" and regain the strong growth patterns of previous years.

Source: "Retailing: Mid-Life Crisis," *Newsweek,* 5 January 1981, pp. 47–48. Copyright 1981, by Newsweek, Inc. All Rights Reserved. Reprinted by Permission.

cessing may arise from transportation specialists. The retailer must realize this specialist's impact on the entire channel and its value as a source of information.

Financial institutions, of course, perform financing and risk-bearing functions. Whether the retailer can find a source of funds to purchase inventory or provide for store expansion has obvious impact on the retailer. Positive relations with financial institutions in addition to credit ratings can enhance the retailer's ability to secure financial support.

SUMMARY

It is vitally important for the retailer to be constantly aware of competitive behavior and channel interrelationships. The competitive audit and an integrated appraisal of the channel situation and potential changes are necessary to adequately evaluate the task environment. In the following chapters the final aspect of the task environment, consumers and their behavior, will be discussed.

KEY CONCEPTS

Competitive audit	Retailer-sponsored VMS
Intratype competition	Wholesaler-sponsored VMS
Intertype competition	Franchising
Three-subset approach	Channel conflict
Positioning	Channel cooperation
Strategy profile	Channel power
Marketing intermediaries	Channel evolution
Conventional channel	Wheel of retailing
Vertical marketing systems (VMS)	Retail accordion theory
Corporate VMS	Dialectic process
Administered VMS	Natural selection process
Contractual VMS	Retail life cycle (RLC)

REVIEW QUESTIONS

1. What is the task environment and why is it important to retailers?
2. What is the purpose of a competitive audit?
3. What are the differences between conventional channels and vertical marketing systems?
4. Explain the retail-sponsored, wholesaler-sponsored, and manufacturer-sponsored (franchising) VMS.

5. What circumstances would make it advantageous for a retailer to join a franchise system?

6. How does power enter into channel management?

7. How do the five theories of retail institutional change interrelate?

LEARNING EXERCISES

1. Develop a competitive audit for two local retail trades.

2. Contact a local franchiser to determine the provisions of the franchise agreement.

3. Question several local retailers to determine the extent of actual competitive analysis.

4. Develop a retail profile for three retailers who are direct competitors. What is the differential niche for a fourth retailer who may desire to enter the market?

5. Compare the types of channels of distribution for three types of retailers.

DECISION SITUATION 5.1: **Saveway B**

In Saveway A (Decision Situation 4.1) an opportunity to build a new store near a new housing area was presented. Saveway management decided not to take this opportunity until at least four hundred houses were built. The fact that they already had 40 percent of the market was a major reason not to expand. However, the situation has now changed.

As part of its continual monitoring of competitors' actions, Saveway learned that a national competitor had bought a parcel of land near the area. Construction of a new store was to begin within six months. The new store would likely capture most of the business from the new development. Saveway does have an option to purchase land across the highway from the competitor's proposed location.

QUESTIONS

1. Should Saveway exercise its option or stick with the original plan?

2. How soon should a store be started if one is to be started?

3. What reaction would you expect from the competitor if Saveway starts a store?

DECISION SITUATION 5.2: **City Auto Parts**

Mark Smith, the owner of City Auto Parts, has been approached by a large parts wholesaler about becoming part of a VMS sponsored by the wholesaler. Mark would have to purchase all his parts from the wholesaler and agree to certain conditions of the contractual agreement.

City Auto Parts has been profitable for all of its eight years of operations. Last year Mark earned $47,000 from the business. He expects even higher earnings this year. (Profits are up almost 10 percent over the same time last year.) According to the wholesaler, every parts store that has joined the VMS has increased its profits.

QUESTIONS

1. What factors should Mark consider in making this decision?

2. What are the advantages and disadvantages of joining the VMS?

3. Would you join if you were Mark?

NOTES

1. Bert C. McCammon, Jr., "Future Shock and the Practice of Management," in *Attitude Research Bridges the Atlantic,* ed. P. Levine, Marketing Research Series 16 (Chicago: American Marketing Association, 1975), p. 77.

2. Philip Kotler, *Marketing Management,* 4th ed. (Englewood Cliffs, N.J.: Prentice-Hall, 1980).

3. Charles W. King and Lawrence J. Ring, "Marketing Positioning Across Retail Fashion Institutions: A Comparative Analysis of Store Types," *Journal of Retailing,* vol. 56, no. 1 (Spring 1980), pp. 37–55.

4. Jerry L. Wall, "What the Competition Is Doing: You Need to Know," *Harvard Business Review,* November–December 1974, pp. 23–28.

5. Robert Hershey, "Commercial Intelligence on a Shoestring," *Harvard Business Review,* September–October 1980, pp. 22–30.

6. Jerry L. Wall, *op. cit.*

7. Bert C. McCammon, Jr., "Perspectives for Distribution Programming," in *Vertical Marketing Systems,* ed. Louis P. Bucklin (Glenview, Ill.: Scott, Foresman, 1970), pp. 32–51.

8. *Ibid.*

9. U.S. Department of Commerce, *Franchising in the Economy, 1976–1978,* (Washington, D.C.: Government Printing Office), 1978.

10. "Franchising: Opening the Doors to Expansion," *Retail Week,* 1 February 1981, p. 29.

11. Michael Etgar, "Selection of an Effective Channel Control Mix," *Journal of Marketing,* July 1978, pp. 53–54. Reprinted with permission from *Journal of Marketing* (published by the American Marketing Association).

12. Robert F. Lusch, "Sources of Power: Their Impact on Intrachannel Conflict," *Journal of Marketing Research,* November 1976, pp. 382–390.

13. *Ibid.*

14. Michael Etgar, "Differences in the Use of Manufacturer Power in Conventional and Contractual Channels," *Journal of Retailing,* vol. 54 (Winter 1978), pp. 49–62.

15. Joseph P. Guiltinan, "Planned and Evolutionary Changes in Distribution Channels," *Journal of Retailing,* vol. 50, no. 2 (Summer 1974), pp. 79–91.

STRATEGIC RETAIL MANAGEMENT MODEL

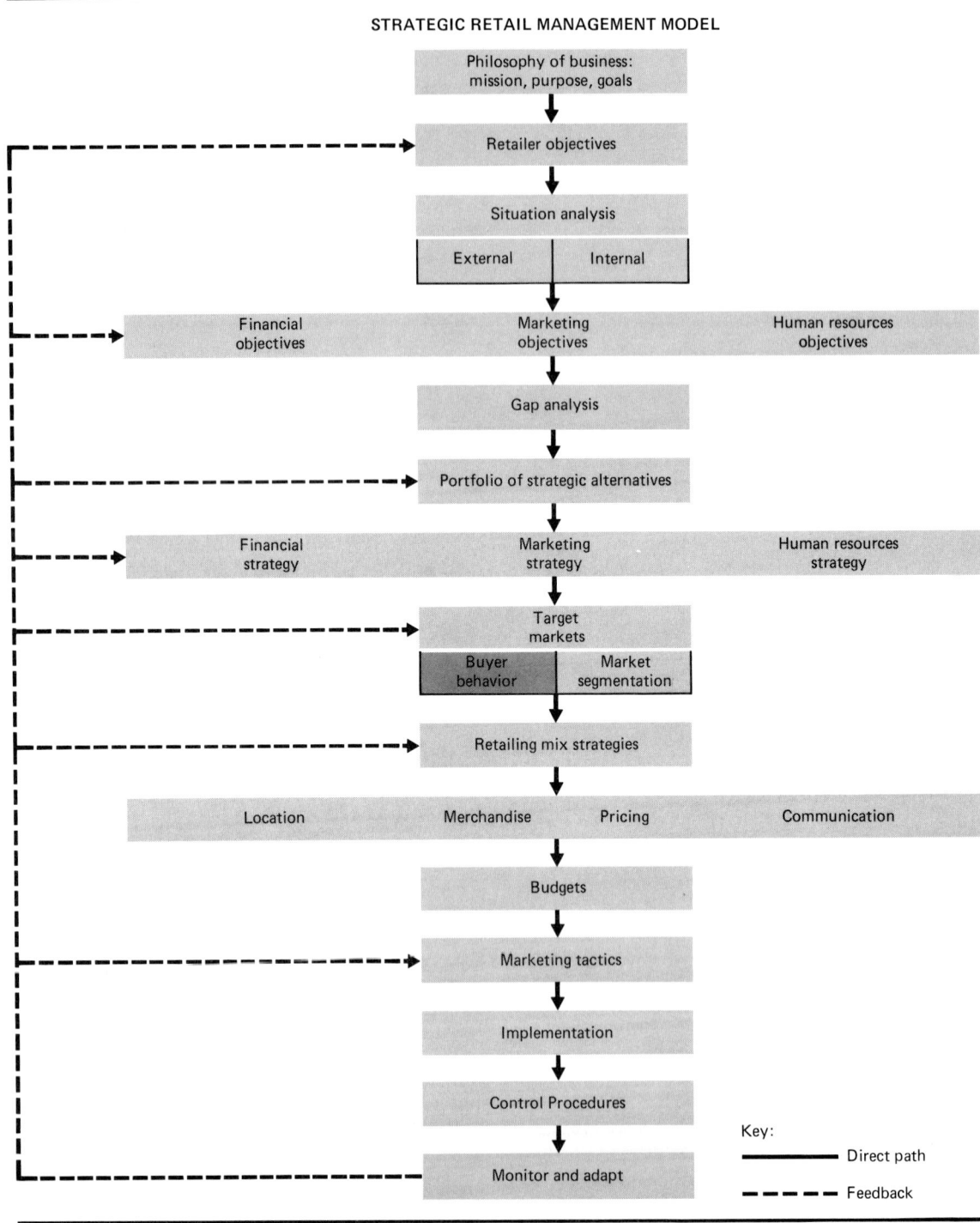

Chapter 6
Buyer Behavior

LEARNING OBJECTIVES

1. To understand the role and importance of buyer behavior and its interaction with retailing strategy.

2. To understand the basic buyer decision process in choosing a retail store.

INTRODUCTION

The consumer is the focal point of all retailing decisions. Without a thorough knowledge of consumers and their behavior patterns a retailer will have difficulty deciding on a course of action, whether it be selecting which merchandise to carry or which appeal to use in advertising. The retailer develops a strategy based on consumers' behavior and also evaluates the effectiveness of retailing efforts on the basis of consumers' reactions. Thus the consumer is the starting point for retail decision making as well as the final indicator of its success.

As is the case for all factors in a dynamic environment, consumers change over time. Many products and retail services that were popular and profitable years ago are not offered by retailers today. Similarly, today's successful retail strategies may not be viable even a few years from now. As indicated in Strategy in Action 6.1, adjusting to changing consumer behavior patterns is an integral part of strategic retail management.

A CONSUMER BEHAVIOR MODEL

A model illustrating consumers' behavior in selecting retail stores is depicted in Fig. 6.1.[1] The model is organized around two factors: the predecision state and the decision process.

STRATEGY IN ACTION 6.1

Changing to Meet Consumer Needs

Drugstore chains such as Revco, Walgreen, and Pay Less are opening larger stores to capitalize on the consumer's need for convenient, one-stop shopping. The expanding merchandise mix in departments like hardware, soft goods, and automotive supplies has improved the drug chains' gross margins.*

Several changes have occurred in the retail merchandise mix of men's shoes because of a new relaxed attitude toward business attire and the desire on the part of men for a more wearable, multipurpose shoe. A new classification called the "casual/dress" shoe has been developed and is quickly dominating men's shoe merchandise mixes.†

Many consumers desire to purchase the status symbols of a society, but lack the funds necessary to do so. Because of this, Sears uses its Cheryl Tiegs line of women's apparel to appeal to the 25-to-40-year-old who wants a "budget-priced" status symbol.‡

Sources:
*Adapted from "Trend Shifts to Larger Stores," pp. 28–32. Reprinted by permission from *Chain Store Age/Executive* © July 1981. Copyright Lebhar-Friedman, Inc. 425 Park Avenue, New York, NY 10022.
†Adapted from "Why a New Hybrid in Shoes Is Making Big Strides." Reprinted from *Retail Week*, 15 July 1981, pp. 36–37.
‡Adapted from "Brenner Brings Cheryl Tiegs' Fashion to Staid Old Sears," pp. 28–35. Reprinted by permission from *Chain Store Age/Executive* © August 1981. Copyright Lebhar-Friedman, Inc. 425 Park Avenue, New York, NY 10022.

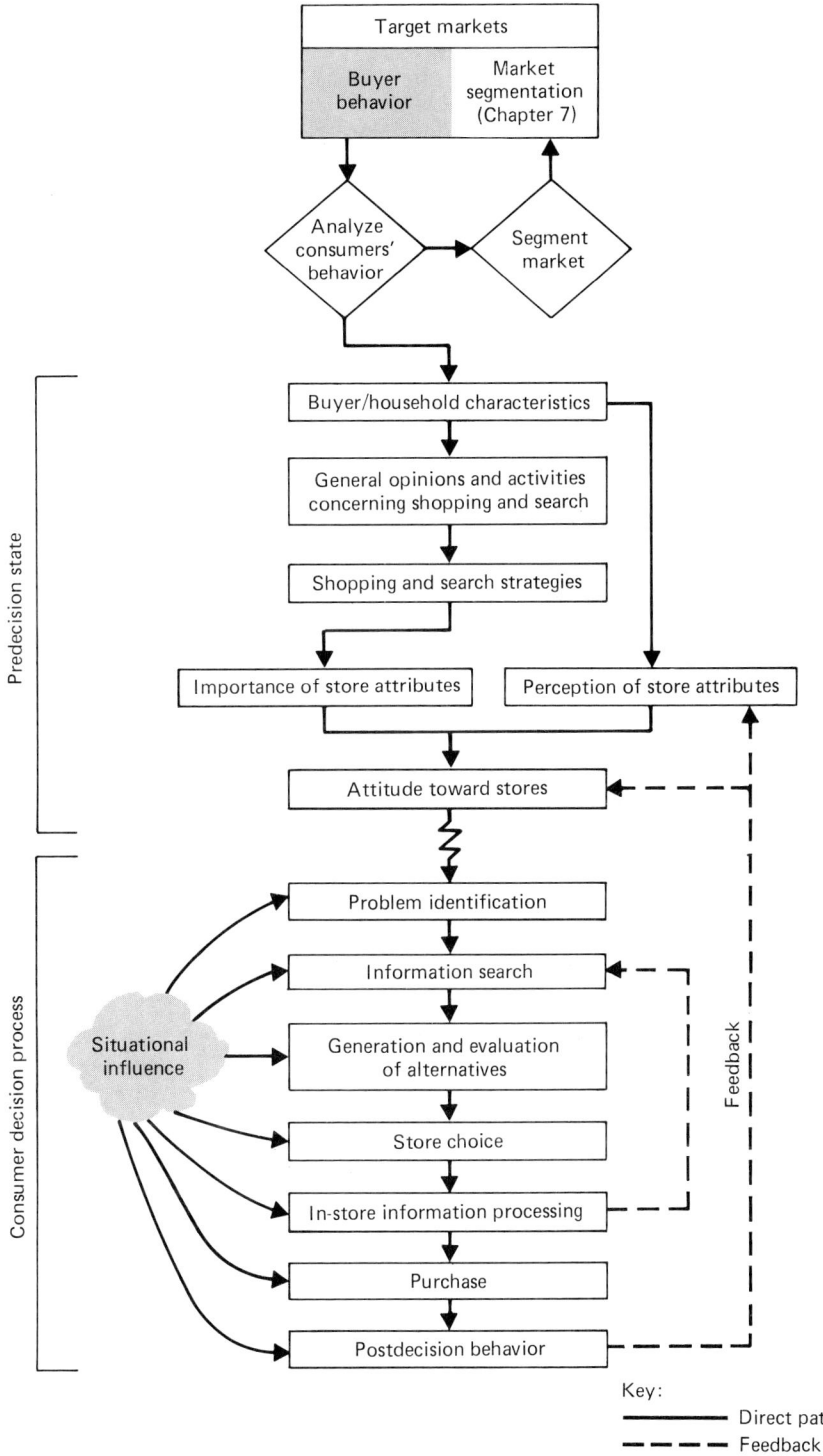

Figure 6.1
Consumer behavior and decision model

The **predecision state,** consisting of buyer/household characteristics, opinions and activities concerning shopping and search, shopping and search strategies, importance of store attributes, perception of store attributes, and attitudes toward stores, is the existing base from which the consumer begins the process of selecting a retail store. This state is characterized by consumers' personal characteristics and their present level of knowledge and attitudes toward retailers.

The **consumer decision process** begins when consumers add new information to their predecision-state knowledge, and it results in their selection of a retail store. Consumer decisions begin with problem identification and proceed to a search for information, which results in generating and evaluating possible store choices. Once the choice of a store is made, the consumer may process in-store information, which may lead to a purchase. Finally, the consumer engages in postdecision behavior, which provides feedback for the predecision state.

HOUSEHOLD/BUYER CHARACTERISTICS

Household/buyer characteristics form the basic framework for understanding how store choices are made. They can be classified as internal and external consumer variables. The **internal variables**—needs, motives, personality, perception, learning, and attitudes—directly influence the choice of a retail store. External variables—family, reference groups, social class, and culture—influence the internal variables.

Internal Variables

Internal variables—in the form of needs, motives, personality, perception, learning, and attitudes—directly influence the retail choice decision.

Needs. The bedrock of all behavior is **needs,** which initiate the process of behavior and provide a general base for behavior. The behavior an individual selects is an attempt to satisfy his or her needs, but needs do not spell out which behavior a person should select.

Table 6.1 presents the elementary aspects of two different theories of needs: Abraham Maslow's hierarchy, probably the best-known and best-articulated theory, and the theory of David McClelland.

The importance of consumer needs to the retailer is that the retailer must "anchor" to a consumer need and may even become involved in resolving consumers' conflicts about their needs. Consumer needs are satisfied by objects in the environment; the stronger the need, the greater desire to obtain the object. If the consumer has not made an association between a retailer's offering and a felt need, preferably a strongly felt need, the retailer will find it difficult to move the consumer to a purchase. Whether the need is for convenience, security, or esteem, the retailer must develop the relationship between satisfaction of the need (or a combination of needs) and a

Table 6.1
Two theories of needs

Needs	*Needs*
Physiological — food, water, shelter, sex, etc.	Affiliation — desire to be accepted and liked by others
Safety and security — protection, order, stability, etc.	Power — desire to influence, guide, and control others
Belongingness and love — affection, friendship, etc.	Achievement — desire to achieve personal goals
Esteem — prestige, success, self-respect, etc.	*Theory*
Self-actualization — self-fulfillment	Degrees of three needs; one increases at the expense of the other two
Theory	*Examples of Application*
Prepotency; satisfy needs in hierarchial order, beginning with physiological	Power — retailer may promote that you as a customer are important and control the transaction
Examples of Application	Achievement — retailer may emphasize the "reward of personal success" that the store satisfies
Belongingness — retailer may emphasize friendliness and acceptance	
Esteem — retailer may position store as "prestige store"	

Sources: Left-hand column: Data based on Hierarchy of Needs in "A Theory of Human Motivation" in *Motivation and Personality*, 2nd Edition by Abraham H. Maslow. Copyright © 1970 by Abraham H. Maslow. Reprinted by permission of Harper & Row Publishers, Inc.
Right hand column: David C. McClelland, *The Achieving Society*, Princeton, N.J.: Van Nostrand, 1961.

purchase from the retailer. A bank, for example, may satisfy security needs or belonging needs through the exterior and interior building design, FDIC affiliation, safety-deposit boxes, a practice of knowing customers by name, and a policy of discreetly handling overdrawn checking accounts or late payments on loans.

Consumers select the needs or combination of needs that must be satisfied. Each consumer purchase and store selection relates to satisfying needs, but not all consumer needs can be satisfied, for a variety of reasons, many of them related to availability of funds. The consumer has conflicting alternatives about need satisfaction that influence product and store selection. The retailer must become part of the consumer's process of resolving that need conflict by indicating the importance of the need the retailer can best satisfy. A drugstore owner with a location advantage, for example, should emphasize the importance of convenience and easy access in selecting a drugstore. Obviously, the retailer must understand which needs are important to the consumer before such a strategy can be effective.

Motives. Motives, predispositions to behave in a certain way, give direction to needs and identify goals to achieve. For motives to be "acted out," **motivation** must take place. Motivation requires (1) that an unsatisfied need be recognized, (2) that the goal or object in the environment be identified as a potential satisfier of that need, and (3) that the consumer have sufficient desire to acquire the desired goal.

The retailer has three options to developing consumer motivation: to increase the need level of the consumer, by emphasizing the importance of needs the retailer can satisfy; to make the goal object of motivation more desirable; and to increase the energy level or desire of the individual. The second and third options are interrelated. If the desirability of the goal object (product, store, and/or service) increases, the energy or desire level of the consumer will increase. The point at which the consumer is motivated to behave is known as the **motivational threshold.**

The consumer is brought to the motivational threshold through **incentives,** which are advantages or benefits to the consumer from using a retail store. There are two types of incentives, intrinsic and extrinsic. *Intrinsic incentives* are benefits or attributes that arise from the retail store itself. *Extrinsic incentives* are "rewards" or benefits that are obtained by the consumer for shopping at a particular store. These incentives must be valuable to the consumer and be linked with satisfying the consumer's needs. Table 6.2 gives some examples of intrinsic and extrinsic incentives.

Personality.   For our purposes **personality** can be defined as patterns of interaction with the environment. Since personality explains our overall behavior patterns, it should at least partially explain retail store selection.

The theories of personality are varied and numerous. The most widely researched theory of consumer decision making is **trait theory,** which proposes that personality is made up of varying degrees of certain traits. Each person has different degrees of aggression, compliance, responsibility, sociability, change-orientation, flexibility, and other traits. Personality is the combination of these traits, reflected in a person's patterns of behavior. Although widely researched, trait theory has not proved to be of great benefit in understanding consumer behavior. Consequently, many retailers have turned to lifestyle characteristics for a partial explanation of consumer behavior.

Table 6.2
Examples of intrinsic and extrinsic retail incentives

INTRINSIC INCENTIVES	EXTRINSIC INCENTIVES
Low price, saving money	Able to purchase other products
Convenience, saving time	More time for higher-value activities
Wide assortment, better selection	Better decision making
Friendly personnel	Psychic value of personal relationship
Cleanliness	Positive feeling of riskless decision
Quality image	Positive psychological feeling about self

Lifestyle, one manifestation of personality, can be defined as a mode of living consisting of how people spend their time (activities), what they consider important in their environment (interests), and their beliefs about themselves and the world around them (opinions).[2] The acceptance and usage of lifestyle theory has been enhanced by the relative ease of measurement of activities, interests, and opinions (AIO). In a typical lifestyle survey, several statements followed by a six-point agree-disagree scale are used to measure AIO dimensions. Table 6.3 shows some specific elements of the activities, interests, and opinions that make up lifestyle along with some common AIO measures.

Lifestyle research has had wide application in marketing, particularly in the areas of automobile, dog food, cosmetics, and cable TV purchases. Little research has been conducted in the area of retailing, however. Bearden, Teel, and Durand found that unique shopper profiles could be developed for patrons and nonpatrons of convenience, department, discount, and fast-food retailers.[3] Shoppers in convenience food stores were predominantly male, and they were better-educated, younger, heavier media users, less traditional, less outgoing, less socially conscious, and with a higher income than shoppers in other kinds of stores. Fast-food patrons

Table 6.3
Lifestyle dimensions and AIO measures for fashion-conscious consumer and information seeker

Dimensions[a]

Activities: work, hobbies, social events, vacation, entertainment, club membership, community, shopping, sports

Interests: family, home, job, community, recreation, fashion, food, media, achievements

Opinions: oneself, social issues, politics, business, economics, education, products, future, culture

AIO Measures[b]

Fashion-Conscious Consumer

    I usually have one or more outfits that are of the very latest style.

    When I must choose between the two, I usually dress for fashion, not for comfort.

    An important part of my life and activities is dressing smartly.

    I often try the latest hairdo styles when they change.

Information Seeker

    I often seek out the advice of my friends regarding which brands to buy.

    I spend a lot of time talking with my friends about products and brands.

    My neighbors or friends usually give me good advice on what brands to buy in the grocery store.

[a]*Source:* Joseph T. Plummer, "The Concept and Application of Life Style Segmentation," *Journal of Marketing,* January 1974, p. 34 (published by the American Marketing Association).

[b]*Source:* William D. Wells and Douglas J. Tigert, "Activities, Interests, and Opinions," *Journal of Advertising Research,* August 1971, p. 35. Reprinted from the *Journal of Advertising Research,* © Copyright 1971, by the Advertising Research Foundation.

were younger, better-educated, heavier media users, more outgoing, more socially conscious, and with a higher income than other shoppers.

It appears that lifestyles generally are becoming more open and liberal, which means people are placing more emphasis on leisure, informality, and saving time. We saw some of the implications of these changes for retailing in Chapter 4.

Perception. **Perception** is the interpretation of stimuli received from the environment through the five senses. Interpretation is the means by which the consumer forms an understanding of the retailing environment and a perspective for behavior. Consumer actions are based upon *perceptions* of the retailing environment, not necessarily on the *reality* of the environment. A consumer may, for example, patronize a retail grocery store because of his or her perception that the store has low prices when in reality another store may have lower prices. Of course, perception and reality are sometimes the same. It is the retailer's function to establish the consumer's perceptions through communication.

Consumers' self-concept or **self-perception** also influences their behavior in the retailing environment. Consumers attempt to act out a combination of real self (what one is) and ideal self (what one would like to be) in the marketplace.[4] The perception individuals have of themselves (conservative, intelligent, worldly, sophisticated, and so on) is a factor in their selection of a retail store. Consumers attempt to match their self-concept with the store image most appropriate to their self-concept. A person who perceives himself or herself as an audiophile would most likely purchase from a stereo specialty store rather than a discount or department store. The retailing implications are clear: The retailer's communication and merchandising strategies affect the store's image and the ability of the consumer to identify with the retailer. An unclear or incomplete image is quite a hindrance to successful retailing, as W. T. Grant Company and other retailers have discovered.

Learning. Developing as an individual is a process of **learning.** The same is true for consumer behavior. The amount and variety of information that a consumer must learn to make a decision about retail stores are immense. Merchandise offerings, the quality of the offerings, prices, store hours, personnel quality, services available, and locations, are some of the factors that can be involved in store selection. Obviously, learning is quite important to the consumer and to the retailer in each of their respective decisions.

Learning can be defined as the "result of a combination of motivation, strongly perceived experience, and repetition upon behavioral tendencies in response to particular stimuli or situations."[5] According to this definition, learning involves three aspects: motivation, strong experience, and repetition. Appropriate levels of motivation are conducive to learning. In some instances, a high level of motivation followed by a reward for behavior may bring about learning, whereas in other instances a low level of motivation or involvement is most appropriate.

A **perceived experience** influences motivation. The satisfaction or sanction that results from a behavior changes a person's tendency to behave in a similar manner in the future. A positive experience in trying a particular restaurant will increase a person's tendency to patronize that restaurant again. Conversely, the dissatisfaction of not saving money at a particular grocery store may reduce the motivation to shop there again.

Repetition of the positive reward for the particular stimulus is necessary for learning. Going to a department store that offers quality merchandise and friendly personnel enhances the learning experience. The more often the experience is repeated, the stronger the positive association will be. Over time, learning leads to habitual behavior. A habit is simply a permanent connection between a stimulus and a response. Habits are commonly formed by consumers to lessen the time and risk involved in the decision process. Habitually shopping at one retail store or chain is identified as *store loyalty*, which is obviously a retailing goal. However, it is possible to repeat experiences too often in which case fatigue or dislike for the store may result. The consumer may then seek new learning experiences.

The "learning" goal of the retailer is to bring about a positive association of reward (or achieved goal) from the consumer patronizing the retail store. Two aspects of learning are involved in achieving this retailing goal, stimulus generalization and discrimination.

Stimulus generalization occurs when a response to one stimulus is extended to other, similar stimuli.[6] The experience of purchasing from one pizza restaurant may be generalized to all pizza retailers. A favorable outcome may result in favorable responses toward all pizza retailers. This is not particularly advantageous for any one pizza retailer. Generalization, however, may be an advantage for the retailer in the case of generalizing from Sears as a retailer of high-quality hardline products to the quality of software products that Sears offers.

Discrimination is the ability of the consumer "to learn to distinguish between and respond differently to similar but nonidentical stimuli."[7] Consumer discrimination is a major goal of retailers. Through discrimination, consumers restrict their responses to certain retailing stimuli. To achieve consumer discrimination, retailers must establish some differences between their store and competing retailers. The better the retailer is able to differentiate on the basis of merchandise, communication, prestige, location, or other factors, the more likely is consumer discrimination in favor of patronizing that retailer's store. The differential advantage aspects of retailing strategy (discussed in Chapter 2) are quite pertinent to achieving discrimination. In addition, the value of establishing a strong, clear store image and competitive position are relevant to achieving the goal of consumer discrimination and to hindering stimulus generalization by the consumer.

Attitudes. A widely accepted definition of **attitudes** describes them as "learned predispositions to respond to an object or class of objects in a consistently favorable or unfavorable way."[8] A consumer's attitudes toward a retailer are his or her tendencies to evaluate and behave in a consistent manner relative to that retailer. According to traditional attitude theory, attitudes are composed of *cognitions* (beliefs) about an object, *affect* (feelings) toward an object, and *behavioral intentions* toward an object. All three of these attitude components should be consistent with one another: if a consumer has positive feelings toward a retailer, the consumer should also have positive beliefs and behavioral tendencies toward the retailer. The converse is also true.

Attitude formation and attitude change are important areas for a retailer's consideration. Unfortunately, this area is not well defined and there is no general agreement on attitude formation theory. The most current thought about attitude formation and change proposes a high- and low-involvement model that influences the formation and change of attitudes.

The **high-involvement model** applies when the consumer is interested in the store selection process and considers it important. In this model, a consumer's attitudes are formed as follows: (1) beliefs about retail stores result from active learning, (2) the consumer evaluates stores, and (3) the consumer makes a store selection decision.

The **low-involvement model** applies when the consumer is uninterested in and does not view the retail store selection process as important. The sequence of attitude formation is the following: (1) beliefs about retail stores are formed by passive learning, (2) the consumer makes a store selection decision, and (3) the consumer may or may not evaluate the store afterward.[9]

Because attitudes are formed differently in the two models, the decision process is consequently different in the high- and low-involvement states. In addition to high and low involvement, theorists have proposed that the consumer's perception of differences between stores enters into the decision process. Figure 6.2 is a matrix demonstrating the combinations of degree of involvement and perceptions of differences between stores.

High-involvement decision making means that the consumer actively seeks information and uses it to make or support a decision. In this model, once attitudes are formed toward the retailer, they may not be changed easily, and conventional approaches to marketing will be effective for the retailer.

The low-involvement model suggests that weaker attitudes are formed and may be changed more easily. Possible retailing strategies to attract low-involvement consumers include linking the retailer to some issue the consumer feels is important; linking the retailer to some significant personal situation; linking the retailer to personally significant advertising; changing the importance of the benefits to the consumer patronizing the retail store; and introducing an important characteristic in the retail store.[10]

High involvement   Low involvement

	High involvement	Low involvement
Significant perceived differences between stores	*Decision sequence* Beliefs Evaluation Behavior *Nature of decision* Complex decision making	*Decision sequence* Beliefs Behavior Evaluation *Nature of decision* Variety seeking
Few perceived differences between stores	*Decision sequence* Behavior Evaluation Beliefs *Nature of decision* Dissonance (doubt) reduction	*Decision sequence* Beliefs Behavior *Nature of decision* Inertia

High involvement   Low involvement

Figure 6.2
Four types of attitude formation and consumer behavior

Source: Adapted from Henry Assael, *Consumer Behavior and Marketing Action* (Boston: Kent Publishing Company, 1981), p. 80. © 1981 by Wadsworth, Inc. Reprinted by permission of Kent Publishing Company, a Division of Wadsworth, Inc., 20 Providence Street, Boston, MA 02116.

External Variables

The **external variables** that influence consumer behavior—family, reference groups, social class, and culture—generally have their impact in an indirect way. They typically affect the choice of a retail store by influencing the internal variables, the needs, motives, personality, perception, learning, and attitudes. Retailers, of course, are also external influences on the consumer decision process, but since much of the text is devoted to retail decision making and its impact on consumers, we will not discuss it separately in this chapter.

It is generally accepted that the strongest external influences on consumers' behavior are those that communicate effectively. The influence of the family on consumer behavior is strongest, followed by reference groups, social class, and culture.

Family. The **family** can be viewed as a buying unit and as an influence on personal behavior. An individual's family certainly influences his or her internal variables, especially perceptions and attitudes. Interaction with other family members influences an individual's store selection process through the exchange of specific information and the development of decision criteria and image and positioning relationships.

Much of the knowledge retailers have concerning the family and its retail decision making focuses on the family as a unit. Family decisions vary according to situation and product, and this area has not been researched extensively. Some generalizations, however, can be inferred. Although family decision patterns are changing, the store selection decision for living room furniture, televisions, and outside entertainment is normally made by husband and wife jointly. Store selection for children's and wife's clothing and supermarkets is usually made by the wife. The choice of insurance agents is usually the husband's decision.[11] Keep in mind that these family decision roles are in the state of flux because of changing lifestyles.

For the retailer to use the family unit as a variable in making strategic decisions, the family life cycle offers insight into family decision patterns. Several family life cycle patterns have been proposed over the years, varying with changes in lifestyle patterns and family orientations. The most current version is that of Murphy and Staples, presented in Table 6.4.[12] The table shows a five-stage family life cycle and the variations within each stage.

Young singles have few financial burdens, and consequently their discretionary income is quite high. Generally, young singles are recreation-oriented and spend on travel, cars, and clothing. Younger families spend heavily on consumer durables and other needs of establishing a family. As children become part of the family, more expenditures are related to them. Older families without dependent children begin spending for themselves and may move into different surroundings such as condominiums or apartments. Each stage offers unique opportunities to the retailer for merchandise

Table 6.4
Family life cycle

1. Young single	*c.* Middle-aged married with children
2. Young married without children	Young
	Adolescent
3. Other young	*d.* Middle-aged divorced with children
a. Young divorced without children	Young
b. Young married with children	Adolescent
Infant	*e.* Middle-aged married without dependent children
Young (4–12 years old)	
Adolescent	*f.* Middle-aged divorced without dependent children
c. Young divorced with children	
Infant	
Young (4–12 years old)	*5.* Older
Adolescent	*a.* Older married
	b. Older unmarried
4. Middle-aged	Divorced
a. Middle-aged married without children	Widowed
b. Middle-aged divorced without children	

Source: Patrick E. Murphy and William A. Staples, ''A Modernized Family Life Cycle,'' *Journal of Consumer Research*, June 1979, p. 16.

selection, promotion, and location decisions. The alert retailer will identify the changes taking place in the family life cycle and will consider their impact in formulating a retailing strategy.

Reference Groups. Consumers look to others for help in defining and understanding their environment. **Reference groups** are "groups whose perspective an individual assumes in forming attitudes and overt behavior."[13] Reference groups not only provide environmental perspective to consumers in decisions about purchasing products, but they also influence decisions about the choice of retail stores through shared perspectives of the retail environment. Members of a reference group are expected to behave in certain acceptable ways (norms), and the group will exert pressures, either directly or indirectly, to make all members conform to the expected behavior patterns. A church group may influence the individual to the extent of not patronizing retail stores that sell alcoholic beverages. A teenager may be influenced in the choice of clothing establishments by the influence of peers.

Various types of reference groups exist with differing degrees and directions of influence. Influence can be positive or negative and it can be very strong or almost nonexistent. The degree of influence is a result of the reward the individual obtains from associating with the reference group. The greater the reward, the more likely the individual is to conform or be influenced by the reference group.

Membership groups are reference groups in which the consumer often has face-to-face contact with group members: family, peers, work groups, shopping groups, and formal social groups. There are positive membership groups and disclaimant membership groups.

Nonmembership groups are reference groups of which the consumer is not a member or does not have face-to-face contact with members. An *aspirational group* is one in which the individual would like to be a member. An *avoidance group* influences an individual to avoid attitudes and behavior patterns associated with that group.

Positive influence is exerted by positive membership groups and aspirational groups. Negative influence is exerted by disclaimant and avoidance groups. A consumer does not have to be a member of a group to be influenced by the group nor does the group have to actually exist or have the behavioral characteristics the consumer attributes to it. In other words, a consumer may purchase from a particular store because he or she perceives that well-educated, refined people purchase at that store, regardless of whether such a group actually exists. Table 6.5 presents a breakdown of types of reference groups with some examples of the influence they may have.

Retailers can use their knowledge of reference groups very effectively, mainly by using the positive influence groups—positive membership groups and aspirational groups—to affect consumers' decisions. Not all

Table 6.5
Reference groups and their influence in consumer behavior

REFERENCE GROUP	TYPE OF INFLUENCE	EXAMPLE OF INFLUENCE
Membership Group		
Positive membership group	Positive	Mother influences daughter's selection of a clothing store
Disclaimant group	Negative	Worker avoids retail stores of co-workers
Nonmembership Group		
Aspirational group	Positive	Lower-level managers shopping at "upper-level" managers' store
Avoidance group	Negative	Younger person avoids shopping where "older people" shop

decisions about choice of store are influenced by reference groups. If we can generalize at all from product research about the influence of reference groups, we can say that stores that are related to conspicuous product purchases are influenced by reference groups. Bourne suggests that "where reference-group influence is operative, the [retailer] should stress the kinds of people who [shop the retailer], reinforcing and broadening where possible the existing stereotypes of users. The strategy . . . should involve learning what the stereotypes are and what specific reference groups enter into the picture, so that appeals can be 'tailored' to each [market segment]."[14]

Social Class.   In any social system, members are organized according to a hierarchy. The prestige and power enjoyed by some is not enjoyed by all members of the social system. This social stratification arranges groups, or **social classes,** in a society relative to their perspectives of the environment and their lifestyle patterns. Generally members of the same social class tend to have similar goals and decision-making patterns and to interact among members of that social class.

A number of methods have been proposed to determine social class. The method most often referred to, and probably the best known, is Warner's Index of Status Characteristics, which consists of occupation, source of income, house type, and dwelling area.[15] From this index, a six-class hierarchy was developed: upper-upper, lower-upper, upper-middle, lower-middle, upper-lower, and lower-lower class. Table 6.6 presents a simplified overview of the different patterns among the social classes.

The particular lifestyle patterns of each social class are further reflected in the shopping behavior and store selection of members of that class. Lower-class shopping behavior has been characterized as not well organized, somewhat impulsive, utilitarian,[16] and acquisition-oriented,

Table 6.6
Social class characteristics, goals, and motivation

1. *Upper-upper* or "social register" consists of locally prominent families, usually with at least second- or third-generation wealth. Basic values: living graciously, upholding family reputation, reflecting the excellence of one's breeding, and displaying a sense of community responsibility. About $\frac{1}{2}$% of the population.

2. *Lower-upper* or "nouveau riche" consists of the more recently arrived and never-quite-accepted wealthy families. Goals: blend of upper-upper pursuit of gracious living and the upper-middle drive for success. About 1% of the population.

3. *Upper-middle* are moderately successful professional men and women, owners of medium-sized businesses, young people in their twenties and early thirties who are expected to arrive at the managerial level by their middle or late thirties. Motivations: success at a career, cultivation of charm and polish. About 10% of the population.

4. *Lower-middle* are mostly nonmanagerial office workers, small business owners, highly paid blue-collar families. Goals: respectability and striving to live in well-maintained homes, neatly furnished, in more-or-less "right" neighborhoods, and to do a good job at their work. They will save for a college education for their children. About 30–35% of the population.

5. *Upper-lower* or "ordinary working class" consists of semiskilled workers. Although many make high pay, they are not particularly interested in respectability. Goals: to enjoy life and living from day to day, to be at least modern, and to work hard enough to keep safely away from the slum level. About 40% of the population.

6. *Lower-lower* are unskilled workers, unassimilated ethnics, and the sporadically employed. Outlooks: apathy, fatalism, "get your kicks whenever you can." About 15% of the population, but only about 7% of the purchasing power.

Source: Irving J. Shapiro, *Dictionary of Marketing Terms* (Totowa, N.J.: Littlefield, Adams and Company, 1981), pp. 234–235.

with discussion occurring about shopping decisions primarily in the family,[17] and with poor knowledge of prices and product alternatives.[18] Lower-class shoppers have been found to be sensitive about fitting in with the store image and being treated well by store personnel.[19] Middle- and upper-class shopping behavior has been characterized as fairly well organized, more confident, and more symbolic and less utilitarian in decision criteria,[20] such shoppers tend to enjoy the act of shopping, discuss shopping with friends (not just family),[21] are better informed concerning prices and product alternatives,[22] and tend to feel more comfortable in a wider range of stores, both geographically and socially.[23] Table 6.7 presents some of the findings related to store choice and social class.

The retail store also has an image as part of a social class, and the consumer perceives himself or herself as fitting in or matching the social image of retail stores. Each retailer must be aware of his or her store's appeal and develop a retailing mix to attract the targeted social class. The retailer emphasizing price may attract all social classes for products such as toys, cookware, tires, and power tools, which are not strongly connected to consumers' self-images. Clothing, furniture, and home-interior products are a few products that relate more directly to social class, which retailers should analyze carefully in developing a store image.

Table 6.7
Social class and store choice

SOCIAL CLASS	STORE CHOICE CHARACTERISTICS
Lower class	Prefer face-to-face contact[a]
	Friendly clerks[a]
	Local stores[a]
	Mass merchandisers[b]
	Downtown stores[b]
	Discount stores for high- and low-risk products[c]
	Store credit
Middle-upper class	New stores and experiences
	Discounters for lower social risk products[c]
	Specialty stores for high-social-risk products[c]
	Purchase from catalog, mail, and by telephone[d]
	High-fashion store (upperclass only)[b]

[a]Pierre Martineau, "Social Class and Spending Behavior," *Journal of Marketing,* October 1958, pp. 121–129.

[b]Stuart U. Rich and Subhash C. Jain, "Social Class and Life Cycle and Predictors of Shopping Behavior," *Journal of Marketing Research,* February 1968, pp. 34–44.

[c]V. K. Prasad, "Socioeconomic Product Risk and Patronage Preferences of Retail Shoppers," *Journal of Marketing,* July 1975, pp. 42–47.

[d]Peter L. Gillett, "In-Home Shoppers: An Overview," *Journal of Marketing,* October 1976, pp. 81–88.

Culture. Because of the widely encompassing nature of culture, its boundaries are not easily defined. A society's language, knowledge, laws, religions, technology, art, customs, products, and artifacts are all included in its **culture.** Shiffman and Kanuk define culture as the "sum total of learned beliefs, values, and customs which serve to regulate the consumer behavior of members of a particular society."[24]

A study by Vinson, Scott, and Lamont indicates the relationship between cultural values and consumption-specific values.[25] *Global values* are enduring beliefs concerning desired states or modes of behavior within a particular culture. They number in the dozen. *Domain-specific values* are beliefs relevant to economic, social, religious, and other activities; there are hundreds of such values among the members of a society. Evaluations of product attributes are *evaluative beliefs,* of which there are thousands. The retailer can bring about changes most readily in the area of evaluative beliefs about store attributes. Evaluations that are more closely tied to the global values are more difficult to change.

Global values lead to domain-specific values, which lead to evaluative beliefs. Vinson, Scott, and Lamont found, for example, that global values such as politeness and social recognition lead to domain-specific values such as prompt service on complaints.[26] Consumers with such values partially, at least, evaluate retail stores on the basis of how well complaints were handled, how well they were personally treated as customers, and the type of return and guarantee policy the retailer offers. Recognizing the value and belief of interrelationships among consumers can provide the retailer with insight into the combination of attributes that come into play in consumers' decision making and how centrally related they are to the global values of the consumer.

Subcultures. Within the larger culture are **subcultures** that can be thought of as "a distinct cultural group which exists as an identifiable segment within a larger, more complex society."[27] Subcultures tend to adhere to most of the dominant patterns of the core culture, but they possess beliefs, values, and customs that set them apart from the rest of the society.

A wide variety of subcultures exist in the United States. We will consider subcultures identified by age, national identity, and race.

Age subcultures are usually classified as youth and elderly. The youth market has received the most marketing attention for many years, particularly in the areas of clothing styles, records, movies, radio stations, magazines, and recreation. The youth market, consisting of those under the age of twenty-five, primarily teenagers, are a subculture because of some attitudinal differences from the cultural mainstream and consequently some differences in spending patterns. Although there was much attention given to the counterculture movement among young people in the 1960s, it appears that a shift in the direction of more traditional values is now taking place.[28] The values of career, saving money, hard work, and increased control of the future have grown in importance among the younger members of our society.

The youth market has different spending patterns because they have a great deal of discretionary income, money to be spent on "luxuries" such as records, stereo equipment, books, cameras, fashion clothing, personal care products, movies, and travel. Retailers certainly ought to be aware of the influence of the youth market on the sales of these kinds of merchandise.

The elderly subculture has been largely overlooked by marketing efforts. Constituting about ten percent of the population and possessing the fastest growth rates, this segment can hardly be ignored in the future. Historically, this subculture has been overlooked because it has been viewed as underprivileged. However, with increasing incomes, improved living conditions, increased militancy about issues related to the elderly, and a changing view of the elderly in society, the elderly market is gaining the attention of marketers, especially retailers.

The elderly spend more on health care, household maintenance, food consumed at home,[29] reading, and gardening[30] than do other subcultures. Elderly consumers have also been found to be price-sensitive, to have more time and interest in shopping, and to view shopping as a social activity. Retailers have adapted to the needs of the elderly more than other marketers have, by providing senior citizen discounts and other privileges.

The fastest-growing subculture in the United States today is the Hispanic subculture. Made up of Mexican-Americans, Puerto Ricans, and Cubans, the Hispanic subculture is much younger and more urban and its members have lower incomes than other Americans. Higher expenditures for food, high degrees of brand loyalty for national brands, and conservatism characterize their shopping behavior.[31] Urban retailers in the major Hispanic markets (California, Texas, Florida, and New York) must be aware of this subculture's influence on the market and develop retailing mixes to meet its particular needs.

The largest *racial* minority in the United States is the black subculture, which constitutes 12 percent of the total U.S. population. Like the Hispanic subculture, the black subculture is younger and more urban, with lower incomes than the rest of Americans. The differences between the black subculture and the mainstream culture are not as great as are the differences between the Hispanic subculture and the mainstream culture.

While it is difficult to generalize behavior patterns to an entire subculture, research has shown that blacks tend to spend more for clothing, personal care, home furnishings,[32] milk, soft drinks, and liquor[33] than do other segments of the population, and they spend less on medical care, food, transportation,[34] and expensive leisure products.[35]

Some research indicates that blacks are more innovative in purchasing products with high social visibility. Clothing is a primary example; some retailers claim to look to black consumers as a guide to what white consumers might be wearing in the future.[36]

Among blacks and whites of similar incomes, blacks prefer discount stores to department stores. This difference disappears among upper-income blacks and whites.[37] In choosing a particular retailer, blacks are more likely than whites to be concerned with a friendly atmosphere, convenience, and service.[38] Consequently, many purchases made by the black subculture are made in neighborhood stores.

GENERAL OPINIONS AND ACTIVITIES CONCERNING SHOPPING AND SEARCH

Consumers develop general opinions concerning the importance and value of searching and shopping for information. Some consumers avidly read newspaper advertisements for grocery store specials, while others see it as a waste of time. Other factors, such as store specials, brand names, convenience, quality of information given by the store, and chain versus independent ownership can enter into opinions and activities concerning shopping and search.

Over the years retailers have sought to categorize how consumers make decisions about shopping and choice of store. Most agree that people shop for a wide variety of reasons, many of them noneconomic or social.[39]

Table 6.8 presents a summary of shopper typologies that can result in differing store choices.

The opinions of consumers are reflected in where they shop. Some consider the local retailing environment to be satisfactory, while others may desire different surroundings. The selection of a store can be influenced by the choice of the total shopping environment, which can range from the physical distance traveled for shopping to the convenience of purchasing products within the consumer's home. Four shopping environments are discussed below.

Outshopping

Some consumers shop outside of their hometown for various reasons, including wider merchandise selection, more pleasing shopping facilities, and better shopping atmosphere. Such consumers, referred to as outshoppers, tend to be younger and male, to have recently moved into a community, and to have less than a college education. Outshopping is usually planned and for specific purposes. One study found that outshoppers were more cosmopolitan and active, they liked traveling, and they tended not to be displeased with hometown stores.[40] It appears that those with broader retail perspectives seek a more pleasing environment than is offered locally. It must be noted that the outshopper is in the minority, with only 20 percent of consumers willing to travel more than ten miles to shop.

Table 6.8
Shopper typologies

Economic shopper (33%)
1. Interested in shopping efficiency.
2. Price, quality, assortment of merchandise are important.
3. Store personnel are instruments for purchasing goods.

Personalizing Shopper (28%)
1. Personal relationships to store personnel quite important (wants to be treated as a friend).
2. Price, quality, and merchandise of secondary importance.

Ethical Shopper (18%)
1. Motivated by what "ought" to be done (shop small store, help local merchants).
2. Price and assortment are secondary considerations.
3. Generally higher socioeconomic groups.

Apathetic Shopper (17%)
1. Convenience outweighs all criteria.
2. Price, quality, assortment of secondary importance.
3. No attachment to store personnel.
4. Generally lower socioeconomic groups.

Source: G. P. Stone, "City Shoppers and Urban Identification: Observations on the Social Psychology of City Life," *American Journal of Sociology,* July 1954, pp. 36–45. © 1954 by the University of Chicago.

**Shopping
Center
Shopping**

Shoppers that frequent shopping centers are searching for physical surroundings that offer wider variety of merchandise, perceived lower prices,
knowledgeable sales help, and, for some, a source of entertainment.[41]
Younger, better-educated, and higher-income people tend to patronize
larger shopping centers more often than smaller shopping centers.

Retail strategies in the planning of shopping centers have taken this
factor into consideration, and necessary ingredients in a successful shopping center are wider merchandise lines through more stores and a true
balance of stores. The ability to shop and enjoy the atmosphere and possibly
other attractions of the shopping center are other positive features desired
by consumers.

Downtown Shopping

Generally, downtown shopping has not enjoyed growth as shopping centers
have, although there are some advantages to downtown shopping and
downtown locations for retailers. For some market segments downtown is
more convenient and, in most cases, public transportation is more available
and effective in downtown areas than in suburban areas. Many larger downtown areas have been revitalized and they now offer the consumer excitement and entertainment with variety and appeal, which many shopping
areas may find difficult to match.

In-Home Shopping

For an apparently growing segment of consumers, the appropriate shopping
environment is their own home. In-home shoppers are motivated largely by
convenience, merchandise assortment, and the "personalized" nature of
purchasing individually rather than as "one of many" in a store.

The in-home shopper is more flexible, visits stores more frequently,
is not dissatisfied with store shopping, perceives less risk, and is more
self-assured and more cosmopolitan in shopping behavior than are other
shoppers.[42] Reynolds suggests that catalog shoppers, one type of in-home
shopper, do not consider time an important shopping variable.[43]

The retailer who notes these trends may desire to offer some type of
in-home shopping service to his or her customers. The in-home segment,
although still small, will probably continue to grow, especially as in-home
shopping becomes more convenient with the increased use of cable television and other forms of in-home shopping techniques.

SHOPPING AND SEARCH STRATEGIES

Consumer opinions concerning shopping and search lead to various personal strategies. One consumer's strategy for grocery shopping may consist of
going to a well-known chain store and purchasing the lowest-priced product in the product categories desired. Another consumer may perceive the
preceding strategy as ludicrous and may go to several stores for the lowest-
priced items, after having spent two hours organizing newspaper advertise-

ments and coupons and mapping a travel route to minimize travel expenses. These consumers may also have different strategies for purchasing furniture or legal services. A combination of consumer characteristics and opinions concerning shopping and search are reflected in strategies consumers use.

The degree of shopping and search is a function of many variables. One of the key variables is **perceived risk,** which involves the perception of uncertainty in purchasing from a retail store. When a consumer cannot predict the outcome of purchasing at a particular store, some perceived risk is involved. The amount of perceived risk is influenced by the importance of the purchase decision. The more important the purchase to the consumer, the higher the level of perceived risk. Perceived risk relates to the personal or social consequences of a purchase. Personal or social risk (sometimes called *sociopsychological* risk) involves the possibility of ego damage or social embarrassment from making the wrong decision. Purchasing furniture that does not match or clothing that is no longer fashionable are examples of sociopsychological risk.

Performance and financial risk deals with the functional purposes of the product. Toys that do not take normal wear and tear or stereo equipment that does not produce quality sound are two examples of performance and financial risk.

The possible choice of an unfashionable clothing store (sociopsychological risk) or the possibility of purchasing from a retailer that will not or cannot repair merchandise or will not accept merchandise returns (performance risk) enters the purchase decision in the form of perceived risk. Thus the consumer faces risk from both the product or service decision and the store decision. In some instances, product risk may be high and store risk low, while in other situations the opposite may occur. High and low risk may also occur together.

Risk theory proposes that beyond a certain level of perceived risk the individual consumer will not make a decision. To lower perceived risk to an acceptable level for decision making, the consumer gathers information.[44] Consumers with high levels of perceived risk engage in an extended search strategy, possibly involving a number of information sources. A low level of perceived risk results in a strategy of limited or perhaps no search for the consumer. Sources of consumer search relate to the perceived value of the information provided by the source. If a consumer perceives that retail stores provide biased information, he or she might turn to family members or friends for information. Generally, consumers tend to seek the easiest information sources first and continue until the risk is perceived to be reduced sufficiently to allow a decision to be made.

The retailer should attempt to reduce consumers' perceived risk. Each of the possible product/store risk pairings suggest different strategies for the retailer. In a situation where product risk is high, emphasis on the product and its characteristics is appropriate. High perceived store risk can be reduced by an emphasis on store name, longevity, name merchandise, or lib-

Table 6.9
Retail methods of reducing perceived risk

TYPE OF RISK	RISK-REDUCTION METHOD
Psychological/social	Prestige image
	Personal assistance
	Carry well-known brands
	Return policy
	Classification merchandising
	Expert endorsement
Performance/financial	Reduced price
	Guarantee or warranty
	Money-back guarantee
	Time payment plans
	Product testing
	Carry well-known brands
	In-store demonstrations
	Liberal return policies
	Small package size
	Product samples

eral return policies. It is apparent that the retailer in the low product risk/low store risk pairing has an advantage over a retailer in the high product risk/high store risk pairing. Table 6.9 suggests a number of methods the retailer may use in reducing perceived risk.

IMPORTANCE OF STORE ATTRIBUTES

Consumers develop strategies for shopping and search, but the strategy does not specifically identify which store will be chosen for a purchase. The specific attributes of the store are important in establishing store choice. The consumer uses the importance of store attributes combined with perceptions of various retail stores to develop attitudes toward each retailer.

Each retail store possesses a wide range of attributes, such as location, size, image, atmosphere, merchandise, services, and the disposition of personnel. The retailer integrates the various attributes to attract consumers. Of course, not all consumers desire similar store attributes. While some consumers may consider price important, others may consider name brands and variety of merchandise important. The consumer's perceptions of what attributes are important will influence his or her choice of store and, thus, they are important to the retailer in focusing and developing a retailing strategy.

Hansen and Deutscher completed an empirical investigation of the attributes that were important in consumers' choice of store.[45] Table 6.10 shows the importance of department store and grocery store attributes. Although each type of store carries different products, "dependable products" was the most important attribute for consumers. Product quality, value for the money, ease in finding desired products, and fast checkout also were important for both types of stores. Adjustments and helpful personnel were important in the selection of a department store, while the level of stock and ease in moving through the store were important in grocery store selection. These findings are not surprising given the type of purchases made in a department store and a grocery store.

Table 6.10
Importance scores of store attributes, department stores versus grocery stores

STORE ATTRIBUTES	DEPARTMENT STORES (N = 267)		GROCERY STORES (N = 215)	
	RATING*	RANK	RATING*	RANK
Dependable products	9.58	1	9.50	1
Fair on adjustments	9.38	2	8.64	12
Store is clean	9.03	10	9.33	2
Easy to find items you want	9.14	5.5	9.27	3.5
High value for money	9.25	3	9.10	6
Fast checkout	9.14	5.5	9.27	3.5
High-quality products	9.15	4	9.23	5
Helpful sales personnel	9.12	7.5	8.94	8
Easy to return purchases	9.12	7.5	7.77	26.5
Fully stocked	8.93	11	9.05	7
Courteous sales personnel	8.91	12	8.79	11
Easy to move through store	8.80	15	8.88	9
.	.	.	.	.
.	.	.	.	.
.	.	.	.	.
Store is liked by friends	4.57	41	4.07	37
Many friends shop there	4.58	40	4.18	38
Easy to get credit	5.41	36	2.58	39
Lay-away available	5.30	37	2.09	40
Easy to get home delivery	6.83	34	1.93	41

*The importance of each attribute was rated from 0 (no importance) to 10 (very important).

Source: Robert A. Hansen and Terry Deutscher, "An Empirical Investigation of Attribute Importance in Retail Store Selection," *Journal of Retailing,* Winter 1977/78, pp. 63–64. Reprinted with permission, *Journal of Retailing.*

It is imperative that the retailer understand which attributes are important for those consumers the retailer desires to attract. The attributes may vary for different groups of consumers. Some research on the retailer's part is often necessary to determine which store attributes are important to his or her target market.

PERCEPTIONS OF STORE ATTRIBUTES

The consumer's perceptions of store attributes influence store selection. The basis for consumer behavior is the consumer's perceptions of the store attributes, not necessarily the reality of the attributes. Although reality and consumer perceptions of store attributes are most often correlated, there can sometimes be a disparity between the two. A high-fashion clothier may not be perceived by some consumers as high fashion, or a discounter with the lowest prices in town may not be perceived by some consumers as having the lowest prices.

The attributes of the retailer are used by consumers to make a store choice, but to simplify the process consumers will combine these attributes into a **store image.** This image is a composite the consumer uses to categorize retail stores. The consumer's categorizations provide indications of his or her behavior toward stores in the environment. Hansen and Deutscher found that the dimensions of retail store image are quite extensive, with as many as nine dimensions and twenty components.[46] These are presented in Table 6.11.

STRATEGY IN ACTION 6.2

Expanding the 7–11 Image

Southland Corporation has been quite successful with its 7–11 convenience stores. Recently, however, Southland expanded the image of 7–11 beyond the traditional classification of the "convenience store." The broader image 7–11 is attempting to achieve is as a "specialty retailer." With its enlarged image 7–11 hopes to position itself not only against other convenience stores but also against supermarkets, gas stations, fast-food chains, drugstores, liquor stores, and delicatessens.

Opportunities and potentials today go beyond the convenience store concept, believes Bruce Krysiak, Southland's new vice-president for marketing. The fact that 7–11 can be at the forefront of the convenience store expansion results from its size and strength in the industry. Convenience is the strong motivator that 7–11 hopes to build on. Expansion into broader merchandise lines such as fast foods, gas, delicatessen items, and other products along with the promotional emphasis on this expansion is their first attempt at enlarging the traditional convenience store image. Convenience can be associated with a wider variety of products, Southland believes. Its new image of a "specialty retailer" is an attempt to capitalize on this concept.

Source: Adapted from Tom Bayer, "Seven–Eleven Takes Steps to Move Beyond Image," pp. 4, 78. Reprinted with permission from the 7 December 1981 issue of *Advertising Age.* Copyright 1981 by Crain Communications, Inc.

Table 6.11
Store image: Dimensions and components

DIMENSION	COMPONENT
Merchandise	Quality
	Selection
	Style
	Price
Service	Lay-away plan
	Sales personnel
	Easy return
	Credit
	Delivery
Clientele	Customers
Physical facilities	Cleanliness
	Store layout
	Shopping ease
	Attractiveness
Convenience	Location
	Parking
Promotion	Advertising
Store atmosphere	Congeniality
Institutional	Store reputation
Posttransaction	Satisfaction

Source: R. Hansen and T. Deutscher, "An Empirical Investigation of Attribute Importance in Retail store Selection," *Journal of Retailing,* Winter 1977/78, p. 67. Reprinted with permission, *Journal of Retailing.*

Specific types of retail stores have particular components that constitute the store image. Department stores are perceived according to dependability of products, honesty in making adjustments, and high value for the money, while the major components of a grocery store image are dependability of products, cleanliness, and ability to locate desired merchandise.[47] The retailer must identify which components are important to its targeted market and how well the store has achieved success among that market with those components. Perceptions of a particular retail store can be different within different market segments. Thus one store image may not be valuable to determining how all consumers will perceive a store; the retailer must determine the store image based on the various segments of the market.

A store image can stand alone with no comparison to other stores' images, but in reality consumers usually compare the store image with other, competing stores. The consumer "positions" each relevant store in relation to the others according to the major image dimensions and components. Figure 5.2 gives an example of department store positions. The position established through retailer communication and other communication gives the consumer a basis for comparison and decision making. It suggests which retailers are similar, which have done a better job of retailing, and which will enjoy larger market shares. Of course, images and position change, and both should be researched periodically.

ATTITUDES TOWARD STORES

The importance of store attributes and a consumer's perceptions of these attributes form the consumer's attitudes toward a retailer. Some stores enjoy positive consumer attitudes and the loyalty that usually goes with positive attitudes. Other retailers may have the problems associated with negative attitudes or no consumer attitudes.

Consumers organize stores into desirable (positive), neutral, and undesirable (negative) groups according to the attitudes they have formed.

The group of possible retailers to patronize is called the consumer's **evoked set.** Out of this evoked set a consumer will choose one or a combination of retailers. The evoked set concept is important to the retailer because if the retailer is not in the consumer's evoked set, the retailer obviously cannot be the consumer's final choice. A consumer's evoked set is fairly small, probably less than seven stores for each type of merchandise. A typical evoked set for grocery products might consist of Kroger, Safeway, and a local retailer, while the remaining grocery retailers would not be considered. The final consumer decision would then be a selection of one of the three stores in the evoked set. Obviously, store image and position play a major role in the consumer's selection of an evoked set. The retailer can become part of the consumer's evoked set by favorable comparison with other retailers on store attributes or by emphasizing certain store attributes or changing the perceptions of consumers.

The neutral set of stores is often referred to as the **inert set.** A retailer is sometimes part of the inert set because of lack of awareness on the consumer's part. This situation may be remedied through effective promotion and possibly future location decisions. Stores that the consumer considers undesirable form the **inept set.** This set consists of stores rejected either because of an unpleasant experience or negative feedback from other consumers.

THE CONSUMER DECISION PROCESS

The predecision state is the consumer's present mental organization of the retail environment. If a problem is identified by the consumer, possibly new information may be processed and a store decision made. Three levels of decision making are commonly identified, with each level determining the extent to which the consumer needs to obtain new information for making a decision. The three levels of decision making are extensive problem solving, limited problem solving, and routinized response behavior.[48]

Extensive problem solving occurs when the consumer has many retailers to choose from, has not formulated any decision criteria, and has little information on which to base a decision. This could be identified as a high perceived-risk situation. **Limited problem solving** is characterized by fewer retailers to choose from (some having been eliminated), established decision criteria, and lack of some information. **Routinized response behavior** involves past experience with the retail store category, established decision criteria, and sufficient information for decision making. Little perceived risk is involved in a decision of this type.

Extensive problem solving usually requires high degrees of information search. Limited problem solving calls for some search, and routine response behavior usually requires no information search. The degree to which the predecision state affects the final store choice can be related to the level of consumer problem solving. The predecision state plays the major role in routinized response, with problem identification or recognition leading directly to store choice. With extensive problem solving, the consumer in the predecision state lacks sufficient information and must conduct a search for information.

The extensive problem-solving process will be examined in the remainder of this chapter. The process consists of six steps: problem identification, information search, generation and evaluation of alternatives, store choice, purchase, and postdecision behavior. Although the extensive problem-solving process is the basis for discussion, remember that many of the consumer's decisions can become routine through the experience of decision making.

The consumer proceeds through the decision process and is influenced by internal and external variables, as mentioned earlier in this chapter. Retailers have recently begun to realize that the situation faced by the consumer at the decision point can influence the decision process.

PROBLEM IDENTIFICATION

A problem exists when the actual and desired states as perceived by the consumer are sufficiently different. In effect, the consumer has a goal and must decide how to achieve it. The retailer who understands the importance of consumer needs, motivation, and perceptions can ascertain whether consumers have already identified a problem that the store can help solve. If not, the retailer can develop a strategy that helps the consumer identify or recognize the problem. Obviously, the retailer's selection of merchandise offerings and the retailer's image are important factors at this stage.

The problem-identification stage of the consumer decision process can be complex. The consumer can have problems relating to product, brand, or

store choice. Examples of possible problem-identification and decision sequences are product-brand-store, store-product-brand, product-store-brand,
and all three simultaneously.

Although the sequence of problem identification can be different, the
decisions about product, brand, and store can separately or in combination
be extensive, limited, or routine decisions. The consumer may know which
product and brand are desired but may not know where to purchase. This
may require limited problem solving for the store problem, but routine response behavior for the product and brand. The sequence for purchasing
groceries might be store-product-brand, with all being routine decisions.
Purchasing a suit might involve extensive problem solving for brand selection and limited problem solving for store choice, in that order.

INFORMATION SEARCH

Once a problem has been recognized, the consumer needs information to
identify alternative solutions to the problem and to establish criteria for
decision making. The degree of problem solving necessary to arrive at a
store choice determines the amount of information search the consumer
must undertake. Of course, this relates to the predecision set, the amount of
information the consumer presently has and the consumer's opinions and
strategies relative to shopping and search.

The search pattern the consumer employs is a rather simplistic one,
although in detail it might appear to be complex. Initially, the consumer
searches internal sources for information. If these sources are insufficient,
the consumer proceeds to external sources, which are usually evaluated on
the basis of the value of perceived information and the cost of using that
source. Hirshman and Mills found that less than half of all retail consumers
engaged in an active search when making retail shopping trips.[49] Generally,
consumers move from easy-access sources to more difficult sources. At this
point, friends, family, neutral sources, and retailers can become sources of
information and influence the decision process. The Hirshman and Mills
study also found that newspaper advertising was the most often used source
in retail store selection. Family and friends are the most accessible sources
of information and have high credibility, but they may not possess enough
of the desired information to enable the consumer to make a decision. The
amount of information a consumer gathers is related to the perceived risk
and experience with the product and store. The greater the risk and less
experience, the more information the consumer must gather. A consumer
moves in the direction of simplification of the problem through routine
response behavior, and thus requires less information as the process progresses.

The search process should enable the consumer to gather sufficient
information to generate alternative stores and sufficient information to evaluate the stores on the important store attributes.

GENERATION AND EVALUATION OF ALTERNATIVES

The consumer search process should provide the consumer with sufficient information to select a small number of stores, the evoked set, from which to choose. The consumer generates alternatives by comparing the important store attributes with his or her perceptions of whether the store actually possesses those attributes. The stores that come closest to being the consumer's "ideal store" as measured by important store attributes are selected for final consideration. It is possible at this point that the consumer may reenter the search process to obtain more information for selecting one store from the evoked set.

In a routine decision this set of alternatives would already exist. In fact, the final choice would probably exist. This step of generating alternatives would be unnecessary in the routine response situation.

Evaluation of alternative store choices involves matching the ideal store attributes with the perceptions of store attributes. The closest match dictates the strongest positive attitude and, consequently, the most likely store choice. In the attributes mentioned in Table 6.10 for department stores, dependable products, fairness about adjustments, and high value for the money were rated most important. Given a hypothetical situation, the department store that is perceived to have the highest of all of these attributes would be chosen by the consumer. Of course, in reality, different store choices are made because different consumers disagree on the importance of certain attributes and have differing perceptions of attributes.

The implications for retailers are clear: Increased patronage or positive store choices arise from highly positive attitudes, which are formed by consumer perceptions of store attributes. Increased patronage can be brought about by altering the importance of various attributes or perceptions to the consumer. The 7–11 example in Strategy in Action 6.2 is a good illustration of this.

It is possible that events or surroundings at the point of decision or decision implementation can influence the store choice and can sometimes alter the store selected.

Situational Influences

Retailers have recently begun to realize that the situation of the consumer at the decision point can influence store choice and/or other behavior. Table 6.12 presents a summary of situational influences.

Each of these factors may affect consumer decisions. Not all decisions are influenced by the consumer's situation at the time of the decision, but many will be influenced to varying degrees. The following discussion considers how the retailer might influence the consumer's decisions.

Physical Surroundings. There are numerous features in the actual purchase situation that may consciously or subconsciously influence the consumer. Within the retail store, factors such as layout, in-store displays, price reduction notices, lighting, carpeting, noise, colors, and merchandise ar-

Table 6.12
Situational variables in consumer retail decision making

1.   Physical surroundings
     Physical features of situation including location, decor, sounds, aromas, lighting, weather, merchandise arrangement

2.   Social surroundings
     Other persons present, their apparent roles, their characteristics, and interpersonal interactions relevant to the product and store decision

3.   Temporal perspective
     Time-related characteristics of the situation including time of day, day of week, season of year, time since last purchase, time before or after pay day, time since last meal, amount of time one has to shop

4.   Task definition
     The task as defined relative to the intent of requirement to select, shop, or obtain information; purchasing for yourself versus other, personal use versus gift

5.   Antecedent states
     Personal, mental, or physical condition immediately antecedent to the current situation, including momentary moods or conditions such as cash on hand, fatigue, or anxiety

Source: Russel W. Belk, "Situational Variables and Consumer Behavior," *Journal of Consumer Research,* December 1975, p. 159.

rangement may all influence the consumer's decision. The retailer can use these factors, singly or in combination, to enhance the store image and lower the consumer's perceived risk.

The physical surroundings outside of the store may influence store choice as well as product choice. Mittelstaedt, Grossbart, and Curtis have found that in making the store choice the consumer uses a shopping area image or environmental map.[50] Each area such as downtown, shopping centers, or other cities, can be identified in consumer environmental mapping.

Social Surroundings.   The individuals with a consumer at the time of decision can influence the choice. Family members may influence the choice of a restaurant or the movie to see. Shopping with friends may determine what clothing a consumer purchases. Studies have shown that a child shopping with his or her mother influences the selection of cereal products.[51] Research has also indicated that perceived crowded conditions pressure the consumer to move through the decision process more quickly. It is evident that differing combinations of people will result in different decisions.

Temporal Perspective.   Time is an important factor in the consumer's decision process. One study showed a relationship between the time lapse since a meal was eaten and the amount spent on groceries.[52] Fast-food restaurants and convenience food stores have flourished by servicing the convenience and time needs of consumers. Most retailers recognize various seasonal aspects of selling and develop their retailing mixes accordingly. More subtle time factors may also be involved. Identifying and relating promotional timing to pay days may be effective. The suggestion that it has been a long time since the family has been out for an evening or taken a vacation may enhance consumers' motivation. Certain days of the week may require longer hours of operation to accommodate differing consumer perceptions of time. Eleven o'clock on weekend nights may not seem too late to shop or get a snack. With more two-income families, retailers may find that later and odd-hour shopping becomes the norm of behavior.

Task Definition. In many situations a person acts as purchasing agent for others, as in the case of the husband or wife purchasing groceries for the family. Whether the consumer is purchasing for himself or herself or others may influence the decision process. In buying a watch for himself, for example, a person may purchase a lower-priced brand at a discount store, but when purchasing a watch as a gift the consumer may purchase from a department store or specialty store and be willing to spend more. A husband taking his wife out for her birthday would probably choose different retailers than for a more ordinary night out.

The retailer can identify the various tasks of the consumer and plan retailing strategy accordingly. Special favors for birthdays, graduations, or anniversaries—cards, a free cake, or a small memento—may add to the store image and sales of the retailer.

Antecedent States. Events occurring immediately before a decision is made may alter the consumer's decision pattern. Fighting traffic, arguing with someone, having a headache, or being anxious over a purchase decision are all factors that may influence the consumer's decisions. Although the retailer can do little to eliminate these antecedent conditions, he or she can be cognizant of them and attempt to alleviate or lessen their impact. Courteous sales personnel, quiet surroundings, adequate parking, organized store layout, and efficient checkout procedures can all aid in making the retail experience pleasant for the consumer. The pharmacist who fills a prescription quickly may increase in stature in the eyes of the ill patient who must wait for the prescription to be filled. The auto repair shop that diplomatically handles an agitated consumer's complaint about the cost of repair bills may gain a loyal customer for the effort.

STORE CHOICE

The store choice is the best match between the ideal store attributes and the consumer's perception of the store's attributes. In some instances, the store choice decision is the beginning of a number of other decisions that follow in sequence. One such sequence is the store-product-brand or product-store-brand sequences mentioned previously.

IN-STORE INFORMATION PROCESSING

Once the consumer arrives at the retail store, he or she begins in-store information processing. Some consumers use the retailer as a source of information for evaluating the store or selecting a product and/or brand in the store.

The effectiveness and efficiency with which the retailer can provide in-store information to the consumer may have a profound effect upon the consumer's choice of a store. It is apparent that store personnel play a key role at this phase of the decision. Well-informed, courteous, and accessible store personnel are essential.

In-store influence can serve a number of purposes. The manufacturer or retailer can use it to switch the consumer to its brand. Additional in-store information can induce a consumer to purchase, not simply to switch brands. In-store information can also bring about additional purchases or unplanned purchases on the part of the consumer.

Researchers have found that many purchases are unplanned, including 61 percent of all health and beauty aid purchases, 51 percent of pharmaceutical and vitamin purchases,[53] and more than 50 percent of all food items purchased in supermarkets.[54] In another study, 39 percent of department store shoppers and 62 percent of discount shoppers were found to buy at least one unplanned item per shopping trip.[55]

The implications to the retailer are evident: Total sales volume is influenced not only by external communication but also through in-store factors. The factors that are most influential in bringing about unplanned purchases are point-of-purchase displays, price and promotional deals, and store layout. Strategies for each of these are discussed in Chapters 15–19. Here our concern is their influence on the consumer.

Point-of-Purchase Displays.   In-store displays bring attention to product areas or products that may otherwise be passed over by consumers. One study indicated a 30 percent increase in cheese purchases when an in-store display was used. The same study found that most of the sales increase came in the first two weeks of display usage. New displays were necessary to stimulate increased sales. The study also found that display height was important; an intermediate height of eight and a half feet was most effective in generating additional sales.[56]

In-store displays very often are developed in conjunction with price reductions. The impact will vary by product category and brand selected for reduction, but impressive sales increases have been found. Chevalier found a 268 percent increase in Clorox bleach sales, a 709 percent increase in sales of Scotties facial tissues compared to a 291 percent increase for sales of a store brand, and an increase of more than 1000 percent for Ivory liquid detergent when in-store displays and price reductions were combined.[57]

Price and Promotional Deals.   Frequently price reductions and promotional deals (samples, coupons, and gifts) are accompanied by some type of display or attention-getting device such as larger or different-color price tags. This makes it difficult to measure the impact of price or promotion independently, but some findings suggest a short-term price impact. Cotton and Babb found increases of regular purchases of cottage cheese (38 percent), ice cream (46 percent), and processed cheese (69 percent) during an in-store price reduction.[58] Several researchers concluded that deal-prone consumers had higher incomes, were more frequent users of the product category, and more likely owned a house and a car than consumers not susceptible to in-store promotional deals.[59]

Store Layout. Consumer movement patterns within a store can influence unplanned purchases. Product visibility and ease of access may also induce a consumer to purchase. The image of a retail store is affected by its layout. A consumer's decision about whether to remain in a store or exit as quickly as possible can be partially determined by store layout and organization. Store layout is examined in more detail in Chapter 18.

PURCHASE

When sufficient information exists for a consumer to match desired product attributes/perceived attributes and desired brand attributes/perceived attributes, the consumer can make a purchase decision. A purchase decision necessitates other decisions, such as when and how to make the purchase. The retailer should develop a strategy to best accommodate the consumer's desired purchasing patterns.

At the actual time of purchase the retailer can aid or hinder the satisfactory completion of the entire store selection process. Expediting the purchase transaction for the consumer can elicit a positive feeling after the purchase. The retailer should consider factors such as ease of checkout, credit or check approval, treatment by sales personnel, and courteous handling of any problems that may arise. The actual purchase situation influences the entire store choice process because that may be the last personal contact an individual has with a retailer and the impression will probably stay with the consumer and may influence future decisions about store choice.

POSTDECISION BEHAVIOR

The consumer's choice process does not end with a decision but continues to the point at which the consumer is comfortable with the decision. Postdecision behavior involves several elements. Some level of satisfaction or dissatisfaction occurs and the consumer may have some doubts about the store choice decision, referred to as **postpurchase dissonance.**

The degree of satisfaction relates the expectations of the consumer to the actual outcome of purchasing from the retailer. If the expectations are exceeded or met, satisfaction will result. An extremely high degree of satisfaction will most likely bring about repeat visits to the retailer and store loyalty to the exclusion of other retailers. Even moderate levels of satisfaction may result in the same behavior, but other retailers may remain as possible substitutes. Dissatisfaction or outcomes below expectations can result in a number of courses of action on the consumer's part. High levels of dissatisfaction may move the consumer to have no further interaction with the retailer, in which case the consumer eliminates the store from his or her evoked set. Moderate levels of dissatisfaction may cause the consumer to gather more information and/or add more stores to the evoked set.

Dissatisfaction can occur with the store, a specific brand, or both. It is possible that a consumer will experience dissatisfaction with a specific brand offered by the retailer, yet be satisfied with the store; if so, the consumer would not change store choice. Although the consumer's store choice behavior may not change, the retailer should be cognizant of consumer dissatisfaction with certain brands when making merchandising decisions.

Doubt may be a result of dissatisfaction or of the knowledge that unchosen stores had positive attributes that were not taken advantage of by the consumer. Dissonance will most likely occur when the purchase is important socially or economically and/or many retailers with similiar characteristics exist. The consumer normally reduces postpurchase dissonance by rationalizing the decision, seeking information from the retailer to support the decision, attempting to influence others to visit or shop the retailer, and looking to others that patronize the store.[60]

Rationalizing the decision might involve finding reasons why the store was chosen: friendly sales personnel, pleasant atmosphere, or other factors. Consumers may seek support from the retailer by considering advertisements that point to the positive aspects of the chosen store. Seeking and exchanging information with others that patronize the selected store can reduce doubt if positive information is obtained supporting the store choice. Finally, the consumer may reinforce his or her choice by attempting to influence others to patronize the same store.

The repetition of a behavior such as patronizing a store leads to loyalty. This repetitive behavior will occur when the consumer's postdecision feelings toward the store are positive. Thus it is imperative that the retailer be aware of and consider the postpurchase behavior of the consumer. Simple retailing efforts such as sending a card or letter thanking consumers for their patronage or purchase of a suit, furniture, or a car can have a very positive influence on future store choice decisions.

All of the consumer's postdecision behavior provides information for future decisions. Whether the consumer continues to purchase from a retailer or switches to another retailer will largely depend on the consumer's assessment of his or her experience. The consumer decision process is circular, with the decision providing new information for consideration in the next decision. The eventual outcome of extensive problem solving is the movement toward routine response behavior.

SUMMARY

The retailer exists to serve the needs of consumers and by doing so may make a profit. This chapter dealt with consumers, how they make decisions, and what the retailer can do to influence consumer decisions. The more a retailer understands the consumer decision-making process and what influences that process, the more effectively and efficiently the retailer can develop retailing strategies to serve the consumer.

Different consumers place importance on different attributes in making a store choice and have differing perceptions of the stores in their environment. Different groups of consumers therefore have differing consumer behavior patterns. Each consumer group will react to retailing strategies with a different pattern. For the retailer to develop effective strategies, the retailer must understand how groups will react to the strategies. The following chapter discusses the market segmentation process and how the retailer should select a group or segment of consumers for which to develop a retailing strategy.

KEY CONCEPTS

Predecision state	Family
Consumer decision process	Reference groups
Internal variables	Social class
Needs	Culture
Motivation	Subculture
Motivational threshold	Perceived risk
Incentives	Store image
Personality	Evoked set
Trait theory	Inert set
Lifestyle	Inept set
Perception	Extensive problem solving
Self-perception	Limited problem solving
Learning	Routine response behavior
Stimulus generalization	Problem identification
Discrimination	Information search
Attitudes	Evaluating alternatives
High-involvement model	In-store information processing
Low-involvement model	Postdecision behavior
External variables	Postpurchase dissonance

REVIEW QUESTIONS

1. Why should the retailer study consumer behavior?
2. How do the internal consumer variables and the external consumer variables affect behavior?
3. Why is the consumer's perception of a retail store important to the consumer and the retailer?
4. How can the retailer make the consumer learning process more effective?
5. What are attitudes? Why are they useful? Why is it beneficial to identify high- and low-involvement attitude formation?
6. How do extended problem solving, limited problem solving, and routine decision making differ? Which would most likely decide the purchase of a house? A pack of gum? Why?
7. Describe the consumer search process. How can the retailer influence consumers at this stage?
8. What occurs during the consumer decision?
9. Why may a consumer engage in postpurchase behavior?
10. How does the situation affect consumer decision making?

LEARNING EXERCISES

1. Question several retailers about how they use their understanding of consumer behavior to determine point-of-purchase displays, sales promotions, store layout, advertising, and pricing.
2. Analyze the differences in consumers' perception of some local retailers' store images compared to the images the retailers have of their own stores. Are the perceptions different? Why?

DECISION SITUATION 6.1: **GENTLEMAN'S QUARTERS**

The Gentleman's Quarters caters to young 30-to-45-year-old, male professionals with incomes over $35,000. The typical customer is married with two children, and most have wives who work outside the home, which raises the average family income to over $50,000. On a typical visit, these customers are likely to spend several hundred dollars.

Women also shop at Gentleman's Quarters. Typically they purchase items for gifts, such as shirts, sweaters, or accessories. In fact, women were the primary purchasers of these items.

QUESTIONS

1. With the customer profile described above, what characteristics should Gentleman's Quarters have?
2. Describe the decision-making process these customers are likely to follow.

3. What factors are likely to be most important to these customers when selecting a store in which to shop?

DECISION SITUATION 6.2: **LECTRONICS INC.**

Lectronics is an electronics store that sells mostly high-quality stereo equipment. Sales other than stereo equipment are "accidents" that the store does not count on making. The owner is planning to change this heavy dependence on stereo equipment; she has signed contracts to carry small computers and the accompanying software packages. Electronic games will also be featured.

The owner is anxiously awaiting the delivery of the computers but is concerned about whether she can sell the computers and exactly how to go about it.

QUESTIONS

1. What kind of consumers are likely to be interested in the new computers?

2. Describe the most likely decision-making process of computer customers.

3. What are the major differences between the decision-making process of computer customers and stereo customers? Do you think these differences will cause Lectronics any problems?

NOTES

1. Some of the basic concepts of this model were derived from Kent B. Monroe and Joseph B. Guiltinan, "A Path-Analytic Exploration of Retail Patronages Influences," *Journal of Consumer Research*, June 1975, pp. 19–29.

2. Joseph T. Plummer, "The Concept and Application of Life Style Segmentation," *Journal of Marketing*, January 1974.

3. William O. Bearden, Jesse E. Teal, and Richard M. Durand, "Media Usage, Psychographic, and Demographic Dimensions of Retail Shoppers," *Journal of Retailing*, Spring 1978, pp. 65–73.

4. Glenn C. Walters, *Consumer Behavior* (Homewood, Ill.: Richard D. Irwin, 1978).

5. Leon Shiffman, Stephanie Schas, and Leon Winer, "Risk Perception as a Determinant of In-Home Consumption," *Journal of the Academy of Marketing Science*, Fall 1976, p. 95.

6. Kenneth E. Runyon, *Consumer Behavior*, 2nd ed. (Columbus, Ohio: Merrill, 1980), p. 235.

7. *Ibid*, p. 234.

8. Gordon W. Allport, "Attitudes," in *A Handbook of Social Psychology*, ed. C. A. Murchinson (Worcester, Mass.: Clark University Press, 1935), p. 798.

9. Michael L. Rothchild, "Marketing Communications in Nonbusiness Situations or Why It's So Hard to Sell Brotherhood Like Soap," *Journal of Marketing*, Spring 1979, pp. 11–20.

10. Henry Assael, *Consumer Behavior and Marketing Action* (Boston: Kent Publishing, 1981).

11.   Harry L. Davis and Benny P. Rigaux, "Perception of Marital Roles in Decision Processes," *Journal of Consumer Research*, June 1974, p. 54.

12.   Patrick E. Murphy and William A. Staples, "A Modernized Family Life Cycle," *Journal of Consumer Research*, June 1979, pp. 12–22.

13.   Francis S. Berkman and Christopher Gilson, *Consumer Behavior*, 2nd ed. (Boston: Kent Publishing), 1981, p. 114.

14.   Francis S. Bourne, "Group Influence in Marketing and Public Relations," in *Some Applications of Behavior Research*, ed. Rensis Likert and Samuel P. Hayes (Paris: UNESCO, 1959).

15.   W. L. Warner, Marchia Meeker, and Kenneth Eells, *Social Class in America* (Chicago: Harper and Row, 1960).

16.   Sidney J. Levy, "Social Class and Consumer Behavior," in *Buyer Behavior*, ed. John A. Howard and Lyman E. Ostlund (New York: Knopf, 1973).

17.   Stuart U. Rich and Subhash C. Jain, "Social Class and Life Cycle as Predictors of Shopping Behavior," *Journal of Marketing Research*, February 1968, pp. 34–44.

18.   Andre Gabor and S. W. J. Granger, "Price Sensitivity of the Consumer," *Journal of Advertising Research*, December 1964, pp. 40–44.

19.   Pierre Martineau, "Social Class and Spending Behavior," *Journal of Marketing*, October 1958, pp. 121–129.

20.   Levy, *op. cit.*, p. 155.

21.   Rich and Jain, *op. cit.*, p. 45.

22.   Gabor and Granger, *op. cit.*, p. 44.

23.   Martineau, *op. cit.*, p. 121.

24.   Leon G. Shiffman and Leslie L. Kanuk, *Consumer Behavior* (Englewood Cliffs, N.J.: Prentice-Hall, 1978), p. 330.

25.   Donald E. Vinson, Jerome E. Scott, and Lawrence M. Lamont, "The Role of Personal Values in Marketing and Consumer Behavior," *Journal of Marketing*, April 1977, pp. 44–50.

26.   *Ibid.*

27.   Shiffman and Kanuk, p. 365.

28.   Daniel Yankelovich, *The New Morality: A Profile of American Youth in the 70's* (New York: McGraw-Hill, 1974).

29.   Herbert Zeltner, "You Can Sell to the Older Set if You Watch These Trends," *Advertising Age*, 22 August 1977, pp. 33ff.

30.   Kenneth L. Bernhardt and Thomas C. Kinnear, "Profiling the Senior Citizen Market," in *Advances in Consumer Research*, vol. 3, ed. Beverlee B. Anderson (Atlanta: Association for Consumer Research, 1976), pp. 449–452.

31.   Assael, *op. cit.*, p. 274.

32.   Raymond A. Bauer and Scott Cunningham, "The Negro Market," *Journal of Advertising Research*, April 1970, pp. 3–13.

33.   Raymond O. Oladipudo, *How Distinct Is the Negro Market?* (New York: Ogilvy and Mather, 1970), pp. 30–34.

34.   Bauer and Cunningham, *op. cit.*, p. 10.

35.   Kelvin A. Wall, "Positioning Your Product in the Black Market," *Advertising Age*, 18 June 1973.

36.   Shiffman and Kanuk, *op. cit.*

37.   Lawrence P. Feldman and Alvin D. Star, "Racial Factors in Shopping Behavior," in *A New Measure of Responsibility for Marketing*, ed. Keith Cox and Ben M. Enis (Chicago: American Marketing Association, 1968).

38.   Dennis H. Gensch and Richard Staelin, "The Appeal of Buying Black," *Journal of Marketing Research*, May 1972, pp. 141–148.

39. G. P. Stone, "City Shoppers and Urban Identification: Observations on the Social Psychology of City Life," *American Journal of Sociology,* July 1954, pp. 36–45.

40. Fred D. Reynolds and William R. Darden, "Intermarket Patronage: A Psychographic Study of Consumer Outshoppers," *Journal of Marketing,* October 1972, pp. 50–54.

41. "Why They Shop Some Centers," *Chain Store Age Executive,* May 1978, pp. 31–41.

42. Peter L. Gillett, "In-Home Shoppers: An Overview," *Journal of Marketing,* October 1976, pp. 81–88.

43. Fred D. Reynolds, "Analysis of Catalog Buying Behavior," *Journal of Marketing,* July 1974, pp. 47–51.

44. Raymond A. Bauer, "Consumer Behavior as Risk Taking," in *Dynamic Marketing for a Changing World,* ed. R. S. Hancock (Chicago: American Marketing Association, 1960), pp. 389–398.

45. R. Hansen and T. Deutscher, "An Empirical Investigation of Attribute Importance in Retailing Store Selection," *Journal of Retailing,* Winter 1977/78, pp. 59–73.

46. *Ibid.*

47. *Ibid.*

48. John A. Howard and Jagdish N. Sheth, *The Theory of Buyer Behavior* (New York: John Wiley, 1969).

49. Elizabeth C. Hirschman and Michael K. Mills, "Sources Shoppers Use to Pick Stores," *Journal of Advertising Research,* February 1980, pp. 47–51.

50. Robert A. Mittelstaedt, Sanford L. Grossbart, and William W. Curtis, "Consumer Perceptions and Retail Mapping: Research Findings and Preliminary Theory," in *Consumer and Industrial Buyer Behavior,* ed. Arch Woodside, Jagdish N. Sheth, and Peter D. Bennett (New York: Elsevier North Holland, 1977), pp. 95–110.

51. Charles K. Atkin, "Observation of Parent-Child Interaction in Supermarket Decision Making," *Journal of Marketing,* October 1978, pp. 41–45.

52. R. E. Nesbitt and D. E. Kanouse, "Obesity, Hunger, and Supermarket Shopping Behavior," in *Perspectives in Consumer Behavior,* rev. ed., ed. H. H. Kassaijian and T. S. Robertson (Glenview, Ill.: Scott, Foresman, 1973), pp. 118–121.

53. "Marketing Emphasis," *Product Marketing,* February 1978, pp. 61–64.

54. David T. Kollatt and Ronald P. Willett, "Customer Impulse Purchasing Behavior," *Journal of Marketing Research,* February 1967, pp. 21–31.

55. V. K. Prasad, "Socioeconomic Product Risk and Patronage Preferences of Retail Shoppers, *Journal of Marketing,* July 1975, pp. 42–47.

56. M. Chevalier, "Substitution Patterns as a Result of Display in the Product Category," *Journal of Retailing,* Winter 1975/76, pp. 65–72.

57. *Ibid.*

58. B. C. Cotton and Emerson M. Babb, "Consumer Response to Promotional Deals," *Journal of Marketing,* July 1978, pp. 109–113.

59. R. Blattberg, T. Buesing,, P. Peacock, and S. Sen, "Identifying the Deal Prone Segment," *Journal of Marketing Research,* August 1978, pp. 369–377.

60. Shiffman and Kanuk, p. 164.

STRATEGIC RETAIL MANAGEMENT MODEL

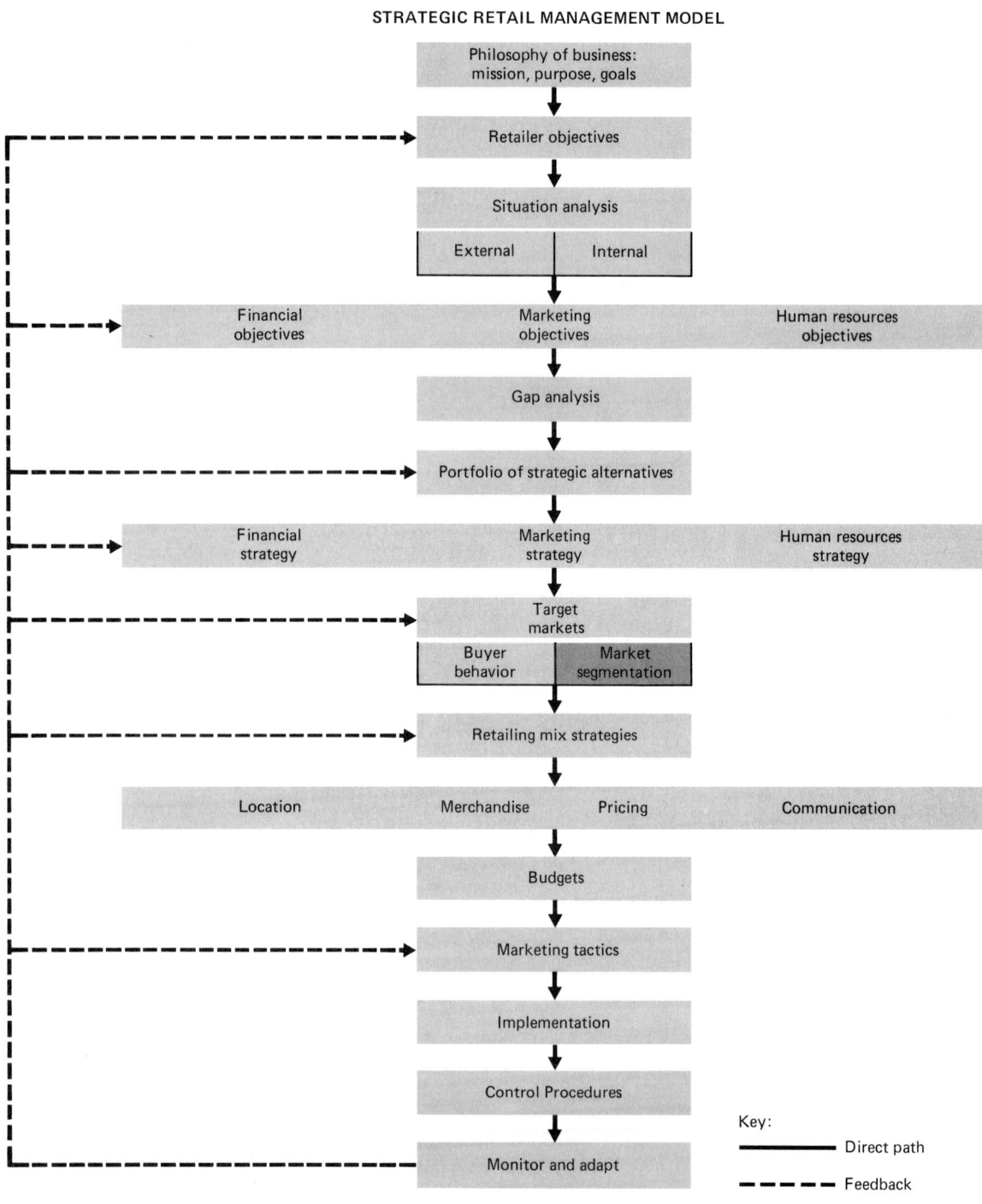

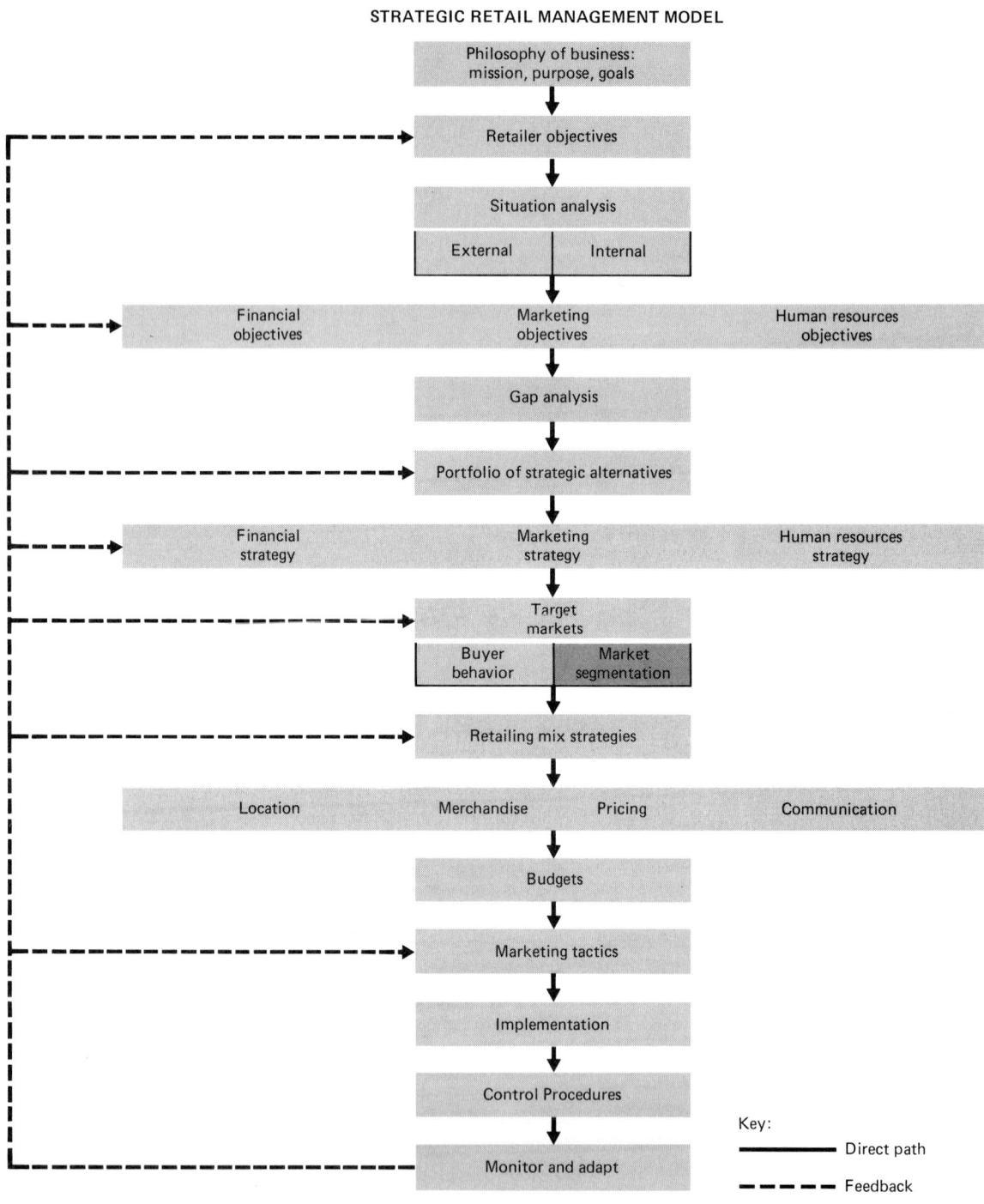

STRATEGIC RETAIL MANAGEMENT MODEL

Philosophy of business:
mission, purpose, goals

Retailer objectives

Situation analysis

External | Internal

Financial
objectives | Marketing
objectives | Human resources
objectives

Gap analysis

Portfolio of strategic alternatives

Financial
strategy | Marketing
strategy | Human resources
strategy

Target
markets

Buyer
behavior | Market
segmentation

Retailing mix strategies

Location | Merchandise | Pricing | Communication

Budgets

Marketing tactics

Implementation

Control Procedures

Monitor and adapt

Key:
———— Direct path
– – – – Feedback

Chapter 7
Market
Segmentation

LEARNING OBJECTIVES

1. To become familiar with the role and importance of market segmentation.

2. To gain an understanding of a strategic approach to selecting market segments.

INTRODUCTION

Developing a retailing strategy requires knowledge and understanding of consumers' behavior. The foregoing chapter on consumer behavior identified patterns for *segments* of buyers rather than for individuals. The reaction to a retailer's strategy will not be the same for all segments of the market. The retailer must determine which segments can be influenced most effectively given the strengths and weaknesses of the particular store.

While it is recommended that a planned approach to market segmentation be implemented, many retailers simply allow the market to segment itself. In essence, the retailer develops a strategy based on personal perspectives of the market's needs. The market segments that respond positively to the retailer's strategy are the segments the retailer then uses for future strategy decisions. Unfortunately, for many new retailers the market does not respond and segment itself, and for these retailers failure usually results.

A retailer's strategy can be made much more effective if the appropriate segment responses are identified prior to development of a strategy. In this chapter we focus on the concept of **market segmentation** or **market opportunity analysis (MOA),** which includes the basis for segmenting markets, how to identify market opportunity, and how to apply a retail strategy to the chosen market segment (see Fig. 7.1).

UNDERSTANDING MARKET SEGMENTATION

The retail market can be viewed from several perspectives, including the economist's, the marketer's, and the psychologist's. The economist views the market as homogeneous, with all buyers being similar and the market acting as a total unit. The psychologist perceives the market as consisting of individuals, each behaving somewhat differently. The marketer identifies groups of behavior patterns. Neither the economist's nor the psychologist's perspective gives the retailer a valid base from which to develop strategies. While the economist might provide the retailer with an efficient perspective, it is not a very effective one, and the converse is true for the psychologist's perspective. The marketer provides the retailer with a mid-range perspective offering effectiveness and efficiency in developing retailing strategies. Whether the retailer is "subdividing" the economist's broader market or "aggregating" the psychologist's individual market, the effect is the same. The retailer is attempting to identify subsets of consumers who can conceivably be selected as a target market and reached with a distinct retailing mix.[1] By segmenting markets, retailers can deploy their resources more efficiently and plan their strategies more effectively because they will know the needs and behavior patterns of the targeted segments.

Some examples of selected target markets, a result of market segmentation, and the consequent retailing strategy should help explain the use of segmentation in retailing. Strategy in Action 7.1 relates the successful use of segmentation in two separate retail situations and two different segments.

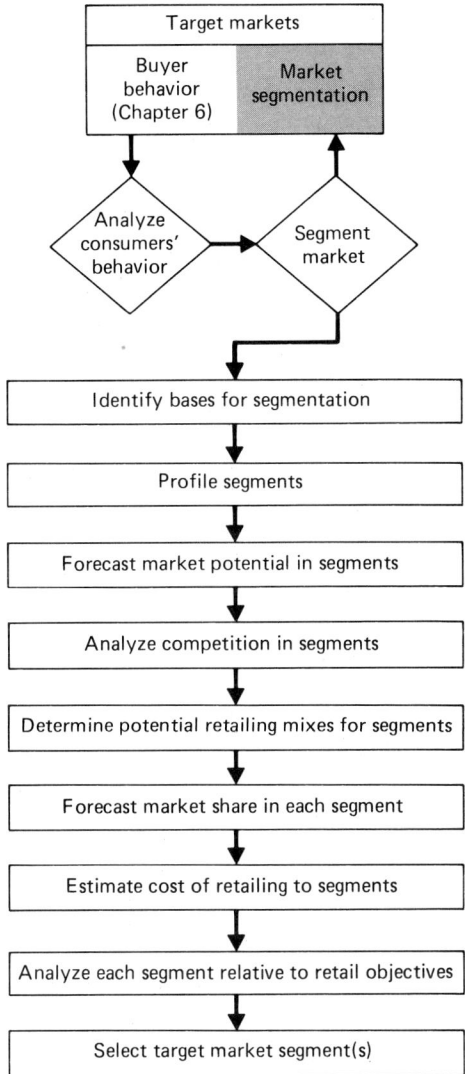

Figure 7.1
Market segmentation and opportunity analysis decision model

WHEN NOT TO SEGMENT

Although segmentation is widely recommended, there are situations in which segmenting markets may not be appropriate, as Young, Ott, and Feigin point out.[2] Two of the situations they relate are relevant to retail segmentation: (1) when the market is so small that retailing to a portion of it is not profitable, and (2) when heavy users make up such a large proportion

STRATEGY IN ACTION 7.1
Retailing to Market Segments

Mervyn's, an operating company with the Dayton Hudson Corporation, has consistently paced the company in growth rate. Walter T. Rossi (Vice President and General Merchandise Manager of Men's, Boys', Children's, and Domestics) defined Mervyn's customer as "usually a woman who is shopping for her whole family in our store. The mean income of our family shoppers is $20,000. The breakdown would be about 25 percent professional, 25 percent housewives, 15 percent blue collar, 15 percent clerical and 20 percent other." Because Mervyn's believes its customer is very sportswear-oriented, it does not carry tailored clothing at all but does have some dress furnishings. Its strength is in the casual area, with the strongest classifications being jeans, knit tops, and cut and sewn sport shirts.*

Hill's, a discount chain, defines its target market by income, occupation, and geography. Anyone above the 10 percent and below the top 25 percent income in the United States who has a blue-collar occupation is part of Hill's target market. Geographically, Hill's has concentrated on what is defined as "America's industrial heartland and the Appalachian Ridge." Historically this segment has been ignored by mass merchandisers like Sears and upscale chains like Target; Hill's is attempting to fill that void in the retail market. A blue-collar atmosphere and everyday low prices have attracted a very loyal customer to Hill's.†

Sources: *Adapted from "Mervyn's Deceptively Simple Approach," *Retail Week,* 15 July 1981, pp. 38–39.
†Adapted from "Hill's: Traditionalist in an Upscale Era," pp. 37–39. Reprinted by permission from *Chain Store Age/Executive* © August 1981. Copyright Lebhar-Friedman, Inc. 425 Park Avenue, New York, NY 10022.

of the sales volume that they are the only relevant target. The former situation suggests that the segmenting of a market would make any one segment too small to be profitable, while the latter situation proposes that any segment besides the heavy users would be meaningless because they would not offer an opportunity for profit.

Some products or services are purchased or used so infrequently that the market is necessarily small, as in the case of the consumer market for automobile tires and batteries. To sell effectively in such a market, the retailer must appeal to all segments.

In certain instances, such as in expensive clothing or jewelry markets, very few consumers account for most market sales. The retailer then has little choice but to direct his or her marketing efforts to this small, high-volume group.

CRITERIA FOR SEGMENTATION

A market can be segmented in a variety of ways, but the segmentation base chosen must be measurable, accessible, and substantial. A base from which segments can be easily *measured* and identified may be preferred to one that is complex and difficult to interpret. Personality variables, for example, are somewhat difficult to measure and relate to store choice, while demographics are easy to measure. The segmentation base should also provide segments that can feasibly be reached with, or are *accessible* to, a retailing mix. Segments that cannot be reached with promotion or that have no reaction to price offer little benefit to the retailer. Fashion leaders or price-sensitive consumers may be identifiable but inaccessible through advertising because they have no distinct media habits. *Substantiality* concerns the size of the segments developed from the segmentation base. The segments must be large enough to make the retailing effort potentially profitable. If the resulting segments are unprofitable, the segmentation base is useless. Segmenting by using narrow income categories or developing a clothing store for extremely large consumers would not provide large enough segments to be profitable.

THE SEGMENTATION PROCESS

Segmentation is a fairly recent practice among retailers, and a generally accepted procedure has not been developed. The market segmentation process presented and discussed here follows an outline recommended by Cravens, Hills, and Woodruff.[3]

The objective of segmenting markets is to identify a segment or segments of the market that offer the retailer an opportunity to more effectively use his or her resources relative to other retailers. An ideal competitive situation is one in which the retailer competes on the basis of his or her strengths relative to other retailers' weaknesses. The nine-step process of segmentation, presented in Fig. 7.1, is an excellent procedure for achieving this objective.

All nine steps are interrelated: The results of each step affect subsequent steps. The process begins with the selection of variables for segmenting the market. After segmenting the market (step 1), the retailer profiles the segments using other segmentation variables (step 2). The potential demand is then analyzed for each of the segments (step 3). Forecast demand is not necessarily a good indicator of potential market success in each segment because the retailer will compete with different numbers and types of retailers in each segment. An analysis of competition (step 4) in each segment gives the retailer an indication of who the competition may be. The retailer next develops potential retailing mixes for each segment (step 5). For some of the segments the retailer may be able to market effectively, and for others the retailer may have weaknesses in the retailing mix. By combining the competitive analysis with the potential mixes the retailer could offer, the retailer can forecast the share of the market in each segment that can potentially be obtained (step 6). The cost of serving each segment is estimated for the potential retailing mix for each segment (step 7). At this point the retailer has established the potential revenue for each segment (step 6) and established the costs of retailing to each segment (step 7). After analyzing each segment relative to the retailer's objectives (market shares, profit, and the like), the retailer can select as a target market those segments that will enable him or her to accomplish the set goals (steps 8 and 9).

Identify Bases for Segmentation

There is no one tried-and-true method of selecting a segmentation base. The retailer may desire to segment using one base, such as geography, or segment on several bases, such as age, education, and lifestyle. In practice a combination of segmentation bases is usually used.

Selecting the appropriate segmentation base often requires analysis to gain insight, but in certain situations the segments may readily suggest themselves. Furniture retailers, for example, can easily decide to segment consumers by family life cycle, social class, or income. Clothing retailers might segment markets by age, occupation, and fashion consciousness. Segmenting the market for restaurants may prove to be more difficult with benefits, demographics, or psychographics as possible segmentors.

Some common bases used in segmenting markets are geography, demographics, behavioral characteristics, and store benefits. Table 7.1 lists bases and some of their components used in segmentation.

Geographic Segmentation.   Segmenting with geographic factors enables the retailer to analyze markets for location, merchandising, and other decisions. With the shift in population to the West and South in the United States, the retailer needs a method for making location decisions. Safeway, the largest grocery chain in the country, has concentrated in the West. For the retailer with stores in various geographical locations, the knowledge of geographical behavior patterns and product preferences can be valuable in planning. Preferences for certain products may vary by region, such as skiing equipment in northern or mountain areas or more formal clothing in urban areas.

Geographical segmentation also relates to city size. A retailer may develop a strategy of entering markets on the basis of population. Wal Mart, a regional discount chain, follows a strategy of locating in towns of less than 25,000 population and, preferably, the county seat. This strategy has been quite successful. In many communities Wal Mart is the "largest and most significant retailer in town." Several retailers, such as Sears and McDonald's, have certain merchandise and store features for different-size population centers. Larger stores with a wider range of merchandise serve larger cities, and smaller stores with less merchandise selection are built for smaller cities.

Demographic Segmentation.   Probably the most widely used segmentation base among retailers is demographics. When compared with the three criteria for segmentation, it is evident why demographics are employed so often. Demographics are sometimes used by themselves or combined with other segmentation variables. In most instances retailers use at least one demo-

Table 7.1
Segmentation variables for retailing

VARIABLE	SUGGESTED COMPONENTS
Geographic	
Region	Pacific, Mountain, West North Central, West South Central, East North Central, East South Central, South Atlantic, Middle Atlantic, New England
County	A, B, C, D
City or standard metro. statistical area size	Under 5,000; 5000–19,999; 20,000–49,999; 50,000–99,999; 100,000–249,999; 250,000–499,999; 500,000–999,999; 1,000,000–3,999,999; 4,000,000 +
Density	Urban, suburban, rural
Climate	Northern, southern
Demographic	
Age	Under 6, 6–11, 12–19, 20–34, 35–49, 50–64, 65 +
Sex	Male, female
Family size	1–2, 3–4, 5 +
Family life cycle	Young, single; young, married, no children; young, married, youngest child under six; young, married youngest child six or over; older, married, with children; older, married, no children under 18; older, single; other
Income	Under $3,000; $3,000–5,000; $5,000–7,000; $7,000–10,000; $10,000–15,000; $15,000–25,000; $25,000 +
Occupation	Professional and technical; managers, officials, and proprietors; clerical, sales; artisans; supervisors; operatives; farmers; retired; students; unemployed
Education	Grade school or less; some high school; high school graduate; some college; college graduate
Religion	Catholic, Protestant, Jewish, other
Race	White, black, Oriental
Nationality	American, British, French, German, Scandinavian, Italian, Latin-American, Middle-Eastern, Japanese.
Social class	Lower-lower, upper-lower, lower-middle, upper-middle, lower-upper, upper-upper
Behavioral	
Lifestyle	Straights, swingers, longhairs
Personality	Compulsive, gregarious, authoritarian, ambitious
Purchase occasion	Regular occasion, special occasion
Usage rate	Light user, medium user, heavy user
Loyalty status	None, medium, strong, absolute
Benefits sought	
	Economy, convenience, prestige

Source: Adapted from: Philip Kotler, *Marketing Management: Analysis, Planning, and Control,* 4th ed. © 1980, p. 199. Reprinted by permission of Prentice-Hall, Inc., Englewood Cliffs, N.J.

graphic variable for segmentation. As Table 7.1 shows, there are many de-mographic variables, many of which we discussed in previous chapters.

Because spending and behavioral patterns change naturally as a person ages and gains experience, age is one of the most commonly used demo-graphic variables for segmentation.

Younger children as a retail market segment may not offer much po-tential as individuals because they have little of their own money to spend, but they are certainly an influence in some decisions. McDonald's has done an excellent job of combining children's and parents' criteria in the restau-rant decision process by providing low prices, fast service, and convenience along with the Ronald McDonald character and certain menu and atmos-phere aspects that appeal to younger children.

Much has been written about the "tween-teen" market, a viable market because the individuals in it have discretionary income and more inde-pendent decision-making patterns than young children. Several categories of products depend heavily on this segment of ten-to-twenty-year-olds, in-cluding records, pin ball, video games, and cosmetics. Moschis has found that this group can be motivated through price appeals but is not greatly influenced by store-related attributes.[4]

Young adults, consumers from their early twenties to mid-thirties, will increase rapidly as a group during the 1980s.[5] This market segment pur-chases a wide range of products, from recreational goods to home furnish-ings. Larger incomes and a wide diversity of personal and family needs combined with a growing number of two-income earners in the young fam-ily make this group a highly sought-after market segment.

Older adults, from mid-thirties through late fifties, offer the retailer a different set of opportunities. The impact of older children can greatly alter this age group's spending patterns. A second or third car may be necessary, and increased expenditures for food, clothing, and education occur as chil-dren enter their teenage years. Even with the burden of increased expenses, this group has some discretionary income for travel and durable goods be-cause during these years workers attain their prime earning potential.

More married couples are choosing not to have children and thus would not be part of the traditional "family with children" category. Very little research has been completed on this segment. However, indications are that they spend more on travel, recreation, and home furnishings than do families in their thirties through fifties with children.

As individuals move from occupations to avocations, their consuming habits change. People in their fifties have more time for themselves and their personal pursuits when their children leave home. Products related to leisure activities and hobbies may become important. As individuals cease working full-time, the movement to hobbies, recreation, and vacations be-comes more evident.

The *role of women* in our society has changed appreciably in the past twenty years. Clothing styles, occupations, decision making, and educa-tional choices have all changed in relation to women's changing roles. The changing social relationships for females have had and will continue to have an impact on how retailers segment them and market to them.

A *family* can be segmented on two bases: size and stage of the family life cycle. Larger families generally incur more expenditures for necessities and less for discretionary items. Larger families are heavy users of products such as paper towels, toothpaste, and food products. As pointed out in Chapter 4, the trend in the United States is toward smaller families. The family life cycle concept discussed in Chapter 6 proposes a changing pattern of expenditures throughout the life of the family and combines several of the variables discussed independently, such as age, family size, income, and number of children. Each stage identified in the family life cycle could be a segment for the retailer.

Rising *incomes* in the United States offer the retailer an opportunity to develop new markets. Much of this increased income has come about because of two-income families. K mart has started offering Izod sport shirts, Minolta cameras, Seiko watches, and Calvin Klein jeans to attract consumers with increasing incomes.[6]

Occupational groups have largely been categorized as blue collar and white collar. Generally, blue-collar workers are identified as lower class while white-collar occupations are associated with middle and upper social classes and with some on-the-job decision making. White-collar segments practice longer, more abstract, and better planning, which suggests more of a demand for travel and investments such as savings accounts.

As an individual's *education* increases, his or her perceptions and interests in the environment change. Broader perspectives, expanded interests, and better decision-making capabilities usually accompany higher levels of education. More interest in magazines, books, cultural activities, and national and international events exist among better-educated segments. Education is difficult to isolate as a variable because of its association with income. Better-educated segments, in most instances, have higher incomes, which allows them more freedom in product and store choices. As discussed in Chapter 4, the better-educated, higher-income, two-income family is a growing force in the retail environment.

Certain *religious beliefs* offer segmentation opportunities for retailers. Christian book stores, Jewish food stores, and other retailers have developed entire outlets based around religion. Other, more indirectly religious factors may be associated with forms of clothing styles and some food product preferences. Some religions have geographic concentrations—Catholics in urban areas of the East and the northeast central United States, Jews in New York, and Baptists in the South.

Race, nationality, and social class as segments have identifiable behavioral habits (see Chapter 6) that make them viable bases for segmentation.

Behavioral Segmentation. Behavioral characteristics are used to segment markets by attitude, usage rate, or other similar patterns rather than on inferred behavior from demographic or geographic characteristics.

Sometimes referred to as volume segmentation, *usage rate* divides the market according to light, medium, and heavy users of retail stores or services. In many instances, heavy users may constitute a small percentage of all users but make a large percentage of all purchases or store visits. Heavy users of department stores have been found to be younger, better-educated, and with higher incomes than light users. In addition, they were found to be more fashion-conscious, more cosmopolitan, more liberal, more innovative, more interested in particular sports, and more interested in cooking.[7] The heaviest users of large shopping centers have been characterized as singles under the age of thirty who attended college and had a higher income[8] than light users. The heavy-user segment has value only as it relates to other characteristics such as demographics or psychographics. If the heavy user has similar characteristics to light or medium users, the usage rate segmentation base is not meaningful.

Store loyalty refers to a consumer's pattern of behavior relative to any one store or chain. Research shows that older, more affluent shoppers have strong loyalty to major department stores.[9] The value of segmenting by loyalty status is that the retailer has an indication of the strength of appeal to customers and the strength of competing retailers. Extremely loyal customers are an obvious asset, and customers extremely loyal to competing retailers may indicate the extent of the difficulty in attracting new customers. Not only must the retailer know the degree of customer loyalty, but he or she should also determine the reasons for the loyalty. The most intensely loyal customers may patronize a department store because of the national brands carried and the wide selection of merchandise, for example. The retailer should also relate loyalty status to demographics and other behavioral characteristics.

Benefit Segmentation.   Reasons for patronizing retail stores may differ within each market segment. If the market can be segmented on a benefits-sought basis, the retailer can identify factors within the retailing mix that would make it more appealing to certain segments. Some argue that benefit segmentation is valuable because it directly facilitates merchandise planning, positioning, and advertising communications.[10] Benefits for particular retailers may differ based on the product category. For grocery stores, segments might be defined by convenience, price, variety, national brands, and so on. Department store shoppers would be interested in merchandise selection, services, quality, store personnel, and other benefits. Those consumers that frequent large shopping centers look for variety of merchandise, better prices, and more knowledgeable sales people as benefits. For any of the benefit segments to be effective, they must relate to demographic variables, which provide information on media, location, and merchandise decisions.

The retailer must determine how many segmentation "stages" will be employed in segmenting markets. Some recommend segmenting by attitude, then lifestyle, and finally media patterns.[11] The results of those three segmentation stages are an indication of the segments with positive, neutral, or negative attitudes toward a retail store, how the store fits into their life-styles, and how each segment can be reached. Others recommend using benefits to segment markets.[12]

We have seen that demographics, geography, product preferences, and media habits can be used as bases for segmenting markets. The choice of a segmentation base depends on the retailer's perception of what base or bases will best give an indication of the retailing strategies that should be developed.

Profile Segments

Once the market segmentation bases have been chosen and the market segmented, consumer profiles must be developed for each segment. The segments are profiled on bases other than the segmentation bases. This profile gives the retailer a clearer picture of each segment and of the possible reactions of each segment to a particular retailing mix. Table 7.2 depicts a profile of two market segments. The market is segmented geographically and then profiled using demographics, behavioral characteristics, and benefits sought.

Each of these profiles gives a more precise indication of the market segments and how they might respond to a retailer's marketing efforts. Members of the suburban segment in Table 7.2 appear to be more frequent purchasers of clothing, to be more style conscious, to have higher incomes, and to be seeking variety and styling from a store. A retail mix that satisfies this segment would most likely not satisfy the urban segment's needs, although each may offer opportunity to the retailer.

Table 7.2
Hypothetical segment profiles for men's clothing store

	GEOGRAPHIC SEGMENTS	
PROFILE VARIABLES	URBAN	SUBURBAN
Demographic	Young, lower income, blue-collar occupation, high school education	Middle-aged, moderate to high income, white-collar occupation, college degree
Behavioral	Conservative, high store loyalty, not style conscious, limited variety of clothes, purchasing occasions limited (back-to-school, birthday)	Slightly liberal, low store loyalty, style conscious, wide variety of clothes, frequent purchases
Benefits sought	Economy, personal shopping relationship with store personnel	Variety, current styles

Forecast Market Potential in Each Segment

Selecting and profiling the market segments should improve the retailer's perspective of the potential demand in each segment. Factors such as the number of consumers and households in each segment, the frequency of purchase, dollars spent in the product category, and probability of purchase will indicate to the retailer the amount of potential demand. A movie theater may want to determine the potential demand within each segment in order to choose movies to show, location, and atmospherics of the theater. Such a market is segmented in three age groups in Table 7.3.

In this simplified example, the 10–25 age group looks most promising. It is important to note that if the behavior characteristics (movies attended per year) were not known for each segment, the 26–50 group might have been chosen simply on the basis of size.

Analyze Competition in Each Segment

The degree to which the retailer can obtain potential volume in each segment is related to the ability to compete in each market segment. Thus an analysis of the competition in each segment is necessary to determine a retailer's opportunity. A competitive analysis consists of identifying compe-

Table 7.3
Segment potential

AGE SEGMENT	MOVIES ATTENDED/ YEAR	SIZE OF SEGMENT	AVERAGE TICKET PRICE	TOTAL POTENTIAL
10–25	10	10,000	$4.00	$400,000
26–50	4	15,000	$5.00	$300,000
50+	1	8,000	$5.00	$ 40,000

tition for each segment by size, market share, and number of retailers. Each competitor's retailing strategy should be profiled by segment in a way similar to the competitive audit technique discussed in Chapter 5. The outcome of this process will give the retailer an indication of what type of competitive environment he or she faces in each segment.

Some segments with great potential may not be attractive because of the strength of the competition, whereas smaller segments may offer substantial opportunity because of little or no effective competition. This illustrates a concept in marketing known as the **majority fallacy,** which suggests that many retailers attempt to market to the largest market segment, consequently making it difficult to compete. The recommendation is also to look to smaller, less competitive segments for opportunity.

Determine Potential Retailing Mixes for Each Segment

In this step the retailer determines what retailing mixes could be offered to each segment. Some segments can be attracted by merchandise characteristics, such as quality and stylish clothing for the suburban segment in the example in Table 7.4. If a retailer's strength is an ability to offer high-quality and stylish clothing, that retailer may be able to market effectively to the suburban segment. It may be more difficult for that retailer to attract the urban market segment because of lack of expertise in clothing lines to fit its needs. Table 7.4 shows the potential retailing mixes that could be offered to the two market segments.

The purpose of this step is to identify the requirements necessary to compete in each segment and to match the requirements with the retailer's strength. The ideal situation is one in which the retailer could deploy his or her strengths in a segment where little effective competition is present.

At this point the retailer has segmented the market, identified how consumers behave in each segment, how much potential exists, who is competing and how they are competing, and finally what the retailer can offer to consumers in each segment. The next step is to estimate how well the retailer can compete in each segment.

Table 7.4
Potential retailing mixes for men's clothing, by geographic segment

MIX ELEMENT	URBAN SEGMENT	SUBURBAN SEGMENT
Product	Narrow line of standard, conventional clothes	Wide line of quality, stylish clothes
Location	City locations	Suburban shopping centers
Promotion	Radio, newspaper	Radio, newspaper
Price	Middle range, highly competitive, 35–40% margins	Higher prices, 45–50% margins
Services	Limited, direct clothing services	Range of services

**Forecast
Market Share
in Each Segment**

To forecast expected share of each segment, the retailer must compare the retailing efforts of potential competitors with what he or she can offer to the segment. Of course, this will take some thought and analysis. The effectiveness of all the retail efforts must be compared with the segment profile developed in the second step of the process. The relative ability of the retailer to satisfy the needs of each segment will determine the forecast market share for each segment.

Comparing what the retailer's potential competition has to offer against the profiled behavior and characteristics of the various market segments will provide some indication of the ability to achieve market share within each segment, as illustrated in Fig. 7.2.

For each segment the retail competition's offerings may differ, and for each segment the retailer's mix may differ. In some instances the competition may be overwhelming, whereas in other segments the retailer may have strong competitive advantages such as location or price. Based on the differential advantage the retailer possesses, forecasts can be estimated to indicate potential segment share. A strong location advantage may translate into certain share points. Coupled with a moderate price advantage, it may indicate a large share of the segment, perhaps 60 percent. However, poor parking

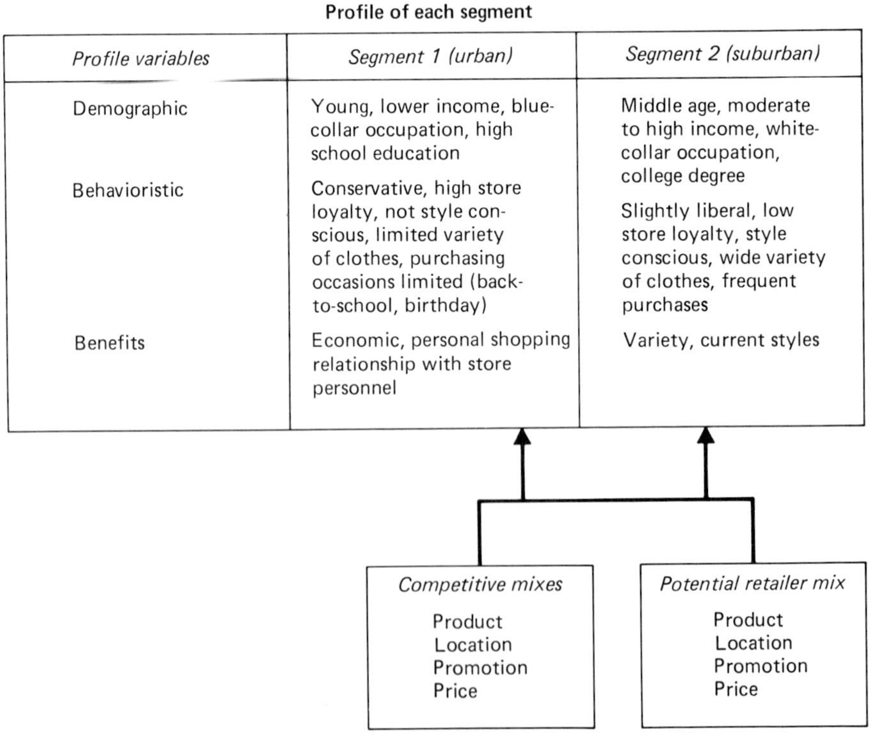

Profile of each segment

Profile variables	Segment 1 (urban)	Segment 2 (suburban)
Demographic	Young, lower income, blue-collar occupation, high school education	Middle age, moderate to high income, white-collar occupation, college degree
Behavioristic	Conservative, high store loyalty, not style conscious, limited variety of clothes, purchasing occasions limited (back-to-school, birthday)	Slightly liberal, low store loyalty, style conscious, wide variety of clothes, frequent purchases
Benefits	Economic, personal shopping relationship with store personnel	Variety, current styles

Competitive mixes	Potential retailer mix
Product	Product
Location	Location
Promotion	Promotion
Price	Price

**Figure 7.2
Comparison of competition and hypothetical mix**

facilities and weak interior decor may reduce this estimate to 45 percent of the segment. This process is more involved than this illustration indicates, but the basic concept behind the forecast share should be evident.

The outcome of this step should be some indication of expected revenue for each segment, as shown in Table 7.5 for the movie theater example we considered in Table 7.3. Competition is strong in the 10–25 segment and the retailer's perceived strengths appeal to the 26–50 and 50+ age markets. Using these calculations, the retailer can see that the 26–50 market appears to be the most attractive segment.

Estimate Costs of Retailing to Each Segment

Before a final decision can be made on which segments to select for a marketing effort, an analysis of the costs of serving each segment is necessary. The fifth step of the segmentation process, determining potential mixes, provides the bases for estimating costs. This is not a simple task. The process involves assigning the dollar costs to the potential marketing mixes. Table 7.4 shows the hypothetical retailing mixes for which costs need to be estimated. Certainly the suburban segment would be more expensive to attract, because of the necessity for wider lines of merchandise and more services, but they may bring in higher revenues. At this point the retailer should be able to determine the potential contribution from each segment by comparing costs and sales forecasts.

Analyze Each Segment Relative to Retailing Objectives

The retailer may have a range of objectives to achieve, and the selection of segments to serve may not be a straightforward process. More than likely, potential profit for each segment will be a determining goal. If this is the case, the retailer would simply select the segments that offer the greatest profit potential. However, a retailer may set a share of the market objective along with certain growth possibilities in the future. Other goals may involve only partial exploitation of the market or other limited strategy goals related to segments selected. The final selection of segments relates to what the retailer wishes to accomplish in the market.

Select Target Market Segment(s)

The results of matching retail goals to certain segment outcomes determine the specific segments selected. Obviously, the best match will determine the segment or segments the retailer will market to.

Table 7.5
Expected revenues, by age segment

AGE SEGMENT	MOVIES PER YEAR	SIZE OF SEGMENT	AVERAGE TICKET PRICE	FORECAST SHARE	EXPECTED (FORECAST) REVENUE
10–25	10	10,000	$4.00	33⅓%	$133,000
26–50	4	15,000	$5.00	50%	$200,000
50+	1	8,000	$5.00	80%	$ 32,000

RETAILING MIX STRATEGY FOR MARKET SEGMENTS

The results of the market segmentation process provide the retailer with an indication of the opportunitites and characteristics of the market to be served. One additional step is needed to complete the entire market opportunity analysis. This step is to make a decision regarding the retailing mix strategy for responding to the needs of the chosen segments. There are four possible retailing mix strategies: undifferentiated, differentiated, concentrated, and aggregated.

Undifferentiated Retailing Mix Strategy

The strategy of **undifferentiated retailing mix** is based on broad appeal to as many segments as possible. The retailer is not fine-tuning the retail offering to any one segment but hoping to attract a sufficient number of consumers from all segments with one retailing mix. This strategy might be compared to the concept of economy of scale. Costs can be kept down because of the standardization of the retailing mix, but the "sameness" of the mix does not satisfy many of the consumers in each segment completely. One writer has compared this strategy to slicing a layer horizontally off a cake (or market)—broad appeal but no depth.

An undifferentiated approach is appropriate in situations where the responses from the selected segments are expected or found to be similar. None of the segments will be satisfied in depth, but all will be appealed to in some degree. Another situation in which the undifferentiated strategy may be used is when the retailer wishes to appeal to the largest market segment. Usually, because of the large size of the segment, diverse behavior patterns exist. One retailing mix cannot satisfy all possible responses, and anticipating similar responses and offering one mix seem to constitute a compatible framework.

Differentiated Retailing Mix Strategy

A retailer that decides to appeal to several of the chosen segments with different retailing mixes for each is practicing **differentiated retailing mix strategy.** This strategy is based on satisfying specific consumer needs in depth. Each segment requires particular products, promotion, price, and location, separately or in combination. The selected segments need not have a completely different retailing mix, but changes in the mix to meet certain needs and bring about positive consumer responses are necessary. One segment may require one product line while another segment may require part of another product line. Some consumer segments may respond to customer services such as free delivery or check cashing, while other segments may not. Various retailing mixes must be designed to attract different segments.

The differentiated strategy is more costly than the undifferentiated strategy because of the separate retailing mixes, but because each segment is served in depth there is a better chance for long-term loyalty to develop toward the retailer. A retailer might choose to use the differentiated approach when the selected segments are perceived as having different responses and meeting the criterion of substantiality. The different forecast responses, of course, require different retailing mixes.

Concentrated Retailing Mix Strategy

The undifferentiated and differentiated retailing mix strategies involve all the segments that meet the retailer's goals. A **concentrated retailing mix strategy** concentrates the retailing effort on one or a few segments. Rather than attempt to attract all of the segments, the retailer decides to deploy his or her strengths to obtain a large share of one or a few market segments. As discussed earlier, more profits might be achieved through a large share of a smaller market than through a small share of a larger market. Numerous retailing examples of concentrated strategy could be cited, from clothing specialists concentrating on juniors, maternity, or tall men to food retailers specializing in ethnic foods.

The concentrated approach has several strong positive aspects, but it also leaves the retailer vulnerable to market shifts and future competitive pressures. The positive aspects of employing the concentrated strategy are the effective use of the retailer's strengths, whether they are location, product lines, or market knowledge; the cost-effectiveness of specializing in one or a few segments; and the possibilities of higher rates of return on investment. As the term suggests, a concentrated strategy keeps a retailer focused on what he or she does best. On the negative side, the concentrated approach increases the retailer's risk. The retailer may be strong in the chosen segments, but a market shift or increased competition may make it difficult to compete. A smaller segment may be able to support one or a few retailers, but when a number of retailers enter the segment some will probably suffer. Early entrants will most likely not suffer greatly if they have kept up with market changes, but the possibility of losing everything because there is no support from other segments may present too much risk for many retailers. As discussed earlier, higher potential profits usually accompany higher levels of risk.

Aggregated Retailing Mix Strategy (Countersegmentation)

A relatively new retailing mix strategy has developed as a combination of the undifferentiated and differentiated strategies. Retailers use this strategy to combine the cost efficiencies of the undifferentiated strategy with the marketing effectiveness of the differentiated strategy.

Countersegmentation is a result of hypersegmented or oversegmented markets. When markets become oversegmented, the possibility of achieving a profit by retailing to these segments becomes less likely (recall the segmentation criterion of substantiality discussed earlier). A reduction in target segments through countersegmentation can be achieved in two different ways: (1) eliminate market segments by dropping products or services, or (2) fuse segments that have similar response tendencies. Eliminating products or services forces the segments to satisfy their needs through the remaining offerings. Segments combine or aggregate because specific offerings are not made to each segment. When the retailer combines segments that appear to have similar response tendencies, he or she then develops separate retailing mix strategies for each fused group of segments.

The retailer can use the aggregated strategy to cut costs and improve effectiveness, although it is possible that depth of market penetration may not occur in the combined segments. This strategy offers the retailer with limited resources the possibility of marketing to a number of segments without a drastic change to the standarization of undifferentiated, the cost of differentiated, or the risk of a concentrated strategy.

Conditions appropriate for each of the four strategies vary, but generally the similarities of market segment responses to retailing efforts and the resources of the retailer determine which strategy is most appropriate. Figure 7.3 depicts the four strategies used for a hypothetical six segments. As the figure shows, the strategies are interrelated. The aggregated strategy combines the strengths of the undifferentiated and differentiated strategies, while the concentrated strategy may be viewed as an extreme version of the differentiated strategy.

To illustrate the differences involved in the retailing mix strategies, we can use a hypothetical supermarket example. A supermarket offering a wide range of groceries, produce, meat, and general merchandise, located in high-traffic areas, and emphasizing a general theme such as price or variety would be classified as using an undifferentiated strategy. A differentiated strategy in a supermarket might be reflected in specialized offerings for certain segments, such as a delicatessen for young adult shoppers, hot lunches for blue-collar workers, or special prices on large purchases of meat for large families. Each of these specialized offerings would be promoted and emphasized for each segment. A concentrated strategy might result in a specialized offering of just meat or ethnic food. The supermarket reduces its retail offering to take advantage of the demands of one segment. The aggregated or

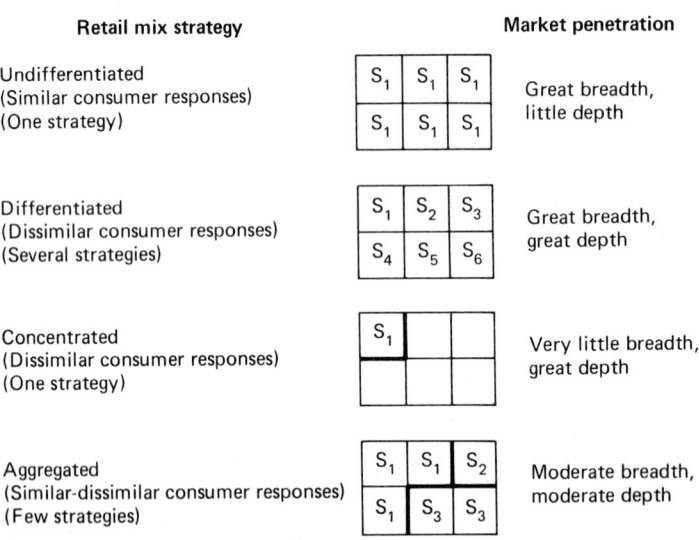

Figure 7.3
Retail mix strategies for six selected market segments

countersegmentation strategy might consist of offering generic grocery products or box stores, both of which combine segments to offer a more general product to the consumer. This short example illustrates how each of the retailing mix strategies is applied and how selection of one strategy affects the functional strategies of location, merchandise, price, and communication.

SUMMARY

This chapter discussed how a retailer proceeds in selecting what members of the market to attempt to attract. After identifying the segments that offer the most opportunity the retailer must determine how many of these segments can be appealed to and how many diverse retailing mixes are necessary to attract them. The text presents specific guidelines for designing appropriate retailing mixes for the chosen segments or target market.

KEY CONCEPTS

Market segmentation

Market opportunity analysis (MOA)

Segmentation process

Segmentation bases

Geographic segmentation

Demographic segmentation

Behavioral segmentation

Benefit segmentation

Majority fallacy

Undifferentiated retailing mix strategy

Differentiated retailing mix strategy

Concentrated retailing mix strategy

Aggregated retailing mix strategy (countersegmentation)

REVIEW QUESTIONS

1. How are market segmentation and market opportunity analysis related?
2. Why should a retailer segment markets?
3. Discuss the market segmentation process and the reasons for organizing it in the manner presented.
4. Discuss the various market segmentation variables relative to measurability, accessibility, and substantiality.
5. What benefits might be sought by college students in a grocery store; department store; clothing store? How might the benefits sought by elderly couples differ?
6. What are the advantages of profiling market segments?
7. Why should a retailer analyze competition in the segmentation process?
8. What is the value of developing hypothetical retailing mixes for each market segment?

9. Why would a retailer select segments on a basis other than profit potential?

10. How do the strategies of undifferentiated, differentiated, concentrated, and aggregated retailing compare with one another?

LEARNING EXERCISES

1. Question three retailers about the market segment(s) that they appeal to. Determine how they chose those market segments. Compare their procedure with the procedure discussed in this chapter. How and why are they different?

2. Determine, through questioning, the most commonly used variables in segmenting markets in retailing groceries; clothing; fast foods; furniture.

DECISION SITUATION 7.1: **BLAIR'S RESTAURANT**

Blair is planning to open a restaurant in her hometown, which has a population of 30,000. After attaining a business degree at the university in the town, Blair took a few restaurant management courses at a trade school and worked for six months in a restaurant in a nearby city. Blair is sure that she can manage the restaurant, but she is not sure of the type of restaurant she wants to open.

The university is the dominant feature of the town. There are about 16,000 students at the university; about half live in dorms, the others in apartments. Only about 1,000 live more than ten miles from the town. Almost half the city residents are connected with the university; 3,000 are employed by the university. The median family income in the city is $27,000. Only 30 percent of the students qualify for financial aid. A study Blair did in a marketing research course indicated that the adult townspeople ate dinner out in the town an average of twenty times a year, about half the time at fast-food restaurants. They typically spent about $12 when they ate in conventional restaurants and $3 when they ate at fast-food restaurants. They ate lunch out an average of six times a month and spent about $3.50 per meal.

Students ate out much more often. Nondormitory students ate dinner out once a week and spent about $5.50 per meal. Dorm students ate dinner out twice a week and spent $6 each time. Dorm students normally ate lunch in the school cafeteria. Nondorm students ate lunch out three times a week and spent $2.50 each meal.

QUESTIONS

1. What other data would you want about these two target markets before deciding on what kind of restaurant to open?

2. Which market do you think is best? Why?

3. What strategies would you use to reach the selected market?

4. Could you appeal to both markets? How?

DECISION SITUATION 7.2: **HENRY'S CASUALS**

Henry has been operating a chain of ten family casual wear shops. Some of the stores are doing well, but several are not. The overall profitability is somewhat disappointing, and Henry is considering several changes for the stores.

Presently Henry tries to sell casual clothes to all buyers in each city where a shop is located. He feels that his medium- to higher-priced lines allow this practice. However, he wonders if it would be advisable to try to divide the total market into segments and try to appeal to one or more of the segments.

QUESTIONS

1. Do you think Henry should segment the market? Why?

2. What basis of segmentation would you recommend to Henry? Why?

3. How would you select a segment or segments of the market as the target market?

NOTES

1. Philip Kotler, *Marketing Management* (Englewood Cliffs, N.J.: Prentice-Hall, 1980), p. 195.

2. Shirley Young, Leland Ott, and Barbara Feigin, "Some Practical Considerations in Market Segmentation," *Journal of Marketing Research,* August 1978, pp. 405–412.

3. David W. Cravens, G. E. Hills, and Robert B. Woodruff, *Marketing Decision Making,* rev. ed. (Homewood, Ill.: Richard D. Irwin, 1980).

4. George Moschis, "Teenagers' Responses to Retailing Stimuli," *Journal of Retailing,* Winter 1978, pp. 80–93.

5. "Going After the Mightiest Market," *Time,* 14 September 1981, pp. 56–61.

6. Jeremy Main, "K-Mart's Plan to Be Born Again, Again," *Fortune,* 21 September 1981, pp. 74–85.

7. Melvin R. Crask, "Department Stores vs. Discount Stores: An Academic's Point of View," in *Competitive Structure in Retail Markets: The Department Store Perspective,* ed. R. W. Stampfl and E. Hirshman (Chicago: American Marketing Association, 1980), pp. 33–42.

8. "Why They Shop Some Centers," *Chain Store Age Executive,* May 1978, pp. 31–35.

9. *Ibid.*

10. Young, Ott, Feigin, *op. cit.,* p. 406.

11. Nariman K. Dahalla and W. H. Mahatto, "Expanding the Scope of Segmentation Research," *Journal of Marketing,* April 1976, pp. 31–34.

12. Young, Ott, Feigin, *op.cit.,* p. 406.

STRATEGIC RETAIL MANAGEMENT MODEL

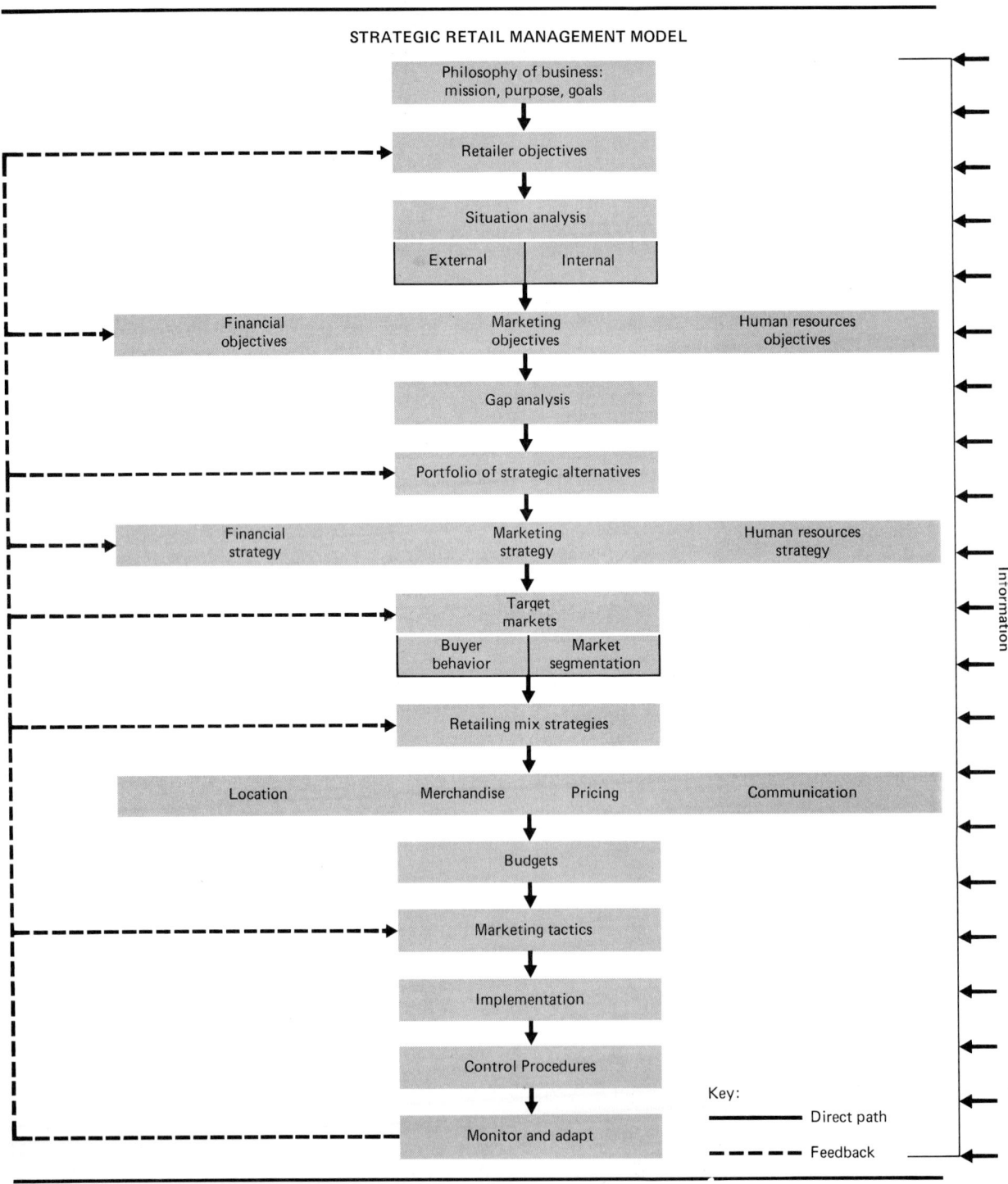

Chapter 8
Information Management

LEARNING OBJECTIVES

1. To develop an appreciation for the role of information management in strategic decision making.

2. To understand the process for information organization and acquisition.

INTRODUCTION

The retailer can make effective decisions only if the appropriate information is available. Effective strategic planning requires that the retailer assemble and organize different types of information from a wide variety of sources. Assembling and organizing information is called **information management**.

Information management bridges the gap between the retailer's environments and strategic planning activities. The role of information management and the retail information system (discussed later in this chapter) is to provide the retailer with input needed to formulate effective strategies. Figure 8.1 demonstrates the overall flow of information in a basic information management system. The retailer uses past experience and information obtained from internal and external sources as an information base for developing retailing strategies. Implemented strategies impact the macro-, task, and organizational environments. Information acquired from the environment provides the retailer with a base for determining the effectiveness of retailing strategies, which in turn becomes part of the information base for future strategies.

Importance of Information Management

Information management is becoming more important to retailers, mainly because of the ever-changing environments to which retailers must adapt. The retail consumer has changed dramatically over the past decade. As we saw in Chapter 4, smaller families, more households, higher incomes, and more single-parent households have become evident during that time. More two-income families have changed retail shopping and purchasing patterns. The implications for retailers in terms of store hours, store layout, merchandise selection, pricing, and other decision areas are enormous. Without information about these consumer changes and about changes in the other environments discussed in Chapters 4, 5, and 6, the retailer would have difficulty making appropriate decisions.

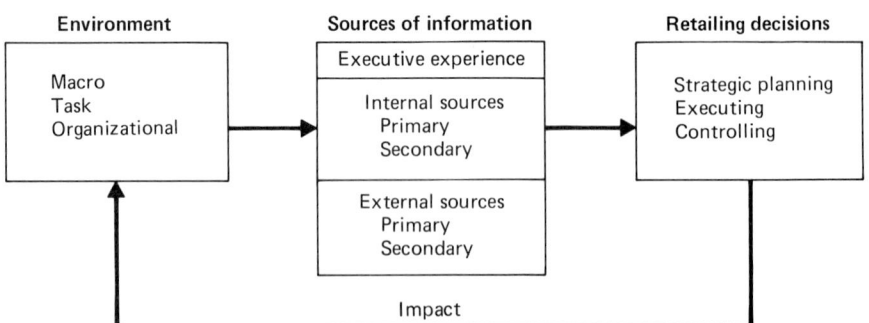

Figure 8.1
Information management system

Source: Adapted from Philip Kotler, *Marketing Management: Analysis, Planning, and Control,* 4th ed., © 1980, p. 603. Reprinted by permission of Prentice-Hall, Inc., Englewood Cliffs, N.J.

STRATEGY IN ACTION 8.1
Using Information

After four years of testing and marketing research, Lowe's, the nation's second-largest retailer of building materials and home-improvement products, has developed a strategy to remodel its stores and expand its geographic base. Lowe's two-year program, RSVP, is a response to consumer shopping preferences obtained from its research efforts. Each store will be redesigned to make it more appealing to the do-it-yourself customer. By altering the store's internal and external appearance, Lowe's is attempting to cater to more of the home-supply industry, which is forecast to grow rapidly in the 1980s. Lowe's further wants to reduce its vulnerability to the economic changes associated with the professional builder and the new-home construction industry.*

I. Magnin, a predominantly women's clothier catering to the affluent, is increasingly expanding into the men's clothing area. Its eventual goal is to "make I. Magnin's name as synonymous with men's wear as it is with women's wear." Based on market research with branded men's wear and I. Magnin's private label, a strategy was developed to make inroads into the men's clothing market through the use of private-label merchandise. The research indicated that I. Magnin's higher-priced private label outsold the competing, branded product. The conclusion was that the customer identifies the I. Magnin name with quality and value for the price; thus the strategic emphasis on private labels.[†]

Source: *Adapted from "Lowe's Proceeds with Ambitious Retrofit Plan," pp. 99–103. Reprinted by permission from *Chain Store Age/Executive* © January 1981. Copyright Lebhar-Friedman, Inc. 425 Park Avenue, New York, NY 10022.
[†]"I. Magnin, an Aggressive Stance." Reprinted from *Retail Week*, 15 March 1981, pp. 18–20.

A second reason for the increasing importance of information management is that retailing itself is changing. New merchandise, new types of stores (computer centers, warehouse grocery stores), and new operating procedures (most involving the computer) were unknown only several years ago. Competitive information about merchandise lines, pricing strategies, and promotional techniques are all necessary for making effective decisions.

The importance of adequate information is illustrated in Strategy in Action 8.1. In the first example, Lowe's used external information sources to redesign its stores. This is an application of a penetration strategy. The second example relates to the use of internal and external information sources to formulate a market development strategy.

Information Management Problems

Most companies, including retailers, have not yet adapted to the intensified information requirements for effective strategic marketing. Information management problems are numerous and they include factors such as (1) inadequate information, (2) wrong type of information, (3) information too late for a decision, (4) information forwarded to the wrong people in the organization, (5) inaccurate method or lack of a method to ensure the accuracy of information, and (6) too much information (information overload).

Many retailers view the information problem as one of inadequate primary information. When a problem arises or a lack of information is identified, often a retailer's initial impulse is to conduct a market survey, sometimes at great expense. In most cases this is an overreaction to the problem that often leads to ineffective use of resources. With proper information management techniques, the retailer's information can be managed more effectively and with less waste of resources.

The essence of strategic retail management is having the appropriate information at the right place, at the right time. Decision making requires combining previous experience with data gathered from external and internal sources. The retailer's personal experience provides concrete, historically tested information and possible solutions to current problems, but experience is limited as a base for retail decision making. First, it is narrow and specific to the individual. While the retailer may experience a wide range of decision-making situations, he or she cannot possibly organize and bring to bear all of this experience at the appropriate time. Even more important, situations and environments change. The correct solution to last year's problem may not be the correct solution today. A changing environment may result in different outcomes for different alternatives, and current information must be combined with the retailer's experience in order to make effective retail decisions.

The remainder of this chapter is organized around the information management decision model depicted in Fig. 8.2. The basic steps are (1) organize the information function, (2) establish information needs, (3) identify sources of information, (4) gather information, and (5) analyze information and make decision.

ORGANIZE THE INFORMATION FUNCTION

The retailer must structure or organize information so it can be retrieved for decision-making purposes. The more organized and accessible information is, the more likely it is that it will be used in decision making by the retailer. A **retailing information system** can be used by the retailer to organize and retrieve information. A retailing information system is a set of well-defined rules, practices, and procedures by which people, equipment, or both operate on given data inputs to generate information according to the needs of retail decision makers in a given business situation.[1]

The information function should be organized to supply information *when it is needed.* Certain information is needed continuously while other information is needed only periodically.

Continuous information is needed for two basic types of problems: routine tactical decisions and long-run strategic planning. Routine decisions are needed for structured problems such as those pertaining to daily operations control and management control activities in order to ensure that resources are employed effectively and efficiently in accomplishing predetermined objectives.

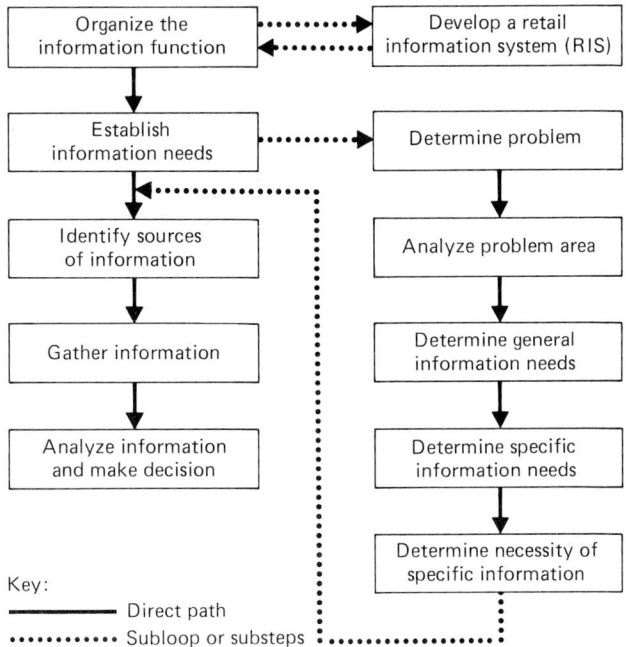

Figure 8.2
Information management decision model

Information for routine decisions is normally available internally (sales, expenses, profit margins, merchandise turnover, inventory levels). This information can be generated daily for each department with a computerized information system.

Continuous information is also needed for long-run strategic planning. We discussed this aspect of the retailing information system in Chapter 4 in relation to scanning and monitoring the environment. In long-run strategic planning, the focus is on external data and includes demographic and economic information, some social, legal, and political information, and possibly information about technology and the natural environment. Continuous information on competition, channels, and other intermediaries should also be provided.

Periodic information is often needed to address special problems. Periodic information is supplied by marketing research, a technique for gathering internal and external data. Marketing research can be used to gather data for almost any type of problem when data in addition to continuous data are needed.

The sophistication of retailing information systems varies according to each retailer's needs. Smaller retailers usually can be served adequately with a relatively simple system *as long as it is organized properly*. Larger retailers can usually benefit from employing a computer-based information system.

Retailers who have developed computer-based retail information systems have experienced other specific benefits in addition to dramatically increased speed and accuracy. They have also noted improved salesperson productivity; improved sales, payroll, and commission data capture; improved inventory management; reductions in sales audit costs, bad debt, inventory levels, markdowns, and shrinkage; and an increase in accounts receivable cash flow. Retailers having computerized information systems include Lerner Shops (a 670-store women's apparel chain), Zayre (a 290-store discount chain), and Dunham's (a 4-store department chain).[2]

Figure 8.3 presents a general format for a computer-based retailing information system. The flow begins with the *retail manager* requesting information from the *computer center* (via a terminal or from computer personnel). The manager may need to make a pricing decision and request

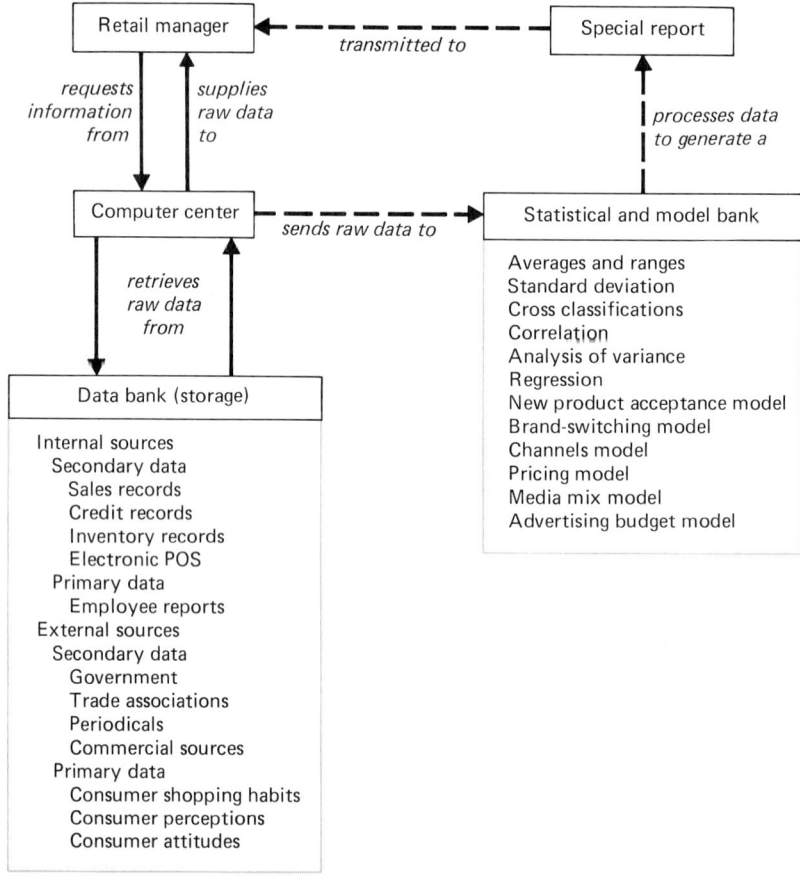

Figure 8.3
Computer-based retail information system

information on merchandise costs and price comparisons with competing retailers. Depending on the nature of the request, the computer center may simply retrieve *raw data* from the *data bank* and transmit it directly to the manager. However, if additional analysis or forecasting is needed, the raw data serve as input to a variety of *statistical packages and models.* This processing stage transforms the raw data into a *special report,* which is transmitted to the retail manager. Examples of special reports include departmental profit comparisons, sales breakdown and comparison by employee, and the relationship between advertising expenditures and sales for the past ten years.

A retailing information system is only as effective as the *quality and quantity* of the information it generates for decision making. Acquiring and storing unnecessary information is a waste of resources, and not storing the appropriate information is just as ineffective. One of the keys to successfully managing information is having the appropriate information available for decision making, and the way to ensure that is to determine what the retailer's information needs are.

ESTABLISH INFORMATION NEEDS

The amount and type of information that can be gathered for retailing decisions are nearly limitless, but not all of the potential information is of equal value in making decisions. Each retailer must determine the amount and type of information to gather, given his or her specific time and financial constraints. This is the core problem in information management: *gathering information appropriate for satisfying the retailer's specific decision needs.*

Figure 8.4 depicts the five-step process that can be used to establish information needs, in this case in making a merchandise turnover decision.

The first step is to *determine the problem* by considering the existing situation, objectives, and alternative courses of action. In the situation depicted in the figure, one of the three major merchandise lines does not meet the turnover objective of 5.0. The alternative courses of action are to make no changes, to add a new line, or to continue searching for another new merchandise line.

Step 2 calls for the retailer to *analyze the problem area.* At this point the retailer has outlined the problem but does not have an adequate structure to determine exactly what information is required to make a decision. This step involves the development of a working model of how turnover occurs and how the retailer can accurately forecast the outcomes of the three alternatives generated in Step 1. While the working model may be crude and simple, it should force the retailer into thinking through the factors that influence turnover and the information that is important to this decision. In Fig. 8.4, since average inventory cannot be decreased, those factors that influence sales must be included. From this perspective, merchandise turn-

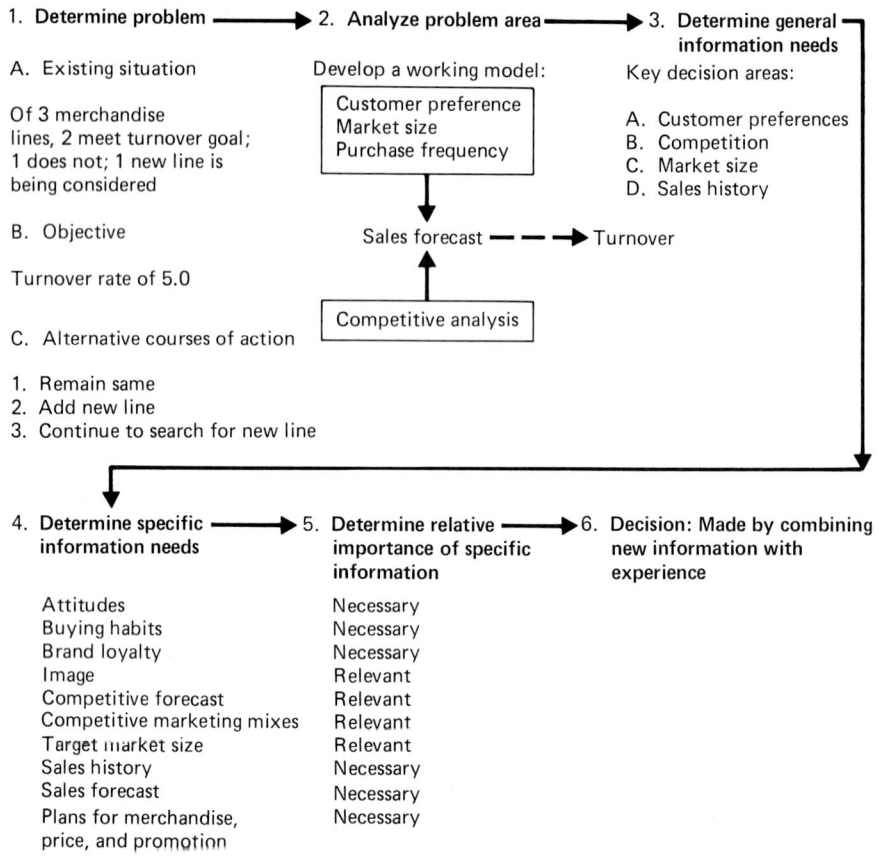

Figure 8.4
Information identification process

over (specifically sales) is influenced by the retailing mix, strength of competitors' retailing mixes, customer preferences, market size, and frequency of purchase. This analysis and modeling give the retailer a rough consumer decision model from which to forecast turnover for new product replacements being considered. For comparison purposes, a consumer preference for the existing product in the merchandise line and a forecast for future turnover figures should be established. Past sales figures would supply this information.

Step 3 involves *determining general information needs*. Once the retailer determines the factors that influence merchandise turnover, he or she has an indication of the general information needed. In the example in Fig. 8.4 the necessary information includes data on retailing mix, competitors' retailing mixes, customer preferences, market size, and sales histories.

Step 4 is to *determine specific information needs*. To identify customer preferences in Fig. 8.4, the retailer must gather information on customer attitudes, buying habits, brand loyalty, and product image. Information should be sought regarding competitors' sales forecasts and competitive retailing mixes for the products in the turnover decision. Market size should be determined through an analysis of the retailer's target market and specific product market. Finally, information concerning the sales history, trends in the product line, and forecast sales for the existing three product lines could be sought.

Step 5 involves *determining the relative importance of specific information*. While the information listed in Step 4 for making the merchandise turnover decision is interesting, it is not all of equal value. Before deciding which information to gather, the retailer should evaluate the relative necessity of each type. In Fig. 8.4, the information determined in Step 4 was categorized in Step 5 as being *necessary*, *relevant*, and *not essential*. The information designated as *necessary* for the turnover decision is customer attitudes, buying habits, and product loyalty; sales histories and forecasts; plans for merchandise, price, and promotion. Other information might be gathered if it is not very costly or time-consuming to acquire.

Essentially, the information identification process forces the retailer to work through the decision and develop a model of the problem and the information necessary for making a decision. Establishing information needs is the foundation for the remaining aspects of information acquisition. The importance of this process to the total information management process cannot be overemphasized. It helps reduce the common information problem encountered by retailers of not having enough information or not having the appropriate information to make a decision. Once the information necessary for making the decision is established, the retailer must determine sources for that information.

IDENTIFY SOURCES OF INFORMATION

Sources of information must be established for at least the necessary and relevant information. Many retailers go directly to expensive sources for information, but in many cases, this is unnecessary and time-consuming.

There are *four sources for information acquisition*. **Internal sources** exist within a retail organization and consist of primary and secondary sources. **External sources** (or sources outside the retail organization) also can be primary or secondary. **Secondary data** are data that were gathered originally for another purpose. **Primary data** are gathered to solve current problems. All four sources can offer the retailer information for decision making and should be considered in problem solving.

A well-organized retailing information system can provide much of the information necessary for making many retailing decisions. It not only organizes information but can also prevent the retailer from gathering unneeded and costly primary data. The information search task should begin with internal secondary sources because they are inexpensive and available.

External secondary sources should be consulted next, followed by internal primary sources. External primary sources are the last sources to pursue because more time and expense are involved. The information search task is complete when sufficient information is available to solve the problem, regardless of whether all sources have been pursued.

Internal Sources

Retailers gather large quantities of internal data to make routine decisions. Figures about sales, inventory, costs, profits, and margins are just a few. Much of these data may not be in the form necessary for decision making but they should not be overlooked as sources of information.

Internal Secondary Sources.   Internal secondary data are plentiful to the retailer, and with some manipulation they can provide a good information base for decision making.

Analyzing *cash register tapes* may provide daily sales information about type of sale, product line, quantity purchased, size of sale, and sales clerk recording the transaction. While this information may be valuable, it is also time-consuming and laborious to compile if done only periodically.

Sales slips or *written customer order forms* provide more complete information than sales tapes. Sales data by order, time, and so on can be gathered. Further information about repeat purchases, location of customers, and related purchases may also be obtained.

Credit records can also be a source of information. Frequency of purchase, location of customers, and other data can be acquired from credit records.

Accounting records, which are readily available and require little manipulation, offer the retailer a source for sales history analysis and forecasting.

An important source of secondary information within the retail store is *previous research* completed for other purposes. Although such studies may not directly concern the existing problem area because of environmental changes, they can provide valuable sources of information, primary-data-gathering designs, and historical perspective for the current problem. At the least they can give some indication of what *not* to do.

Electronic point-of-sale (POS) systems enable the retailer to gather a more comprehensive set of data on a continuous basis. In combination with scanning equipment (UPC or OCR-A), point-of-sale equipment can identify the merchandise item, find the price, record the sale, and provide inventory information for retail decisions. The uses of POS data in retail decision making are limited only by the retailer's imagination. POS data can provide the retailer with information on specific merchandise movement hourly, daily, weekly, by sale time period of any length, and by salesperson. The impact of reducing a price for a day or week can be identified easily using POS data. Evaluating promotion or coupon offers by day, store, geographic location, and other factors can be done. The retailer can have improved inventory control through reduction of the amount of merchandise lost, immediate reordering, and closer approximation of inventory to sales figures. Numerous comparisons by store, department, salesperson, location, credit and cash sales, and regions can be made using POS data. Table 8.1 relates other possible uses for POS data.

A retail publication, *Stores*, suggests that more small retailers are taking advantage of computers. The knowledge required to use computers has become less technical and the advent of minicomputers has made electronic technology accessible and feasible for many small retailers. A retailer can start off with one minicomputer, add on others as he or she can afford them, and eventually have a system equivalent to a large mainframe computer. The minicomputers are easy to operate, and viewscreens, printers, and other options can be added. Such a system produces a variety of merchandising, financial, and personnel reports for management use. Fast-selling items can be tracked down during the work day. Using employee numbers entered during each transaction, the system can develop several types of productivity reports about the salespeople. Time lag in processing data has been cut drastically by such systems.[3]

Westerfield cautions that electronic data processing is not as simple and easy to implement as might be supposed from the previous discussion. He suggests that organizing and administrating the data processing activities are essential. Selecting which functions will benefit most from electronic systems is necessary prior to implementation. It is also necessary to develop staff qualifications to meet the retailer's long-term organizational needs.[4]

Table 8.1
Point-of-sale scanning data as an information source

AREA OF APPLICATION	EXAMPLES
Evaluation of merchandising programs	Product use rates/repeat purchase patterns
	In-store mix of promotions
	Store demographics
	Store-by-store variables
	Drawing board versus execution
Measurement of price elasticity	Size/price relationships
	Incremental price change comparisons
	How price-conscious are customers?
Shelf space allocation	"Equivalization" of data—how important?
	Market size
	Essential product availability
Automated reordering systems	Precision of data
	Merchandise loss factors
	Store-by-store differences

Source: Courtesy A. C. Nielsen Company.

STRATEGY IN ACTION 8.2
Electronic Data for Retail Decisions

F. W. Woolworth Company has installed a distributed data processing (DDP) system to control sending and receiving operations in its distribution centers. The DDP system, which is similar to other retailer's systems, consists of two or more physically distinct processors — minicomputers — that are functionally autonomous but that are dependent on a centralized computer. The DDP system enters, verifies, and processes data close to the user and transmits data between locations only as required. All information is not processed centrally and only that information relevant for each decision area is transmitted to that area.*

Even small retailers have implemented electronic mechanisms to record and analyze data. Bailey's, a men's wear store in New Mexico, purchased a minicomputer several years ago. The results included less time spent on record keeping and savings of $150 per month on banking services. The computer is designed for businesses with annual sales over $100,000. The accounts receivable program includes daily transactions, monthly finance charges, customers' monthly statements, a sales checklist, and month-to-month activity.†

Sources: * Adapted from "DDP Clicks with Chains," pp. 46–47. Reprinted by permission from *Chain Store Age/Executive* © October 1980. Copyright Lebhar-Friedman, Inc. 425 Park Avenue, New York, NY 10022.
† Adapted from "Small Computer Earns Its Way in Small Town Store," *The Office,* July 1978, pp. 81–82.

Internal Primary Sources. Employees of the retail organization are an excellent, but often underutilized, source of information. Salespeople, cashiers, checkers, delivery people, and credit and office personnel all come into contact directly or indirectly with customers. They hear many comments about the store, from pricing to merchandise display. In some cases, criticisms or compliments may be directed to personnel and in other instances they may be overheard or received secondhand. However the comments are received, they may be indicators of success or problems. Certainly a few comments should not necessitate radical change, but this source can provide information for improvement in store operations.

A mechanism for receiving employee information must be developed; it does not occur naturally. Many techniques can be used to encourage employee participation in providing information. Informal methods such as weekly or monthly meetings, conversations, or interviews are possibilities. More formal techniques such as comment forms or a suggestion box may also be used. The retailer must establish that employees' contributions are important and that management is eager to listen. This atmosphere is not easy to create and it may take time and effort to develop it. A bonus may be offered to employees who provide information that results in more effective decisions. At the very least employees' suggestions or information should be acknowledged by management and the effects of the employees' communications made known to them. Employees who feel they have contributed to the retail organization can obtain a great deal of satisfaction. The retailer benefits from this satisfaction in addition to having a good internal source of information.

External Sources   Although internal information is more accessible and often less costly, sources outside the retail organization may have to be consulted to gain adequate information for decision making. External sources run the spectrum from library sources to simulation of customer behavior. External secondary sources should be searched first because they are more available and less expensive than primary sources. If this information, when combined with the internally generated information, is insufficient, external primary sources must be used.

External Secondary Sources.   Secondary data search or usage is normally a part of any research process or retail decision. There is a wealth of information available for the retailer in external secondary sources, much of it at no expense.

The advantages of secondary data include quick access and low costs, they extend the retailer's time and money resources, and they offer information on a scope otherwise unavailable to most retailers.

The problems with secondary data include unavailability of data to meet the retailer's specific needs, different definitions, different units of measure, questionable accuracy, and the time lag between data gathering and the retailer's actual need for the data. In many cases, retail decisions can be made using only secondary data, but the disadvantages of secondary data sources should be kept in mind.

There is an enormous amount of external secondary data available. Government sources (both federal and local) provide a wide range of data specifically oriented toward retail decision making. Federal publications include the *Census of Retail Trade*, compiled in years ending in 2 and 7. (The *Census of Retail Trade*, the *Census of Wholesale Trade*, and the *Census of Selected Services* together make up the *Census of Business*.) Statistics on the type, location, sales, payroll, and size of establishment are part of this census. However useful these census statistics, there is a time lag of three years or so between data gathering and publishing.

The *County and City Data Book* (a supplement to the *Statistical Abstract of the United States*) provides recent figures for county, city standard metropolitan area, and urban-area data on population, vital statistics, sales by type of retail establishment, payroll, and many other items. These data are derived from various censuses and government departments.

Every two years the Department of Commerce publishes *Business Statistics* (a supplement to the *Survey of Current Business*). This volume contains monthly or quarterly data on all of the statistical business indicators for the previous four years and annual data since 1929.

A monthly governmental periodical that provides current statistics on the U.S. economy and its operation is the *Business Conditions Digest*, which contains about six hundred economic time series in a form convenient for business analysis.

A monthly catalog of U.S. government publications is available to interested citizens. The catalog lists many current publications of the federal government. The *Business Service Checklist*, printed weekly by the U.S. Department of Commerce, updates the publications of the Department of Commerce. The annual supplement is an accumulation of the weekly publication.

The Small Business Administration (SBA), a federal agency, publishes a wide range of pamphlets and books that offer management, technical, and marketing advice to small firms. Some of the SBA titles include "Business Plans for Retailers," "Inventory Control," "Furniture Retailing," "Advertising — Retail Stores," and "Starting and Managing a Small Business of Your Own." These publications and a listing of all SBA publications can be obtained from the U.S. Government Printing Office or from SBA field offices throughout the country.

Many local government agencies provide data for retailers without charge. City or county planning commissions can provide demographic data, retail sales data, housing starts, home values, spending patterns, and other data pertaining to the local area. Planning commissions also do forecasting in most of these areas. Traffic departments of local governments can supply data on traffic counts and patterns and projected changes in traffic patterns.

Trade associations offer the retail member a wide variety of information in the form of publications, which are often available to nonmembers for purchase. The National Retail Merchants Association (NRMA), a retail trade association, produces a diversified list of publications for its members. Research studies and management aids are published in the areas of merchandising, information systems, credit management, store planning, security and shrinkage, operating results, and research, among others. NRMA also has a lengthy checklist of subjects for retail planning. Table 8.2 lists some of these checklists.

The American Retail Federation has recently issued a report, "Retailing and the American Economy," that combines information from several documents. Facts on retail sales, retail employment, profit margins, consumer expenditures by type of retailer, taxes paid, and other figures on retail operations are included in this report.

Many trade associations serve the needs of specialized groups of retailers. The Food Marketing Institute, National Home Furnishings Association, National Sporting Goods Association, and Retail Jewelers of America are only a few of such specialized retail trade associations. There are literally hundreds of trade associations; a comprehensive list of them can be found in the *Encyclopedia of Associations*, published by Gale Research Company, Detroit.

Table 8.2
Selected National Retail Merchants Association checklists for retailers

The Art of Sales Forecasting	48 Ways of Merchandising to a Profit	Peak Period Checklist
Bad Check and Counterfeit Money Checklist	Fuel Shortage Guidelines	Personnel Recordkeeping
Blueprint for Strengthening a Weak Department	Grievance Handling and Discipline— The Importance of Documentation	Reducing Controllable Payroll Costs
Checklist on Customer Service— The Salesperson as a Key to the Store's Success	Inventory Taking and Reconciliation	Revised Chart of Accounts for Expenses
	Leased Department and Agreement Checklist	Safety Checklist
Code of Fair Debt Collection Expense	Legal Considerations of the Employment Interview	Selling Energy Conservation to Everyone: A Creative Approach
Deal from Strength, Mr. Small Retailer	Meeting the Consumer Affairs Challenge: A Consumer Affairs Checklist	Store Housekeeping and Maintenance Checklist
Developing a Sound Insurance Program		Supply Conservation Checklist
Effective Ways of Keeping in Stock	Merchandise Inventory Control for Smaller Stores	Television Checklist for Retailers
Energy Conservation Checklist	The Merchant's Checklist for More Profitable Performance	Transportation Checklist and Advice
Equal Employment Opportunity Act		Update on Social Security: Checklist
Equal Pay Act	Motivation: Key to Productivity	Wage and Hour Inspections: Do's and Don'ts
50 Ways to Improve Merchandise Turnover	Open to Buy Systems for Smaller Stores	

Many periodicals provide useful information to retailers. Some concern business in general while others pertain specifically to retailing. The following list is not inclusive but should give the reader a glimpse of the wealth of information available from periodicals. Articles in these periodicals cover such topics as strategic planning, market segmentation, pricing, advertising effectiveness, store location, personnel policies, and many others. Depending on the individual source, the articles may have a theoretical perspective, such those in the *Journal of Marketing Research* or *Journal of Retailing*, or a practical orientation using specific business examples, such those in *Business Week, Chain Store Age Executive,* and *Retail Week.* Table 8.3 gives some of the major periodicals, with a short description of the orientation of each one.

A retailer may often require the services of private organizations to gather data for decision making. In some cases the charges for these services may be considerable; this points out the importance of determining exactly what information is necessary to make a decision. Commercial data can be purchased from various private organizations. Table 8.4 gives a partial list of these firms and the types of information they supply.

Guides or indexes provide an excellent starting point in the search for external secondary data. The following guides are available in most libraries: *Business Periodicals Index, Sources of Business Information, Data Sources for Business and Market Analysis,* and *Marketing Information*

Table 8.3
Periodical sources of external secondary data

Advertising Age: Weekly magazine of advertising, with applications to retailing

Business Week: Weekly magazine, with articles on all phases of business

Chain Store Age Executive: Monthly magazine catering to chain store information

Dun's Review: Monthly periodical analyzing current topics in business

Forbes: Biweekly publication that discusses industries, companies, business personalities, and investments

Fortune: Semimonthly magazine, with articles on all phases of business

Journal of Advertising Research: Bimonthly that includes articles on advertising in retailing

Harvard Business Review: Bimonthly publication with articles on all aspects of business

Journal of Marketing: Quarterly concerned with developments in all areas of marketing

Journal of Marketing Research: Quarterly dealing with research developments in all areas of marketing

Journal of Personal Selling and Sales Management Semiannual publication with articles on sales and sales management effectiveness

Journal of Retailing: Quarterly covering developments in all aspects of retailing

Marketing Times: Bimonthly publication presenting current marketing topics

Progressive Grocer: Monthly publication emphasizing trends in food retailing

Retail Week: Biweekly periodical presenting articles on trends in retail product categories and current topics in retailing

Sales and Marketing Management: Monthly publication of interest to retailers; contains an annual survey of buyer power by county (based on income, retail sales, and population in each county)

Stores: Monthly publication with emphasis on store management

Other periodicals: Regular publications for retailers in areas such as hardware, supermarkets, franchise, furniture, and department stores

Source: Reprinted with permission of Macmillan Publishing Co., Inc. from *Retail Management* by Barry Berman and Joel R. Evans, p. 170. Copyright © 1979 by Macmillan Publishing Co., Inc. Adapted from the original.

Guide. Goeldner and Disks have written an informational article entitled "Business Facts: Where to Find Them," which appeared in *MSU Business Topics.*[5] This article is another excellent source with which to begin a secondary information search.

External Primary Sources. Data gathered specifically to solve a particular problem or make a current decision can come from a variety of sources. Although suppliers and competitors can be valuable sources of primary data, consumers are the most common external primary data sources.

Primary data offer the retailer both advantages and disadvantages as sources of information. Basically, the advantages and disadvantages of primary data are opposites of those of secondary sources. The advantages center on the timeliness of the data and ability to control measuring techniques, method of data gathering, information sample, and overall accuracy of the research. Disadvantages of external primary sources include the cost and

Table 8.4
Commercial sources of external secondary data and decision information

SOURCES	USE OF DATA
A. C. Nielsen: Conducts a retail index service; generates continuous data on food, drug, cosmetic, tobacco, toiletry, other products sold in food stores and drugstores.	Market share based on consumer purchases, changing market share, evaluation of price and promotion changes
Audits and surveys: Provide physical audits of merchandise in stores.	Merchandise line of competition, merchandise movement
Market Research Corporation of America: Examines purchasing behavior via a large consumer panel; computes consumer and store data.	Consumer habits, changes, demographic relationships to purchases, geographical purchases
R. L. Polk: Provides mailing lists and automobile registrations.	New automobile purchasers, related products*
Selling Area—Marketing, Inc. (SAMI): Gathers information on flow of products to retail outlets.	Market share based on channel movement, effectiveness of promotion on movement of merchandise*
Standard Rate and Data Service: Collects information on advertising rates for various media; consumer data include income, retail sales, etc.	Information on advertising rates and costs, media usage for advertising and segmentation
Dun and Bradstreet, Inc.: Information about specific customers and credit ratings.	Extension of credit
Daniel Starch and Staff: Magazine and newspaper readership data.	Awareness and impact of advertising*
American Market Research Bureau: Target Group Index covers purchase, usage, and demographics and psychographics for 400 product categories.	Demographic and psychographic consumer segmentation, identification of purchasing and usage behavior*

*More applicable to large retailers.

Source: Reprinted with permission of Macmillan Publishing Co., Inc. from *Retail Management* by Barry Berman and Joel R. Evans, p. 170. Copyright © 1979 by Macmillan Publishing Co., Inc. Adapted from the original.

time involved in gathering the data and limitations in research scope that the retailer can undertake.

External primary data sources should be the final information source utilized. If the secondary sources and internal primary sources are insufficient in providing adequate information, then gathering external primary data will be required.

GATHER INFORMATION

A fully operational retailing information system facilitates the gathering of most types of information. Gathering external primary data requires additional time and activities. The four basic methods for gathering external primary data are survey, observation, experimentation, and simulation.

Survey Method

The **survey method** is a technique whereby information is gathered from respondents through the communication process. Because of the versatility of the survey method it is the most common technique used by retailers. Survey information is gathered by personal interview, telephone, or mail. Some type of questionnaire is usually developed as a mechanism for gathering survey data.

Survey Data–Collection Methods

Survey Data–Collection Methods. The **personal interview,** a face-to-face method, makes it possible to gather a wide range of data, to get considerable detail, and to ask a number of questions. A higher response rate is obtained from personal interviews than from telephone or mail techniques. On the negative side, the personal interview is expensive and *interviewer bias* is possible, especially if untrained interviewers are used.

The **telephone survey** is relatively inexpensive and requires a short time to gather data. It allows person-to-person contact for explanation and probing in the questioning process, but the time allotted to the interview must be kept short because of the possibility of the respondent terminating the interview by hanging up the telephone. Of course, certain types of information, such as picture interpretation, cannot be obtained using the telephone. The telephone does offer a quick, inexpensive method for gathering simple types of information.

Mail questionnaires offer the retailer the possibility of reaching nearly all respondents over a wide geographical area. Economy and versatility make mail questionnaires a widely used technique. Interviewer bias is also eliminated. Problems do exist with mail questionnaires, including the following: obtaining addresses or mailing lists for sampling, the relative shortness of the questionnaire to ensure interest on the part of the respondent, inability to probe and explain questions, and nonresponse rates that run as high as 80 percent or more for some surveys. This introduces problems of *nonresponse bias,* or bias against those not answering the questionnaire. It is entirely possible that those answering a questionnaire are more interested in the subject, more educated, or more articulate. Their responses may not be similar to nonrespondents' answers and may give the retailer erroneous data for decision making. A number of methods can be used to decrease nonresponse, such as introductory letters, personally addressed questionnaires, stamped return envelopes, incentives (money, coupons, gifts, contest entry), assurance of anonymity, and, if possible, short easy questions and answers.

Each survey method has strengths and limitations. The choice of a data-collection technique is often a compromise between cost, time, and accuracy. Certain data requirements must be met for effective decision making and they should form the bases on which to select a data-gathering technique. The need for highly accurate information may dictate the use of an expensive technique such as personal interviewing. Time requirements must be lengthened accordingly. If budget constraints are quite restrictive, the telephone may be the most appropriate method. The retailer must keep in mind the objective of the primary research process — accurate data for decision making — in choosing a survey method.

Questionnaire Design. The organization and design of the questionnaire follows from the information required and the data-gathering method chosen. The questionnaire design must focus on obtaining the appropriate information in as clearly interpretable a form as possible.

Two major design issues involve questionnaire structure and level of disguise. **Questionnaire structure** refers to the degree of standardization of the questions. A highly structured questionnaire consists of questions and allowed responses predetermined by the researcher. A highly unstructured questionnaire involves little predetermination of answers. The questions asked are less definite and may even be developed during the data-gathering process.

Questionnaire disguise refers to how apparent the purpose of the questionnaire is to the respondent. A disguised questionnaire is one in which the purpose of the study is hidden from the respondent. Nondisguised questionnaires consist of direct questions concerning the research topic.

The retailer has four possible structure/disguise combinations to choose from: structured/disguised, structured/nondisguised, unstructured/disguised, and unstructured/nondisguised. These relationships are illustrated in Fig. 8.5.

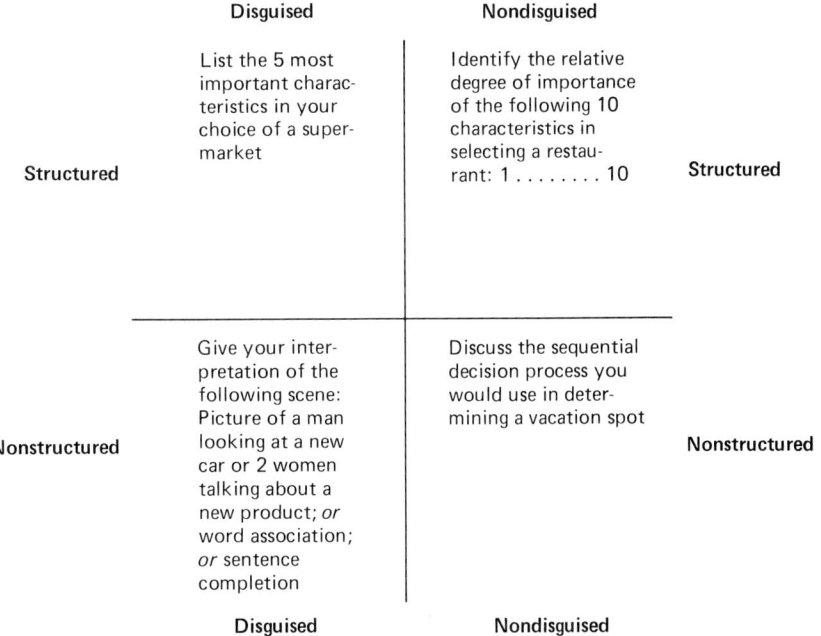

Figure 8.5
Structure and disguise relationships in questionnaire design

The disguised questionnaire may be used when the consumer does not know the information at the conscious level or is unwilling to provide it. In most situations, however, nondisguised questions can be used.

A structured questionnaire is appropriate when the specific information is known and the options are straightforward. If time is restricted, a structured questionnaire can use the time most efficiently. A structured questionnaire is appropriate, for example, for determining how far shoppers drive to shop at a retail store. Unstructured questionnaires are suitable in situations where the expected answers are not well defined.

Each type of questionnaire can be effective depending on the specific situation. Identifying the reseach situation and consumer's possible answers dictates the selection of the questionnaire design.

Measurement Techniques.   The effectiveness of a questionnaire will greatly affect the quality of data gathering. Poorly worded questions, leading questions, and broad, open-ended questions may not give the retailer information for decision making but only result in an inefficient use of resources. Use of proven techniques can decrease the incidence of wasted effort. Many of the studies retailers conduct are attitude studies. There are several widely accepted attitude measuring techniques, including semantic differential, Likert scales, and multidimensional scales.

The **semantic differential** is a technique consisting of two bipolar adjectives anchoring a seven-point scale. Figure 8.6 gives an example of a semantic differential. This indirect technique for measuring attitude has had wide use in retailing to measure store images, merchandise, personnel, store appearance, and other aspects. The semantic differential has a number of advantages, including efficiency and ease in obtaining attitude data from a large sample. Attitudes can also be measured in both direction and intensity. A set of responses can provide a comprehensive picture of the respon-

---

STRATEGY IN ACTION 8.3

Using Attitude Research: Retailer Images

Hamburgers—a 23 unit, Baltimore-based mostly men's specialty chain—has expanded rapidly within the past few years and needed reassurance their image had not been altered by the rapid expansion through acquisition process. Within the past four years Hamburgers had acquired a three-store operation in Delaware, a six-store specialty business in New England, and had plans to open three new stores of their own in the Baltimore area. They engaged a marketing research firm to determine whether their image of a quality clothier was still intact after the many recent changes. Survey methods using attitude measuring techniques were used to gather the data. Fortunately, the research indicated the image of a quality store still existed among consumers.

Source: "Expanding a Classy Name." Reprinted from *Retail Week,* 15 April 1981, pp. 24–32.

dent's attitude toward the subject. The technique can be replicated, which makes it possible to detect changes in trends such as store image.

A second popular method of gathering attitude data is the use of **Likert scales.** These scales are constructed by developing a statement and asking the respondent to indicate the response, ranging from strongly agree to strongly disagree, that best reflects his or her attitude. Figure 8.6 also includes an example of a Likert scale. Likert scales are popular because they are easy and quick to construct. This technique is a "summated scale," which means the respondent's attitude is determined by adding the scores from all of the items. By comparing respondents' scores, the retail decision maker can use the Likert scale as a quantitative method of analysis.

The semantic differential and Likert techniques are unidimensional methods of attitude measurement. Unidimensional techniques may not be sufficient in some instances to describe a consumer's attitude. A technique known as **multidimensional scaling** has been developed to measure more complex issues and has received growing recognition in retailing. The problem of identifying competitor's positioning in the competitive audit (Fig. 5.2) was an example of the use of multidimensional scaling. The procedure for developing the multidimensional space is quite complex and is based on the respondent's selecting similar pairs of objects, say stores or products, and ranking preferences among those objects.

Figure 8.6
Semantic differential and Likert scales

SEMANTIC DIFFERENTIAL

Well-known store	— — — — — —	Unknown store
Items easy to find	— — — — — —	Items difficult to find
Clean	— — — — — —	Dirty
Convenient	— — — — — —	Inconvenient
Courteous personnel	— — — — — —	Discourteous personnel
Low prices	— — — — — —	High prices

LIKERT SCALES

* 1. This store has helpful salespeople.
      Strongly agree   Agree   Neutral   Disagree   Strongly disagree

   2. This store carries well-known brands.
      Strongly agree   Agree   Neutral   Disagree   Strongly disagree

   3. This store has informative advertising.
      Strongly agree   Agree   Neutral   Disagree   Strongly disagree

   4. I have a difficult time finding a parking place at this store.
      Strongly agree   Agree   Neutral   Disagree   Strongly disagree

* 5. This store has courteous salespeople.
      Strongly agree   Agree   Neutral   Disagree   Strongly disagree

*Questions 1 and 5 can be summed to determine the customer's attitude toward the retailer's sales personnel.

Sampling. In order to gather primary data, the retailer must select respondents to answer the survey questionnaire. Collecting data from all possible respondents (a census) is too costly and time-consuming, but a sampling of the population is appropriate. The manner in which the sample is selected will influence the representativeness of the data collected.

A sample selection procedure known as *probability sampling* gives each member of the population a chance of being selected. While this procedure is complex and time-consuming, it gives the retailer answers that are representative of the actual population. *Nonprobability sampling* may be more convenient and less costly, but it does not have the accuracy of a probability sample. Table 8.5 provides a short description of the two types of sampling.

As a matter of practice, many retailers rely on *store or shopping center intercepts* (that is, talking to people face to face at a store or shopping center) to gather primary data. The advantages of this method are low expense and speed. However, if it is carried out ineffectively the intercept method can result in poor data and misinformation. Sudman contends that the sampling techniques for most retailers using the intercept method are nonprobability methods, which do not represent the actual behavior or feelings of the store or shopping center population.[6]

Taking precautions can improve the quality of the data gathered via the intercept method. Sudman recommends a cluster sampling technique to identify the various shopping areas at which sampling can take place. Choosing where and when to sample the selected clusters (shopping centers) must be determined. Sampling near the entrance of the shopping center or store is recommended because respondent cooperation will be higher at that point and less bias will result. The sampling time is also of primary

Table 8.5
Selected sampling techniques

Probability Sampling Techniques

1. *Simple random sample:* Select from list of population on a random basis (for example, give every credit customer a number and then select numbers from a random number table).

2. *Stratified random sample:* Group population into subsets; select from subsets (strata) of population on a random basis (for example, stratify population by sex and randomly select a certain number of males and of females to survey).

3. *Cluster sampling:* Group population into subsets; select subsets (clusters) to sample.

Nonprobability Sampling Techniques

1. *Convenience sample:* Select sample at convenience of interviewer ("person on the street" or whoever is convenient to interview).

2. *Judgment sample:* Select a sample based on judgment of expert (retailer may select people representing "typical customer").

3. *Quota sample:* Select sample in proportion to some population characteristic(s) (quota by sex, income, age to represent population characteristics by sex, income, and age).

importance in reducing bias. Sampling days and times might be selected randomly. Bias could otherwise result simply because different shopping habits would bring certain types of customers to the center or store on particular days or at particular times. The final precaution is to weigh the data for how often the respondent shops and to develop an estimate of nonshoppers' behavior. These precautions are not expensive or time-consuming, and they can greatly improve the quality of the data gathered using the intercept method.

Observation Method

A research technique quite applicable to the retail situation is **observation**. Rather than questioning respondents, the observation technique employs simple recording of behavior. Observing the consumer can be done personally or with mechanical devices.

Respondent cooperation is not required, and interviewer and questioning biases are not present in the observation method. Observation does, however, limit sample selection because the respondents must be part of the setting being observed and only limited information can be gathered because no questioning is involved.

Personal Observation.   Personal observation involves watching and recording consumers' behavior while not interacting with them. The observer may pretend to be stocking shelves or pose as a customer in order to observe others' behavior. This direct observation can be used to determine shopping patterns or movement in the store. Some researchers have used this technique to observe child-parent interaction in selecting cereals. Traffic counts are commonly done using this method.

Mechanical Observation.   Data can also be gathered using mechanical techniques such as movie cameras that film consumer behavior or salesperson-consumer interaction or electronic sensors for making traffic counts.

Unobstrusive Observation.   Another useful method for data gathering is observing things rather than people. Periodically observing the number of free samples or coupons taken in a time period or observing the carpet or tile wear to determine traffic patterns are some uses of unobtrusive measures.

Experiments

An **experiment** is used as a data-gathering technique to establish a cause-and-effect relationship. Factors can be manipulated under controlled conditions to allow the desired relationship to be tested. For example, the price could be changed on a product from $1.99 to $1.69 for one week to see the effects this has on sales of the product. All other factors such as advertising, shelf location, and personal selling would remain constant over the one-week period. By isolating the cause (price) and effect (sales), a relationship between the two can be established. Sales from the previous week would be compared with sales during the experimental week to measure the effect of the price change. Similar experiments could be undertaken with shelf location, store displays, store hours, advertising, and so on.

While experiments have an advantage over the survey and observation methods for testing cause and effect, experiments are not easily conducted in retailing. High costs, artificiality, and problems in controlling for all extraneous variables in the experimental setting make experiments difficult to conduct.

Simulation

Simulation techniques offer the retailer exciting potential for analyzing retail systems or processes. Simulation is the process of conducting experiments on a model of a system, a model being anything used to represent reality. The essentials of simulation are (1) a mathematical model of the process or system being studied and (2) a sample of inputs.[7] The inputs may be actual data or hypothetical data. Changes are entered into the simulation system to determine the effect on the system or process. In most cases the simulation is computer-based. Examples of the use of simulation in retailing are bank-teller scheduling, design of inventory reorder rules, and parking facility design. In simulation of bank-teller scheduling, the changes entered into the model would be variations in the number of customers requiring service and the results would show the changes required in scheduling tellers.

Research Specialists

Because many retailers, especially small retailers, lack the time, money, and/or detailed knowledge necessary to gather primary data, specialists or retailing research agencies are sometimes hired by retailers. Selection of the appropriate specialist is important for the retailer because of the wide range of services offered and because of the varying ability of different specialists to relate to the retailer's specific problem-solving needs. Some outside specialists offer services covering the whole spectrum of retail decision making from analyzing problems through recommending solutions. Other specialists offer a very narrow range of services, perhaps limiting their offerings to data gathering or designing a questionnaire. As with gathering primary data, the retailer should not contract for more services than are necessary or for an insufficient amount of services. Table 8.6 provides some guidelines to the retailer in selecting a research specialist.

While hiring a research specialist may be expensive, it is a better method than attempting to gather data with only partial knowledge of the

Table 8.6
Guidelines for selecting a research specialist

1. Identify service offerings (from specialist) and select only those relevant to problems.
2. Consult other retailers or firms about reputation.
3. Request samples of previous research.
4. Identify specifically what will and will not be done by the specialist.
5. Request a detailed outline with time estimates before agreeing to service.
6. Request a presentation of proposed research.

process, which can waste time and money. The key is to acquire additional information when it is needed for improved retail decision making.

MAKE THE RETAIL DECISION

The purpose of acquiring information is to enlarge the retailer's information base. Once the information has been acquired, whether from internal sources or external sources, the retail decision maker must apply it to the problem and select the best alternative solution. The quality of the decision a retailer makes is only as good as the information on which the decision is based. It is vitally important to the retailer to acquire and organize, through a retailing information system, the most relevant and essential information for decision making. The information function should be viewed as any other retailing function in terms of strategic planning and management. A planned orderly acquisition of retailing information will greatly facilitate the retailer's ability to develop strategic retailing decisions in the other functional areas.

SUMMARY

Information management is a way of integrating new information with existing information. The retailing information system enables the retailer to bring various pieces of information together in an organized manner for effective decision making. Recalling sales figures and employee performance while adding newly acquired information on customer attitudes provides tremendous capability to the retail decision maker.

In a sophisticated retailing information system, countless possibilities for data manipulation exist for the retailer. The capabilities of the retailing information system offer the retailer greatly expanded information bases for decision making. The retailer must constantly adapt to the changing environment, and the higher the quality of information the retailer has about the environment, the better his or her retail decisions will be.

KEY CONCEPTS

Information management	Mail questionnaire
Retailing information system	Questionnaire design
Internal information sources	Questionnaire structure
External information sources	Questionnaire disguise
Secondary information sources	Semantic differential
Primary information sources	Likert scales
Survey method	Multidimensional scaling
Personal interview	Sampling
Telephone survey	Observation

Personal observation   Experiments
Mechanical observation   Simulation
Unobtrusive observation

REVIEW QUESTIONS

1. What is the relationship between strategic planning and information management?
2. Explain the value of a retailing information system to a retailer.
3. Although it is valuable in making decisions, why isn't the retailer's experience sufficient for decision making?
4. Explain how the retailer decides what information to gather for decision making.
5. Why should the retailer go to internal secondary sources first and external primary sources last?
6. How will the use of electronic point-of-sale equipment aid the retailer's decision making?
7. What are the advantages of external secondary sources? Disadvantages?
8. Describe situations in which the survey method, observation, experimentation, and simulation would be appropriate.
9. What are the advantages and disadvantages of the personal interview, telephone survey, and mail questionnaire?
10. What are the advantages of probability sampling over nonprobability sampling?

LEARNING EXERCISES

1. Contact three local retailers, each in a separate store classification. Determine how each retailer manages the information function.
2. Select two retailers using electronic POS equipment. Determine how they have used the new data generated by their systems in making retail decisions.
3. Design a questionnaire to determine the store image of a local supermarket, department store, and discount store.

DECISION SITUATION 8.1: **MICK'S**

Mick's is a chain of 12 children's wear shops. The owner, Mick, wants to find out what kind of store image the shops have, and she contacted a research firm to see what the cost of a research project would be.

The firm's proposal was to conduct two hundred interviews at each branch store using an intercept methodology. An individual hired by the research firm would stand at the store and question customers as they entered. A semantic differential on twenty-five items would be used to gather raw data. Extensive demographic data would also be gathered on all respondents. The cost of this study is $3 per interview plus $3,000 for the analysis of the data.

QUESTIONS

1. What major problems do you see with the proposal as presented?

2. Can internal sources yield any of the data that the research firm plans to collect?

3. Do you think Mick should accept the research proposal?

4. What changes, if any, would you recommend in the proposal?

DECISION SITUATION 8.2: **DARYL'S MARKETS**

Daryl recently placed scanning checkouts in his fifteen grocery stores. He is now reaping many benefits but apparently not all that are possible.

Daryl has a set of reports prepared each night by the computer. The reports make a stack about six inches high and, so far, he has not made it through the entire report. As a result, he has missed some information that could have helped his decision making.

Another problem is that some personnel are not using the data. For instance, buyers are making little use of the computer. They still count items in their departments and buy as they always have. One of their complaints is that it takes longer to "figure out" the report than it does to order the old way. Daryl sometimes feels the same way himself.

QUESTIONS

1. Does Daryl have a good information management system? Why or why not?

2. What changes would you recommend in the reports Daryl receives?

3. What would you do about employees who do not use the computer? Why do you think they refuse to use the data?

NOTES

1. Donald F. Heany, *Development of Information Systems* (New York: Ronald Press, 1968), p. 7.

2. "MIS: Finding What You Need," *Chain Store Age Executive*, April 1981, pp. 46–48.

3. Marian Burk, "Mini Computers: Who Needs Them?" *Stores*, October 1978, pp. 26–28.

4. William U. Westerfield, "Avoid EDP Surprises," *Chain Store Age Executive*, December 1980, p. 11.

5. C. R. Goeldner and L. M. Disks, "Business Facts: Where to Find Them," *MSU Business Topics*, Summer 1976, pp. 23–26.

6. Seymour Sudman, "Improving the Quality of Shopping Center Sampling," *Journal of Marketing Research*, November 1980, pp. 423–431.

7. William C. Emory, *Business Research Methods* (Homewood, Ill.: Richard D. Irwin, 1976), p. 322.

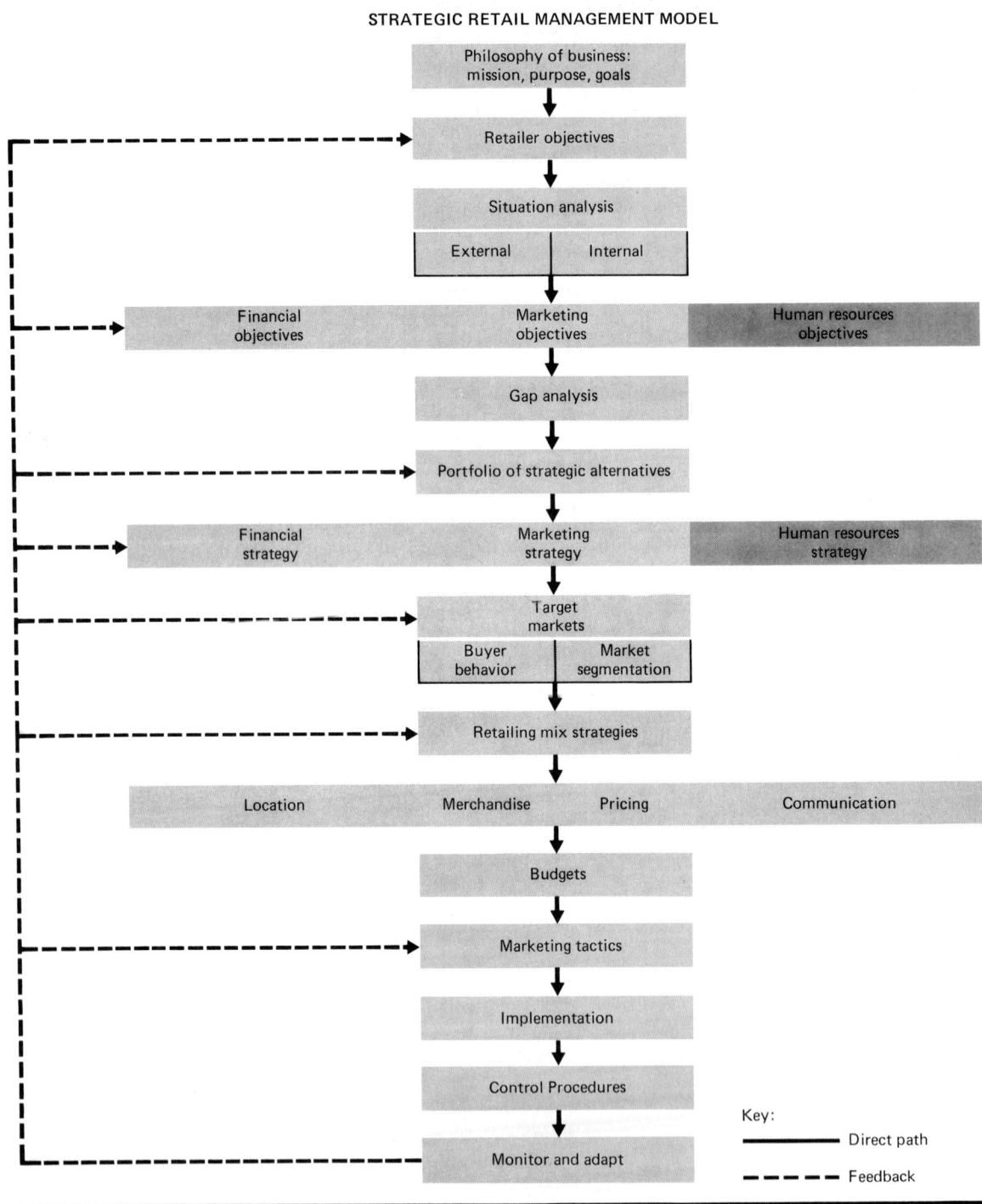

STRATEGIC RETAIL MANAGEMENT MODEL

Philosophy of business:
mission, purpose, goals

Retailer objectives

Situation analysis

| External | Internal |

| Financial objectives | Marketing objectives | Human resources objectives |

Gap analysis

Portfolio of strategic alternatives

| Financial strategy | Marketing strategy | Human resources strategy |

Target markets

| Buyer behavior | Market segmentation |

Retailing mix strategies

| Location | Merchandise | Pricing | Communication |

Budgets

Marketing tactics

Implementation

Control Procedures

Monitor and adapt

Key:
——— Direct path
– – – Feedback

Chapter 9
Human Resource Decisions

LEARNING OBJECTIVES

1. To understand the role and importance of strategic human resource planning.

2. To understand the planning processes necessary for organizing and staffing a retail organization.

INTRODUCTION

Having the right personnel and handling them correctly are necessary ingredients for retailing survival and success. The retailer's strategies, policies, and procedures are implemented by *people*. The best-laid plans cannot be effective without effective personnel.

Organizing, selecting, and training of personnel should be considered an integral part of the strategic planning process. Far too often, retailers map strategies, policies, and procedures with little regard to the people involved in retailing. Plans may be made that totally disregard the people who must carry out those plans. Conversely, people may be hired with little thought of their ability to adequately implement plans. Human resources, like any other resource, must be allocated in a way that allows the store's objectives to be achieved.

To minimize the risks associated with improperly organizing, hiring, and training personnel, the sequential decision model shown in Fig. 9.1 is recommended. This process focuses on determining *what* is needed from personnel and then determining *how* to obtain performance. The specific steps in the process are the following:

1.   Review all other plans.

2.   Determine the goals of organizing.

3.   Select the type of organization.

4.   Determine the organizational relationships.

5.   Determine the human resource goals.

6.   Determine personnel policies and procedures.

7.   Determine the type and number of employees.

8.   Hire the needed employees.

9.   Train the employees.

10.   Evaluate the employees.

11.   Monitor and adapt.

As with any process, following these steps does not guarantee good personnel, but the process should help achieve a reasonable congruency between human resources and the retailer's overall strategic plans.

REVIEW ALL OTHER PLANS

The strategic human resource plans must be compatible with the retailer's other strategies and plans. The target market definition, for example, may influence the type of sales force needed. Consider a retailer who specializes

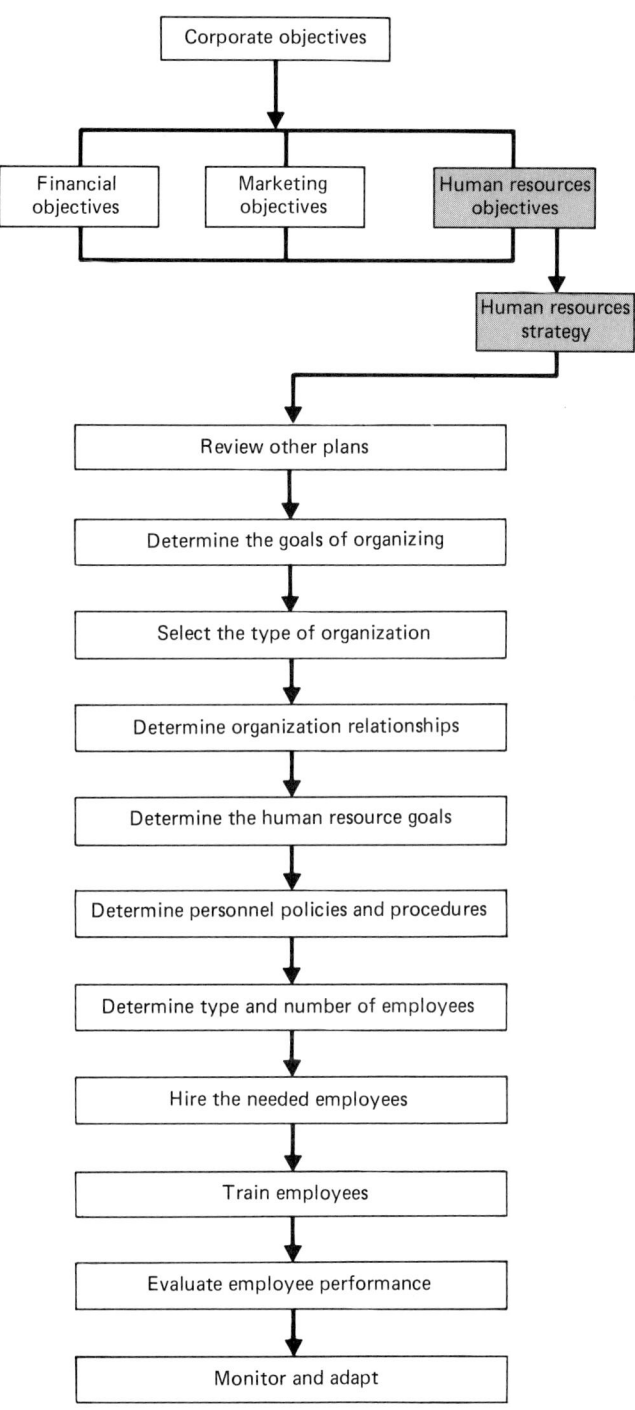

Figure 9.1
Human resource decision model

in jeans for high school and college students; for compatibility with custom-ers, the retailer should probably hire mostly high school and college students.

The products carried can also influence the type of employees needed. A retailer of high-quality sound systems probably needs more knowledgeable salespeople than a retailer who sells ordinary radios and stereos.

A retailer must also consider the desired image of the store in determining human resource practices. If a clothing retailer desires a high-quality, high-priced, conservative image, personnel who can and will portray that image should be recruited. Other factors that must be examined include financial constraints, community characteristics, and the available labor pool.

Retailers often change strategies but fail to make adjustments in organizational structure or personnel. Any change in strategy should be followed by a review of the store's human resources to determine whether they still fit in with the new strategy.

DETERMINE THE GOALS OF ORGANIZING

After reviewing other strategic plans, the retailer should determine the goals of organizing, the second step in human resource planning. *Organizing* can be defined as

> activities in the managing process which consist of selecting and combining suitable resources (personnel and capital) and integrating them into a structure of relationships that enables [retailers] to carry out the planned activities in a coordinated and controlled way.[1]

This chapter focuses specifically on the organization of personnel (rather than of capital). The basic reason for organizing is to provide a structure through which the management of activities can occur. The resulting **organizational structure,** which defines the authority and responsibility of a store's personnel, can aid or hinder the achievement of the retailer's other goals.

To help ensure that the structure is appropriate, the retailer must determine specific goals of organizing. Several different organizational forms can achieve the basic goal of providing a vehicle through which to manage or control retail activities. One major determinant of an appropriate structure is whether the retailer prefers centralized or decentralized management.

Centralized versus Decentralized Control

Retailers must determine the level at which various decisions will be made in the retail organization. If the major decisions are made by relatively few people at higher levels, **centralized control** is being practiced. When decision-making authority is more widely dispersed throughout the organization, **decentralized control** is being used.

The centralized versus decentralized decision is particularly important to chain stores. In these multiunit organizations, the issue is whether decisions will be made at the home office or at the individual stores. If close coordination and similarity are desired (such as that necessary to portray a consistent nationwide image), centralized control is called for. If a chain has good, competent store managers and serves a wide geographical area, decentralized control has an advantage because each manager is familiar with local market conditions.

Different chains have tried varying degrees of centralization, with varying degrees of success. Opportunities for centralization are likely to increase as better individual store data become more readily available from the expanded use of computers.

The retailer's control objective helps shape the organizational structure. If centralized control is desired, the firm's headquarters will have relatively more managers than if decentralized control is desired. Conversely, decentralized control calls for an organization with smaller headquarters staff and somewhat larger staff at the individual stores. Note that this issue has little impact on operating employees. A related, though different, concept that does affect operating employees is whether tight or loose control is a goal.

Tight versus Loose Control

A retailer must determine the degree of control desired, primarily regarding employees. There are many variables to consider when making this decision.[2]

Tight control offers several advantages to the retailer, most revolving around the potential for achieving a high degree of internal coordination. Retailers who use part-time or noncareer personnel are likely to need relatively tight control. Some jobs, such as a cashier, might also require more direct supervision. A problem with tight control is that it can inhibit employee development.

The primary advantage of **loose control** is enhanced employee development owing to greater involvement with and control over assigned duties. Many retailers complain that employees, including management employees, do not have enough initiative. Using loose control tends to foster more initiative among employees. The major problem with loose control is that employees may make mistakes or not perform tasks exactly as the retailer might like. The retailer must therefore make a trade-off between coordination and employee development.

The decision regarding degree of control has a direct impact on the retail organizational structure. Tight control requires that a manager have relatively fewer employees to supervise, and, consequently, more layers of management are required.

There are other goals that should be enumerated for organizing a particular store. Including the determination of goals for organizing in the human resource planning process provides a starting point. No structure

Reorganizing Sears

What will the acquisition of Coldwell Banker—the country's largest real estate sales firm—mean to Sears?

"It's like chicken soup," says Stu Robbins, retail analyst for Paine Webber. "It can't hurt. But it's not expected that Coldwell Banker's real estate knowledge will markedly change either Sears expansion strategy or the economics of that expansion."

"From Sears's point of view, Coldwell Banker is small potatoes," observes Dave Taylor, an analyst for Donaldson, Lufkin and Jenrette. "Coldwell Banker had less than $6 million in net income last year, compared with $600 million for Sears. There's not going to be a lot of impact on the bottom line."

On the other hand, the merger could mean worlds of opportunity to Coldwell Banker. For one thing, the real estate company will have access to Sear's prodigious credit card holders' lists, which include more than half the households in the United States. Every one of those households is a prospective client for Coldwell Banker, which owes 35% of its $346 million in revenues in the fiscal year ended January 30, 1981, to residential real estate transactions.

Also, both Sears and Coldwell Banker have experimented with video merchandising techniques. Sears took part in a test in Coral Gables, Florida, and has big plans for video, while the real estate broker is engaged in an electronic sales program in Los Angeles. More than one industry observer has pointed to the benefits that should accrue to Coldwell Banker as Sears further develops its video capabilities, which already include a videodisc version of its catalog.

"What Sears is positioning itself for is a complete circle of homeowner services," says analyst Bernard Sosnick of Rothschild Unterberg Towbin. "Sears will be able to provide not only a new house, through Coldwell Banker, but also mortgage financing, homeowners' insurance, home improvement merchandise, a new washing machine and the credit to buy the washing machine."

"The fact that this is all possible on a national basis is significant," says Taylor. "You may be able to walk into a Sears store or an Allstate office and arrange to sell your house in the East—while looking for another one somewhere else. It seems that there will be some link-up to Allstate—it makes sense."

"What this tells me is that Sears's management now wants to capitalize on its good will and established organizations," says analyst John Landschulz of Mesirow and Company. "Of course, this rests on the assumption that they have control of their current operation—but they do."

"Obviously, they are looking for a synergistic effect," says Michael Kelly, president and CEO of The Center Cos., a Minneapolis-based shopping center developer. "It's hard to say what form it will take, but there will certainly be changes. Change is a natural part of any merger."

The selection of C. Wesley Poulson, Coldwell's chairman, as the replacement for Preston Martin as chairman and CEO of Seraco, Sears's real estate and financial services subsidiary, is one indication that Kelly is right. But Coldwell's precise post-merger relationship with Homart, the mall developer within Seraco, is still a subject for speculation.

Coldwell Banker has not been heavily involved with shopping center tenanting. For a while, the company worked closely with Ernest W. Hahn, the El Segundo, California-based developer, but it is not known primarily as a broker of retail space.

Of the $169 million in commercial real estate revenues that Coldwell amassed in fiscal 1981, only $46.2 million was attributed to non-office building activities. Although this was up 14% from $40.4 million the year before, it still represented only 13.4% of total corporate revenues.

"I don't think Sears will want to shape Coldwell Banker into more of a shopping center broker. I don't think management looks at it that way," says Landschulz. "The action is in office complexes right now. The acquisition will help to broaden Sears' real estate business. Coldwell Banker should complement Homart, but they are really different businesses."

According to Kelly, however, developers are keeping a watchful eye on the situation, expecting that some integration of capabilities between Homart and Coldwell Banker is a good bet. After all, Coldwell Banker is expert at securing new tenants, property maintenance, supervision, and accounting—all areas which have come to the fore as the result of the slowdown in new center development. Even if nothing more than advice is exchanged, the interaction should be beneficial to both real estate entities.

The hope is that the whole will become greater than the sum of its parts, but the new and improved Sears is far from a fait accompli. It still remains for management to determine exactly how integration will be effected, and where, and when.

"Video sales of private homes, for instance, will require some pretty centralized operations," says Landschulz. "I think Sears has the organization to handle it—but Sears will have to decide whether the use of video is a distinct advantage over current methods."

Nor will such *complex integration* take place overnight, says Landschulz. "It's going to take time for these acquisitions to fold in and really develop, but Coldwell Banker and Dean Witter will be the growth elements within Sears."

"Sears will feel its way along with Coldwell Banker," says Stu Robbins. "Sears will be slow to alter a good thing. It's already the largest real estate broker in the country, but Coldwell Banker has very fine management. There won't be any massive changes."

"Sears will basically continue to let Coldwell Banker do its own thing," agrees David Taylor, "which it has done very successfully. There is the potential for some opportunistic link-ups, but you won't see them right away. Sears may create a task force to study the possibilities, or start with some experimentation in 1982. But things won't fall into place until 1983, and that's speculation."

Source: "Chicken Soup and Small Potatoes," pp. 71–72. Reprinted by permission from *Chain Store Age Executive,* © January 1982. Copyright Lebhar-Friedman, Inc. 425 Park Avenue, New York, NY 10022.

can be set until the goals for the structure are understood. Setting these goals begins to shape the organization. With these goals firmly in mind, the retailer is ready to consider the various structural alternatives.

SELECT THE TYPE OF ORGANIZATION

The third step in human resource planning is to select the type of organization to establish. A retailer can choose from several different types of organizational structures, according to how the store is departmentalized or divided for managerial purposes. Although any of the types discussed below can be used in a retail operation, the *needs* of the particular retailer should be the determining factor.

One excellent method of analyzing the organizational needs of the business is the **stage method.**[3] The stage method involves examining the complexity of the business and selecting a structure capable of handling that complexity without being too complex itself.

Thompson and Strickland identify four stages of operational complexity, ranging from a simple owner-operator business to large, multiunit, multiproduct, multimarket enterprises. Table 9.1 contains brief descriptions of the four stages. Stage I businesses need only the simplest type of structure. Stage IV retailers need more complex structures and, in fact, usually must combine several types, as discussed below.

The principal point of the stage method is that the structure should be no more complex than is necessary for smooth operation. A store that is managed by the owner and has eight employees can have a very simple structure—the owner on one level and eight subordinates on a second level. A retailer as complex as Sears requires a complex structure and many layers of management.

Although analysis using the stage method can help a retailer determine a general type of structure, it does not determine the specific type of organization to use. Selecting the best specific structure is predicated on a thorough understanding of the various specific types, which include functional, geographic, product, matrix, and hybrid organizations. (As you read the following sections, bear in mind that most retailers combine two or more of these structural types to form a *hybrid* structure.) Figure 9.2 presents examples of several types of organizational structures.

Functional Organization

As the name implies, a **functional organization** is structured according to the functional activities required. A retail store organized around divisions such as operations, merchandising, and credit is an example of a functionally organized store (see Fig. 9.2A). Almost all retailers other than the smallest are at least partially organized by function.

Table 9.1
Organizational stages

STAGE	DESCRIPTION
I	Small, owner-operated business (Bill's Pharmacy, Brad's Shoes); usually the owner is the only real decision maker.
II	Large single-unit retail store; usually more than one decison maker, often called department or division manager.
III	Regional or local chain consisting of several stores; usually more than one *layer* of mid-level managers; some managers are at the corporate or home store and others at the various units.
IV	Nationwide or worldwide retailers; multiple layers of specialized and general managers; normally there are corporate, regional, and local managers; some managers will be in specialized areas (credit, accounting, etc.) while others will be general merchandising and operating managers (Sears, K mart, J. C. Penney are examples of this stage).

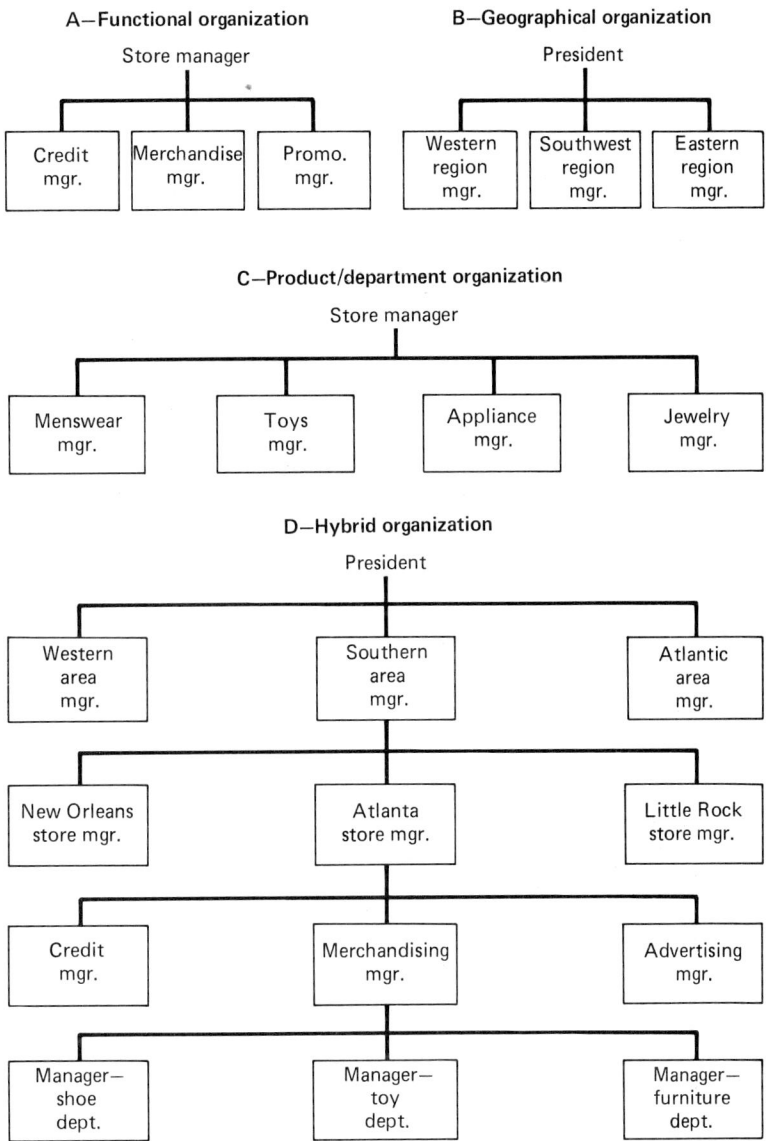

Figure 9.2
Sample organization charts

A key advantage of functional organization is that it allows specialization in each functional area (for example, an expert in consumer credit may handle all credit operations). This specialization can also cause certain problems, primarily when the specialized personnel are not able or willing to comprehend the interrelationships and trade-offs necessary between the various functional areas. The credit manager may institute tight credit policies and procedures that are good for the performance of the credit area, but those responsible for merchandising efforts might insist on looser credit policies to attract a wider target market. Such conflicts are inevitable in most functionally organized firms; when conflicts are allowed to mature, the functional organization becomes the antithesis of a strategically managed store. Most of these conflicts can be solved effectively if special care is taken to see that functional managers understand the overall organization and realize that their area does not operate in a void.

Geographic Organization

Retail firms with widely scattered units normally must develop a **geographic organization** structure. If a geographic structure is needed, each unit can operate independently or various units can be combined into territories or regions. A purely geographical structure is not usually possible; some other structure must also be used. Figure 9.2B presents an example for geographic organization.

An advantage of the geographic organization is that the unit or regional managers are in a better position than are headquarters personnel to understand local customers. Coordination of plans and activities between units or regions is usually the primary problem. The advantages and disadvantages of this type of structure are related to those discussed under centralized/decentralized control earlier in this chapter.

Product or Departmental Organization

A **product (or departmental) organization** is one that is organized according to product types. Departments such as men's wear, women's wear, and appliances, (Fig. 9.2C) are common in product organization. The product structure is used to organize the merchandising operations of almost all retail stores. Note that the pure form of this structure (wherein each department handles all planning and operations functions) is seldom used.

A key advantage of the product organization is that each departmental manager can become extremely familiar with the department's operations and merchandising situation. Unless coordinated effectively, problems can develop regarding the interrelationships between departments. Merchandise decisions in women's wear, for example, also affect the men's wear department; the store would have difficulty maintaining a high-quality image in women's wear and an inexpensive image in men's wear.

The *boutique structure* is a special form of product organization, but boutiques are designed according to *customer shopping patterns*. A store may put all equipment related to jogging in a "jogging boutique" instead of scattering the merchandise in a variety of departments such as shoes, clothing, and sporting goods. Similarly, a store might put all children's clothes, shoes, furniture, and toys into a children's boutique. This type of organization can work well because it is designed around the customer's shopping habits. It enhances suggestion selling and allows better coordination of offerings in groups.

**Matrix
Organization**

A **matrix organization** is one that attempts to combine the advantages of functional and product organizations. Figure 9.3 presents a diagram of a matrix organization. The matrix structure is a relatively new organization type that offers some distinct advantages and disadvantages.

The primary advantage of the matrix organization is that every decision area has a specialist in a control position. For a decision involving credit procedures for appliances, the credit manager can give directions for the credit aspects, while the appliance department manager can provide input regarding the credit procedure's impact on appliance merchandising. The key disadvantage is that every employee has more than one boss. This problem can be minimized if authority and responsibility are clearly defined for all the managers and the managers do not try to usurp other managers' authority and responsibility. Better managers are a definite prerequisite for an effective matrix structure.

**Hybrid
Organization**

Few retailers can be organized using only one of the pure types. Retailers that utilize more than one type of structure are creating **hybrid organization** (see Fig. 9.2D). A large retailer may have a functional structure at the top, a geographic structure at the middle level, a functional/product structure at the operating level, and a matrix structure for special projects and decisions. Overall, this retailer has a hybrid organization structure.

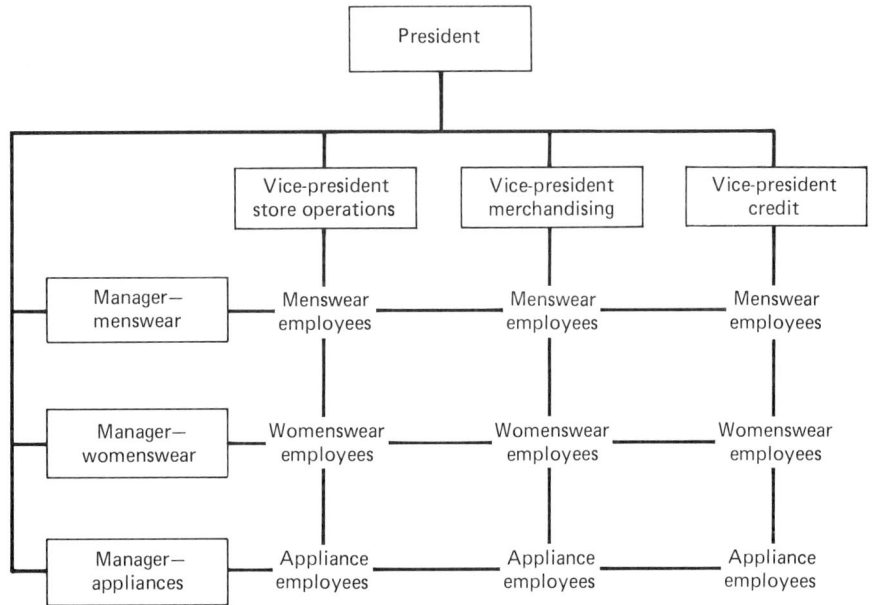

**Figure 9.3
Matrix organization**

To develop an effective hybrid organization, the retailer must consider the needs and goals of organizing for the entire business and also for each level or division within the organization. A retail operation of any size will in most cases have to use a hybrid structure to take advantage of the strong points of each pure type and to minimize the disadvantages. One hybrid structure developed specifically for retailing is called the Mazur plan.

The **Mazur plan** has served as the retail version of a hybrid organization since the 1920s. Although many modifications to the original plan have evolved, the basic features of the plan are still incorporated into the organizational structure of many retailers. A diagram of the basic Mazur plan is shown in Fig. 9.4. The basic Mazur plan can be easily adjusted to include factors such as multiple-unit operations and specialized departments. The Mazur plan can be used for each store in a retail chain, with the position Store Manager becoming Store Manager, Store A.

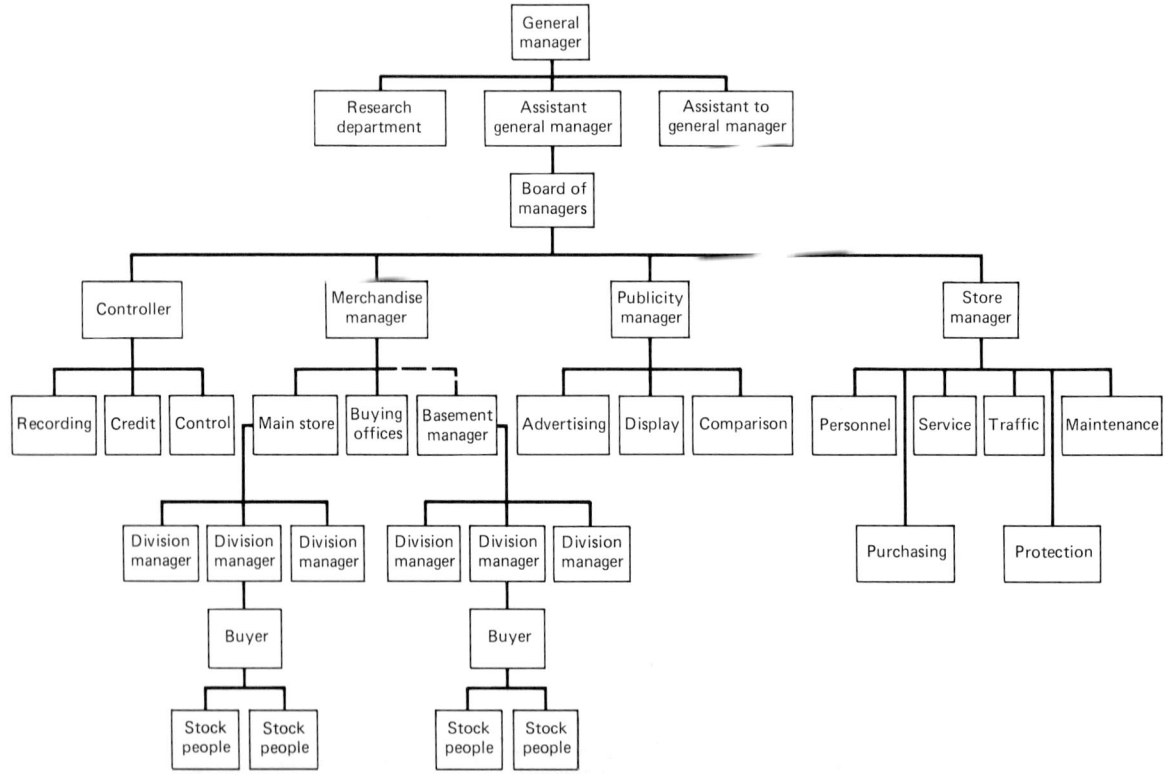

Figure 9.4
The Mazur plan of retail organization
Source: After Paul Mazur, *Principles of Organization Applied to Modern Retailing* (New York, Harper & Brothers, 1927), frontispiece.

DETERMINE THE ORGANIZATIONAL RELATIONSHIPS

The fourth step in human resource planning is to determine the organizational relationships desired by the retailer. The retailer must select the organization that is most appropriate in light of his or her goals, size, and complexity. The determination of the type of organizational structure to use leads to formally structuring the organizational relationships.

Formal organization is the name given to the structure of an organization's positions and relationships. Once the type of organization has been determined the general structure of the formal organization is set, with some adjustments for specific positions and relationships. A retailer should make whatever changes are necessary in the formal structure to achieve his or her specific goals.

Too often small retailers do not specifically define their formal organization, but all retailers, even small ones, should draw up a chart of their organization. The chart is a diagram of managerial interrelationships. Formal organization charts result in responsibility assignments and make it easy to identify gaps in the structure. Even if a chart is used to depict the management structure, various problems can arise as a result of the informal organization.

The **informal organization** refers to the power relationships that exist in a retail organization. It exists in all businesses and can and should be influenced by retailers. A retailer can help determine who will have power beyond the authority relationships defined by the formal structure.

Once the desired organization (both formal and informal) is determined, a retailer is in a better position to select personnel because the organizational structure helps determine the specific requirements for each position. But some other activities must occur before good hiring decisions can be made.

DETERMINE THE HUMAN RESOURCE GOALS

The fifth step in human resource planning (and the first step leading to the actual hiring of employees) is to determine the human resource goals. There are many factors to be considered in establishing these goals. The retailer should be sure that the review of other plans, the first step in human resource planning, has been completed. Many of those plans and strategies have a direct impact on the human resource goals. A retailer who desires to be a full-service, prestigious specialty store would need more competent and knowledgeable personnel than would a self-service, bargain-price retailer.

In addition to goals regarding the desired characteristics of personnel, the retailer should establish goals about the treatment and handling of employees. Goal statements of this type include salary, stability of employments, requirements for promotion, and the like.[4]

DETERMINE PERSONNEL POLICIES AND PROCEDURES

It is important that a retailer determine personnel policies and procedures *before* personnel are hired. The policies and procedures should influence the hiring process and may actually be a selling point in hiring the right personnel.

Written Policies

Personnel policies that are known only to people in the personnel area are not particularly effective. A *policy manual* is an excellent vehicle for distributing this information to employees. All personnel policies may not be included in the manual (salaries, for instance, might not be included), but most items should be covered. The purpose of the manual is to avoid problems and misunderstandings that can result from lack of communication about the policies.

Three issues that should be included in the personnel manual are *fringe benefits, promotion opportunities and requirements,* and *grievance procedures.* Consider an employee who thinks that all employees get a two-week vacation each year because a co-worker had a two-week vacation. If employees must have five years' service to get a two-week vacation and the employee in question only has one year of service, a misunderstanding could occur that could result in ill will and possibly even loss of the employee. If leave policy is explained in a manual, a misunderstanding is less likely. The reasons for including promotion opportunities and requirements and grievance or complaint handling are similar—to avoid misunderstandings that may hinder the work effort.

Many other items can be included in the personnel manual.[5] When constructing a manual, the retailer should analyze manuals prepared by other businesses, especially other retailers. Particular attention should be devoted to sections that deal with personnel problems the retailer has previously experienced.

Compensation

The retailer should determine the appropriate compensation structure before employees are hired. From the retailer's perspective, a good compensation plan is simple to administer, is reasonable in terms of costs and benefits, and facilitates control of employees. From the employee's perspective, the compensation plan should provide a regular income, reward for above-average performance, and fairness.[6] Although compensation levels for specific positions may not be determined at this point, the retailer should establish salary *ranges* for the various positions. The organizational structure determined earlier provides some guidance in selecting salary ranges.

Four factors that should be considered when establishing compensation plans are (1) the quality of employees desired, (2) prevailing local wage rates, (3) the type of compensation plans established, and (4) legal requirements. The first two factors are fairly straightforward. A retailer will normally have to pay higher wages for better employees and meet prevailing area wage rates. The other two factors can be a bit more complex.

There are three basic types of compensation plans: straight salary, straight commission, and a combination of salary and commission. *Straight salary* means that the employee is paid according to some measure of time ($4.25 per hour, $1,100 per month). It is most often used for management, clerical personnel, and salespeople who are expected to perform many non-selling duties.

Straight commission plans typically pay employees some fixed percentage of sales volume or profits. Although commission plans can provide greater motivation in certain circumstances, they can create problems such as employees not wanting to perform duties that are not directly related to the duties on which commissions are based.

The *combination salary and commission* plans pay a specified amount based on time and a commission based on sales or profits. These plans offer a good compromise to retailers, but they can become a source of irritation if they are poorly conceived. The retailer must consider what duties employees are expected to perform when selecting the compensation plan for the organization.

Two primary legal considerations are minimum wage and the Equal Employment Opportunity Commission (EEOC).[7] The part of minimum-wage laws that causes the most trouble for retailers involves white-collar or exempt employees. These employees are exempt from minimum-wage and particularly overtime standards. To be exempt, an employee must earn a minimum salary ($155 per week in 1980) and perform some supervisory or managerial duties. Some retailers violate the rules by calling all employees management so that they can avoid paying overtime rates.

EEOC regulations specify that employers give equal pay for equal work. Although a simple regulation, it has caused many problems for retailers. A central issue is determining what constitutes equal work. A firm must document that individuals who receive different salaries actually perform different work. This can be done by carefully preparing the job description. Retail firms, which typically employ many women, must stay informed concerning current developments in the area of equal opportunity regulations. When setting specific wages retailers must be careful not to place women and other minorities at the low end of the range.

DETERMINE THE TYPE AND NUMBER OF EMPLOYEES

The organizational structure selected by the retailer largely determines both the number and the type of employees to hire. The seventh step of the strategic human resource planning process involves a more complete definition of the number of employees to hire and the qualities to look for in those employees.

Task analysis and the preparation of job descriptions can be very helpful in determining the type and number of employees. These tools are presently underutilized in retailing.

Task Analysis

Task analysis is an analysis of the store's operations in order to define and describe all of the tasks or activities that must be performed. Examples of tasks required in most retail stores include stocking, greeting customers, wrapping or bagging merchandise, and marking merchandise.

Task analysis usually begins with a broad perspective of overall operations and gradually becomes more and more detailed until specific activities are defined. The retailer might first consider the key functional areas of buying, merchandising, accounting and credit, and so on, and define the specific tasks necessary in each area.

Once the tasks are defined, they must be divided into groups of activities that can be handled by individual employees. These groupings form the basis of the job descriptions.

Job Description

Task analysis leads directly to **job description.** Each position within the firm should have a description of the requirements for that job and all of the activities that the person hired in that position will have to perform. Table 9.2 contains two job descriptions. (Another example is provided later in Table 12.1.)

Job descriptions are very important for several reasons. First, they aid in the proper hiring and placement of employees. Second, they may be helpful if an equal rights suit is brought against the firm. Job descriptions may be used to define equal jobs. (Note that the salesclerk positions in

Table 9.2
Sample job descriptions

JOB	LEVEL	DUTIES
Salesclerk (Toy Department)	I	Greet customers who enter toy area.
		Help customers make toy selection.
		Check inventory of electronic games.
		Check customers' purchases.
		Handle minor complaints and returns.
		Direct customers to customer service area for major complaints and returns.
		Help keep aisles clear of merchandise.
		Help clean checkout area.
Salesclerk (Toy Department)	II	Greet customers who enter toy area.
		Help customers make toy selection.
		Direct customers to Salesclerk I for checkout.
		Help keep aisles clear of merchandise.
		Get electronic games from storage as directed.

Table 9.2 are similar but different enough to have different salaries.) The retailer should be very careful in writing up job descriptions and should accurately portray every position. If one employee with a similar job title is given extra duties and a higher salary, those duties should be written into the job desciption to explain why that employee makes more money. Third, the job description is necessary when introducing an employee to a job. Fourth, superior-subordinate relationships are identified in the job descriptions. Once the descriptions have been completed, the personnel department should be ready to begin hiring employees.

HIRE THE NEEDED EMPLOYEES

If a retailer has followed the recommended procedure to this point, the eighth step in the human resource planning process, the hiring of employees, should be fairly easy to complete. An organization that has a well-defined structure and job descriptions faces a simplified hiring task. The retailer knows the kinds of employees that are needed before entering the personnel market.

There are six major steps in the employee hiring process: (1) determine the source of employees, (2) determine the methods to reach potential applicants, (3) have the prospective employees complete application forms, (4) interview the applicants, (5) investigate the applicants' backgrounds, and (6) make the selection decision.

Determine Sources of Employees

The information contained in the various job descriptions should give a retailer a good idea of the sources to use for recruiting employees. Some positions require certain education levels; the retailer will know from the job descriptions whether to recruit at universities, junior colleges, or high schools. The retailer can also investigate the local labor pool; if local applicants do not have adequate qualifications, the retailer will have to expand the search. Often the retailer needs several different education levels and both local and nonlocal labor. Once the sources of potential employees are determined, the retailer needs to analyze the alternative methods for reaching them.

Determine Methods to Reach Potential Applicants

The sources or locations of prospective employees determine the methods necessary for reaching them. If the retailer has determined that a college degree is mandatory for an entry-level position, the retailer may begin recruiting on university campuses. Not all positions will need college graduates and the retailer will find other methods for recruiting for those positions.

At one time, many retailers' entire recruiting effort consisted of simply putting a "Help Wanted" sign in the window. This practice is still appropriate for some positions, but the problem with this practice is that the retailer

STRATEGY IN ACTION 9.2

Retail Hiring, Revisited

The skills required for retail managers are rapidly changing, and this is reflected in the type of credentials sought by retailers hiring new management trainees. An ideal candidate for a retail management position is "aggressive, dynamic, a high-energy self-starter, has some mathematical ability and a genuine desire to get into the field." The retail manager of tomorrow will also need an ability to analyze and interpret information quickly.

To attract people with these combinations of skills, retailers are increasingly seeking college graduates and MBAs. These two groups have historically shown little interest in retailing careers, but things are changing. As retailers are seeking management trainees with increased levels of education, college graduates appear to show increased interest in retailing.

A variety of reasons have been identified to explain these changes, including increased salaries and "career-pathing." The top-level MBA attains salary levels in the upper-twenty- to lower-thirty-thousand-dollar range as a retail trainee. Career-pathing seems to be the key, however, to attracting highly qualified MBAs. This means the path on which the trainee moves is well defined and usually designated in a particular time frame. One of the greatest incentives a retailer can offer an MBA is the projection of where that person will be in five or ten years.

During the early 1970s many large retailers hired a number of MBAs, only to see many resign. Retailers believe the changes they have made in their training programs and the increased sophistication of retail management make it unlikely that history will be repeated.

Source: Adapted from Lisa Keith, "The Renaissance Retailer." Reprinted from *Retail Week,* 15 March 1981, pp. 22–24.

is not actually recruiting employees—the applicant must come to the retailer. Good employees may be difficult to find this way. The most common recruiting method used by retailers is newspaper advertising.

Once the retailer knows the type of employees needed, he or she should find and utilize the methods capable of reaching those people. Specific methods necessary to reach various types of potential employees are discussed in more detail in the Glasser text.[8]

Have Prospective Employees Complete Applications

It is important that all prospective employees complete an application. The retailer needs certain information about all job applicants. Equal rights laws require that information be maintained about certain categories of applicants, regardless of whether they are hired. Beyond the legal requirements, retailers should keep a complete list of those people who have applied. Even if the retailers cannot hire an individual at the time of application, the application should be kept on file for future reference.

A normal application blank that can be bought at many business supply houses will suffice for most retailers. Any special information that an individual retailer needs can be included in the standard form. A retailer should be careful to avoid asking for information that violates EEOC regulations. Some information that should definitely be sought includes past work experience, education, and references.[9]

**Interview
Applicants**

All potential employees not rejected because of information on the application should be interviewed. The interview may be thought of as an extension of the application, a chance for the retailer to gain additional information and insight about the applicants. Since employees help form the retailer's image, relevant factors such as appearance and personality can be examined during the personal interview. Retailers must also comply with EEOC regulations during the interview.[10] The interview can also be used to convince the applicant of the benefits of working for the retailer.

Information to Seek. One important piece of information to make note of during the interview is the appearance of the applicant. Other information must also be ascertained. Very often the retailer can at least partially determine the attitudes of the applicant, his or her aspirations, and an indication of whether the applicant intends to be an interim or permanent employee. This latter point is especially critical if the position requires substantial training and investment.

The applicant should also be given a chance to elaborate on any points that were inadequately covered on the application blank, such as why he or she left previous jobs. Most applicants can give more information during the interview than they can write on a standard application form. Although the personal interview is helpful in determining the quality of an applicant, there are some problem areas with personal interviews that must be considered.

Potential Problem Areas. The primary problem with personal interviews involves requesting information that is not considered legal under the EEOC guidelines. The retailer cannot directly ask applicants if they intend to get married or have children and other similar questions. Although many retailers do ask these types of questions, they may be viewed as discriminatory and should be avoided. This type of information may be provided voluntarily by an applicant. In fact, one way of conducting a personal interview is to ask as few direct questions as possible and allow the applicant to volunteer information.

Another problem area involves the lack of a written record of what was said. An applicant may not tell the complete truth in the personal interview, and it is more difficult to verify accuracy of information supplied orally. If a manager does not ask illegal questions and verifies as much as possible the answers obtained during the interview, the interview itself can be a tremendous aid in selecting good employees. It cannot and should not be used alone; rather, it should be used in conjunction with other tools and activities.

**Investigate
Applicant's
Background**

Before any hiring decision is made, the retailer should investigate each applicant's background. Part of this investigation should be focused on verifying the information contained on the application blank and gained through the personal interview. This background check should be as complete as possible. Certainly all previous employers should be asked about the applicant, conviction records should be examined, and educational data should be checked. This does not mean an applicant who has received a bad recommendation from a previous employer or who has a conviction record in the past should be immediately ruled out. Depending on the circumstances, such people may make excellent employees. The investigation should go as far back as possible so the retailer can gain an understanding of what to expect from the applicant on the job.

An actual example may help describe some of the problems a retailer can have if a good background investigation is not conducted. The owner of a small pharmacy in Louisiana hired a new pharmacist after calling only his present employer. The owner felt that that reference and the application information were good enough to make the applicant a job offer. The new pharmacist turned out to be a terrible worker. He frequently filled prescriptions incorrectly and even forgot to lock the store at closing time the first time he was left alone by the owner. Additional investigation revealed that the pharmacist was considered incompetent by all previous employers. The good recommendation was given by a pharmacy owner who wanted to rid himself of an incompetent worker. A thorough investigation of *all* previous employers would have relieved the owner of the onerous task of firing a middle-aged man with several children.

Make the
Selection Decision

After the retailer has gained sufficient information about an applicant, he or she can make the selection decision. This decision is much easier if the retailer has followed the human resource planning process. The retailer should compare the particular job description to the applicants' qualifications for the position. There may be no perfect fits, and the retailer may have to determine what constitutes a "close enough" fit. The retailer may find that several applicants are "close enough." This subjective decision can be improved and made more objective if the retailer knows exactly what skills the store needs and what skills the applicants possess.

Many retailers view selection decisions as having only two outcomes — hire the applicant or do not hire the applicant. Actually, the retailer may decide not to hire the applicant for the present position but to file the application for future consideration. Applicants who have good, but not presently needed, qualifications can be handled this way. The file can be a good source for previously screened potential employees.

If the retailer makes the decision to hire an applicant, the applicant must be assimilated into the work force. This usually involves some type of training.

TRAIN THE EMPLOYEES

Retail training programs often leave much to be desired, especially those for non-management personnel. Department stores in one study were found to spend an average of only 12.5 hours on training salespeople. Almost half of that time (6 hours) was spent teaching the employees to use the cash register and explaining policies and systems. The stores spent an average of 1 hour on instructions about how to sell merchandise. Most training programs utilized on-the-job training only.[11] These statistics indicate an alarming lack of training, and smaller retailers usually give even less training.

All newly hired personnel need some type of training. Even employees with experience in similar retail jobs need at least an introduction to a new job. A four-step process is recommended to ensure that proper training is provided: (1) assess the training needs, (2) determine appropriate training methods, (3) conduct the training, and (4) evaluate and adjust the training.

Assess the Training Needs

To assess the training needs of a newly hired employee, the retailer must compare the skills needed to do a job with the skills possessed by the employee. Any deficiencies must be addressed by the training process.

The assessment is important because giving a worker too much or too little training can create problems. Most retailers understand the problem of too little training. Too much training, however, can result in an over-qualified and unhappy worker. Overtrained workers may feel that they are being prevented from achieving their potential. There is a good possibility that such a worker will soon quit.

To assess training needs more accurately, some retailers have set up *assessment centers*. Although smaller retailers typically cannot afford such a center, they may be able to hire outside sources to help assess workers and jobs. Even these outside assessment centers are not available to some retailers, in which case the retailers must attempt to assess the training needs themselves. As previously stated, a good starting point is a comparison between the job description and the application form.

Determine Appropriate Training Methods

Once the training needs have been determined, the retailer can begin the process of determining which training methods to use. The specific training methods should be based on the assessment and the statement of training needs. If the training needs are not great, less formal and less developed training methods can be used. However, if the training needs are great, then more advanced and complex types of training will be required. Although there are many training methods, three basic types are on-the-job training, classroom training, and correspondence training.[12]

On-the-Job Training. On-the-job training is frequently used in retail establishments. Unfortunately, on-the-job training sometimes means *no* training. If done properly, it provides instruction while the employee is performing actual job functions. It can be done by having a more experienced employee instruct and guide the new employee. Someone (the owner or a member of the personnel staff) should make sure that the new employee is actually getting training while working.

On-the-job training should never result in the employee's being placed on the job with no real instruction or direction. This sink-or-swim attitude usually results in the employee's taking a long time to become trained and possibly never becoming trained.

Classroom Training.   Some retailers use classroom training to give the employee a better introduction to the job, to the retailer, and to the initial parts of training. Although retailers do not use this method very often, larger retailers should at least consider the method as a way of giving more information to the trainee in a quicker way than is possible with on-the-job training. The classroom training can take two different forms, external and internal.

External classroom training occurs when someone from outside the firm is hired to conduct the training. This kind of training is available from universities and a variety of specialized consulting firms. A problem with external training is that the employee often learns very little about the specific store. The advantage of external training is that the employee is exposed to several ways of performing an activity. The external training can be costly and is normally appropriate for management-level positions, rather than lower-level jobs. Sales personnel can also benefit greatly from training in sales techniques in a classroom situation.

Internal classroom training consists of classroom exercises conducted by the retailer's personnel. Perhaps the principal advantage of internal training is that the retailer has a chance to train the employee in his or her own method of doing business. Internal classroom training of some type is normally recommended at least as an introduction for the employee to the job and the company. If possible, the internal training should be conducted far enough away from the work situation to avoid interruption of and by normal store activities.

Correspondence Training.   Correspondence training, as the name implies, involves some type of correspondence course. If a retailer uses this type of training, some controls are needed to make sure that the employees are actually participating in the training. That is, the retailer may have to check to see that employees perform the tasks necessary to complete the training. For small retailers who often cannot afford to set up their own training programs, correspondence training can be particularly beneficial.

Conduct the Training

After the retailer has assessed the training needs and selected the appropriate training method or methods, the actual training can be conducted. The best-planned training program will not be effective unless the retailer makes sure that the trainee understands the need for training. One way to do this is to show the employee what the training program can do for the employee.

For a training program to be truly effective, the employees must transfer the information gained in training to the actual work situation. The retailer can make sure this occurs (particularly for classroom training), by combining the classroom training with on-the-job training. Perhaps the most effective training program is one in which classroom or correspondence training teaches the employee how to do the job and on-the-job training is used to show the employee how those procedures actually work on the job. This process should result in the best transfer of information from the training manual or from the training lecturers to the actual work of the business.

Evaluate and Adjust the Training

The training program established by the retailer should be evaluated periodically and any necessary adjustments should be made. If the training program is an expensive one, it should be watched closely. If it is not achieving the desired results, the entire package may need adjustment. The training needs may have been misjudged, the training methods may be inappropriate, or the training sessions themselves may have been deficient. Any of these problems should lead the retailer to a total or partial adjustment of the training system. There are several ways to evaluate the program and determine whether adjustments are needed.

Follow-up Testing.   One way of determining whether the training program is reasonably effective is to implement a testing procedure immediately following the program. The testing procedure should check that the training objectives have been fulfilled. The retailer should also determine whether the trainees have the proper skills and abilities after completing the training program. If the trainees do not seem to have the abilities that they need, additional training may be indicated. If additional training does not seem to be the answer, then the entire training program may have been inadequate.

Ongoing Evaluations.   Another way of determining whether the training program has been effective is to run continual checks to see if problems emerge after the trainee goes into the work situation. Even employees who seem to know the necessary information and have the necessary skills and abilities after completing the training may not be able to perform adequately in the actual job situations.

Several factors can cause this apparent gap between training and performance. One is an inadequacy of the training program. Another is that employees may not be following the procedures presented in the training program, but may have adopted the procedures of co-workers. Either of these symptoms indicates a problem with the training program.

The performance of all employees should be checked on a continuing basis. These appraisals can often indicate new problems that can be handled through additional training. Not all training needs can be met in the initial training of a new employee. Older employees also may need refresher training.

EVALUATE EMPLOYEE PERFORMANCE

The tenth step in human resource planning is to evaluate employee performance.[13] Most preceding steps were aimed at new employees, but this step focuses on all employees.

It is necessary for a retailer to evaluate the effectiveness of all resources, including human resources. To properly evaluate personnel performance, the retailer should (1) specify desired performance, (2) determine actual performance, (3) motivate employees to achieve better performance, and (4) take corrective action.

Specify Desired Performance

The first step in evaluating personnel performance is to specify the desired performance. This task is more difficult than it seems at first glance. Most retailers have a general idea of what they expect from an employee, but a *specific* statement of desired performance is needed for an evaluation. This specific statement informs the employee what is expected, reduces the likelihood of discrimination suits, and provides a sound basis for employee evaluation.

The job description should serve as the basis for determining desired performance. Even using the job description, exact performance levels for many retail employees are difficult to specify. For instance, a retailer may have ten salesclerks responsible for greeting customers, selling goods to those customers, and checking customers' purchases. These activities are not easily quantified, but the retailer can compare the performance of the ten employees in certain areas. The focus might be the checking-out activities. The merchandise checked out can serve as a reasonable measure of how well most of the tasks are performed. Electronic cash registers and point-of-sale equipment can easily match employees with the transactions they complete. The retailer can establish a total sales goal for each clerk and monitor it with the point-of-sale equipment.

In a similar fashion, the retailer can examine all the positions within the firm to determine what measures of performance are appropriate and what levels of performance to establish as goals. The retailer should be careful to establish appropriate measures and levels of performance. If either is incorrect, the entire evaluation process may not work as well as desired. For jobs involving nonquantifiable tasks, the retailer can state the specific job elements that will be evaluated subjectively.

Determine Actual Performance

Determining actual performance is relatively easy once the desired performance is established. In the salesclerk example used earlier, the retailer can total each clerk's sales and then compare this figure to the goal or to the other salesclerks' totals. It is important that what the retailer plans to measure can actually be measured and can be used to separate good performers from bad performers. After actual performance is measured and compared to desired performance, the retailer should attempt to move performance levels in the desired directions.

Motivate Employees to Achieve Better Performance

Most retailers worry more about cost minimization than about performance maximization of their human resources. This is the case even when research indicates that stores with a competent and motivated sales force can increase their profitability.[14]

Although a small percentage of personnel does not require motivation from management, most employees do. The retailer has three basic options for attempting to motivate personnel. First, the overall *organizational climate* can have a strong impact on motivation. The organizational climate is the employees' perception of their opportunities, value, and rewards for a good performance.[15] Motivation tends to be greater when personnel feel valuable or important to the retailer and see opportunities for promotion or other direct and indirect rewards.

Second, *sales quotas* may be established for salespeople. A quota specifies how much each person should sell during the year or season. Quotas may be positive or negative and they can be tied to compensation. A positive quota provides a reward to those who achieve it, in the form of increased commissions or bonuses. A negative quota involves penalties, the extreme of which would be dismissal.

Third, other *positive incentives* are available to the retailer, including special recognition, sales contests, honors and awards, profit-sharing plans, and vacations with pay. David Sirota claims that retail managers can best motivate employees by fulfilling employees' goals, which are job security, money, and safety, the desire to work in an effective and efficient organization, the desire to be rewarded for their contributions, and respect.[16]

Take Corrective Action

Unless retailers are willing to take the necessary actions to reward good performance and correct bad performance, the entire evaluation process is useless. Four specific actions that should be considered as a result of an evaluation (1) promote the employee, (2) support the employee, (3) give the employee directions or remedial training, and (4) terminate the employee. All of these actions and almost all of the evaluation processes are best handled in face-to-face meetings between supervisors and employees. Three specific benefits of these meetings have been identified:

1. The retailer is led to formulate specific and uniform standards.

2. The retailer is encouraged to make more systematic evaluations.

3. The meetings tend to have a positive influence on performance.[17]

Employees who perform at rates higher than necessary or expected should be considered for promotions or other rewards, such as bonuses or raises. If the reward is promotion, an evaluation should be made as to whether the employee can perform at the higher-level job or whether additional training is needed before the promotion is given. The retailer should attempt to make sure that employees are not promoted beyond the level of competence.

Those employees who perform adequately but not exceptionally should be supported by management so that their performance does not drop. Management might consider additional training for some of these employees to try to make them exceptional employees.

If an employee's performance is below standard, the first action should be remedial training or discussions aimed at improving performance. It is possible that an employee's lack of performance is caused by factors that can be corrected by training and/or directions. Employees whose performance appears beyond correction should be terminated.

Decisions to terminate employees are difficult but sometimes necessary. An employee whose performance is repeatedly low and who does not respond to less severe efforts must usually be fired. Some retailers do not like to fire people. While this concern for the employee may be admirable, it can also be expensive. Management is paid to make difficult decisions, including those that involve termination.

There is one caution about termination: *Have good reason.* It is very easy for almost any employee to complain of discrimination when fired. The best defense is to have documented proof that the employee was not performing adequately. Few courts will fail to consider evidence that the employee was not performing adequately and that the retailer attempted to aid the employee in improving performance.

MONITOR AND ADAPT THE ORGANIZATION

The final step in strategic human resource planning is ongoing monitoring and adapting to meet current needs. Any organization and the personnel within the organization can become stagnant or even regressive as the environmental situation evolves. Consequently, the organization and the personnel should be continually evaluated to ensure that they are meeting the current and anticipated needs of the retailer. Continuous monitoring and adapting can often prevent the need for major abrupt overhauls, such as massive layoffs or firings, major changes in organizational structure, or major changes in the training program. In other words, the retailer will be much more successful with an evolutionary adaptation process rather than a revolutionary adaptation process.

SUMMARY

Having the correct organization structure, the right personnel, and the proper training are essential for retailing survival and success. To help assure that human resources are utilized properly, the retailer should perform eleven activities: (1) review all other plans, (2) determine the goals of organizing, (3) select the type of organization, (4) determine the organizational relationships, (5) determine the human resource goals, (6) determine personnel policies and procedures, (7) determine the type and number of employees, (8) hire the needed employees, (9) train the employees, (10) evaluate the employees, (11) monitor and adapt. Although the implementation of these eleven steps does not assure proper use of human resources, it should increase the likelihood that they will be used efficiently and effectively.

KEY CONCEPTS

Organizational structure
Centralized control
Decentralized control
Tight control
Loose control
Stage method
Functional organization
Geographic organization
Product (departmental) organization
Matrix organization

Hybrid organization
Mazur plan
Formal organization
Informal organization
Task analysis
Job description
On-the-job training
External classroom training
Internal classroom training
Correspondence training

REVIEW QUESTIONS

1. Discuss the requirement that human resource plans mesh with other plans of the retailer.
2. Discuss the reasons a firm might select centralized, decentralized, tight, and loose control.
3. Why would a retailer be likely to use a hybrid organization type?
4. Why does an informal organization form in any organizational structure?
5. Why should a retailer have a written personnel policy manual?
6. Why should a retailer use job descriptions?
7. Discuss some methods of reaching potential employees.
8. Why must all employees have some training?
9. Discuss the process a retailer should go through in improving inadequate performance of employees.

LEARNING EXERCISES

1. Ask a retailer for a copy of his or her organizational chart. (If one does not exist, ask the retailer to describe the organization.) Ask an employee to describe the organizational chart. Explain any differences.
2. Ask two retailers to explain their training and evaluation processes. Do you think that these activities are adequately handled? What changes would you suggest?

DECISION SITUATION 9.1: **BRUCE'S FINE FURNISHINGS**

Bruce Jacobson, owner of Bruce's Fine Furnishings, has a problem. When he started his furniture business fifteen years ago, managing the one store was easy. Bruce did most of the work of management, including making all major decisions. The business has grown since then, and there are now five stores located near

Corpus Christi, Texas. Bruce has also agreed to buy four additional stores in the Victoria, Texas, area. The stores will be as much as 175 miles apart and there will be about two hundred employees. Bruce doesn't think the loose, informal organization he now uses will work anymore. He is not sure what the new organizational structure should be. He also plans future acquisitions that would give him stores in the San Antonio area. Eventually Bruce plans to have about fifteen stores and employ over three hundred people.

QUESTIONS

1.   What are some factors for Bruce to consider in selecting a new organization?

2.   What stage of development is Bruce's business in?

3.   Design a basic organizational structure that Bruce might use.

DECISION SITUATION 9.2: **SHELLY'S SOUND**

Shelly has worked for several years in a store selling stereo equipment. Recently she decided to open her own store in a location across town. Shelly is confident of her ability but has some misgivings about selecting and managing her employees. Shelly plans to employ five full-time and four part-time workers. She plans to sell three top-of-the-line brands of stereo equipment. (Shelly prefers to say she will carry from "the very best to exceptionally good" equipment.) She will have the highest-quality products of any of her three primary competitors in a city of about 500,000.

Shelly is considering hiring six college students and three more permanent employees. She is not sure how to train or compensate the employees. She also is not sure whether she should control the employees tightly or loosely. She would prefer not to have to supervise them tightly. She is sure that the quality of her employees will be critical to the success of the business.

QUESTIONS

1.   What do you think of Shelly's hiring plans?

2.   How should Shelly train her employees?

3.   What compensation scheme would you recommend?

4.   Would you recommend tight or loose control of the employees?

5.   What criteria should Shelly use to select the employees?

NOTES

1.   Mervin Kohn, *Dynamic Managing: Principles, Process, Practice* (Menlo Park, Calif.: Benjamin-Cummings Publishing Company, 1977), p. 176.

2.   Many management texts have one or several chapters that deal with the tight-versus-loose-control controversy. A representative text is Harold Koontz, Cyril O'Donnell, and Heinz Weirich, *Management,* 7th ed. (New York: McGraw-Hill, 1980).

3.   For a more complete discussion of the stage method see Arthur A. Thompson, Jr., and A. J. Strickland III, *Strategy and Policy Concepts and Cases*, rev. ed. (Plano, Tex.: Business Publications, 1981), pp. 154–158, or David Meredith, "Maintaining Productivity While Implementing Formal Systems in a Maturing Firm," in *Productivity in General Merchandise Retailing*, ed. Stanton G. Cort, (New York: National Retail Merchants Association, 1980), pp. 85–94.

4.   Rollin Glasser, *Retail Personnel Management* (New York: Lebhar-Friedman Books, 1977), is a text that discusses specific human resource goals related to retailing.

5.   See Glasser, *op. cit.*

6.   Philip Kotler, *Marketing Management* (Englewood Cliffs, N.J.: Prentice-Hall, 1980), p. 562.

7.   See a business law or personnel text for a more complete discussion of laws affecting retail personnel, or see Glasser, *op. cit.*, pp. 39–69.

8.   Glasser, *op. cit.*, pp. 71–95.

9.   *Ibid.*, pp. 100–104.

10. See Dion Friedland, Richard Israel, and Edith Lynch, *People Productivity in Retailing* (New York: Lebhar-Friedman Books, 1980), pp. 23–35.

11. Irving Burstiner, "Current Personnel Practice in Department Stores," *Journal of Retailing*, vol. 51, no. 4, Winter 1975/76, p. 11.

12. See Glasser, *op. cit.*, pp. 139–169.

13. See Friedland, Israel, and Lynch, *op. cit.*, pp. 113–160.

14. Gilbert A. Churchhill, Jr., Neil M. Ford, and Orville C. Walker, Jr., NYU Conference, 1980, as quoted in *Marketing News*, 22 August 1980, p. 14.

15. Kotler, *op. cit.*, p. 570.

16. David Sirota, "Structuring the Management Organization to Enhance Production of the Retail Workforce," in *Productivity in General Merchandise Retailing*, ed. Stanton G. Cort (New York: National Retail Merchants Association, 1980), p. 50.

17. Kotler, *op. cit.*, p. 574.

PART III

THE RETAILING MIX

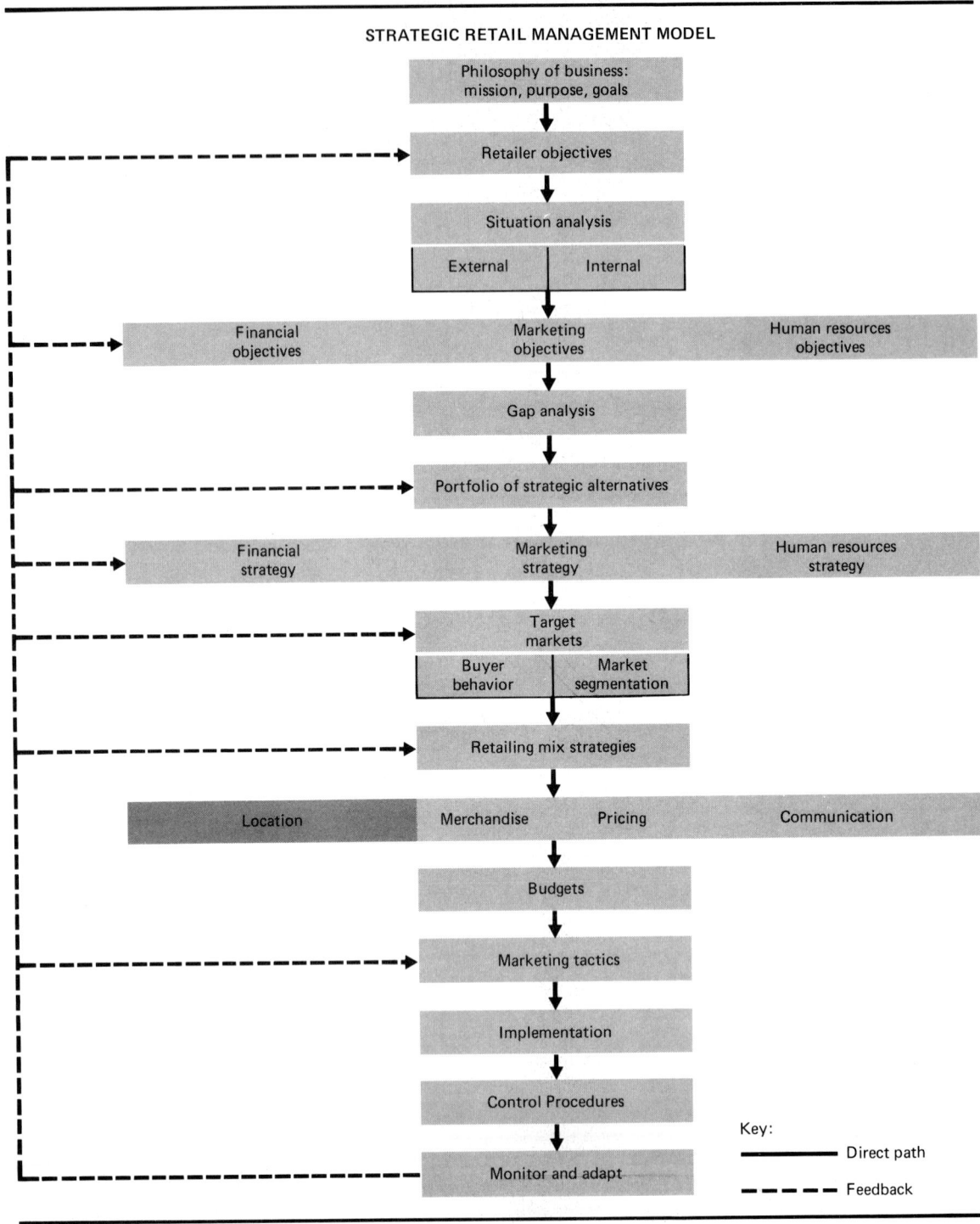

STRATEGIC RETAIL MANAGEMENT MODEL

Philosophy of business:
mission, purpose, goals

Retailer objectives

Situation analysis

| External | Internal |

Financial objectives | Marketing objectives | Human resources objectives

Gap analysis

Portfolio of strategic alternatives

Financial strategy | Marketing strategy | Human resources strategy

Target markets

| Buyer behavior | Market segmentation |

Retailing mix strategies

Location | Merchandise | Pricing | Communication

Budgets

Marketing tactics

Implementation

Control Procedures

Monitor and adapt

Key:
——— Direct path
— — — Feedback

Chapter 10
Store Location Decisions

INTRODUCTION

One of the retailer's most important strategic decisions is the location of the store. Retail stores, whether small or large, are probably affected more by their location than is any other type of business. Mistakes in locating a store are usually difficult and expensive to overcome. Some poor locations cannot be offset, regardless of adjustments in other elements of the retailing strategy. Further, the retailer's location, unlike some other aspects of a store, is relatively permanent, even when the land and building(s) are leased.

Location consultant Howard Green gives three principal reasons for the importance of location:

1. Increasing competition as stores proliferate and retailers scramble to offer consumers a wider range of goods and services.

2. A slowdown in population growth and new shopping center construction, which reduces the number of available locations and means that retailers cannot afford to pass up solid opportunities.

3. Higher store-development expenses. As the costs of land and construction continue to rise, the penalty for making poor site selections becomes harsher. In addition, landlords are requiring longer lease periods.[1]

To help ensure that a good location is chosen, a strategic planning process such as shown in Fig. 10.1 should be utilized. The process has five major steps:

1. Review all other plans and information.

2. Determine needed location characteristics.

3. Determine the area in which to locate.

4. Select the site.

5. Monitor and adapt.

REVIEW ALL OTHER PLANS AND INFORMATION

As is the case in making all strategic decisions, all existing plans and information must be examined. The retailer's overall strategy helps determine an appropriate location and, conversely, the location has a major impact on other strategies of the business. The target market, the competition, and the desired store image all must be reviewed before the location decision process begins. These basic decisions, which were discussed in earlier chapters, form the foundation of the location decisions and strategy.

Many of the activities associated with strategic planning for a new store only exist on paper until the location is selected. The location decision

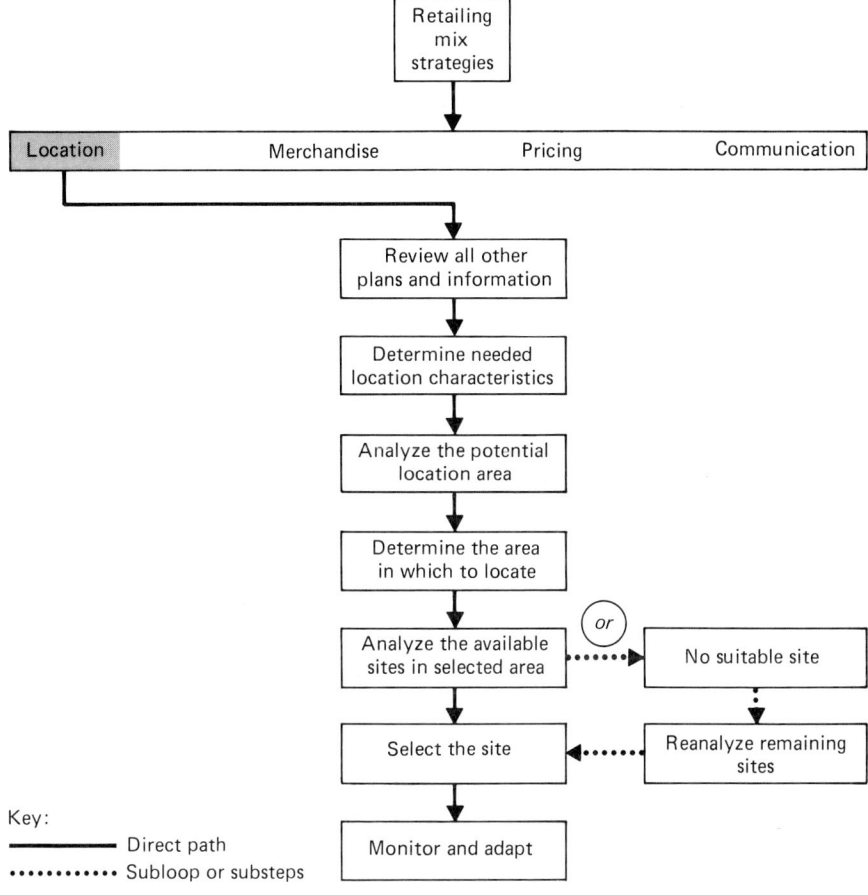

Figure 10.1
Location decision model

is often the first strategic plan implemented. It is also likely to be one of the first decisions that must be backed with money. Major elements of the strategic plan such as the target market, the competitive position, and the desired image can and often are changed in the early stages of planning. Once the location is selected (whether it is bought, built, or leased), the retailer makes a commitment to the strategic plans. Further changes or adjustments become more difficult. A change in the target market, for example, may not be possible once the location is selected. If a retailer chooses a location in a shopping center dominated by low-priced stores and factory outlets, it is probably too late to decide that his or her store will be a shop catering to fashion-conscious women willing to pay high prices.

As can be seen from the preceding example, the location may dictate potential customers, the resulting merchandise selection, the general price level, and numerous other elements of the business. The one part of the previously developed plans that should have the greatest impact on location is the target market of the store.

The target market is the group of customers that a store wishes to attract. The target market must be analyzed, studied, and understood before proceeding with many other plans and actions. Few decisions of the retailer are more closely tied to target market analysis than the location decision.

Once a location is selected, that location can deliver a set of customers, who will be the previously selected target market *if* the location is appropriate. If the location is not appropriate, the customers may be entirely different from those desired or there may possibly be too few customers to survive. Location also helps determine a store's image: A good location helps foster the desired store image whereas an improper location decision can lead to an undesirable image.

Any potential site has characteristics that will meet the needs of some target markets and, therefore, some retailers. A target market has characteristics that can be best met by certain locations. The task for a business locator, then, is to match location characteristics desired by the target market with characteristics of various locations.

DETERMINE NEEDED LOCATION CHARACTERISTICS

Good locations generally possess certain common characteristics. The retailer must exercise caution when making comments about or interpreting general location characteristics. Serious mistakes can be made if general location guidelines or suggestions are forced on all situations and stores.

General Characteristics

One way of selecting the location of a business is to analyze the factors or characteristics of a good retail location. Nelson developed a reasonably complete listing of factors that might influence the location decision. A brief summary of Nelson's location checklist is given in Table 10.1. The checklist proposed by Nelson can act as a guide for selecting a site. Kotler suggests that a firm might be able to quantify the location decision based on Nelson's ideas.[2] In fact, many large retailers do use sophisticated models to determine locations.[3]

The analysis of general characteristics can range from the sophisticated quantitative models (some of which are discussed in the appendix to this chapter) to just driving around and selecting a site. Whatever technique is used to analyze the characteristics of sites, it should be a carefully designed process.

Location Characteristics and the Target Market

As mentioned earlier, the target market is a principal determinant of the desired location characteristics. Once the target market has been selected by a retailer, the characteristics needed in the location are at least partially

Table 10.1
Retail location factors

I. *Trading area potential*
A. Public utility connections (residential)
B. Residential building permits issued
C. School enrollment
D. New bank accounts opened
E. Advertising lineage in local newspapers
F. Retail sales volume
G. Sales tax receipts
H. Employment — specific
I. Employment — general

II. *Accessibility*
A. Public transportation (serving site)
B. Private transportation (serving site)
C. Parking facilities
D. Long-range trends (transportation facilities)

III. *Growth potential*
A. Zoning pattern
B. Zoning changes
C. Zoning potential
D. Utilities trend
E. Vacant land market (land zoned for residential use)
F. Land use pattern (in areas zoned for other than residential)
G. Retail-business land use trend
H. Retail-building trend (building permits issued for new retail business construction)

I. Retail-improvement trend (permits issued for remodeling, expansion, etc. in existing properties)
J. Retail-location trend (changes in occupancy of retail business locations)
K. Income trend for average family unit
L. Plant and equipment expenditure trend
M. Payroll trend

IV. *Business interception*
A. Location pattern — competitive businesses between site and trade area

V. *Cumulative-attraction potential*
A. Neighboring business survey

VI. *Compatibility*
A. Compatibility factors

VII. *Competitive-hazard survey*
A. Competitive pattern–competitors within one mile of site (nonintercepting)

VIII. *Site economics*
A. Cost and return analysis
B. Site efficiency
C. Natural description
D. Adjacent amenities (for both vacant land and existing building sites)

Source: From *The Selection of Retail Locations* by Richard L. Nelson. Copyright © 1958, McGraw-Hill Book Company. Used with the permission of McGraw-Hill Book Company.

defined. If the target market consists of individuals interested primarily in convenience, the store will have to be located in an accessible location near the customers. Conversely, convenience may be relatively unimportant for customers who are looking for quality merchandise. A serious location mistake is likely when retailers do not adequately define and analyze their target market.

Location Characteristics and the Retailer's Strategy

The elements of the retailer's overall strategy (other than the target market) also affect the location decision. The analysis runs parallel to the target market analysis. That is, first determine the strategies, then select the location. Once the location is selected, some elements of the store's strategy may have to be changed to remain congruent with the location.

A retailer might decide to feature low prices as a primary promotional technique. One location possibility is an out-of-the-way location, possibly even an out-of-town location. The store's promotion might have as one theme "Come out of town — out to lower prices." The location reinforces the idea that the retailer is doing whatever he or she can do to give the customer lower prices.

Likewise, more prestigious locations can help promote a high-quality strategy. A downtown location may lead to promotion based on the theme "Come to our downtown store—where beautiful people shop."

Since the retailer's other strategies are so interrelated with the target market, it is imperative that all strategies be related to the target market and to each other so that a basic strategy or philosophy is formed before selecting a location. If the location is chosen before the basic strategy is selected, the location will largely dictate the strategy that must be used.

DETERMINE THE AREA IN WHICH TO LOCATE

Once the desired location characteristics are determined, the retailer is ready to begin selecting the location. A retailer should make the final decision in two stages. The first stage of the decision is the selection of an area. The steps necessary to select an area include (1) perform a trading area analysis, (2) determine the sales potential of the areas, (3) determine the city or area growth and development trends, and (5) match the area characteristics to the needed characteristics.

Perform Trading Area Analysis

The first step in selecting an area in which to locate is to perform an analysis of the trading area of the areas being considered. Trading area analysis is applicable to both the selection of the area and the actual site. General trading areas are examined for the macro or area location. More site-specific trading area analysis is done after the macro location is selected. The following relates to both the macro and site decisions. The trading area has been defined as

> A district whose size is usually determined by the boundaries within which it is economical in terms of volume and cost for a marketing unit or group to sell and/or deliver a good or service.[4]

In other words, the trading area is the area in which a store's customers live. It is important that a retailer look at the trading areas of several potential location areas.

There are several degrees of trading areas for a potential location. The **primary trading area** contains most of the customers for a location, normally 55 to 70 percent. This is obviously the area in which the retailer should concentrate. The **secondary trading area** contains most of the remainder of the customers, approximately 15 to 25 percent. All other customers are in the **fringe trading area**.[5]

If a store already exists, the trading area of the store can be analyzed in a rather direct manner. A survey may be performed, license plates can be checked, credit cards can be analyzed, or checks can be examined. These direct methods cannot be used to determine the trading area of a store that does not yet exist. For this location decision, it is the *expected* trading area that must be determined. The following sections deal with methods of predicting trading areas.

Characteristics of Trading Areas. Each trading area examined will have certain characteristics that help in determining the appropriateness of a location. Much of the information needed about the characteristics of a trading area is available from secondary sources.

The *Census of Population*, the *Survey of Buying Power*, and *Editor & Publisher Market Guide* are three excellent sources of information about the population of an area.[6] These three sources provide information such as population, income levels, employment, education, and age of the residents of an area. Except in the *Census*, the data are arranged by city. This makes some of the information difficult for retailers to use if they have not yet decided in which city to locate. Chambers of commerce, city planning commissions, newspapers, and other organizations may be able to provide some valuable information such as updates of the census and breakdowns of city-wide data. All potential sources should be examined so that appropriate data will not be omitted from the analysis.

The exact type of data needed and important characteristics to be reviewed will vary from retailer to retailer. A fast-food store may only look at population figures, while some restaurants may need to know population, income, and educational levels of the areas. The selection of a target market defines the characteristics that will be most important to the retailer. The retailer should then select an area whose residents possess these characteristics.

Retail Gravitation.   Retail gravitation refers to the pulling ability of a given location. Reilly proposed what is known as the **Law of Retail Gravitation** in 1929.[7] (This and other models are presented in the appendix.) The formula for Reilly's law is as follows:

$$\text{Breaking point, miles from A} = \frac{\text{Distance between A \& B in miles}}{1 + \sqrt{\dfrac{\text{Population of B}}{\text{Population of A}}}}.$$

Reilly's law is most useful to a retailer making the choice of a city in which to locate. Its usefulness in other situations, such as choosing between two shopping centers, is limited.

Several attempts have been made to improve the general formula. Most of these have centered on defining distances in *time* rather than in *miles*. Another improvement that could be made is replacing *population* with *store quality*. The original model assumed that the quality of shopping was defined by population.

Huff has developed a probabilistic model to try to improve on Reilly's law[8] (see the appendix). Huff's model deals with intracity drawing power rather than intercity drawing power. Although it has some variables that are difficult to establish, it can be used to map trade areas by probability contour lines.[9]

The various gravitation models should lead to one point—the definition of the areas from which customers are likely to come. Actually, the models may also help distinguish both the primary and secondary trading areas. These trading areas may be of any shape and can often be approximated by examining maps and the location of competitors.

Defining the trading areas is only the first step in trading area analysis. After the areas are defined, they must be analyzed further.

Determine the Sales Potential of the Areas

The most important outcome of analyzing the macro location is obtaining an estimate of the sales potential for the trading areas examined. The sales potential is determined by the economic characteristics of the area and the competition in the area.

Economic Characteristics.   One of the main reasons for performing the trading area analysis is to determine the economic characteristics of an area, both for the current time period and for the future. Income, occupational type, and education are all part of the economic characteristics of the area. One aspect that should not be overlooked is the economic base of an area.

The **economic base** refers to the sources of income for the area under examination. Normally, a relatively wide economic base is preferred because with a wide base (consisting of several nonrelated industries) a general downturn of drastic proportions is less likely. If an area is dominated by one industry, a downturn in that industry will have a large impact on retailers in the area. Retail sales in agricultural areas, for example, are determined by the profit made by farmers. If severe drought conditions occur (such as in 1980), retail sales will suffer drastically. Michigan retailers suffer badly when auto sales slacken. Since finding areas where one firm or industry does not dominate may be difficult, a retailer should try to find areas that are dominated as little as possible.

All the economic characteristics of an area should be reviewed at this point. The idea is to try to develop a feel for the demand that an area will provide. Once the demand has been examined, the supply of goods in the area must be examined.

Level of Saturation.   The supply of goods in an area is determined by the number and quality of stores in the area. The **index of saturation** has been developed to help rate areas as to potential customers, retail expenditures, and the size of retail facilities in square feet. The index is calculated for a specific product category or service. The basic formula is as follows:[10]

$$\text{Index of saturation (for a specific product in a specific area)} = \frac{(\text{Customers in area}) \, (\text{Expenditure/customer})}{\text{Total square feet allocated in area to the product}}.$$

All the parts of the formula relate to a particular product in the area under question. The resultant index number is extremely useful in comparing areas. An area with a high index is generally preferable. Higher index numbers indicate that demand in the area is not being satisfied by the retail space as completely as in areas with lower index numbers. The index number is an estimate of the potential sales per square foot of allocated space.

Suppose two areas are being considered as the site for a new sporting goods store. Area A contains 20,000 people who spend about $10 per year on sporting goods. Total space allocated to sporting goods in Area A is 500 square feet. Area B contains 50,000 people spending $10 per year on sporting goods. There are 2,000 square feet allocated to sporting goods in Area B. Area A has an index of 400 (20,000 × $10/500). Area B has an index of 250 (50,000 × $10/2,000). All else being equal, Area A would be the preferred area.

Note in the above example, however, that Area A has a relatively small amount of space devoted to sporting goods. A new sporting goods store of only 1,500 square feet would decrease the saturation index dramatically, to 100 for Area A (20,000 × $10/2,000) and 142 for Area B (50,000 × $10/3,500). After addition of the proposed 1,500-square-foot store, Area B would be more attractive than Area A. Consequently, when comparing areas that differ a great deal in population or allocated space, the retailer should calculate the saturation index both *with* and *without* the proposed store.

The index of saturation is a good measure of relative desirability of areas. The index does leave out one very important variable—the strength of competition. A retailer usually has to judge the strength of the competition in each area being considered. There are no exact measures for judging strength, but one measure is the degree of outshopping that occurs. In determining whether an area has enough doctors (a retailer of services), a doctor may look at the number of prescriptions filled in the area but written by doctors outside the area. Most retailers cannot find such a direct indication, but other indicators are often present. Customer loyalty and satisfaction with existing competitors, for example, can be determined through research.

Regardless of the specific method used to estimate sales potential, the decision regarding the area in which to locate should also be based on an analysis of city or area growth patterns.

Determine City or Area Growth Trends

Since a location is a relatively permanent factor, the location decision must be made with both the present and the future in mind. The direction and nature of growth must be examined to strategically locate a store. Each city or trade area has different growth patterns. Some cities grow concentrically, others grow along major traffic arteries, and others may grow in what appears to be a rather haphazard manner.[11]

Looking at land ownership, zoning regulations, and present land use patterns may give hints to future area growth patterns. Talking to long-time residents, real estate people, city planners, and influential business or civic leaders may give even greater insight. Essentially, any data that can possibly indicate future growth and development trends must be sought. Even a simple drive through residential and business areas may help a retailer recognize patterns.

After completion of the analysis of potential areas, the retailer should be ready to select the best area in which to locate. The selection decision should be based on the characteristics that an area possesses and the characteristics that have been determined to be desirable.

Match the Area Characteristics to the Needed Characteristics

The aim of location analysis is to match the characteristics of a location to characteristics desired by the retailer. The proper matching is not a small feat. Each potential area will normally have some but not all of the desired characteristics. A retailer must often decide which set of characteristics is most important. A key to the preceding sentence is the word *set*. Often analysts are tempted to rate each specific characteristic and then to select the area that has the most high-rated characteristics. This procedure fails to recognize that each location has a set of characteristics. The entire set, not just individual parts of the set, must be rated. An area may have the three characteristics considered most necessary but may lack several desirable but less important characteristics. This deficiency may cause the area to be inferior to one that is less outstanding in the three primary characteristics but that does have *all* the characteristics desired.

As can be seen, the retailer is looking for the *best fit* of what is available and what is needed in a location. The process involves several difficult but necessary decisions. The more the retailer understands the target market and the store's strategy, the more likely it is that he or she will make a proper decision.

The decision about the trade area is the beginning of the location process. After completing this step, the specific site must be selected. Some parts of this analysis are very similar and other parts are different from the trade area selection procedures.

SELECT THE SITE

The specific site a retail outlet is to occupy is as important to the profitability of the store as the macro location decision. The best area location decision can turn into disaster by selection of the wrong site within the area. The site should be examined as closely as possible to try to minimize the chance of a mistake.

Types of Sites

One of the earliest decisions that must be made is the type of site desired. This decision should be made carefully, taking into account the store's target market and basic strategy. All sites have certain advantages and all have disadvantages. The aim of the site-type analysis is to select the type that best suits an individual retailer.

Shopping Center Sites. One type of site is in a planned shopping center. These sites generally offer several advantages. They tend to help draw customers, and a retailer who cannot draw enough traffic standing alone may be able to draw enough in conjunction with other businesses. Other advantages of locating in a shopping center include sharing of some costs, declining appeal of central city locations, ability to offer climate-controlled shopping, better accessibility, and large number of parking spaces, among others.

There are many reasons for the growth in popularity of shopping centers. Some trends such as a growing desire for convenient, one-stop shopping appear to indicate that shopping centers will continue this growth in popularity.

If a retailer decides to locate in a shopping center, the type of center must be chosen. For many years there have been three basic types of shopping centers—regional, community, and neighborhood. Today a new type, the super-regional, has emerged. The general characteristics of regional, community, and neighborhood centers are shown in Table 10.2.

The **super-regional center** is the largest type of shopping center. It includes three or more full-line department stores and 1,000,000 or more square feet of total space.[12] In many ways the super-regional and regional centers are very much alike except for size.

Both the super-regional and **regional centers** are very large. A customer is able to go to either one and find goods to fill almost all needs. Both centers are best suited for businesses that sell shopping goods. Customers

Table 10.2
Characteristics of shopping centers

	NEIGHBORHOOD	COMMUNITY	REGIONAL
Average gross floor area	40,000 square feet	150,000 square feet	400,000 square feet
Range in gross floor area	30,000–75,000 square feet	100,000–300,000 square feet	400,000 to over 1,000,000 square feet
Coverage of minimum site area	4 acres	10 acres	40 acres
Minimum support	1,000 families: 7,000–20,000 people	5,000 families: 20,000–100,000 people	70,000–300,000 families: 250,000 or more people
Leading tenant	Supermarket or drugstore	Variety or junior department store	One or two department stores

Source: Walter D. Stoll, "Characteristics of Shopping Centers," *Traffic Quarterly,* April 1967, p. 161.

can shop for these items in one location and easily make comparisons of price, quality, or other factors. Some convenience stores may choose to locate in regional or super-regional centers. Customers patronize these stores primarily as an afterthought while shopping for other goods. Some specialty stores are also located in regional or super-regional centers.

The **community center** is smaller than a regional center but larger than a neighborhood center. The community center often consists of a supermarket, a drugstore, a hardware store, a small department store, and several convenience stores. The emphasis is on shopping goods but there are usually convenience stores that do not depend completely on shoppers attracted by the larger stores. Community centers are often good locations for dress shops, shoe stores, and other clothing stores.

The **neighborhood shopping center** is the smallest type of center. It will contain stores similar to the community center, but without a department store. The stores usually sell convenience goods. Shoppers at these centers often go to only one store for specific merchandise. They are interested in convenience more than price, quality, or other factors. Normally stores are not in direct competition with each other in a neighborhood center.

One of the chief reasons for selecting a shopping center site is the increased drawing power of several stores. Larger stores such as the department stores in regional or super-regional centers have much greater ability to draw customers, and these customers will often shop at both the department stores and smaller stores. In effect, a store located in a shopping center has a larger trading area than it would have standing alone.

Some problems with shopping center locations are higher rent and control by the center owners or major tenants. Typically, major shopping centers have higher rent per square foot than other locations. (This is a generalization and is not always the case.) The extra rent may be well spent, however. Often part of the rent is a percentage of sales and lower rents are usually granted to outlets with lower sales potential.

The control exercised by the center owners and major tenants has become less of a problem in recent years. The Federal Trade Commission (FTC) ruled in 1973 that developers and anchor tenants cannot place stringent limitations on smaller stores regarding merchandise lines, advertising policy, hours and days of operation, expansion, and merchant association membership.[13] Even with this ruling, the center may request or demand certain concessions in the rental agreement.

Free-Standing Sites. A retail outlet that has no adjacent retailers with which it shares traffic is a free-standing store. Large retailers can best utilize this type of location. The major problem is attracting enough customers to remain visible. Customers, especially those interested in one-stop shopping, will often not shop at isolated stores unless they contain a wide selection of merchandise or have a national reputation.

A relatively new form of free-standing store is one that locates at the edge of a shopping center. The shopping center chosen for this practice is usually large. The retailer using this practice establishes a store near the center with the hopes of attracting some of the center's customers. A store using the technique should be sure that it is near a major entrance or exit. The store signs should be large, attractive, and visible from the shopping center.

Strip Sites. Often free-standing stores are built near each other; the result is a strip-site development. Such a site has many characteristics in common with shopping centers, but the stores are not connected or under common ownership.

Strip sites are often utilized by automobile dealerships, fast-food restaurants, and similar businesses. College towns usually have strip developments near the campus that cater to the students. Major problems with strip sites include lack of parking, confusion among the various parking lots and traffic congestion owing to lack of traffic planning.

Central Business District Sites. The area of a city that has or has had the greatest concentration of retail stores is the central business district. It is similar to the strip development in that stores select individual sites that are near each other.

The central business district was, and in some cases still is, the main retailing district in a city. The downfall of some central cities has led to a change in retailing in the central city. There are many reasons that customers have stopped shopping downtown, among them are lack of parking, traffic congestion, high actual or perceived crime rates, and the movement of residences into the suburbs.

Several cities have attempted to rejuvenate their central business districts. Some of these attempts have been successful, and others have not.[14] The successes have shown that customers can be drawn downtown again. The failures indicate that consumers have to be given something to convince them to drive farther than the shopping malls, and it has to be more than a few new store fronts and an advertising campaign urging people to shop downtown. It is unfortunate that many fine downtown buildings are not being utilized as they should be. The nonuse is a waste of valuable resources.

Economic Considerations

A retailer should pay careful attention to economic considerations before making a location decision. The true determinant of the quality of a location is the benefits of the location compared to the costs. In selecting a location, the retailer has to judge such factors as the traffic passing by an outlet, the accessibility of the location, and provisions for parking. These three factors form a basis for projecting the economic benefits of a site when there are no other more direct measures.

When direct measures are available, they should be utilized. Direct measures of the quality of a location are possible only when an outlet already exists at a site. Even then it may be difficult to separate the impact of the site on the success of a business from the impact of other elements of the retailing mix. Often even the retailer who has past records of a business at the same site must also rely on the traffic, accessibility, and parking factors to analyze the site.

Traffic.   The traffic associated with a site refers to the number of cars or people that pass the site. The traffic count gives a number of autos or people who might be induced to stop and shop at a site. All else being equal, a site with a high traffic count is more desirable than a site with a low count. There are, however, several exceptions to this general rule.

One exception, discussed in the next section, is that too much traffic makes ingress and egress difficult. Also, traffic count is not as important to specialty shops, which customers will seek out regardless of location. Stores selling shopping goods will generally be most interested in high traffic counts.

There are several ways to obtain traffic counts. The traffic control department in a city often has vehicular traffic counts for various streets and especially for intersections. Physical counts are sometimes necessary, and they are not very difficult.

Physical counts are usually necessary for pedestrian traffic. These are especially important if a shopping center location is being considered. A retailer should check the people passing the specific site being considered, not the number of people entering the center. Some sites on side "streets" of malls do not have the same traffic as sites on the main arteries.

An element that may become increasingly important in traffic studies is the presence of mass transit. As automobile driving becomes more expensive, more people may begin to use public transportation. This trend should be considered in location decisions. A site that is not accessible by public transportation may lose both vehicular and pedestrian traffic.

In any type of traffic count, a retailer should attempt to determine whether the vehicular or pedestrian traffic is made up of potential customers. If most of the traffic is not in the target market, then a high count is not helpful. Suppose a retailer of children's clothes discovers a site in the selected area that has a very high vehicular traffic count. If 75 percent of the vehicles passing contain businesspeople going to work, the location may not be as good as a location with half the traffic most of which consists of parents taking children to and from school.

Accessibility.   All the traffic in the city will be of little use if a site is not easy to enter and exit. Many site analyses are misleading about accessibility. Too much traffic may limit accessibility. This may be particularly true of intersection locations when one or both streets are divided. Such a location is indicated in Fig. 10.2. The service station A did not have a good location.

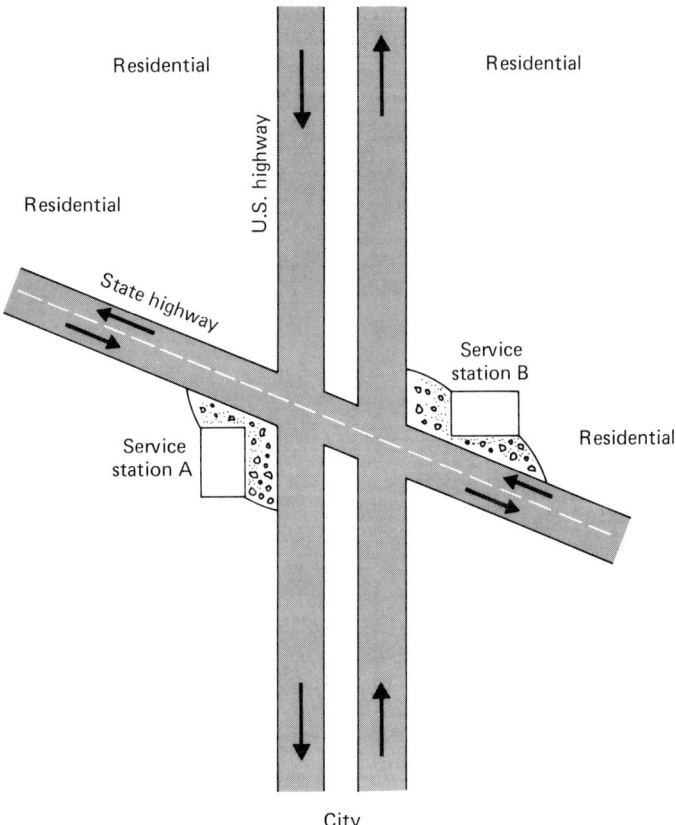

Figure 10.2
Accessibility differences at an intersection

The traffic count was extremely high and the station was accessible in the morning as people went to work, but most people bought gas on the way home in the afternoon. Station A was not at all accessible to out-bound traffic. Station B was successful because it was accessible when people wanted to buy gas.

Small differences in sites can also make large differences in the accessibility of a site. Such a situation is depicted in Fig. 10.3. Location A has poor accessibility. To reach location A a driver must exit the highway on a ramp that seems too far away or else circle the block (a distance of about 2 miles). Location B, which is adjacent to A, is a much better site. A driver can exit and drive right into the entry of the business. Site C is even better. During rush hour it is sometimes difficult to get into Site B even though the service road has a Yield sign, but Site C can be entered easily, regardless of traffic conditions.

Almost anyone can think of sites similar to those described here. These accessibility problems are easy for a retailer to see after a site is chosen. They are often not as apparent before the store is established. Sometimes a site will become less desirable because of changes in traffic patterns, not necessarily as drastic as changing a major route. Accessibility problems can

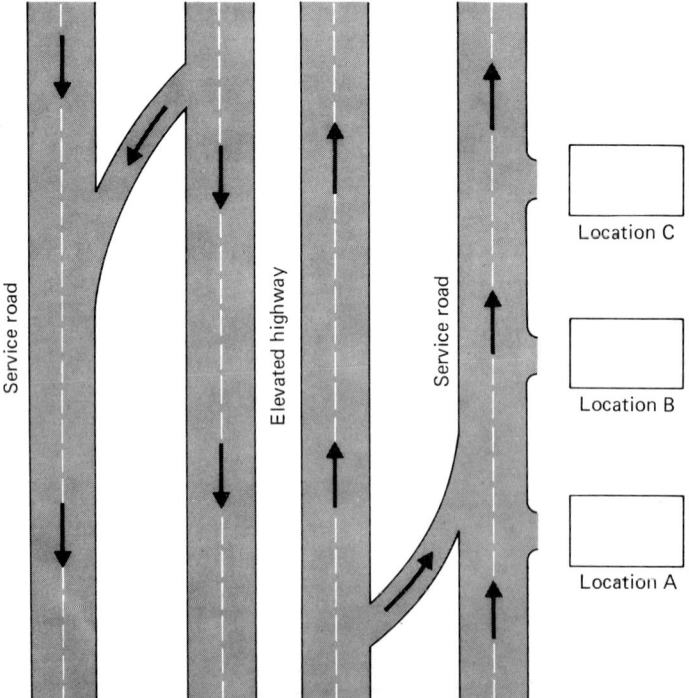

Figure 10.3
Accessibility differences resulting from off-ramps

occur when streets are made one-way, for instance. Retailers should investigate potential problem areas to determine if any changes are imminent. Changes made years after a site is selected are difficult to predict and avoid, however.

Parking.   Many customers will shop only where they can reasonably expect to find a parking space. One reason for the growth in shopping centers is the fact that free parking is available. Central business districts, free-standing stores, and strip developments often are plagued with too little parking or expensive parking. A retailer selecting a non–shopping center location (and even some shopping center locations) should be careful that the parking is sufficient now and will be sufficient in the future. Safe, secure, and accessible parking is demanded by most if not all customers. The customer will not often tolerate inadequate or unsafe parking.

Cost of the Site.   Too often the costs of sites are considered first and foremost in the site selection decision, but the cost of a site should be considered as a relative measure. The best measure of true cost is the percentage of total sales spent on the rent or mortgage. A location that costs $2 per square foot and produces sales of $40 per square foot is preferable to a location that costs $1 per square foot and produces sales of $5 per square foot. The cost of the site should be considered, but only in light of the benefits a site delivers. A site with little traffic, poor accessibility, and little parking is probably expensive regardless of the stated price of the site.

Locations that have more benefits are likely to be priced higher. A careful analysis is required to see if the higher-priced site really has lower costs. Obviously if two sites have very similar characteristics, the lower-priced site should be selected. In essence, price should be considered only after rating the benefits of a site. The retailer should not save a few dollars (or even a few thousand dollars) up front and lose many more dollars owing to lack of sales later. The fixed-cost site expense becomes small when spread over many years of high sales.

Aesthetic Considerations

There are some considerations that make their way less directly into the income statement. The location and appearance of the location may help establish the image of a store. A natural food store in a "plastic" setting may lose some of its identity. The same store in a location with trees, rocks, or other natural objects can probably foster a suitable image more easily.

The strategy and target market of the outlet help define what is aesthetically pleasing to customers. The site, if properly selected, may be one of the prime differentiating points of a store.

Barriers

Barriers affect delineation of trade areas and estimates of market potential. The barriers may be physical barriers or they may be psychological. A psychological barrier might be a neighborhood that is viewed as undesirable. A visitor to the area might not recognize the boundaries of the barrier, but the boundaries are there. These barriers are difficult to overcome, and sites affected by them should be avoided.

Physical barriers may be railroad tracks, poor roads, rivers, or a heavily traveled cross street. Whatever the barrier is, the retailer should note it during the locating process. Barriers that are harmful should be avoided. Any barrier is difficult if not impossible for the retailer to overcome.

Nonavailability of Sites

A retailer may discover that there are no sites in the selected area that meet the needs of the store or that zoning or other laws prohibit the use of a good site. When this occurs the retailer must either change the site requirements, try to have the ordinance changed, or select a different area. Great care should be taken before changing the site requirements. If the requirements were realistic in the beginning, the retailer should not discard them. To settle for a poor site is not usually good practice.

Sometimes a better solution is to go back to the step where the area was selected and reconsider the area. Often it is better to have a good site in a marginally worse area than to have a bad site in a slightly superior area. There are often several similar trading areas and one of these should have a good, available site. The retailer should not accept what is available unless the site comes very close to meeting his or her requirements.

Location Anomalies

How to select a good location is a difficult topic to understand. One reason is that there are some businesses that seem to have poor locations but are doing well. Other businesses seem to have good locations and are not doing nearly as well as they should. The key to the above statements is the word *seem.*

Near a Texas city is a very successful restaurant. The restaurant is about a one-hour drive from the city. The food quality and price are similar to many restaurants in the city. The restaurant is not elaborately decorated and, in fact, is somewhat rundown. To the casual observer, the restaurant has no distinguishing characteristics. Its location seems to make it almost undesirable. Careful analysis gives insight into why the restaurant is successful, however. People who go to the restaurant seem to consider it an "outing." The difficulties of getting to the restaurant constitute its distinguishing characteristic. People often tell friends how great the restaurant is, which may be a rationalization, but for whatever reason, the restaurant is successful. Its location is favorable *for that particular business.* Other restaurants that tried to locate near the successful restaurant were unsuccessful. Apparently only one restaurant could use this strategy.

Almost everyone can think of similar examples. The location that appears to be bad is not bad when all factors are considered. The anomalies only seem that way. Some retailers can turn a "bad" location into a good location, or at least overcome the deficiencies by astute manipulation of the retailing mix variables.

Conclusion:
Selecting the Site

The factors discussed above must be considered in the selection of a retail site. Other factors that should also be considered include drainage, garbage pickup, utility availability, and the like. One method that can help a retailer organize and evaluate the site selection factors is creating a checklist or rating form structured similarly to Table 10.1. The difference would simply involve substitution of the relevant site selection factors for the particular retailer.

MONITOR AND ADAPT

As with all other elements of the strategic retail management system, a retailer must monitor the situation and factors that lead to the selection of a specific site. New information or circumstances may force the retailer to adjust the location.

The retailer should be constantly aware of trends that develop. A city may begin growing in a different direction. A new housing development may arise. A new highway or street may change traffic patterns. A new shopping center may void a location advantage. Any of these changes and a multitude of others may affect the location. If the impact is great enough the location may have to be changed. There are also other things that can be tried when a location begins to lose its effectiveness.

Branch Stores

One step short of total relocation is the opening of a **branch store.** If the original location was good, the store may be ready for a branch. The branch location should be chosen in much the same manner as that of the original store. A new consideration is that the branch not take a major portion of its customers from the original store.

Large retailers often have branch stores in most major shopping centers as well as a downtown store. A small retailer can consider this philosophy on a smaller scale. A well-located home store and one or more well-located branches may help the retailer become a major force in an area.

Branch stores may become necessary when the competition moves into new locations and begins taking some of the retailer's business away. In this situation the retailer is trying to avoid a competitive threat rather than take advantage of a specific opportunity.

A branch or several branches also offer several advantages not specifically related to location. Branches may lower the average distribution and advertising cost of the business by spreading them over several stores. Merchandise can be moved between stores to allow for slight differences in customer preferences and to keep "fresh" merchandise in all the stores.

Other Retailing
Mix Adjustments

Rather than moving to a new location, a retailer may make adjustments in other parts of the retailing mix. Extra promotion or reduced prices may bring lost customers back. These adjustments have a cost associated with

STRATEGY IN ACTION 10.2

Locating the "Perfect 10"

The "perfect 10" for the Rite Aid drug chain is a 10 percent annual net increase in the number of new stores over the previous year. This year the chain plans to add 87 new drug stores to expand to 965 units, a 9.9 percent increase over last year. Next fiscal year Rite Aid has an objective of opening 100 new stores, or 10.4 percent of its current outlets. The 10 percent growth figure has been achieved the past five years.

When the chain consisted of "only" 500 stores the 10 percent objective was simpler to achieve. However, with the planned increase of around 100 stores per year, site selection has become an acute problem. Historically, regional shopping malls and strip centers were the mainstay of Rite Aid's location strategy. With the need to expand more rapidly than these two types of retail settings would allow, the chain is relying more on freestanding location sites.

Rite Aid seeks a real estate parcel of approximately 30,000 square feet for a "freestander." Around 6,500 square feet are used for store selling space and remaining space is largely allocated to parking for 30 to 35 cars. Obviously, the location of the 30,000 square feet lot is important. The location must be situated on a main traffic artery and accessible to an area with a high population density. The smallest trade area that Rite Aid considers is 8,000 to 10,000 people. However, if a strong independent pharmacy or a chain is already in the area, the opportunity becomes less viable.

The freestanding strategy offers some advantages and disadvantages to Rite Aid. On the plus side, with a freestander the store can be positioned between an existing shopping center and the population base. Customers are already passing by the store. Of course, the freestander also allows location in more sites and requires small parcels of land. On the negative side, freestanding locations cost more in rent, about $3,000 per year compared to a shopping center.

An interesting sidelight to Rite Aid's location decisions is their lack of interest in the Sunbelt. While many retailers have moved into the Sunbelt region, Rite Aid management contends that this area is too overstored with too many competitors vying for the best location sites.

Source: "Rite Aid: Looking for a Perfect 10," pp. 84–89. Reprinted by permission from *Chain Store Age Executive*, © January 1982. Copyright Lebhar-Friedman, Inc. 425 Park Avenue, New York, NY 10022.

them, but the costs of making the changes may be less than the costs of opening a new store. When location becomes a disadvantage rather than an advantage, some action must occur.

KEY CONCEPTS

Trading area analysis	Community center
Primary trading area	Neighborhood center
Secondary trading area	Strip development
Fringe trading area	Central business district
Reilly's Law of Retail Gravitation	Traffic
Economic base	Accessibility
Index of saturation	Location barriers
Super-regional center	Branch stores
Regional center	

REVIEW QUESTIONS

1. If college students are a retailer's target market, what are some characteristics the location should possess? Suppose the target market were young married people. Would your answer change? How?

2. Discuss how a retailer might use Reilly's law or a variation of it to define a trading area.

3. Discuss the use of the index of saturation and some problems with its use.

4. Discuss some of the advantages and disadvantages to small retailers of locating in large (regional) shopping centers.

5. What are the advantages and disadvantages large stores might realize in locating in large shopping centers?

6. Discuss some problems with and reasons for rejuvenating the central business districts.

7. Discuss the difference between traffic and accessibility. Which is most important?

8. Discuss the merits of and problems with using price, merchandise, and promotion to compensate for a poor location.

LEARNING EXERCISES

1. Think of two or three relatively large cities in your area. Try to map the trading area of each city using Reilly's law. Are these trading areas reasonably accurate from other observations that you can make?

2. Think of locations that seem to be poor but that are attracting large numbers of customers. Why do you think this contradiction occurs for these retailers?

DECISION SITUATION 10.1: **CHRIS'S DRUGS**

Chris, the owner of Chris's Drugs, is considering moving to a new location. The present location is on Main Street of a small Louisiana town. About 80% of the town's retail stores are within three blocks of Chris's. The building is over seventy years old and needs substantial reconditioning (carpets, fixtures, doors, and so on). These are projected to cost $20,000. The store is enjoying considerable success, with a yearly profit of about $75,000. Prescription drugs account for about $30,000 profit. The other $45,000 comes from nonprescription drugs, cosmetics, small appliances, jewelry, veterinary supplies, and other similar goods.

Chris is considering a new location because a new clinic to house all five of the town's doctors has been built near the town's only hospital. A site near the clinic (which is about one mile from Chris's present location) is available at a reasonable price. The lot and building that Chris wants would cost about $70,000. Most patients would have to pass the new location after leaving the clinic. Chris thinks he could increase his share of the prescription market from the present 25% to 40% by making the move. Chris would also have a store building designed specifically for a drugstore.

QUESTIONS

1. What are the significant variables for Chris to consider?

2. What other information would be helpful in making the decision?

3. If you were Chris, would you make the move? Why?

4. Would a branch store be possible? What factors favor branching?

DECISION SITUATION 10.2: **NANNY'S FASHIONS**

Evelyn has decided to open a store carrying infants' and children's clothes. She plans to carry a wide selection of better-quality clothes and will have two or three national brands in most lines. Her major problem involves where to locate the store. She is considering three different locations.

One location is a vacant building near the downtown section of a city of 300,000 people. The store was once a drugstore and is in good condition. There is ample street parking, although customers will have to "feed the meter." The cost of the store is about $5 per square foot. The building's owner will make the repairs and changes Evelyn wants.

Another site is in a small shopping center near an older housing area. The residents of the housing area earn an average of $18,000 per year and have an average age of 40. The shopping center has a large supermarket, a hardware store, a branch of a small regional department store, a Sears catalog store, and a video game store. All are reasonably busy, especially the game room. The cost of this site will be about $6 per square foot.

The third site is in a major shopping mall. The center has almost 100 shops including a Sears, a Penney's, and a large regional department store. The department store carries some of the same brands Evelyn will carry. The center is at the intersection of two of the busiest streets in town. Most residents consider this the best shopping center within one hundred miles. The cost of this site is $10 per square foot and a maintenance fee of 3% of gross income. Evelyn will have to be open when the center is open. The extra hours will require at least two additional clerks.

QUESTIONS

1. What are the principal advantages of each site? What are the disadvantages?

2. What are the characteristics of the customers that you would expect each site to attract?

3. Which site would you select?

4. If Evelyn plans a store of about 2,000 square feet and an average markup of 50 percent, how much additional revenue will she need to pay for the mall site?

Appendix
Mathematical
Location Models

A relatively nonmathematical discussion of location decisions and strategy was presented in Chapter 10. Location decisions can also be approached in a more quantitative manner. This appendix is designed for those who prefer a more mathematical treatment. Practical application of these techniques is becoming increasingly feasible as more and more retailers gain access to computer technology and substantial data bases become more readily available. Most consulting firms that specialize in location and most large, multi-unit retailers presently use some or all of these models (or variations of them).

All of the models discussed in this appendix are attempts to quantify critical location factors such as those discussed in Chapter 10. The models are simply techniques for organizing and summarizing location information to facilitate analysis and evaluation of retail location. The four specific techniques or models discussed are

- Reilly's law

- Huff's model

- Spotting technique

- Regression model

REILLY'S LAW

Reilly's law represents the earliest attempt to quantify the location decision.[15] It focuses on predicting the size of a city's trade area. The original model simply uses the population of the city to predict the size of the city's trade area. (A market center other than a city might also be used.)

Paul Converse reformulated the original model to allow calculation of the breaking point between two cities under consideration. The *breaking point* between two cities is the "dividing line" between the trade areas of the cities. The formula is

Breaking point (miles from City A)

$$= \frac{\text{Distance between A \& B (in miles)}}{1 + \sqrt{\dfrac{\text{Population of B}}{\text{Population of A}}}}$$

As an illustration, assume that City A and City B are 80 miles apart and that the population is 200,000 in City A and 1,800,000 in City B. The breaking point would be calculated as follows:

$$\text{Breaking point} = \frac{80}{1 + \sqrt{\dfrac{1,800,000}{200,000}}} = \frac{80}{1 + \sqrt{9}} = 20 \text{ miles.}$$

Therefore, the trade area of City A would extend 20 miles toward City B and the trade area of City B would extend 60 miles toward City A. To define the total trade area of City A (in all directions), calculations for City A and many other cities could be made. The results of these calculations could then be plotted on a map; lines connecting the plotted breaking points would graphically define the total trade area for City A. The total population of the trade area could then be determined.

Although Reilly's model can be useful, there are also a few shortcomings. Driving *time* may be more important than driving *distance*. The quality of retail shopping in a city may be more important than population for actually determining trade area. These and other problems can be partially alleviated by adjusting the formula. A more serious shortcoming is that the model works best for intercity analysis with rural areas between each city. David Huff has developed a model that is more useful for *intracity* analysis.

HUFF'S MODEL

Huff's model is based on the assumption that a consumer expects a shopping trip to be more successful if a large number of items are carried by the shopping center. (Note that *shopping center* in this context refers to any shopping area within a city, either planned or unplanned, including the central business district.) Since a consumer wants a shopping trip to be successful, the consumer is willing to travel greater distances to gain access to more goods and services. The formula to express this relationship is[16]

$$P(C_{ij}) = \frac{\dfrac{S_j}{T_{ij}^{\lambda}}}{\displaystyle\sum_{j=1}^{n} \dfrac{S_j}{T_{ij}^{\lambda}}},$$

where

$P(C_{ij})$ = Probability that a consumer residing in area i will travel to shopping center j.

S_j = Square footage of selling space devoted to a desired class of goods by shopping center j.

T_{ij} = Travel time or distance between area i and center j.

λ = Empirically estimated parameter to reflect the effect of travel time on the specific type of goods desired.

The steps involved in obtaining the data for the equation are

1. Divide the area under consideration into smaller areas or statistical units to define the i values.

2. Determine the selling space of each shopping center in the area under consideration to define the S_j values.

3. Determine the travel times or distances between the areas selected in Step 1 and the centers under consideration to define the T_{ij} values.

4. Estimate the value of λ. A model developed by Huff and Blue is frequently used as a method of estimating this value.[17]

5. Calculate the probability of shopping at a shopping center, $P(C_{ij})$, for each statistical unit selected in Step 1 using the formula.

6. Map the trading area of the shopping center by connecting each statistical unit with like probabilities.

To illustrate this calculation for one statistical unit, assume

S_1 = 20,000 square feet
S_2 = 30,000 square feet
T_{11} = 3 miles
T_{12} = 4 miles
λ = 2 (assumed).

Therefore,

$$P(C_{11}) = \frac{\dfrac{20,000}{3^2}}{\dfrac{20,000}{3^2} + \dfrac{30,000}{4^2}} = 0.54.$$

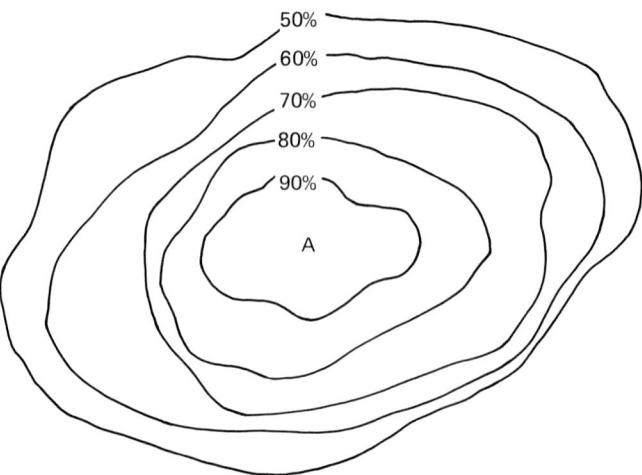

Figure A10.1
Trade area map for shopping center A in probability contours

This calculation means that there is a 54% probability that a customer in statistical area 1 will choose to shop at shopping center 1 for the goods in question. To map the trading area for shopping center 1, the probabilities for every statistical area would be calculated; the areas with similar probabilities (i.e, between 50% and 60%) would be connected to yield a probability contour map such as shown in Fig. A10.1.

It is important to note that the trading area for each product category is likely to be different. Consequently, a separate calculation should be made for each product category.

As mentioned above, when analyzing the trading area of a given shopping center, separate calculations must be made for each statistical area and for each major product category. When analyzing an entire city for the purposes of selecting a new location, calculations must also be made for each key shopping center. For example, if a city has 10 major shopping centers and the analysts choose only 200 statistical areas, 2000 calculations (10 × 200) would be necessary *for each product category*. The number of potential calculations combined with the likelihood of the probability contours changing shape rapidly (because of the opening of a new center or a major new subdivision, for example) highlights the practical difficulties of using Huff's model.

Note that other relevant variables, such as store image,[18] can also be incorporated in the model.

SPOTTING TECHNIQUE

The **spotting technique** was proposed by Applebaum.[19] The spotting technique is related to Huff's method of delineating trade areas, although it is less rigorous. Applebaum proposed that each store is surrounded by three zones: the primary trade area, the secondary trade area, and the fringe (or tertiary) trade area. He defined the *primary trade area* as the area that contains 50–60% of the retailer's customers. The *secondary trade area* contains 10–20% of the customers. The remaining customers are in the *fringe trading area.*

The first step of the spotting technique involves defining a series of geographical bands (often a quarter of a mile wide) around the store under consideration. Consumers who live in these bands are interviewed to determine their shopping patterns relative to the specific store. The *drawing power* of the store is defined by the proportion of respondents in each band who normally shop at the store. This information forms the basis for defining the primary, secondary, and fringe trading areas.

When looking for a new site, a retailer can use the spotting technique in delineating existing competitors' relative drawing power. Gaps in the primary and secondary areas of competitors are likely to indicate good sites.

REGRESSION MODELS

There are several specific models that use **regression analysis** as a basis for estimating market potential within a trading area. The data necessary to operationalize these models are derived from examining the location factors that have a significant influence on sales. Chains are the primary users of regression models, although location consultants may have a customized model for various retail trades.

The regression model might be stated as follows:

$$\text{Estimated sales} = a + b_1X_1 + b_2X_2 + b_3X_3 \ldots + b_nX_n.$$

The X_i values represent the location factors, such as household income, number of people in specific age groups, vehicular traffic, pedestrian traffic, consumption patterns, quantified accessibility score, and so on. The a and b_i values are coefficients developed in the model-building process.

To build a regression model, the various location factors must be selected and evaluated for many stores. This evaluation results in the coefficients a and b_i for each location factor. Additional sites can then be evaluated by measuring or estimating each factor for the new site and plugging these values into the regression model. The site with the highest score should be the best site.

SUMMARY

The techniques presented in this appendix represent some quantifiable general models and methods that can facilitate the location decision. Any of these and other available techniques can help retailers perform more logical evaluations of the various location factors. However, those who use these models, figures, and calculations must realize that they represent present and historical data. Future conditions may obviously be different and cannot be adequately considered in the models.

As a further warning, a battery of sophisticated techniques will not guarantee a good decision. There are many nonquantifiable variables in any location decision. The location suggested by any or all of the models may not be the best location. Rather than providing the decision, these models and techniques should be used to provide input for the retailer's decision-making process. In other words, the retailer should also exercise good judgment.

NOTES

1.   Howard L. Green, as reported in "Selecting a Store Site, the Computer Way," *Chain Store Age Executive*, vol. 57 (March 1981), p. 46.

2.   Philip Kotler, *Marketing Management Analysis, Planning and Control*, 2nd ed. (Englewood Cliffs, N.J.: Prentice-Hall, 1972), pp. 617–618.

3.   "Computer Analysis Aids Strategic Site Location," *Stores*, vol. 58 (July 1976), pp. 25–27.

4.   Ralph S. Alexander, *Marketing Definitions: A Glossary of Marketing Terms* (Chicago: American Marketing Association, 1960), p. 22.

5.   Barry Berman and Joel R. Evans, *Retail Management: A Strategic Approach* (New York: Macmillan, 1979), p. 195.

6.   Summaries of the information provided by each are given in Berman and Evans, *op. cit.*, pp. 204–210.

7.   William J. Reilly, *Method for the Study of Retail Relationships*, Research Monograph No. 4 (Austin: University of Texas Press, 1929).

8.   David Huff, "A Probabilistic Analysis of Consumer Spatial Behavior," in *Emerging Concepts in Marketing*, Winter Conference Proceedings, ed. William S. Decker (Chicago: American Marketing Association, 1972, pp. 443–461.

9.   David Huff, *Determination of Intra-Urban Retail Trade Areas* (Los Angeles: University of California Real Estate Research Program, 1962).

10. Bernard J. LaLonde, "New Frontiers in Store Location," *Supermarket Merchandising* (February 1963), p. 110.

11. These patterns are more completely explained in Chauncy D. Arris and Edward L. Ullman, "The Nature of Cities," *Annals of the American Academy of Political and Social Sciences*, vol. 242 (November 1945). A later, more condensed version appears in Joseph Barry Mason and Morris Lehman Mayer, *Modern Retailing Theory and Practice* (Dallas, Tex.: Business Publications, 1978), pp. 477–479.

12. Dennis H. Tootelian, "The Suburban Centre," a case in *Marketing Management: Cases and Readings*, ed. Dennis H. Tootelian, Ralph M. Gaedeke, and Leete A. Thompson (Santa Monica, Calif.: Goodyear Publishing Company, 1980), p. 163.

13. Joseph Barry Mason, "Power and Channel Conflicts in Shopping Center Development," *Journal of Marketing*, vol. 39 (April 1975), pp. 28–35.

14. Many articles have appeared on this subject. A partial list includes "Downtown— The Road Back: Who Is Doing What to Revitalize Downtown," *Stores*, vol. 58 (July 1976), pp. 3–5; "Downtown Malls Debated," *Chain Store Age Executive*, vol. 53 (May 1977), pp. 56–57; "How to Evaluate Downtown Development," *Stores*, vol. 62 (Fall 1980), pp. 61–62; and "Big Stores Vote for Downtown Again," *Business Week*, September 1976, pp. 13–22.

15. Reilly, *op. cit.*

16. David L. Huff, "Defining and Estimating a Trading Area," *Journal of Marketing*, vol. 28 (July 1964), p. 35.

17.   David L. Huff and Larry Blue, *A Programmed Solution for Estimating Retail Sales Potential* (Lawrence, Kans.: Center for Regional Studies, 1966).

18.   Thomas J. Stanley and Murphy A. Sewell, "Image Inputs to a Probabilistic Model: Predicting Retail Potential," *Journal of Marketing*, vol. 40 (July 1976), pp. 48–52.

19.   William Applebaum, "Methods for Determining Stores' Trade Areas, Market Penetration and Potential Sales," *Journal of Marketing Research*, vol. 3 (May 1966), pp. 127–141.

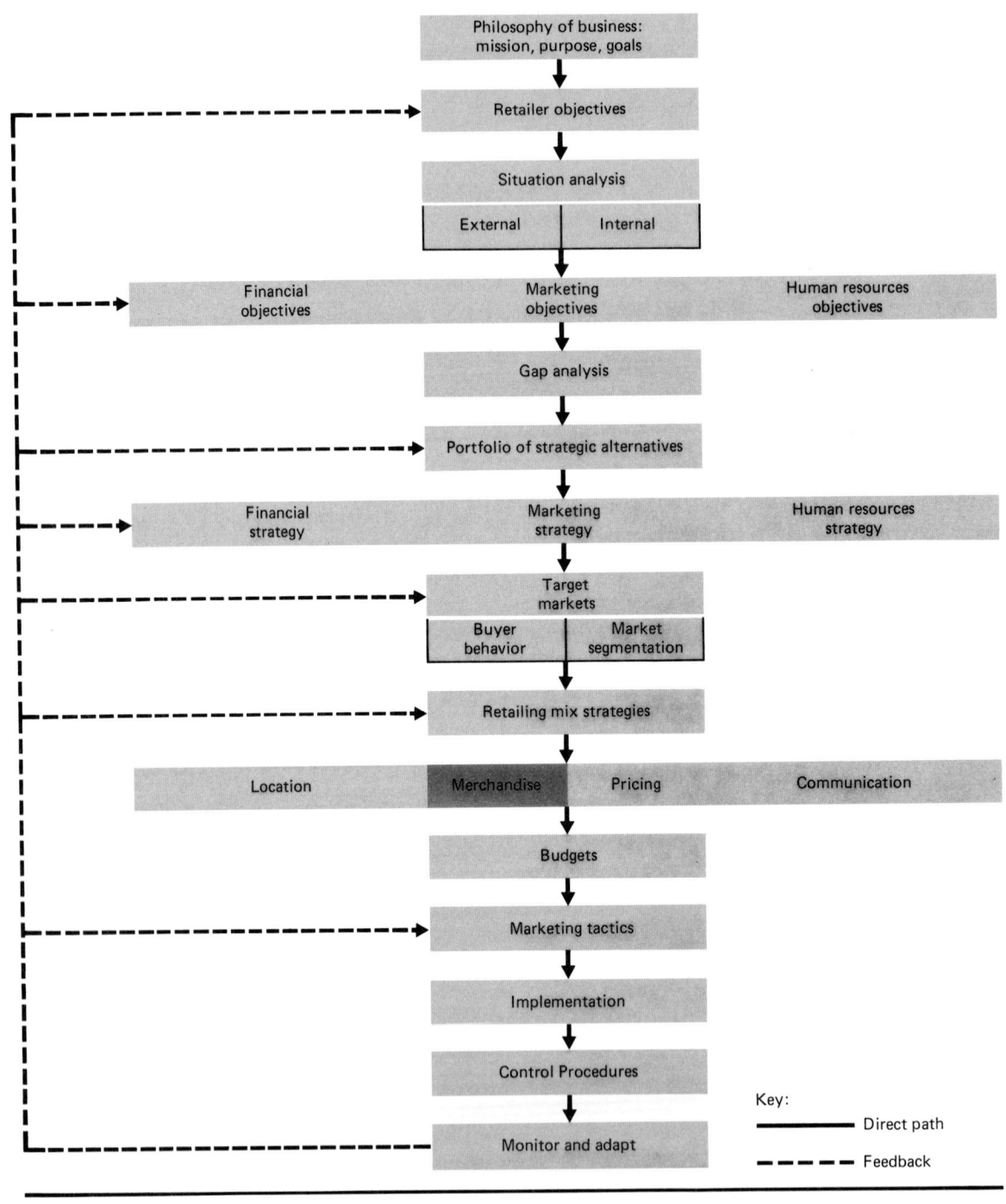

STRATEGIC RETAIL MANAGEMENT MODEL

Philosophy of business:
mission, purpose, goals

Retailer objectives

Situation analysis

External | Internal

Financial objectives | Marketing objectives | Human resources objectives

Gap analysis

Portfolio of strategic alternatives

Financial strategy | Marketing strategy | Human resources strategy

Target markets

Buyer behavior | Market segmentation

Retailing mix strategies

Location | Merchandise | Pricing | Communication

Budgets

Marketing tactics

Implementation

Control Procedures

Monitor and adapt

Key:
———— Direct path
- - - - Feedback

Chapter 11
Merchandise Planning and Budgeting Decisions

LEARNING OBJECTIVES

1. To understand the strategic merchandise planning process.

2. To understand the fundamentals of merchandise budgeting.

INTRODUCTION

"Goods well bought are goods well sold" is one form of an old retailing adage. Despite its triteness, it lingers on because it remains appropriate. Although consumer buying decisions may be influenced by a variety of retailing strategy variables (such as price, location, personnel, and so on), a major key to successful retailing involves matching the store's merchandise and service offerings to the needs, preferences, and expectations of the target customers.

The retailer has three major concerns relative to merchandising: planning, buying, and controlling. The focus of this chapter is on strategic merchandise planning. Buying and controlling are discussed in Chapters 12 and 13, respectively.

This chapter first introduces basic merchandising terminology, then considers the overall process for strategic merchandise planning. Finally, the specifications necessary to generate the merchandise budget, a primary output of merchandise planning used for buying and controlling activities, are addressed.

MERCHANDISING TERMINOLOGY

It is helpful to understand the basic merchandising terminology used by retailers before attempting to learn the strategic merchandise planning process. Table 11.1 defines and describes the key merchandising terminology used in this chapter. It is especially critical to distinguish between variety, assortment, and depth. Table 11.2 presents examples of these concepts for two retailers.

MERCHANDISE PLANNING

As shown in the strategic merchandise planning and budgeting decision model in Fig. 11.1, merchandise planning activities can be divided into five broad steps:

1. Review all existing information and plans.

2. Formulate merchandise philosophy.

3. Determine merchandise objectives.

4. Formulate merchandise budget.

5. Prepare the buying plan.

REVIEW ALL EXISTING INFORMATION AND PLANS

The first step in merchandise planning involves a thorough review of all existing information and current plans. A retailer's merchandise has a major influence on other retailing factors. The pricing and communication strate-

Table 11.1
Merchandising terminology

TERM	DESCRIPTION
Product	A salable unit, normally a tangible object or service. Examples include a hammer, purse, coffee, hair cut, and so on.
Product line	All of the products and services offered by a retail organization. Retailers collect and assemble various manufacturers' product lines into a retail product line.
Variety	Used to describe a retailer's product line. Refers to generically different product groups or classifications. For example, a donut shop might have an extremely narrow variety (or *breadth*) consisting of donuts and drinks (two product groups).
Assortment	Used to describe a retailer's product line. Refers to the range of choice or alternatives within a particular variety or product group. For example, the donut shop with narrow variety might have a wide assortment of donuts, such as 42 different kinds.
Assortment factors	The various specifications used to select an assortment for a particular variety: brands, size, weight, color, and so on.
Depth	The degree of support or number of units carried for a particular merchandise item.

Source: Drawn from many sources. See, for example, Joseph Barry Mason and Morris Lehman Mayer, *Modern Retailing* (Plano, Tex.: Business Publications, 1981), pp. 298–302. © BUSINESS PUBLICATIONS, INC., 1978 and 1981.

Table 11.2
Variety, assortment, and depth for two retailers

	DARYL'S SHORT STOP		RYAN'S SUPER FOODS	
QUESTIONS	ANSWER	EXAMPLES	ANSWER	EXAMPLES
What kind of *variety?*	Relatively *narrow;* limited to fast-moving food, beverage, and nonfood items	Items normally carried in a convenience food store	*Wide;* "complete" line of food and beverage items plus many categories of nonfood items	Items normally carried in a large, full-line supermarket
What kind of *assortments* in each product category?	*Narrow*	For catsup: one brand — Hunt's; two sizes — 14 oz. and 32 oz.	*Wide*	For catsup: four brands — Hunt's, Heinz, Del Monte, and Ryan's house brand; four sizes for each brand — 14 oz., 20 oz., 24 oz., and 32 oz.
What kind of *depth* for each *assortment factor?*	*Shallow* for many items but *deep* for selected items	Stocks 3 cases of Hunt's 14 oz. catsup and 1 case of Hunt's 32 oz.	*Deep* for many items but *shallow* "slow-movers"	Stocks 3 cases for each brand; less than a case for strawberry syrup, cocktail onions, Korean noodles, etc.

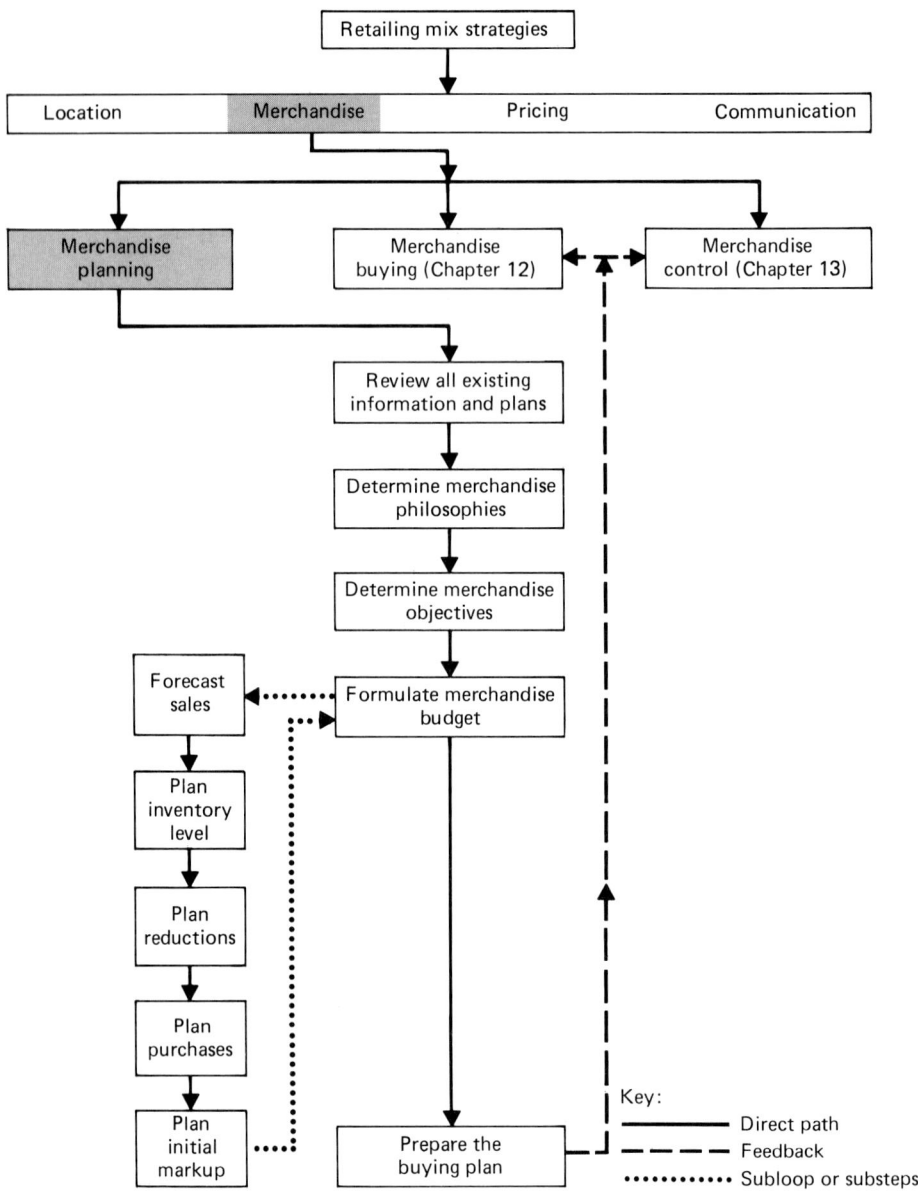

Figure 11.1
Merchandise planning and budgeting decision model

gies will be heavily dependent on merchandise. Conversely, merchandise must reflect the retailer's overall business philosophy and be compatible with all retailing strategies.

Although all information and strategic plans must be considered, particular attention should be devoted to the target customers, competition, marketing objectives, and financial objectives. *Customers* are the key to a successful retail business. Customers visit a particular retail store because they anticipate need satisfaction. Retailers satisfy customers' needs primarily with merchandise and services. Therefore, knowing the target customers well enough to supply them with an offering they are willing to purchase is the first key.

A second key involves knowledge of *competition*. All retailers occupy a position relative to their competition, regardless of whether they plan it. The merchandise a retailer carries is a major determinant of the store's competitive position.

A third key for review is the store's *marketing objectives*, usually stated in terms of sales (sometimes including market share). In general, the merchandise plan or budget details how merchandise can contribute to accomplishing the overall marketing objectives.

The fourth key is the store's *financial objectives*. Although various financial objectives can be stated, profit- and cash-related objectives are

STRATEGY IN ACTION 11.1

Changing Merchandise for a Changing Market

Jordan Marsh, a fourteen-store division of Allied Stores Corporation, faced the same problem that all retailers confront, how to adapt to changing demographics and downtown shopping patterns. Their solution was to completely rebuild the downtown Boston flagship store. The store's size was halved to 850,000 square feet, which meant eliminating some departments and reducing the size of other departments. The physical redevelopment of the store also required an altered merchandising philosophy.

Consumer research completed at the time of renovation indicated that consumers were responding more to higher-quality goods, regardless of the price. These studies also showed that Boston had large segments of people in the 25 to 44 and 55 to 64 age groups, both of which are considered quite affluent.

The results of substantially reducing floor space and the existing demographics brought about a different merchandising direction. Merchandise was upgraded. As an example, decorator-type furniture with names such as Drexel, Heritage, and Henredon were added to the merchandise lines. Designer names became much more common in men's and women's apparel. There is a 3,000 square foot area devoted just to designer-label men's wear. Professional women's clothing is offered under departments entitled "Investments." A Gucci Shop and a Baccarat Shop featuring sculptured china from France were also opened at the same time.

In adapting to consumers' changing wants, Jordan Marsh also added a home computer department. According to executives, the department is off to a good start.

Elliot J. Stone, president of Jordan Marsh, comments, "We have to make important statements in our merchandise to show that we back what we believe." Jordan Marsh has done that in restructuring their downtown Boston store.

Source: "Jordan Marsh Reflects Boston Profile," p. 72. Reprinted by permission from *Chain Store Age Executive,* © March 1982. Copyright Lebhar-Friedman, Inc. 425 Park Avenue, New York, NY 10022.

common. Ideally, marketing and financial objectives are in harmony. Sometimes, however, subsequent strategy planning will uncover points of conflict. A marketing objective that calls for an increase in sales may necessitate a corresponding increase in merchandise inventory, for example. This increase in inventory requires cash, which could be in conflict with financial objectives calling for cash conservation.

FORMULATE A MERCHANDISE PHILOSOPHY

The retailer's second major step is to formulate a basic merchandise philosophy, which can be viewed as a broad, overall guide for making further merchandise decisions. Six components must be considered: variety, price-quality dimensions, brand dimensions, turnover, gross margin return on investment, and stock balance.

Variety

The retailer's philosophy about variety is perhaps the major determinant of what business the retailer is in. Remember that variety refers to the number of generically different product classifications. One retailer may have a variety consisting only of shoes. This retailer obviously runs a shoe store. Another retailer may also carry shoes but have additional product categories such as men's suits, slacks, sport coats, shirts, and ties. This retailer's variety makes his store a men's store. Each of these variety patterns represents a different degree of the **specialized merchandising philosophy**.

Retailers can also choose a **scrambled merchandising philosophy**. This involves increasing breadth of variety to include products outside the traditional domain. Many drugstores also carry garden equipment and supplies, food, and hardware; supermarkets often carry calculators, cameras, watches, plants, and even TV sets. Retailers engaged in scrambled merchandising usually have wide breadth and depth in their major merchandise lines, but only a scattered assortment of other product lines. These other lines are typically highly profitable owing to either high volume or high profit margins.

Neither scrambled nor specialized merchandising has an inherent advantage over the other. Depending on the situation, either policy can be used successfully. In fact, there appears to be a trend *both* ways, toward increased specialization *and* toward greater scrambling, with fewer stores attempting a middle-of-the-road approach. This trend is called *retail polarization*. The variety philosophy must be integrated with the retailer's overall retailing strategy because the merchandise variety is the most visible indication of the retailer's business strategy.

Price-Quality Dimensions

The second component of the retailer's merchandise philosophy is price-quality dimensions. At the extremes, the retailer can carry high-quality merchandise at high prices or low-quality merchandise at lower prices. Most retailers fit somewhere between these two extremes. There is no "best" approach. The retailer must choose the price-quality approach that is most attractive to his or her target customers. A men's wear outlet with target market criteria of college education and over $30,000 income might carry higher-quality and higher-priced merchandise. Another retailer might carry the same quality but at lower prices. Still another men's wear outlet with a less prosperous target market might feature lower prices associated with lower-quality merchandise. The price-quality philosophy chosen by the retailer will have a large impact on the other philosophy components.

Brand Dimensions   From the retailer's standpoint, there are three basic types of brands: (1) manufacturers' and wholesalers' brands, (2) private brands, and (3) generics.

Manufacturer brands are initiated by producers such as Del Monte and Westinghouse. *Wholesaler brands* are initiated by wholesalers such as the Topmost brand by General Grocer. The retailer's advantages in carrying these types of brands include the opportunity to tap customer brand loyalty, to take advantage of the manufacturers' or wholesalers' promotion efforts, and perhaps identification with the positive image of certain brands.[1]

STRATEGY IN ACTION 11.2

Woolco's Merchandise Strategy

Many retailers feel that environmental changes such as slower economic growth, higher energy prices, and more working women have created a new breed of consumer. Further, these new consumers "will need to be lured by value, particularly in quality products, and by ease of shopping."

Woolco's strategic reaction to these changes has been to move toward adopting an "upscale" discount store concept. The resulting "upscale merchandising" strategy consists of offering higher quality merchandise than the traditional discount store while maintaining discount prices. The strategic adaptation involves both merchandise paring and upgrading.

Departments carrying big-ticket items such as furniture and large home appliances are getting pared. Departments with high labor needs are also getting pared, such as pet centers, key-making, and blinds-cutting. The merchandise variety in many departments has also been reduced to eliminate slow-moving lines and make popular lines more visible.

Woolco is also reclaiming several departments that have previously been leased to other operators, such as womenswear, shoes, and automotive centers. Woolco is also bolstering its apparel lines, which provide the most sales per square foot and are among the most profitable departments. Specific changes involve increased variety of apparel, greater visibility for the apparel departments, and increased emphasis on better-known brands. In addition, infantwear has been relocated toward the front of the store because of its good growth potential.

Note: See Chapter 18 for Strategy in Action box on Woolco's layout strategy.

Source: Marjorie Leedy, "Sparring Starts for Scarcer Retail Dollars," *The Clarion-Ledger,* 20 September 1981, p. C-1.

Private brands are owned by the retailer. These brands are normally produced by a manufacturer, who may also produce a manufacturer's brand, but the manufacturer is not usually identified on the product. Using a private brand gives the retailer the opportunity to obtain products of a specified quality at the lowest cost, to develop more efficient promotion, to generate higher gross margins, and to improve the store image. Examples of private brands include Kenmore (Sears) and Ann Page (A&P).[2]

Generics (also called "no-frills" and "no-brand") are characterized by lack of a specific brand name, plain labels, low cost, and minimal advertising. A wide variety of generics are available in categories such as food, beverages, household products, and health and beauty aids.[3]

The retailer must decide whether to carry each of these types of brands and determine the balance between types. These decisions must be integrated with other merchandise philosophies and overall strategy.

Turnover

The retailer's **turnover** (or turnover rate) is *the number of times the average inventory is sold and replaced during a period of time* (usually a year).[4] Three alternative methods of calculating turnover rate are shown in Table 11.3.

Since turnover relates sales to average inventory, it is a ratio that provides an indication of the velocity or speed with which the merchandise flows through the store. A high turnover rate indicates that merchandise is selling well relative to the average amount of inventory kept in stock. A low turnover indicates that goods are not moving very quickly relative to average inventory.

Note that a low turnover rate is not necessarily bad. Table 11.4 shows turnover rates ranging from 29.4 for gasoline service stations to 3.3 for hardware stores. Whether a particular retailer's turnover rate is too high or low is determined by comparison with trade practice and by relating turnover to other philosophies and strategies.

The retailer's turnover philosophy (that is, higher or lower than average turnover) must be compatible with the retailer's other philosophies and strategies. High turnover rates, for example, are not normally compatible with a high price/high quality philosophy. To fully develop a reasonable turnover philosophy, the retailer should also develop a gross margin philosophy.

Gross Margin Return on Investment (GMROI)[5]

The **GMROI** concept can serve as a measure of the relative efficiency of the retailer's investment in inventory. It is a measure of return on *inventory* investment before expenses. The computation is made using gross margin (or gross profit) and inventory investment. The GMROI ratio is

$$GMROI = \frac{GM}{AI_c},$$

where,

GM = gross margin dollars or sales minus cost of goods sold
AI_c = average inventory investment (at actual cost).

Table 11.3
Turnover rate calculations

Sales dollar basis

$$T = \frac{S}{AI_r}$$

where

T = turnover rate
S = net sales dollars
AI_r = average inventory in retail dollars*

Cost basis

$$T = \frac{S_c}{AI_c}$$

where

S_c = sales at cost or cost of goods sold (CGS)
AI_c = average inventory at cost

Unit basis

$$T = \frac{S_u}{AI_u}$$

where

S_u = number of units sold
AI_u = average inventory in units

Example: Assume a retailer sells 300 blouses in a year. The blouses cost a total of $3,600 and the retailer had net sales of $6,000. The average inventory was 50 blouses that cost $600 and were valued on a retail basis at $1,000.

$$T = \frac{S}{AI_r} \qquad T = \frac{S_c}{AI_c} \qquad T = \frac{S_u}{AI_u}$$

$$= \frac{\$6000}{\$1000} \qquad = \frac{\$3600}{\$600} \qquad = \frac{300}{50}$$

$$= 6 \qquad\qquad = 6 \qquad\qquad = 6$$

*Note that

$$AI_r = \frac{I}{n_I},$$

where

I = sum of available inventory figures
n_I = number of available inventory figures.

Thus, in the above example, if the retailer obtained periodic inventory figures of $800, $1000, and $1200:

$$AI_r = \frac{I}{n_I} = \frac{\$800 + \$1000 + \$1200}{3} = \frac{\$3000}{3} = \$1000.$$

GMROI does not indicate clearly the relationship we want to emphasize—the relationship between gross margin and turnover. This relationship can be developed by changing the average inventory from the cost to the retail basis. Hence, GMROI at retail can be calculated as follows:

$$GMROI\text{-}R = \frac{GM}{AI_r} = \frac{GM}{S} \times \frac{S}{AI_r} = GM\% \times T,$$

Table 11.4
Examples of turnover rates

TYPE OF RETAILER	MEDIAN STOCK TURNOVER RATE
Building materials dealers	5.2
Hardware stores	3.3
Garden supply and mobile home dealers	4.2
General merchandise stores	4.2
Food stores	13.1
Motor vehicle dealers	6.9
Gasoline service stations	29.4
Apparel and accessory stores	3.4
Furniture and home furnishings stores	3.6
Eating and drinking places	18.4
Drugstores and proprietary stores	4.9
Liquor stores	7.1

Source: From the book, *Almanac of Business and Industrial Financial Ratios,* 1980 edition, by Leo Troy. © 1980 by Prentice-Hall, Inc. Published by Prentice-Hall, Inc., Englewood Cliffs, New Jersey 07632.

where:

$\qquad AI_r$ = average inventory investment (at retail)
$\qquad S$ = sales
$\qquad T$ = turnover rate.

The **GMROI-R** concept is a way to gauge the relative contribution of diverse products by combining gross margin and turnover. It may be more easily calculated by those retailers who take periodic inventory only and who do not have inventory cost figures readily available.

Although GMROI-R is a logical way to relate gross margin and turnover, it is not a measure of return on inventory investment, as is GMROI. The reason is found in the ratio's denominator. The AI of GMROI-R is not the actual investment (or cost) in inventory; it is the retail value of inventory. GMROI-R will generally yield the same interpretation as GMROI, such as when considering multiple-purchase alternatives. Table 11.5 shows GMROI and GMROI-R calculations for a hypothetical retailer.

As can be seen in Table 11.5, analysis of the single factors of sales or gross margin would indicate deletion of Brand A. However, further analysis using GMROI and GMROI-R demonstrates that Brand A is actually the most efficient brand in utilizing investment dollars. In this situation, use of GMROI or GMROI-R could have prevented a mistake; the deletion decision now calls for further analysis of factors such as customer attitudes and expectations, space availability, other opportunities, funds available, and so on.

Table 11.5
Examples of GMROI and GMROI-R calculations

Situation

For a number of reasons, a women's apparel retailer is considering dropping one of the three brands of ladies' handbags currently carried in stock. The following data were accumulated:

	BRAND A	BRAND B	BRAND C
Sales	$1000	$1200	$1500
GM-dollars	400	480	600
AI_c	120	180	300
AI_r	200	300	500
Calculations			
GM percentage (S ÷ GM × 100)	40%	40%	40%
Turnover (S ÷ AI_r)	5.0	4.0	3.0
GMROI (GM ÷ AI_c)	367%	267%	200%
GMROI-R (GM% × T)	200%	160%	120%

GMROI-R can also be used to demonstrate a fundamental merchandise strategy trade-off between gross margin and turnover, as shown in Table 11.6. Retailers in the same trade can achieve identical GMROI-R ratings with drastically different strategies. On one extreme, a retailer can pursue a high turnover rate while accepting a relatively low gross margin per unit, that is, a small margin on many units. The opposite extreme is a low turnover rate and relatively high gross margins.

This fundamental trade-off has far-ranging strategic implications for other retailing mix variables and for the retailer's expense structure. The retailer who pursues high turnover, such as a supermarket, must normally lean toward lower prices, highly visible locations, much advertising and sales promotion, wide variety, and assortments of proven good sellers. Retailers with lower turnover, such as jewelry stores, but high gross margins

Table 11.6
Examples of the gross margin and turnover trade-off

GROSS MARGIN %	×	TURNOVER RATE	=	GMROI-R
20.0		10		200
25.0		8		200
33.3		6		200
50.0		4		200
100.0		2		200

are usually characterized by high prices, high merchandise quality, high service level, more personal selling, narrow variety, and wide or deep assortments.

Stock Balance

The sixth component of merchandise philosophy involves formulating a **stock balance** philosophy. The retailer must decide how to employ the three merchandise dimensions—variety, assortment, and depth. The combination of these three dimensions forms the retailer's stock balance.

Because of constraints such as space and financial limitations, most retailers must be highly selective in tailoring inventories to create a stock balance that meets the demands of customers and the firm's objectives. Sporting goods retailers cannot usually offer a variety that includes all possible categories of sporting goods. Further, for the product categories they carry, few can offer an assortment that includes items for every possible assortment factor (all brands, sizes, and models of fishing rods, for instance). As a result, retailers must be prepared to make judicious trade-offs between variety, assortment, depth, and investment.

Typically, the variety and total investment factors are relatively fixed for a given planning period, with total investment in inventory being the most difficult factor for most retailers to adjust. Table 11.7 depicts examples of the various trade-off situations faced by retailers.

Maintaining a reasonable stock balance is a general merchandise philosophy for all retailers. Each retailer should transform this general philosophy into a more specific goal that provides ongoing guidance.

Conclusion: Merchandise Philosophy

The retailer's merchandise philosophy should serve as an overall guide for planning merchandising strategy. The six basic components are variety, price-quality dimensions, brand dimensions, turnover, gross margin return on investment, and stock balance. Retailers should use these components to construct a logical, consistent statement of philosophy. Examples of two diverse philosophy statements are presented below.

> *Example 1:* For a ski clothing outlet: "We carry a narrow variety consisting of ski clothing. Only high-quality merchandise is carried. As a result, prices are somewhat higher than average, which leads us to a higher than average gross margin percentage and lower than average turnover. Our stock balance emphasizes wide assortments."

> *Example 2:* For a full-line sporting goods store: "We carry a wide variety of sporting goods. Popular prices (with corresponding quality) are emphasized. Turnover and gross margin are about average for the trade. The wide variety and wide assortments for selected product categories are emphasized."

The philosophy components must be compatible with each other and appropriate for the target market.

Table 11.7
Merchandise tradeoff alternatives*

KEY CONSTRAINT	DESIRED ACTION	FORCED TRADE-OFF ALTERNATIVE
Fixed investment dollars	Expand variety	Reduce assortment, maintain depth for remaining assortment factors *or* Maintain assortment, reduce depth supporting selected items
	Expand assortment for a product group	Reduce variety *or* Reduce depth
	Expand depth for a product item	Reduce variety *or* Reduce assortments
Fixed variety	Reduce total investment	Reduce assortment *or* Reduce depth
	Increase assortment for a product group	Increase investment *or* Reduce depth
Fixed investment dollars and fixed variety	Increase assortment for a product group	Reduce depth
	Increase depth for a product item	Reduce assortment

*Including all possible trade-off alternatives is well beyond the space limitations for this table. The intention is to provide a sample of common situations sufficient to guide the reader in defining additional trade-off situations.

DETERMINE MERCHANDISE OBJECTIVES

The third step of merchandise planning is to determine specific merchandise objectives. Although specific statements can be formulated for each of the six merchandise components, the two key factors that should be translated into specific objectives are turnover and GMROI-R. Both can be quantified and viewed as measures of effectiveness for merchandise strategy planning. Since GMROI-R incorporates the gross margin percentage (GM%) and turnover (T), GMROI-R is emphasized in an example below. (Recall that GMROI-R = GM% × T.)

Consider Margo's, a woman's clothing retailer that emphasizes current fashions and has a rather affluent target market. Margo's has achieved a gross margin of 37 to 38 percent and a turnover rate of 2.5 for the last several years. Given this information along with a conviction that she had gained experience and skill in buying, Margo felt she could reduce the cost of goods sold, which would improve the gross margin. Further, several previous buying mistakes had resulted in some merchandise inventory that would not sell. Margo felt that getting rid of this merchandise (thereby reducing the average inventory) would increase the turnover rate. As a result of this analysis Margo stated her merchandising objectives as achieving a gross margin of 40 percent, turnover rate of 2.5, and, therefore, a GMROI-R of 100.0.

Specific GMROI-R objectives can also be set for major departments or product categories. Margo could develop GMROI-R objectives for dresses, blouses, accessories, coats, and so on. Some categories could have GMROI-Rs greater than the store average of 100.0, while others could be lower.

FORMULATE THE MERCHANDISE BUDGET

With broad merchandise philosophies and specific objectives established, the fourth major step in merchandise planning is to formulate the **merchandise budget.** The merchandise budget is a plan containing the dollar amounts a retailer expects to sell and buy during the planning period. The planning period can be a year for retailers with stable sales or a selling season for those with distinct seasonal sale fluctuations. The merchandise budget should be constructed for specific **merchandise control units** (MCU). An MCU is a group of products viewed as a unit for buying, selling, and planning purchases. The retailer can define MCUs to include the entire store, each department, or specific product categories.

The specific format of the merchandise budget depends mainly on the needs of the planner. Various retail trade associations often supply standardized forms for their membership to use in planning budgets. Table 11.8 shows an example of a simple merchandise budget as of the middle of a season.

As can also be seen in Table 11.8, the merchandise budget does not indicate which specific items to purchase. Rather it provides the dollar value of goods to be purchased for the selected control units. Specific assortments and depth are selected in the next major step, *after* the merchandise budget has been completed.

Before getting into the specific activities necessary to generate a complete merchandise budget, the reader must understand the essential differences between the **cost basis** and **retail basis** of valuing merchandise. On the cost basis, merchandise is valued at cost plus freight-in. On the retail basis, merchandise is valued according to current retail prices. Many retailers employ the retail basis simply because cost data are frequently not available at the end of a monthly accounting period. Visualize a display of men's shirts containing 400 to 500 items. This assortment could easily represent the remainder of thirty or more purchase orders (and costs). Cost data for the individual shirts are simply unobtainable without a computer. Fortunately, as you will see, calculations from the retail basis are quite satisfactory for merchandise decisions.

At various places in this textbook, a given group of goods may be described in one of three ways: in units, in cost dollars, or in retail dollars. A group of 500 items held in inventory (I) can be described accurately by:

- Units: I_u = 500 units

- Cost dollars: I_c = $10,000

- Retail dollars: I_r = $20,000

Other groups of merchandise often described in this manner are "items sold" and "planned purchases."

As depicted in the decision model (Fig. 11.1), there are five basic activity steps involved in formulating a complete merchandise budget:

1. Forecast sales.

2. Plan inventory level.

Table 11.8
Example of seasonal merchandise budget

	FEB.	MAR.	APR.	MAY	JUNE	JULY	TOTAL
Sales							
Last year	$10,000	$11,000	$12,000	$13,000	$12,000	$11,000	$69,000
Budgeted for this season	11,000	12,000	13,000	14,000	13,000	12,000	75,000
Adjusted budget			12,000	13,000			
Actual sales	10,000	11,000	12,000				
Inventory (beginning)							
Last year	$21,000	$23,000	$25,000	$25,000	$23,000	$16,000	$ 5,000
Budgeted for this season	23,000	25,000	27,000	25,000	25,000	17,000	5,000
Adjusted budget							
Actual inventory	23,000	26,000	29,000				
Reductions							
Last year	$ 500	$ 500	$ 500	$ 600	$ 600	$ 600	$ 3,300
Budgeted for this season	500	500	500	600	600	600	3,300
Adjusted budget							
Actual reductions	525	470	495				
Purchases							
Last year	$12,000	$13,000	$12,000	$11,000	$ 5,000	-0-	$53,000
Budgeted for this season	13,000	14,000	13,000	12,000	5,000	-0-	57,000
Adjusted budget			8,000				
Actual purchases	13,000	14,000	4,000				
Open-to-buy (OTB)			4,000				

Notes: All figures at retail; adjustments are for middle of April.

3. Plan reductions.

4. Plan purchases.

5. Plan initial margins.

Forecast Sales

The first step in merchandise budgeting is to develop a **sales forecast.** An accurate sales forecast is one of the most important ingredients of strategic merchandise planning and is also important for all other retailing strategy variables. Note that merchandise planning requires accurate forecasts, especially for the various merchandise control units, while financial strategy requires accurate total sales figures.

Determining storewide forecasts and MCU forecasts can be approached from either a *build-up* or a *breakdown* perspective. The build-up approach involves first making forecasts for each MCU and simply summing the MCU forecasts to arrive at the storewide forecast. The breakdown approach calls for first making a storewide forecast and breaking this figure down into the component MCU forecasts. Either approach can yield accurate forecasts when used properly. The best hedge against an inaccurate forecast is to use both approaches independently. Any discrepancies should be investigated and resolved.

The basic forecasting procedure discussed below can be employed for either the build-up or breakdown approach. Quantitative or statistical techniques such as trend analysis, time series analysis, and multiple regression are used by some retailers to develop sales forecasts. Discussion of these techniques is beyond the scope of this work, but it is important to understand that these techniques should be used to *assist or facilitate* an overall, logical forecasting procedure.

For convenience, the example used to illustrate the sales forecasting procedure is for a single merchandise control unit.

1. *Begin with last year's sales figure.* The retailer must begin the sales forecasting procedure with known, concrete information. Therefore, the entire forecasting procedure is anchored to last year's sales. The remaining steps are designed primarily to modify this base figure. It is perfectly acceptable to forecast sales for a particular selling season rather than for a year when sales are seasonal.

2. *Analyze sales trends.* Sales trends for the entire season must be analyzed, usually using three to five years of data. The purpose is to determine the historical growth rate (which can be negative) and adjust this growth rate for price increases to arrive at a projected *real growth rate* in sales. The real growth rate is then used to get an accurate sales forecast that does not include expectations for price increases. Table 11.9 shows an example of the data used in this analysis.

3. *Analyze factors that will affect all competitors equally.* This step calls for a review of the environmental analysis to determine those factors that could influence equally the sales of the retailer and all relevant compet-

itors. Essentially, changes in the *total market demand* are estimated. Both the general (or national) and the local environments should be analyzed. Examples of national trends that might be relevant are the economy, interest rates, trends in lifestyles, and governmental regulations. Local factors might include new industries, old industries leaving, new home starts, and the like.

The lawn mower retailer in Table 11.9 might discover three factors that are likely to influence sales. First, new safety regulations are expected to add 5 percent to the cost of every mower. Second, a large new industry is moving into town, which is expected to increase total demand for lawn mowers by 5 percent. Third, 1982 was an extremely dry year, resulting in minimal grass growth, which reduced wear and tear on lawn mowers. But

Table 11.9
Example of sales data needed to analyze sales trends for sales of lawn mowers*

MONTH	SALES 1980	SALES 1981	SALES 1982	% CHANGE 1980–81	% CHANGE 1981–82	PROJECTED % CHANGE 1983[a]	PROJECTED % CHANGE ADJUSTED FOR PRICE CHANGES[b]	SALES FORECAST 1983[c]
Jan.	$ 1,000	$ 1,200	$ 1,300	+20.0%	+8.3%	+10.0%	+5.0%	$ 1,365
Feb.	1,000	1,200	1,300	20.0	8.3	10.0	5.0	1,365
Mar.	2,000	2,200	2,400	10.0	9.1	9.5	4.7	2,513
Apr.	10,000	12,000	12,500	20.0	4.2	10.0	5.0	13,125
May	11,000	12,000	13,000	9.1	8.3	9.0	4.5	13,585
June	10,000	10,200	10,400	2.0	2.0	2.0	1.0	10,504
July	10,000	10,400	10,500	4.0	1.0	2.0	1.0	10,605
Aug.	7,000	7,200	7,400	2.9	2.8	2.8	1.4	7,504
Sept.	11,000	11,200	11,500	1.8	2.7	2.7	1.3	11,650
Oct.	5,000	5,500	5,600	10.0	1.8	5.0	2.5	5,740
Nov.	2,000	2,100	2,200	5.0	4.8	5.0	2.5	2,255
Dec.	2,000	2,100	2,200	5.0	4.8	5.0	2.5	2,255
Total	72,000	77,300	80,300	9.15[d]	4.84[d]	6.08[d]	3.0[c]	82,466[e]

*A simplified "indexing system" is also popular. Seasonal or annual forecasts are finalized before considering monthly forecasts. The annual forecast is then divided into monthly forecasts via the indexing system, which assigns each month its historically normal share of sales. The authors prefer to consider the monthly figures initially for purposes of clarity.

[a]These figures can be derived by judgment or sophisticated quantitative techniques.

[b]Analysis of prices for 1980–1982 revealed that one-half of the increases in sales volume were due to price increases. The "projected percentage change adjusted for price changes" represents the *real growth rate* in unit sales expected for 1983 over 1982.

[c]The monthly and season's MCU forecasts represent expected sales *if there are price increases by the retailer*. Any expected price increases are reintroduced to adjust the sales forecasts later in this technique.

[d]Average figures.

[e]Discrepancies due to rounding errors.

the spring of 1983 is predicted to be extremely wet, causing maximum grass growth. Consequently, sales of lawn mowers in late spring and early summer 1983 are expected to be up by 10 percent.

4. *Analyze factors that will affect only the retailer's store.* Whereas Step 3 involves forecasting changes in the *size of the pie*, Step 4 involves forecasting changes in the retailer's *share of the pie* by further analysis of the external environment. The two key factors to address are *target market* and *competititve strategy*. Although the target market can easily be analyzed in Step 3 from the standpoint of overall population, population shifts, and so on, analysis can be delayed until Step 4 to interpret the effects of trends *directly* on the retailer's defined target customers. Specific factors to investigate are changes in number of the targeted age group, targeted income level, lifestyle trends, and so on. Competitive factors include the entry or exit of competitors and changes in competitive strategy, such as location, product line, prices, and advertising.

The lawn mower retailer might discover that the size of the targeted age group has expanded 5 percent (excluding the influx of residents with the new industry). Although no changes in competitors' strategies are expected, a major new competitor has entered the market, and the retailer might anticipate a 20 percent decrease in unit sales from what they would otherwise be.

5. *Modify intermediate sales forecast.* The intermediate sales forecast developed in Step 2 should now be modified with the information derived in Steps 3 and 4. Table 11.10 presents this modification for the lawn mower retailer.

6. *Use judgment to finalize monthly forecasts.* Finalizing the monthly sales forecasts involves judgment. The primary focus is again on environmental factors, but specifically on those factors that could effect the *distribution* of monthly sales. Factors the lawn mower retailer should evaluate might include the number of selling days per month (compared to last year), the number of peak selling days per month (Saturdays, Mondays) and the timing of the last frost of the year (early or late). To simplify the lawn mower example, assume that the retailer discovered nothing that would cause a significant shift in monthly sales.

Plan Inventory Levels

The second step of formulating the merchandise budget is to *plan the inventory levels for each month*. Since sufficient merchandise must be carried in inventory to satisfy expected sales, accurate monthly sales forecasts in Step 1 are crucial. More specifically, inventory planning should focus on three objectives: (1) to satisfy customer demand, (2) to adjust inventory levels to variations in seasonal sales, and (3) to control inventory investment and achieve a turnover rate that enhances achievement of profit objectives.

There are five commonly used methods for planning inventory levels. Note that all focus on planning beginning-of-the-month (BOM) inventory levels and that a given month's BOM is also the end-of-the-month (EOM) inventory figure for the preceding month. The EOM on March 31 will also be on the BOM on April 1.

1. *Judgment.* Some retailers (too many) use nothing but **judgment** to plan their inventory levels. These inventory plans are simply rough estimates based on experience and intuition. Although pure judgment may be sufficient for extremely small inventory levels, and perhaps for very small retailers, more formal methods followed by judgment provide a more sound basis for inventory planning.

2. *Safety stock method.* The **safety stock method** (often referred to as the basic stock method) is recommended for stores with relatively low turnover and stable monthly sales. The BOM is calculated as follows:

BOM = Forecast monthly sales + Safety stock.

The safety stock is a cushion or hedge for the retailer against forecasting errors, "unforecastable" sales fluctuations, and shipping delays. For example, if the retailer in Table 11.10 wanted a 10 percent safety stock, the BOM for January would be $1419 ($1290 + $129).

Table 11.10
Modification of intermediate sales forecast

MONTH	INTERMEDIATE SALES FORECAST[a]	SALES CHANGES DUE TO UNIT SALES CHANGES[b]				ADJUSTED SALES FORECAST	PRICE INCREASE[c] 5%	NEW SALES FORECAST[d]
		NEW INDUSTRY (5% INCREASE)	TARGETED AGE (5% INCREASE)	NEW COMPETITION (20% DECREASE)	WET YEAR (10% INCREASE)			
Jan.	$ 1,365	$ +68	$ +68	$ −272	$ 0	$ 1,229	$ +61	1,290
Feb.	1,365	+68	+68	−272	0	1,229	+61	1,290
Mar.	2,513	+126	+126	−504	0	2,261	+113	2,374
Apr.	13,125	+656	+656	−2,624	+1,312	13,125	+656	13,781
May	13,585	+679	+679	−2,716	+1,358	13,585	+679	14,264
June	10,504	+525	+525	−2,100	+1,050	10,504	+525	11,029
July	10,605	+530	+530	−2,120	0	9,545	+477	10,022
Aug.	7,504	+375	+375	−1,500	0	6,754	+378	7,132
Sept.	11,650	+582	+582	−2,328	0	10,486	+524	11,010
Oct.	5,740	+287	+287	−1,148	0	5,166	+258	5,424
Nov.	2,255	+113	+113	−452	0	2,029	+101	2,130
Dec.	2,255	+113	+113	−452	0	2,029	+101	2,130
Total	$82,466	$+4,122	$+4,122	$−16,488	$+3,720	$77,942	$+3,934	$81,876

[a]From Table 11.9.

[b]Note that in this example the percentage changes are not cumulative; rather, each is applied directly to the intermediate sales forecast.

[c]The 5% price applies to all sales and is therefore cumulative.

[d]The new sales forecast will be finalized later through judgment.

The safety stock method and the following methods provide a BOM inventory level. The activities necessary to replenish and maintain satisfactory assortment and depth throughout the month are based on BOM, EOM, and actual sales figures.

3. *Percentage variation (or deviation) method.* The **percentage variation method** provides for lower inventory fluctuation for stores with high inventory turnover rates. This method incorporates only one-half of the forecast percentage variation from average stock. The formula is

$$\text{BOM} = \text{Average inventory} \times \tfrac{1}{2}\left(1 + \frac{\text{Forecasted month's sales}}{\text{Average monthly sales}}\right).$$

"Average inventory" can be determined by transposing the turnover formula:

$$T = \frac{S}{AI}$$

into the following formula:

$$AI = \frac{S}{T},$$

where:

$$AI = \text{average inventory}$$
$$S = \text{sales}$$
$$T = \text{turnover.}$$

To illustrate with the data in Table 11.10, assume the retailer desired a turnover rate of 6. Then:

$$AI = \frac{\$81,876}{6} = \$13,646,$$

and

$$\text{Average monthly sales} = \frac{\$81,876}{12 \text{ months}} = \$6823.$$

Then, for January:

$$\text{BOM} = \$13,646 \times \tfrac{1}{2}\left(1 + \frac{\$1290}{\$6823}\right).$$
$$= \$8,113$$

Note that a fraction other than $\tfrac{1}{2}$ can be used to adjust the amount of sales deviation accounted for in the inventory levels.

4. *Week's supply method.* The **week's supply method** assumes that the inventory levels should always be proportional to sales. It involves forecasting and planning sales on a weekly basis and is appropriate for merchandise that needs to be planned weekly.

The number of weeks to be stocked is calculated as follows:

$$\text{Number of weeks' supply} = \frac{52 \text{ weeks}}{\text{Turnover rate}}.$$

For a grocery store with a turnover rate of 15, the number of weeks' supply is 3.47 (52 ÷ 15). The 3.47 also means that the retailer expects or desires *one* turnover every 3.47 weeks. A retailer with relatively stable sales would then multiply 3.47 by average weekly sales. A retailer with large fluctuations in weekly sales, however, would have to make so many subjective adjustments that the initial calculations would become meaningless.

5. *Stock-to-sales ratio.* The **stock-to-sales ratio (SSR)** assumes that the retailer must maintain a fixed proportion of inventory to sales. The overall logic of the SSR can be seen in the calculation of an average SSR for the year. This is done as follows:

$$\text{SSR} = \frac{12}{\text{Turnover rate}}.$$

For the lawn mower retailer, with a desired turnover rate of 6, the SSR is 2 (12 ÷ 6). Remember that a turnover rate of 6 means that the retailer's average inventory will turn over or sell every two months. Therefore, the BOM should be sufficient to cover two months of sales. Consequently, in this example, average inventory should be twice as large as sales, or SSR should be 2. The SSR is multiplied by the forecast sales for a particular month, or

$$\text{BOM} = \text{SSR} \times \text{Forecast month's sales.}$$

The yearly SSR is actually an "average" figure. Specific monthly SSRs are more useful to most retailers. Past experience with a retailer's own inventories and sales and trade information can be used to establish individual SSRs for each month. Table 11.11 presents actual SSRs for department and specialty stores.

The SSR method is easy to apply and is best used when monthly planning is performed, SSRs are available, and turnover objectives are realistic.

Comments on Inventory Planning Methods. Although they can provide the retailer with sound guidance, inventory planning methods *cannot* wholly substitute for sound judgment. Each method yields a single, beginning inventory level and does not account for the dynamic nature of retailing. The retailer must maintain a view of the forward movement of the selling season or of expectations for subsequent months. Perpetual environmental scanning must be employed to allow for continuous adjustments to changes in the business environment, availability of supply, prices, and other environmental factors.

Inventory levels will seldom fluctuate in direct proportion to sales fluctuations. Inventory planning methods usually "dampen" the effect of sales changes on inventory levels.

Table 11.11
Stock sales ratios # for fiscal year ended January 1980

	DEPARTMENT STORES					SPECIALTY STORES		
	UNDER 1 MILLION	1–5 MILLION	5–10 MILLION	10–20 MILLION*	OVER 20 MILLION	UNDER 1 MILLION	1–5 MILLION*	OVER 5 MILLION
February	6.55	6.52	5.98	6.86	4.99	6.95	4.65	4.89
March	5.52	5.30	4.42	4.94	4.14	5.33	3.90	4.37
April	6.33	5.87	4.92	5.30	4.01	5.44	3.56	4.61
May	6.15	5.85	5.10	5.53	4.26	5.12	4.07	4.98
June	5.75	5.11	4.89	5.57	4.64	4.71	4.04	4.57
July	5.46	5.06	5.33	6.70	4.97	5.40	4.28	5.06
August	5.67	5.43	4.98	5.70	4.59	4.51	4.05	4.43
September	6.57	5.17	5.06	4.98	4.44	4.96	4.02	4.41
October	5.42	5.39	5.28	5.33	4.01	5.49	4.01	5.14
November	3.06	4.77	4.12	4.60	3.71	5.43	3.60	4.61
December	3.07	2.67	2.55	3.17	2.25	2.87	2.36	2.65
January	7.00	6.95	5.93	6.88	5.88	6.10	4.35	5.62

*Less than ten stores.

#Median.

Source: Merchandising and Operating Results of 1979 (New York: Financial Executives Division, National Retail Merchants Association, 1980), pp. xix.

Certain types of merchandise have minimum inventory levels. Merchandise that must be fitted to customers' physical dimensions, such as clothing and shoes, have minimum levels below which merchandise levels cannot fall, regardless of sales volume. In any situation, the retailer must maintain an adequate assortment for the customers' perusal.

Activities necessary for maintaining and controlling inventory levels are discussed in Chapter 13.

Plan Merchandise Reductions

The third step of formulating the merchandise budget is to plan for merchandise **reductions.** There are three main types of reductions: markdowns, shortages, and discounts.

A **markdown** is a reduction in price made available to all customers. There are four basic reasons for markdowns: (1) planning or buying errors, such as wrong sizes, colors, styles; (2) external price changes, such as for supplier price decreases and decreases in competitors' prices; (3) promotional reasons, such as special sales and multiple-unit pricing; and (4) conventional markdowns, such as for damaged goods.

Shortages are typically discovered during a physical inventory. They are caused by shoplifting, employee pilferage, unreported breakage, and natural inventory spoilage (drying, rotting, warping).

Discounts are price decreases offered to special groups of customers, such as employees, clergy, and the elderly. Discounts are typically treated as markdowns.

Reductions are inevitable. They must be incorporated into merchandise budgeting because they have the effect of reducing the retail value of merchandise available for sale. A reduction of $100 has the same dollar impact on the inventory value as $100 in sales. Units must be replaced because the physical inventory has changed. We can view reductions, sales, and EOM as "uses" of available merchandise, whereas BOM and purchases are "sources" of merchandise for a given month.

To grasp the impact of ignoring reductions in merchandise budgeting, consider the following simplified example. Suppose a retailer has a BOM for candy of $100 and desires to end the month with $100. If half of the candy is sold, the retailer would obviously have to purchase another $50 worth of candy. But, what if $50 worth of candy was missing because of shoplifting? If the retailer did not incorporate this reduction in inventory level, the actual EOM would be $50 (from the new purchases). (The actual technique for incorporating reductions is shown later in this chapter.)

There are two major activities necessary to plan reductions.

1. *Determine total reductions for the planning period.* Determining total reductions for a planning period involves examining past experience and trade data to arrive at a base figure. This base figure can be adjusted for any anticipated strategy changes, price trends, amount of old merchandise carried over, and any other factor that could cause a reduction. The total reduction can be expressed in terms of dollars or percentage of sales.

2. *Distribute reductions to months.* Distributing the planned reductions to the appropriate months can occur simply by applying the reduction percentage to each month's forecast sales. A great deal of judgment is also needed to account for those months that are most likely to experience large reductions, especially markdowns. The lawn mower retailer of Table 11.10, for example, expects sales to trail off in August but to regain strength in September. This sales resurgence might be due to large markdowns during a month-long clearance sale. If so, a much larger proportion of reduction dollars should be allowed for September. (Markdowns are discussed in more detail in Chapter 14.)

Plan Purchases and Open-to-Buy (OTB)

The fourth step in merchandise budgeting is to plan the amount of purchases (on retail base) needed during the month and to set up the **open-to-buy (OTB)** figure. OTB is the amount of merchandise a buyer is responsible for buying at a specific time during the month. At this point, all the variables necessary to calculate planned purchases have been planned or forecast and no judgment is necessary.

Perhaps the simplest way to describe planned purchases or merchandise is with a "sources and uses" technique. Essentially, the retailer faces this situation for a given month:

Uses of Merchandise:

1. For *Sales* (from Step 1)

2. For *EOM* (from Step 2; same as BOM for next month)

3. For *Reductions* (from Step 3)

Sources of Merchandise:

1. From *BOM* (from Step 2)

2. From *Planned purchases* (to be calculated)

These sources and uses can be easily converted into a solution format, such as this one for the lawn mower retailer:

$1,290	Sales, January
+$8,113	EOM, January or BOM, February
+ 65	Reductions, assume 5% of sales
9,468	Total uses for January
− 8,113	Source, BOM January
$1,355	Planned purchases for January (retail base)

Although OTB is used by buyers, it is appropriate to explain the calculation at this point. At the beginning of January, the buyer must acquire all of the planned purchases for January; thus, OTB is equal to planned purchases, or $1,355. As purchase commitments are made during the month, the OTB is reduced equivalently. The simple formula is

OTB = Planned purchases − Purchase commitments.

Assume that goods valued at $1,000 are ordered on January 10. When this order is placed, the OTB is reduced to $355 ($1,355 − $1,000). This procedure is followed until all necessary purchases are made and the OTB is zero.

Exceptions to this OTB procedure can occur when sales of a product exceed expectations. When this situation develops, the merchandise budget and the OTB should be increased.

Plan the Initial Markup

The fifth step of merchandise budgeting is to plan the initial markup required to achieve the desired net profit objective (before taxes). The following formula is used:

$$MU_I = \frac{E + P + R}{S + R} \times 100,$$

where:

MU_I = Initial markup required
E = Expenses
P = Profit
R = Reductions
S = Sales.

The lawn mower retailer might calculate MU_I as follows:

$$MU_I = \frac{\$22,000 + 8,000 + \$4,646}{\$81,866 + 4,646} \times 100 = 40\%.$$

Table 11.12
Example of merchandise budgeting process

	SALES FORECAST[a]	BEGINNING INVENTORY[b]	REDUCTIONS[c]	PURCHASES
January	$ 1,290	$ 8,113	$ 65	$ 1,355
February	1,290	8,113	65	2,439
March	2,374	9,197	119	13,900
April	13,781	20,604	689	14,953
May	14,264	21,087	713	11,742
June	11,029	17,852	551	10,573
July	10,022	16,845	501	7,633
August	7,132	13,955	357	11,367
September	11,010	17,833	1,101	6,525
October	5,424	12,247	271	2,401
November	2,130	8,953	107	2,237
December	2,130	8,953	107	[d]

If desired profit = $8,000 and expenses = $22,000, MU_I = 40%.
[a]From Table 11.10.
[b]Assumptions: (1) percentage variation method used, and (2) desired turnover rate is 6.
[c]Average monthly reductions are 5 percent of sales, except for clearance sale in September, which increases reductions to 10 percent.
[d]Cannot calculate without the ending inventory.

The initial markup must be sufficient to cover expenses, desired profit, and reductions (thus the numerator, E + P + R). Note, however, that the initial markup is not *maintained* over the course of the planning period because of reductions. Consequently, the MU_I percentage is expressed in terms of *sales as if no reductions occur,* or *original retail price* (thus the denominator, S + R). Markups are explained in more detail in Chapter 14. (An example of the merchandise budgeting process is shown in Table 11.12.)

PREPARE THE BUYING PLAN

The fifth and last major step of merchandise planning is to prepare the buying plan. Although not all retailers will prepare a formal buying plan, very few can operate without having at least some idea of what to purchase. The basic purpose of the buying plan is to provide guidance for buyers.

Preparation of the buying plan begins with the dollar amount authorized for inventory investment and the variety decision; both investment and variety are relatively fixed at this stage of planning. Consequently, the major decisions involved in preparing the buying plan are focused on planning **assortment** and **depth.**

Most retailers use some form of an **ideal stock list** to serve as their buying plan. The ideal stock for a particular retailer is stock that satisfies all

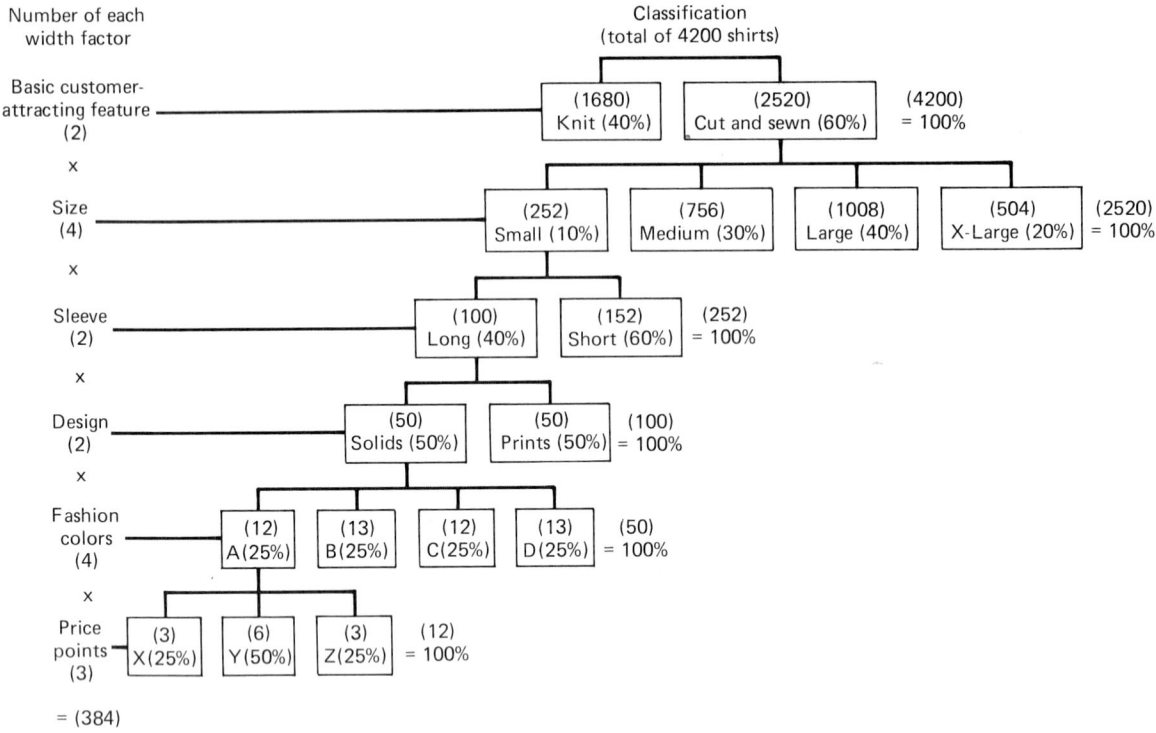

Figure 11.2
Model stock—sport shirts

Note: The percentage in each factor is the expected importance of that component. Numbers represent the percent share of the 4,200 total; for example, 60 percent × 4,200 = 2,520, 10 percent × 2,520 = 252, and so on.

Source: Joseph Barry Mason and Morris L. Mayer, *Modern Retailing,* 2nd ed. (Plano, Tex.: Business Publications, 1981), p. 316. ©BUSINESS PUBLICATIONS, INC., 1978 and 1981.

the major considerations of balance. Therefore, the ideal stock list is a document that lists the merchandise items that should be on hand during a particular planning period. The ideal stock list can be expressed in dollars and/or units. Its degree of exactness can vary, depending on the type of retailer. Some retailers use a **basic stock list,** which can list the exact items to stock. The basic stock list is appropriate for staple goods with relatively constant demand. Other items, such as fashion goods, may call for a **model stock list.** This list contains key assortment factors, such as major price lines, size distribution, material, and so on. In reality, the concept of the model stock list can be used for merchandise other than just fashion merchandise. A model stock list for sport shirts is shown in Figure 11.2.

A UNIQUE MERCHANDISING SITUATION: SERVICE RETAILERS

The greatest difference in strategic planning between service and merchandise retailers is in the area of merchandise. Merchandise buying and control (covered in Chapters 12 and 13) have extremely limited applicability in service retailing, but several concepts discussed in this chapter can be quite useful to service retailers.

Before discussing the relevant points from this chapter, it is critical that the reader understand the similarities between a *merchandise offering* and a *service offering*. Perhaps the key similarity is from the consumer's perspective: both service and merchandise offerings are attractive to the consumer because of the satisfaction the consumer anticipates. This implies that the consumer is interested in an exchange to obtain satisfaction from the offering. Many factors involved in planning the offering (whether it is tangible merchandise or an intangible service) are similar.

Now let us modify and apply portions of the merchandise planning process discussed in this chapter to the service retailer's situation. (Note that many concepts discussed in this chapter are not particularly useful to the service retailer and are therefore not mentioned below.)

Review All Existing Information and Plans

This first step of merchandise planning is certainly applicable for service retailers. Target customers, competition, marketing objetives, financial objectives, and other factors must be reviewed by the service retailer.

Formulate a Merchandise Philosophy

In this second step, at least two of the merchandise philosophies are relevant, if modified: variety and stock balance. Recall that variety refers to the number of generically different product classifications. *Service variety* would therefore refer to the number of generically different service classifications. Although most service retailers are limited to a relatively narrow variety of services (consider a chimney-sweep service, a dance studio), some have much more latitude regarding the variety decision. A beauty shop might offer any combination of facials, manicures, cosmetic consulting, dress or fashion consulting, or even shoe care and whirlpool facilities in addition to standard hair care services.

Stock balance involves the decision of how to employ variety, assortment, and depth. *Service balance* involves the same three factors as they apply to the service offering. Note that even retailers with a narrow variety must still make decisions regarding assortment and depth. An automobile repair shop might offer a narrow variety of services (repair and maintenance of autos and light trucks) but offer a wide assortment of services, ranging from body work to major overhauls to changing tires.

Determine Merchandise Objectives

Although relating this third step to service retailers is stretching the point somewhat, service retailers should have some type of objective for each service offered. The relevant objective for each service might be stated as sales volume or, perhaps, gross margin (to calculate gross margin, the cost of goods sold equivalent would consist of labor cost, other direct costs such as supplies, and an overhead allocation). The service retailer with multiple offerings would need sales objectives for each offering.

Formulate Merchandise Budget

Although the service retailer obviously does not need a merchandise budget, most of the activities suggested by the merchandise budgeting process are relevant. First, the service retailer must forecast sales, just as the merchandise retailer does. Second, although the service retailer does not need to plan an inventory level, plans must be made regarding human resources (scheduling and allocating time for personnel) and capital resources (as they pertain to individual services offered).

Third, reductions must be planned. The service retailer will normally be more concerned with markdowns (for promotions) and discounts (say for the elderly).

Fourth, planning the initial markup is also relevant. Recall that the four components of the initial markup formula are desired profit, expenses, reductions, and forecast sales. The service retailer should use all of these amounts, just as the merchandise retailer does. The critical difference involves applying the markup percentage. Whereas the merchandise retailer would apply the markup percentage to the cost of the merchandise, the service retailer could apply it to the relevant labor cost figure (as is done on a much less sophisticated basis by many service retailers).

KEY CONCEPTS

Specialized merchandising philosophy	Week's supply method
Scrambled merchandising philosophy	Stock-to-sales ratio
Turnover	Reductions
GMROI	Markdowns
GMROI-R	Shortages
Stock balance	Discounts
Merchandise budget	Open-to-buy (OTB)
Merchandise control units (MCU)	Depth
Cost basis	Assortment factors
Retail basis	Ideal stock list
Sales forecast	Basic stock list
Safety stock method	Model stock list
Percentage variation method	

REVIEW QUESTIONS

1. Develop the strategic merchandise planning model.
2. Discuss the potential trade-off between variety, assortment, depth, and investment.
3. Discuss the trade-off between gross margin and turnover.
4. Develop the merchandise budgeting process.
5. Compare the cost basis and retail basis of valuing merchandise.

6. Develop the retail sales forecasting process.
7. Discuss five procedures for planning inventory levels.
8. Discuss reduction planning.
9. What is a buying plan?

LEARNING EXERCISES

1. Analyze ten local retailers to determine whether their apparent philosophy is to emphasize variety, assortment, or depth.
2. For the same ten retailers, analyze their apparent philosophy toward turnover versus gross margin.

PROBLEMS

1. What is EOM_c if $EOM_r = \$90,000$, $BOM_c = \$50,000$, $BOM_r = \$100,000$, and purchases were $30,000 at cost and $50,000 at retail?

2. Given:
   Planned sales, May = $10,000
   Planned sales, June = $12,000
   Planned sales, July = $14,000
   Basic stock = $1,000
   Average stock = $20,000
   Average sales per month = $15,000
   a) Use basic stock method to find BOM for May, June, and July.
   b) Find the purchases necessary for May and June.
   c) Use the percentage-variation method to find BOM for May, June, and July.

3. Use the week's supply method to find BOM, if average monthly sales = $40,000 and T = 6.

4. Given:

EOM	$18,000
Planned sales	$ 8,000
BOM	$24,000
Reductions	$ 500

   Find planned purchases.

5. Given:

BOM	$23,000
EOM	$25,000
Planned sales	$11,000
Reductions	$ 900
Goods ordered	$ 9,000

   a) Find planned purchases.
   b) Find open-to-buy (OTB).

6. Given:

EOM	$300,000
BOM	$280,000
Planned sales	$ 70,000
Reductions	$ 6,000

   Find planned purchases at cost.

7. Given:

Net sales	$200,000
Reductions	$ 30,000
Expenses	$ 50,000
Profit	$ 20,000

   Find the initial markup percentage.

8.   Find turnover if sales are $640,000 and I_r is $350,000.

9.   Find turnover if cost of goods sold is $100,000 and I_c is 20,000.

10. Find turnover if sales are $100,000, I_c is $15,000, and MU_r is 40%.

11. Find average inventory if sales are $90,000 and T = 3.

12. Find turnover if three months' sales are $32,000 and I_r = $64,000.

13. A retailer had sales of $60,000 with a turnover of 5. How much will average inventory have to change to achieve a turnover rate of 6?

14. Which retailer is better off, Retailer A with GM of $200,000 and average inventory of $100,000 or Retailer B with GM of $125,000 and average inventory of $60,000?

15. Develop a merchandise budget (sales forecast, beginning inventory levels, reductions, planned purchases, and initial markup) for the following data:

   a) Sales last season:

March	$5,000
April	7,500
May	8,000
June	7,500

   b) Annual rate of sales growth = 15%.

   c) Normal annual increases in price = 10%.

   d) A major competitor has left the area; expect a 25% increase in unit sales.

   e) The week's supply method is used to calculate beginning inventories.

   f) Expected turnover rate is 10.

   g) Reductions are normally 6 percent of monthly sales.

   h) Desired profit = $6,000.

   i) Expenses = $10,000.

DECISION SITUATION 11.1: **BRAD'S MARINE**

Brad's Marine is the largest boat dealer in the South. It has been a very profitable business for over twenty years. Many customers travel several hundred miles to buy boats from Brad. The large volume allows Brad's to sell boats for a little less and to carry a wide assortment of boats and motors. The owner does not think that he can increase his share of the boat market appreciably without taking action that might hamper profitability. However, the pattern of sales is somewhat troubling.

Almost all of the sales occur between March and September. Most of the August and September sales are on boats that have been drastically reduced. Essentially, all profits are generated between March and July 4. Brad's main revenue in the fall is from boat and motor repairs, with some boat equipment sales coming at Christmas.

Brad would like to utilize his large showroom differently during the fall. He is certain that something other than boats and motors will be the answer.

QUESTIONS

1. What product or products would you suggest for Brad to try to sell in the fall?

2. What problems would be encountered with selling the products you recommend? (Consider personnel, location, promotion, and so on.)

3. Do you think Brad should try any products or just accept the seasonal nature of his sales?

DECISION SITUATION 11.2: **SUPER SUPERS**

Super Supers (SS) is a chain of forty supermarkets in the Midwest. The merchandising manager, Laura Turner, is contemplating adding a line of generic products. SS's average customer earns $17,000 to $22,000 a year, has two children, and spends about $200 a month at SS. (These figures were provided to Laura by a research project performed by a student group from State University.) The customers in the survey considered themselves to be price conscious but also wanted high-quality products.

SS already carries three national brands and a private brand for most items. The private brand was produced by various national and regional firms and labeled with Super Supers' label. A wholesaler has approached Laura with a proposal to supply generics at a lower price than the private labels. Laura is not sure what action to take.

QUESTIONS

1. What are the pros and cons of taking the generics?

2. Should SS have three national brands, a private brand, and a generic label for some items?

3. What would you recommend, assuming SS makes the same profit margin on each item?

NOTES

1. William M. Pride and O. C. Ferrell, *Marketing* (Boston: Houghton Mifflin, 1980), p. 197.

2. *Ibid.*, p. 198.

3. Robert Dietrich, "Generics at Age Three, Still Growing or Past Their Prime?," *Progressive Grocer*, March 1980, p. 197.

4. Joseph Barry Mason and Morris Lehman Mayer, *Modern Retailing* (Plano, Tex.: Business Publications, 1981), p. 255.

5. Daniel J. Sweeney, "Improving the Profitability of Retail Merchandising Decisions," *Journal of Marketing*, January 1973, pp. 60–68.

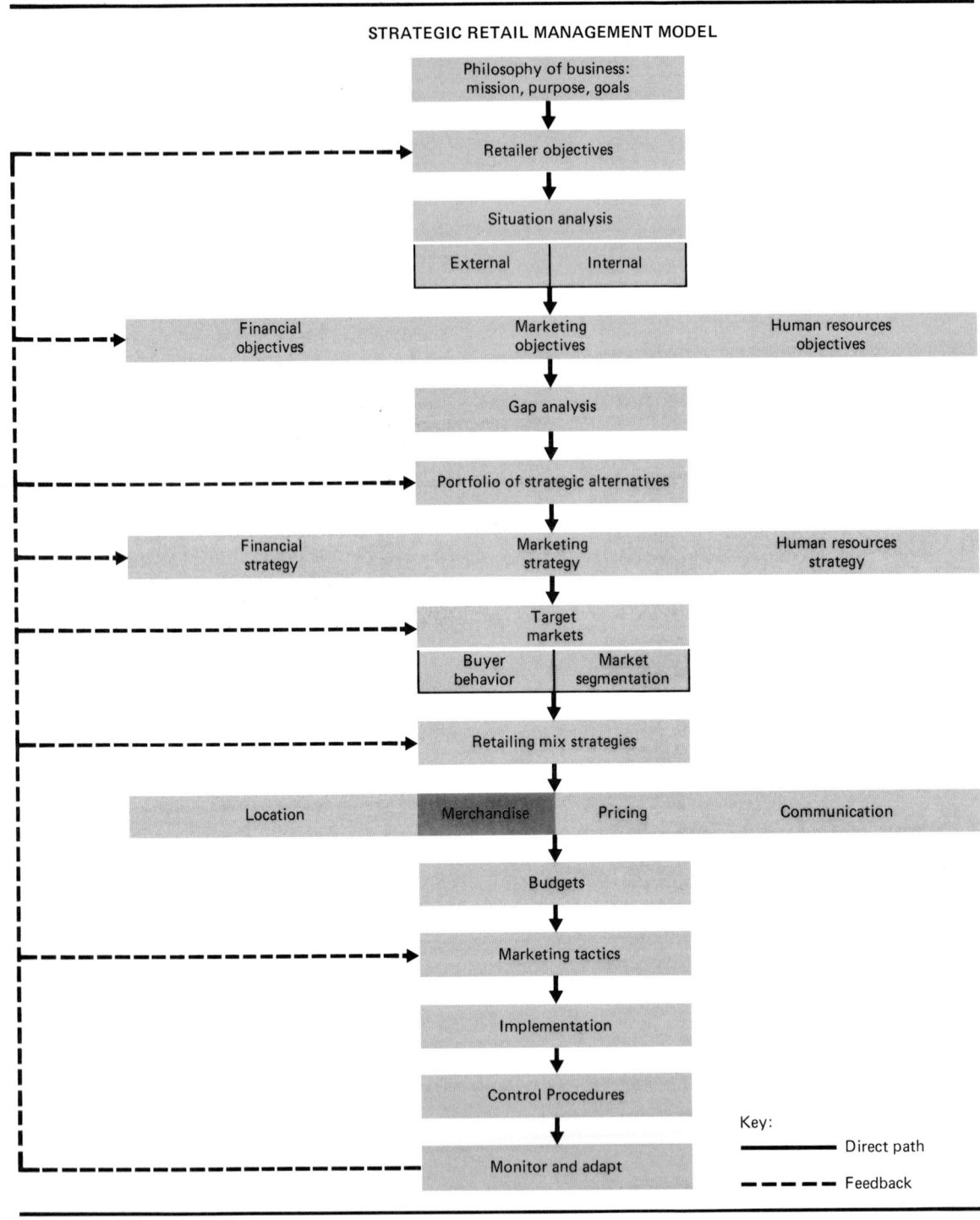

STRATEGIC RETAIL MANAGEMENT MODEL

Philosophy of business:
mission, purpose, goals

Retailer objectives

Situation analysis

| External | Internal |

Financial objectives — Marketing objectives — Human resources objectives

Gap analysis

Portfolio of strategic alternatives

Financial strategy — Marketing strategy — Human resources strategy

Target markets

| Buyer behavior | Market segmentation |

Retailing mix strategies

Location — Merchandise — Pricing — Communication

Budgets

Marketing tactics

Implementation

Control Procedures

Monitor and adapt

Key:
——— Direct path
- - - - Feedback

Chapter 12
Merchandise Buying Decisions

LEARNING OBJECTIVES

1. To appreciate the role and importance of good buying practices.

2. To understand the fundamentals of the basic buying process.

INTRODUCTION

Buying decisions are not as strategic in nature as many other topics covered in this text. Buying is, however, the implementation phase of strategic merchandise plans. Although some retailers do not consider buying as important as many other activities, "getting the best buy" is one of the most critical elements of a successful retail operation. Further, buying is more than just ordering because there can be great differences in the offerings of various suppliers. An examination of a typical retail store's income statement can help emphasize the importance of good buying.

A specialty store with sales of two million dollars might have an income statement similar to the following:[1]

Sales	$2,000,000	100%
Cost of goods sold	$1,200,000	60%
Labor	380,000	19%
Other costs	380,000	19%
Total Costs	1,960,000	98%
Pretax earnings	$40,000	2%

If the firm wanted to increase pretax earnings to $80,000, several alternatives could be pursued. Sales could be doubled, labor could be cut by almost 10.5 percent, other costs (promotion, building, and so on) could be reduced by about 10.5 percent, the cost of goods sold could be reduced by about 3.3 percent, or a combination could be tried.

Analysis of these figures indicates the tremendous leverage potential of cost of goods sold. In fact, every 1 percent decline in cost of goods sold ($12,000) results in a 30 percent increase in profits ($12,000 ÷ $40,000). Since increased efficiency in buying practices has a direct impact on cost of goods sold, a substantial opportunity exists for enhancing retail profits.

If the above example does not entirely convince you of the importance of good buying, consider that the best merchandise plans will fail if the correct merchandise is not on the shelves as planned. A retailer usually cannot make up for goods bought at excessive prices or delivered at the wrong time, even by using sophisticated merchandising techniques. Heart-shaped boxes of candy do not sell well after February 14, regardless of the price or promotional techniques used. A buyer who buys from a supplier who delivers this candy on February 16 has made a serious, costly mistake. (In this chapter the term *buyer* is used generically. That is, it refers to the person who buys merchandise for the retailer, regardless of official position or title. Some stores, especially department stores, have a position called buyer. The assignment of buying to an official position is discussed in the following section.)

To minimize cost of goods sold and avoid major buying errors, a sequential *merchandise buying decision model* is recommended (see Fig. 12.1). The basic steps in the process are

1. Review the merchandise plans.

2. Determine the precise character and amount of desired merchandise.

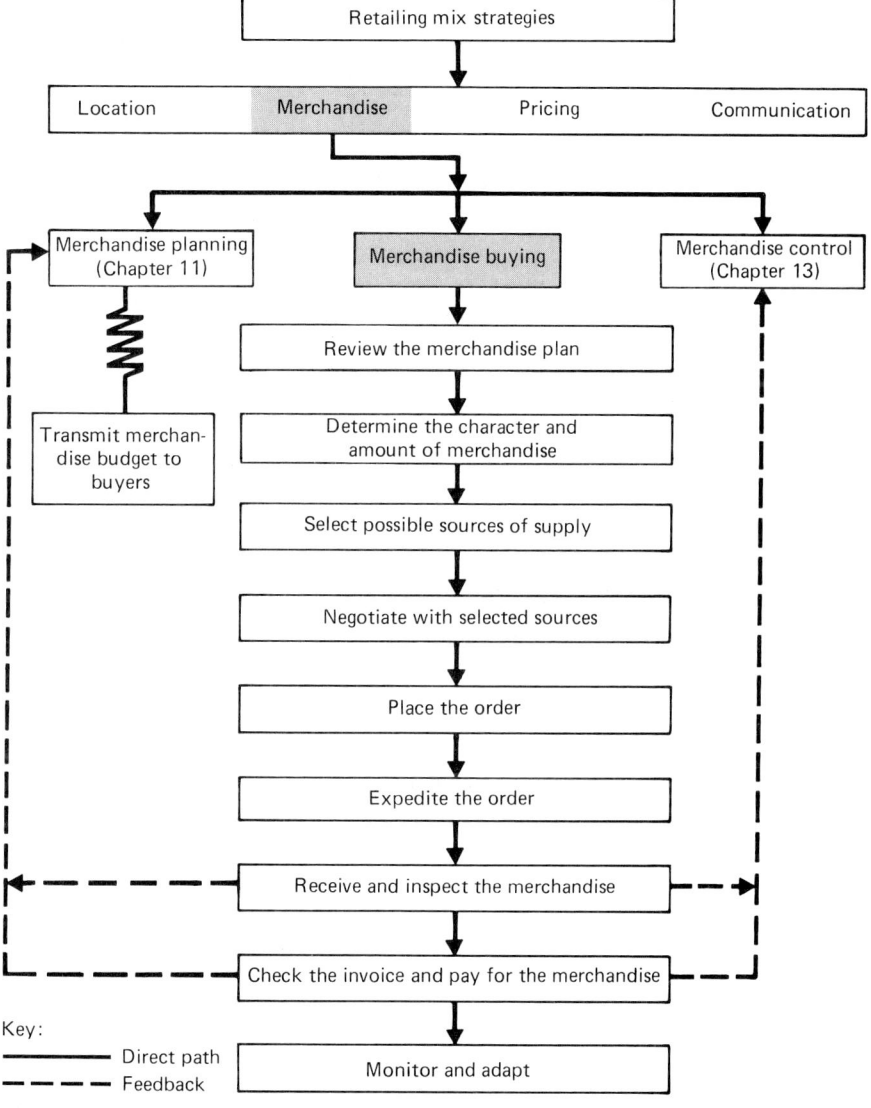

Figure 12.1
Merchandise buying decision model

3. Select possible sources of supply.

4. Negotiate with selected sources.

5. Place the order.

6. Follow up on the order.

7. Receive and inspect the merchandise.

8. Check the invoice and pay for the merchandise.

9. Monitor and adapt.

ASSIGNMENT OF BUYING RESPONSIBILITY

Buying may be done by the owner of a small store, by a clerk assigned to buy certain items, by department managers, or by any other individual or group designated by management to handle this function. The exact title given this person is not important in our understanding of the strategic buying process. It is important to understand the decisions regarding who buys what merchandise, what other duties the buyer has, and how much freedom this buyer has in making decisions.

Who Buys What? To determine who buys what, the retailer must decide the *degree of specialization* for each buyer. On one extreme, an individual may buy all the merchandise for the entire store. This practice is normally used only in small stores, where the owner is likely to handle all of the merchandise planning, buying, and controlling. In that case, congruency of the merchandising activities is an advantage. A problem encountered by retailers using this method is the time required to properly handle the total merchandising function. When this time is added to the retailer's time spent managing other activities associated with a retailing operation, some managerial functions are likely to suffer. Buying is often one of the neglected activities. Proper selection of suppliers and negotiations with suppliers are often replaced by automatically using the "usual" supplier and accepting that supplier's terms without question.

The other buying extreme involves assigning responsibility for a product or narrow product class (perfume, greeting cards) to an individual. A major advantage of this arrangement is that the buyer can maintain closer checks on merchandise and may become very skillful at buying the narrow range of products. Buying is only one part of the person's job, and lack of buying training and experience will usually cause problems. Another problem with the method is that the person may not understand the interrelationships between his or her product and the store's other merchandise. Good merchandise plans can help lessen the impact of this lack of understanding. Usually when clerks are given buying responsibility they place orders with predetermined vendors, at a predetermined time, for a predetermined quantity. In those cases, someone else has actually made the purchasing decisions and the clerk simply fills out the order.

A better situation for retailers who are large enough to afford it is the use of specialists, individuals whose primary job is to negotiate the best deals possible for the store. The buying specialists can be trained to utilize good buying techniques and can become experts in *how* to buy. Even if a retailer cannot afford a group of buying experts, a few employees can be trained in the buying process.

Other Duties of Buying Personnel

Except in very large retail institutions, the people who buy may perform other duties as well. Even when employees' primary jobs are buying, they often can give aid with other activities, such as merchandise planning and control.

Some retailers also want buying personnel to be involved in selling efforts. This practice is often useful, especially if the buyers are also involved in planning and control. The sales floor is the final test of the adequacy of merchandising activities. There is probably no better place for buyers and other merchandising personnel to develop an understanding of customer wants and merchandising problems. A buyer and merchandise planner need to know how a *customer* views relative product merit as much as they need to know how *experts* view relative product merit. Customer contact is the best source of this information. A buyer who is not assigned sales floor duties is well advised to make some visits to the floor anyway.

Any number of other duties might be assigned to the buying personnel. The retailer should realize, however, that the more duties assigned to a buyer, the less time the buyer can devote to actually buying. Also, the degree of freedom a buyer has in making a decision influences the number of other duties that he or she can handle effectively.

Freedom in Buying Decisions

Some buyers are little more than order processors. Merchandise planners determine exactly what is to be ordered, from whom it is to be ordered, and (along with merchandise control) when it is to be ordered. The narrow-responsibility buyer depicted in Table 12.1 is such a buyer. Under these conditions, the buyer needs little training, experience, or ability. Actually, the buyer only places the order. If clerks are expected to buy some items, this system (which provides little, if any, freedom to the buyer) may be the optimum system.

If more qualified buying personnel are used, it is often advantageous to allow the buyer greater flexibility in making the buying decisions. The broad-responsibility buyer in Table 12.1 is such a buyer.

The merchandise planners who set the rules in a low-freedom system cannot usually know the exact conditions that will exist when their plans are put into effect. Good buyers should be allowed the opportunity to take advantage of unexpected changes. A buyer may discover, for instance, that

Table 12.1
Sample job descriptions for buyers

TITLE	DESCRIPTION
Buyer, Men's Wear Suits	
Narrow responsibility	Use model stock plan to buy men's suits
	Negotiate with supplier selected by merchandise planner for suits
	Expedite orders placed with selected supplier
	Physically count suits once a month and send report to merchandise control and merchandise planners
	Reorder as directed by merchandise planners
Broad responsibility	Determine stock plan based on merchandise budget
	Negotiate with and select suppliers of men's suits
	Expedite orders and update evaluation of suppliers
	Use counts of suits supplied by men's wear department head to reorder suits when needed (reorders exceeding planned purchase or budget by more than 20% must be approved by store manager)
	Prepare reports on actual purchases for merchandise planning and control

the wholesale price of an item has temporarily dropped since the merchandise plans were developed. In this case the buyer possibly should be allowed to increase the units purchased to take advantage of the temporary low price. Similarly, a buyer may discover that wholesale prices are about to go up, in which case the buyer may wish to adjust the plan. A buyer may find that a new supplier has entered the market. Even if the plans specified a source, the buyer should have at least the opportunity to investigate the new source. Obviously, situations calling for some freedom require that retailers hire buyers who are competent and understand the store's markets and strategies. A buyer who lacks this competence should have little, if any, freedom to make adjustments to merchandising plans. The organizational character and type are principal factors influencing the freedom of buyers.

Once a retailer has made the assignment of buying responsibility, the persons given that responsibility should utilize a buying process like the one described in the remainder of this chapter. Following the process will help ensure that goods placed on the floor are the correct goods, at the correct cost, and at the correct time.

REVIEW THE MERCHANDISE PLANS

Throughout this text, at almost every major step of the strategic retail management decision process, the retailer has been advised to review all other plans. In buying merchandise, a thorough review of the *merchandise plans* is the critical review. The buyer should also know something about how the merchandise plans were developed, but the matching of merchandise selection and the other elements of strategy should have been accomplished when the merchandise plans were developed. To minimize problems, the merchandise plan should be reviewed as completely as possible. The buyer needs to know not only what merchandise is to be bought but also *why* that merchandise was selected. As the buying process progresses, some aspects of the plan may need adjustment. Without a good understanding of the plans and their derivation, the buyer cannot make the adjustments in a reasonable manner.

The merchandise budget, which forms the basic merchandise plan, may not be entirely accurate when the buying actually takes place. If the budget calls for $2,000 to be spent on an item that was budgeted to cost $20 per item and the per item price is now $22, should the buyer spend $2,000 or $2,200? The buyer's knowledge of whether it is more important to buy 100 items or stay within the budgeted amount of $2,000 is critical. A possibly more critical situation involves the unavailability of some items that appear in the merchandise plan. Suppose a store has planned and budgeted $1,000 to buy a high-quality version of an item, $3,000 for moderate-quality versions, and $700 for a lower-quality version. What should be done if only $2,500 worth of the moderate-quality version is available? The buyer may want to increase the purchase of either the higher or lower-quality version, buy less than budgeted, or buy a substitute item. Knowledge of the logic of the merchandise plan will help the buyer in making the decision. After the merchandise plans are reviewed, the buyer should make a more exact statement of the quantity and kind of merchandise desired.

DETERMINE THE PRECISE CHARACTER AND AMOUNT OF DESIRED MERCHANDISE

If a buying plan exists (see Chapter 11), much of the work of this step may have already been done. This step involves listing the exact items or the exact characteristics of the items to be bought and the exact amount to be ordered, stated in units to the extent possible. (In some cases specification of the number of units may be left until actual price negotiations are completed.) The goods should also be described as accurately and precisely as possible.

Some goods may be described by product numbers, sizes, and the like. A buyer for an appliance store may be told that $25,000 should be budgeted for the inventory of color televisions. The buyer should allocate the budgeted amount to specific television sizes, brands, cabinet styles, and other specific variables. Eventually, the buyer will have enough information to specify product numbers and then order the sets from the appropriate suppliers by product number.

Other goods may be described initially only by the desired characteristics. A buyer may be told to purchase thirty sets of patio furniture and may decide to buy twenty iron and ten wooden sets. More exact specifications could be determined during the negotiating process (described later in this chapter). Also, a buyer may specify a total number or dollar amount of merchandise by some general characteristic. Costume jewelry, for example, could be described as "$400 worth of gold-colored jewelry that will sell between $1 and $4 per unit, with a minimum of fifty pieces."

The description of merchandise is not an easy task. Chapter 11 discussed some of the factors that must be considered when selecting specific merchandise. When a buyer has broad responsibilities, much of the analysis must be performed by the buyer. Some of the more important factors to consider are sales growth potential for the product, compatibility of the product with other offerings, whether the product gives a competitive edge, and the potential profitability of the item. When buyers analyze these factors, they are performing part of the merchandise planning function, and a review of the material presented in Chapter 11 is necessary. Precise merchandise descriptions make the selection of suppliers and the negotiations with suppliers easier.

SELECT POSSIBLE SOURCES OF SUPPLY

In some cases, the source of supply may be predetermined. The buying plan may indicate a specific product from a specific manufacturer. If this is the case, the third step in the buying process is not necessary for that item. Often, however, the item will not be so precisely defined or there will be multiple sources even for a tightly defined product. In those cases, several sources of supply should be considered. The major areas involved in properly determining potential sources of supply include: (1) the type of vendor, (2) the number of vendors, (3) factors to look for in a supplier, (4) past vendor performance, (5) vendor-initiated contacts, (6) buyer-initiated contacts, (7) leased departments, and (8) foreign sources.

Types of Vendors   Generally the differences in vendor types involve the kinds of tasks each vendor will perform and the variety, assortment, and depth each vendor offers. The basic types of vendors from which the retailer can select are wholesalers (see Table 12.2) and producers.

The type of vendor to utilize should be carefully considered. In practice, many retailers simply use the vendors that call on them. This may cost the retailer money since the retailer may be paying for services that are not used. The selected vendors should be monitored to see that the needed services are being performed and that unneeded services are not being paid for.

Any of the vendors may be selected by the retailer as a supplier. The key to selecting the proper type of supplier is to look for those that perform the functions or deliver the services the retailer wants. Generally, the more

Table 12.2
Characteristic types of middlemen serving retailers

TYPE OF MIDDLEMAN	CHARACTERISTICS
Service (regular) wholesaler	Serves as the retailer's buying agent by assembling and collecting goods, storing goods, providing fast delivery, extending credit, and furnishing market information. These services appeal especially to small and medium-sized retailers.
Limited-function wholesaler	Charges less because he provides less service since he generally does not grant credit or offer delivery service. Offers only fast-moving items; may do business only by mail.
Rack jobber	Supplies mainly nonfood items to supermarkets, sets up displays, maintains merchandise assortment, and receives payment only on goods actually sold; thereby guarantees a pre-specified percent markup to the outlet.
Broker	Receives a commission to bring retail buyers and suppliers together; does not handle merchandise or take title to goods. Handles only a few lines, mainly grocery specialties, dry goods, fruits, vegetables, drugs, and hardware.
Commission agent	Similar to broker, except that he handles merchandise although he does not take title to it; supplies mainly large retailers with dry goods, grocery specialties, and fruits and vegetables.
Manufacturer's agent (representative)	Renders services similar to those of a salesman; is restricted to a limited territory and by limited authority to negotiate price and terms of sale; sells only part of his client's output.
Selling agent	Similar to manufacturer's agent, except that a selling agent is responsible for disposing of entire output of his client.
Auctioneer	Product is placed on display and sold to highest bidder. Used mainly to sell livestock and fruits and vegetables to small restaurants, large chains, or other wholesalers.

Source: From *Retail Management: Satisfaction of Consumer Needs,* 2nd ed. by Raymond A. Marquardt, James C. Makens, and Robert G. Roe, p. 225. Copyright © 1979 by the Dryden Press, a division of Holt, Rinehart and Winston. Reprinted by permission of Holt, Rinehart and Winston, CBS College Publishing.

functions or services the supplier performs, the more he or she will charge for merchandise. The descriptions of a service wholesaler and a limited-service wholesaler in Table 12.2 exemplify this point. Some retailers may want few, if any, services from suppliers. In fact, large retailers may perform all the "wholesaler" functions themselves and deal directly with producers. A smaller retailer will normally deal with wholesalers. Although the large retailer can perform many wholesaler functions, these functions must be cost-efficient. The large retailer may want to investigate periodically whether using wholesalers would actually be cheaper. After the type of supplier is selected, the retailer must determine how many to use.

Number of Vendors to Use

The decision involving the number of vendors to use is more complex than it might seem at first. Using a small number of suppliers (perhaps even one) has certain advantages, while using several sources has other advantages. When the retailer attempts to balance advantages and disadvantages, he or she may find that the decision may vary from one item (or item type) to another or from one time period to another. Listed below are some advantages of using limited sources and of using many sources. Generally, an advantage for one can be considered a disadvantage for the other.

Advantages of using a small number of suppliers include the following:

1. Possible cost savings from quantity discounts.

2. Possible free delivery or other concessions if the retailer is considered an "important" customer.

3. Less time needed for negotiations.

4. Possible savings on transportation costs.

5. General goodwill that may occur from agreeing that someone will be a sole supplier.

6. Possibly a greater consistency of product.[2]

Almost all the advantages begin with the word *possible* because none of the potential advantages are assured. Probably the most significant advantage of using one supplier, or at least a relatively small number of suppliers, is that it makes the buyer's job a little easier. (This may only be an advantage for the buyer, not necessarily for the retailer.)

Advantages of using several suppliers include the following:

1. Possible lower costs owing to supplier competition.

2. Less reliance on one supplier who may have trouble filling an order because of strikes, fires, or other problems that may not affect all suppliers.

3. Less problem with "creeping costs," which refers to a supplier's giving a good price to become a sole supplier and gradually increasing costs to a higher-than-market price.

4. Less chance of "supplier slippage," which occurs when a supplier gives good service in order to become the sole supplier and then give less service.[3]

The general advantage of several sources is less reliance on one supplier, who may be or become a less than ideal source. The buyer may have to work harder but may be able to get better deals.

The decision about the number of suppliers is one that has to be made. For the small retailer, a limited number of vendors, maybe even one, may be the best (or only) choice. Larger retailers can usually benefit more than smaller retailers from multiple sources. The decision is not easily quantified; it requires judgment about what will really happen after the decision is made. Whether many or few sources are used, the buyer should look for certain characteristics in a supplier.

Factors to Look for in a Supplier

Suppliers should be examined to see whether they can deliver the desired goods on time, at a good price. The buyer should also look further than the strictly economic aspects of supply. Sears, for instance, has been accused of "making 'unconscionable profits' on garments made under substandard wage and health conditions at Manhattan sweatshops. . . ."[4] Headlines such as these may mean that retailers, especially large, visible retailers, have to check not only the price and delivery but also the "social desirability" of a supplier. There are many ways of trying to quantify some of the intangible characteristics of a supplier; price alone should not be the deciding factor. One way of examining other factors is called factor ratings.

Factor Ratings.[5] Essentially, **factor ratings** are exactly what the name implies—evaluating and rating a potential source on certain factors important to the retailer. The specific factors are different for different goods. Some factors that might be rated are price, promised delivery date, product quality, terms of sale, services provided, performance history, and general management. Each factor that is considered important is listed with a weight. The weight is normally a subjective evaluation, expressed as a percentage, that represents the importance the buyer thinks that factor has in the decision about buying from a source. A buyer of bath towels, for instance, may decide that the primary factors and appropriate weights are price (30%), variety of colors (20%), variety of patterns (20%), promotion by the manufacturer (10%), delivery (10%), and performance history (10%).

Each competing supplier is rated on those factors. A rating scale of 1 to 10, with 10 highest, might be used. Table 12.3 is an example of how a factor rating for the towels might look.

Table 12.3
Factor rating for towel vendors

FACTOR	WEIGHT	RATINGS		WEIGHTED RATING	
		FIRM A	FIRM B	FIRM A	FIRM B
Price	0.30	10	5	3.0	1.5
Colors	0.20	8	10	1.6	2.0
Patterns	0.20	4	10	0.8	2.0
Promotion	0.10	2	10	0.2	1.0
Delivery	0.10	2	10	0.2	1.0
History	0.10	4	10	0.4	1.0
Total weighted rating points				6.2	8.5

The firm with the highest total weighted rating points should be the selected vendor. In the example in Table 12.3, firm B would be selected as the towel supplier. The more factors that are considered important in selecting a supplier, the more helpful a rating system can be. Without a method of relating various factors, the buyer may not make a good decision. If the weight is correctly determined (that is, if it is in line with the importance of that factor to the total decision), the factors will be properly related to one another. If the ratings are appropriate, they can be used to compare competing firms. If both the ratings and weights are proper, the firm rated highest will be the best source.

Problems with Rating Systems.   You probably noted that the above discussion contained many "if's." A buyer who can rate and weight properly can gain significant benefits from a rating system, but accurate rates and weights are by no means assured. Inaccurate estimates may be worse than no estimate because once a rating is written down it is very easy to consider the number absolute.

Rating systems often cannot adequately handle extreme variations between suppliers on some factors. Suppose that firm B in the example in Table 12.3 had had an extremely bad delivery problem. Even if rated 0 on this factor, firm B would still have the highest weighted rating (7.5). If the buyer could not be assured of reasonable delivery, firm B would not be a good choice regardless of the weighted rating. This problem can be partially handled by a rule that requires a certain minimum rating on *all* factors.

The rating system of analyzing vendors offers great potential. A buyer who can give reasonable weights and ratings (and can also use some logic) can benefit from such a system. The rating system can be time-consuming and counterproductive if not properly used. We recommend the judicious use of a rating system by buyers. One source of information for good rating systems is records on each vendor, which should be kept by the retailer.

Vendors' Past Performance Records

Whether a rating system or a less formalized system is used to investigate vendors, records of past performance are a tremendous aid in selecting possible vendors. To make the best use of records, they should be kept carefully and accurately. Most retailers keep some records on past suppliers, and with a little extra work after the receipt of goods the records can be even more useful.

A file that contains copies of all purchase orders, invoices, and descriptions of how the supplier performed on each order should be kept on each supplier. The *performance descriptions* can be most useful in selecting possible sources. They should contain at least four sections.

First, the performance descriptions should summarize any difference between what was ordered and what was received. This summary should indicate whether a supplier sent less than was ordered, more than was ordered, or incorrect merchandise.

Second, the performance descriptions should contain a summary of any discrepencies between promised delivery dates and actual delivery dates. To obtain business, some suppliers may promise delivery dates they cannot meet. Knowing that a particular supplier is normally two weeks late in shipping can help the buyer determine when an order needs to be placed and whether to use the supplier.

A third major element of the performance description is a summary of all terms of sale that a supplier may give. Suppliers often grant negotiated concessions. A buyer who knows the concessions a supplier has made in the past is in a better negotiating position.

Fourth, the description should enumerate any extenuating circumstances that have affected a supplier. A source that did not perform well on a past order may have had good reason. Excusable poor performance should not rule out future use of a supplier. Continued poor performance, even if excusable, should lead to the removal of a source as a possible supplier.

The performance descriptions should eventually lead to concise statements of performance for each supplier. The statement may be something like "Quick delivery, higher price, cash-on-delivery, few discrepancies in orders." This evaluation would indicate not only whether a supplier should be considered but also when a supplier should be considered a prime possibility.

The vendor records obviously help only when the supplier has been used previously. A buyer should be continuously looking for new and better sources. Generally there are two ways to find new sources—contacts *initiated by the vendor* and those *initiated by the buyer.*

Vendor-Initiated Contact

Many retailers rely primarily on vendor-initiated contacts. As the name implies, the vendor brings to the retailer's attention the products the vendor has to offer. There are two principal types of vendor-initiated contacts: calls by **sales representatives** and **catalogs**.

Sales Representatives. Many suppliers have field representatives that call on retailers. The representative may simply talk to the buyers or the representative may examine the merchandise on the retailer's shelves and make recommendations to the buyer about what to buy. The retailer should make every effort to give sales representatives a chance to see the buyer. The representative may have information that the buyer does not have. Although talking to representatives can be time-consuming, a buyer who makes a practice of not seeing them is not performing a key aspect of his or her job.

The buyer should ask the representative questions about the supplier's products, services, and practices. Often the order is negotiated and finalized when the representative calls on a store, but a buyer should recognize that a deal made with a sales representative is not necessarily a contract. For the agreement reached between the buyer and sales representative to be legally binding, the sales representative must have an agency relationship with the supplier. Often such a relationship does not exist, and the representative's firm decides whether to abide by the agreement. The only way for a buyer to be absolutely certain that a sales representative has an agency relationship is to contact the supplier. (In practice, most firms will abide by an agreement made by a representative.)

Catalogs.   Catalogs are a convenient source of buying information that some suppliers send to retailers. In fact, for product classifications that have good supplier catalogs, such as furniture, the catalog can be used in the merchandise planning stage. Catalogs should be filed so the buyer can refer to them when necessary. They also can be used by the retailer's salespeople to sell customized merchandise. This practice benefits the retailer since custom-ordered items do not require investment in inventory.

Buyer-Initiated Contact

A buyer should not simply sit in the store and wait for potential suppliers to make contact. A good buyer constantly looks for suppliers who can do a better job than present suppliers. The buyer often has to make the initial contact. Attitudes such as "If I am not important enough for them to call on, then I won't buy" are counterproductive. A representative may inadvertently or intentionally not visit a retailer. The "mistake" of the representative should not deter the buyer from looking for the best possible deals through whatever means are necessary.

It is especially critical that new and small retailers devote adequate time and attention to seeking potential suppliers. Possible sources of help in discovering potential suppliers include other retailers, chambers of commerce, state development agencies, and the Yellow Pages of nearby large cities.

Two special types of buyer-initiated contacts deserve special attention: **central markets** and **resident buying offices**.

Central Markets.   New York, Dallas, Chicago, Los Angeles, and San Francisco are central markets for apparel and general merchandise. They are called central markets because vendors for apparel and general merchandise are concentrated in the area. Sometimes many potential suppliers have displays located in one building, as in the Merchandise Mart in Chicago. Vendors may also hold temporary trade shows or markets for specific merchandise in various cities. A toy market held in a hotel in Memphis is an example of a temporary market.

Basically, when a buyer "goes to market," the buyer has an opportunity to meet with many firms in a short period of time. There is no other way for a buyer to see as much merchandise as possible from as many suppliers as possible in a short time. The biggest problem with central markets is that they can create a type of "information overload" for the buyer. If the buyer has a good merchandise plan and is reasonably careful in following the plan, however, the central market will not become a bewildering array of people and products. Even a small retailer can take advantage of some markets. In businesses such as furniture, fashions, and gifts it is practically essential that some trips be made to the central markets to see what new and different items are available. The central market is valuable from both the buying and the planning aspects of merchandise.

Resident Buying Offices. Resident buying offices are specialists who work with both manufacturers and retailers to facilitate the transfer of information and goods. The four primary types of resident buying offices are shown in Table 12.4.

Retailers who cannot or do not send their buyers or planners to market on a frequent basis can particularly benefit from a resident buying office. The office, which is normally paid on a commission basis, can send information about prices, availability, and trends for the retailer to use in planning and can also arrange group purchases by noncompeting stores. These services can enhance the buying performance of many retailers, especially small and medium-sized ones.

Leased Departments   Leased departments are a form of buying. A **leased department,** as the name implies, is a department that is leased to another firm. If a retailer is not

Table 12.4
Primary types of resident buying offices

TYPE OF OFFICE	CONTROLLED BY	EXAMPLES
Cooperatively owned, associated type	Stores that own it Stores it serves Directors, who are usually executives of member firms	Associated Merchandise Corp. Specialty Store Association Frederick Atkins, Inc.
Divisional resident office, syndicated type	A division of a corporation that owns a chain of department stores	Allied Purchasing Corp. Associated Dry Goods Corp. Gimbel's, Macy's, May Co. buying offices
Specialty, independent buying office	Completely independent relationship, sets own policies, handles both hard- and soft-line goods	Arkwright Independent Retailers Syndicate Felix Lilienthal and Co. Mutual Buying Syndicate
Company-owned buying office	Its management (buying primarily women's, men's, infant's, children's wear)	Jack Braustein, Inc. William Van Buren, Inc.

Source: Winston Borgen, *Learning Experiences in Retailing* (Pacific Palisades, Calif.: Goodyear Publishing, 1976), p. 156.

competent in a product area that is necessary in his or her store, the leased department can be an attractive alternative. The retailer is paid a part of the revenue of the department that is leased and the running of that department is the responsibility of the leasing firm. The retailer deciding to lease is willing to take a portion of the profits of a well-run department rather than all the profits of a department that is not so well run. Discount stores such as K mart often use leased departments for items such as cameras and jewelry. Any department can be leased, but specialty departments such as cameras or food services are those most often leased.

Foreign Sources

Foreign sources should also be considered as suppliers. By **foreign sources** we do not mean goods made in a foreign country for or by a domestic firm. We mean goods made by foreign firms. Some larger retailers can deal directly with foreign manufacturers or importers. Smaller firms often come into contact with foreign sources through wholesalers or agents. Central markets and resident buying offices are good contact points with importers. Federal and state agencies also can help a retailer locate foreign sources.

There are many types of suppliers and ways of discovering them. A good buyer will attempt to reach enough potential sources to be assured of good prices, deliveries, and other services. After the potential sources are selected, the buyer should negotiate with those vendors for the best contracts available.

NEGOTIATE WITH SELECTED SOURCES

A good buyer should always attempt to negotiate the best deals possible from the sources he or she selects. In fact, a good buyer negotiates with several firms to see which can and will give the best deals.

The buyer must know how far to go in negotiating with suppliers. A buyer should not play one firm's offer against another. It is proper to ask for concessions and to ask one source for the same concessions that another is giving. It is not proper to continue asking each supplier for more and more concessions. A buyer can step over the invisible ethics line when he or she plays sellers against one another in a relentless manner to get a better deal. In general, as long as a buyer is acting in good faith to aid his or her firm, the supplier will be willing to negotiate. Buyers who try to take advantage of suppliers may find that future negotiations are not possible. In other words, a buyer may pay at a future date for improper negotiating on the present contract.

The best deal is not based solely on price. As was shown in Table 12.3, price can be outweighed by other factors. Often the list price itself is not even a negotiating point. Negotiation points may include discounts, datings, or others instead.

Terms of Sale   A principle negotiating point involves the **terms of sale**. Although the list price may not be negotiable, most suppliers can negotiate about discounts and dating, which change the real cost of the item to the retailer.

Discounts. Discounts may be given to a retailer who meets certain qualifications. A buyer should inquire into the kinds of discounts a supplier will give and attempt to get as much of a discount as is legally possible. Some caution must be exercised because of the Robinson–Patman Act.

The **Robinson–Patman Act** (1936) makes it illegal for the seller to negotiate a net price that may lessen competition or create a monopoly. Discounts are not illegal under Robinson–Patman, but the discounts have to be justified. A buyer who demands and receives an illegal discount can be prosecuted under the act. Generally, if the same discounts are allowed to all buyers and the discounts are reasonable, no legal problems exist.

One type of discount often used is the **quantity discount**. As the name implies, these discounts are given for purchase of larger quantities of an item. Quantity discounts are given by many suppliers and a buyer should try to get such a discount. Buyers may even be able to get cumulative quantity discounts, which mean the seller allows a discount based on units bought during a time period rather than on one order. Quantity discounts are often investigated by the Federal Trade Commission (FTC) under the Robinson–Patman Act. To be legal, the discount must be based on savings to the supplier because the buyer buys in large quantities.

Trade discounts may also affect retailers. Trade discounts are discounts given because of the functions performed by some member of the distribution channel. A supplier may list the price of an item in a catalog or representative's price list as "100/40-10-10." This means that the retail price is normally $100 and that a channel member performing the normal retail functions gets a 40 percent discount. A retailer automatically gets this discount. It also means that a channel member who performs other functions for the supplier gets the 40 percent discount plus an additional 10 percent discount. A channel member who performs still other functions such as storage and transporting would get an additional 10 percent discount. These are called *chain discounts*. If a retailer can negotiate a deal such that the store performs the regular retail functions plus enough other functions to get the first additional 10 percent discount, the cost of the merchandise would be $54 rather than the $60 most retailers would pay. The calculations are as follows:

Regular retailer	$100 - (\$100 \times 0.4) = \$60$
Retailer performing additional functions	$60 - (\$60 \times 0.1) = \$54$

A buyer can try to get a better trade discount on any order. The Robinson–Patman Act can affect trade discounts also, but if the discount is given for functions actually performed, there should be no legal difficulties.

Seasonal discounts are often offered to retailers. A seasonal discount is usually given for buying an item during the off-season. The retailer is, in essence, being paid for carrying goods when they normally do not sell well. Some retailers may be able to make good use of such discounts, but seasonal discounts can cause problems for a retailer. If the merchandise is truly off-season, the retailer can tie up money that could be better used on merchandise that will sell. A toy retailer may get a good discount by taking delivery of toys in February, but it is a long time from February until Christmas. There are many costs associated with having nonselling goods in inventory.

A variation of the seasonal discount is a discount given for ordering early, but not necessarily taking possession of the goods or paying for them early. These discounts are given because early orders allow for better planning by the supplier. They can easily benefit both parties. Seasonal discounts normally do not lead to any legal problems.

Cash discounts are offered by most suppliers, they are given for prompt payment by the retailer. A rather standard discount is stated as *2/10, net 30*. This means that the entire bill is due in thirty days but if the bill is paid within ten days, a 2 percent discount will be given. After thirty days the vendor can charge interest. Although cash discounts of 2 percent may seem small to many retailers and students, it is actually an excellent discount. When one considers that the 2 percent is for only 20 days (30 − 10), the annual interest rate is about 36 percent [(360/20) × 0.02].

Another way to think of the impact of cash discounts was hinted at early in this chapter. If a retailer is earning a 4 percent return on sales before taxes, has a cost of goods sold amounting to 60 percent of sales, and is not taking cash discounts, that retailer could achieve about a 30 percent increase in pretax profits by taking discounts that average 2 percent (0.60 × 0.02 = 0.012; 0.012/0.04 = 0.3, or 30 percent). Some discounts are for more than 2 percent. Cash discounts normally do not cause legal problems if they are granted to all buyers. A retailer may be able to negotiate some cash discount concession, especially through datings.

Datings.   The official date of a transaction, the date on the invoice, can be very important because it determines when discounts can be taken and/or when payment is due. There are two basic types of dating, immediate and future.

Immediate dating and **cash on delivery (COD)** have the same meaning—the retailer must pay when the goods are received. Normally COD is used only when the supplier has had no dealings with the retailer or when the retailer is in such a poor financial position that the supplier must ask for immediate payment to protect his or her interest. A retailer who has financial problems and must pay COD is at a serious disadvantage. Cash discounts may not be allowed to COD buyers. A larger problem, however, involves cash flow. If the retailer has to pay for goods when received, cash is flowing out and cannot flow back in until the merchandise is sold. The interest paid to finance the inventory may offset any profit on the merchandise. This cash-flow problem may prove fatal to already financially weak firms.

Future dating is much better for the retailer. Essentially, future dating furnishes the retailer interest-free inventory financing. The net 30 dating discussed earlier is a normal method of future dating. It is usually given to a retailer without negotiation, and a buyer may be able to negotiate better future-dating terms. The terms *2/10, 30 days extra* may be granted. This means that the regular terms of *2/10, net 30* do not begin for thirty days. Thus the buyer has forty days to take the discount and sixty days to make final payment without interest. (This type of **extra dating** may be for longer periods of time, such as sixty days, ninety days, and so on.)

A similar dating is **EOM** or **end-of-month dating.** EOM indicates that the "regular" terms do not start until the end of the month. If goods are bought on June 2 with *2/10 EOM* terms, the retailer can take the discount until July 10 and must pay in full by July 30. Most suppliers have a specific cut-off date for determining to which month the EOM applies. A supplier might decide that goods bought after the twenty-fifth of the month be put on the next month. In that case, a retailer who bought goods with *2/10 EOM* terms on May 28 could take the discount until July 10.

Advance dating is another type of future dating. This method simply states a date on which regular terms begin. Goods bought in January, for instance, may have terms stated in the invoice such as *2/10 net 30 as of July 1*. This means that the discount can be taken until July 10 with full payment due by July 30. **Seasonal datings** are similar to advance datings, the difference being that the date is based on seasons. A toy supplier may allow retailers to order and receive goods early and date the invoice December 1 or even January 1. This helps the supplier to get early orders and shipments and allows the retailer to actually sell some, if not most, of the merchandise before paying for it.

One last type of dating is **receipt of goods (ROG).** As the name implies the regular terms apply beginning on the date the goods are received by the buyer. On goods ordered March 30 and delivered June 5, for example, the 2/10 discount could be taken until June 15.

The importance of negotiating good future datings cannot be overemphasized because of the large potential impact on cash flow and profits. The cash-flow implications should be fairly obvious. If the buyer can negotiate a future dating that allows an extra sixty days to pay, the retailer may not have to finance the inventory at all. The inflow of cash from sales may occur partially or totally before the outflow of payments to suppliers occurs.

The impact on profits can be equally beneficial. Suppose a retailer negotiates a dating that allows sixty days before payment is due. Also suppose that interest rates are 18 percent at the retailer's bank. If the retailer orders $100,000 worth of merchandise (after discounts), the savings on interest would be about $3,000 (1.5 percent per month times $100,000 times 2 months). This savings would go directly to pretax profits because no additional costs are incurred. As the amount ordered and the interest rates rise, so do the potential savings.

Other Negotiating Points

Although discounts and datings are the two principal negotiating points, there is any number of other items that may be negotiated: the potential list of negotiating points is as long as the innovativeness of the buyer and the supplier. The following four points follow discounts and datings in importance in negotiating: transportation, promotion, price guarantees, and exclusive distributorships.

Transportation Terms.   There are two general types of transportation terms used in sales contracts. In **free on board (f.o.b.) destination** (or store), the vendor pays all transportation costs and assumes transportation risks. Other f.o.b. designations, such as **f.o.b. shipping point,** mean the buyer pays all or part of the transportation charges. The buyer should be certain that it is clear who will pay what charges and who assumes transportation risks. As freight charges increase, this aspect of negotiation is likely to become more important. In fact, it is possible that in certain situations transportation costs might be higher than the cost of the merchandise being shipped. A good buyer will try to shift the burden of cost and responsibility to the vendor or at least try to ensure that the vendor will help keep transportation costs down.

Promotional Terms.   A buyer may negotiate a monetary allowance for the store's advertising of the supplier's product. This allowance can be in the form of a discount, of a cooperative advertising allowance (see Chapter 16), or of a guarantee that the supplier will spend a specified amount on advertising in the retailer's market area. Other promotional aids such as signs and displays may also be negotiated. The retailer may even be able to negotiate for the services of the supplier's representative or celebrities for special promotion. A beauty consultant hired by or representing a certain supplier may give in-store demonstrations, for example. An athlete who endorses a manufacturer's products may visit stores for special promotions at little or no cost to the retailer. Obviously, if such terms can be negotiated into an agreement, the retailer will benefit.

Price Guarantees.   Sometimes a retailer can negotiate for a price guarantee, an assurance from the vendor that if the price of an item drops between the time of an order and some future date (usually the delivery date) the buyer will be charged the lower price. Price guarantees can often be negotiated if seasonal merchandise is ordered early. The guarantee assures the buyer of paying no more than the contract price, and possibly less. On merchandise other than seasonal merchandise, a buyer may have to allow the seller an **escalator clause,** that is, the right to increase the price, in order to get the price guarantee. In times of inflation it is often not worth the risk of an increased price to get a price guarantee. For this reason, price guarantees are most useful on seasonal merchandise ordered early.

Exclusive Distributorships. As the name implies, an exclusive distributorship is established when a supplier gives a retailer the sole right to sell an item in a given market. For certain merchandise, this arrangement can be beneficial to the retailer. If customers look for the item by brand name, the retailer with an exclusive agreement will almost automatically gain some sales. Exclusive distributorships are often granted for fashion merchandise, sporting goods, appliances, and auto parts. Any branded merchandise is a candidate for exclusive distributorship negotiations. The supplier may demand certain rights, such as some control over price and presentation, when granting an exclusive distributorship.

Many other factors can be negotiated. Any "special" offered by a supplier should be carefully evaluated by the buyer to see that it is worth the price the supplier expects. The buyer should remember that whatever specials or services are offered will be reflected in the price, but the price may not be reduced just because the buyer does not use a service that a vendor customarily gives.

PLACE THE ORDER

The fourth step in the buying process is the placement of the order. Although this step may sound simple, it is a critical one. The order actually forms the contract; any mistake may be legally binding. Even if the vendor does not hold the retailer to a mistake, extra costs can and do occur when improper orders are placed. Even if the vendor agrees to take back incorrectly ordered merchandise, for instance, not having the correct merchandise in stock may be costly to the retailer. To minimize the possibility of mistakes, all orders should be written, preferably on a purchase order form of the buyer.

Necessity for a Purchase Order

The principal reason for using a **purchase order** for all orders is that it becomes the foundation of a legally binding contract. It is the offer by the retailer to buy merchandise according to the stipulated terms. As the beginning point of contract and often as the only written document of contract, it is important that the buyer know exactly what the "fine print" on the agreement states and, therefore, should use purchase orders developed for the retailer, not those supplied by the vendors. The Uniform Commercial Code (UCC) states that for contracts for more than $500, some written notation is necessary.

Some buyers contend that it is a lot easier to call a vendor and place a telephone order or to let a vendor's sales representative fill out an order blank supplied by the vendor. Under normal circumstances either of those methods of ordering works fine, but problems with the "fine print" on a supplier's order blank can develop. Problems of large proportions normally do not develop, but the retailer should not risk any problems if possible. The retailer's purchase order, although sometimes a bit difficult to use, should be used on all orders. It is a reasonably easy means of protecting the retailer from a supplier's accidental or intentional mistake related to merchandise ordered, payment terms, delivery terms, or other important terms.

Electronic Ordering

With increased use of computers in retailing, electronic control of inventories and **electronic ordering** may become the rule rather than the exception. Electronic ordering may consist of a computer printing a purchase order to be signed by the buyer, or it may be the buyer's computer communicating with the seller's computer, in which case the order is "untouched by human hands." The latter method is technically possible today, but many buyers and sellers want some input into the ordering process. (Computer possibilities are discussed more completely in Chapter 13.)

Some buyers think the buying process has ended when the order is placed. This is not true. The buying process does not end until the needed merchandise is in the store ready to be sold. After the order is placed, the

---

STRATEGY IN ACTION 12.1

Electronic Purchase Order Systems

During the 1960s computerized inventory control and ordering systems made inroads into large retail organizations. The 1980s will see the growth of electronic ordering systems. Sears, Penney's and K mart are currently using electronic purchase order (EPO) systems. F. W. Woolworth has a system under review and many other retailers are in the process of considering such systems. The major advantages for retailers of an EPO system are shorter lead times and lower inventory levels.

K mart has about two hundred vendors linked up to a direct electronic purchase order system. The system works something like this: (1) a store manager sends the store order to K mart headquarters electronically, (2) the order is then "homogenized" in the ordering system, (3) by the following morning a consolidated purchase order for the various K mart stores is available.

Each vendor has an assigned path and time slot for calling K mart headquarters to obtain orders. If the vendor misses the assigned time a repeat request can be made later on an unassigned line. The vendor pays for the phone call and transmission of the order. Merchandise is sometimes shipped the day following the initial store order.

K mart now has about 80 percent of its vendors and 95 percent of its volume on electronic purchase order for some departments. K mart has the capacity to add 150 new vendors to the vendors already on the system.

Source: Adapted from "At K mart: Nearly 200 Vendors Now on a Direct Electronic Purchase Order System; How It Is Working," pp. 50–52. Reprinted from *STORES* Magazine, © National Retail Merchants Association, Copyright, 1981.

buyer must expedite the order, receive and inspect the merchandise, and check the invoice and pay for the merchandise.

EXPEDITE THE ORDER

The buyer should not assume that after the order for merchandise is placed everything will happen as it should. **Expediting,** or order follow-up, may be necessary. The buyer should make sure that the vendor actually receives the order and that the vendor intends to fill the order as written. These two things should be ascertained a short time after issuing the order, usually within one week. A later check, the exact timing of which depends on the goods, should be made to determine the status of the order. This check is usually done in the middle of the period between ordering and shipping of the goods. Its primary purpose is to discover if the vendor is going to have any major problems filling the order. If there seems to be a problem, other status checks or possibly using other suppliers may be called for. One last status check should be made near the promised shipping date. This check is to determine if the goods were or will be shipped on time. Normally at this stage it is too late to change suppliers if the order has not been processed properly. The main purpose of the last check is to determine the arrangements that will be necessary to receive the goods.

RECEIVE AND INSPECT THE MERCHANDISE

The sixth (and sometimes neglected) step in the buying process is the receipt and inspection of ordered merchandise. The entire receiving process is more often considered part of merchandise control (and is discussed as such in Chapter 13), but it should also be considered part of the buying process. The main reason for buying personnel to be somewhat involved is that receipt of the goods is the completion of the vendors side of the agreement, and the buyer should be knowledgeable about the manner in which the vendor does this. Damaged or faulty goods cannot be easily sold, and having damaged or faulty goods may be the same as having no merchandise. A vendor that habitually delivers wrong or faulty merchandise should be informed of the errors and possibly not dealt with in the future. Much of the information the buyer needs to keep the vendor records accurate and current is derived from the receipt and inspection process. Even if the buyer is not responsible for receipt and inspection, he or she should receive reports and do some investigation of the merchandise that is actually received. If there is a problem with the merchandise, the buyer should be involved in the rejection or adjustment process. Since the buyer should know the specific requirements of the contract for the merchandise and the circumstances surrounding the contract, the buyer is in the best position to negotiate any problems that may develop.

STRATEGY IN ACTION 12.2

Postdistribution: The Way of the Future

The question of channel functions and activities performance has been discussed for years. Which channel member should perform which functions and when the functions should be performed are vital questions in determining the efficiency and effectiveness of a channel of distribution. One of the options retailers must decide on is whether to use predistribution or postdistribution. *Predistribution* is what the manufacturer does for the retailer. Sorting merchandise and shipping directly to specific retail stores by the manufacturer are examples of predistribution. *Postdistribution* involves the receiving of merchandise in bulk from the manufacturers. The retailer then sorts and sends merchandise on to the specific stores.

The chain retailers are heavily committed to postdistribution. Department stores are moving in that direction and specialty stores are beginning to use postdistribution more commonly. The benefits of postdistribution are supposedly reduced inventory and payroll costs and faster distribution. Don DeSancties, a consultant, claims the predistribution method is "too cumbersome." A few of the retailers using postdistribution are K mart, Target, Mervyn's, Petire, The Gap, and Casual Corner. Some retailers continue to advocate predistribution. Among these are Lerner Stores, Brooks, Fashions, and Mothercare.

Source: Jules Abend, "Distribution: Post or Pre?," pp. 37–41. Reprinted from *STORES* Magazine, © National Retail Merchants Association, Copyright, 1981.

CHECK THE INVOICE AND PAY FOR THE MERCHANDISE

The payment for goods received is normally handled by the accounting department, but it can be considered the last step in the buying process. The buyer should double-check the purchase order, the invoice, and the merchandise received. Omitting this check makes it easy for a fraudulent vendor to operate.

Some dishonest vendors, for instance, will send a bill to accounting when no merchandise has been delivered. Unless a control process is in effect, the bill is often paid. Another fraudulent practice is to ship and bill for merchandise that has not been ordered. Although there are several ways to cross check, one way is to allow or require that buyers help control this dishonest practice.

By being involved with the payment process buyers can be sure that accounting is taking advantage of all negotiated discounts. An accounting office that fails to take advantage of every possible discount cannot be tolerated. The buyer may have negotiated hard and long for good terms only to lose those advantageous terms because of a slow payment process. Since the buyer is often judged on the net cost of merchandise bought, the buyer must be sure that a co-worker's oversight does not add unnecessary costs.

After the merchandise is received and the vendor is paid, the buying process is finished, but two other important concepts are involved in the buying process: title to goods and special buying arrangements.

TITLE TO GOODS

Determining the point at which the **title** or ownership of goods passes from the vendor to the retailer is important. Liability for damage depends on legal ownership. If the goods are damaged during shipment or even while in the store, it is necessary to know who legally owned them. Returning merchandise that is unsold can also be affected by legal ownership.

Normal Title Transfer

Title to goods is normally transferred at the f.o.b. location. Although it should be spelled out in the contract, if the f.o.b. location is not specified the title is considered to transfer when the vendor releases the goods to a common carrier. (There are other possibilities from a legal standpoint, which are too complex for inclusion in this text. The Uniform Commercial Code (UCC) covers most of these conditions.) If the goods are damaged in shipment, the retailer's recourse is against the common carrier. There are other conditions under which the retailer does not gain title to goods even when they are for sale in the store. Some of these are discussed below.

Consignment Buying

Title to goods bought on **consignment** remains with the vendor. In that case, the retailer does not normally have the risk of obsolescence or nonselling merchandise. Consignment also frees the retailer from some inventory costs because the goods usually are not paid for until after the retailer has sold them. The potential benefits to the retailer are fewer risks and fewer dollars tied up in inventory. The potential benefits to the vendor are a greater ability to control retail prices and the possibility that retailers will accept more and/or marginal items because of the lack of risk. There are also some problems with consignment sales, however.

Sometimes vendors may not want to remove nonselling merchandise from the store. Combined with the possibility of the retailer's accepting more merchandise initially, this may mean that a store's selling space is cluttered with nonselling or slow-selling merchandise. The vendor must cover the risk and pay the inventory carrying cost in some manner, often through reduced retailer margins or higher retail prices.

The advantages and disadvantages of buying on consignment must be carefully examined. Retailers should neither accept nor reject consignment merchandise out of hand. Some consignment buying, especially of new product lines or new product areas, can be beneficial. Too much consignment buying can result in the retailer's being little more than the agent of a supplier.

Memorandum Buying

Using **memorandum buying,** the retailer takes title to goods but has a return privilege similar to that under consignment. The retailer pays the inventory cost and the vendor assumes obsolescence risks. If a retailer wants more control over the prices and presentation of an item but is unsure of the salability of the item, memorandum buying may be an attractive alternative.

SPECIAL BUYING ARRANGEMENTS

This chapter has discussed what might be called the normal buying process. Some firms use other arrangements to supplement and/or replace the normal process. Three such arrangements are committee buying, group buying, and the central buying office.

Committee Buying

Some retailers have appointed **buying committees,** which are generally more useful in formulating major merchandise strategy than in the actual purchase of merchandise. The primary reason for using a buying committee is to involve more key people and, hopefully, arrive at better overall merchandise strategy. As is the case with most committees, some retailers find committee buying effective and others do not.

Central Buying Office

Some large retail organizations have centralized their buying function by using **central buying offices.** Rather than having personnel at each store or outlet do the buying for that unit, large chains often have one buyer or a committee of buyers who buy certain merchandise for all units of the chain. Staple merchandise is most often bought in this manner. Essentially the same buying process used by an individual retailer is used by the buying office, on a larger scale. The primary advantage of using central buying offices is the opportunity to get good prices or terms because of increased buying power.

Group Buying

Group buying is a non–chain store's answer to the central buying office. Several retailers who get together to pool their purchases to get better prices or terms are practicing group buying. Group buying has the potential to save retailers money because of consolidated buying power. Before joining a buying group the retailer should realize that he or she will lose some autonomy. The group may decide to buy Brand A when the individual retailer and that retailer's customers would prefer Brand B. This difference in customer preferences is one good reason that buying groups and central buying offices usually concentrate on staple items, for which there is little brand loyalty.

MONITOR AND ADAPT

Since buying is only one element of strategic merchandise decisions and this chapter was related only to buying, we discuss the monitor-and-adapt phase here only as it relates to the buying process. Other monitor-and-adapt decisions related to merchandise are discussed in Chapters 11 and 13.

The primary monitoring and adapting activities specifically related to buying involve vendors and deals received from vendors. The vendor records kept by the buyer provide the best data for evaluating previous vendor performance and they generally provide a good base for predicting future performance. Some vendors may be omitted from future consideration because of their past performance. Other possible suppliers may need to be added to the list of potential sources as their existence becomes known.

The best way for a retailer to determine whether he or she is getting good deals from vendors is to relate his or her buying arrangements to those of other retailers. Although it is difficult if not impossible to make a direct comparison, a retailer can examine competitors' retail prices to see if there appear to be any discrepancies. If competitors consistently offer substantially lower prices and remain profitable, they may be getting better prices or terms from vendors. Whatever the reason, the retailer should attempt to discover why competitors are able to offer lower prices.

The retailer should also monitor the environment to see whether new buying arrangements or channels of distribution are developing. It may be possible to reduce the cost of merchandise substantially by adapting to new channel arrangements. A retailer is in too dynamic a field and the buying of merchandise is too important to ignore such opportunities.

KEY CONCEPTS

Factor ratings	Extra dating
Vendor performance records	End-of-month dating (EOM)
Sales representatives	Advance dating
Catalogs	Seasonal dating
Central market	Receipt of goods dating (ROG)
Resident buying office	Free on board (f.o.b.) destination
Leased departments	F.o.b. shipping point
Foreign sources	Price guarantees
Terms of sale	Purchase order
Robinson–Patman Act	Electronic ordering
Quantity discounts	Expediting
Trade discounts	Consignment buying
Seasonal discounts	Memorandum buying
Cash discounts	Committee buying
Immediate dating	Central buying office
Cash on delivery (COD)	Group buying
Future dating	

REVIEW QUESTIONS

1. Discuss the importance of buying decisions.
2. Develop the framework of the buying process.

3. Discuss why some sales experience may be desirable for a buyer.

4. Discuss some ethical and legal considerations involved with negotiating.

5. Should a retailer use many or only a few suppliers?

6. Discuss vendor rating systems.

7. Discuss the importance of maintaining vendor performance records.

8. Discuss the need for and the forms of buyer-initiated contacts.

9. Discuss why the best deal does not always have the lowest price.

10. If you were a buyer of perfume and were convinced that a competitor was getting a lower net price, what actions would you consider?

LEARNING EXERCISES

1. Ask three retailers whether they visit central markets. Determine their opinions of the markets. (If possible, visit a market with a retailer and give your opinion.)

2. Ask three or four retailers about the concessions they attempt to negotiate from suppliers. If possible, ask some sales representatives what concessions they are normally willing to grant. Explain any differences.

DECISION SITUATION 12.1: **GENTLEMEN'S, INC.**

Richard Wade, the general manager of Gentlemen's, is deciding on a vendor for higher-priced suits for his chain of eighteen men's wear stores. The chain is known for selling high-quality suits at reasonable prices. Three brands of higher-priced suits ($350–$500) are presently carried. High inventory costs and slack sales have convinced Richard to carry only two brands. The problem is which brand to drop.

There are some differences among the three manufacturers. Brand A is a well-known, high-quality brand. It is produced by an older firm that uses primarily traditional fabrics, cuts, and patterns. The firm gives few concessions on terms. For items ordered nine months prior to a season, it will allow sixty days after shipment for payment. Any suits rush-ordered during the season are charged an extra 10 percent and COD is demanded. Only defects found within seven days of receipt may be returned.

Brand B is also a high-quality suit. The manufacturer produces both traditional and "fashion" suits. It is willing to give terms on many orders. Datings of several months are often granted, especially on less traditional cuts and patterns. There have been some problems with not receiving the exact suits ordered although the suits received are usually acceptably close to those ordered.

Brand C suits are not made quite as well as Brands A and B. The quality problems are usually very minor and not detectable by customers. Gentlemen's earns a slightly higher margin on these suits and can often get good quantity and seasonal discounts. Deliveries are sometimes made a few weeks after they are promised and on several occasions a few "dogs" (suits that are difficult to sell because of patterns or cuts) are added to the order. The firm gives credits of 70 percent of wholesale price on the next order for suits not sold and returned.

QUESTIONS

1. What are the advantages and disadvantages of each brand?

2. Compare the three brands using factor ratings. Which firm would you drop?

3. What other information would you want before making a decision? How could you get this information?

DECISION SITUATION 12.2: **MARILYN'S**

Marilyn is considering an interesting offer on some costume jewelry for her gift shop. A jobber with whom Marilyn has had no dealings has offered her a "one-time, introductory offer." Basically, if Marilyn agrees to take a group of products and pay cash, she will be granted a good price reduction. The package is to include an assortment of costume jewelry, selected by the vendor, worth $4,000 at retail. The entire package will cost Marilyn $1,500 rather than the normal $2,000. Marilyn must pay cash, accept delivery next month (April), and there can be no returns unless the merchandise is broken when delivered.

QUESTIONS

1. What are some risks Marilyn must accept if she takes the offer? Can any of these risks be reduced? How?

2. If Marilyn's jewelry sales are mostly in November and December, should she take the offer?

3. Would you take the offer?

NOTES

1. The percentages used in the example are rounded from figures given in *Financial and Operating Results of Department and Specialty Stores, 1979* (New York: National Retail Merchants Association, 1980), pp. 108, 109. The idea of presenting the data in this manner was taken from Michiel R. Leenders, Harold E. Fearon, and Wilbur B. England, *Purchasing and Materials Management*, 7th ed. (Homewood, Ill.: Richard D. Irwin, 1980), p. 9.

2. Leenders *et al.*, op. cit., p. 234.

3. *Ibid.*, p. 235.

4. "Sears Accused of Selling Illegal Clothing," *Jackson Clarion-Ledger*, 7 April 1981, p. 4A.

5. For a more complete discussion of factor ratings, see Leenders *et al.*, pp. 529–534.

STRATEGIC RETAIL MANAGEMENT MODEL

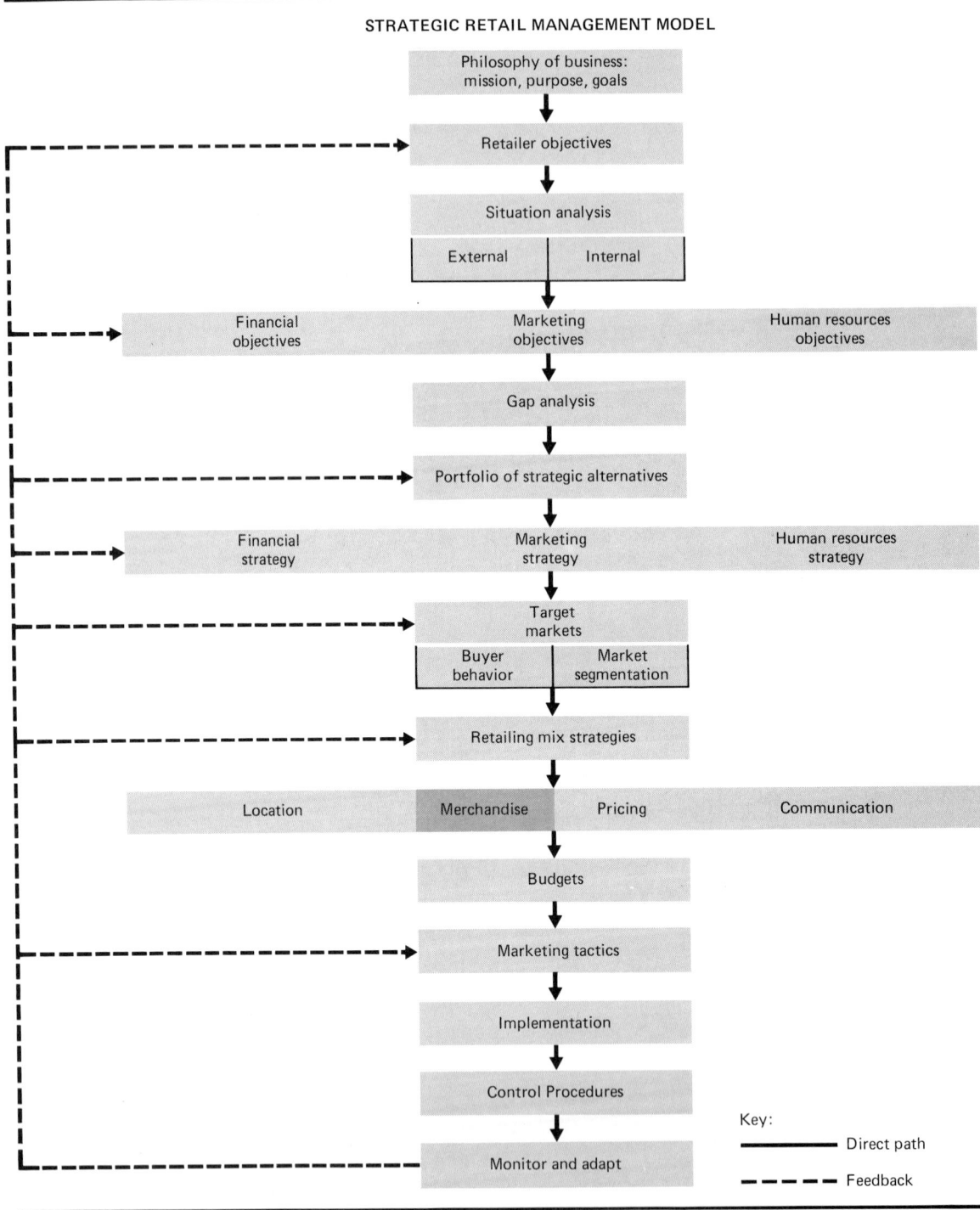

Chapter 13
Merchandise Control

LEARNING OBJECTIVES

1. To appreciate the role and importance of good merchandise control.

2. To understand the basic merchandise control process.

INTRODUCTION

This chapter is concerned with controlling the merchandise situation by comparing actual results with the strategic merchandise plans. To be effective, the strategic merchandise plans must be implemented and operated as envisioned by the planners. Deviations from the plans do occur, however, and they must be detected so the necessary adjustments can be made. If the merchandise control function is handled properly, the strategic merchandise plan will be followed reasonably well and adjustments can be made as necessary.

Effective control exists when (1) there are measurable standards, (2) actual performance and desired performance are compared, and (3) corrective action is taken when necessary. These three conditions of control can be transformed into three general control questions: (1) What merchandising results do we want (standards)? (2) How can we determine whether we are getting the desired results (performance comparison)? and (3) What should we do when the desired and actual results do not match (corrective action)?

Merchandise control, like many other aspects of strategic retail management, can be viewed as a decision-making process. The key elements of this process are organized around the *merchandise control decision model* shown in Fig. 13.1. The major steps necessary for exercising proper control are the following:

1. Review all existing plans and goals.

2. Determine the objectives of the merchandise control system.

3. Select the merchandise and inventory control systems.

4. Implement the control system.

5. Determine the receiving procedures.

6. Determine return procedures.

7. Monitor and adapt.

REVIEW ALL EXISTING PLANS AND GOALS

To ensure that merchandise control procedures and activities are compatible with the retailer's overall strategic plan, all existing plans and goals should be reviewed. The retailer's existing plans and goals combine to form the standards, at least part of the performance comparison, and to an extent the manner in which corrective action will take place.

The strategic merchandise plan forms the cornerstone of the standards. With very little adjustment, the merchandise buying plan discussed in Chapter 11 can serve as a standard for the retailer. The merchandise budget is also an integral part of the standards. Forecast sales, planned turnover

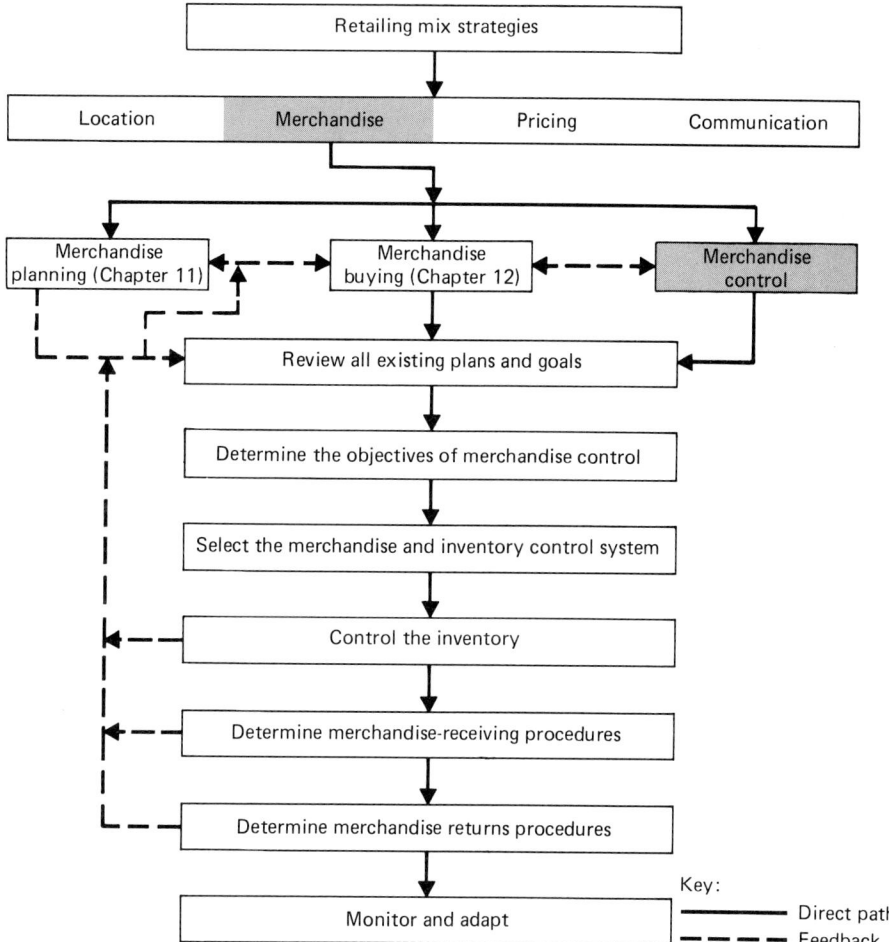

Figure 13.1
Merchandise control decision model

rates, planned maintained markups, and other elements of the merchandise buying plan enter into the formation of the desired performance standards.

The above-mentioned elements that form the merchandise control standards also help determine how to compare the standard and actual performance. The manner in which the various parts of the merchandise plans are stated determines how actual performance must be examined. If the plan states that the inventory of black, size 9 shoes should consist of ten pairs, then the *number* of pairs of black, size 9 shoes must be counted.

These plans also influence corrective procedures. The store's desired image, organization, and merchandise plans strongly affect the corrective actions that must occur if performance deviates from the plans. Consider a retailer who desires a high-quality, fashion image. If some merchandise is old and not selling, the retailer may decide to protect the store's image by selling the merchandise to another retailer rather than display outdated merchandise at a low price. A store with a different image might use the same merchandise in a promotional sale. The organizational structure will likely determine who will make corrective decisions, such as changing the plans or adjusting actual performance. The objectives of merchandise control and the selection of control systems are a direct result of answering the three control questions.

DETERMINE THE OBJECTIVES OF THE MERCHANDISE CONTROL SYSTEM

The basic objective of the merchandise control system is to provide accurate, timely, and concise information regarding the amount of merchandise in inventory and the condition of that merchandise to various personnel throughout the organization. Table 13.1 shows the types of information needed by various personnel.

Since many of the actual merchandise control activities take place at the departmental level, it is imperative that higher-level management set the specific objectives the various departments should strive to achieve. Higher-level managers should determine, for example, the performance desired on each of the elements listed as needed information in Table 13.1 and any other element that is considered necessary for a specific store. Higher-level management must monitor the entire store to see that each merchandise control unit (department, section, or other division) is in fact maintaining adequate control in its area of responsibility. Once the retailer has determined the area of responsibility and information needs of each employee and manager, the objectives for merchandise control have been essentially determined. The retailer can then select the specific types of merchandise control and inventory control to be used.

Table 13.1
Types of information needed by users of merchandise control information

USERS	NEEDED INFORMATION
Buying	Inventory level, receipts, return, conditions of received merchandise, discrepancies between purchase orders and invoices
Accounting	Inventory level, changes in inventory, discrepancies between invoice and receipts, returned merchandise
Finance	Inventory investments, changes in inventory investments
Merchandise managers	Inventory level, turnover, age of inventory, condition of inventory, fast-moving merchandise, slow-moving merchandise
Warehouse managers	Merchandise needed on sales floor, expected shipments

SELECT THE MERCHANDISE AND
INVENTORY CONTROL SYSTEM

The third step in merchandise control is to select the merchandise and inventory control systems. Although many authors treat the selection of these systems as separate and distinct decisions, they are so interrelated and interdependent that they must be made simultaneously. To understand how to make the decisions, however, a brief description of merchandise control and inventory control is necessary.

**Merchandise
Control**

There are two basic or pure types of merchandise control—dollar control and unit control. A third type is a combination of dollar and unit control. All three have certain advantages and disadvantages.

Dollar Control. As the name implies, **dollar control** is based on the *dollar value of merchandise*. Control of the dollar value of merchandise is needed because the merchandise plans are often expressed in dollars to be spent on specific items, categories of items, and/or departments. If the plans are stated in dollars, the control system must also be formulated in dollars. The dollar value usually is stated on the retail base. For example, "$100 of shoes" means that when the shoes are sold, $100 will be realized. (Review Chapter 11 to understand the difference between the cost basis and retail basis.) With dollar control, monitoring is usually concentrated on sales volume (in dollars) and inventory investment. The *units* sold and held in inventory are not formally monitored.

For dollar control (and planning) to be effective, the merchandise must be categorized, and the categories used for the merchandise control function must be the same as those used in merchandise planning. If a model stock plan similar to that in Fig. 11.2 is used, the same merchandise classifications must be used for control purposes. (Figure 11.2 is expressed in units, but it could be, and sometimes is, in dollars.) The categories are normally based on departments, item groups within departments, standard merchandise classifications, or price lines. The standard merchandise classifications in *Department and Specialty Store Merchandising and Operating Results,* an annual publication of the National Retail Merchants Association, offer several advantages. A principal advantage is that an individual store's results can be compared with national averages. Whatever classification scheme is used, the category should be narrow enough for effective monitoring and control.

Dollar control offers several advantages to the retailer, the primary one based on the difficulty of maintaining accurate records for unit control. Retail stores have so many products that keeping up with unit sales and units in inventory is not always practical. Dollar control, especially if narrow classifications are used, can give a reasonably accurate picture of what merchandise is selling and the overall condition of inventory. Dollar control is also necessary for financial control, because inventory investment is a major asset. The main disadvantage of dollar control is that when used alone it provides little insight into the specific merchandise that is and is not selling.

Unit Control.   As the name implies, **unit control** means that merchandise units (rather than dollars) are monitored and controlled. Unit control must be used when the merchandise plan is expressed only in units.

Unit control offers several advantages to a retailer. A good unit control system can pinpoint slow- or fast-moving items early enough for corrective action to be taken. Lack of stock (*stockouts*) and excessive inventories can be minimized. To obtain the full benefits of a unit control system, a perpetual inventory must be maintained, which means that changes in inventory are updated after each transaction. The difficulty and expense of maintaining a perpetual inventory system are the primary disadvantages of unit control. (Perpetual inventory is discussed later in this chapter.)

Combination Control.   To gain maximum control of the merchandise situation, a combination of dollar control and unit control should be used. Most retailers would benefit from controlling both the dollars invested in inventory and the units in inventory. Although combination control gives the retailer the advantages of both dollar and unit control, many of the disadvantages also remain. The primary problem involves the difficulty and expense of operating two somewhat parallel control systems. The advantages often outweigh the disadvantages, however.

Combination control is particularly useful for important items or item classes. The principal determinants of the importance of items are the cost of the items, the profits derived from the items, and customer response to stockout of the items.[1] Items that are costly may need combination control because overstocking these items can create serious financial problems related to inventory investment. Items that generate high profits through either high margins or high turnover may need combination control because stockouts may cause substantial loss of profits. Items that customers absolutely expect a retailer to have may need combination control because stockouts of these items may cause the customer to discontinue patronizing that store. For important items, combination control, at least on an informal basis, is required, and each retailer must determine which items within the store are most important. The computer has made the cost and complexity of combination control more manageable.

Inventory Control

Most of the merchandise control procedures and activities are focused on inventories. The two basic methods of inventory control are periodic and perpetual, but before we discuss these methods, a brief look at two *inventory valuation* methods, LIFO and FIFO, is necessary.

LIFO (last-in, first-out) and FIFO (first-in, first-out) are *not* inventory control methods; they are inventory valuation methods. With LIFO, the cost of the last merchandise bought (last-in) is used to determine the cost of goods sold; with FIFO, the cost of the oldest units in inventory (first-in) is used to determine the cost of goods sold.

During inflationary periods, the last goods purchased generally cost more than those purchased earlier. Therefore, LIFO would result in lower reported profits. The benefit of lower reported profits is lower taxes and the resulting enhancement of cash flow. Thus, LIFO would likely be favored if costs are expected to continue to rise. It should be noted, however, that if LIFO valuation is chosen, the Internal Revenue Service does not permit changing back to FIFO when prices begin to fall. If prices do begin to fall, LIFO results in higher reported profits and taxes.

It is also important to recognize that few, if any, merchandising decisions are affected by the choice of valuation method. The contention that inventory decisions are changed because of the differences in reported profits owing to the valuation method is invalid. Regardless of the valuation method used, *no more and no fewer units are sold*, and the retailer therefore should feel no impact on inventory decisions.

If any control-related figures, such as inventory turnover, are affected by a change in the method of valuation, the figures should be adjusted to a constant basis. If costs are increasing and the valuation method is changed from FIFO to LIFO, for example, the average inventory will decrease and, with constant sales, the inventory turnover rate will increase. This "improvement" in the turnover rate is an illusion. No *real* changes have occurred.

This is not intended to disparage the importance of the LIFO versus FIFO decision. Rather, we wish to stress that inventory valuation methods do not influence inventory control. The valuation methods can have a large impact on the financial picture of the firm, and, as such, inventory valuation should be viewed as an accounting decision, not a merchandising decision.

Periodic (or Physical) Inventory. One method of monitoring inventory is to count the stock on hand on a specific date, usually once or twice a year. Most retailers consider this "taking inventory" a necessary, though unenjoyable, task. The physical inventory count is necessary to determine the value of the ending inventories and, consequently, cost of goods sold.

Generally, different retailers use different specific procedures to take the physical inventory. Smaller retailers may find it advantageous to hire a firm that specializes in taking inventories. Most larger retailers, however, have specific, detailed plans specifying who, how, and when the count is to be taken.

The physical or periodic inventory method can be used with dollar, unit, or combination merchandise control. The problem with periodic control is that the information may not be timely enough for many decisions. Since it is costly and time-consuming to perform the count, many retailers perform only one count per year. This may be enough for accounting purposes, but it is not enough for decision-making and control purposes. Also, unusual circumstances occurring just before the count can give a somewhat distorted picture of the true or normal inventory situation. The practice of reducing inventory through special sales immediately before the count, for example, may result in an abnormally low inventory. This may be beneficial for tax purposes (most states and the federal government have a tax on goods-in-inventory), but the distorted inventory figures can be misleading to management. The distortion and time lag can be remedied by taking frequent physical inventories or by using a perpetual inventory method.

Perpetual Inventory.   The perpetual inventory provides up-to-date information at all times. The information is usually provided in both dollar and unit terms.

Although the perpetual method provides information for accounting purposes, the primary benefit is enhanced managerial control. Recall that the second necessary condition for effective control is a comparison of results to a standard. With a perpetual inventory, the current results (or inventory situation) can be determined at any time and compared with standards (or plans). In effect, perpetual inventory methods allow continual inventory control, which is not possible with periodic inventory methods. The primary drawbacks of perpetual methods are that they are more complex and expensive than periodic methods. Perpetual inventories can be maintained either by hand or by computer.

Hand methods of keeping a perpetual inventory are very time-consuming and difficult. Sales tickets or tapes, merchandise receipts, transfers, and all other merchandise-related documents must be kept accurately. These records must then be tabulated and assimilated into a workable control format. Each merchandise item must be handled separately. Since many retail stores have literally thousands of products, it is practically impossible to keep perpetual inventories by hand on all items in inventory. A retailer can, however, use hand methods on items that are extremely important to the store.

There are two computer-based methods for handling perpetual inventory. One involves batch processing of tags attached to each item (tag system) and the other involves various point-of-sale systems.

The **tag systems** involve attaching a tag that contains information such as department, style, size, product number, and so on on each item. The exact information on the tag depends on the control information needed by the specific retailer. The more specific the information, the greater the potential for control. When an item is sold, the tag or part of the tag is removed. The coded information on the tag is then tabulated by a computer, which can be programmed to prepare whatever reports are needed for effective control. The batch processing of the tags means that the reports will typically lag behind activity by a few days. A big advantage for retailers who do not own or lease computers is that the tags can be processed by computer service companies, eliminating the need for an investment in computer hardware.

STRATEGY IN ACTION 13.1
The Limited's Two-Way Communication System

A recent advancement in the "new technology" of retailing is a point-of-sale (POS) electronic cash register with two-way communication capabilities. The two-way system allows a store to communicate with the store's main office during working hours. The store's main office computer can also poll the individual store's point-of-sale register. This two-way system enables the chain to monitor prices being recorded into the individual POS registers. Price verification is instantaneous and if a wrong price is entered by a store clerk, the home office computer automatically changes it and informs the clerk of the change. Shrinkage can be reduced significantly with this system.

The Limited, a moderate-priced chain emphasizing contemporary or higher-fashion styles, is implementing a two-way communication system. Acquiring the two-way method was part of The Limited's search for increased POS flexibility and improved inventory control.

Source : "The Limited: A Dramatic Turnaround," pp. 39–41. Reprinted by permission from *Chain Store Age/Executive* © September 1981. Copyright Lebhar-Friedman, Inc. 425 Park Avenue, New York, NY 10022.

A newer means of performing perpetual inventory involves the use of **point-of-sale (POS)** equipment. For these systems, the information is often printed on a tag and also coded on a magnetic or sensitized strip. A scanning device is used to "read" the strip into the computer. Other systems involve manually entering product codes into the cash register along with the price at the point of sale. With any of these systems, the information is sent directly to the computer for processing.

Two special types of codes for computer-assisted perpetual inventories are the universal product code (**UPC**) and the optical character recognition (**OCR-A**),[2] which we discussed in Chapter 4. The UPC, which is used primarily in the food industry, requires that the manufacturer place a code on the package. The UPC code, a series of vertical lines, is now on most products sold in supermarkets. When read by the optical scanner, the product's code is sent to the retailer's computer, which in turn sends the product description and price back to the checkout register. To change prices, the supermarket manager simply changes the computer program; each product does not have to be re-marked. Many supermarkets are now using this system. The OCR-A works in a similar manner. With either system, the amount of inventory for any product classification in the store can be determined at any time.

Combinations of Merchandise and Inventory Control Systems

As we stated at the beginning of this section, merchandise and inventory control systems are so interrelated and interdependent that their selection must be considered simultaneously. Table 13.2 shows six possible combinations of merchandise and inventory control systems. Each retailer must

Table 13.2
Merchandise and inventory control system alternatives

INVENTORY CONTROL METHODS	MERCHANDISE CONTROL METHODS		
	UNIT CONTROL	DOLLAR CONTROL	UNIT AND DOLLAR CONTROL COMBINATION
Periodic	Periodic/unit	Periodic/dollar	Periodic/combination
Perpetual	Perpetual/unit	Perpetual/dollar	Perpetual/combination

choose the combination that yields the best control for his or her particular firm.

For a variety of reasons, four of the merchandise/inventory system pairings are not particularly useful to most retailers. The periodic/unit and the perpetual/unit systems do not yield the dollar information required for tax purposes. In addition, the periodic/unit control system fails to deliver the primary benefit of unit control systems — up-to-date information on the number of merchandise units in inventory. The perpetual/unit control system cannot be justified from a cost-benefit standpoint; the small amount of information generated relative to a perpetual/combination system is generally not worth the cost.

Although perpetual/dollar control systems are adequate for tax purposes, they are not nearly as good as some other control systems. (A perpetual/combination control system, for example, has basically the same cost but yields much more information.) Periodic/combination systems yield more information (in units and dollars) than the simpler periodic/dollar system. The cost typically is also greater and the unit information is not useful to decision makers unless it is provided very frequently, which is not feasible.

We suggest, therefore, that the periodic/dollar control system can be useful for many retailers, especially smaller retailers. Its advantages are that it is relatively inexpensive to operate, it yields the information necessary for tax purposes, and it is not unduly complex. The major shortcoming of periodic/dollar control is that it does not yield much usable information to decision makers such as buyers and merchandise planners. Buyers need up-to-date information on the status of the inventories for which they are responsible. If this information is not provided by the formal control system, an informal system must be developed by the buyer, such as "biocular analysis" (that is, the buyer goes to the sales floor and looks at the shelves whenever necessary). This is a major reason that some stores use department managers as buyers.

The most logical and productive alternative is the perpetual/combination control system. Although it is the most expensive system to operate, it also yields more information than any other control alternative. A well-designed perpetual/combination system can provide almost any data necessary for maximum control. If a retailer can afford the initial cost of installing the necessary equipment, this system allows the best control of merchandise. New point-of-sale equipment is constantly being introduced, often at lower prices. Any retailer should at least investigate the possibility of a computer-assisted perpetual/combination system of control. Even with this system, a periodic count of the stock is necessary to account for any discrepancies between the records and the physical inventory.

After the merchandise and inventory control system has been selected, the retailer is in a position to effectively control the inventory. The system chosen yields the data needed to control the inventory, but effective control also calls for the performance of several other activities.

IMPLEMENT THE CONTROL SYSTEM

Proper control of inventory is essential for any retailer. Too much inventory costs money while too little inventory costs sales. Inventory carrying costs have increased as interest rates increase. If a retailer carries just $20,000 excess inventory for a year, the interest expense of carrying this excess could be $3,600 at 18 percent, or more at higher interest rates. A retailer with a normal margin of 40 percent would have to sell $6,000 worth of additional merchandise just to cover interest costs. Such figures cannot be tolerated by any retailer, whether large or small.

Perhaps the key inventory control issue is the determination of how much inventory is enough. Unfortunately, there are no formulas or "magic" methods to answer the question. Coming to grips with this issue involves establishing specific guidelines and exercising sound judgment. Inventory turnover and inventory aging are often used as guidelines for controlling inventory.

Inventory Turnover

Inventory turnover is a widely used control concept, discussed in Chapter 11. Turnover is also extremely important to inventory control, and we will review it here with emphasis on how turnover can be utilized for control purposes.

Turnover is a standard used by many retailers, often developed from the retailer's own records or from trade figures. (Selected trade averages were shown in Table 11.4.) The standard may be expressed as a desired turnover rate for the entire store, for departments, or for smaller categories. Generally, much better control can be achieved with narrower merchandise categories. After establishing the turnover standard, the retailer should compare actual turnover rates to the standard and investigate any deviations from the standard.

Generally, a retailer should calculate turnover rates (see Table 11.3) on a regular basis, such as monthly. Frequent calculations will allow the retailer to take any necessary corrective actions as soon as possible. If the turnover rate for a department is eroding gradually, the retailer may want to take corrective action before the turnover rate becomes completely out of line with the standard.

Consider a retailer who has decided that the optimum turnover for the store is between 8 and 8.5 times per year. Further, the store's turnover rate has generally held around 8.5, but for the last four months the turnover rates (expressed on an annual basis) have been 8.45, 8.3, 8.25, and 8.1. This trend is depicted graphically in Fig. 13.2. Although the actual turnover is still between the desired limits, the retailer should at least consider taking some action now because if the trend continues it will soon be outside the limits. A control chart similar to that shown in Fig. 13.2 is a very useful tool for analyzing trends related to control.

Inventory turnover rates used alone can sometimes be misleading. The retailer must also consider several other factors, such as the relationship between turnover and gross margin.

Gross Margin/Turnover.   The *turnover versus gross margin trade-off* is one of the most important factors for the retailer to consider. Chapter 11 discussed this trade-off in some detail. Here we will review some of the key points as they affect control.

It is critical for retailers to establish a profitable balance between turnover and gross margins. If a retailer uses trade averages to establish turnover standards, he or she can usually expect to obtain gross margins similar to trade averages. Departures from the trade average turnover rates also usually require departures from the gross margin average. The median turnover for a furniture store (as depicted in Table 11.4) is 3.6 times a year. If an individual furniture retailer decides to operate as a discount furniture store, he or she can expect turnover rates to be higher than normal and gross margin percentage to be lower than normal. A low-margin retailer must turn the inventory over more often than a high-margin retailer to make the same profit.

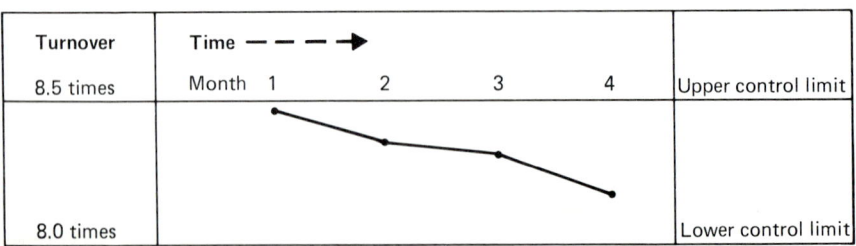

Figure 13.2
Control chart for turnover

The retailer should also remember the turnover/margin trade-off when taking corrective action. Suppose a retailer desires a turnover of 6 times per year and discovers that the inventory is only turning over 5 times a year. Should the retailer try to bring the turnover figure back to the desired level by increasing sales using lower prices (and lower margins)? More data are necessary to properly answer the question. It is possible that turning the inventory 6 times at a lowered margin would be less profitable than turning the inventory 5 times at a higher margin. Before taking corrective action, the retailer must examine possible problems and outcomes. A corrective action that lessens profitability is usually not a good correction.

Interpreting Turnover.   There are several problems with use of inventory turnover rates. One of these is proper interpretation of the turnover rate. Often the retailer must examine more than just the turnover figure before taking action. Suppose a retailer finds the trade average turnover is 8 times a year. If the retailer's actual turnover is 10 times, what action should the retailer take? Since the turnover rate is calculated by dividing average inventory into annual sales, one corrective action is to reduce sales, possibly by cutting hours of operation. This solution would likely lead to another problem—lower profits. Another possible solution is to increase inventory; this solution is appropriate only if a larger inventory is needed, such as to reduce stockouts. Another solution is simply to "laugh all the way to the bank." If normal margins are maintained and the turnover rate is higher than normal, the store is performing better than "normal" and there is no problem.

Another interpretation problem arises from an analysis of trade averages. The turnover rates in Table 11.4 are the *median* turnover rates for that type of store, not the *ideal* turnover rates. The retailer may find it more profitable to maintain turnover rates either higher or lower than the median, depending on the gross margins obtained. Sometimes turnover figures for the trade are also given for the most and least profitable quartiles. These figures can be easier to use since the most desirable direction from the median may be indicated. The retailer can also benefit from comparing actual turnover to trade average turnover for categories of retailers according to geographic region, square footage, sales volume, city population, and so on.

This discussion is not intended to be an argument against use of turnover as a control method. Rather, it is intended to show that proper inventory control involves more than a consideration of turnover rate alone.

Inventory Aging   While inventory turnover indicates the number of times the *entire* average inventory is sold during the year, **inventory aging** can give a better picture of how well *specific* inventory items are selling. Inventory aging simply means determining how long each item has been in inventory. In a small store it can be as simple as looking at various items and recalling how long the items have been in stock. Larger stores typically need a more elaborate method, such as assigning certain personnel to check certain items. Aging can be aided by coding the date an item went into inventory on the price tag or on the item itself. The aging of inventory is greatly simplified with computerized perpetual inventory systems.

The principal benefit of determining merchandise age is that the retailer can see whether items are moving at the desired rate. Although this is done by almost all retailers, at least on an informal basis, a regular, formal check of the merchandise is beneficial for all retailers, especially those selling perishable, fad, or fashion items. For those items moving too slowly, the retailer can plan special sales events, cut future orders, or remove the items entirely from the store selection. For items moving faster than expected, order size or frequency can be increased. Both slow and fast movements necessitate some type of adjustment in the inventory plan. Note that the correction may be to *change the standard* rather than to adjust the performance. The dynamic nature of retailing may force the retailer to use an alternative to the normal control process of adjusting performance.

One important outcome of inventory aging involves reordering. Examining the speed and volume of merchandise movement helps the retailer determine whether to reorder, how much to reorder, and when to reorder.

Reordering

The inventory control process is also concerned with the quantity and the timing of reordering goods. The *merchandise budget* is essentially a forecast of these activities, but *inventory control* is concerned with adjusting this forecast to reflect current conditions. The merchandise budget in Table 11.12 shows *planned purchases,* the amount of merchandise that should be bought for a given month, if the sales and reduction forecasts are correct. Any deviations from forecast sales and reductions must be reflected in the open-to-buy (OTB), and the inventory control process should be designed to make the necessary adjustments. Once the retailer gains a clear picture of how a product is actually selling, he or she can make a more accurate assessment of how much and when to reorder.

Reorder Amount. The amount of merchandise reordered each time directly affects the average inventory. Reordering too much merchandise at a given time will increase the costs associated with carrying goods in inventory. These inventory **carrying costs** include interest expenses on the inventory investment, storage expense, obsolescence or spoilage expenses, and opportunity costs (owing to inefficient use of selling space or capital). The *opportunity cost* may make carrying costs higher than some retailers realize. If a retailer could earn 15 percent return on an alternative investment and averaged $10,000 too much inventory for a year, the opportunity cost is $1,500. This amount would need to be apportioned to the individual items in question but would add to the carrying cost. Basically, any cost associated with having an item in inventory can be called a carrying cost.

Reordering too little merchandise increases **ordering costs.** Small orders require as much time to process as large orders and have a greater possibility of resulting in a stockout. Some of the costs normally considered ordering costs are the expense of preparing an order (buyers', stock checkers', secretaries' salaries and other similar costs), receiving costs, and portions of marking and transportation costs. (However, the portion of these costs to be allocated to a specific order is not easily determined.)

A quantitative method that utilizes ordering costs and carrying costs to arrive at the most advantageous order size is called the **economic order quantity (EOQ)** model. Figure 13.3 is a graphic representation of the EOQ model. Carrying costs increase as the order size (and, consequently, the average inventory) increases. Ordering costs decrease as the quantity ordered increases and, consequently, the number of orders decreases. Since the total cost of having the goods in inventory is a combination of ordering costs and carrying costs, the minimum *total costs* occur at the order size that has *equal* carrying costs and ordering costs.

The precise EOQ can be found mathmatically using the following formula:

$$Q = \sqrt{\frac{2(SO)}{IC}},$$

where:

Q = economic order quantity
S = forecast annual sales in units
O = ordering costs per order
I = carrying cost as a percentage of average inventory
C = unit cost of an item.

The EOQ formula gives the "exact" order quantity that results in the lowest total cost of inventory, *assuming* the figures are accurate. Herein lies the undoing of the EOQ formula: the figures are seldom exact. Annual sales, for example, is a forecast figure and, therefore, subject to forecasting errors.

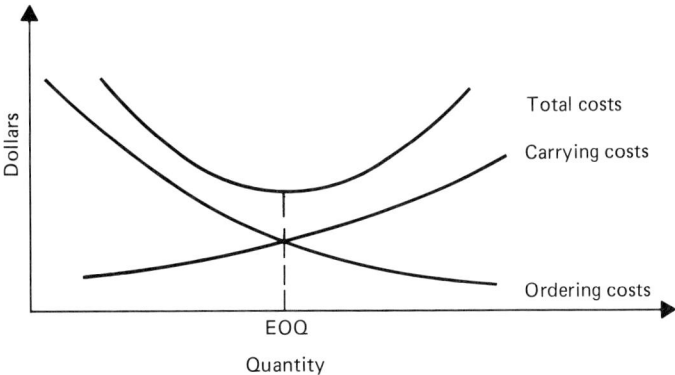

Figure 13.3
Economic order quantity model

Ordering costs for a specific order are also difficult to determine because many costs (such as salaries of the employees involved) are at least partially fixed but are treated as variable costs in the formula. The same is true of carrying costs. Additional problems are encountered when discounts are available, demand is uncertain, or price increases are anticipated. With these problems, the retailer might question the value of the EOQ model.

The primary contribution of EOQ is not the specific EOQ figure derived from the formula; this figure is not always as accurate as it appears. The *concept* of the EOQ model is valuable to retailers, however. The key idea is to balance two costs (ordering and carrying) that move in opposite directions with changes in the amount ordered. A retailer who understands the concept and the components of ordering and carrying costs can make better decisions about order size. It is also important to note that, in the region about the true EOQ, the total cost curve is often rather flat. As a result, if the retailer calculates an EOQ that is relatively close to the true EOQ, total costs will probably be acceptable.

The **order-up-to-level** model incorporates the spirit of the EOQ concept and can be used effectively by retailers.[3] This model uses the desired level of inventory investment, turnover, desired frequency of reordering, and other costs to determine maximum and minimum inventory levels. Figure 13.4 is a graphic representation of this model. The quantity to be ordered is determined by subtracting the merchandise on hand from the predetermined order-up-to-level for maximum quantity. If 13 units are on hand, the order point (14 units) has been reached, and 17 units should be ordered to reach the order-up-to-level quantity (30). The amount ordered will normally approximate the EOQ.

The order-up-to-level can be calculated using techniques like those presented in Chapter 11 relating to planning inventory levels. Essentially, the order-up-to-level is the maximum inventory the retailer wants to carry for an item. (The order point can be calculated as described in the next section of this chapter.)

A special case of determining how much to order involves fashion and fad items, which can gain the favor of customers quickly and experience intense sales growth. They also lose their appeal and sales with equal suddenness, however. Since profits are often quite high on these items, not having the items can result in high opportunity costs. Producers often do not make many units of these goods (they do not want to be caught with a lot of merchandise in their inventories either); therefore, future deliveries cannot be assured. Conversely, the risk of ordering too many units is also great because of the potential for a short life cycle. Because of the unstable sales situation, no order quantity model is particularly effective for these goods. The merchandise planners must use intuition (based on experience and knowledge of customers) to decide whether to carry these goods. If the merchandise sells well, another intuitive decision on the reorder amount must be made.

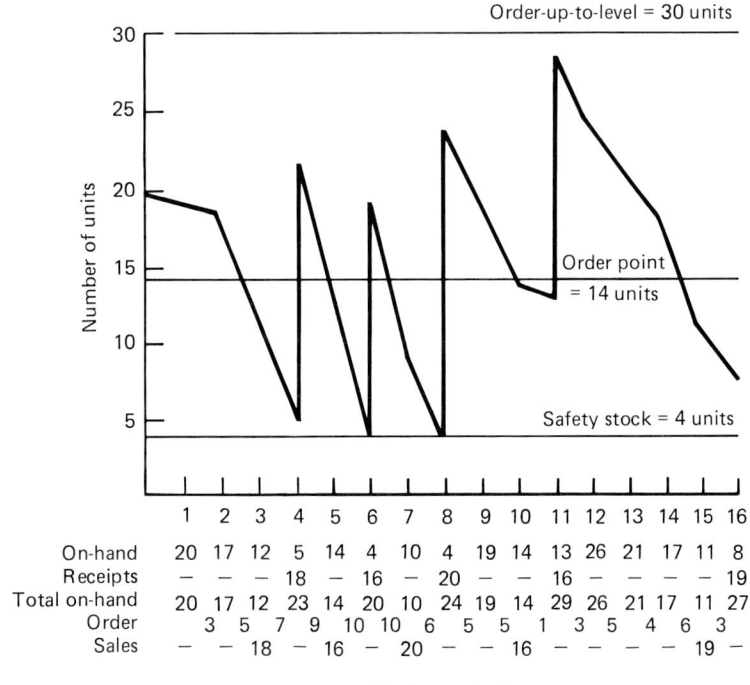

	1	2	3	4	5	6	7	8	9	10	11	12	13	14	15	16
On-hand	20	17	12	5	14	4	10	4	19	14	13	26	21	17	11	8
Receipts	—	—	—	18	—	16	—	20	—	—	16	—	—	—	—	19
Total on-hand	20	17	12	23	14	20	10	24	19	14	29	26	21	17	11	27
Order		3	5	7	9	10	10	6	5	5	1	3	5	4	6	3
Sales	—	—	18	—	16	—	20	—	—	16	—	—	—	—	19	—

Review periods

Figure 13.4
Order-up-to-level model
Source: William R. Davidson, Alton F. Doody, and Daniel J. Sweeney, *Retailing Management,* 4th ed. (New York: Ronald Press Co., 1975), p. 366.

Reorder Timing.   Determining reorder size is only part of the reorder problem. A closely related decision involves when to reorder. Ideally, a retailer should place an order when the stock on hand is equal to the expected sales between the order date and the delivery date. This must be adjusted for orders already placed but not received and for variations in expected sales. It is therefore necessary to know the length of time between order and receipt of goods, the status of previous orders, and the expected demand.

Chapter 12 discussed the need for accurate vendor records and status checks (or expediting) of orders. This information is vital for determining when to reorder. The vendor records should show normal delivery times and the status of all orders, including promised delivery dates of previously ordered merchandise. If good vendor records exist and reliable vendors are used, the adjustment of reorder times in light of existing orders and normal delivery time should be relatively simple.

Safety stock is merchandise held in inventory to deal with unpredicted changes in demand or minor supply problems. Experience with suppliers and customers form the basis for determining the amount of safety stock needed. Less reliable sources and/or erratic demand require more safety stock. Each retailer must analyze each merchandise item to determine the amount of safety stock.

The safety stock can be used to help determine the **reorder point** for each merchandise item. A reorder point is a specific inventory level that, when reached, triggers a reorder. The calculation of reorder points is relatively simple if the delivery period, normal demand rates, and safety stock are known. Suppose that a retailer has determined that demand for an item is normally 10 units per week, that the normal delivery time is two weeks, and that safety stock is needed to cover one week's sales. The retailer should place an order when 30 units remain in inventory (expected sales during delivery period + safety stock, or 20 + 10). This situation and three demand possibilities are shown in Fig. 13.5. Longer delivery periods or as yet unfilled orders only make the calculations a little more complicated, but the same general format can be used.

With the aid of point-of-sale computer devices and the order point model, reordering can become an automatic process for many merchandise classifications. The order point can be programmed into the computer and, as soon as that point is reached, a purchase order can be printed.

Regardless of whether computer or manual systems are used, the *frequency of orders* should be analyzed. Orders placed too frequently may mean that order size is not large enough, perhaps because forecast sales are being exceeded. In this situation, the merchandise budget and plans may need adjustment. Infrequent ordering also can provide an early warning. If the merchandise budget indicates that a good will be reordered each month

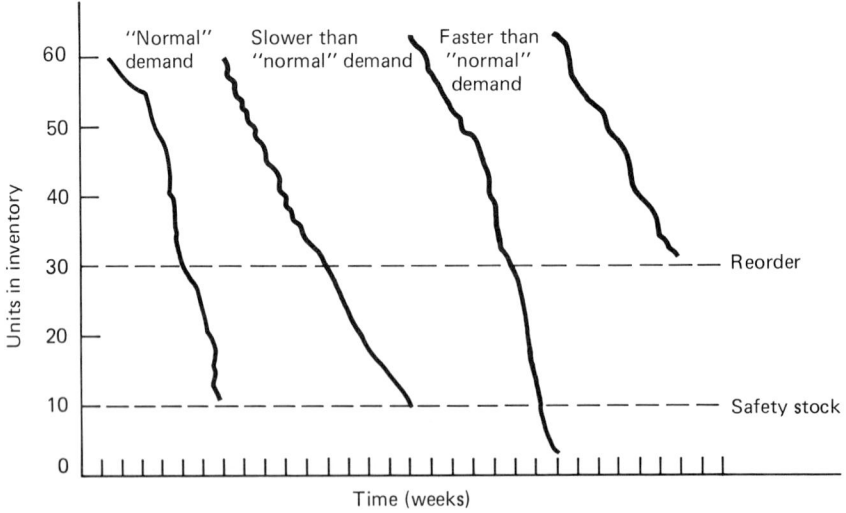

Figure 13.5
Reorder points

(see Table 11.12) and it is not being ordered, some adjustment may be necessary in the reorder point, the merchandise budget, or some other element of the retailing mix, such as promotion.

Our discussion of inventory control has implied that the retailer can calculate the exact inventory level at any time, but this implication is not necessarily correct. The retailer may know the exact number of units in beginning inventory, the exact number of goods purchased and actually placed in inventory, and the exact number of goods that have been sold, and still have fewer goods in the actual inventory than in the "paper" inventory. A physical count of the inventory may reveal, for example, that there are only 80 units when the computerized perpetual inventory system computes 100 units. This problem is due to inventory shrinkage.

Inventory Shrinkage

Inventory shrinkage is that part of reductions (discussed in Chapter 11) that includes shoplifting, internal theft of goods, erroneous calculations, and spoilage. Shrinkage results in less merchandise actually in inventory than the retailer's records indicate. If records are kept carefully, the shrinkage is likely to be caused by shoplifting or employee pilferage.

According to Ronald G. Assaf, chairman and president of the leading electronic surveillance manufacturer, shrinkage as a percentage of sales is *larger* than profit as a percentage of sales for apparel retailers (shrinkage = 3 percent; after-tax profit = 2.5 percent; some stores have 8 percent shrinkage).[4] Also, the National Retail Merchants Association estimates that shrinkage costs amount to 15 percent of the retail price.[5] The magnitude of these figures and indications that the problems are increasing stress the need to bring shrinkage under control.[6] A retailer must control both theft by employees and theft by shoplifters if shrinkage losses are to be reduced.

The most obvious way to avoid internal losses begins with better hiring practices. Admittedly, it is rather difficult when hiring someone to anticipate whether that person will steal from the store, but the retailer does have several measures available before and during employment. One practice is to administer polygraph tests to employees before hiring and periodically to all employees. This technique is growing in popularity, especially in convenience stores and stores in the lower end of markets. There are several problems with using polygraphs, however, such as accuracy, employee resistance, and the possibility of court intervention. The tests are sometimes viewed as an invasion of privacy or even as an unwarranted search of employees. If a retailer is experiencing heavy internal shrinkage, polygraphs should be considered as a potential deterrent.

In Chapter 9, retailers were admonished to thoroughly examine applicants' backgrounds. Part of that check should be aimed at uncovering previous convictions for theft and any other information that might indicate a high potential to steal. Legal regulations do not allow a retailer to ask applicants directly about arrests or other minor problems with the law, but with inventory shrinkage losses as high as they are, retailers must gather and use as much information about applicants as they legally can.

Another method to reduce employee theft is work rules. One possibility is to not allow employees to ring in their own purchases or purchases of relatives. Another helpful rule is to have someone check all packages before employees leave the store. Another might be that employees must obtain receipts for all products consumed (such as candy) while on breaks. These and related rules must be applied consistently to all employees if they are to be effective. The rules cannot eliminate all theft, particularly when employees cover for each other, but good work rules combined with greater vigilance by management can help reduce theft.

The area of inventory shrinkage that receives the most attention from retailers is shoplifting. There are several techniques useful in reducing shoplifting costs. One of the best methods of reducing shoplifting is to prosecute shoplifters. A recent survey indicated that stores that prosecute tend to have lower shrinkage than stores that do not prosecute.[7] There are several problems with prosecuting everyone caught shoplifting, however. More than half of all shoplifters who are apprehended are between thirteen and nineteen years of age,[8] and the value of stolen merchandise is often relatively small. These two factors often make it difficult to obtain a conviction, which has led some people to suggest that a nationwide code be adopted for state shoplifting laws.[9]

Another method that can help reduce shoplifting is a tagging system, usually called *electronic article surveillance or (EAS)*. EAS involves placing a tag on each merchandise item and having some type of scanning device at exits. If the tag has not been removed by a sales clerk when the customer pays for the merchandise, the scanning device sounds an alarm. The success of EAS in some stores has been astounding. Gimbel's in Philadelphia realized a 70 percent reduction in shrinkage after it installed EAS equipment.[10] Although EAS equipment catches many shoplifters, its real value probably is as a deterrent because amateur shoplifters (which some people feel make up the majority of shoplifters) are often afraid to try to beat the system. Improvements in EAS tags may soon allow their use on practically all types of merchandise.

There are many other techniques that can help reduce shoplifting, including *television cameras, mirrors, store layout, packaging, employee training,* and *fitting room surveillance*. Any method that makes a potential shoplifter afraid of getting caught should be considered.

Determining the methods to use in controlling shrinkage and how far to go in prosecuting suspects are definitely parts of the strategic planning process, and the retailer must review other plans and information. Customers may dislike EAS tags in stores selling expensive merchandise, for example. It may be that the cost of controlling shrinkage, both in equipment expense and lost business, is greater than the benefits that can be gained from the control.

As a general rule, most stores should try to make their shoplifting control procedures as discreet as possible but with enough visibility of the processes to discourage at least amateur shoplifters.

STRATEGY IN ACTION 13.2

Preventing Shrinkage, Employee Style

Retailers have experimented with a wide variety of methods to reduce merchandise shrinkage with various degrees of success. One of the more innovative, and apparently successful, methods has been developed by the Price Chopper supermarket chain located in upstate New York. Price Chopper used a people-oriented program based on voluntary employee participation to reduce shrinkage.

Each store manager asks for employee volunteers to join to establish Help Establish Loss Prevention (HELP) committees. Volunteers are screened by using personal interviews and written exams along with the current employee files to determine if they should be part of a HELP committee. A typical committee might consist of the produce manager, meatcutter, cashier, part-time stockperson, and a person from the maintenance area.

Eight hours of formal training on loss prevention, taught by the director of loss prevention for Price Chopper, is enriched by sixteen hours of on-the-job training for new volunteers. There are supposedly certain telltale signs that identify shoplifters. Apparently in supermarkets shoplifters are not too deceptive and are usually amateurs. Spotting and preventing customer shoplifting is made much easier when employees are properly trained to identify suspected shoplifters.

Keeping employees interested and maintaining self-respect among volunteers is vital to the continued success of HELP. Recognition for accomplishments and changing committee duties keep volunteers from becoming bored with the program. Although no figures were reported, Price Chopper has reduced merchandise shrinkage "drastically below the national average" with this program.

Source: "How Price Chopper Mobilizes an Employee Vigilance Network," *Progressive Grocer,* November 1979, pp. 57–60. Reprinted with permission.

With losses running as high as they are, all stores are going to have to examine the shoplifting problem much closer. If a store discovers that shoplifting losses are large and/or growing, the store must consider instituting some type of control procedures, which can range from simply watching customers a little closer to the installation of various electronic equipment.

Analysis of inventory turnover, inventory age, reordering history, and shrinkage is designed to inform management about how the inventory is adding to or detracting from the success of the store. The analysis should be aimed at producing timely, concise, and accurate reports, which often can be used to check past and present activities and to forecast future activities.

Reports to Merchandise Planning and General Store Management

Reports transmitted from inventory control to merchandise planners and/or general management (the same individual may carry all three titles) should be timely, concise, and accurate. The reports should be aimed at alerting merchandise planners and general store management about the condition of inventory and any changes needed to bring actual inventories in line with desired levels. In some retail organizations, those in charge of inventories may have authority to take corrective action, but sometimes the actions must be performed by or approved by higher management.

The three elements — *timeliness, conciseness,* and *accuracy* — must be evaluated and approached carefully. There are often trade-offs necessary between the elements. For fashion or fad merchandise, for example, timely information may take precedence over absolute accuracy. As previously discussed, certain decisions for these goods are based largely on intuition and the decisions must be made quickly if they are to be effective. Suppose an apparel store buys a new high-fashion item and sales for the first two days are very strong. Two days of good sales does not mean a trend is established, but merchandise planners and buyers may need a head start if any of the items are going to be reordered. Decisions, or at least the decision-making process, need to be initiated if there is a possibility that the new fashion item will be "in" this season.

For other items, timeliness might not be the key element. The accuracy gained from observing inventory for several weeks could be more important for some other merchandise. Inventory control should always strive for accuracy in any report, even those in which timeliness is of prime importance.

Conciseness is a deceptively difficult element to achieve in a report, but it can be achieved in both individual reports and the overall set of reports by carefully examining the question "Who needs to know what?" Indiscriminate collection, analysis, and dissemination of inventory data is both time-consuming and costly. Before the data are collected, a decision regarding the usefulness of the data must be made. Before the data are analyzed, a decision must be made about how the analysis will be used. Before the data are given to an individual, a decision regarding that person's need for the information must be made.

Achieving conciseness may become more difficult in the future. Computers can store and analyze incredibly large amounts of data quickly and accurately. The marginal cost of making additional copies of computer-generated reports and adding bits of information to the reports is seemingly small. With the increasing use of computers, retailers have a tendency to generate reports containing vast amounts of data and give these reports to everyone who might need the information. This practice can easily lead to information overload, that is, the information an individual needs to make a decision is hidden in far too much data. This is not an effective use of a computer. The machine can be programmed to summarize and give only necessary information to those who need it. If an individual *needs* additional data, these data can be provided in an additional report. The key point is that computers can be extremely useful in providing timely, accurate, *and* concise reports only if conciseness is demanded of them.

Although controlling the inventory is probably the most time-consuming and important part of merchandise control, there are other activities that must also be considered, one of which involves the procedures used for the receipt of merchandise.

DETERMINE MERCHANDISE RECEIVING PROCEDURES

The receipt and inspection of incoming merchandise were discussed in Chapter 12 as part of the buying process. These activities are also part of merchandise control. In a sense, the receipt of merchandise occurs when the merchandise moves from the retailer's buying component to the control component. This overlap of responsibility is appropriate for the receiving activities. The buyer usually is involved only to see that the vendor performed as agreed. Control staff are more involved with the actual work of receiving.

An early decision about merchandise receiving for multiunit retailers is whether centralized receiving will be used. Many retailers prefer *centralized receiving*, which means vendors send merchandise to central warehouses operated by the retailer (see Strategy in Action 12.2). At the warehouse, normal receiving procedures (discussed below) are used. The goods are then shipped from the warehouse to the individual branches. This practice can result in greater discounts, more control, lower freight costs, reduced inventories, and lower payroll costs.

Decentralized receiving means that the goods are shipped from the vendor to each of the various branches. Sometimes the supplier may perform some of the receiving-related duties, such as marking (see Strategy in Action 12.2). Some reasons for this practice include fewer duplicated activities and anticipated cost savings.

There are four principal parts of the receiving process: *record keeping, storage, marking,* and *inspection*.[11] They must be performed whether centralized or decentralized receiving is used.

Record Keeping

The cornerstone of any control system is good records. One of the most important activities in receiving is to keep accurate, up-to-date records of merchandise received and distributed to the selling floor.

Essentially the records should contain a description of exactly what goods have been received, the condition of the goods, the storage location of the goods, and any other pertinent data desired. Corresponding records are needed about the movement and distribution of the goods into the sales area.

Most small stores and some large stores use a manual record-keeping system. A list of merchandise to be received and placed in the store is given to the receiving department. As goods arrive, counts, condition, and dispositions of the items are noted. The records can be maintained in this manner, but it is difficult to produce up-to-date reports for management because the system is sometimes too slow to provide information to all those who need it in a timely manner.

To overcome some of these problems, many retailers are beginning to use computer-based systems. A retailer using a computer-based perpetual inventory system can easily maintain the receiving records on the computer. The primary advantage of these systems is the potential for generating timely data. As the merchandise is received and checked, records are updated immediately. Consequently, an up-to-date status of merchandise on hand can be obtained easily and quickly. This can be extremely useful for certain items, such as appliances and seasonal merchandise. If a customer wants a particular appliance, for example, the salesperson can quickly find out what is in the warehouse, even if it was just received. (Some point-of-sale terminals can interact directly with the receiving records and display the desired information.) Timely information about seasonal merchandise can be even more important. It is possible to appear to be out of stock for fast-selling merchandise when a new shipment is being processed or is sitting in a warehouse. Many sales can be lost before floor personnel even know the merchandise is in. Sales can slow down before the merchandise is delivered from the warehouse to the sales floor. Such situations can occur with a computer-based system, but the potential for timely information makes such occurrences much less likely.

Storage

Storage is another important part of the receiving operations. (Sometimes it is called **warehousing** and is considered an activity separate from receiving.) Merchandise is often held in storage before it is actually placed on the sales floor. It is important that the goods be placed in storage facilities that guard against spoilage. Almost any kind of merchandise can spoil if not properly stored. Garments, for instance, that are exposed to sunlight can "spoil" through fading. Care should also be taken to ensure that the merchandise is protected from theft.

Another important part of storage involves being able to find the merchandise while it is being stored. Many retailers have "lost" merchandise in their own storage facilities for long periods of time. When this occurs, money is tied up in merchandise that cannot possibly be sold. The "lost" items can easily become out of season, out of fashion, or spoiled before they are located. Misplaced merchandise causes profits to suffer.

Marking

Marking, the placing of the prices and other information on an item, is another activity that can be part of the receiving process. It is beyond the scope of this text to cover all the marking procedures and methods that a retailer can use.[12] The use of computer equipment has both helped and hurt the marking process.

Many goods, especially grocery items, are precoded by the manufacturer, such as with UPC symbols. This precoding can obviously help the retailer in that the merchandise does not have to be marked again. On the other hand, customers cannot interpret the code, but they usually want to know the price they will have to pay. Some firms have put their prices on the shelves rather than on each item to save marking costs, but this does not alleviate the problem entirely. If the price displayed by the POS at the time of sale does not agree with the price marked on the shelf, the customer may get angry. Thus, even more care may be needed to accurately mark coded items.

The amount of information marked on the items or tags should be determined early. Information needed by inventory control should be marked. This is especially true if point-of-sale or other machine-assisted inventory control is to be used.

Inspection

An element of receiving alluded to earlier is **inspection.** Incoming merchandise must be inspected to see that the proper quantity and quality of merchandise are received. The merchandise received must be compared to the merchandise that was ordered and to the vendor's invoice and any discrepencies reported to the appropriate personnel. Proper inspection procedures must also be followed. If the merchandise is not the correct quantity or quality, a return procedure is usually implemented. Damaged goods are a particular problem. If they are not discovered during inspections, the retailer may not be able to return the damaged merchandise.

DETERMINE MERCHANDISE RETURN PROCEDURE

The sixth major step in merchandise control is to develop merchandise return procedures. The need to return merchandise can occur for two basic reasons: (1) the merchandise cannot be sold, perhaps because of damage or (2) the wrong merchandise was received. The issue of returning goods that were ordered and properly received but that cannot be sold is normally negotiated at the time of purchase.

The return procedures usually involved in the receiving process are those designed for merchandise of improper quantity or quality. Speed in returning, or at least in notifying the supplier that a problem exists, is very important. If a retailer does not give timely notice, courts may hold that the goods have been accepted and cannot be returned. In essence, courts may decide that the supplier offered the goods and, by not returning the goods or notifying the supplier of the intention to reject the shipment, the retailer accepted the offer. If this occurs, the retailer may have to pay for the goods even if they were not ordered.

A special problem may occur in relation to the receipt of improper goods. Suppose a retailer orders items of a stated quality and receives items of a different quality. Further suppose that the items are selling well. Should the retailer return the items or sell the items even though they are different from those ordered? Often the retailer must keep the items received so that the store will have some of them on hand. Even under these circumstances, buying, accounting, and the supplier should be immediately notified so that merchandise plans, budgets, and payments may be adjusted. The accounting department should not be overlooked. The store should only pay for the merchandise that is received, and only receiving can inform accounting as to what was received.

MONITOR AND ADAPT

The last step in merchandise control is to monitor and adapt the overall merchandise control process to see that the process is working as desired. Key factors to monitor include the number of stockouts, excessive price reductions (to sell slow-moving merchandise), profitability, and any other factor that indicates the normal control procedures are not working as designed. If a problem is discovered, further investigation is needed to determine exactly why the control system is failing.

One reason might be that the entire control process is not suitable for the particular retailer. This would call for an overhaul of the control system itself. A retailer using a control system based on periodic/dollar control, for example, may discover that perpetual/combination control would be more efficient and effective.

Another reason for the control process not functioning properly is incorrect implementation. Sometimes the system may be appropriate but the individuals who implement the process may not be performing effectively. This problem calls for adjustments such as training or possibly replacement.

A third type of problem involves the cost of the system relative to its effectiveness in getting the job done. A control system that costs more than it provides is not a good system. If a retailer could reduce yearly inventory carrying costs by $8,000 by adding a computer and an operator who costs $15,000, the benefit ($8,000) is not great enough to cover the cost ($15,000). If the cost is less than the benefit, however, a change is indicated. (Note that the cost of computer-based merchandise control systems is decreasing rapidly while the potential benefits are increasing; consequently, retailers are well advised to consider computer capabilities to help control merchandise.)

Whatever the reason, a merchandise control system that does not control as desired should be investigated and changes should be made, if necessary. Careful consideration should be given to maintaining effective and efficient control systems.

KEY CONCEPTS

Dollar control	Carrying costs
Unit control	Ordering costs
Combination control	Economic order quantity (EOQ)
Periodic inventory	Order-up-to-level
Perpetual inventory	Safety stock
Tag systems	Reorder point
Point-of-sale system	Inventory shrinkage
UPC	Storage (warehousing)
OCR-A	Marking
Inventory turnover	Inspection
Inventory aging	

REVIEW QUESTIONS

1. Discuss the three conditions necessary for control.
2. Develop the strategic merchandise control process.
3. Discuss the differences between dollar control and unit control.
4. Discuss the relative usefulness of data yielded by periodic and by perpetual inventory systems.
5. Discuss why periodic/dollar and perpetual/combination control systems are the most practical to use. How should a retailer select between the two?
6. Discuss the potential applications and usefulness of computer-based merchandise control systems.
7. Discuss the use of inventory turnover in analyzing a retailing firm.
8. Discuss the EOQ model and problems with its use.
9. Why should the number and length of merchandise control reports be limited?
10. Why should goods be carefully inspected before being accepted?

LEARNING EXERCISES

1. Ask a local retailer who uses a computerized inventory system what kinds of data the system yields. (Get copies of reports if possible.) Also ask a retailer who does not use a computerized system about the information his or her system yields. Do you think each system is being used as effectively as possible? Compare the costs and benefits of the systems, if possible.
2. Talk to three local retailers about their inventory shrinkage. How big a problem is it? What do they do to control it? Do you see how it can be reduced?

DECISION SITUATION 13.1: **TURNER'S**

Turner's, a small chain of six stores selling up-scale women's clothing, is beginning to experience some growing pains. Until recently Leigh Turner (the merchandise manager) thought that the merchandise was being controlled adequately. After a recent inventory she is not so sure. For one thing, the total inventory investment was several thousand dollars higher than planned. Also, clerks indicated during the taking of inventory that they "found" items that customers had been looking for earlier; the lost sales appeared to be substantial.

After long and careful analysis of the inventory and a check with the branch managers and many clerks, Leigh concluded that the six stores combined had at least $75,000 more average inventory ($40,000 at cost) than was needed. She also concluded that at least $20,000 of sales were needlessly lost because of misplaced merchandise and that better timing of reductions and proper selection of sales merchandise would have resulted in $15,000 more profit.

Looking at these figures, Leigh wonders if the chain is large enough for a computer.

QUESTIONS

1. What benefits would you expect a computer system to provide? What problems would you expect?

2. If the computer could help solve the inventory problems, how much could Turner's spend on a computer?

3. Would you recommend a computer? (Support your decision.)

DECISION SITUATION 13.2: **PEGGY'S BOUTIQUE**

Peggy's is a moderately priced women's wear store. Annual sales have grown during the first ten years to $700,000. The store's annual profits are about $60,000. Peggy has been successful and hesitates to change the store more than necessary. Recently, however, shrinkage seems to have become more of a problem. Peggy believes that at least $10,000 is being lost to shoplifting. She thinks that little, if any, merchandise is being stolen by employees.

Peggy is considering the installation of electronic article surveillance devices and the imposition of strict rules about the number of items to be carried into dressing rooms. She is afraid that these measures will upset some regular customers, but she is also afraid that some of her regular customers are taking small items on occasion. She saw one customer who spends over $1,000 a year at the store take an inexpensive item, but she said nothing.

QUESTIONS

1. What reactions are likely if Peggy installs the EAS equipment?

2. What means other than EAS would you recommend?

3. What action should Peggy take if someone is caught shoplifting? Should exceptions be made for "good" customers?

NOTES

1. A more complete description of the three determinants and a model for using them can be found in Garry D. Smith and Danny R. Arnold, "Retail Inventory Planning: A Tri-Axis Approach," *Proceedings, Small Business Institute Directors Association National Conference,* 1981, ed. Kenneth D. Douglas and Steve Teglovic, Jr., pp. 309–316.

2. See *Universal Vendor Markings: A Voluntary System for Retail and Vendor* (New York: National Retail Merchants Association, 1976).

3. William R. Davidson, Alton R. Doody, and Daniel J. Sweeney, *Retail Management* (New York: Ronald Press, 1975), p. 365.

4. Valerie Seckler, "Article Surveillance Gaining as Retailers Combat Pilferage," *Chain Store Age Executive,* April 1980, p. 63.

5. *Ibid.*

6. Figures in *Merchandising and Operating Results* (New York: National Retail Merchants Association) for several years indicate an upward trend for almost all product and store categories.

7. "Retail Security Survey", *Retail Week*, 1 January 1981, p. 14.

8. John Friedman, "Code Suggested for State Shoplifting Laws," *Chain Store Age Executive*, February 1981, p. 37.

9. *Ibid.*

10. Seckler, *op. cit.*

11. There are other elements that may be considered part of the receiving function. For a discussion of these activities see Delbert J. Duncan and Stanley C. Hollander, *Modern Retailing Management* (Homewood, Ill.: Richard D. Irwin, 1977), pp. 370–393.

12. For a discussion of some procedures and methods of marking, see Duncan and Hollander, *ibid.*, pp. 380–388.

STRATEGIC RETAIL MANAGEMENT MODEL

Philosophy of business:
mission, purpose, goals

↓

Retailer objectives

↓

Situation analysis

| External | Internal |

↓

Financial objectives — Marketing objectives — Human resources objectives

↓

Gap analysis

↓

Portfolio of strategic alternatives

↓

Financial strategy — Marketing strategy — Human resources strategy

↓

Target markets

| Buyer behavior | Market segmentation |

↓

Retailing mix strategies

Location — Merchandise — Pricing — Communication

↓

Budgets

↓

Marketing tactics

↓

Implementation

↓

Control Procedures

↓

Monitor and adapt

Key:
——— Direct path
- - - - Feedback

Chapter 14
Pricing Decisions

LEARNING OBJECTIVES

1. To understand the role and importance of pricing for retailers.

2. To understand the major steps and considerations involved in strategic price planning.

INTRODUCTION

Pricing is one of the most important elements of the retailing mix; for some retailers it is *the* most important element. Prices must be in close harmony with all other retailing mix strategies. Items priced too high may not be salable even if the rest of the retailing mix is outstanding. Items priced too low might be sold, but the low prices might not yield a satisfactory profit. Price is the only element of the retailing mix that yields revenue directly; the other elements are actually costs. Because of continuing inflation, the importance of price to consumers (and therefore to retailers) is likely to continue and perhaps even increase.

Despite the importance of price, many retailers do not handle pricing well. Part of the problem is that price decisions can be made quickly by relying solely on simple multiplication. This common practice of devoting too little attention to pricing strategy leads to several common mistakes: pricing is too cost-oriented, prices are not adjusted often enough to take advantage of changing market conditions, and pricing strategy is not integrated adequately with other retailing mix strategies.

Most retailers can benefit from approaching pricing decisions using a logical, organized *pricing decision model* (see Fig. 14.1). Most of this chapter is devoted to developing this strategic price planning process. The discussion is organized around the following steps:

1. Review all existing information and plans.

2. Formulate pricing objectives.

3. Determine pricing strategy and tactics.

4. Prepare for normal price adjustments.

5. Monitor and adapt.

REVIEW ALL EXISTING INFORMATION AND PLANS

The first step of strategic price planning involves a review of the external and internal environmental analyses and of the current status of other strategic plans. Many factors, such as cost, store image, and supplier plans, can influence the pricing strategy.

Target Markets

The target markets chosen by the retailer must be analyzed to determine customers' attitudes and behavior toward prices. Low prices are required to reach some customers, while other customers are more inclined to pay higher prices for certain merchandise. Some customers, for instance, are primarily interested in convenience and will pay higher prices to get it. Stores such as 7–11 and Store 24 are primarily aimed at such customers.

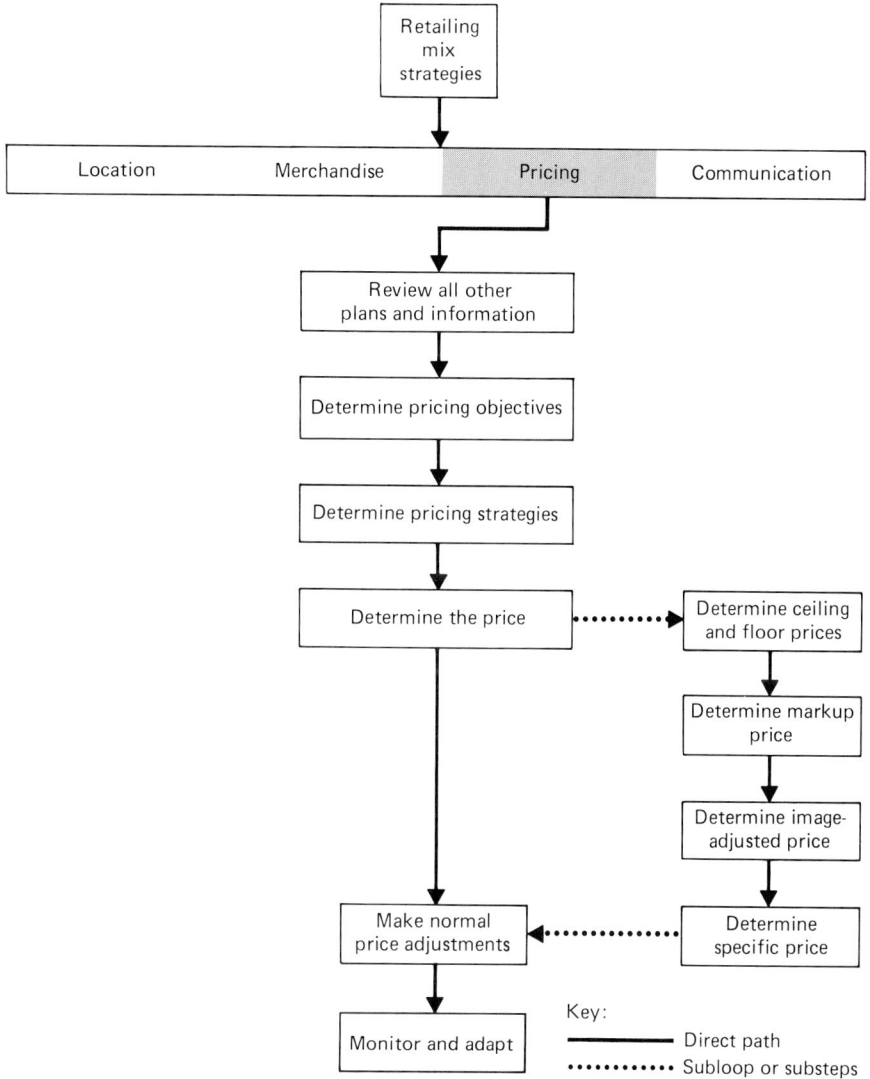

Figure 14.1
Pricing decision model

Other customers will spend hours shopping for "deals." Low prices are a principal attracting force for these customers. Some customers may even look hard to find higher prices. Stores with a prestige image depend on these customers. The ability of customers to pay, along with their predispositions to pricing levels, should be examined when analyzing the target market. The point is that by analyzing the target market the retailer can develop a better understanding of the role and importance of price.

STRATEGY IN ACTION 14.1

Consumer Price Perceptions and Grocers' Reactions

How do shoppers react when presented with new information about relative prices at food stores in their city? Do their reactions indicate that time is of secondary importance to money?

Some answers are suggested by a study of the effects of weekly price reporting which was carried out in late 1979–early 1980 under funding by the Agricultural Marketing Service of the U.S.D.A. and the Agriculture Economics Department of Purdue University.

Prices were collected for a marketbasket of 100 items in each of eight cities to construct a comparative price report. Over the three-month period of the study, newspapers in four of the cities served as controls for the experiment.

Here are some highlights of this unusual study.

The most important consideration for shoppers in choosing a supermarket is convenience of store location. Price consistently ranked second, followed by product quality and specials or sales. Rated lower were variety, ease of shopping, courtesy of clerks and, least important, store services.

Shoppers are fairly skilled at identifying the lowest price store in their city (i.e., the lowest price as measured by our 100-item marketbasket), and almost as adept at pinpointing the store with the highest prices. Consumers seem better informed on prices than we guessed initially.

Shoppers say they do not believe all stores have the same prices. They do agree, however, that, over time (for a group of items), costs are about the same at all stores in their city.

Beat the Clock

Consumers rate saving money above saving time. They also admit they could save money by exerting more time and effort in food shopping. Why don't they make the extra effort to cut costs? Because shoppers are likely to follow the economically rational rule—time is money.

Consumers also understand something about retailers' merchandising strategy. They believe that when a store offers an item at a particularly low price, the grocer probably makes up for it by raising the price of another item.

Consumers are split fairly evenly on the question of whether there is one store in their city which has the lowest prices week after week.

Shoppers choose a variety of stores; they agree that they are mobile enough to shop at almost any store in their city. (Our survey was carried out in metro areas of less than 400,000 people.)

Consumers are reluctant to ask the store manager to lower the price of an item they believe is too high. (The shopper was asked to imagine she found the price of hamburger in her regular super to be 20 cents higher than in another store.)

Weekly newspaper food ads are perceived to be somewhat more useful than the weekly shopper report which lists prices at eight local supermarkets. This may be due to the fact that shoppers were making "market list" or "menu" decisions rather than "store" decisions. That is, they already knew which store they were going to shop at, so the store ad conveyed more useful information than the price report, which only listed costs of 26 individual items.

The price report is used most often to understand how prices vary among supermarkets in an area, and also to compare how prices change from week to week. While the price report has a tendency to make consumers more sensitive to price as a criterion for store choice, the effect is fairly subtle.

How do these findings relate to the everyday business of running a store, meeting the needs of customers and calculating the proper merchandising mix? Retailers are faced with a knowledgeable consumer who balances a large number of factors before deciding which store to shop at. Today's consumer also has an accurate picture of price patterns among competing supermarkets, and is better equipped to choose the lowest price stores.

Tailor Merchandising Strategies

To appeal to these better informed shoppers, retailers should adopt a merchandising strategy acknowledging that price is important, but not the overriding issue. The price factor must be part of the blend which includes quality, convenience, variety, and courtesy.

A merchandising strategy must be flexible, too, since consumers' choice criteria are likely to change as economic and transportation conditions change. Newspaper ads will remain as shoppers' key channel for supermarkets' information messages.

What role does the major infusion of price information, such as in our experiment, play in consumer buying trends? Seemingly, a minor one, as long as food markets remain competitive and any price differences among stores are accepted by consumers as justified or small enough to be unworthy of extra effort. We found no evidence that shoppers' views of stores — or reasons why they chose a particular supermarket — were significantly altered by the new price information.

Source: Robert D. Boynton, "Shoppers Do More Than Just Pick Lowest Price," *Progressive Grocer,* February 1982, p. 29. Reprinted with permission.

Competition

The retailer should already have analyzed the price strategies of his or her competitors (see Chapter 5); this analysis should be reviewed carefully and extended if necessary. Competitors' price strategies can have a major impact on retail pricing strategies. Consider the retailer's competitive position in the market. Price is a major determinant of position in many retail trades. If a market is saturated with high-price stores, a retailer with a low-price strategy might be able to gain a competitive advantage. Other retailers may be forced to follow price strategies that are high, low, or moderate, depending on the strength of major competitors.

Legal Considerations

Legal considerations are a major constraint on pricing decisions. Retailers must be careful not to intentionally or inadvertently violate pricing-related laws. Although the monetary fines for violating these laws are obviously undesirable, the negative publicity associated even with accusations of such violations may be much more damaging to the retailer in the long run. Some of the laws discussed below pertain only to interstate commerce, while others are in effect only in certain states.

Pricing-fixing. There are two types of price-fixing: horizontal price-fixing and vertical price-fixing.

Horizontal price-fixing is an agreement among merchants at the same level of distribution (retailers, wholesalers, manufacturers) to charge certain prices. Both the Sherman Antitrust Act and the Federal Trade Commission Act declared these agreements to be illegal. The practice is illegal regardless of why it occurs or of the impact on previous prices. Even prestige retailers such as Saks Fifth Avenue, Bergdorf Goodman, and Bonwit Teller have been accused of horizontal price-fixing. Although they managed to settle out of court, the negative publicity was detrimental to all three stores.[1]

The control of retail prices by manufacturers is known as **vertical price-fixing** or fair trade.[2] Until 1975, many states allowed manufacturers to forbid retailers from charging lower prices than specified by the manufacturer. This practice was made illegal in the United States by the Consumer Goods Pricing Act of 1975. A manufacturer can now maintain direct price control only by providing merchandise on a consignment basis or possibly by threats to withdraw the right to sell the products from retailers who discount the product.

Minimum Price Laws. Minimum price laws have been passed by several states. The primary focus of these laws is the prevention of **predatory pricing.** Retailers are prohibited from pricing an item at less than its direct cost plus a fixed nominal percentage to cover overhead and/or shipping costs. One purpose of these laws is to protect small retailers from unfair competition by larger retailers. Certain large retailers have been known to price items below total costs in order to obtain an abnormally large share of the market and drive out weaker retailers. After driving out competition, the predatory retailer can raise prices to original levels or higher. The primary intention of these laws is to protect the consumer from higher, monopolistic prices.

The use of **loss leaders** is also limited by minimum price laws. Loss leaders are items sold at below cost to generate profitable sales on other items. Again, the primary aim of the law is to prevent predatory pricing.

Unit Pricing. Several states have passed laws requiring that items be priced by some conventional unit of measurement (such as cents per ounce). These laws are designed to help consumers faced with a vast array of different-sized packages. Few consumers can easily make price comparisons between two products when one is in an 8.2-ounce can and the other is in a 7.6-ounce can. Unit pricing laws require that the total price and the price per ounce (or some appropriate unit) be given for all sizes of products. The unit price is often posted on the shelf rather than on each product.

Some research indicates that unit pricing benefits both the retailer and the consumer.[3] One retailer reported that unit pricing can pay for itself because of improved space management, better inventory control, and fewer price-marking errors.[4] These and similar findings appear to indicate that unit pricing should be considered by retailers even when it is not mandated by law.

Price Advertising. The Federal Trade Commission has issued various rules concerning the advertising of prices. One segment of the rules deals with the advertising of price reductions.

The intent of the price-reduction guidelines is to prevent a retailer from indicating that an item is on sale at a reduced price when it is actually being sold at a non-reduced price. The retailer must prove that the advertised "original retail price" is a real, bona fide price that other customers have paid. Likewise, if a retailer's claims compare his or her prices with a competitor's prices, the retailer must be able to prove that the comparison is real and involves competitive stores selling under similar circumstances. If a retailer is accused of misleading or fraudulent price advertising, the burden of proof is on the retailer to prove the advertisement is legitimate and truthful.

Another group of price advertising guidelines deals with **bait-and-switch advertising,** the practice of advertising an item at a low price and then being out of stock or trying to get the customer to "trade up" to a higher-priced version. If the retailer does not have "enough" of a reduced-price item, some indication (limited quantity, four only, or the like) must be made in the advertising, or the retailer must offer rainchecks. An obvious problem is how many is enough to have on hand. The retailer must make a good-faith effort to have a sufficient quantity even if the exact number is difficult to determine. There is also a problem with knowing when too much pressure is being put on a customer to buy a higher-priced product. A salesperson may show a potential customer a higher-priced item and explain the benefits of that item. The salesperson cannot degrade the reduced-price item or indicate that it is of obviously inferior quality. Sears received a great deal of negative publicity when it was accused of bait-and-switch in 1976.

Administered Prices. Prices for certain categories of goods, such as milk, gasoline, and alcoholic beverages, are heavily regulated or **administered** by federal, state, and local governments.[5] It is critical for each retailer to be aware of any applicable regulations. Failure to follow price regulations can bring litigation or cries of price-gouging, neither of which is desirable.

FORMULATE PRICING OBJECTIVES

The review conducted in the first step of the pricing decision process should provide a solid foundation for formulating pricing objectives. A key factor in formulating these objectives is the role of price in the retailer's overall strategy.

Establish the Role of Price

Price must be assigned a specific role in the retailer's overall strategy. Because price can greatly enhance or detract from the overall retailing strategy, a retailer must be extremely careful in integrating price with other elements of the overall strategy.

Price can assume one of two roles in retailing strategy. First, price can be used in a differentiating role, in which case the prices of merchandise are relied on by the retailer to establish and support the desired store image. The retailer may differentiate by using either high or low prices. Service Merchandise, for example, a catalog showroom discount store, uses low prices on name brands as a major basis for appealing to customers. Conversely, Neiman Marcus uses high prices to help differentiate itself from competitors.

Price can also have a nondifferentiating role, in which case price is *not* a major competitive factor. Rather, the retailer stresses other retailing mix elements to attract customers, while prices tend to remain near competitive levels.

STRATEGY IN ACTION 14.2

Supermarket Frills

Lunds supermarkets, a six-store Minneapolis retailer, has expanded its services into areas not normally associated with grocery store retailing. Among some of the services offered by Lunds are (1) a book department, (2) hostesses to help customers find items, offer menu suggestions, give out recipes, and follow up customers' requests, and (3) prepared recipes using their own stock for customer sampling.

Lunds believes that there is a segment of the population who wants a broad range of services, wide aisles, a large selection, and top-quality fresh foods. Results of these "frills" have brought a "continual growth pattern" for Lunds.*

Shopwell, Inc., a seventy-one store supermarket chain in the New York City area, has also developed an up-scale "frills" strategy to convey the idea of the "excitement of good eating." Shopwell is opening what it calls food department stores known as the Food Emporium. These new stores carry gourmet items such as fresh pasta, cookies, lobster, individually wrapped fruits from New Zealand, fresh milk chocolate, Bahlsen cookies from West Germany, and all varieties of game available on order.

Each store is organized into boutique-style departments with names like "The Fruit and Vegetable Stand," "Seafood Cove," and "The Butcher Shop." All of the departments offer personalized service to the customer.

Although only affluent areas can support this type of store, company executives believe that a market segment exists for this type of retailing. Shopwell also hopes for higher gross margins from the Food Emporium stores to help alleviate the chronic low-margin problems faced by the chain.†

*Source: "Frills Pay Off for Lunds." Reprinted by permission from *Sales & Marketing Management* magazine. Copyright 1981. 14 September 1981, pp. 21–22.
†"Shopwell: Upscale with Its Food Emporiums," pp. 33–36. Reprinted by permission from *Chain Store Age Executive* © February 1981. Copyright Lebhar-Friedman, Inc. 425 Park Avenue, New York, NY 10022.

The role selected for price establishes important boundaries and guidelines for pricing decisions. The role of price should be made explicit by formulating the objectives that price is expected to fulfill.

Choose Specific Price Objectives

Specific pricing objectives should be predicated on the retailer's basic orientation toward growth, profit, coping with competition, and enhancing cash flow and other retailing mix elements and overall strategy. Table 14.1 presents various pricing objectives organized according to these orientations.

Retailers should have a set or hierarchy of pricing objectives. The primary, bottom-line objective should be profit. Other secondary pricing objectives (both short and long run) should focus on achieving the primary profit objective. The retailer may face a situation in which long-run profits are possible *only* if the firm can survive a current cash flow crisis. This situation would call for pricing objectives that enhance cash flow. (Note that cash-flow pricing objectives can call for lowering or raising prices, depending on the demand elasticity of the retailer's offerings.)

Beware of Conflicting Objectives

Not only should pricing objectives be compatible with other retailing strategy, they must be consistent with one another. Many retailers are inclined to seek maximum profit and sales (revenues) simultaneously, for example. Although this is a laudable set of objectives, accomplishing these dual objectives is practically impossible. As shown in Figure 14.2, at high levels of unit sales, costs are likely to increase at a rapid rate while the price reduc-

Table 14.1
Potential pricing objectives

Growth	*Cash flow*
Sales or profit growth	Rapidly recover new product development costs
Market share growth	
Profit	*Enhancement of other strategy elements*
Return on investment	Provide a promotional theme
Maximize (or optimize) short- and long-run profits	Make a product "visible" and create interest
	Fill out the firm's product line
	Contribute to the product's and firm's image
Competitive	Build traffic
Discourage entrants and speed exit of marginal firms	Be regarded as "fair" by vendors and customers
Maintain price leadership	
Discourage price cutting and stabilize market prices	
Rapidly establish market position	

Source: Adapted from Alfred R. Oxenfeldt, "A Decision-Making Structure for Price Decisions," *Journal of Marketing* 37 (January 1973), pp. 48–53. Reprinted with permission from *Journal of Marketing* (published by the American Marketing Association).

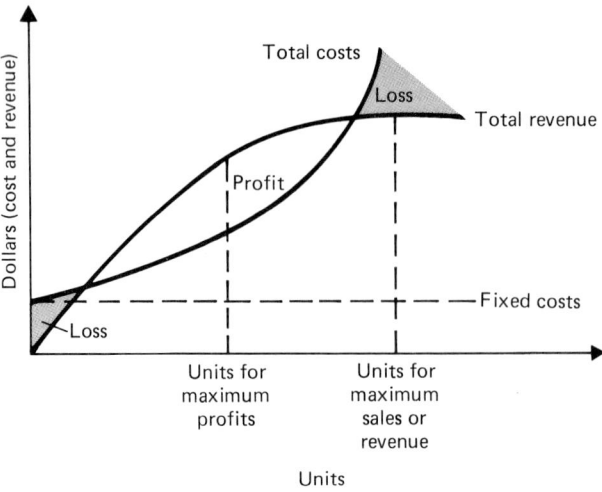

Figure 14.2
Maximum profit and revenue

tions needed to increase unit sales may actually cause the total revenue to
decline. The key point is that *maximum profit and maximum sales are not
likely to occur at the same unit sales quantity.* Retailers must guard against
such conflicting objectives.

DETERMINE PRICING STRATEGY AND TACTICS

The third step in the pricing decision process involves developing basic
pricing strategies and specific pricing tactics to accomplish the pricing objectives defined in Step 2. The focus of this step is on a pricing procedure
that incorporates the major pricing approaches used by retailers and other
crucial pricing considerations. Before developing the procedure, we will
briefly discuss two pricing philosophies and three basic pricing approaches.

Basic Pricing
Philosophies

There are two decisions involving pricing philosophy that a retailer must
make early in the pricing process, price level and price flexibility decisions.

Skimming versus Penetration.   Although skimming or penetration decisions have limited usefulness in retailing, they are relevant in a few specific
situations. The question of skimming or penetration involves the retailer's
approach to obtaining and maintaining market share for particular items. If
a retailer foresees good long-run profit potential for a particular item, a large,
solid market share would be desirable, and the most compatible pricing
strategy would be **penetration pricing.** Penetration pricing involves placing
relatively low prices on items, which should result in relatively high initial

sales and market share. The high market share and relatively low profit per unit usually help prevent new competitors from entering the market.

Conversely, some items may provide good profits only to those retailers who are first to offer the item. Some consumers are willing to pay higher prices to be the first in their group to have certain items, such as fad items and those with short fashion cycles. For these kinds of items, the retailer might use a **skimming** strategy by charging higher prices when a product is first introduced and perhaps reducing the price to meet competition later. Skimming can also be used by vertically integrated firms to help recover development costs earlier.

One Price versus Flexible Price.   Another factor that can affect the price placed on an item is whether the firm has a one-price or a flexible-price policy. A **one-price policy** simply means that customers will expect to pay and will pay the price that is marked on an item. Most retailers in the United States operate under a one-price policy. Automobile and furniture retailers are two major exceptions. For these two types of retailers, the customer does not expect to pay and usually does not pay the marked price. This is a **flexible-price policy**.

A business using a flexible-price policy can, to a degree, be less careful in placing the original price on an item than can a firm using a one-price policy. (The price cannot be so high that it scares the customer into not buying, however.) If a customer thinks the price is too high, the customer can offer a lower amount. The final price is determined through the negotiating process. In a sense, the price the retailer places on the item is just the upper negotiating limit. Sometimes a code is used so the salesperson will know the range in which he or she is allowed to negotiate. Generally, a flexible-price policy requires better sales personnel. Also, in the United States customers are not accustomed to the practice for most goods and may not be willing to negotiate. On the other hand, a store that fosters haggling or "horse trading" may get a favorable response from the uniqueness of the idea or because people may enjoy arguing.

Basic Pricing Approaches

There are three basic approaches to pricing: (1) demand-oriented pricing, (2) cost-oriented pricing, and (3) competition-oriented pricing.

Demand-Oriented Pricing.   **Demand-oriented pricing** is based on economic price theory and, in its purest form, embodies the concept of **marginal analysis**. Essentially, retail profits are maximized at the price that results in the sale of the number of items at which the marginal cost of selling the item is equal to the marginal revenue received from the item. This relationship is shown graphically in Fig. 14.3. In the figure, the price P_m results in maximum profit.

If profit maximization were the pricing objective, marginal analysis would theoretically provide the best pricing approach. Unfortunately, mar-

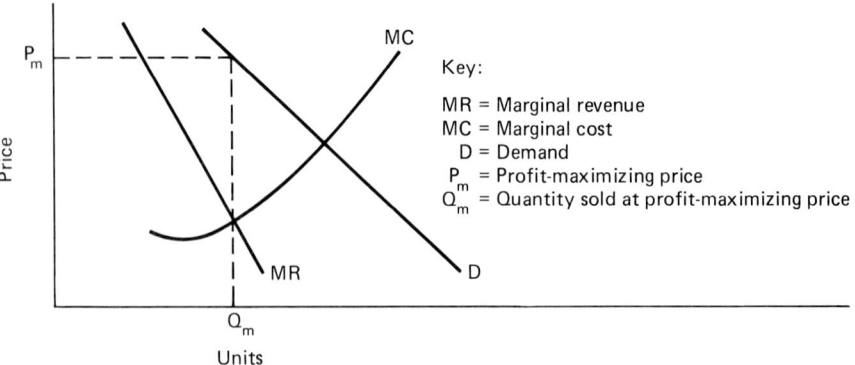

Figure 14.3
Demand-oriented pricing

ginal analysis is extremely difficult to implement because of the near impos-
sibility of accurately determining marginal cost, marginal revenue, or even
demand for a product. Also, demand for some products may rise as price
rises (backward-bending demand). The theory is useful, however, because it
highlights the concept that additional revenue does not necessarily result in
additional profits for the retailer.

Demand-oriented pricing can also be used in a less-than-pure form. A
retailer may analyze the demand for a product or service in a qualitative
manner, that is, the retailer may simply estimate how high a price customers
are willing to pay or how many customers are willing to pay a specific price.
Services are often priced in this manner. Resort accomodations, for example, are more expensive during peak periods because more people are willing to pay the higher prices. Also, more desirable concert or athletic event
tickets can be high priced because enough people are willing to pay the
higher prices.

Cost-Oriented Pricing. **Cost-oriented pricing** involves determining price
by adding a fixed percentage (or dollar amount) to the cost of an item. This
approach is normally referred to as **markup pricing** and is discussed more
fully later in this chapter.

Competition-Oriented Pricing. As the name implies, a retailer using
competition-oriented pricing exclusively will price merchandise strictly
according to the price charged by competition, with little or no attention
given to other factors. The retailer's prices can intentionally be higher,
lower, or the same as competition. Convenience stores often have a practice
of charging 10 to 15 percent more for most items than area supermarkets.

There are several reasons a retailer might decide to price above, at, or
below the competition. Generally a store that can be differentiated by factors

such as location, hours of operation, or overall image can price items above the competition. Stores with poorer locations, high volume, or low overhead may be able to or have to offer prices below the competition. Most stores will price goods at or near the competition.

A Suggested Retail Pricing Procedure

Each of the three pricing approaches possesses certain advantages and disadvantages. Retailers need an overall pricing procedure that incorporates the advantages of all three approaches. The procedure developed below utilizes certain aspects of all three along with other key considerations. The procedure has five distinct steps, each of which can be illustrated on a graphic retail pricing model (see Fig. 14.1).

The five steps in the procedure are (1) determine the floor price, (2) determine the ceiling price, (3) determine the markup price (ORP), (4) adjust the price to fit the store image, and (5) adjust the price for the store's consumers and policies.

Determine Floor Price. The **floor price** is the direct cost (including transportation charges) of an item to the retailer. A lower price may be charged, if legal, but this would occur only in special situations, such as in the use of items as loss leaders or in clearance sales.

One example will be used throughout this section to illustrate the steps in the pricing procedure. Consider a sporting goods retailer, Kelly's Sports Shop, which is taking on a new line of tennis racquets. These racquets are top-of-the-line quality and Bill Kelly, the owner, must determine how much to charge for them. Assume that the invoice price per racquet is $38 and transportation cost per racquet is $2. Kelly's floor price would therefore be $40 per racquet.

Determine Ceiling Price. The **ceiling price** is the price charged by a direct competitor for similar merchandise. The retailer would normally not want to charge a price substantially higher than the ceiling price. The ceiling price is somewhat "softer" than the floor price, however, in that the retailer can more easily justify pricing above the ceiling. The key point, however, is that unless the retailer can justify prices higher than the ceiling, the ceiling forms a realistic upper limit for the price. The floor and ceiling prices in combination form a realistic range of prices.

Assume that Kelly discovers that the highest price charged by his competitors for similar-quality tennis racquets is $85. Kelly's ceiling price is therefore $85. Kelly's *realistic price range* for the racquets is shown in Fig. 14.4.

The use of ceiling and floor prices forces the retailer to consider the key aspects of both a cost-oriented strategy (floor price) and a competition-oriented strategy (ceiling price). A different means of determining the ceiling price is to check the prices charged by several competitors rather than

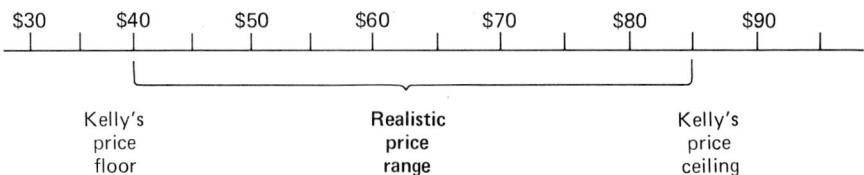

Figure 14.4
Retail pricing range model

just the highest-priced competitor. A ceiling price determined with this method will sometimes result in information that is more useful in adjusting prices as described in later steps.

Determine the Markup Price.   After the realistic price range is determined, the retailer must determine the first estimate of the price. This is normally found by using a percentage markup. Simply stated, markup is the amount added to cost to arrive at a price. Some retailers, especially small retailers, use only this step. Many just double the cost and add a dollar, for instance. This practice is not sufficient. Retailers (even those who use only markup) should first select the specific markup percentage to use.

There are two general methods for determining the markup percentage. One is to look at *historical markup percentages*, which may be based on trade averages or on the retailer's own historical markup percentages. Determining prices in this manner presents several problems. They are obviously "old," they are average figures, and they do not take into consideration factors such as expenses of the retailer, changed conditions, or pricing objectives. Prices determined using historical markups can serve as useful benchmarks, however.

The other method of determining the markup percentage is based on a retailer's *desired net profit*. Price is obviously a major determinant of target return. *Target return pricing* involves finding an initial markup percentage and the corresponding prices that will achieve the desired profit.

The retailer should actually calculate two target return markup percentages: one for the entire store or department and one for the specific item being priced. The store or departmental target markup is an average markup for all items; many items will have markups higher or lower than the average. The retailer's burden is to decide which items will be above and which below the average markup. Some means of making this decision are discussed in later steps.

The well-organized retailer will also be able to calculate a target return markup percentage for the specific item. The formula for **initial markup percentage** (MU_I) was first mentioned in Chapter 11 (markup computations are discussed in more detail in the Appendix to this chapter).

$$MU_I = \frac{E + P + R}{S + R} \times 100,$$

where:

E = expenses
P = profit
R = reductions
S = sales.

The MU_I must be large enough to cover expenses attributable to the product item, desired profit, *and* expected reductions. Note that MU_I will not actually be achieved during a period because of reductions; the **markup percentage maintained** (MU_m) as of the end of the period may be *less than* MU_I because of reductions. This concept is illustrated in Fig. 14.5.

Assume that Kelly estimates the following information for the new tennis racquets: E = $2,248, P = $2,000, R = $900, and S = $9,000. Kelly's MU_I would be computed as follows:

$$MU_I = \frac{\$2,248 + \$2,000 + \$900}{\$9,000 + \$900} \times 100 = 52\%.$$

The relationship between **original retail price (ORP),** sales, MU_I, and MU_m is shown graphically in Fig. 14.5. Kelly would achieve the target return of $2,000 by establishing the original retail price for the racquets at $83.33, computed by the following:

$$ORP = Cost + MU_I$$
$$ORP = \$40 + 0.52(ORP)$$
$$0.48(ORP) = \$40$$
$$ORP = \$83.33.$$

Before the ORP calculated by the target return approach can be accepted as final, the retailer must exercise judgment. Can enough units be

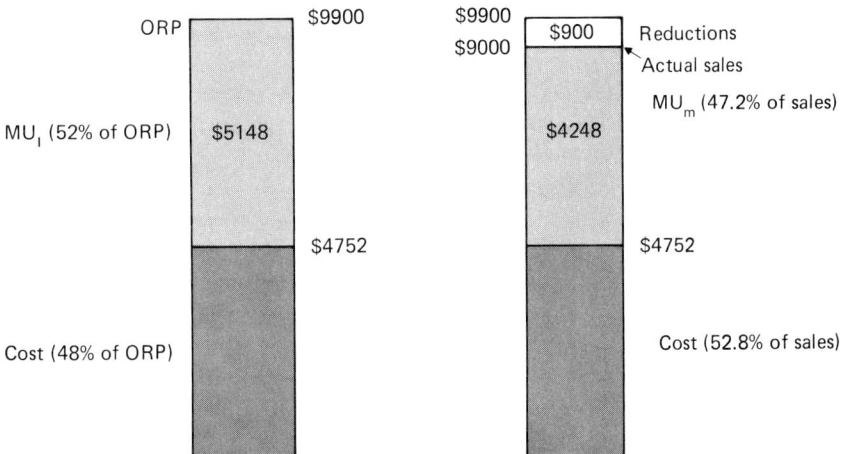

Figure 14.5
Relationship between ORP, MU$_I$, and MU$_m$

sold at the ORP to actually yield the forecast sales figure? Kelly, for example, must sell about 119 racquets ($9,900/$83.33) to obtain $9,000 in actual sales (at an average selling price of $75.63 after reductions). If Kelly does not consider this situation realistic, some factor must be adjusted, such as expense reduction, lower target return, fewer reductions, or ORP. If Kelly thinks the ORP of $83.33 is realistic, then the $83.33 is another factor to include on the retail pricing model.

If the percentage markup determined using the target profit method is substantially different from the historical markup percentage, the situation should be examined, focusing on why the difference occurred.

The price and markup percentage determined in this step should not be viewed as final. Although many retailers use markup pricing as the only method of arriving at a price, further analysis is necessary to arrive at the right price. The ORP determined here is the first estimate of the price.

Adjust Price to Fit Store Image. The first adjustment that should be performed on the normal markup price (ORP) is an adjustment based on the image of the retail store. During the initial and continuing environmental scanning process (Chapter 4), the relationship of the store and its competitors should be noted. The target market, the location, the promotion, and the product lines carried also help the retailer determine the image of the store. The image that customers have of a business is a powerful determinant of the price that can be charged. Economists would say that a store that has achieved an image that allows the retailer to charge a higher price has effectively shifted the demand curve to the right. In simpler terms, a retailer that can in some way differentiate or make the store different can charge higher prices than his or her competitors.

There may be an advantage to having a price higher than the competition. There is a large body of research that indicates that consumers associate price and quality.[6] Whether the association is correct is not important from the retailer's perspective. What is important is that many customers think the relationship is valid.

The adjustments to the normal markup price can be in either direction. One potential situation is presented in Fig. 14.6(A). If Kelly has an image of offering lower prices, the normal markup price ($83.33) is a realistic price to place on the item. If he has an image that indicates the store's prices should be about equal to the competition, he might place a price higher than the normal markup price but not higher than the competition (possibly $85). The equal-image retailer might also charge the normal markup price ($83.33) but feature the price in promotion. The store can get its normal markup (52 percent) and still have a price advantage. A third possible situation is an image that indicates a price higher than the competition. If a store has a high-price image, it should not normally price items below the competition. Therefore, Kelly can, and probably should, price the item to attain more than the normal markup (possibly $90). Items priced like this last

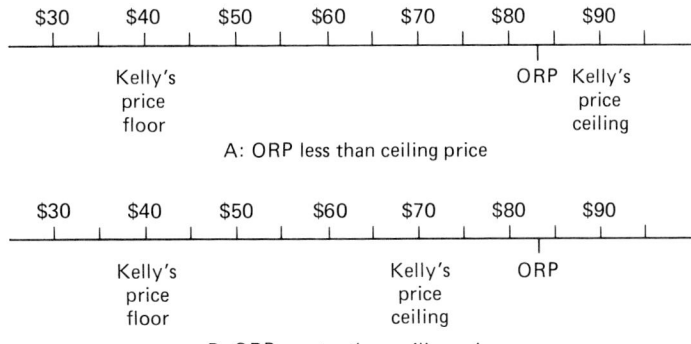

Figure 14.6
Pricing to fit store image

example make excellent sale merchandise. Kelly can lower the price (say to $85.00 from $90) and still attain the normal markup or more.

A very different situation is presented in Fig. 14.6(B). In this situation the retailer would have to charge more than the competition to get the normal markup (52 percent). If the store has a high-price image, the higher price will cause few if any problems ($83.33 can be used as the price). Some major problems can occur if the store has a lower-price image. It would probably not be wise to price above or at the competition price. The obvious reason is that some customers compare prices. If a store is positioned as a lower-price store but charges a higher price on many items, customers may become confused and the retailer's image may deteriorate. Even pricing at the competition risks this possibility. The store might decide not to carry the item. Otherwise the retailer will usually have to accept the lower markup dictated by the image of the store. A price of $68.95 may be used.

Adjust Price for Consumer Preference and Store Policy. This step results in determining the specific price to place on an item. The step calls for adjusting the price for several consumer and store policy considerations.

Odd/Even Pricing. Often, the use of **odd prices** ($.49, $.99, $1.99, $13.95, and so on) gives the consumer the impression of low prices. Research is inconclusive on whether the method really works. Lambert's research suggests that the illusion of lower prices occurs under some circumstances.[7] Part of the theory dealing with odd prices is that the consumer will perceive that an item priced at $49.95 is less than $50. If the price were $49.20, the consumer would think the same and would not recognize the difference between $49.95 and $49.20. Also, theory indicates that the consumer will think that a retailer who deals with the cents has cut prices as low as possible.

Even prices are thought to evoke prestige images in consumers. Higher-priced items in a class are often given even or whole dollar prices. Although the research is inconclusive, many retailers use odd prices to connote low prices and even prices to connote quality or prestige.

Odd or even prices can easily be assimilated into the pricing model. The retailer need only raise or lower the price to either an odd or an even one. The resulting price should not be a great distance from the image-adjusted price.

Price Lining. Another pricing practice often used is **price lining.** Retailers who use price lining select a limited number of key prices or *price points.* Belts may be priced at $7.50, $10, and $15. A retailer may decide that belts that cost less than $5 will be sold for $7.50, belts that cost $5.01 to $7.50 will be sold for $10, and belts that cost $7.51 to $10 will be priced at $15 and so on. One practical reason to use price lining is that sales clerks and stock persons have to remember fewer prices. Hise and Gable indicate that retailers use price lining because it is easy to administer but do not really understand the effects on sales or profits.[8]

Price lining should be incorporated into the pricing procedure. The retailer simply adjusts the price (after considering image) to the nearest predetermined price line. The retailer should review the margin and demand to see if price lining has resulted in lower sales and/or profits.

Multiple-Unit Pricing. As the name indicates, **multiple-unit pricing** (2 for $.99, 6 for $1.59, and so on) is the practice of providing discounts for purchases of two or more units of an item. The idea behind multiple-unit pricing is to sell more total goods by getting the customer to buy more at one time. The technique probably works best for a retailer such as a grocery store that is relatively inconvenient but has a lower-price image. It is more likely that the customer in such a store will buy more items because the customer makes fewer trips to that store. A more convenient store may sell more initially, but if the customer is stockpiling and does not buy on the next shopping trip, the additional sales evaporate. For any store, multiple-unit pricing works well for moving slow-selling or seasonal merchandise. Sales such as "buy one, get another for a penny" are variations of multiple-unit pricing.

Multiple-unit pricing can fit easily into the pricing model presented in this text. All a retailer need do is determine the image-adjusted price and price two or more items in question at a little less than two or more times the image-adjusted price.

Interrelated Demand. The last factor that may affect the ORP of an item to be considered here is **interrelated demand.** The demand for two or more goods may be related, and sales of one item may affect sales of another item. When this situation occurs, the prices of the goods should be determined together.

Loss leaders work best if there is some interrelated demand. A shoe store may reduce the price of shoes to sell more shoes *and* more handbags, which are regularly priced, since shoes and handbags are complementary goods. The main point for the retailer to remember is that for items whose demand is interrelated, the price that would normally be charged may need adjustment.

Summary of the Pricing Model. The model presented here has several advantages. The principal advantage is that final price should allow for adequate profits at a price that is reasonably close to that of the competition. When this cannot occur, the model indicates that a problem exists. The solution is easier to find when the nature of the problem is known.

Another implied advantage of the procedure is that while yielding a specific price for an item, it also yields information that can be used to adjust markup percentages when the complete procedure is not used. If a retailer uses the procedure to price ten items in a department and discovers that the markup (on retail basis) is about 55 percent on all the items, other items in that department may be priced with the 55 percent markup instead of using the entire procedure. This method is not recommended for important items in a department but it is acceptable for some items.

The principal disadvantage to the model is the seeming length of the process. In actuality, the time and effort required are much less than this discussion indicates. The floor price (cost of the item) has to be known to the retailer. The ceiling price (competitors' price) can be discovered more easily than might be expected. Many retailers, either small business owners or heads of departments, do look at the prices of competitors or similar stores when the chance arises. Also, checks of newspaper or other advertising can give an approximation of the competition's prices. Some competitors may print catalogs that provide easy access to the prices of numerous items. The information is available. The entire sequence of steps does not have to be used for every product. A retailer may know that for a certain type of item a major competitor prices the item at a little below the normal markup. Without checking the competitor's price on every item within the type, the retailer will know that his or her prices either must reflect a smaller markup or be higher than competitors'.

On the whole, the procedure offers more help than problems. Retailers would do well to formalize their pricing process.

PREPARE FOR NORMAL PRICE ADJUSTMENTS

The fourth step in the pricing decision process involves pricing adjustments that occur during the normal course of business operations. The basic pricing procedure is aimed at establishing the initial price and standard markup. The hope is that the price is one that will achieve the sales objectives of the firm, that is, all the goods on hand will sell at the initial price and customers will be able to buy the item when desired. An economist would say that an equilibrium price has been achieved. A retailer knows that that situation does not happen often. Usually the price is either too high or too low, resulting in some goods remaining in inventory or a stockout situation. Each of these conditions requires that the price be adjusted either up or down.

The effects of a change in price on the quantity sold can be large or small, depending on the **price elasticity of demand.** Price elasticity relates the change in units bought (or demanded) and the change in price. It can be represented as:

$$\text{Price elasticity} = \frac{\text{Percent change in quantity demanded}}{\text{Percent change in price}}$$

The price elasticity is negative as long as the demand curve for an item slopes downward and to the right. If elasticity is more than -1, a decrease in price will result in more total revenue to the firm. There is one major problem with price elasticity: it is not a practical base on which to adjust prices.[9] The concept, however, is useful. A decrease in the price of an item whose demand is highly price-elastic will generate a disproportionately large rise in the units sold. An increase in the price will result in a disproportionately large decrease in the units sold. Thus, an idea of or feeling for the price elasticity of demand is necessary before making price changes. Both price increases and price decreases are sometimes needed.

Reasons for Price Reductions

There are four primary reasons for **price reductions.** The retailer should incorporate planned reductions as part of the strategic pricing decision process. If the reductions are handled properly, they will have a minimum negative impact on profits and may even have a positive impact. To understand markdowns or price reductions, the retailer must understand the reasons they happen.

Seasonal Merchandise. Almost all retail outlets have some seasonal merchandise. Consumers are accustomed to seeing special sales events at the end of each selling season. Fall swimwear sales and spring coat sales are typical examples. Seasonal merchandise must be either sold or carried over until its season recurs. Carrying over merchandise can be an expensive process for the retailer. Insufficient space to store the merchandise may cause the retailer to decide to sell the merchandise regardless of the original cost of the item.

Over-Bought Merchandise. The best forecasting and merchandise planning may still result in some mistakes. When too much of an item is bought, the retailer may have to reduce the price to reduce the inventory. These reductions are often less than the seasonal sales events. When it becomes obvious that too much of an item has been purchased, a retailer should consider a reduction. This gives the retailer some mid-season promotional opportunities.

Damaged Merchandise. If merchandise is damaged before being received by the retailer, a credit for the damage should be demanded from the shipper or the manufacturer. Sometimes the damage occurs in the store. In that case, the merchandise may be sold at a reduced price. Floor models or demonstration models, for example, must often be sold at a lowered price. By using floor models or demonstration models that more price-conscious buyers are likely to be interested in, the retailer can reduce the risk of not being able to sell the merchandise without excessive price reductions. Family-type automobiles are normally used as demonstrators rather than flashy sports cars for that reason.

Leader Merchandise. Often merchandise is put on sale simply to create business. Loss leaders are an extreme example of leader merchandise, but the retailer does not have to lose money when the price is reduced. The items that are best suited for leader merchandise are those that a large part of the target market buys at relatively frequent intervals. Actually, any item that has a reduced price can be leader merchandise, regardless of the reason for the reduction. Strictly leader merchandise is reduced only to draw customers to buy other regularly priced merchandise.

Need for Price Reductions

The reasons for taking price reductions also imply why those reductions are necessary. Of principal importance here is a discussion of the need to take reductions on seasonal and over-bought merchandise. Either of these types of goods can be carried over until the next season or until they are sold at the regular price, but the retailer assumes several risks by deciding to carry over merchandise.

One risk is the **risk of obsolescence.** The merchandise may be fashion merchandise, or new, improved versions may replace the merchandise, either of which (not to mention other similar situations) can cause the merchandise to lose value to consumers. The longer the merchandise is held, the lower its value may become. Thus if a retailer decides to hold the price or to carry the merchandise over, there is a risk that larger price cuts will be necessary at a later date. The merchandise may be unsalable at practically any price if it becomes totally outdated.

Another risk that is assumed is the **financial risk** of carrying excess inventory. Money needed in the business is tied up in non-selling items. Financing for salable merchandise must come from some source. This financing will cost actual money and will force some opportunity cost on the firm. The opportunity cost may stem from not buying merchandise that can sell during the current period because of a lack of funds. Also, an opportunity cost may occur because space is occupied by slow or non-selling merchandise.

An example may help illustrate the costs associated with carrying over merchandise. Suppose a men's clothing store discovers in March that ten overcoats remain in stock. The coats were originally priced at $100. The store manager thinks eight could be sold if the price were reduced to $60. Doing this gives the store $480 to spend on new merchandise that can be sold in the spring and summer. If this new merchandise is marked up 40 percent (on retail) and sold at that price, the store's profit margin is $320. Since this transaction would not involve a substantial increase in expenses, the store has a profit of $320 from selling the original coats for a reduced price. If the coats were not sold and the spring merchandise was bought through borrowing, the interest expense would reduce the profit. If interest rates were 1.5 percent per month (below the prime rate at times) and the spring merchandise is held for an average of three months, the interest cost would be $21.60. Again, this lessens the profit. If there were many items carried over (even small stores may have over $10,000 worth of such merchandise), the cost could be astounding.

One final risk may be **inventory spoilage.** If we allow the term *spoilage* to encompass deterioration of appearance, this cost may be great. Suits or other clothes left hanging on racks in storage rooms may look like they have been hanging in storage rooms for lengthy periods. Reductions, possibly greater than would have been necessary, must occur. The coats used in the example above are not worth much if they become soiled while in storage. Also, dated merchandise gives a negative appearance even if the merchandise can be sold.

In summary, when reductions become necessary, they should be taken. The risks of carrying goods over are normally greater than the benefits. If a mistake was made in ordering merchandise, the cost of the merchandise should be considered a sunk cost. Consequently, the original cost should not enter into the decision-making process. Also, merchandise on clearance sale may induce customers to shop and buy other nonsale merchandise.

Timing of Price Reductions

Reductions should be taken as soon as it becomes apparent that they will be necessary to sell certain merchandise. A retailer can develop a feel for the timing or can age the inventory to get an even better understanding. Some indications that a reduction will be necessary may occur soon after merchandise is received. If customers are looking at merchandise but not buying, a price problem is likely to exist. Sales personnel may get early and clear indication that a store's customers consider certain merchandise overpriced.

If a retailer can get information early, small price reductions can be tried. A typical pattern is to reduce the price by 10 to 20 percent as soon as a pricing or stocking problem is discovered. Such three-day to two-week sales events can be promotional. If these reductions do not bring the stock into the desired position, other more drastic reductions (25 to 40 percent) may be tried. Later, final clearance sales with reductions of 50 percent or more may become necessary. With proper timing, the merchandise may be placed on sale at a price that yields a profit. If the timing is wrong, the items may need clearing at a price that is below cost.

A retailer should be careful not to always follow a set pattern of reductions. Customers may determine the pattern and wait for the reductions. A customer may determine that a retailer places goods at 20 percent off for two weeks and then reduces the price by 50 percent. If the customer sees several items that are appealing at 20 percent off, he or she may wait, thinking that at least one of the desirable items will be left when the price is further reduced. The retailer's automatic reductions may become counterproductive.

A last point on both the need to take reductions and the timing of the reductions is to *take the reduction when necessary*. The size of reductions should be large enough to get rid of non-selling merchandise. The earlier the reductions are taken, the less the reductions are likely to be. Reduction (or markdown) calculations are illustrated in detail in the Appendix to this chapter.

Price Increases

Price increases are also sometimes necessary, but a retailer will create much consumer dissatisfaction by changing prices upward after the merchandise goes on the shelf. Arguments are still being heard on this subject. One argument that supports price increases is that current prices must reflect current replacement costs. Suppose a retailer has a product that cost $100 and is priced and sold for $150. If the product now costs the retailer $200, how much is the profit? Obviously a retailer could go broke making the "profit" of $50 ($150 − $100). When prices to retailers are rising rapidly, retailers must consider the replacement cost of inventory.

Regardless of the reasoning used by retailers, consumers do not like the practice. If a retailer is going to increase prices on products already marked, the original price should be obliterated completely to create the least negative reaction. This practice should be used as sparingly as possible. If the retailer expects costs to increase, he or she should consider the alternative of setting the original price a little higher than normal.

Cautions about Price Adjustments

Any price adjustment should be viewed with caution. A price change can mean different things to different consumers. Oxenfeldt has identified several possible consumer interpretations of *price decreases:* (1) the item is flawed or is to be superseded by a later model, (2) the peak season is past, (3) the retailer has financial difficulties that might lead to warranty and repair problems, and (4) quality has been reduced.[10] Perceptions of *price increases* might include: (1) the item may be unavailable if not purchased soon, (2) the item has high quality, and (3) the seller is greedy and gouging the public.[11]

The variety of possible interpretations indicates that price adjustments can create problems among customers. Potential customers may get entirely incorrect ideas as to the cause of price adjustments. A price reduction on leader merchandise, for instance, may be interpreted as a reduction or as lowering of quality and the promotional value can be entirely lost.

Large price reductions may also be viewed in a bad light by customers. Excessively high markdowns may cause the consumer to question the seller's integrity,[12] but items that the consumer expects to find on sale probably do not elicit negative reactions.

The array of potential reactions by consumers helps stress the need for establishing proper initial prices as well as the need to coordinate all other activities in the retailing mix so that price adjustments are minimized.

MONITOR AND ADAPT

As with all other elements in the strategic planning process, pricing must be monitored to see that prices placed on items are achieving the desired results. To price items properly and to monitor the process of price setting, four rules are essential: (1) know your costs, (2) know your demand, (3) know your competition and your market, and (4) know your business targets.[13]

Three specific items that should be monitored are the *profitability* of the firm, department, and/or item; *markdowns* taken; and the number of *stockouts*. If any of these items is out of line, the price should be checked to see if it is a cause or a contributing factor. Other elements of the retailing mix may be the problem, and the investigation should include all the elements of the retailing mix.

When problems are discovered in the pricing process, actions should be taken to adapt the pricing process. The adaptations may involve adjustments to new customers, adjustments to new competitors, adjustments to the firm's image, or any other adjustments that are necessary. The ongoing environmental scanning process should discover changes in the environment, either external or internal, that necessitate changes in the retailer's pricing process.

KEY CONCEPTS

Horizontal price-fixing	Skimming
Vertical price-fixing	One price policy
Predatory pricing	Flexible price policy
Loss leaders	Demand-oriented pricing
Unit pricing	Marginal analysis
Bait-and-switch advertising	Cost-oriented pricing
Administered prices	Markup pricing
Penetration	Competition-oriented pricing

Floor price	Multiple-unit pricing
Ceiling price	Interrelated demand
Initial markup percentage	Price elasticity of demand
Markup percentage maintained	Price reductions
Original retail price (ORP)	Risk of obsolescence
Odd/even pricing	Financial risk
Price lining	Inventory spoilage

REVIEW QUESTIONS

1. Discuss the interrelationship of the target market and pricing.
2. Discuss the interrelationship of pricing strategy and competitor's prices.
3. What is the difference between bait-and-switch advertising and a salesperson showing customers higher-priced items than those advertised?
4. If simple markup pricing is not considered adequate, why is it the only method used by some retailers?
5. Why would a retailer not want to use only competitive pricing?
6. Why should markdowns be considered when setting the initial price of an item?
7. Why might it be inadvisable for a retailer with a high-price image to charge a relatively low price for an item?
8. Discuss why a retailer should take price reductions when they are necessary.
9. Discuss factors that should lead a retailer to reduce prices on items.
10. Discuss why a retailer should be cautious in making large price reductions.

LEARNING EXERCISES

1. Choose three local retailers selling similar products who you think will price items differently. One should be what you consider a low-price retailer, another a moderate-price retailer, and the last a high-price retailer. Select three specific items and price the items. Were your images correct?
2. Ask three local retailers to explain the role price plays in their strategy. Check other elements of the retailing mix for consistency. If there are inconsistencies, what changes would you recommend?

DECISION SITUATION 14.1: **CHARLOTTE'S RESTAURANT**

Charlotte, the owner of a small restaurant, has just received some distressing news. McDonald's plans to begin constructing a new restaurant near Charlotte's next month. Charlotte's serves a limited menu of hamburgers and related items, much like McDonald's. The restaurant has earned Charlotte and her two young daughters an income of about $27,000 a year in the past. She is afraid that McDonald's will cut deeply into her profits.

To offer prices similar to McDonald's, she will need to reduce her price by 10 percent, which would reduce gross revenues by almost $30,000. Charlotte does not know whether to reduce prices to McDonald's level. If she does not, she may lose many of her customers. If she does, her profits will vanish.

QUESTIONS

1. What are the significant variables for Charlotte to consider in her pricing decision?

2. Does Charlotte have to reduce her prices to compete?

3. If you were Charlotte, would you reduce the price?

4. What else can Charlotte do to compete with McDonald's?

DECISION SITUATION 14.2: **SPORTS SHOP, INC.**

The Sports Shop, Inc. is a store that sells sporting goods, primarily fishing tackle. The store has not been successful since its formation four years ago. It has been near break-even for the last two years but has never made a profit. Ryan, the owner-manager, has tried many cost-reduction measures. Only he and his wife work at the store, which was started after he retired from the fire department.

Since Ryan thinks expenses have been minimized, he wonders if his prices are the problem. The store has strong competition from three other angling-oriented shops, two full-line sporting goods stores, four discount stores, and six department stores. Ryan's pricing strategy has been to undercut the other angling stores by about 5 percent on most items. He is price-competitive with the discount stores on slow-moving equipment, such as tackle boxes and better rods and reels. He prices smaller, faster-moving items above most of his competitors because he feels that customers compare prices only when the price is relatively high. Ryan is beginning to question his assumption because his sales of higher-priced items are out of proportion to his sales of lower-priced items.

QUESTIONS

1. What is your opinion of Ryan's assumption about price-shopping?

2. A price comparison between the Sports Shop and K mart revealed that Ryan sold ice chests for 10% less, a name-brand rod and reel combination for 8% less, a top-of-the line tackle box for 15% less, a fast-selling lure for 20% more, and a quality fishing line for 30% more. Would you change the pricing strategy?

3. What pricing strategies would you recommend to Ryan?

Appendix
Markup and Markdown
Calculations

Every retailer needs practice to become skillful with markup and markdown calculations. This appendix is designed to provide guidance and practice for these calculations. The following symbols are used throughout the appendix:

$$C = \text{cost}$$
$$ORP = \text{original retail price (in the procedure presented earlier this}$$
is the price before adjustments for image and so on are made)
$$SP = \text{actual selling price}$$
$$MU = \text{markup}$$
$$R = \text{reductions}$$
$$MD = \text{markdowns}$$

Combinations of the following subscripts will be used to identify MU:

$$MU_R = \text{MU on retail base}$$
$$MU_C = \text{MU on cost base}$$
$$MU_I = \text{initial MU}$$
$$MU_m = \text{maintained MU}$$
$$MU_\$ = \text{dollar MU}$$
$$MU_\% = \text{MU percentage}$$

For example, $MU_{IR\%}$ is initial MU percentage on retail base.

Some retailers find it convenient to perform markup and markdown calculations with formulas. The more common relationships are presented in formula form below:

$$ORP = C + MU \tag{1}$$

$$MU_{M\$} = MU_{I\$} - R \tag{2}$$

$$SP = C + MU_{M\$} \tag{3}$$

$$MU_{\%C} = \frac{MU_\$}{C} \tag{4}$$

$$MU_{\%R} = \frac{MU_\$}{ORP} \tag{5}$$

$$ORP = \frac{C}{100\% - MU_{\%R}} \tag{6}$$

$$ORP = \frac{MU_\$}{MU_{\%R}} \tag{7}$$

$$C = \frac{ORP}{100\% + MU_{\%C}} \tag{8}$$

$$MU_{\%C} = \frac{MU_{\%R}}{100\% - MU_{\%R}} \tag{9}$$

$$MU_{\%R} = \frac{MU_{\%R}}{100\% + MU_{\%C}} \tag{10}$$

$$MD_\% = \frac{MD_\$}{S} \tag{11}$$

$$\text{Off-retail \%} = \frac{MD_\$}{ORP} \tag{12}$$

These formulas and their algebraic variations can be used to solve any type of markdown problem. To some, however, the markup formulas (4–10) can be rather troublesome to use. For those who prefer to avoid formulas, a markup box is described below.

THE PROPORTIONAL MARKUP BOX

The markup box is designed to help the retailer perform markup calculations. Its foundation lies in the idea of proportionality regarding the three ways of stating formula (1). Consider an item purchased for $50 and priced at $75 and the three ways of stating formula (1):

$$\text{ORP} = \text{C} + \text{MU}$$
$$\$75 = \$50 + \$25 \text{ (in dollars)}$$
$$150\% = 100\% + 50\% \text{ (as \% of cost base)}$$
$$100\% = 66.7\% + 33.3\% \text{ (as \% of retail base)}$$

Each of the three numerical equations is accurate, but each uses a different base. Notice that each variable remains directly proportional to the other two variables in each equation. This proportionality is the key to the markup box.

The basic markup box before adding specific data is drawn as follows:

	$	%C	%R
C		100	
+			
MU			
=			
ORP			100

The fundamental markup formula is positioned vertically so that the top *row* of squares is for cost figures, the middle row for markup figures, and the bottom row for retail price figures. All of the figures in the first *column* are stated in dollars, the middle column is for percentages on the cost base, and the last column is for percentages on the retail base.

It is critical that the two 100s be included as part of the initial setup. The C/%$_C$ square will always be 100% because the remainder of the squares in the column are expressed in terms of cost. Similarly, since the %$_R$ column is expressed in terms of a retail base, the ORP/%$_R$ square will always be 100%.

The markup box can be filled in with the data from the above example:

	$	%C	%R
C	50	100	33.3
+			
MU	25	50	66.7
=			
ORP	75	150	100

When one of the squares is unknown, it can be found using simple algebra. Seven types of markup computations are presented below. The detailed steps for using the model are described in the first problem; the same procedure can then be used for each succeeding problem. The formula-derived solution is also presented.

Problem 1   If MU = $40 and C = $70, find MU$_{\%C}$.

Step 1. Set up the markup box.

	$	%C	%R
C		100	
+			
MU			
=			
ORP			100

Step 2. Fill in known squares and indicate target square with a ?.

	$	%C	%R
C	70	100	
+			
MU	40	?	
=			
ORP			100

Step 3. Add or subtract to complete columns, where possible.

	$	%C	%R
C	70	100	
+			
MU	40	?	
=			
ORP	110		100

As you will see below, this step does not help in solving this particular problem. However, it is necessary for many problems and should always be performed.

Step 4. Form an imaginary rectangle (or square) of markup squares that has three *known* corners and the unknown target square.

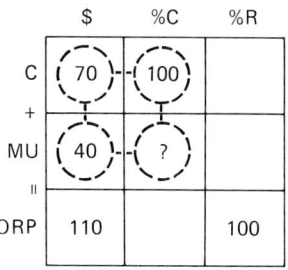

If the first three steps have been performed correctly, this step can always be performed.

Step 5. Cross-multiply the variables from step 4. This involves pulling the numbers from the imaginary rectangle and setting them up in an algebraic equation:

$$\frac{70}{40} = \frac{100}{?}$$
$$70\,(?) = 40\,(100)$$
$$70\,(?) = 4000$$
$$? = 57.14\%$$

The unknown, $MU_{\%C}$, is therefore 57.14%.
Formula (4) can also be used to compute $MU_{\%C}$:

$$MU_{\%C} = \frac{MU_\$}{C} = \frac{40}{70} = .5714, \text{ or } 57.14\%.$$

Problem 2   If $MU_\$ = \$40$ and $ORP = \$150$, find $MU_{\%R}$.

	Markup box	Formula (5)

$$\frac{40}{150} = \frac{?}{100}$$
$$150(?) = 40(100)$$
$$150(?) = 4000$$
$$? = MU_{\%R} = 26.67\%$$

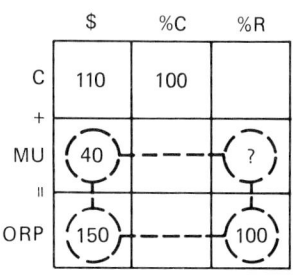

$$MU_{\%R} = \frac{MU_\$}{ORP}$$
$$= \frac{40}{150}$$
$$= 0.2667$$
$$MU_{\%R} = 26.67\%$$

Problem 3   If $MU_\$ = \$50$ and $MU_{\%R} = 75\%$, find ORP.

Markup box   Formula (6)

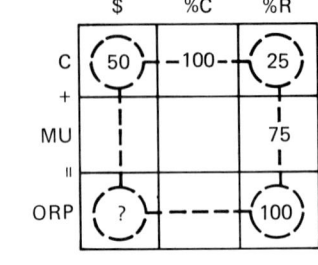

$$\frac{50}{?} = \frac{25}{100}$$

$$25(?) = 50(100)$$

$$25(?) = 5000$$

$$? = ORP = \$200$$

$$ORP = \frac{C}{100\% - MU_{\%R}}$$

$$= \frac{\$50}{100\% - 75\%}$$

$$= \frac{\$50}{25\%}$$

$$= \frac{50}{0.25}$$

$$ORP = \$200$$

Problem 4   If $MU_\$ = \$30$ and $MU_{\%R} = 33\%$, find ORP.

Markup box   Formula (7)

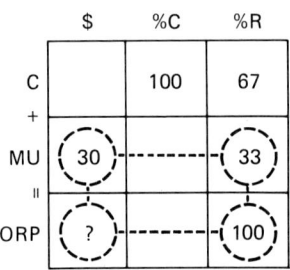

$$\frac{30}{?} = \frac{33}{100}$$

$$33(?) = 3000$$

$$? = ORP = \$90.91$$

$$ORP = \frac{MU_\$}{MU_{\%R}}$$

$$= \frac{\$30}{33\%}$$

$$= \frac{30}{0.33}$$

$$ORP = 90.91$$

Problem 5   If $ORP = \$125$ and $MU_{\%C} = 40\%$, find C.

Markup box   Formula (8)

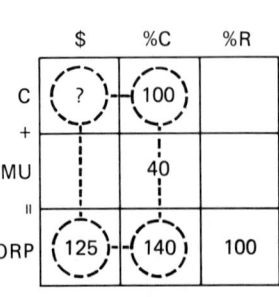

$$\frac{?}{125} = \frac{100}{140}$$

$$140(?) = 125(100)$$

$$140(?) = 12,500$$

$$? = C = \$89.29$$

$$C = \frac{ORP}{100\% + MU_{\%C}}$$

$$= \frac{\$125}{100\% + 40\%}$$

$$= \frac{\$125}{140\%}$$

$$= \frac{125}{1.40}$$

$$C = \$89.29$$

Problem 6   If $MU_{\%R} = 75\%$, find $MU_{\%C}$.

Markup box

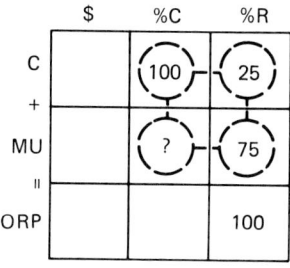

Formula (9)

$$MU_{\%C} = \frac{MU_{\%R}}{100\% - MU_{\%R}}$$

$$= \frac{75\%}{100\% - 75\%}$$

$$= \frac{75\%}{25\%}$$

$$= \frac{0.75}{0.25}$$

$$MU_{\%C} = 3.0 = 300\%$$

$$\frac{100}{?} = \frac{25}{75}$$

$$25(?) = 100(75)$$

$$25(?) = 7500$$

$$? = MU_{\%C} = 300\%$$

Problem 7   If $MU_{\%C} = 75\%$, find $MU_{\%R}$.

Markup box

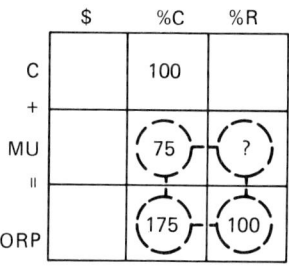

Formula (10)

$$MU_{\%R} = \frac{MU_{\%C}}{100\% + MU_{\%C}}$$

$$= \frac{75\%}{100\% + 75\%}$$

$$= \frac{75\%}{175\%}$$

$$= \frac{0.75}{1.75}$$

$$MU_{\%R} = 0.4286 = 42.86\%$$

$$\frac{75}{175} = \frac{?}{100}$$

$$175(?) = 75(100)$$

$$175(?) = 7500$$

$$? = MU_{\%R} = 42.86\%$$

Note that the markup box procedure was the same for each of the seven problems, whereas each problem required a different formula. The retailing student should seek to understand each method and choose one or the other to practice to develop skill in that method.

Also note that the markup box is *not* designed for markdown and off-retail computations. Formulas (11) and (12) must be used.

REVIEW PROBLEMS

These problems do not include adjustments to price owing to image, customer preferences, or store policy. The prices determined or used include only the markup considerations in the suggested pricing procedure.

1. A retailer desires an initial markup on retail of 40%. The item costs the retailer $10. What initial price should be placed on the item?

2. An item is priced at $15. The markup on cost is 50%. What was the cost of the item to the retailer?

3. The markup on retail for an item is 30%. What is the markup on cost of the item?

4. An item costs a retailer $8. The item sells for $11. What is the markup on retail? On cost?

5. A retailer buys $300 worth of item A. The initial markup is 40%. Ten percent of the merchandise must be sold at a 20% reduced price. What is the maintained markup?

6. An item has a markup on cost of 30%. The initial price is $14. What is the cost of the item?

7. An item has a markup on retail of 35%. The cost of the item is $10. The price of the item must be reduced to $12. What is the off-retail percentage?

8. An item is initially priced at $18. The actual selling price is $17. The initial markup on retail is 40%. What is the maintained markup in dollars?

9. An item costs $54. The initial markup on retail is 30%. The initial price is decreased by 20%. What is the maintained markup?

10. The maintained markup at retail on an item is 25%. The item cost the retailer $135. The initial markup on cost was 60%. What was the initial price of this item?

11. Men's hose may be purchased for $9.50 per dozen and women's hosiery for $13.50 per dozen.
    a) If the hose are marked up 70% on cost and the hosiery are marked up 90% on cost, what retail price will be set per pair?
    b) If a markup of 45% on retail were applied, what prices would be set per pair?

12. An item carries a markup on retail of 37%. What is the equivalent markup percent on cost?

13. A retailer prices a chair so that the markup amounts to $36. This is 42% of retail. What are the cost and retail figures?

14. A snowsuit costs a retailer $4.80. If a markup of 45% of retail is required, what must the retail price be?

15. A cotton blouse costs a retailer $6.60. If a markup of 30% on cost is desired, what will the retail price be?

16. A retailer has been pricing merchandise at 45% on cost. What is the equivalent markup percent of retail?

17. A markup of 38% retail is equivalent to what markup percent on the cost base?

18. The retail price is $92; the cost markup is 34%. What is the cost?

19. A retailer prices a dress so that the markup amounts to $72. This is 50% of retail. What are the cost and retail figures?

20. What should the initial markup percent be in a department that has the following planned figures: expenses, $12,000; profit, $3,000; sales, $45,000; markdowns, $700; stock shortages, $300?

21. An item has been marked down to $3.95 from its original price of $5. What is (a) the markdown percentage and (b) the off-retail percentage?

22. Department A has taken $2,100 in markdowns to date. Net sales to date are $70,000. What is the markdown percentage to date?

23. Sales of $60,000 were planned in a department in which expenses were established at $18,000; employee discounts, $600; and markdowns and shortages, $3,400. If a profit of 4% were desired, what initial markup would be planned?

24. An item that was originally priced at $14 has been marked down to $11.50. What is (a) the markdown percentage and (b) the off-retail percentage?

NOTES

1. Daniel Kahn, "5th Avenue Stores Offer $5.2 Million to Settle Suit," *Newsday*, (10 July 1976), p. 9.

2. James C. Johnson and Louis E. Boone, "Farewell to Fair Trade," *MSU Business Topics*, vol. 24 (Spring 1976), pp. 22–29, is the basis for this section of the text.

3. J. Edward Russo, "The Value of Client Price Information," *Journal of Marketing Research*, vol. 14 (May 1977), pp. 193–201.

4. Esther Peterson, "Consumerism as a Retailer's Asset," *Harvard Business Review*, vol. 51 (May–June 1973), p. 97.

5. Marshall C. Howard, "Government, the Retailer and the Consumer," *Journal of Retailing*, vol. 48 (Winter 1972–73), pp. 48–62, provides a good review of the restraints placed on retailers by the legal system.

6. Benson P. Shapiro, "The Psychology of Pricing," *Harvard Business Review*, vol. 46 (July–August 1968), pp. 14–25, is a classic article on the subject. There have been many studies with similar findings.

7. Zarrel V. Lambert, "Perceived Prices as Related to Odd and Even Price Endings," *Journal of Retailing*, vol. 51 (Fall 1975), pp. 13–22.

8. Richard T. Hise and Myron Gable, "Analyzing Price-Lining Policies," in *Proceedings: Southern Marketing Association*, ed. Henry Nash and Donald Robin, 1976, p. 40.

9. Andre Gabor, *Pricing Principles and Practices* (London: Heinemann Educational Books, 1977), p. 138.

10. Alfred R. Oxenfeldt, *Pricing for Marketing Executives* (San Francisco: Wadsworth Publishing Company, 1961), p. 28.

11. Philip Kotler, *Marketing Management: Analysis, Planning and Control* (Englewood Cliffs, N.J.: Prentice-Hall, 1980), p. 401.

12. Nonyelu Nwokoye, "An Experimental Study of the Relationship between Responses to Price Changes and the Price Level for Shoes," in *Advances in Consumer Research*, vol. 2, ed. M. J. Schlinger, 1975, p. 701.

13. Kent B. Monroe, *Pricing: Making Profitable Decisions* (New York: McGraw-Hill, 1979), pp. 272–273.

STRATEGIC RETAIL MANAGEMENT MODEL

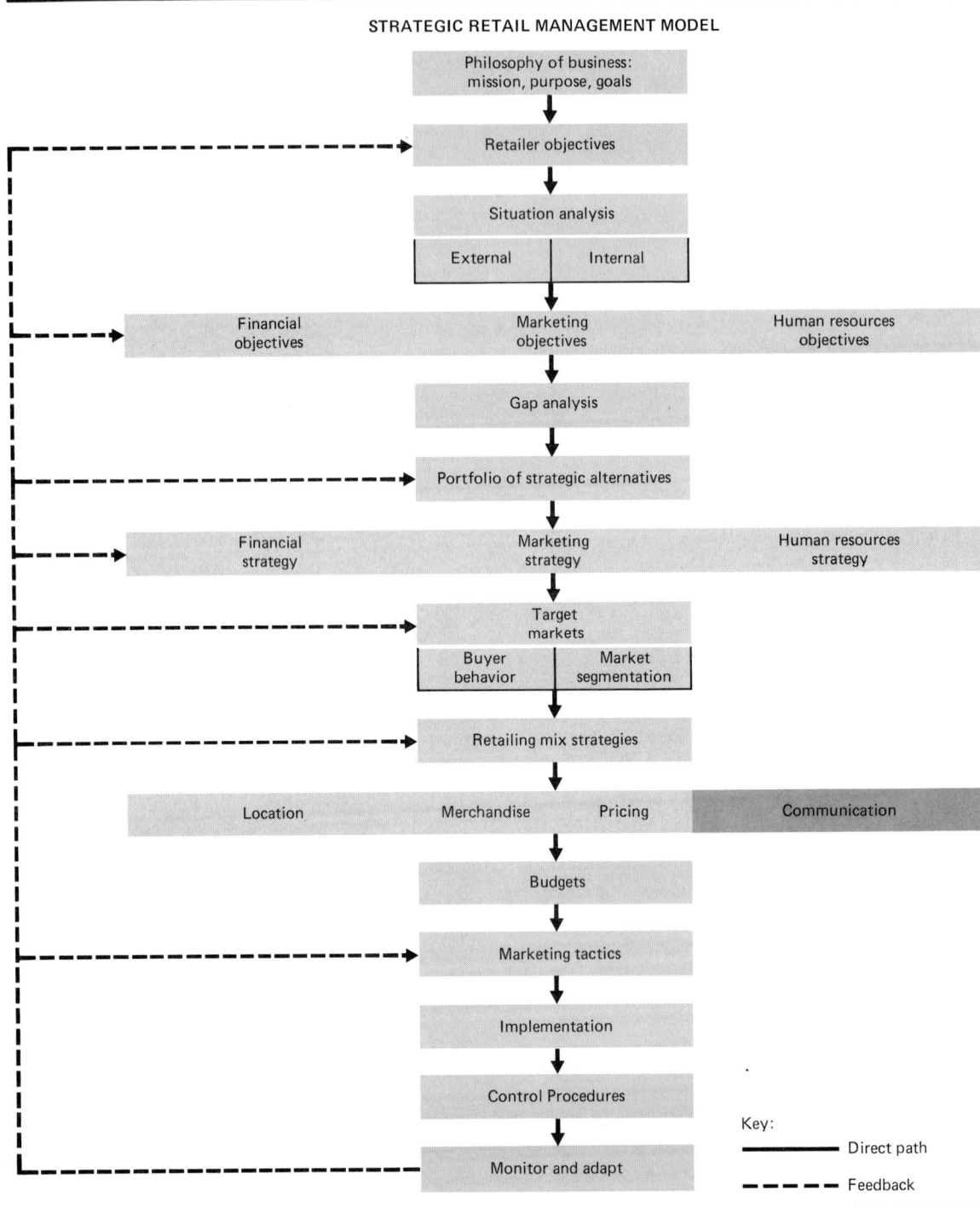

Chapter 15
Communications and Promotion Decisions

LEARNING OBJECTIVES

1. To understand the strategic communications planning process.

2. To understand the need for integration, coordination, and monitoring the communications program.

INTRODUCTION

Successful retail marketing calls for more than stocking good merchandise, pricing it attractively, and making it easily accessible to target customers. The retailer must also persuade target customers that they can obtain satisfaction by visiting and buying at the store. Attracting customers is accomplished by designing and disseminating information about the store's existence, merchandise, prices, and location and about how these features can benefit the customer.

This chapter is an introduction to communications and promotion decisions and strategy formulation, highlighting the broad steps involved in planning the overall communications and promotion strategy. Strategy formulation for the specific forms of promotion is discussed in the following four chapters.

THE RETAIL COMMUNICATIONS MIX

Communicating with target customers is accomplished by use of available communication tools. There are three distinct views of the tools of the **communications mix.**

The narrow view of the communications mix defines the tools as consisting only of the conventional promotion tools: **advertising, personal selling, sales promotion,** and **publicity.** These four tools are defined as follows:

- *Advertising.* Any paid form of nonpersonal presentation of ideas, goods, or services by an identified sponsor, with predominant use made of the media of mass communication.

- *Personal Selling.* The process of assisting and persuading a prospect to buy a good or service or to act upon an idea through the use of person-to-person communication.

- *Sales Promotion.* Those marketing activities, other than personal selling, advertising, and publicity, that stimulate consumer purchasing and dealer effectiveness, such as displays, shows and exhibitions, demonstrations, and various nonrecurrent selling efforts not in the ordinary routine.

- *Publicity.* Any form of nonpaid commercially significant news or editorial comment about ideas, products, or institutions.[1]

The intermediate view holds that the communications mix consists of the promotional tools plus store atmosphere, layout, and customer services. The broad view adds the other elements of the retailing mix: merchandise, price, and location.

The broad view assumes that a retailer's success is heavily dependent on the store image and market position. **Store image** is the subjective attitudes consumers have toward the store. **Market position** is the relationship of a retailer's store image to the store images of all competitors, with emphasis on those characteristics most important to consumer decision making.

The philosophical base supporting the broad view can be expressed two ways. From the retailer's perspective, once the retailer has chosen a desired store image and market position, he or she should use all the retailing mix tools to reinforce the image and position. From the customer's perspective, all retailer-controlled factors that can influence the customer's likelihood of visiting and buying at a retail store should be considered part of the communications mix.

We are proponents of the broad view of the communications mix. We view all factors that can influence the retailer's ability to obtain and retain customers as communication factors. To facilitate the organization of this textbook, however, merchandise, pricing, and location are treated as functional areas of retailing. Thus, we use the intermediate view to structure strategic communications planning.

STRATEGIC COMMUNICATIONS PLANNING

As shown in the *strategic communications decision model* in Fig. 15.1, communications planning can be divided into eight broad steps:

1. Review all existing information and plans.
2. Review general communications theory.
3. Determine overall communications objectives.
4. Develop communications strategy profile.
5. Formulate communications budget.
6. Develop strategic plans for each communications strategy variable.
7. Integrate strategic plans for each element.
8. Monitor and adapt.

The remainder of this chapter is devoted to describing each of these steps. It is also important to note that these steps are rather broad and might be covered in other chapters as well. Step 6, for instance, encompasses Chapter 16 (advertising), Chapter 17 (personal selling and sales promotion), Chapter 18 (atmosphere and layout), and Chapter 19 (customer services).

REVIEW ALL EXISTING INFORMATION AND PLANS

As in planning strategy for the other functional areas of retailing, the first step of strategic communications planning is to review all existing information and plans. The retailer must keep in mind two key points. First, the

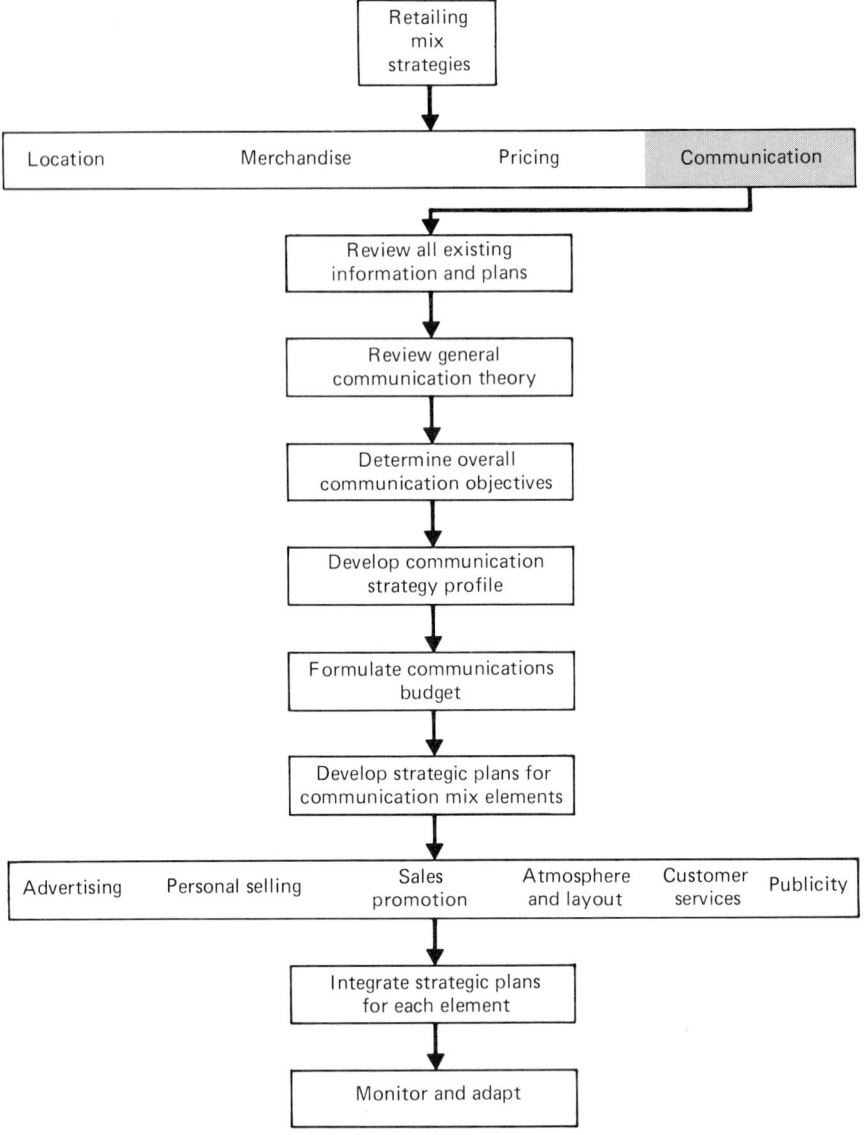

Figure 15.1
Communications decision model

information in the environmental analysis may need to be interpreted or expanded to fit specific communications planning needs. Second, plans for other retailing strategies are not likely to be finalized, but they should be at a more advanced stage than that for communications because communications strategy involves disseminating information about merchandise, price, and location.

STRATEGY IN ACTION 15.1

Godfather's Lunch Offer

The fastest-growing fast-food chain during the late 1970s and early 1980s was Godfather's Pizza. Company sales grew from about $6 million in 1976 to $265 million in 1981. The chain had 750 stores at the end of 1981 and planned to open 240 new stores in 1982.

This rapid growth has altered the communication strategy of Godfather's. It has added a corporate communication's department and an advertising and promotion director.

The overall communication strategy is aimed at differentiating Godfather's from other pizza restaurants with the campaign of "There's nobody's pizza like Godfather's Pizza" combined with the slogan "The pizza you can't refuse." Of course, product quality is the emphasis of this strategy. Heavy spot advertising will be used with some regional network and cable television. Advertising is combined with a sales promotion game entitled "Numbers Racket." This communication base is aimed at bringing more families into Godfather's restaurants.

The real battleground for pizza restaurants is the lunch market. Godfather's has developed a smaller pizza and holding ovens to ensure quick lunchtime service and offers a second pizza free if the product is not served within five minutes. The "Five-Minute Lunch" strategy plays off the overall differentiating communication strategy, providing "two offers you can't refuse."

Source: "Godfather's Pulls Family Together for Major Push," pp. 4, 89. Reprinted with permission from the 18 January 1982 issue of *Advertising Age.* Copyright 1982 by Crain Communications, Inc.

The retailer should devote particular attention to several factors. First, he or she must analyze the marketing objectives so the communications strategy can contribute to attaining them.

Second, the retailer should review the desired store image. Although many other controllable and non-controllable factors affect the store's image, communications strategy can often be a dominant factor in presenting the image.

Third, strategic plans for other elements of the retailing mix have a tremendous influence on the firm's ability to communicate with target customers. The communications strategy must be compatible with all other retailing strategy.

Fourth, the firm's target market is the focus of communications strategy. Detailed knowledge concerning the target customers' needs, desires, preferences, buying habits, and media habits is essential for developing good communications strategies.

Fifth, the firm's financial situation usually has a large impact on communications strategy. Although funds spent on communications should be viewed as an investment, all investments (including communications) require dollars. For most firms, the dollars available must come from the firm's normal cash flow because it is extremely difficult to borrow funds with intangible collateral such as advertising. This illustrates the somewhat circular concept that although communications should help bring in sales, sales are needed to justify communications expenditures. The retailer cannot spend dollars that do not exist on communications.

REVIEW GENERAL COMMUNICATION THEORY

The second step of communications planning is to review communication theory. There is little hope for successful communications with target customers without an understanding of basic communication fundamentals and theory. In this section we present the basic fundamentals and theory as they apply to retail communications.

What Is Communications?

Communications can be viewed as "the process of establishing a commonness or oneness of thought between a sender and a receiver."[2] The *commonness of thought* between sender and receiver implies a sharing of meaning. *Meaning* can be viewed as the "set of internal responses and resulting predispositions evoked within a person when presented with a sign or stimulus object."[3] Another implication of the definition of communication is that because it is a *process*, it can be modeled and studied as a *communications flow*.

The Flow of Communication

The communications process can be structured as a graphic model. The communications model depicted in Fig. 15.2 contains eight communications elements. The **sender** and **receiver** are the two parties in communication. The **message** and **media** are the two major communications tools. **Encoding, decoding, response,** and **feedback** are the four major communications functions. These eight components are defined as follows:

- *Sender.* The party sending the message (often called *source*).
- *Encoding.* The process of translating an idea(s) into appropriate signs and symbols.

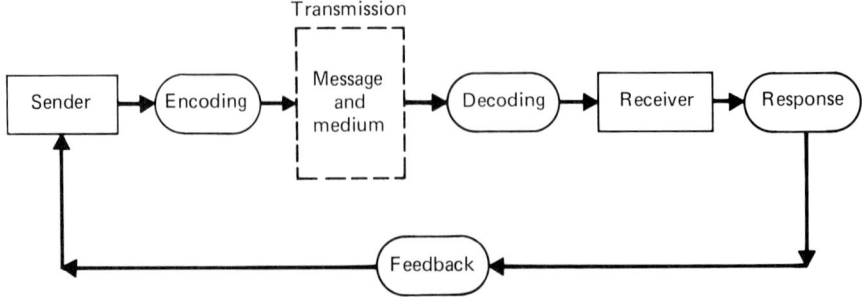

Figure 15.2
A general communications model

- *Message.* The set of signs and symbols representing an idea sent by the sender.

- *Media.* The path or channel chosen by the sender through which the message is transmitted.

- *Decoding.* The receiver's process of assigning meaning to the message's signs and symbols.

- *Receiver.* The party receiving the message (often called *audience* or *destination*).

- *Response.* The receiver's reactions to the message.

- *Feedback.* The part of the receiver's response transmitted back to the sender.[4]

This communications model contains the elements necessary for effective communication, especially when the sender (in this case a retailer) has a specific response objective. In the following discussion, we have modified the general communications model as it applies to retail communications.

The Retail Communication Process

Figure 15.3 depicts a retail communications model and includes various alternatives available to the retailer for each element. The *channels* depicted in Fig. 15.3 are usually considered promotion methods — advertising, per-

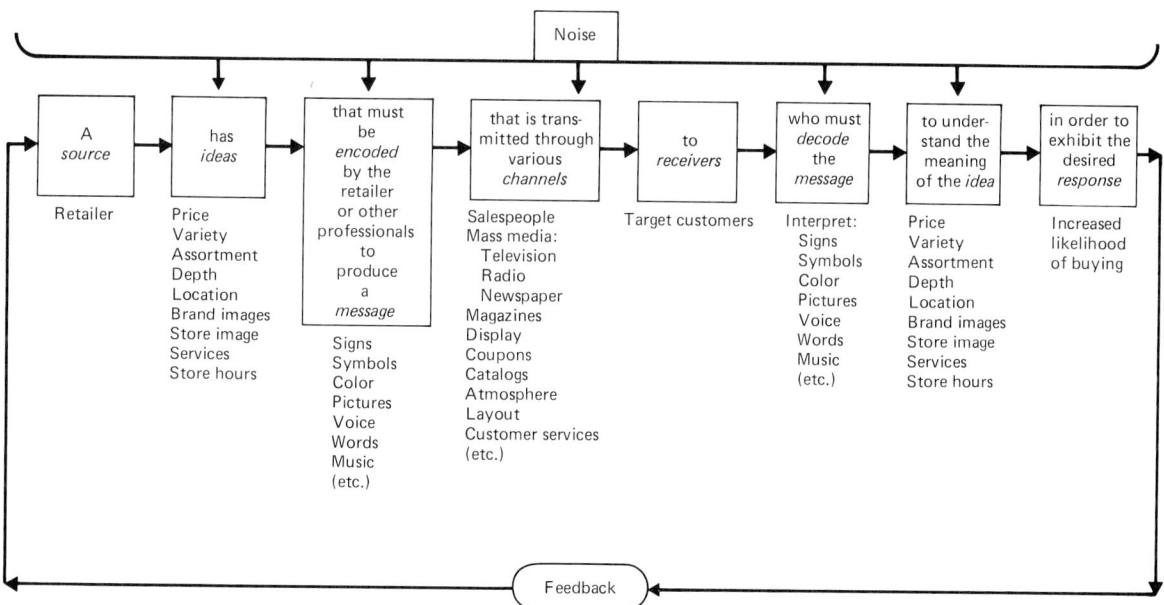

Figure 15.3
A retail communications model

Source: After Fig. 15.1, "The Retail Communications Process" (p. 267) in *Retailing,* 2nd Edition, by R. Ted Will and Ronald W. Hasty. Copyright © 1973, 1977 by R. Ted Will and Ronald W. Hasty. By permission of Harper & Row, Publishers, Inc.

sonal selling, sales promotion, publicity, atmosphere and layout, and customer services—and they are discussed in the following four chapters.

Retail Communications Decisions

Harold Lasswell is credited with the idea that communication involves five major decisions: *who . . . says what . . . in what channel . . . to whom . . . with what effect.*[5] This concept suggests that once the retailer grasps the basic *message flow* from sender to receiver, a *planning flow* must be organized. The planning flow (such as overall strategic communications planning and strategic advertising planning) must be designed to provide answers to the following questions:

1. Who is the target audience? (Receiver)
2. What response should be sought? (Response and decoding)
3. What message should be developed? (Message and encoding)
4. What channel should be used? (Channel)
5. What source attributes should accompany the message? (Channel)
6. What feedback should be collected? (Feedback)[6]

Retail Communications Analysis

Each of the above six questions calls for in-depth analysis.[7] Target audience analysis, for example, involves research into customers' needs, preferences, media habits, and so on.

Target Audience.   A major part of target audience analysis involves determining the store image as perceived by the target audience, or the *audience store image*. The audience store image can often serve as the starting point for formulating communications objectives, especially when the audience store image is not congruent with the retailer's desired store image. If the desired store image is actually supported by the store's characteristics (good services, low prices, wide assortment, and so on), the retailer can address the lack of congruency with the communications tools. (Chapter 8 discusses various image measurement techniques.)

A second factor the retailer must consider is the target audience's ability to process incoming information. Although research in this area is inconclusive, several general comments are possible. The **cognitive information-processing** ability is apparently individual-specific and issue-specific. Individuals with higher intelligence and higher education are likely to be able to handle a more complex set of symbols (the message) than are those with lower intelligence and less education. Regardless of intelligence and education, a target audience that is extremely familiar with a given issue or subject is more likely to be able to handle a complex message than are those less familiar with the issue.[8] Consider a retailer who specializes in stereo components and has a specific target audience consisting of stereo buffs. Because this audience is somewhat familiar with the technical aspects of stereo components, the retailer can use a more complex message. Conversely, if the same retailer wanted to reach an unsophisticated target audience of potential buyers, a complex message would likely be doomed to fail. The key point is that retailers must make sure the message is within the information-processing ability of the target audience.

A third audience-related factor to consider is the target audience's **persuasibility.** Although research is again inconclusive, it appears that people who possess one or more of the following characteristics tend to be more easily persuaded: female, males who feel socially inadequate, lower intelligence, weak self-concept, low or moderate self-confidence, or accepting of external standards as behavior guides.[9] Retailers should study their target market to find specific characteristics that correlate with persuasibility and use these to guide communications planning.

Responses. The retailer must define the desired *response* of the target audience. The bottom-line response is purchase behavior. As we saw in Chapter 6, most consumers go through a series of stages before deciding to purchase a product. Lavidge and Steiner identified six stages in the buying process: awareness, knowledge, liking, preference, conviction, and purchase.[10] The DAGMAR model identifies four stages: awareness, comprehension, conviction, and action.[11]

The assumption of these and other similar **response hierarchy models** is that the consumer moves through the various stages sequentially. It is important to note, however, that the stages can occur in a different order. The various response models can be summarized into three stages: *cognitive, affective,* and *conative,* which can be simplified to *learn, feel,* and *do,* respectively. Most retailers need the last stage, which consists of repeat visits and purchases by loyal customers. Arriving at this final stage can involve a variety of approaches. A home-improvement center might need to focus initially on a *do* that is simply a visit to the store. A large, attractive special sales event might be called for. During and after the initial visit, the retailer can place greater emphasis on *learning* and *feeling* by presenting the customer with merchandise and service attributes and prices and by fostering positive customer attitudes toward returning to the store.

The key issue for retailers is to determine what kind of response stages the desired target customers go through and design the communications strategy to enhance customers' movement through those stages.

Response Keys. Response keys are the variables that have a major influence on a message's ability to create the desired response. These keys can be described as follows:

1. *Exposure:* the physical appearance of a message in the target audience's immediate environment.

2. *Attention:* the mental process of consciously focusing on a given stimulus. *Selective attention* is the human process of choosing to

Table 15.1
Factors affecting attention

STIMULUS FACTORS THAT HELP ATTRACT ATTENTION	INDIVIDUAL FACTORS
1. Large size	1. Permanent interest in stimuli subject
2. Movement	2. Immediate concerns
3. High intensity	3. Span of attention
4. Novelty	4. Fluctuations in attention
5. Contrast with surroundings	5. Attitudes
6. Color	6. Opinions
7. Suddenness of contact with stimulus	7. Needs
8. Position (such as on a page)	
9. Shape	
10. Isolation	
11. Multiple-sensory messages	

Source: Drawn from M. Wayne DeLozier, *The Marketing Communications Process* (New York: McGraw-Hill Book Company, 1976), pp. 37–43.

pay attention to one of several competing stimuli. Table 15.1 summarizes the factors that have an important influence on attention.

3. *Perception:* the process of forming a mental image of a stimulus and assigning meaning to the stimulus.

4. *Comprehension:* the perception by the receiver of the message as *intended* by the sender.

5. *Long-term memory:* the capacity of the receiver to retain the message, a precondition to modifying the receiver's beliefs and attitudes.

6. *Learning:* the process by which some aspect of an individual's behavior or attitudes is changed through the individual's exposure to stimuli.

The retailer must achieve each of these six keys to obtain effective communication.

Message Content. Message content is alternatively referred to as *appeal, theme, idea,* or *unique selling proposition.* The retailer must determine what to say to the target audience to produce the desired response. Although message strategy is discussed in detail in the next chapter, it is appropriate to mention here the three basic types of communication appeals:

1. *Rational appeals:* directed at the rational, logical self-interest of the audience in an attempt to show that the retailer can deliver functional benefits ("We carry the best lawn mower in town").

2. *Emotional appeals:* designed to activate positive or negative emotion that leads to interest and purchase. Fear, guilt, and shame are examples of negative emotional appeals. Love, pride, and joy are examples of positive emotional appeals ("If you don't want to look drab and old-fashioned . . ." versus "If you want to look your best . . .").

3. *Moral appeals:* designed to appeal to the receiver's sense of what is right and proper to do ("Since you want the best for your family . . .").

Message Structure. Message structure can also have a major impact on the persuasive ability of a message. The retailer must consider three structural questions. First, should the message draw a definite conclusion? Usually, yes,[12] but situations unfavorable to stating a conclusion occur when: (1) the communicator is seen as untrustworthy, (2) the audience perceives the message as being simple, and (3) the issue is highly personal. The retailer should also remember that *stimulus ambiguity* can sometimes lead to broader markets by letting consumers draw their own conclusions. An example of a message that draws a conclusion is "The best buy on men's shoes is at—." Second, should both sides of an argument be presented? Should a high-priced retailer mention the high prices along with high quality and service? The general recommendation is to present both sides of an issue when the audience is predisposed against the "second" side (in this case, high prices). Third, should the strongest arguments be presented first or last? Generally, the strongest arguments should be first (when obtaining attention and interest is paramount) or last (when a climactic presentation and conclusion are needed), but *not* in the middle.[13]

Channels. The determination of the best channel for transmitting a message is based on a variety of factors, including the target audience, the message itself, and the desired response. The channels that a retailer can control are personal, mass, and auxiliary channels. **Personal channels** involve direct person-to-person contact with target customers; salespeople are the primary personal channels.

Mass channels are media that carry messages to a target audience without direct contact. They consist of newspapers, magazines, television, radio, direct mail, catalogs, and billboards.

Auxiliary channels include store atmosphere, layout, displays, and customer services. Retailers too often overlook the potential impact of communication from these channels.

A special personal channel is word-of-mouth, the second step of a **two-step flow of communications process**. The first step consists of communications directly from the retailer to the target audience. The second step, word-of-mouth, flows from *opinion leaders* in the audience to other audience members. The influence of opinion leaders can reinforce the retailer's message. The retailer should recognize that word-of-mouth communication is generated by *all elements of the retailing mix*. Retailers can take several steps to stimulate positive word-of-mouth from opinion leaders:[14]

1. Devote extra effort to individuals who appear influential in their groups.

2. Create opinion leaders for the store by supplying selected individuals with attractive terms or by selecting them as store representatives (by placing them on an advisory council, for instance).

3. Build good relations with "community influentials," such as disc jockeys and group presidents.

4. Use testimonials by influential people or interpersonal discussions of the store in mass advertising.

5. Feature advertising that is high in conversational value.

6. Choose salespeople who are of the same general social status as the store's clientele.

Although all retailers should exercise extreme care in fostering positive word-of-mouth, the authors have observed far too many retailers who attempt to rely *solely* on word-of-mouth. Word-of-mouth is normally too slow and random when unaided by other elements of a communications strategy. Word-of-mouth is a form of communication, *not a form of advertising*.

Source Credibility.   While the retailer is the sender of a message, the *source* is the actual spokesperson or deliverer of the message, and, therefore, the source employed by the retailer must be credible to the target market. The key factors underlying source credibility are *expertise, trustworthiness,* and *likability*.

DETERMINE OVERALL COMMUNICATIONS OBJECTIVES

Sales versus Communications Objectives

A basic decision regarding objectives is the choice between sales-oriented and communications-oriented objectives. One school of thought, supported typically by advertising and marketing practitioners, is that the sole objective of promotion is to sell products and, therefore, the retailer should emphasize sales objectives. This school of thought receives support for two primary reasons. Advertising and other marketing practitioners are usually evaluated on sales volume, and the bottom line for all marketing activity (especially in the long run) is profitable sales.

This line of thought has three unfortunate aspects. First, the task of determining the *causal* relationship between promotion (especially advertising) and sales ranges from very difficult to impossible. The promotion tools do help cause sales, but they often receive far too much credit for both successes and failures. An example of the difficulty in determining the exact promotion-to-sales relationship is seen in the "lag effect," that is, the full impact of promotional efforts on sales volume may not be experienced for several months. Second, strict reliance on sales objectives fosters too much managerial emphasis on the short-run perspective and tends to preclude the use of image-building advertising. Third, few advertisements are potent enough to carry a consumer from unawareness all the way to purchase.

The second school of thought is sometimes referred to as the *communication effects* school. Proponents of this view perceive advertising as a tool for communications and, consequently, they see communications-related objectives as superior to sales-related objectives. A primary rationale supporting communications objectives is based on the response hierarchy models. According to these models, different consumers will be in different stages of perception of a given store or product. If the retailer is to enhance the likelihood of consumers' visiting a store or buying a product, he or she must make some consumers aware of the offering, give others a greater understanding of the offering, and create a preference for the specific offering among others. Proponents of communications objectives prefer to analyze consumers to determine their relevant stages in the model and to formulate promotion objectives designed to help move consumers to the next stage.

Critics of communications objectives point to two main problems. First, it is possible to accomplish communications objectives without influencing sales, that is, it is possible to motivate consumers to visit a store without buying. If this situation arises, however, it can usually be traced to an *incorrect* communications objective, a weak product, or a flaw in other parts of the marketing program. Second, it is difficult to evaluate managers who are responsible for the marketing function on any basis other than easily quantifiable data, such as profits or sales.

It should be apparent that the retailer who uses either type of objective exclusively is likely to experience severe problems. Most successful retailers use both sales and communications objectives. There are situations where communications are required and other situations where sales objectives are more appropriate. Advertising is not likely to induce an immediate purchase from a consumer who is in the early stages of problem recognition and definition or who is unaware of the product. Advertising can be expected only to increase the likelihood-to-buy through stimulation of awareness or interest that already exists. Communication objectives would therefore be best in this situation.

Sales objectives might be appropriate when the planning period is short, when the potential buyer is in the conviction stage, and when an attractive offer is intentionally presented so forcefully that buyers could reasonably be expected to make a special effort to obtain the offer. Sales objectives are most relevant to the conative or *do* stage. It must not be overlooked, however, that achievement of sales objectives is accomplished through effective communication of a persuasive message. The burden of the retailer is to determine which approach to use and when to use it.

Of all organizations that advertise, retailers are perhaps in the most unique position regarding objectives. Many times the retailer can formulate sales objectives (such as those for a one-day special promotion) and find out literally the next day if they are achieved. Specific objectives for the various communication forms are discussed where appropriate in the following chapters.

A Suggested Approach

Overall communications objectives can be focused on moving the customer closer to visiting and buying at a retail store. Objectives for each variable in the communications strategy can be derived from an analysis of the target market in terms of consumers' **readiness to buy.** Retailers can often benefit from dividing readiness to buy into *readiness-to-visit* and *in-store buying behavior.* Target customers can be researched and distributed into three readiness-to-visit classes: awareness, knowledge of variety, and store visits. Similar distributions can be made for in-store buying behavior for various relevant purchase quantities.

Consider two similar retailers who use these readiness-to-buy classifications to obtain the results shown in Fig. 15.4. Retailer A found that 80 percent of the target market was aware of the store's existence, 75 percent knew the basic variety offered, and 50 percent had visited the store at least once. This latter 50 percent is composed of 20 percent regular customers, 20 percent who visit periodically, and 10 percent who never returned. Retailer B found that only 50 percent of the target market was aware of the store's existence, the same 50 percent knew the basic variety offered, and 45 percent had visited the store at least once. The 45 percent who had visited the store is composed of 25 percent regular customers, 15 percent who visit periodically, and 5 percent who never returned.

The readiness-to-visit analysis has very different implications for communications objectives and strategies for the two retailers. For Retailer A, the 80 percent awareness might be acceptable, depending on the overall situation. Comparison of awareness and store visits, however, reveals that 30 percent (80% − 50%) of the target market that is aware of the store *has never visited the store.* The implication is that the quality of the promotion messages is suspect. Communications objectives should be focused on

Readiness to visit   In-store purchase behavior

Retailer A

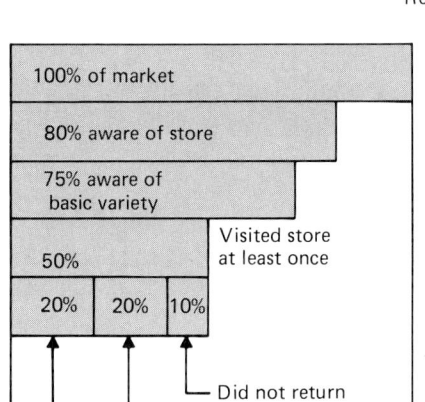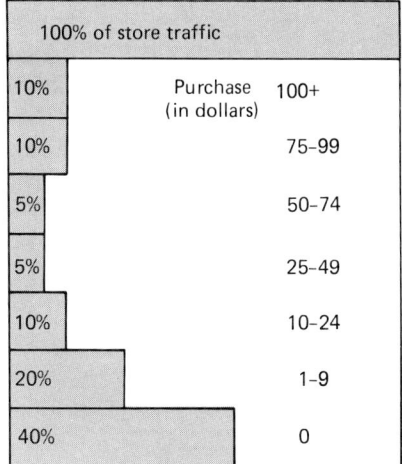

Retailer B

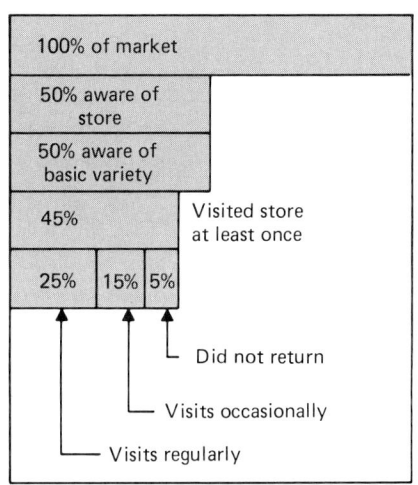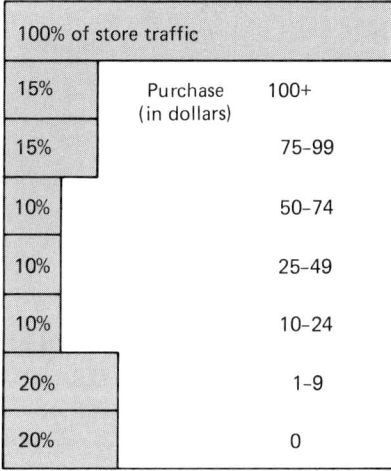

Figure 15.4
Readiness to visit and in-store buying behavior for two retailers

this 30 percent of the market and on the 20 percent who visit occasionally.

Retailer B faces a completely different situation. Most of the target customers who are aware of the store (50 percent) have actually visited the store (45 percent). The key factor is that 50 percent of the target is not aware of the store. Consequently, the focus of communications objectives should be those consumers who are not aware of the store.

Retailer A has a less desirable situation than Retailer B regarding in-store purchase behavior, primarily because of the 40 percent of the customer traffic that leaves without purchasing. If the merchandise and prices are not at fault, then at least one of the in-store communications tools is likely to require a different objective and corresponding strategy. Improvements in personal selling techniques or efforts, displays, atmosphere, or layout might be in order.

The main conclusion for retailers is that communications objectives should be derived from an analysis of how the target market has responded to the store in terms of its readiness to visit and in-store purchase behavior. The retailer can use the approach discussed above or adapt any of the response hierarchy models discussed previously. This step should result in specific objectives for each tool in the communications strategy.

DEVELOP A COMMUNICATIONS STRATEGY PROFILE

Many retailers would at this point develop the communications budget, but it is important to indicate formally the relative importance of each communications tool before allocating dollars to each. Table 15.2 highlights the relative importance of each variable to two different retailers. Examples of the two retailers' **communications strategy profiles** are presented. Retailer A might be a discount furniture retailer who emphasizes mass advertising and sales promotion, with little or no emphasis on the other variables. Retailer B could be a top-of-the-line furniture retailer who emphasizes personal service, often-changed displays of room settings, many free customer services, and direct mail to preferred customers.

Table 15.2
Communications strategy profiles for two retailers

	IMPORTANCE RATING	
COMMUNICATION VARIABLES	RETAILER A	RETAILER B
Mass advertising	5	2
Direct mail	0	3
Personal selling	0	5
Sales promotion	4	2
Display	1	4
"Free" customer services	0	4

Notes: Rating scale is 0 to 5. Display refers to the emphasis given to frequently changing displays.

STRATEGY IN ACTION 15.2

Repositioning and Sharpening Howard Johnson's

Howard Johnson's, a national retailer in the lodging and restaurant industry, is developing a completely new marketing strategy. While sales have grown, the rate of growth has been unsatisfactory for Howard Johnson management. A strategy of upgrading the corporate image and increasing top-of-mind awareness is designed to increase sales growth to a desirable level.

By using an existing strength, nostalgia and good feelings many Americans have toward Howard Johnson's, the company hopes to reposition, clarify, and sharpen its present image. A combination of promotion based on the customer being treated "like your mother would treat you" and changing some of the operational aspects of the lodges and restaurants will be used to increase visibility and clarity. Training personnel, altering services, and heightening the price/value relationship are all part of the strategy.

Howard Johnson management defines their competitive position relative to Holiday Inns, Ramada Inns, and Best Western Motels in the lodging area. They perceive their restaurant competition as Denny's and Shoney's Big Boys at the national level and various regional chains and independent restaurants at the local level. The success of their new strategy will depend on how well Howard Johnson is able to reposition and sharpen its image relative to this competition.

Source: Christy Marshall, "New Leadership at H. Johnson Eyes Traffic Rise," p. 4. Reprinted with permission from the 28 December 1981 issue of *Advertising Age.* Copyright 1981 by Crain Publications, Inc.

Considering the relative importance of each communications strategy tool helps simplify the task of budget allocations. The retailer should also consider extending this profile approach to specific communications variables, especially advertising.

FORMULATE THE COMMUNICATIONS BUDGET

At this stage, only a broad, tentative communications budget can be formulated. Final approval of the communications budget should occur *when the final approval is given to the strategic plan for each communications variable.* This is necessary because the final budget should reflect realistic cost estimates of the tasks required to achieve each objective.

Rough cost estimates can be established for each variable through *objective-and-task* thinking, which involves (1) analyzing the objective for each variable, (2) delineating the tasks necessary for achieving the objective, and (3) estimating the costs of the tasks. The following is a simple example for advertising:

1. *Objective:* Increase target market's awareness of store from 50 percent to 80 percent.

2. *Task:* Since the 50 percent awareness level has been achieved with saturation newspaper advertising, radio advertising must be used to gain the attention of an additional 30 percent of the market. Therefore, 1 million exposures are needed (200,000 different people reached an average of five times each).

3. *Cost:* The average cost per thousand exposures for radio in our market is $6. Therefore, our tentative advertising allocation is $6,000 ($6 × 1,000,000 ÷ 1,000).

It is important to understand that this step results in *tentative* allocations for each communications variable and a *tentative* overall communications appropriation. A much more detailed budgeting approach must be used when planning the strategy for each variable. Detailed approaches are discussed in later chapters along with strategic planning for each variable.

DEVELOP STRATEGIC PLANS FOR EACH COMMUNICATIONS STRATEGY VARIABLE

At this point the retailer is ready to develop the strategic plans for each communications strategy variable. The next four chapters are devoted to this step. To complete our discussion of the strategic communications planning process in a logical manner, however, two additional topics must be addressed.

INTEGRATE STRATEGIC PLANS FOR EACH VARIABLE

The seventh step of communications strategy planning occurs *after* the detailed strategic plans are made for each variable. These detailed plans must be integrated and evaluated in terms of overall efficiency and compatibility. Executive judgment must be exercised to answer the following questions:

1. Will the specific strategic plans for each element of the communications mix accomplish the respective objectives?

2. Will the total input of accomplishing each individual strategic objective accomplish the overall communications objective?

3. Are the individual strategic plans compatible?

4. Are the individual and total budgets acceptable?

Coordination of the elements of the communications mix actually begins with this step (before implementation) and continues throughout the planning period. When multiple communication elements are used, some type of coordination method is necessary. The coordination calendar shown in Fig. 15.5 is a simple but effective tool.

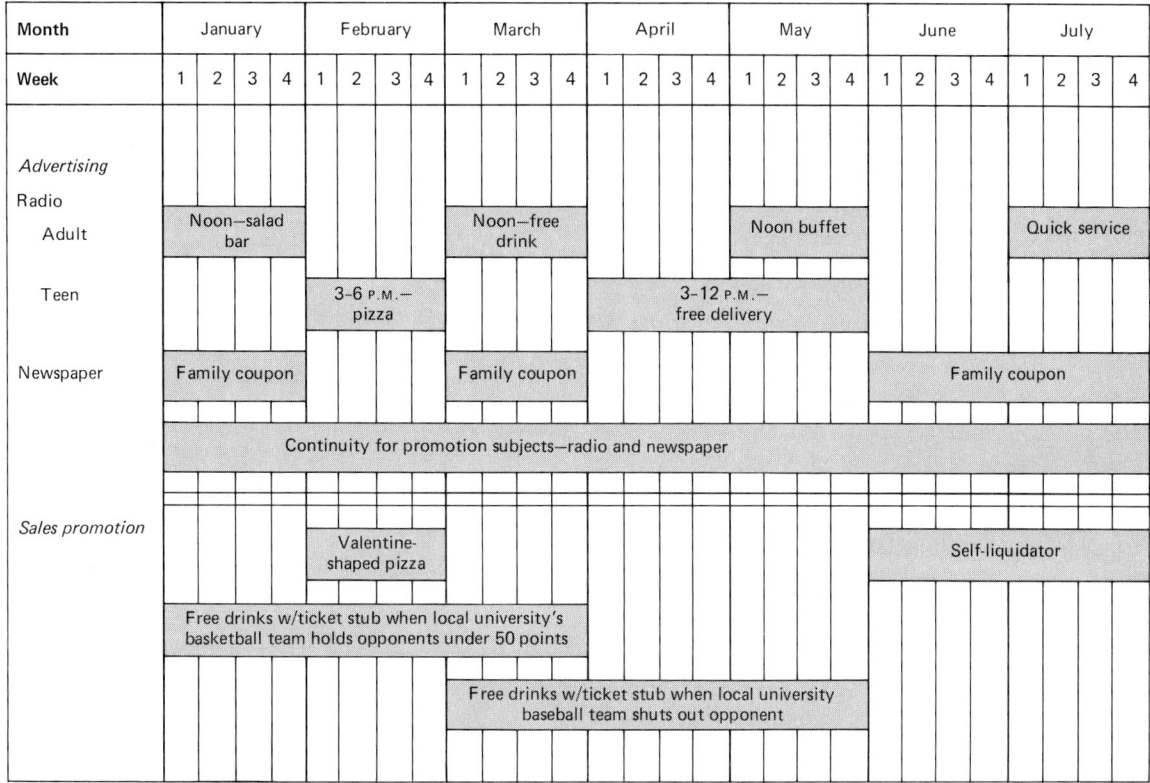

Figure 15.5
Six-month promotion calendar for Crusty's Pizza

COORDINATE, MONITOR, AND ADAPT

Someone must be responsible for coordinating the communications program as it unfolds during the planning period. In addition, the retailer must monitor the environment and the results of the communications program.

Environmental changes can cause the need for adaptations of the communications strategy. A change in any environmental factor on which the communications program was based will very likely require adaptations. The retailer might need to respond to new competitors, new industry, economic shifts, and so on.

The retailer must also monitor communications efficiency. Although good strategic planning can enhance communications efficiency and results, it cannot ensure efficiency and results. Any number of factors can damage the retailer's communications program, from improper objectives to poor production and execution. If a particular communications variable is not yielding acceptable results, the retailer must seek other communications alternatives.

KEY CONCEPTS

Communications mix   Cognitive information processing
Advertising   Persuasibility
Personal selling   Response hierarchy models
Sales promotion   Exposure
Publicity   Attention
Store image   Perception
Market position   Comprehension
Sender   Long-term memory
Receiver   Learning
Message   Personal channels
Media   Mass channels
Encoding   Auxiliary channels
Decoding   Two-step flow of communications
Response   Readiness to buy
Feedback   Communications strategy profile

REVIEW QUESTIONS

1. Contrast the narrow, intermediate, and broad views of the communications mix.
2. Discuss at least five factors that must be reviewed when planning communications strategy.
3. Define communications.
4. Develop and describe the general communications model.
5. Develop and describe the retail communications model.
6. Discuss consumer response patterns using the "learn-feel-do" model.
7. Describe the major response keys.
8. Describe the three basic types of communications appeals.
9. What are the three major issues of message structure?
10. Describe the three major communications channels available to the retailer.
11. Discuss word-of-mouth influence.
12. Present the arguments for sales versus communications objectives.
13. Discuss the causal relationship between sales and promotion.
14. Discuss the determination of communications objectives using readiness-to-visit and in-store buying behavior.
15. Discuss the concept of communications strategy profiles.

LEARNING EXERCISES

1. Choose a variety of local retailers and define the appropriate response stages for yourself and several acquaintances. Use each of the response hierarchy models discussed in the text.

2. Determine the primary response patterns for different types of local retailers.

3. Develop communications strategy profiles for selected local retailers.

4. Develop a communications mix coordination calendar for a local retailer.

DECISION SITUATION 15.1: **ATHLETIC OUTFITTERS I**

Athletic Outfitters is a sporting goods store specializing in recreation and athletic equipment, clothes, and gifts. It is located in a city of 50,000 and is the largest store specializing in recreation and athletic equipment and clothes in the area. The store was opened five years ago when the owner realized that there were no existing stores specializing in these lines in the area. Soon after opening, the owner also realized that no store was selling a complete line of team sports equipment, so he added these products to the merchandise offering. Gifts with an athletic theme were added three years ago. In general, the store has been very successful.

The primary customers of the store were under forty and had family incomes of over $25,000. A large share of the sales were to parents of youngsters participating in various recreational leagues (soccer, baseball, football). Athletic Outfitters supplied the uniforms for virtually all organized sports in the area. Jogging equipment was also a good profit center. Most of the remaining sales came from golf equipment. Slower-moving lines included bowling equipment, camping equipment, skiing equipment, and outdoor clothing. The gift items had low sales but were still profitable.

In reviewing the past five years, the owner was satisfied but wondered if any changes might help profits. One nagging concern was indications that many customers considered the store to be overpriced. Although the store did have prices higher than the two discount stores in the city, the owner felt that customers received good value for their money. He knew he could not compete with the discount houses on price, but no store offered the same high quality and selection. His question was how to convince customers that his products were fairly priced and offered good value.

QUESTIONS

1. What communications mix strategy would you recommend for Athletic Outfitters? Support your answer.

2. Would you make any specific recommendations relative to the high-priced image?

3. If the high-priced image begins to cut into profits, what changes would you recommend?

4. What would you do, if anything, to increase the sales of the slower-moving items?

DECISION SITUATION 15.2: **WESTERN STEAKS**

The owner of Western Steaks was surprised as he read a student research study of his restaurant, which indicated that most of the respondents thought the restaurant was a fast-food operation. Many respondents indicated that they considered the restaurant to be of low quality and not a restaurant that they would choose to visit often. The entire report was almost totally negative.

The owner was surprised because he knew that he purchased only the highest-quality food. In fact, meat and other suppliers indicated that his requirements were the highest in town. Also, he employed an excellent cook and the cook had enough kitchen help to prepare the food adequately. The owner was absolutely sure that the quality of food was not the problem.

The owner wondered if he was failing to communicate properly with the customers. His advertising was limited to a portable sign with flashing lights in front of the restaurant. Various specials were advertised on the sign. Also, limited radio ads were used for certain "special nights," which featured items such as lobster, pheasant, quail, and so on.

The waitresses actually did no personal selling; they only took orders. The owner was usually too busy helping in the kitchen to greet customers. The atmosphere was rather plain. The owner felt that customers valued good food much more than atmosphere and surroundings. The study made him wonder if he was correct.

QUESTIONS

1. What short-run communications mix strategy would you recommend to the owner of Western Steaks?

2. Would you recommend the same strategy for the long run?

3. What is your opinion of the owner's contention that customers prefer good food to good atmosphere?

NOTES

1. *Marketing Definitions: A Glossary of Marketing Terms,* compiled by the Committee on Definitions of the American Marketing Association, Ralph S. Alexander, Chairman (Chicago: American Marketing Association, 1960).

2. M. Wayne Delozier, *The Marketing Communications Process* (New York: McGraw-Hill, 1976), p. 1.

3. David K. Berlo, *The Process of Communication* (San Francisco: Holt, Rinehart, and Winston, 1960), p. 184.

4. Philip Kotler, *Marketing Management* (Englewood Cliffs, N.J.: Prentice-Hall, 1980), p. 470.

5. Harold D. Lasswell, *Power and Personality* (New York: Norton, 1948), pp. 37–51.

6. Kotler, *op. cit.,* p. 471.

7. This section draws heavily on Kotler, *ibid.*, pp. 472–487.

8. Ralph E. Anderson and Marvin A. Jolson, "Technical Wording in Advertising: Implications for Market Segmentation," *Journal of Marketing*, 44 (Winter 1980), pp. 57–66.

9. Kotler, *op. cit.*, p. 474.

10. R. J. Lavidge and G. A. Steiner, "A Model for Predictive Measurements of Advertising Effectiveness," *Journal of Marketing* 25 (October 1961), pp. 59–62.

11. R. H. Colley, *Defining Advertising Goals for Measured Advertising Results* (New York: Association of National Advertisers, 1961).

12. Carl I. Hovland and Wallace Mandell, "An Experimental Comparison of Conclusion-Drawing by the Communication and by the Audience," *Journal of Abnormal and Social Psychology*, July 1952, pp. 581–588.

13. Kotler, *op. cit.*, p. 482.

14. For a more complete discussion of these and related points, see Thomas S. Robertson, *Innovative Behavior and Communication* (New York: Holt, Rinehart, and Winston, 1971), Chapter 9.

STRATEGIC RETAIL MANAGEMENT MODEL

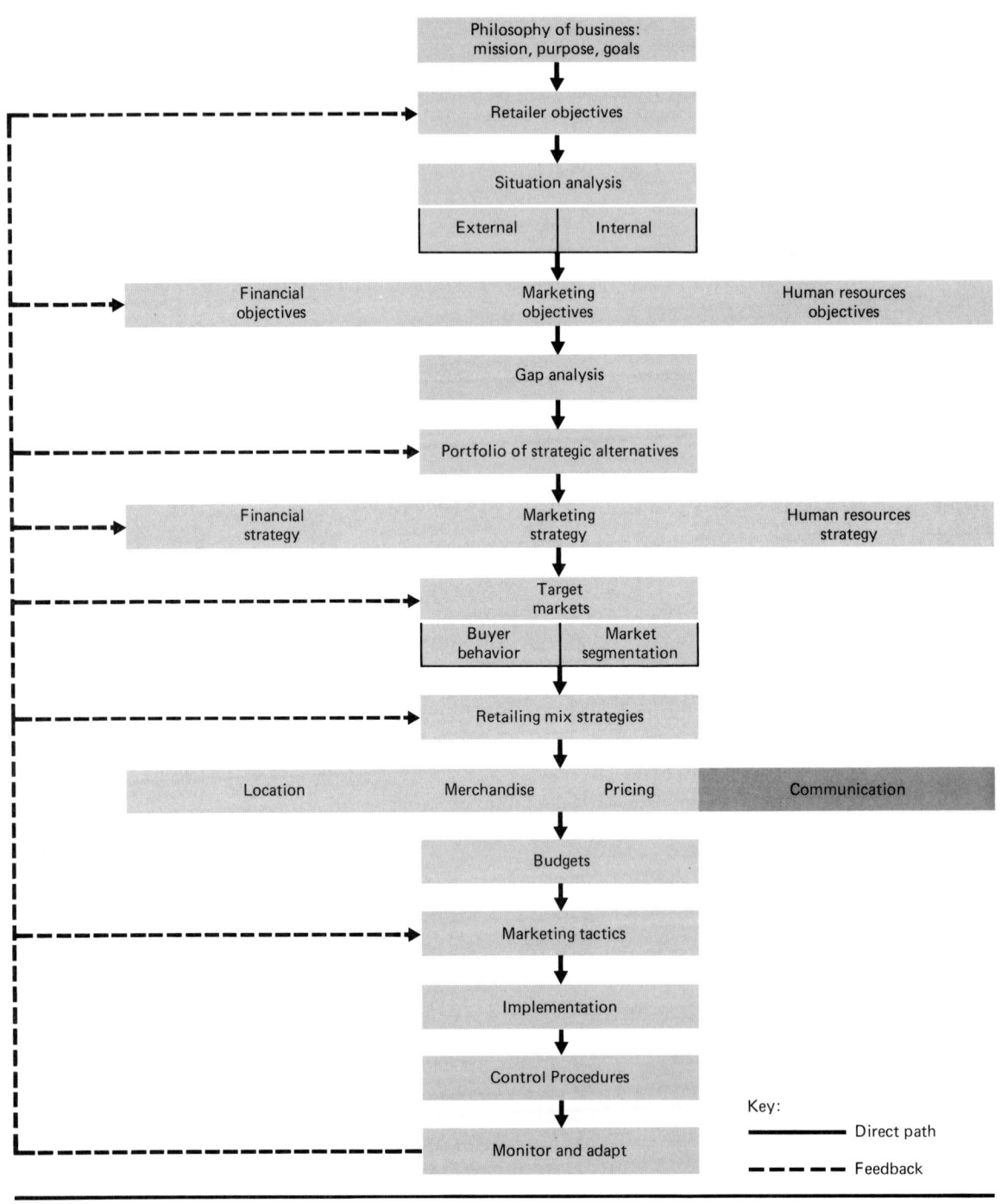

	Philosophy of business: mission, purpose, goals	
	Retailer objectives	
	Situation analysis	
	External	Internal
Financial objectives	Marketing objectives	Human resources objectives
	Gap analysis	
	Portfolio of strategic alternatives	
Financial strategy	Marketing strategy	Human resources strategy
	Target markets	
	Buyer behavior	Market segmentation
	Retailing mix strategies	
Location	Merchandise Pricing	Communication
	Budgets	
	Marketing tactics	
	Implementation	
	Control Procedures	
	Monitor and adapt	

Key:
——— Direct path
- - - Feedback

Chapter 16
Advertising Decisions

LEARNING OBJECTIVES

1. To understand the importance and role of advertising in retailing.

2. To understand and learn the major steps and considerations involved in strategic advertising planning for retailers.

INTRODUCTION

Advertising is one of the major promotion tools available to retailers. It is safe to say that for many retailers advertising is *the* major promotional tool. The largest retail advertisers spend up to 6 to 7 percent of sales revenue on advertising (see Table 16.1).

For some retailers, advertising is a frustrating and money-wasting endeavor. For others, it is a rewarding and profitable business tool. Although a retailer can sometimes obtain effective advertising by sheer luck, most successful advertising programs are based on careful planning. The best way to increase the probability that the time and effort devoted to advertising plan-

Table 16.1
Largest retail advertisers, 1979

STORE TYPE	ADVERTISING EXPENDITURES	ADVERTISING AS % OF SALES	% CHANGE IN ADVERTISING FROM 1978
General Merchandise			
Sears, Roebuck & Co.	$709,312,000	5.2	− 2.2
K mart Corp.	287,095,000	2.3	15.8
J. C. Penney Co.	278,000,000	2.5	− 2.5
Montgomery Ward & Co.	200,000,000	3.8	− 3.4
Federated Department Stores	174,000,000	3.0	5.4
F. W. Woolworth Co.	157,560,000	2.3	10.3
R. H. Macy & Co.	128,480,000	6.3	12.2
Associated Dry Goods Corp.	118,000,000	6.6	25.5
Allied Stores Corp.	103,807,000	4.7	4.9
May Department Stores	84,000,000	2.8	12.0
Supermarkets			
Safeway Stores	136,625,000	1.0	9.3
Kroger Co.	108,000,000	1.2	14.3
Great Atlantic & Pacific Tea Co.	77,000,000	1.2	− 8.3
American Stores Co.	67,000,000	1.1	18.9
Grand Union Co.	47,000,000	1.5	20.5
Jewel Cos.	43,113,000	1.1	− 0.8
Lucky Stores	43,000,000	0.7	22.9
Winn-Dixie Stores	41,260,000	0.8	4.1
Supermarkets General Corp.	30,000,000	1.3	5.3
Stop & Shop Cos.	27,350,000	1.5	6.6

Source: Drawn from Louis J. Haugh, "Top Retailers Increase Ad Outlays by 9%," pp. 5–7. Reprinted with permission from the 29 October 1979 issue of *Advertising Age.* Copyright 1979 by Crain Communications, Inc.

ning actually result in a good advertising plan is to use an organized, logical approach or *planning framework*. Most of this chapter develops a strategic planning framework specifically for advertising. In these first few pages, we briefly describe the purpose of advertising, the reasons advertising is important to retailers, and the retailer's major assumptions about advertising. The strategic advertising planning framework is then presented and discussed in detail.

What Is the Purpose of Advertising?

From a retailing perspective, the purpose of advertising is to enhance consumer responses to the store and its offerings.[1] Whatever the specific objective, advertising is expected to increase the likelihood of consumers' visiting and buying from the retailer. Advertising accomplishes its basic purpose by performing several vital communications functions, such as informing, entertaining, persuading, reminding, reassuring, assisting other company efforts, and adding value.[2]

Why Is Advertising Important to the Retailer?

Advertising activities are important to retailers primarily because of their potential impact on financial factors and on other marketing efforts. The retailer's net profit is influenced directly by advertising. Advertising expenditures are classified as expenses and are thereby direct reductions of

---

STRATEGY IN ACTION 16.1

In-Store Advertising?

For years, candy, gum, magazines, and flashlight batteries have occupied the selling space and possible attention of consumers waiting in supermarket checkout lines. Things have changed. Consumers can now see closed-circuit television commercials from televisions hung from supermarket ceilings. The commercials have no sound track since testing revealed the sound annoyed consumers. To maintain consumer interest, commercials are interspersed with trivia quizzes and household hints.

A number of firms have bought time in the closed-circuit system. Companies that have never used supermarkets for distribution are buying this advertising. NBC television network even advertises its shows in the supermarkets. Although time costs are near prime-time television prices, the demand by advertisers has continued to grow.

On-Line Media, Inc., one of the more successful companies selling the closed-circuit system to advertisers, pays supermarkets rent of $300 per month for installing the televisions. On-Line's goal is to reach one-third of all grocery stores in the United States by 1985. If the present trends continue, many U.S. consumers can watch television while waiting to check out of supermarkets instead of reading the same magazine headlines over and over again.

Source: "Lining Up to Watch TV Commercials," *Newsweek,* 25 January 1982, pp. 58–59. Copyright 1982, by Newsweek, Inc. All Rights Reserved. Reprinted by permission.

net profit. Effective advertising should further influence net profit directly by having an eventual impact on sales volume. Net profit is also affected indirectly by advertising's influence on the timing of sales, which influences cash-flow patterns.

Advertising can have a major influence on the retailer's overall image. A retail store's image or personality can be viewed as the sum of consumer perceptions of the store. Many of those perceptions can be determined largely by the character and quality of the retailer's advertising.

Advertising can have a strong influence on the performance level achieved in other aspects of the retailing program. Advertising designed to improve the sales of slow-moving merchandise, for example, can improve the rate of stock turnover and reduce the frequency and amount of mark-downs.

Consumers have certain expectations about the type and amounts of information provided by advertising. To obtain and retain the patronage of a selected target market, the advertising program must provide information in the form, content, and frequency desired by the target customers.[3]

Retailers who advertise steadily tend to lose a smaller share of their market in bad times (such as recessions), rebound more quickly at the end of such periods, and achieve higher profits during times of sales prosperity.[4]

Although advertising is potentially important to all retailers, it is not equally effective for all retailers. Conditions favorable to successful advertising include the presence of good products, a favorable primary demand trend, a large sales potential, an adequate supply, powerful emotional buying motives, products with significant and/or hidden qualities, and a large advertising budget.[5] Although all of these conditions do not have to be present, the more that exist, the greater the odds for successful advertising.

Assumptions of the Retail Advertiser

A brief discussion of the major assumptions made by the more progressive retail advertisers will serve as a point of departure for the remainder of the chapter. These major assumptions can be summarized as follows:[6]

1. *Advertising is communication.* The purpose of retail advertising is to communicate information (whether rational, emotional, or evaluative) to prospective purchasers or to those people who are likely to have a positive effect on the retailer's ability to attain specific objectives.

2. *Advertising should be persuasive.* Advertising should be convincing to the selected audience and should predispose them to act either immediately or some time in the future.

3. *The basis of effective advertising is knowledge and skill.* This two-fold basis begins with *knowledge* of what is most important to the audience. The second factor is *skill* in translating features of the

store and merchandise into meaningful consumer benefits and communicating these features and benefits to the target audience in a persuasive manner.

4. *Advertising effect is lagged.* The retailer will not necessarily experience 100 percent of the eventual effect of advertising immediately, because consumers are not continuously in the market for all products. Although advertising may effectively predispose a consumer to shop at a specific retail store, the consumer may delay the visit until he or she experiences the needs that the retailer can satisfy.

5. *Advertising effect is cumulative.* The impact of advertising on a given consumer may build up over time as additional relevant information is delivered by the retailer and comprehended by the consumer.

6. *Advertising effect is based on content and repetition.* Advertising content is important in terms of the consumer's perception of the meaningfulness of the message. A meaningful message tends to have a greater effect if it is experienced many times rather than few times.

7. *Advertising also fosters positive momentum.* Stated simply, a retailer has a positive momentum if the number of consumers predisposed to shop at a retail store exceeds the actual number of customers.

8. *The retailer advertiser works with imperfect knowledge.* Retail advertising is ultimately at the mercy of the consumer. It is unlikely that consumers and the manner in which advertising affects consumers will ever be understood completely. The task of the retail advertiser is to increase the probability for successful advertising by learning as much as possible about the consumer, systematically planning advertising, and being creative in developing messages.

PLANNING ADVERTISING STRATEGY

Effective advertising strategies and campaigns are almost always the result of good planning. Unfortunately, far too few retailers know how to go about planning a complete advertising program. The remainder of the chapter focuses on the major decision areas involved in advertising planning.

The advertising decision model depicted in Fig. 16.1 presents the major areas that are involved in advertising planning. To be useful to the retail advertising planner, however, the model must be translated into an "actionable" format. The *strategic advertising planning process* followed in this chapter is composed of seven sequential stages:

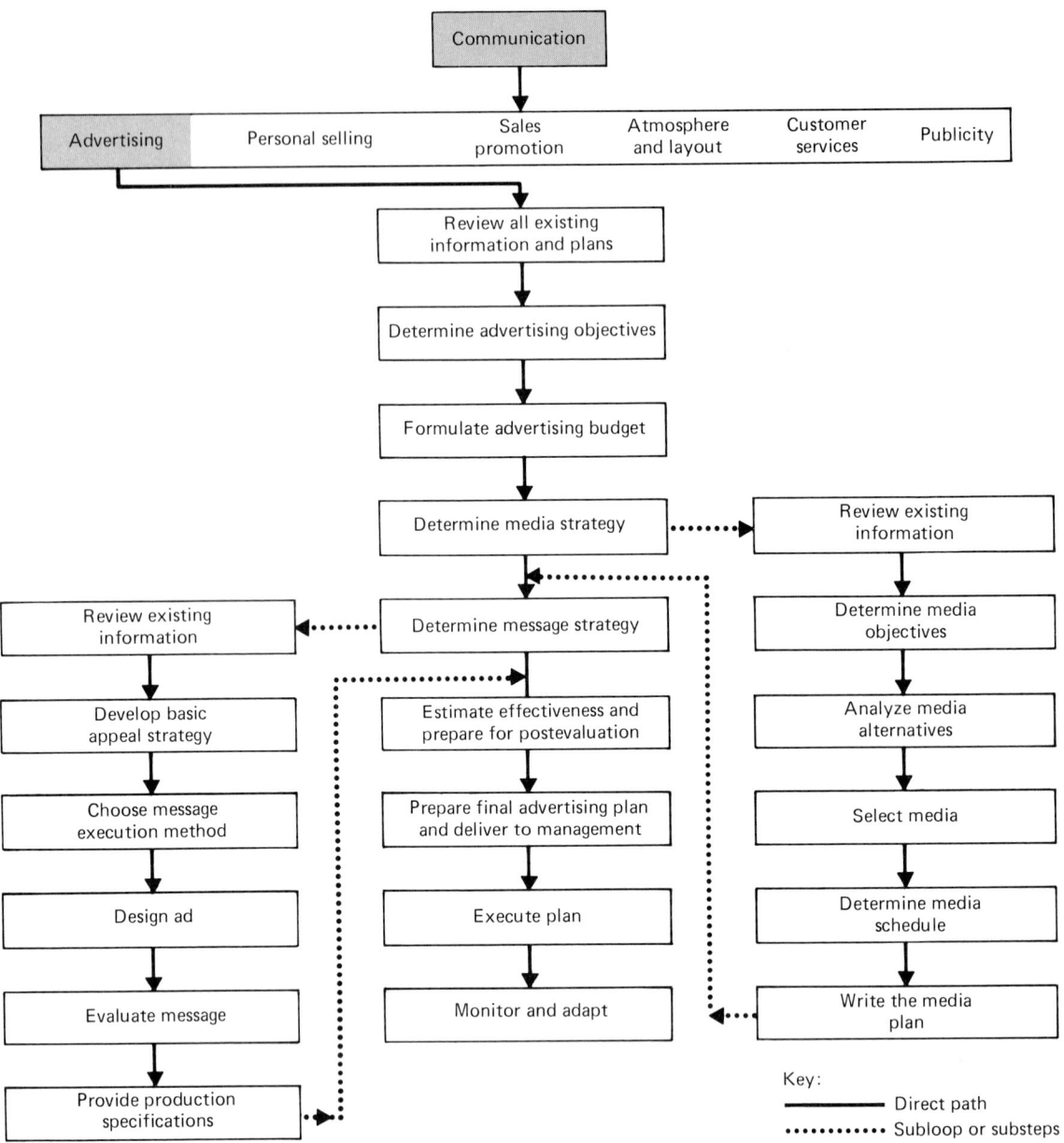

Figure 16.1
Advertising decision model

1. Determine advertising objectives.

2. Formulate advertising appropriation and allocation.

3. Determine media strategy.

4. Determine message strategy.

5. Estimate effectiveness and prepare for postevaluation.

6. Prepare advertising plan for review and execution.

7. Monitor and adapt.

Each of these basic stages contains a varying number of substeps and key considerations.

Just as advertising is not a panacea for the retailer, advertising planning does not guarantee the effectiveness of advertising. It is safe to say, however, that those retailers who use a sound approach to advertising planning, such as the above framework, are much more likely to derive a greater benefit from their advertising efforts than those who do no planning.

It is critical to note that strategic advertising planning should be focused on developing an **advertising campaign** rather than on a specific advertisement. A campaign can be thought of as a collection of comparable advertising executions, even in different media. More formally, a campaign is a series of advertisements with a similar theme, message, and appeal. An apparel shop might plan a three-month campaign consisting of the basic message the "Fashion Center." Many different ads for a variety of media could then be designed with the "Fashion Center" theme used in each. Although each ad might be different in design and execution, the entire series would be considered a campaign. At the end of this period, a new campaign might begin that features the annual clearance sale.

DETERMINE ADVERTISING OBJECTIVES

After the retailer has completed a thorough review of existing information and plans (see Chapter 15), the first major stage in planning advertising strategy is to develop appropriate advertising objectives. Retailers who execute advertising programs with little thought given to goals and objectives are typically no better off than retailers who do not advertise at all, and they can easily be worse off. Before considering specific advertising objectives, the retailer must select the *type* of advertising to use: promotional, institutional, or a combination.

Basic Types of Advertising

Promotional Advertising. **Promotional advertising** is designed to produce immediate results. All of the potential objectives for this form of advertising focus on tangible results such as sales of specific items or visible traffic in the store or a specific department. Many retailers (such as discounters, mass merchandising chains, supermarkets) employ promotional advertising almost to the exclusion of institutional advertising. Most promotional ads are placed in newspapers and usually include prices and other descriptive facts; illustrations are usually of merchandise items.

Institutional Advertising.   Institutional advertising is designed to foster an image, to reach customers at an emotional as well as rational level, and generally to create favorable impressions. Since immediate sales are not the primary objective of institutional advertising, results naturally tend to accrue more slowly than those of promotional advertising and are more difficult to measure precisely. Despite the measurement problem, the use of institutional advertising relative to promotional advertising has been increasing.[7]

Combined Promotional and Institutional.   More and more retailers are combining promotional and institutional advertising techniques. This trend has apparently resulted from retailers' increased awareness that products selected for promotional ads by their very nature tell something about the store, thereby contributing to the store's image. As a result, more care is used in the selection of products and in the overall presentation of the products in advertisements.

Two other developments have also stimulated this trend toward combined ads.[8] First, both the actual and perceived discrepancies between products and their characteristics have diminished. As a result, the store itself tends to become the "product" that people buy and, consequently, the retailer must put more emphasis on the store's atmosphere, reputation, and customer services. Second, as consumers become more and more service-oriented, their buying decisions increasingly hinge on intangible, emotional, and psychological factors. As a result, the retail store must be presented as a vehicle for satisfying psychological needs and wants rather than merely as a source for tangible possessions.

Specific Advertising Objectives

Specific advertising objectives must be determined to serve as a guide for further planning. A classic work in this area is Colley's *Defining Advertising Goals for Measured Advertising Results*, commonly known as **DAGMAR**.[9] Colley contends that the more specific an advertising goal or objective, the better. A specific *task* such as "to create store preferences" should be translated into a specific *objective* such as "to create 35 percent preference for store X among Y thousand consumers in the eighteen- to thirty-nine-year-old range, with annual household incomes of $20,000 plus, by the end of 1983." This latter objective can serve as a guide to further planning and can later act as a standard of measurement for the advertising campaign. The implicit assumption is that if this objective is met, it will be an aid (while

Table 16.2
Advertising objectives and trial budget appropriation

OBJECTIVES	ESTIMATED COST
Hold share of regular trade (via regular radio spots and weekly promotional ads in newspapers)	$10,000
Reinforce seasonal promotions and clearances (via radio and newspaper)	3,000
Promote new youth-oriented department (via radio and campus newspaper)	1,000
Attract residents of new apartment complex in nearby suburb (via series of "welcome" letters)	200
Increase traffic of elderly and retired persons (via sponsorship of health-care programs on FM radio)	2,000
Total trial budget for specific objectives	$16,200
Reserve for unforeseen uses	1,800
Total trial budget appropriation	$18,000

Source: From *Retail Advertising* by William Haight. Copyright © 1976, Scott, Foresman and Company. Reprinted with permission.

interacting with other retailing factors) to accomplishing the overall retailing and organizational objectives. (Examples of a few specific advertising objectives along with budget appropriations are shown in Table 16.2.)

FORMULATE ADVERTISING APPROPRIATION AND ALLOCATION

For a retailer to employ advertising as a business tool, the retailer must accept the proposition that advertising will "pay for itself." This acceptance and the corresponding commitment are manifested in the advertising budget. The advertising budget consists of the **appropriation** (the amount to be spent) and the advertising **allocation** (where or how the amount is to be spent). Budgeting decisions are high-priority management decisions because of their important effect on the organization's financial situation and advertising plans. Too few dollars appropriated or a misallocation of a sufficient number of dollars, for example, are perhaps the quickest ways to ensure the failure of even the most well planned campaigns.

A Suggested Approach

Retailers need a logical, effective approach that is within reach of the time, money, and skill available. The approach described below is adapted from Engel, Warshaw, and Kinnear.[10] It is based primarily on an objective-and-task approach.

Review (or Define) Objectives. Both communications and sales-related objectives can and should be defined, as the situation dictates (see Chapter 15).

Determine Task Alternatives. Several different alternative tasks or activities will usually be available for accomplishing a given set of advertising objectives. An objective involving increased awareness might be accomplished with radio advertising, direct mail, a walk-a-thon, and so on. The retailer should enumerate and evaluate these alternatives in terms of their potential effectiveness. Note that the final decision regarding alternatives such as media selection and message strategy is not made at this time. This step does, however, generate certain constraints for later decisions.

Determine Expenditures. The retailer should now estimate the expenditures necessary to accomplish each delineated task (by contacting media, checking published data sources, and so on). The result of this determination is a trial budget (see Table 16.2). Again, note that some tentative decisions, such as media selection, must be made now that will not be analyzed completely until later. This step is essentially a build-up analysis in that the costs associated with each task are accumulated until a total cost figure is obtained.

Analyze Appropriation as a Percentage of Sales. Calculate the tentative appropriation as a percentage of forecast sales. This percentage, along with previous years' percentages, is useful as a benchmark. The idea is to compare the percentages and analyze any departures from previous years. Note that departures from previous practice are not necessarily mistakes; if a departure can be justified, it is appropriate. The key lies in knowing *why* the appropriation is larger or smaller. New target markets, new product lines or departments, a revised promotion strategy, or new competitors could justify increases in the appropriation, for example.

Compare with Trade Practice. Advertising expenditures as a percentage of sales should also be compared with general trade practices *and* with direct competitors. This comparison is not necessarily to make sure that the retailer matches competitors' expenditures; the retailer's percentage may be higher or lower and still be appropriate. Again, the key is to find out *why* discrepancies exist and to determine if they are justified.

Percentage figures are available for many retail trades in various trade publications and other sources. Although accurate data for individual competitors are more difficult to obtain, comparative subjective estimates are possible.

Analyze in Terms of Firm's Internal Situation and Policies. The appropriation level needs to be fine-tuned to make it consistent with expenditures for other functions and with company policies. Even though some retailers would benefit from borrowing funds to help achieve specific advertising objectives, overall financial liquidity must be maintained regardless of the logic or apparent compelling necessity of achieving the advertising objectives.

A retailing organization is a system of related flows (inventory, personnel, and so on), each making a contribution to the organization *and* requiring resources. From this perspective, there are two hazards to avoid. The primary hazard is suboptimization of a contributing functional flow, such as advertising, by devoting too little effort and money to it. Although not too many retailers err relative to the second hazard, there is always the chance of spending *too much* on advertising. This, too, can create systemwide problems.

Provide for Flexibility.   The advertising allocation and the resulting budget should not be written in stone. The retailer should be prepared to adapt to changing conditions. Markets are becoming more volatile, prices of media continue to increase, and there is always the possibility of a tactical shift by competitors. One relatively common (and effective) technique for providing flexibility is to appropriate a *reserve fund* of 10 to 15 percent of the advertising budget that is not allocated until the need arises (see Table 16.2).

Justify High or Low Allocations.   Extra care should be devoted to justifying those allocations that are high or low relative to last year's budget and to advertising budgets for comparable stores in the same trade, chain, or town. The following are some factors to include in this analysis:

- The position, importance, and objectives of advertising in the store's basic promotional policy.

- The quality and quantity of manufacturers' advertising.

- The age or newness of the store in the area.

- The location of the store (poor locations, for instance, usually require a larger advertising appropriation).

- The nature of the market (population mobility, trends, wealth, and so on).

- The presence of barriers (such as rivers, new traffic arteries, or a new shopping center).

- The quantity, quality, and cost of available media.

- New competition.

- The effect of business cycles on the trading area.

- The perishability of the store's merchandise.

- The size of the store and the variety of merchandise carried.

The presence or absence of any of these factors could be sufficient justification for a budget allocation higher or lower than normal. Retailers should also understand that an advertising allocation that is only slightly low may sometimes be no more effective than not advertising at all.

Finalize the Budget Appropriation.   The retailer is now in a position to finalize the budget appropriation. The word *finalize* is used somewhat loosely because even though the remaining plans and decisions should be made within the budget constraints, new information or events could necessitate changes in the stated objectives or dollars involved.

Cooperative Advertising Allowances

Cooperative advertising allowances deserve mention at this point because they are a potentially lucrative source of advertising funds. These allowances can be used either to obtain more advertising with the same budget or to obtain the same amount of advertising with a smaller advertising allocation. Unfortunately, these funds are far too often overlooked by retailers. In 1980, $1 billion of the $4 billion offered by manufacturers was unspent.[11]

The most common form of cooperative advertising support is **vertical cooperative advertising,** which involves the retailer and the retailer's suppliers (usually manufacturers, but sometimes wholesalers). For advertising the manufacturer's product according to the manufacturer's program specifications, the retailer is reimbursed at a specified rate when the manufacturer receives a tear sheet, a broadcaster's performance affidavit, or direct mailer's invoice. Although rates vary widely, a somewhat standard reimbursement procedure is that the retailer and the manufacturer each pay half the costs.

A variation of vertical cooperative advertising is **promotional advertising allowances.** Promotional allowances are offered by manufacturers periodically to support specific promotional programs or drives. The allowance is usually based on a percentage of the invoice value of the promotional merchandise offered by the manufacturer to the retailer, such as 5 percent off invoice.

Another cooperative advertising form becoming increasingly common is **horizontal cooperative advertising,** or joint advertising. Many variations are possible; all the independent jewelers, pharmacists, realtors, or insurance agents, for example, may join in sponsoring advertising campaigns to professionalize their public image. Shopping center or downtown shopping area associations often advertise for the benefit of all members.

Proper utilization of cooperative advertising can lower costs or increase advertising volume, result in more professional-looking ads, and tie in with the prestige of a manufacturer's national advertising campaign. These potential benefits indicate that retailers should always investigate the availability of cooperative advertising programs.

Allocation Considerations

Allocation involves the distribution of the total advertising appropriation. For smaller stores, the allocation decision can be rather simple, and it can become quite complex for larger, multidepartment establishments. The decision could involve allocations according to merchandise lines, products, departments, geographical areas, customer types, advertising functions, media, and timing.

Department. The allocation techniques for products, merchandise lines, and departments are essentially the same. The required managerial decision involves determining which departments should be represented in the store's advertising and on what basis the total appropriation should be distributed. Standard numerical bases include sales, gross profit, and traffic figures. Table 16.3 shows how a hypothetical store with four major departments might combine each of the three numerical bases for allocation purposes.

Any one of the three bases could be used alone or in combination with any of the others. In the absence of any other information, sales would be an appropriate base to use. This may be all that a small store will need, and sales is a good starting point for any store. The gross profit contributed by each department is a somewhat more logical base because a dollar of sales in a high-profit department is more valuable than a dollar of sales in a low-profit department. Sometimes traffic (as measured by number of transactions or number of customers) should be used because of potential spillover business generated for other departments. In Table 16.3, the percentages for sales, gross profit, and traffic are based on the firm's records. The percentage of advertising allocated to each department is derived from judgment based on the facts. To obtain the percentage of advertising in Table 16.3, the hypothetical planners gave greater emphasis to the contribution to gross profit and the traffic generated than to sales generated.

Sometimes allocations derived similarly to those in Table 16.3 are modified even further by considering growth potential. The situation analysis should yield information on market trends, competition, and so on, sufficient to pinpoint the growth potential of each department. The planners

Table 16.3
Advertising allocation to departments

DEPARTMENT	% OF TOTAL SALES	% OF GROSS PROFIT	% OF TRAFFIC ATTRACTED	% OF ADVERTISING*	ADVERTISING DOLLARS
A	40	35	30	35	5,600
B	30	35	40	40	6,400
C	20	15	10	10	1,600
D	10	15	20	15	2,400
					16,000

*Based on subjective evaluation of the three other percentage columns.

could decide to shift some additional advertising support to a department with high growth potential.

Customer Type.   Whether a retailer must consider allocating advertising on the basis of customer type depends on the existence of more than one customer type and whether different customer types can or cannot be reached with a particular advertising campaign. Examples of customer types that could be included as target markets, but that could require different advertising approaches, are working women/nonworking women, black/white, male/female, and university students/townspeople.

Advertising Function.   Advertising functions that are generally assigned portions of the allocation are media, copy development, production, research, and administrative overhead. As would be expected, media is the most expensive function, with 70 to 90 percent of the typical appropriation.[12] Allocating media dollars requires a consideration of concepts such as reach, frequency, continuity, and size or time (which are discussed later in this chapter). The key to the media allocation is to ensure that it is sufficient to achieve the stated media objectives. Allocations to the other functions of copy development, production, and research are somewhat more difficult to make. Perhaps the key to these allocation decisions is to recognize that a dollar trade-off exists among all four functions.

Geographic Location.   For firms with multiple retail locations, a geographic allocation is necessary (unless advertising decision making is completely decentralized). The key to this decision is an accurate determination of relative sales possibilities for each geographical area. As a general rule, advertising dollars are allocated in proportion to the sales potential of each area.
Several different potentials might be computed for a given area:

1.   Sales volume attainable under ideal conditions, such as if all efforts were perfectly adapted to the environment.

2.   The relative capacity of a market area to support a particular retail trade.

3.   The actual sales a retailer can expect.

With one or more of these potentials as a base, the planner must then consider the relative strength of the competition, the firm's ability to make inroads against the competition, and the impact of a given level of advertising expenditure.

DETERMINE MEDIA STRATEGY

Media strategy is subordinate to both the retailing and the advertising strategy. The result, or output, of formulating media strategy is the *media plan.* The basic function of media strategy is to show how media will be selected and used to attain the advertising and retailing objectives.

Two major factors illustrate the importance of the media strategy. First, media normally represent the largest portion of the advertising budget. Second, although the greatest amount of objective data available for advertising planning involve media, most media decisions are eventually based largely on subjective or judgmental factors. Because of the high cost and subjectivity involved, media planners need an organized, logical approach for developing media strategy. Such an approach involves the following steps:

1. Review existing information

2. Determine media objectives.

3. Analyze media alternatives.

4. Select media.

5. Determine media schedule.

6. Construct media plan.

Media selection and scheduling are the two most critical steps and consequently receive more attention in the following discussion.

Review Existing Information

Before plunging directly into the various media considerations, the media planner must review existing information along with the status of other relevant strategies. Since media strategy must evolve directly from retailing and advertising strategy, the media planner should have a thorough working knowledge of related objectives and plans (even though certain plans may be incomplete at this time). This review is obviously necessary for those media planners who were not involved in the initial strategy planning. Even if the media planner has personally developed all related objectives and plans, it is a good idea to review them in light of media considerations.

The *target market definition* is a good example of a strategic marketing consideration that should be reviewed from a media planning perspective. Since the media selected should be those that will reach the desired target market, the target market definition should be in a form that can give guidance to the media planner. A target market definition that is heavily oriented toward psychographic variables, for example, may be inadequate for proper matching with media audience data. In such instances, the definition must be expanded to include more specific demographic data compatible with available media audience data.

Another factor to be considered at this point is *budgetary constraints*. Selecting media without knowing how much can be spent is obviously a waste of time.

Determine Media Objectives

Media objectives should evolve or flow naturally from the retailing and advertising objectives. They should be simple but clearly specify what media can be expected to contribute to achieving the advertising objectives. The following is an example of how objectives might be stated for a hypothetical outlet:

- *Retailing Objective:* Increase sales volume by 20 percent.

- *Advertising Objective:* Increase consumer awareness of outlet's existence.

- *Media Objective:* Provide continuous pressure in metropolitan area to maintain present awareness level as consumers enter and leave the marketplace. Provide intense and wide pressure for one month, preceding and during special anniversary sales event.

Table 16.4
Comparisons of advertising media

CHARAC-TERISTIC	NEWSPAPERS	MAGAZINES	RADIO	TELEVISION	DIRECT MAIL
Types	Morning, evening, Sunday, Sunday supplement, weekly, special	Consumer, farm, business, local, regional	AM, FM	Network, local, CATV, educational	Letters, catalogs, lists, calendars, brochures, coupons, circulars, newsletters, postcards, booklets, broadsides, samples
Unit of sale	Agate lines, column inches, counted words, printed lines	Pages, partial pages, columns	Programs: sole sponsor, co-sponsor, participative sponsor Spots: 5, 10, 15, 20, 60 seconds	Programs: sole sponsor, co-sponsor, participative sponsor Spots: 5, 10, 15, 20, 60 seconds	By contract
Factors affecting rates	Volume discounts, frequency discounts, number of colors, position charges for preferred and guaranteed positions, circulation level	Circulation, cost of publishing, type of audience, volume discounts, frequency discount, size of ad, position, number of colors, regional issues	Time of day, audience size, length of spot or program, volume discount	Time of day, length of program, length of spot, volume discount, frequency discount, audience size	Cost of mailing list, postage, production costs
Cost comparison indicators	Milline rate = cost per agate line × 1,000,000 divided by circulation	Cost per thousand (CPM) = cost per page × 1,000 divided by circulation	Cost per thousand (CPM) = cost per minute × 1,000 divided by the audience size	Cost per thousand (CPM) = cost per minute × 1,000 divided by the audience size	Cost per contract

Analyze Media Alternatives

Analysis of media alternatives begins with a broad, general perspective that gradually narrows until specific media and vehicles are selected in the following step. To analyze media alternatives, two activities are necessary. First, the retailer should gather enough information to become familiar with the general characteristics of the various available media. Since a lengthy discussion of these characteristics is not feasible in this text, key points are summarized in Table 16.4. Although this review may appear somewhat mundane to the experienced retailer, many retailers are extremely familiar with two or three media alternatives but know very little about others.

CHARAC-TERISTIC	NEWSPAPERS	MAGAZINES	RADIO	TELEVISION	DIRECT MAIL
Market coverage	Single community or entire metro area; zoned editions sometimes available	Varies; local magazines may cover an entire region or metro area; zoned editions sometimes available	Definable market area surrounding the station's location	Definable area surrounding the station's location	Controlled by the advertiser
Type of audience	General; tends toward men, older people, slightly higher income and education; some newspapers have traditional sales days that tend toward women	From general to highly selective depending on editorial content; tends toward better educated and more affluent	Selected audiences provided by stations with distinct programming formats	Varies with time of day; tends toward younger age group	Controlled by the advertiser through use of demographic lists
Particular suitability	All general retailers	If market coverage/audience is appropriate, restaurants, entertainments, specialty shops, mail order	Retailers catering to identifiable groups: teens, commuters, students	Highly personal, owner-oriented businesses; sellers of products or services with wide appeal	New and expanding businesses; those using coupons or catalogs
Major advantages	Flexibility, immediacy, selectivity, low cost	Socioeconomic selectivity, good reproduction, long life	Flexible, personal, selectivity, low cost, high frequency	Dramatic impact, large audience, low CPM, high prestige	Personalized, flexible, little wasted circulation
Major disadvantages	Poor color reproduction, short life, little selectivity	Long lead times, costs, somewhat limited audience	Audio only, short life, divided attention	High total cost, fleeting message, complexity of production	Cost per contract can be high, many consider it junk mail

Source: Information in this table was drawn from a number of sources, including S. Watson Dunn and Arnold M. Barban, *Advertising,* (Hinsdale, Ill.: Dryden Press, 1974); R. Ted Will and Ronald W. Hasty, *Retailing* (San Francisco: Canfield Press, 1977); Barry Berman and Joel R. Evans, *Retail Management* (New York: Macmillan, 1979).

The general objective of this first part of media analysis is to eliminate obviously inappropriate media from further consideration. A retailer might eliminate the shopper, transit, and local magazine categories simply because they are unavailable. Further, direct mail might be eliminated because of the difficulty of obtaining customer names and addresses.

The second portion of this step involves gathering information about specific media directly available to the retailer. The information concerns the audience size and characteristics, costs, and other data needed for the media selection decision discussed in the following step.

Select Media

The overall purpose of media selection is to find the best way to deliver the desired number of exposures or impressions to the desired target market. As in many other business decisions, media selection is complicated by the need to combine objective and subjective data to arrive at an effective and efficient decision. Media selection involves three distinct activities.

Exposure, Reach, Frequency, Impact, and Continuity.   The first major decision area for media selection is the determination of the desired exposure, reach, frequency, impact, and continuity, which can be defined in the following ways:

- *Exposure (E):* One exposure occurs when an individual sees or hears an advertisement. Exposures refer to the total number of times an advertisement is seen or heard by the media audience. Some sources use the term *impressions* rather than *exposures*.

- *Reach (R):* The number of different people (or households) exposed to an advertisement at least once during a particular time period.

- *Frequency (F):* The number of different times the typical person (or household) is exposed to an advertisement during a particular time period.

- *Impact (I):* The qualitative value of an exposure that can be attributed to a specific medium (a food ad would have greater impact in *Good Housekeeping* than in *Handyman*).

- Continuity (C): The degree of regularity or evenness with which exposures are delivered over the relevant time period.

At this point, the media planner should view the advertising and media budgets as fixed (although they could change later), and therefore the total possible exposures can be calculated. If the media allocation is $100,000 and the cost per thousand exposures (CPM) of average quality is $4, the media planner can purchase 25,000,000 exposures ($100,000 × 1,000/$4). If fewer exposures, but of a higher quality, were desired, the media planner might use a $5 CPM to obtain 20,000,000 exposures ($100,000 ×

1,000/$5). In either case, the effect of the exposures (in terms of their contribution to attaining the advertising objectives) is determined largely by the exposures' reach, frequency, impact, and continuity.

Reach and *frequency* are used directly to determine exposures:

$$E = R \times F.$$

In the above example, the planner could use the 20,000,000 exposures to reach 2,000,000 people an average of 10 times during the period. Or 5,000,000 people could be reached an average of 4 times.

Reach and frequency are also used to develop the **gross rating points (GRP).** To do so, reach is converted from *number* of people to the *percentage* of the audience reached. Therefore,

$$GRP = R\% \times F.$$

Thus, if the 2,000,000 people above represented 40 percent of the audience and were reached an average of 10 times, the GRP would be 400 (40 × 10). Similarly, a GRP of 400 could also be attained by reaching 100 percent of the audience (5,000,000 people) an average of 4 times each. Note that media schedules with identical GRPs may be substantially different because of the reach and frequency trade-off. McDonald's seeks a minimum weekly GRP of 350 and a maximum of 600.[13]

As you can see in the above example, there is a trade-off between reach and frequency for a given budget size. Reach can be increased only at the expense of frequency, and vice versa. Balancing this trade-off is critical and must be predicated on the advertising objectives. If the objective involves making a large number of people aware of a special sale, the planner would probably want to emphasize reach. A more complicated message (changing or repositioning the retailer's image) might be effective only through a high degree of repetition and would therefore need greater frequency.

The trade-off decision actually involves more than just reach and frequency. Impact and continuity must also be considered, and trade-offs among all four factors must be evaluated. Since budgetary constraints seldom permit a media planner to emphasize all four factors, one of the four should be selected as the primary media objective and trade-offs evaluated among the remaining three factors. If a large reach is considered more important than high frequency, high continuity, and large impact, the decisions regarding reach will be made first. The second factor in importance would then be optimized, and so forth.

Choosing among the Major Media Types. After making the preceding decisions, the media planner is ready to choose the major media type(s), based on their capacity to deliver the particular reach, frequency, and impact objectives selected. As previously mentioned, the media types have different characteristics, including reach, frequency, and impact values. Television normally has greater reach than radio, magazines, or newspapers. Outdoor advertisements deliver more frequency than magazines. Magazines deliver more impact than newspapers.

In addition to reach, frequency, and impact, the media planner must consider several other factors:

1. *Target Audience Media Habits.* The most effective medium for reaching sports fans, for example, is sports-oriented magazines, TV and radio sports programs, and newspaper's sports sections.

2. *Products.* For a retail advertiser, the products or departments to be advertised can influence the media type chosen because each media type has different potentials for demonstration, visualization, explanation, believability, and color. Product lines like furniture or women's dresses, for example, might be shown to best advantage in print media that have good color reproduction.

3. *Message.* The type of appeal (such as demonstration versus technical data) can have a major influence, especially on eliminating certain types of media.

4. *Cost.* The total cost of a media type relative to the media budget must be considered. The minimum cost for a television commercial is much higher than for a newspaper advertisement. For those media that have costs within reach of the retailer, cost per thousand exposures is actually more important than total cost of the advertisement.

Select Specific Media Vehicles. Once the media types have been selected, the planner is in a position to finally select the specific media vehicles that can deliver the desired message in the most cost-effective way. Comparing media vehicles requires that the planner analyze a great deal of data, both objective and subjective. Some of these data are more or less readily available from sources such as the *Audit Bureau of Circulations, Business Publications Audit of Circulations, Verified Audit Circulation, Standard Rate & Data Service* (the primary source for most media buyers), and the media themselves. Key data from these sources include circulation and costs for different ad sizes, color options, ad positions, and quantities of insertions. Other qualitative data the planner must consider include credibility, image, availability of geographical editions, production quality and assistance, editorial climate, lead time, and psychological impact. The media planner must use these quantitative and qualitative factors to make a final judgment as to which specific vehicles will deliver the best combination of reach, frequency, and impact for the money.

Selecting the media vehicles that are most effective in achieving the media objectives is only part of the selection problem. The planner must also be concerned with the *efficiency* of the various vehicles from a cost standpoint. For many media types the basic measure of efficiency is **cost per**

thousand (CPM). In some situations, cost per million (for newspaper) or cost per hundred (for radio) might be more appropriate.

Although the specific formula will vary from media to media, the basic formula for computing CPM is:

$$CPM = \frac{\text{Cost of ad units}}{\text{Audience in thousands}}.$$

If a radio station charges $100 for a commercial that delivers 25,000 exposures, the CPM is $4.00 ($100 ÷ 25).

The best use of CPM is in comparing two or more vehicles of the same media type, such as newspaper versus newspaper. Comparing the CPMs of two different media, such as radio versus newspaper, should never be done because the nature of the audience and advertisements varies widely across media types.

CPM can be refined to the degree that the denominator (audience) can be defined. Rather than total audience, the number of people in the audience that are actually part of the retailer's desired target market could be used. This refinement results in *cost per prospect*. Further refining could occur if the planner could determine how many people in the target market would actually be exposed to the ad.

Determine Media Schedule

Determining the media schedule involves deciding *when* the various media vehicles will be used. Achieving the optimal timing pattern for advertising expenditure can be viewed as two separate problems: macroscheduling and microscheduling.

Macroscheduling Problems. The **macroscheduling** problem is to determine how to schedule advertising over the course of a year, which is essentially allocating advertising expenditures over time. The primary concern of retailers is usually the seasonal sales patterns for the trade. A secondary, but still important, concern is the seasonal sales patterns for various lines the retailer might carry.

Three interrelated decisions must be made relative to the retailer's seasonal sales patterns. For each decision, the retailer has three basic alternatives:[14]

- *Decision 1:* seasonal or constant or counter-seasonal emphasis

- *Decision 2:* lead or coincide or lag relative to seasonal sales peaks and troughs

- *Decision 3:* more intense or proportional or less intense than seasonal amplitude of sales

Although many retailers follow a seasonal, leading pattern of varying intensity, the other decision alternatives should not be overlooked. A counter-seasonal emphasis might be used, for example, to lessen the severity of a sales trough. A seasonal but lagging pattern might be used when close-out or year-end sales are an especially important part of a retailer's business. Some retailers may follow a constant emphasis for media through-out the year but use seasonal or counterseasonal patterns for specific product lines or departments.

Two factors can be helpful for evaluating these decisions: *degree of advertising carry-over* and the *amount of habitual purchasing*. Carry-over refers to the amount of influence advertising retains as time passes. In general, the greater the advertising carry-over, the greater the lead time relative to seasonal sales peaks and troughs can be; conversely, no carry-over would effectively rule out advertising that leads the season. Habitual purchasing refers to the amount of repeat purchasing regardless of the marketing stimuli. High amounts of habitual purchasing indicate that constant emphasis might be more effective.

Microscheduling Problem. The **microscheduling** problem pertains to scheduling advertising over a relatively short period of time, such as a month.[15] Consider a retailer whose macroscheduling has resulted in a decision to purchase forty spot radio announcements in the month of December. There is a multitude of scheduling possibilities during the month. Figure 16.2 classifies these possibilities into twelve patterns. A *concentrated/level pattern* (1) could mean the retailer advertises only the last two weeks of each month at about the same rate each day and week. A retailer that advertises continually during the month, but with more advertising on the weekends, is using a *continuous/alternating pattern* (8). A retailer that advertises only on weekends but that increases the number of ads each

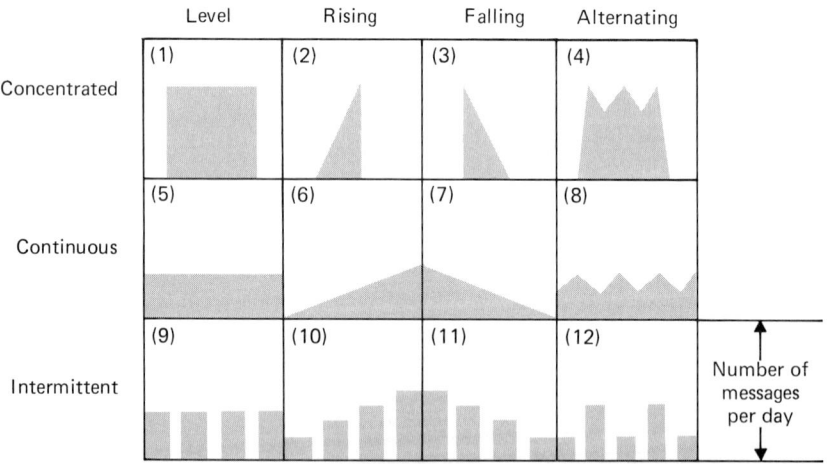

Figure 16.2
Classification of advertising scheduling patterns

Source: Philip Kotler, *Marketing Management: Analysis, Planning, and Control,* 4th ed., © 1980, p. 518. Reprinted by permission of Prentice-Hall, Inc., Englewood Cliffs, N.J.

weekend until the last weekend of the month is using an *intermittent/rising pattern* (10).

The most effective microscheduling pattern for the retailer depends on the retailing and advertising objectives, target customers, and the other retailing strategy decisions. Four other factors should also be considered.

First, *customer turnover* refers to the degree of inflow and outflow of customers in a retailer's market. Although the degree of outflow influences all retailing strategy, the amount of inflow of new customers is especially relevant to microscheduling of media. The greater the inflow, the more continuous the advertising must be to reach these new, potential customers.

Second, *shopping frequency* refers to the number of times during the period an average customer will visit a particular type of store. The higher this frequency, the more continuous the advertising should be to keep the retailer's name in mind.

Third, *forgetting rate* refers to the rate at which customers forget the store name in the absence of other stimuli. A high forgetting rate indicates the need for more continuous advertising.

Fourth, *competitive efforts* can influence scheduling. In many towns a particular day of the week is popular for advertising "specials" in the newspaper. If a retailer's competitors use this pattern, the retailer is almost forced to schedule some advertising on this day.

Construct the Media Plan

The media plan should be put down on paper in an orderly manner. The written plan will serve as a guide to those responsible for its execution. A calendar should be prepared, indicating the media schedule, dollar allocation, and ad space (or time) for each month, week, and day. Note that these six steps actually culminate in two additional activities, *execution* and *monitoring and adapting,* which are discussed later in this chapter.

STRATEGY IN ACTION 16.2

Media Expenditures — K mart 1981

K mart spent about $373 million on advertising in 1981. This figure was a 10 percent increase over the preceding year.

Newspapers play the major role in communication for K mart. The breakdown for media expenditures was newspaper 88 percent, television 8 percent, magazine 2 percent, and radio 2 percent.

K mart advertising emphasizes a wide range of consumables, usables, and edibles at very low prices. K mart believes its store refurbishings and new store openings combined with aggressive advertising will continue to increase sales and bring customers back to K mart "time and time again."

Source: "K mart to 'Keep the Doors Swinging' in '81," p. 10. Reprinted with permission from the 1 June 1981 issue of *Advertising Age.* Copyright 1981 by Crain Communications, Inc.

DETERMINE MESSAGE STRATEGY

The retailer is now ready to plan the *message strategy* (or creative strategy). The basic purpose of the advertising message is to inform, remind, or persuade. All messages will have one or more of these elements, but with one purpose usually dominant. The dominant message is derived from the advertising objectives.

Although certain aspects of planning the message strategy must be performed concurrently with planning the media strategy, when viewed alone, the message strategy development can be organized into six sequential steps:

1. Review existing information.

2. Develop basic appeal strategy.

3. Choose message execution method.

4. Design ad.

5. Evaluate message.

6. Provide production specifications.

Review Existing Information

All existing information should be reviewed from the perspective of creating an appropriate message. The review should at least cover the situation analysis and all current objectives and strategy statements. Particular attention should be devoted to the retailer's own store image, to target customers, and to competitors. The retailer must answer two critical questions: "Why do customers come to my store?" and "Why do other customers *not* come to my store but go to my competitors?" The answer to these two questions should have a great deal of influence on the message strategy.

The reasons that people purchase a particular product from a particular store are not necessarily obvious. It may be for a single reason or a combination of price, brand names, convenience, seasonal needs, ethnic customs, self-concept, and psychological compensation.

Develop Basic Appeal Strategy

The appeal strategy consists of specifications for four components of the message: *objective, content, support,* and *tone.* The appeal strategy should be based on answers to the following types of questions:

- What criteria do consumers use in evaluating this type of store?

- What features or selling points are unique to the store?

- What is the position of the store image relative to the competition?

The message objective should be specific and state exactly what effect the message should have. An example of a message objective is shown in Table 16.5 as part of the appeal strategy statement. In designing a specific message objective, the retailer has five broad alternatives:

Table 16.5
Appeal strategy statement for Wade's Mens's Wear

1. The *objective* of the message is to inform customers about special sale and convince them that they can save money.

2. The *content* consists of emphasizing the following points:
   a) All items are reduced by 40%
   b) Use examples of brand names
   c) Dates of sale

3. *Support* for the "saving" appeal will consist of comparing regular price with sales price for selected popular brand names.

4. The *tone* of the message will be similar to a news announcement, with a sense of immediacy.

1. Affect those forces that influence strongly the criteria consumers use to evaluate stores belonging to the trade category.

2. Add characteristics to those that consumers consider salient for the trade category.

3. Increase/decrease the rating for salient trade category characteristics.

4. Change perception of the store with regard to some particular salient characteristic.

5. Change perception of the competition with regard to some particular store characteristic.

The content of the message is drawn from determining what to advertise, which usually involves specific products, product lines or services, special sales events, or institutional factors. If products are to be used, the retailer must choose between popular items, timely items, items stocked in depth, items that are typical of the store, items that are good values, items in the same price line, newsworthy items, and items being promoted by manufacturers or other stores. Institutional ads can center around store personnel, special instructions or information, comments on local, state, or national issues, anniversaries, cultural issues, sports events, services, name brands, store policies, store visits by celebrities or experts in a field, trade at home, public service, or store expansion and improvements.

Whatever the appeal strategy, it should be evaluated on three criteria: *desirability, exclusiveness,* and *believability.*[16] A message should tell something desirable or interesting about the store. Since other retailers may be making the same claim, the message should include something exclusive or distinctive. Everything that is said must be believable or provable. Appeals that lack any of these three elements are doomed to ineffectiveness.

The sample appeal strategy statement shown in Table 16.5 (also called copy plan, copy strategy statement, and message strategy) is rather simple and short. Other elements that might be included are specific product claims, relative degree of emphasis to be given to each claim, specification of media type and units (30 seconds or 6 column inches), and suggestions for visual devices or action. In any case, the appeal strategy statement should provide sufficient guidance to anyone responsible for designing and producing the message.

Choose Message Execution Method

The impact of an advertisement depends not only on what is said but also on how it is said. In fact, message execution can be decisive for those retailers that are perceived as being similar to their competitors. The retailer must convey the message in a manner that will win the attention and interest of the target audience.

Message execution decisions involve approach, style, and tone. The approach to message execution is the manner in which the retailer attempts to activate buyers to action, by providing information, using commands, or providing people and situations that the audience can imitate. Closely related to execution approach, but more specific, is execution style. Examples of style include fantasy, musical, mood, and scientific evidence. The desired tone of the message might be positive, negative, humorous, arrogant, nostalgic, fear-provoking, or self-deprecating.

Design Advertisement

Designing the ad involves selecting appropriate words and formats. Words must be found that are attention-getting, understandable, powerful, and memorable. They are important for both headlines and copy. Examples of attention-getting words are "new," "save," "improved," and "sale." To ensure that the audience understands what is intended, both the denotative meaning (dictionary meaning) and connotative meaning (emotional or evaluative meaning) must be considered.

Format is especially critical for print ads. Format includes headlines, subheads, copy position, illustrations, color, ad size, and the overall visualization of the ad.

Evaluate Message

The primary objective of evaluating the message strategy is to make sure the overall message is "on strategy" (that is, does it execute the message strategy effectively in terms of appealing to the target audience and registering the message specified in the copy platform?). The ads should be memorable in that they attract and hold attention. They must also register the intended message and hence achieve the persuasive objectives.

Provide Production Specifications

Since most retailers must rely on media personnel or other specialists for the production of an advertisement, production specifications must be provided to those responsible for the production. Specifications for print ads include print type, printing method, dimensions, color, and so on. Specifications for broadcast ads include items such as film or tape, live action or animation, live or recorded, casting, and so on. The retailer must exercise care in developing specifications to avoid unnecessarily adding to the cost of advertising.

ESTIMATE EFFECTIVENESS AND PREPARE
FOR POSTEVALUATION

Good planning and control of advertising depend on obtaining appropriate feedback to determine the effectiveness of the advertising. This feedback can be obtained by pretesting and posttesting.

Pretesting

Pretesting occurs before a given advertisement is produced and circulated. The general objective is to reduce the risk of producing a bad advertisement. For many smaller retailers, the pretesting may consist simply of talking to employees and other people about certain ideas. As the advertising budget rises, the risk also increases from two standpoints: direct loss of money from spending advertising dollars incorrectly, yielding ineffective advertising; and more of an indirect loss from advertising that damages the retailer's image. As the risks increase, the need for more information through pretesting increases.

Posttesting

Posttesting refers to testing individual ads or campaigns after they have been used in the media. Its objective is to evaluate rather than to diagnose. Changes can no longer be made; the task now is to determine what has already happened and to use this information as input to future decisions.

The initial problem that must be considered in posttesting is the criteria to be used. The most desirable measure of advertising effectiveness is sales. Although retailers are probably in a better position to use a sales criterion than any other type of organization because of the short advertising-to-purchase cycle, using sales as the only criterion is very difficult because of the large number of factors in addition to advertising that influence sales. If a retailer experiences poor sales during a special anniversary sale, it could be due to poor advertising, pricing, merchandise, the weather, competitive activity, or a number of other factors. Despite this criticism, retailers should still use sales as a criterion, as long as other factors, such as traffic, inquiries, and the consumer's decision process are also considered.

Although sales results are difficult to relate to a single advertisement, other stages in the typical consumer decision (or buying) process can be measured—for example, the readiness-to-buy stages (see Chapter 15).

At this point, the retailer's preparation for postevaluation involves selecting a measurement criterion and technique and arriving at a quantitative benchmark statement.

It is of utmost importance that the measurement criterion and technique are compatible with the advertising objectives. If the advertising objective is "to increase consumer awareness of store name from 50 percent to 80 percent," the measurement criterion must be *awareness* (not sales or attitudes) and the measurement technique must measure awareness.

The *quantitative benchmark statement* is a statement of the present (pre-advertising) status of the measurement criterion. In the above example, the benchmark was actually contained in the objective, ". . . from 50 percent to 80 percent." The 50 percent awareness level is the benchmark.

PREPARE ADVERTISING PLAN
FOR REVIEW AND EXECUTION

One of the major outputs of strategic advertising planning is the *advertising plan*, which formally establishes advertising objectives and explains how these objectives will be reached. It should also include at least a summary of the advertising budget, media strategy, message strategy, rough copies of the ads themselves, and an impact analysis. An **impact analysis** is an evaluation of the expected influence that the proposed advertising will have on other strategy variables, such as pricing, store image, inventory, and so on.

The advertising plan should be written. The idea that a mental outline of the advertising program is sufficient is a mistake, even for smaller retailers. A written plan has the advantages of explicitly stating the reasoning, permitting better coordination and delegating, and providing a permanent record.[17] Good advertising plans have several other common characteristics. They should be appropriate, feasible, comprehensive, management-specific, time-specific, and dollar-specific, and they should be reviewed regularly.[18]

Once the advertising plan is reviewed and approved, execution can take place. Execution refers to producing the final advertisements and beginning the campaign with the selected media.

MONITOR AND ADAPT

Monitoring involves obtaining the appropriate feedback, from the implementation of the measurement techniques selected and the ongoing general analysis of environmental factors that could force alterations of the advertising plan. Adapting the advertising plan involves adjusting the advertising to combat problems or to take advantage of new opportunities. Quick adjustments are the rule rather than the exception for the fast-paced retail industry. Environmental factors that could force alterations include weather, new fashions, changing customs, competitive activity, special events, and availability of special merchandise.

WHAT ADVERTISING CANNOT DO

Adhering to the strategic advertising planning process presented in this chapter should increase the retailer's chances of developing a good advertising program. Although well-planned advertising can be a powerful and effective tool for the retailer, it is also important to recognize what advertising *cannot* be expected to do. The following are its major limitations:

1. Advertising cannot sell a product (or make a store successful) if the offering does not satisfy a consumer need or want.

2. Advertising cannot be used to sell customers an unsatisfactory or bad product more than once.

3. Advertising cannot move merchandise without adequate support from the other marketing factors and store divisions; advertising cannot wholly compensate for a poor store location, unattractive atmosphere, incompetent personnel, and so on.

4. Advertising cannot be expected to create sales when conditions are unfavorable, such as during the off-season or economic downturns. (However, advertising can sometimes help reduce the severity of seasonal or cyclical dips.)

5. Advertising cannot be expected to succeed to the fullest extent of its potential unless it is used regularly and consistently; timid and sparse advertising efforts often accomplish nothing.

Advertising cannot stand alone as an all-powerful substitute for good merchandise, good service, and other basic retailing factors. Rather, advertising should be viewed as a tool for fostering the accomplishment of the retailer's overall marketing and business objectives.

KEY CONCEPTS

Lagged effect	Exposure
Cumulative effect	Reach
Momentum	Frequency
Advertising campaign	Impact
Promotional advertising	Continuity
Institutional advertising	Gross rating points (GRP)
DAGMAR	Cost per thousand (CPM)
Appropriation	Macroscheduling
Allocation	Microscheduling
Vertical cooperative advertising	Pretesting
Horizontal cooperative advertising	Posttesting
Promotional advertising allowance	Impact analysis

REVIEW QUESTIONS

1. Discuss the purpose and importance of advertising to the retailer.
2. Develop the framework for strategic advertising planning.
3. Develop the framework for formulating the advertising budget.
4. Why should retailers be interested in cooperative advertising?

5. Discuss the various allocation considerations a retailer is likely to encounter.

6. Develop the framework for planning media strategy.

7. Discuss the interrelationships and trade-offs between reach, frequency, impact, and continuity.

8. Discuss the retailer's media scheduling decisions.

9. Develop the framework for planning the message strategy.

10. Contrast pretesting and posttesting.

LEARNING EXERCISES

1. Select newspaper ads for three different retailers. Evaluate each ad to determine whether it is promotional or institutional and what its apparent objective, content, support, and tone are.

2. Using audience data and readership of local media, design a media schedule that would achieve 100 percent reach (locally) and determine the total cost. Evaluate the wisdom of implementing such a plan. Compare it with a similar plan that would reach 80 percent of the population (or homes).

DECISION SITUATION 16.1: **ATHLETIC OUTFITTERS II**

The owner of Athletic Outfitters presented in Decision Situation 15.1 must determine which advertising media to use. His choices include all those presented in Chapter 16. He could have about ten times as many radio ads as television ads for the same money. A weekly newspaper ad would cost about the same as a 30-second TV ad. Outdoor and direct-mail costs vary greatly, depending on the specific location and number of mailouts, respectively. All media cover an area roughly equivalent to the trade area of Athletic Outfitters.

QUESTIONS

1. What combinations of advertisements would you recommend for Athletic Outfitters? Why?

2. How would you recommend the owner develop his advertising budget?

3. What type (format) of radio station would you recommend? Why? What TV programs? Why?

4. What changes in media and scheduling would you recommend for special sale? Why?

DECISION SITUATION 16.2: **SANDWICH KING, INC.**

Sandwich King, Inc. is a reasonably successful regional chain of forty-three sandwich shops. They sell eight types of sandwiches, with the hamburger (with or without cheese) being the overwhelming favorite. Throughout its history the chain has fought to impress on customers the quality of Sandwich King's offerings.

Kelly, the advertising manager, has just been presented with yet another battle involving the quality of Sandwich King's hamburgers. For some reason there was a rampant rumor in some areas that Sandwich King was adding earthworms to its hamburgers. The fact that earthworms were about five times as expensive as beef had apparently not been considered by the rumor passers. Branch managers thought that hamburger sales had been reduced by 20 percent because of the rumors.

QUESTIONS

1. Do you think people actually believe rumors about businesses?

2. Would you recommend an increase in the advertising budget?

3. What message strategy would you recommend to Kelly? Why?

NOTES

1. Philip Kotler, *Marketing Management* (Englewood Cliffs, N.J.: Prentice-Hall, 1980), p. 498.

2. M. Wayne DeLozier, *The Marketing Communications Process* (New York: McGraw-Hill, 1976), pp. 216–219.

3. William R. Davidson, Alton F. Doody, and Daniel J. Sweeney, *Retailing Management* (New York: Ronald Press, 1975), p. 400.

4. William Haight, *Retail Advertising* (Morristown, N.J.: General Learning Press, 1976), p. 104.

5. Otto Kleppner, *Advertising Procedure* (Englewood Cliffs, N.J.: Prentice-Hall, 1979), p. 24, and William M. Weilbacher, *Advertising* (New York: Macmillan, 1979), p. 437.

6. Weilbacher, *op. cit.*, pp. 635–638.

7. Haight, *op. cit.*, p. 104.

8. *Ibid.*

9. Russell H. Colley, *Defining Advertising Goals for Measured Advertising Results* (New York: Association of National Advertisers, 1961).

10. James R. Engel, Martin R. Warshaw, and Thomas C. Kinnear, *Promotional Strategy* (Homewood, Ill.: Richard D. Irwin, 1979), pp. 237–242.

11. "Ad Dollars and Sense," *INC.*, August 1981, p. 93.

12. Robert L. Anderson and Thomas E. Barry, *Advertising Management* (Columbus, Ohio: Merrill, 1979), p. 188.

13. Christy Marshall, "McDonald's '79 Plan: Beat Back the Competition," *Advertising Age*, 1 February 1979, p. 8.

14. Kotler, *op. cit.*, pp. 516–517.

15. *Ibid.*, p. 518.

16. *Ibid.*, p. 505.

17. David W. Nylen, *Advertising* (Cincinnati, Ohio: South-Western Publishing, 1980), p. 65.

18. Rollie Tillman and C. A. Kirkpatrick, *Promotion: Persuasive Communication in Marketing* (Homewood, Ill.: Richard D. Irwin, 1968), p. 385.

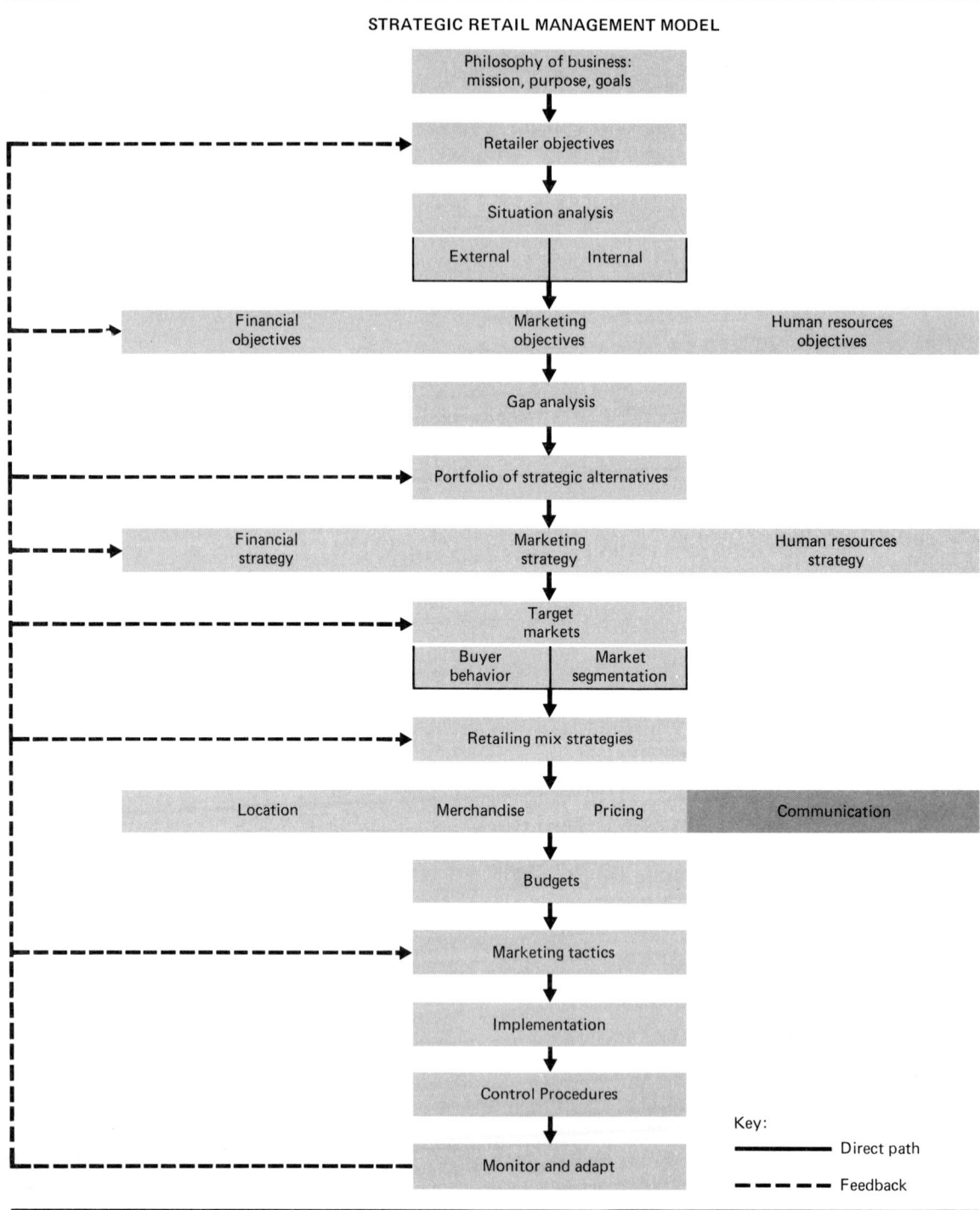

STRATEGIC RETAIL MANAGEMENT MODEL

Philosophy of business: mission, purpose, goals

Retailer objectives

Situation analysis

External | Internal

Financial objectives | Marketing objectives | Human resources objectives

Gap analysis

Portfolio of strategic alternatives

Financial strategy | Marketing strategy | Human resources strategy

Target markets

Buyer behavior | Market segmentation

Retailing mix strategies

Location | Merchandise | Pricing | Communication

Budgets

Marketing tactics

Implementation

Control Procedures

Monitor and adapt

Key:
———— Direct path
— — — Feedback

Chapter 17 Personal Selling and Sales Promotion Decisions

LEARNING OBJECTIVES

1. To understand the role and development of effective retail sales-force strategies and the retail personal selling process.

2. To understand the role and development of effective retail sales promotion strategy.

INTRODUCTION

This chapter continues the development of retail communications strategy. It is divided into three major parts: sales-force strategy and the personal selling process (the two components of strategic personal selling) and sales promotion strategy. Sales-force strategy focuses on the planning process and decisions necessary to develop an effective sales-force strategy from a manager's perspective. The personal selling process is designed to help salespeople match product benefits to customer needs. Sales promotion strategy focuses on the planning process and decisions necessary to develop effective sales promotion programs. The decision models for these three areas are depicted in Fig. 17.1.

SALES-FORCE STRATEGY

The overall **sales-force strategy** and the individual salespeople can have a major impact on the success or failure of a retailer's business. Many of the potential impacts of the sales force can be either positive or negative. Consider the impact of the sales force on store image; a good sales force can have a tremendous positive impact on the store image because of its interaction with customers. Unfortunately, this is not always achieved. In fact, many negative or poor store images can be attributed directly to sales personnel. Table 17.1 lists the major potential strengths and limitations of a sales force.

Table 17.1
Major opportunities and problems with maintaining a retail sales force

Opportunities

Achieving a dollar sales volume impossible with other communication methods

Enhancing the store image

Persuading customers to buy products when other communication methods cannot

Providing information to customers

Providing information to the retailer

Helping maintain store appearance

Problems

Fostering a negative store image

Discouraging self-service

Less ability to attract new customers than other communication tools

Generating higher expenses than other communication tools, without achieving increases in sales

Difficult to attract good salespeople

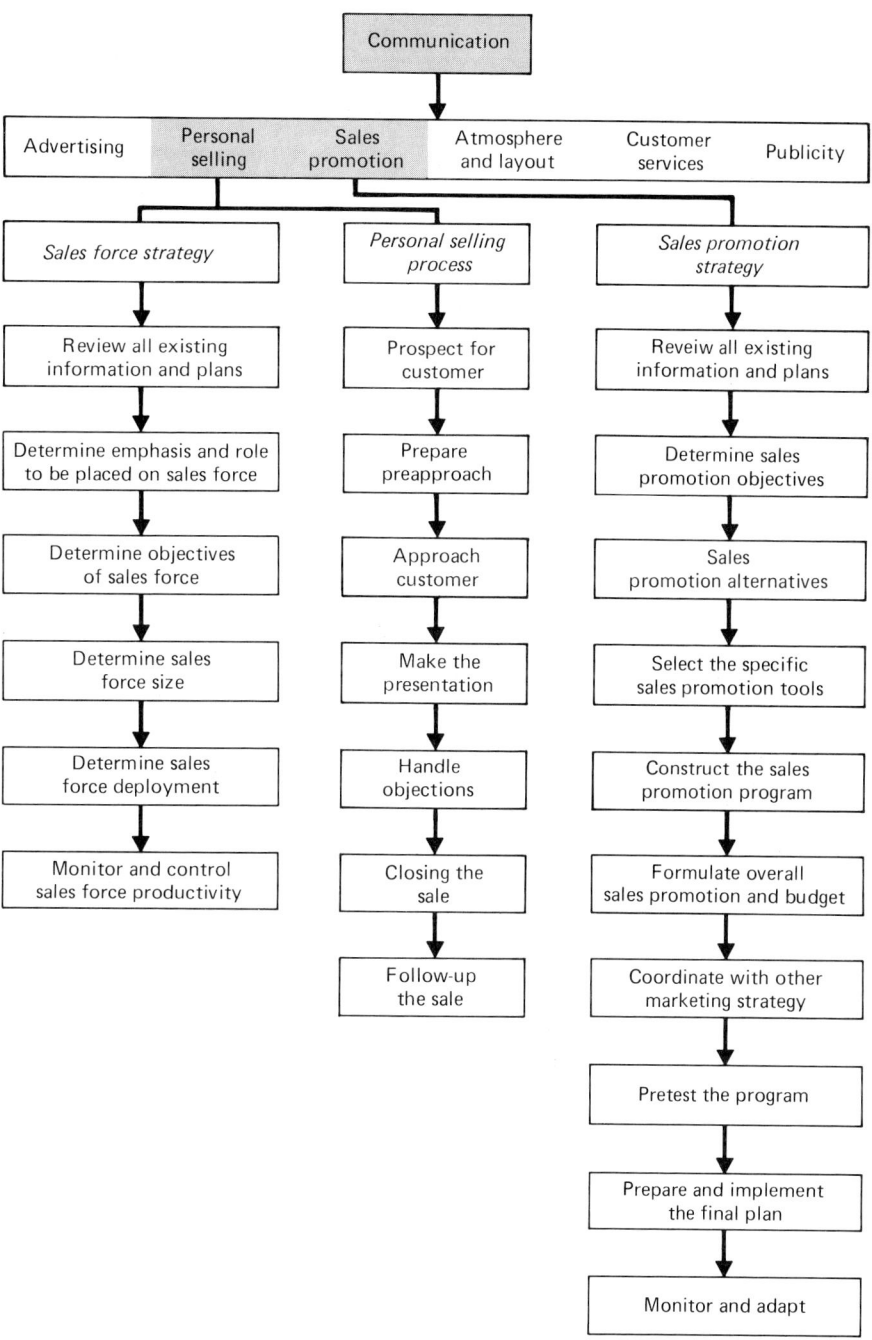

Figure 17.1
Personal selling and sales promotion decision models

The six steps necessary to plan an effective sales-force strategy are the following:

1. Review all existing information and plans.

2. Determine the emphasis and role to be placed on the sales force.

3. Determine the objectives of the sales force.

4. Determine the sales-force size.

5. Determine sales-force deployment.

6. Monitor and control sales-force productivity.

Review All Existing Information and Plans

The review of existing information and plans is extremely important, especially for establishing the role of the sales force in the next step. Key information and plans to review include target market, consumer decision processes, products offered, other communications strategy, competitive strategy, availability of personnel, and the sales volume and patterns expected.

To illustrate the nature of this review, consider the impact of the target customers on sales-force strategy. First, the retailer must determine whether customers need and expect salespeople for the type of merchandise carried. If salespeople are needed, the retailer must attempt to match their characteristics with the customers' characteristics and expectations. Customers usually expect a prestigious apparel store to provide salespeople, and they do not expect these salespeople to dress in overalls and jogging shoes.

Determine the Emphasis and Role of the Sales Force

If the retailer has diligently followed the overall strategic planning framework, the general emphasis to be placed on the sales force should have been determined already (see Chapter 15). If not, the retailer should make this determination now. The initial problem in determining the emphasis on sales force is whether to even have a sales force. The retailer can opt for self-service, full service, or a combination. The key to this choice is to obtain an effective blending or interaction between the customers' needs and desires, the merchandise, and the salespeople.

Note that retailers must make a trade-off between the reduced expense of self-service and the potentially greater sales volume per customer with full service. For customers, the trade-off is between the potentially lower prices with self-service and the facilitated decision making associated with full service.

Self-service. From the retailer's perspective, self-service (or self-selection) is likely to be appropriate if: (1) customers find self-service acceptable, (2) the communication burden can be shouldered by promotion tools other than personal selling, and (3) self-service is compatible with the desired store image. Consumers have demonstrated, for example, that they are willing to serve themselves in supermarkets, gasoline stations, and even in certain clothing stores.

Full Service.   Situations requiring the presence of salespersons possess one or more of these characteristics: (1) customers know little about the product features and benefits (stereo components, for example), (2) price negotiation or trade-in allowances are standard (automobiles), (3) the product is technically complex in design, installation, or usage (washing machines), (4) the product is expensive (jewelry), (5) the risk of the customer's making an incorrect decision is high (home-improvement products), and (6) customers expect a greater level of service because of the price or quality of the store or merchandise.

Combination.   Some retailers can utilize a combination approach in which certain departments are staffed with salespeople while others are self-service. Discount stores, for example, often concentrate on self-service but employ salespeople in departments such as jewelry, shoes, electronics, and cameras (if the departments are not leased to a specialty firm).

Types of Selling.   Retail selling can be categorized into three primary types, depending on the number and nature of functions performed by the salespeople. First, **transaction processing** involves simple checkout or cashier duty. All retailers must have someone to perform this exchange function. Some retailers, however, need their cashiers to perform little or no personal selling. These retailers emphasize self-service operations in which customers are willing to exert effort in serving themselves. Most supermarkets and many discount operations use only transaction processing.

Second, **routine selling** is somewhat more involved than transaction processing. The salesperson actually waits on customers and generally assists customers in their decision making, primarily by providing information. Routine selling is normally effective when the customers recognize that they need something, but do not know exactly what they want and are not willing or able to select the proper merchandise efficiently. Nontechnical merchandise, such as clothing and shoes, often require routine selling.

Third, in **creative selling** the salesperson's role is more involved with finding customers, persuasion, and problem solving. Creative selling requires imaginative selling, often to consumers who have an unfelt or unrecognized need for the salesperson's offering. In these situations, the salesperson cannot simply ask the potential customers if they want the product because few will know whether they want it. Rather, the salesperson must show the customer how he or she can use the product and why he or she should buy it. This approach involves transforming the unfelt need into a felt need and showing how the product's benefits can satisfy that need. One retailer, a plant nursery, used creative selling to build up a $30 million-a-year business. The strategy was to offer homeowners a free sketch of how their landscape *could look.* They "sold" beauty, but earned their profits from the sale of shrubbery.[1] Another retailer (of home improvements) increased sales of awnings and shutters by taking snapshots of homes and showing potential customers the actual photo along with a photo of an "improved" home.

Determine Sales-Force Objectives and Tasks

After determining the overall emphasis and role of the sales force, the retailer is ready for Step 3—determining the objectives and tasks required of the sales force. The outcome of this determination should be a clear statement of sales-force objectives, even though the objectives may be general.

When feasible, specific sales volume objectives should be stated. If the retailer has five full-time salespeople and sales volume has been forecast at $350,000 for the year, each salesperson might be tentatively assigned a sales objective of $70,000. A final sales volume objective for each salesperson could then be derived by adjusting the $70,000 according to the times each salesperson is scheduled to work, his or her experience, or other relevant factors. Note that sales volume objectives can also be established for specific product lines when salespeople handle more than one product line.

Depending on the situation, salespeople may be responsible for any or all of the following tasks (in addition to actual sales presentations): buying, inventory control, greeting customers, determining customer wants and needs, providing information to customers, providing information for retail managers, making sales tickets, accepting payment, wrapping, delivery, housekeeping, stocking, security, creating displays, and handling complaints. The retailer should have salespeople provide only necessary functions; nonessential activities are expensive.

Determine Sales-Force Size

Once the retailer has formulated objectives and tasks for the sales force, he or she should consider the size of the sales force. Several approaches for determining the size of the sales force have been proposed that are adaptable to retailing.[2] These approaches contain many variables that can influence the number of salespeople needed, such as type and number of customers, time needed to serve each customer, type of merchandise, strength of competition, store image, and salespeople's ability and experience. Perhaps two of the most critical variables the retailer should consider are workload and productivity.

A salesperson's **workload** consists of both selling and nonselling activities. Assigning more nonselling duties to salespeople reduces the amount of time available for actual selling. **Productivity** is the relationship between the sales volume (or gross profit) a salesperson generates, the sales potential of the department, and the expense of employing the person.

A simple example illustrates how one retailer might consider workload and productivity for a shoe department. The tentative sales forecast for the department is $100,000 for the year. The average pair of shoes sells for $29; therefore, the expected unit volume is 3448. To attain this volume, a salesperson would have to average selling about 66 units per week (3448 ÷ 52), or 11 pairs per day. The retailer feels this productivity level is within reach of one salesperson, but was concerned about two problems. First, other housekeeping chores, such as stocking, ordering, and so on, must be accomplished. These tasks are absolutely necessary but somewhat beyond the reach of one salesperson. Second, the shoe department experiences several peak periods of activity during the year. One person can handle all of these peaks except the back-to-school peak period and one or two special sales. One alternative is to hire a second full-time salesperson at a cost of about $8,000 per year. This addition would permit accomplishing all housekeeping chores and provide adequate coverage during peak periods. Further, the retailer feels that two salespeople can attain a sales volume of $120,000. The additional $20,000 in sales volume would yield additional gross profit of $8,000 ($20,000 × 40% markup). However, this alternative would result in no additional dollar productivity because of the $8,000 increase in wages. A second alternative involves hiring a part-time employee to help with housekeeping and using temporary employees to help with sales peaks. The total cost of these employees would be $3,000. With the help of the temporary salesperson, the retailer expects sales of $110,000, an increase in gross profit of $4,000 ($10,000 × 40% markup). Since the expected increase in gross profit exceeds the increase in cost by $1,000 ($4,000 − $3,000), the retailer should hire the part-time and temporary help if the desired quality of service can be maintained.

Determine Sales-Force Deployment

Determining sales-force deployment will often be done simultaneously with Step 4 because the size of the sales force and its deployment are closely related. The retailer's essential decision involves where to place salespeople relative to major product lines or departments and how to assign selling and nonselling responsibility.

Deploying salespeople to specific departments can be a complicated task, especially for the larger retailer. Too few salespeople in a sales area can result in lost revenue; too many salespeople in a sales area can result in unnecessary expenses. Effective deployment calls for considering factors such as pattern of customer arrival times, length of service required, average sales to each customer, average customer waiting time, average number of customers, and sales-force cost. *Queuing theory* (or waiting-line theory) can assist the retailer in considering this problem.[3] Stated simply, this theory balances the costs associated with customers waiting in line with the additional direct costs associated with reducing the waiting line (by using more sales personnel).

For smaller outlets, salespeople would typically be responsible for selling all products. For larger outlets, salespeople may be responsible for two or three departments, one department, or perhaps a major product line within a department. Again, the retailer must balance the productivity and workload by analyzing selling responsibilities (or customer needs) and non-selling needs (or retailer needs).

Control of Sales-Force Productivity

Sales-force productivity is usually viewed in terms of sales. Sales-force salaries typically range from 7 percent to 10 percent of sales. Further, payroll expense can run to around 60 percent of operating expenses.[4] Proper control of selling activities and the resulting expense has a critical impact on the retailer's profit. Consider a retailer who has $1,000,000 in sales, a 4 percent net profit ($40,000), and 7 percent sales-force salaries ($70,000). If this retailer allows the sales-force salaries to rise to 10 percent of sales ($100,000) without a corresponding increase in sales, the net profit would fall by $30,000 ($100,000 − $70,000) to $10,000 ($40,000 − $30,000), a 75 percent decrease.

The major activities that can have an impact on improving sales-force productivity are hiring practices, training, compensation, motivation, supervision, and evaluation, all of which were discussed in Chapter 9.

To illustrate the importance of these areas to retail productivity, consider the need for good supervision. The typical breakdown of salespeople's activity is: 35 percent selling, 25 percent sales support, 20 percent delay-idle, and 20 percent out of the area.[5] As you can see from these figures, the proportion of selling to nonselling time is rather unfavorable. The overall utilization of time is a critical problem faced by most retailers. It can be addressed with better supervision and coaching of salespeople, better scheduling of the sales force (via more accurate forecasts of the number of salespeople needed), better deployment, and more efficient layout of work areas.

THE PERSONAL SELLING PROCESS

The key to the **personal selling process** is the matching of product benefits to customer needs and desires. More specifically, the salesperson must help the customer make a series of decisions, such as the following:[6]

1. What do I need? (Need decision)

2. When shall I buy it? (Time decision)

3. Where shall I get it? (Place decision)

4. Which one should I choose? (Item decision)

5. How much should I pay? (Price decision)

Although it is beyond the scope of this text to develop the personal selling process fully, the following subsections present several points critical to the process.

STRATEGY IN ACTION 17.1

Effective Sales Training

As retailers search for methods of increasing productivity, the personal selling area is undergoing greater scrutiny. In addition, retailers believe the consumer of the 1980s desires quality and ego satisfaction in his or her shopping experience. Both of these concerns point to the possibility of more effective use of sales personnel. The effectiveness of sales personnel can be greatly enhanced through improved sales training methods. Many retailers are now placing greater emphasis on effective methods of training their sales staff.

Various methods of sales training have been developed recently, but all of the methods seem to focus on behavior modeling. This approach to sales training includes practical instruction and heavy doses of reinforcement at the supervisory management level. In most programs, the sales trainees watch an example of a selling situation played out by "models," discuss the situation, and then role-play the situation themselves. Reinforcement by trained sales trainers occurs in the training sessions and on the sales floor. Most training executives believe that the reinforcement of good sales behavior is the key to effective training.

J. C. Penney's sales training program incorporates the behavior modeling method through the use of video equipment and in-house production of its own tapes. Before the behavior modeling occurs, each Penney employee is given a product-knowlege, department-specific training period. The combination of extensive product knowledge and behavior modeling should improve sales productivity and consumer satisfaction. Macy's New York uses a similar method that also incorporates the case method.

Source: "A New Realistic Approach to Training Sales Personnel." Reprinted from *Retail Week*, 1 September 1981, pp. 15–22.

Why Do People Buy?	People buy products with particular features to obtain the specific benefits supplied by those features. These specific benefits are the *motive* or reason a person buys. Different customers will have different motives for buying any given product. Table 17.2 presents a variety of motives organized into rational considerations and emotional considerations. To appreciate fully the variety and multiplicity of buying motives, choose a consumer product (soap, lawn mower, diamond ring) and consider which motives would apply for yourself versus someone else, like your parents. Chapter 6 provides a detailed discussion of various buying motives.
The Basic Selling Steps	Successful retail salespeople usually use some type of systematic approach to selling. For our purposes, seven basic steps can be delineated: (1) prospecting, (2) pre-approach, (3) approach, (4) presentation, (5) handling objections, (6) closing, (7) follow-up.

Prospecting. **Prospecting** is the search for new prospects to convert into customers. Because of population mobility, retailers must continually strive

Table 17.2
Buying motives

RATIONAL CONSIDERATIONS	EMOTIONAL CONSIDERATIONS
Cost	Ease and convenience
Durability	Safety and protection
Depreciation	Play and relaxation
Efficiency	Price and prestige
Economy	Love and affection
Degree of labor necessary	Sex and romance
Saving of time and space	Adventure and excitement
Length of usage	Asthetic pleasure
Profit and thrift	Urge to create

Source: Adapted from C. Winston Borgen, *Learning Experiences in Retailing* (Pacific Palisades, Calif.: Goodyear Publishing Company, 1976), p. 291.

to renew their clientele. Some retailers can rely successfully on advertising and other forms of promotion to generate customer traffic, but many retailers can make better use of prospecting than they do now (especially for big-ticket items, such as appliances, tires, and even shoes). Some retail salespeople maintain file cards for "customers sold." These customers (presumably satisfied) can often provide names of new prospects, such as new people hired by their firm or new neighbors.

The retail salesperson should develop a prospect list and then try to determine whether the individuals on the list are really good prospects. This process is called **qualifying.** Although each retail situation is likely to have a different set of qualifying characteristics, the following three criteria are especially critical:

1.   Does the prospect have a need or desire for the product? (A prospect who has just bought a refrigerator does not need another new refrigerator.)

2.   Does the prospect have the ability to pay? (A prospect making over $50,000 a year is a better prospect for expensive furniture than one making $12,000 a year.)

3.   Does the prospect have the authority to buy? (Few husbands will have the authority to purchase a new living room suite without their wives' participation in the buying process.)

In many situations, the retail salesperson will not be able to answer all three of the above questions. For these prospects, the salesperson might assume the individual is a good prospect until the assumption is disproved, perhaps during the first contact.

The retail salesperson should also be alert to opportunities for **in-store prospecting and qualifying.** In-store prospecting involves finding out if the customer is also a prospect for other products. This is often called *suggestion selling*, which is discussed in more detail later in this chapter. In-store qualifying involves determining whether the customer is a good long-term prospect. A businessman is typically a better long-term prospect for suits than is a plumber, for instance.

Pre-Approach.   The **pre-approach** occurs before the salesperson meets the customer. It involves the preparation and information gathering needed to approach a customer. This necessary information includes facts about local customers, the retailer's merchandise (including complementary products), competitors' merchandise, service policies, store layout, store policies, and promotional efforts. Inadequate knowledge of merchandise usually loses sales quickly, for example, but too many salespeople also make the opposite mistake of overemphasizing their knowledge of product features rather than emphasizing customer benefits.

Approach.   The **approach** brings the salesperson into the physical presence of the customer. An effective approach is one that sets the stage for the presentation of the product. The two basic approaches are the **merchandise approach** and the **service approach.** The merchandise approach involves the salesperson commenting on the product the customer is viewing or handling. The service approach is being used when the salesperson offers to assist the customer. Either approach can be used effectively if delivered warmly and sincerely. However, "May I help you?" is an overused service approach that allows the customer to respond with "No!" Contrast this opener with "Have you seen our sale merchandise?" The latter implies service and lessens the opportunity for rejection. Also, the salesperson should vary the exact wording to avoid sounding too mechanical.

Presentation.   The **presentation** is the actual sales pitch in which the salesperson attempts to persuade the customer to buy the product. Although there is no one basic presentation format, many salespeople have benefited from AIDA. AIDA is an acronym for attention-interest-desire-action (discussed in Chapter 15), which can be viewed as a customer's readiness to act or buy. The salesperson must move the customer through the first three stages to the last action stage. Table 17.3 presents selected suggestions for improving the retail sales presentation.

Handling Objections.   **Handling objections** involves overcoming the customer's objections and doubts. Unless there is a perfect product-to-customer match, objections will arise. Salespeople should be able to anticipate common objections and either handle them during the presentation or be prepared to respond after the presentation.

Table 17.3
Suggestions for improving retail sales presentations

1. Work on "selling benefits"—the value (to customer) should be established before discussing price.

2. Work at selling "interest points" about a product or service. For example, you are selling *beauty*. You are selling *simple* application. You are selling *durability*.

3. Do not be afraid to be the listener. Listen to make the customer feel important, to convince customers of genuine service interest, to adjust thoughts to customer's interests, and to understand. Work for two-way communication with the use of questions when necessary.

4. Remember, customers want to be sold well so that they can go home armed and ready with all the reasons they bought.

5. When possible try to show the item in use. "Here is the way it will look on your table," and so on.

6. Wherever possible, involve the customer. Let the customer handle the goods, taste the product, smell the perfume.

7. Talk in a language that the customer understands. Remember that customers may not understand the jargon of the business.

8. Remember that a customer's best value is generally not the lowest-priced item. The presentation should recognize this and justify through factual data any substantial price differences.

9. First, show the customer the merchandise requested. If a certain price range is not requested, show the medium price range and build benefits from there.

10. Handle goods as if they were valuable. Build respect for the merchandise.

Source: Adapted from C. Winston Borgen, *Learning Experience in Retailing* (Pacific Palisades, Calif.: Goodyear Publishing Company, 1976), pp. 298–300.

Closing.   Closing the sale involves obtaining the customer's commitment to buy the merchandise. If the initial steps of the selling process have been handled properly, the close should be relatively easy. The following guidelines can increase the salesperson's odds for closing the sale:[7]

1. Focus on the point of greatest interest.

2. Handle the difficult issues early in the process.

3. Avoid surprises at the close (such as extra charges).

4. Do not isolate or ignore the customer at the close.

5. Display a high degree of self-confidence at the close.

6. Ask for the order more than once.

There are many techniques that can help the salesperson close; six basic techniques are summarized in Table 17.4. Although discussing these techniques is beyond the scope of this text, retailers should provide salespeople with formal training or coaching in these techniques.

Table 17.4
Selected closing techniques

TECHNIQUE	EXAMPLE
Assumption close	"Do you want this purchase added to your charge account?"
Direct close	"Do you want to purchase this?"
Limited-choice close	"Do you prefer the blue or green?"
Summary of benefits close	The salesperson summarizes the key benefits and then uses direct technique.
Standing room	"This is the last unit we will get until March or April."
Silence	

Follow-up. The time period between purchase commitment and customer departure can be quite productive if good follow-up techniques are used. The salesperson can thank the customer, answer any last-minute questions, volunteer tips for using the product, reinforce the customer's decision, and generally attempt to ensure that the customer is satisfied. Remember that it is easier to sell to a satisfied customer than to create or find a new customer.

Suggestion selling should always be considered after the close. It occurs after purchase commitment and involves suggesting other complementary products for the customer's consideration. For the majority of consumer products, other products exist that are closely related or complementary in use. These products provide an excellent opportunity for suggestion selling. Consider a customer purchasing new tennis balls. Complementary products include sweat bands, racquets, racquet covers, ball carriers, grip improvers, shoes, clothing, and caps.

Retailers who can identify customers after they have left the store (charge customers, for instance) should also consider telephone follow-up. An experiment involving jewelry store customers obtained excellent customer responses from calls thanking the individuals for being customers.[8] Sales increased 27 percent over the same month in the previous year (in spite of a 25 percent decrease in year-to-date sales) and there was a sizable increase in the number of customers paying delinquent accounts.

Why Are Sales Lost? Just as the salespeople must understand why people buy, they must also understand the reasons that sales are *not* made to specific customers. Sometimes, there simply will not be a match between the product and the customer. There are, however, many situations in which sales are lost because of factors controllable by the salesperson. Table 17.5 presents nine possible reasons.

Table 17.5
Reasons why sales are lost

Poor qualification of the customer. Information should be obtained from the customer that enables a salesperson to tailor his or her presentation to the prospective buyer.

Salesperson does not demonstrate the product. A good sales presentation should be built around the item shown in use; product benefits can be easily visualized.

Failure to put feeling into presentation. The salesperson should be sincere and consumer-oriented in his or her presentation.

Poor product knowledge. The salesperson should know the major advantages and disadvantages of his or her products as well as those of competitors and be able to answer questions.

Arguing with a customer. A good salesperson should avoid arguments in handling customer objections even if the prospect is completely wrong.

No suggestion selling. A salesperson should attempt to sell related items (such as service contracts, product supplies, and installation) along with the basic product.

Giving up too early. If an attempt at closing a sale is unsuccessful, it should be tried again.

Inflexibility. A salesperson should be flexible in analyzing alternative solutions to a customer's needs as well as in altering his or her message to the requirements of the individual consumer.

Poor follow-up. A salesperson should be sure that the order is correctly written, that merchandise arrives at the agreed upon time, and that the customer is satisfied.

Source: Reprinted with permission of Macmillan Publishing Co., Inc. from *Retail Management* by Barry Berman and Joel R. Evans, p. 444. Copyright © 1979 by Macmillan Publishing Co., Inc.

SALES PROMOTION STRATEGY

Sales promotion was defined in Chapter 15 as those marketing activities, other than personal selling, advertising, and publicity, that stimulate consumer purchasing and dealer effectiveness, such as displays, shows and exhibitions, demonstrations, and various nonrecurrent selling efforts not in the ordinary routine. Sales promotion efforts are generally designed to supplement and complement the other communications activities. Although sales promotion is often viewed as playing a secondary role to advertising and personal selling, it can make a major contribution to retailing objectives and performance.

Sales promotion is composed of a wide variety of tactical promotional tools, as shown in Table 17.6. Most of these tools are short-term incentives designed to stimulate earlier and/or stronger sales responses.

Many practitioners view advertising as a means of building up brand loyalty and sales promotion as a means of breaking down competitors' brand loyalty. There is evidence to support this view for products in the maturity stage of their product life cycle. One study drew the following conclusions:[9]

1. Sales promotions create quicker sales responses than does advertising.

Table 17.6
Basic types of sales promotion

TYPE	FEATURES
Coupons	Stores advertise special discounts for customers who redeem advertised coupons. Customers clip coupons from newspapers and redeem them in the store.
Demonstrations	Products are shown cleaning floors, mixing foods, and so on. Services may also be demonstrated (Evelyn Woods Reading Dynamics, for example).
Stamps	Customers are given free trading stamps based on the dollar amounts of their purchases. These stamps are accumulated and are used to acquire products.
Point-of-purchase	Window, floor, and counter displays that allow a retailer to remind customers and stimulate impulse purchases. Often the materials are supplied by manufacturers.
Samples	Free tastes or smells of items are given to customers.
Contests	Customers compete for prizes by completing a contest (game), such as a crossword puzzle, a slogan, or a football lottery. Winning is at least partially based on a correct answer (skill).
Sweepstakes	Similar to a contest, except that participants merely fill out application forms and the winner is picked at random (chance). No skill is involved. Direct-mail retailers use this tool quite often.
Prizes	The store gives prizes or premiums, such as glasses or silverware, immediately. Usually one piece of a set is obtained with each purchase. Prizes usually free or at minimum cost.
Referral gifts	Gifts are given to current customers when they bring in new customers.
Matchbooks, pens, calendars, shopping bags, and so on	Items that contain the store's name are given to customers.
Skywriting	Attention-getting messages are printed in the sky or pulled behind aircraft.

Source: Reprinted with permission of Macmillan Publishing Co., Inc. from *Retail Management* by Barry Berman and Joel R. Evans. Copyright © 1979 by Macmillan Publishing Co., Inc.

2. In mature markets, sales promotions attract primarily deal-prone consumers rather than new, long-term buyers.

3. Sales promotion does not tend to attract brand-loyal consumers.

4. Advertising appears to be capable of increasing the "prime franchise" of a brand.

Other evidence indicates that sales promotion can build a stronger "consumer franchise" if used properly.[10] To do so, the sales promotion must include a selling message along with the promotional deal.

The best use of sales promotion appears to be in conjunction with advertising. One study showed that point-of-purchase displays produced 15 percent more sales when they were related to television advertising. Further, heavy distribution of free samples combined with television advertising proved more successful than either television alone or television with coupons in introducing a product.[11]

Sales promotions make three basic contributions to retailing strategy:[12]

- **Communication.** They gain attention and usually provide information that may lead the consumer to the product.

- **Incentive.** They incorporate some concession, inducement, or contribution designed to represent value to the receiver.

- **Invitation.** They include a distinct invitation to engage in the transaction now.

To achieve these potential contributions of sales promotion, the retailer needs a systematic, logical approach. The following steps are suggested, and each is briefly discussed below:

1. Review all existing information and plans.

2. Determine sales promotion objectives.

3. Analyze sales promotion alternatives.

4. Select sales promotion tools.

5. Construct sales promotion program.

6. Formulate sales promotion budget.

7. Coordinate with other retailing strategy.

8. Pretest the program.

9. Prepare the final plan and implement it.

10. Monitor and adapt.

Review All Existing Information and Plans

As with all other retailing strategies, sales promotion strategy must be anchored to the existing situation and be compatible with other strategic plans. Although many factors are important, competitive sales promotion activity and advertising strategy are of particular significance. Competitors' heavy use of a particular sales promotion tool, such as coupons or stamps, might severely damage a retailer's market share unless the retailer takes defensive actions. These defensive actions may influence the sales promotion strategy.

Although all sales promotion strategy must be compatible with advertising strategy, it is almost mandatory to use advertising in conjunction with certain sales promotion programs to enhance the probability of success. Sales promotion programs involving elements such as coupons, sweepstakes, and contests, for example, are likely to have little impact without advertising assistance.

Determine Sales Promotion Objectives

Sales promotion objectives must be derived from the communications and promotion objectives, which are in turn derived from the basic retailing objectives.

In general, the sales promotion objectives are usually oriented toward increasing short-run sales, maintaining customer loyalty, supplementing other communications tools, or emphasizing the novelty of an offering.[13] Longer-term objectives are used by some retailers (see Strategy in Action 17.2). To operationalize these general objectives, the retailer has to translate them into more specific objectives, such as:

- Encourage purchase of larger units.

- Encourage purchase of multiple units.

- Encourage trial among nonusers.

- Encourage trial by users of competitive brands.

- Stimulate impulse purchases.

- Increase patronage by regular customers.

- Bolster weak departments.

Review Sales Promotion Alternatives

Although this step may appear rather mundane to the experienced retailer, all retailers should conscientiously perform this review. New variations may be available or old, forgotten alternatives may now be feasible. (The basic types of sales promotion alternatives are shown in Table 17.6).

Select the Sales Promotion Tools

The retailer should now be in a position to undertake Step 4, the tentative selection of the specific sales promotion tools to use. The key criterion for selection is that *the tools selected must have the potential to accomplish the stated objectives*. If the objective is to encourage the purchase of larger units, the tools most appropriate are coupons and cents-off offers on large units. Other critical factors to take into account include the type of market, competitive activity, and the cost-effectiveness of each tool.

Construct the Sales Promotion Program

Since each sales promotion tool is somewhat unique, the specific details of program construction vary widely. The five-step process discussed below is primarily for programs involving monetary incentive. The key decisions involve determining the size of the incentive, conditions for participation, distribution vehicle, duration of program, and timing of program.[14]

STRATEGY IN ACTION 17.2

Sales Promotion: Special Events

Sales promotion has traditionally been identified as a short-term "shot in the arm" for retailers—
something to generate immediate interest. More recently, though, retailers are viewing sales
promotion as an investment that will generate revenue over time. Sales promotion is taking on
more of a long-term strategic role within the retailer's promotional mix.

Bloomingdale's, part of the Federated chain of department stores, has been an innovator in
orchestrating promotionally oriented "sales events." Its management believes the sales promotion
event should be entertaining and have long-term image and patronage impact. One of Bloomingdale's events was entitled "China: Heralding the Dawn of a New Era." This $10 million, 1980
theme consisted of numerous activities and special products, many designed specifically for
Bloomingdale's. Displays, exhibits, designed graphics, merchandise imported from China, and do-
mestically made merchandise using Chinese materials were all part of the sales promotion event.
Moreover, the 1980 Christmas catalog was photographed using China as background settings.

The average percentage spent on special events is only 2 percent of the total promotion
budget for retailers. However, this percentage is beginning to grow as retailers see the long-term
value of these events. A further advantage over other forms of promotion is that local media will
often give space or time to newsworthy promotional events, thereby adding to their impact.

Source: "How Retailers Promote, Entertain," pp. 47–48. Reprinted with permission from the 6 April 1981 issue of *Advertising Age.*
Copyright 1981 by Crain Communications, Inc.

Determine Size of Incentive. The retailer should consider the incentive
sizes that lead to accomplishing the objectives of the program and should
choose the incentive size that is most *cost-effective.* Assuming a fifteen-
cents-off coupon will have a greater response rate than a five-cents-off coupon, the fifteen-cents-off coupon would need a response rate three times as
large to have the same cost-effectiveness. Unfortunately, there are no concrete guidelines to determining the "best" incentive size. The retailer's only
recourse is to maintain accurate records of the cost and response rates of
different sales promotion activities. When sufficient data are available, the
retailer should be able to correlate the data to gain insight into the cost-
effectiveness of various incentive levels.

Determine Conditions for Participation. Conditions for participation
should be established to attract customers in the promotion's target group
and to discourage those who are not (that is, those who are not likely to
become users). Examples of conditions include the requiring of box tops or
labels, filling out an application at the store, valid driver's license, and the
like.

Determine Distribution Vehicle. The retailer must decide how to make the
sales promotion available to the target market. Coupons can be distributed in
a product's package (called in-packs), in the store, in the mail, and in the

advertising vehicle. Each of these vehicles reaches a different audience and has different costs. In-packs normally reach only the users of the product, whereas direct mail can reach anyone, including nonusers, but at a higher cost.

Determine Duration of the Program. The optimal duration of many sales promotion programs appears to be the length of the average purchase or patronage cycle.[15] Shorter duration does not give all the prospects an opportunity to be exposed to the promotion. Longer durations cause the deal to lose some impact, may foster the view that the deal is a permanent price concession, and may raise questions about the brand's quality or store image.

Determine Timing of Program. A definite starting date should be determined. A detailed schedule of activities for each sales promotion program should be carefully constructed to permit coordination of supply and production needs, the sales force, distribution, and other communication tools. A summary schedule or calendar such as the one shown in Fig. 15.5, that includes all sales promotion and advertising programs, should be constructed.

Formulate Sales Promotion Budget

The retailer should already have had a general idea of budgetary constraints. Reasonably accurate costs for a given sales promotion program can now be calculated. Sales promotion programs have two basic cost components: *incentive costs* (costs of premium or cents-off) and *administrative costs* (all other costs such as printing, mailing, promotion, supplies, and additional labor). The cost of a program can be calculated using the following formula:

$$C_{sp} = C_a + (C_i \times U_e),$$

where:

C_{sp} = cost of sales promotion program
C_a = administrative costs
C_i = incentive costs
U_e = expected number of units that will be redeemed or sold.

Consider a retailer who places a coupon in the daily newspaper. If the administrative costs were $500, the coupon was for $2 off, and 500 coupon redemptions were expected, the total cost would be $1,500 ($500 + $2 × 500 units).

Note that the above formula is designed primarily for sales promotion programs that involve some form of monetary incentive. It can also be used for other types of promotion, such as demonstrations. For these, the $(C_i \times U_e)$ component is zero.

If the sales promotion cost is within the budgetary constraints, the retailer can proceed with further planning and implementation. If the cost exceeds the budgetary limitations, the specific sales promotion program or the total promotion budget will have to be reviewed and possibly revised.

Coordinate with Other Marketing Strategy

The sales promotion obviously does not exist in a vacuum; each sales promotion program must be coordinated with other sales promotion programs as well as with the merchandise, price, location, advertising, personal selling, and store image strategies to achieve desired results. The merchandise must be available, the sales promotion must not permanently damage the price structure, the timing with advertising must be right, the sales force must be aware of the program, the program must not be detrimental to the store image, and the program should not cannibalize future sales.

A large, single-unit sporting goods retailer once used a sales promotion/advertising program to help offset cash-flow problems. The program consisted of five to ten off-retail coupons in the newspaper. The coupons appeared each week on Friday, Saturday, and Sunday. At first, this program was quite successful. As the program continued, however, certain undesirable characteristics began to become apparent, primarily with price and store image. The near-continual deals caused many consumers to believe that regular prices must be too high, which damaged the overall store image and hurt the sales of items not on special.

Pretest the Program

Whenever possible, sales promotion programs should be pretested to determine if the tools are appropriate, the size of the incentive is optimal, and the method of presentation is efficient. Note that pretesting can focus only on short-run considerations of effectiveness; the long-run impact on image and profits must normally be judged subjectively. Multiunit retailers can run trial tests for a limited geographical area before launching a full-scale program. Single-unit retailers can ask a group of consumers to rank or rate alternative deals. For programs that have been used previously, an analysis of previous effectiveness can often replace the pretesting.

Pretesting manufacturer-initiated programs is seldom possible, but manufacturer-initiated programs are seldom forced on the retailer. Retailers always have the option to refuse cooperation. Again, the key issue is the impact on the retailer's image and profits. Many retailers are unhappy with the choice of redeeming manufacturer coupons. For some it is a losing proposition. Many retailers would suffer customer wrath, however, if they refused to honor these coupons.

Prepare the Final Plan and Implement It

The retailer is now in a position to collect all of the information and plans generated by this strategic process into the final plan. This final plan should be written and should contain sufficient details to guide those responsible for implementation.

Monitor and Adapt

Each sales promotion should be monitored and evaluated so that appropriate adaptations in future programs can be made. For most sales promotion programs, the retailer can monitor sales, market share, or store traffic. The monitored factor can be evaluated by comparing data before, during, and after the program. When results are less than satisfactory, the retailer might want to interview a sample of consumers to find out why the program was not attractive. Particular attention should be devoted to the after-promotion period. If the promotion merely shifted sales from the after-promotion period to the promotion period, it may not be considered successful, depending on the promotion's objectives.

KEY CONCEPTS

Sales-force strategy	Approach
Self-service	Merchandise approach
Full service	Service approach
Transaction processing	Presentation
Routine selling	Handling objections
Creative selling	Closing the sale
Workload versus productivity	Follow-up
Personal selling process	Suggestion selling
Prospecting	Sales promotion strategy
Qualifying	Sales promotion objectives
In-store prospecting and qualifying	Sales promotion programs
Pre-approach	

REVIEW QUESTIONS

1. Develop the strategic sales-force planning process.
2. Discuss the major strengths and limitations of maintaining a retail sales force.
3. Contrast the workload and productivity approaches for determining the size of the sales force.
4. Develop the strategic personal selling process.
5. Contrast prospecting and qualifying.
6. Discuss the role of sales promotion in the overall communication strategy.
7. Develop the strategic sales promotion planning process.
8. Discuss various types of sales promotion objectives.
9. Discuss the factors involved in constructing a sales promotion program.
10. Discuss sales promotion budget formulation.

LEARNING EXERCISES

1. Choose a local retailer that emphasizes a full-service sales force. Evaluate the possibilities for greater use of self-service.

2. On your next five purchases, analyze the salespeople's use of suggestion selling. If it was not used, could it have been?

3. Cite examples of several sales promotions being carried out by local retailers and discuss the possible objectives, advantages, limitations, and potential effectiveness of each.

DECISION SITUATION 17.1: **ATHLETIC OUTFITTERS III**

On a recent trip to visit relatives, the owner of Athletic Outfitters visited a sporting goods store. On the day he visited, the store was conducting a fishing clinic. Several tournament fishermen were demonstrating and discussing techniques that they used successfully. In a discussion with the owner he discovered that various fishing tackle manufacturers would supply the "experts" for a nominal fee. He also discovered that these demonstration days resulted in very high sales volume.

Although Athletic Outfitters carried little fishing equipment, the owner wondered if he could successfully use the "clinic technique."

QUESTIONS

1. Would you recommend the demonstration for Athletic Outfitters? Why or why not?

2. What types of demonstrations would you recommend? How would you schedule them?

3. Could a technique other than live demonstrations be used? Along what lines?

4. What impact would demonstrations have on the store's image?

DECISION SITUATION 17.2: **CHEVROLET CITY**

Jim Eldon, the owner of Chevrolet City, is considering what actions he should take as the result of a conversation with a local farmer. Jim had asked the farmer why all of his trucks were GMC trucks. The farmer told him that he had tried to buy trucks at Chevrolet City but the salesperson did not seem interested in talking to him. The farmer indicated that only a few months ago he had visited Chevrolet City to shop for a large grain truck and two pickup trucks. When he told a salesperson that he wanted to look at trucks, he was directed to the used-truck lot.

Jim realized what had occurred but did not know how to handle the problem. His salespeople were paid only a commission and had to be productive to earn a good salary. They had to decide quickly many things about a customer, including the type of vehicle a customer could afford. They had read the farmer wrong. He did not have the appearance of a reasonably wealthy individual. Few would guess that he was on the board of the local bank and farmed several thousand acres of land. Jim estimated that the farmer spent $75,000 to $100,000 on trucks each year.

QUESTIONS

1. What can Jim do to get the farmer's business?

2. What should he say to the sales manager and the salespeople?

3. How can an auto retailer do prospecting?

NOTES

1. David D. Seltz, *Handbook of Innovative Marketing Techniques* (Reading, Mass.: Addison-Wesley, 1981), p. 115.

2. Walter J. Semlow, "How Many Salesmen Do You Need?," *Harvard Business Review*, May–June 1959, pp. 126–132; Henry C. Lucas, Jr., Charles B. Weinbert, and Kenneth W. Clowes, "Sales Response as a Function of Territorial Potential and Sales Representative Workload," *Journal of Marketing Research*, August 1975, pp. 298–305; Walter J. Talley, "How to Design Sales Territories," *Journal of Marketing*, January 1961, pp. 7–13.

3. John O. McClain and L. Joseph Thomas, *Operations Management* (Englewood Cliffs, N.J.: Prentice-Hall, 1980), pp. 563–572.

4. *Merchandising and Operating Results of 1979* (New York: Financial Executives Division, National Retail Merchants Association, 1980).

5. Stephen P. Cron, "Control of Retail Selling Costs," *Retail Control*, August 1976, p. 60.

6. C. Winston Borgen, *Learning Experiences in Retailing* (Pacific Palisades, Calif.: Goodyear Publishing Company, 1976), p. 294.

7. Gerald L. Manning and Barry L. Reece, *Selling Today* (Dubuque, Iowa: William C. Brown, 1980), pp. 355–358.

8. J. Ronald Carey, Steven H. Clicque, Barbara A. Leighton, and Frank Milton, "A Test of Positive Reinforcement of Customers," *Journal of Marketing*, October 1976, pp. 98–100.

9. Robert George Brown, "Sales Response to Promotions and Advertising," *Journal of Advertising Research*, August 1974, pp. 36–37.

10. Roger A. Strang, Robert M. Prentice, and Alden G. Clayton, *The Relationship Between Advertising and Promotion in Brand Strategy* (Cambridge, Mass.: Marketing Science Institute, 1975), Chapter 5.

11. Roger A. Strang, "Sales Promotion—Fast Growth, Faulty Management," *Harvard Business Review*, July–August 1976, p. 124.

12. Philip Kotler, *Marketing Management* (Englewood Cliffs, N.J.: Prentice-Hall, 1980), p. 527.

13. Barry Berman and Joel R. Evans, *Retail Management* (New York: Macmillan, 1979), p. 444.

14. Kotler, *op. cit.*, pp. 531–532.

15. Arthur Stern, "Measuring the Effectiveness of Package Goods Promotion Strategies," paper presented at a meeting of the Association of National Advertisers, Glen Cove, N.Y., February 1978.

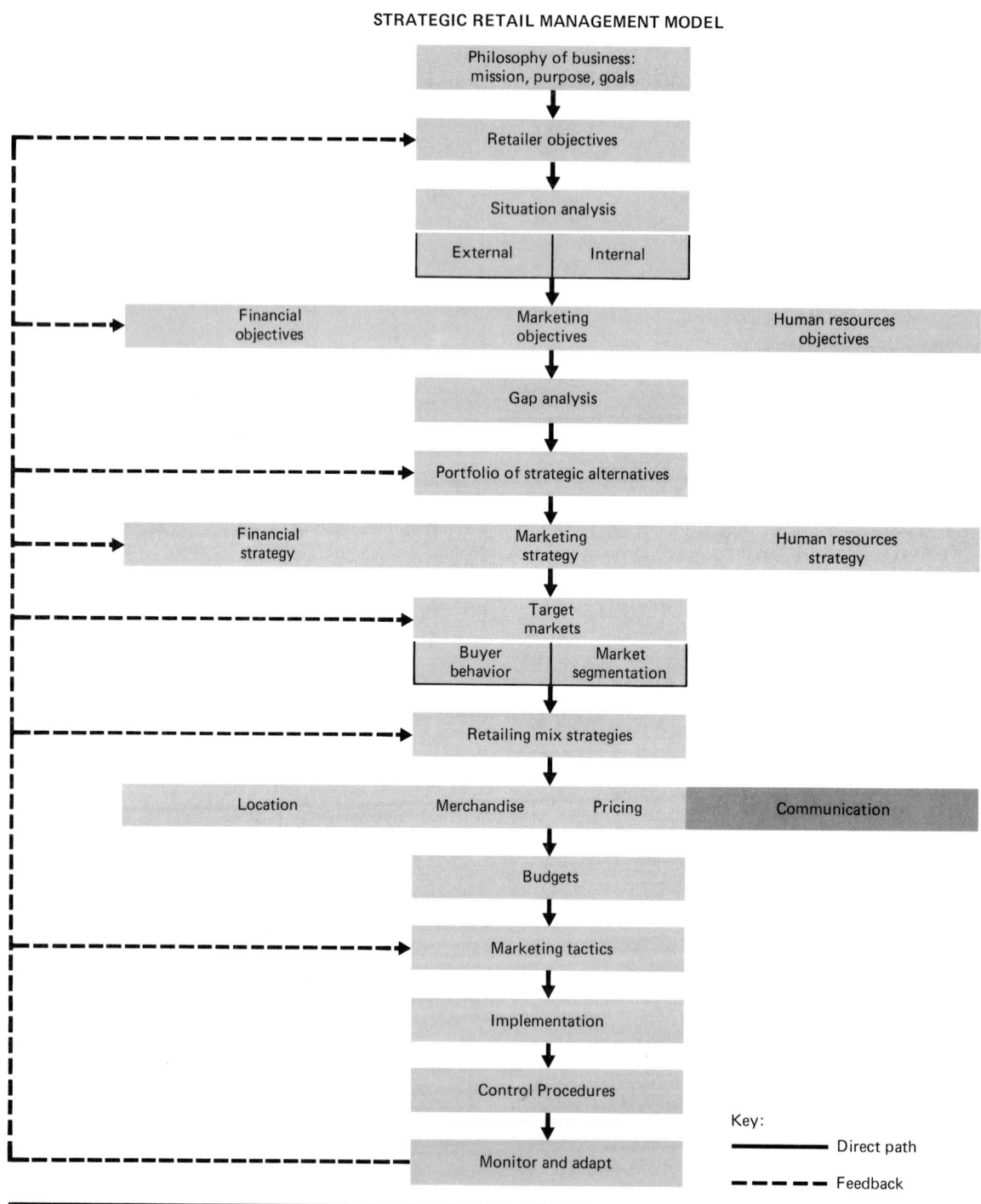

STRATEGIC RETAIL MANAGEMENT MODEL

Philosophy of business:
mission, purpose, goals

Retailer objectives

Situation analysis

| External | Internal |

Financial objectives — Marketing objectives — Human resources objectives

Gap analysis

Portfolio of strategic alternatives

Financial strategy — Marketing strategy — Human resources strategy

Target markets

| Buyer behavior | Market segmentation |

Retailing mix strategies

Location — Merchandise — Pricing — Communication

Budgets

Marketing tactics

Implementation

Control Procedures

Monitor and adapt

Key:
——————— Direct path
– – – – – Feedback

Chapter 18
Atmosphere and Layout Decisions

LEARNING OBJECTIVES

1. To understand the interrelationships of store design, atmosphere, and store image.

2. To understand and learn the major steps and considerations involved in strategic atmosphere and layout planning.

INTRODUCTION

The primary focus of this chapter is on creating a store atmosphere by carefully blending the designs for the store's exterior, interior, layout, and displays.

A retail store's **atmosphere** is the dominant effect created by its design and physical characteristics. **Atmospherics** can be defined as the effort to design the retail store's environment to produce specific emotional effects in buyers that enhance the probability of purchase.[1] Table 18.1 presents the major components of atmosphere.

A store's design and the corresponding atmosphere it creates are important to the retailer for several reasons. First, the store design influences store image through atmosphere, and thus affects the retailer's ability to

Table 18.1
Components of atmosphere

1. *Exterior*
   a. Storefront
   b. Marquee
   c. Entrances
   d. Display windows
   e. Height of building
   f. Size of building
   g. Visibility
   h. Uniqueness
   i. Surrounding stores
   j. Surrounding area
   k. Parking
   l. Congestion

2. *General Interior*
   a. Flooring
   b. Colors
   c. Lighting
   d. Scents, sounds
   e. Fixtures
   f. Wall fixtures
   g. Temperature
   h. Width of aisles
   i. Dressing facilities
   j. Vertical transportation
   k. Dead areas
   l. Personnel
   m. Self-service
   n. Products
   o. Prices (level and manner of displays)
   p. Placement of cash registers
   q. Modernization

3. *Store Layout*
   a. Allocation of floor space for selling, merchandise, personnel, and customers
   b. Product groupings
   c. Traffic flow
   d. Space/product category
   e. Department locations
   f. Arrangements within departments

4. *Interior (Point-of-Purchase) Displays*
   a. Assortment
   b. Theme/setting
   c. Ensemble
   d. Racks and cases
   e. Cut-cases and dump bins
   f. Posters, signs, and cards
   g. Mobiles
   h. Wall decorations
   i. Product positioning
   j. Self-service

Source: Reprinted with permission of Macmillan Publishing Co., Inc. from *Retail Management* by Barry Berman and Joel R. Evans. Copyright © 1979 by Macmillan Publishing Co., Inc.

attract and retain patronage, especially when the target market consists of distinct social classes or lifestyles.[2] Second, the store design provides the environmental context in which the other retailing strategy variables are ultimately offered to the customer. Third, the cost of occupying and operating a physical facility is a major retail expense. Fourth, store design influences the efficiency of retail operations; efficient design can increase selling space, improve customer traffic flow, and facilitate selling of related items. Fifth, store design and atmosphere are excellent tools for achieving a differential competitive advantage, especially in trades where merchandise and/or price differences are small.[3]

The strategic atmosphere and layout decision model is presented in Fig. 18.1. The six basic steps are the following:

1. Review all existing information and plans.

2. Define atmosphere requirements.

3. Design store exterior.

4. Design store interior.

5. Devise interior display.

6. Monitor and adapt.

These steps can help the retailer answer the following questions: (1) Who is the target market? (2) What is the target market seeking from the buying experience? (3) Which atmosphere variables provide what customers are seeking? and (4) Does the resulting atmosphere compete effectively with competitors' atmospheres?[4]

REVIEW ALL EXISTING INFORMATION AND PLANS

The retailer should first review the *target market definition* and all that he or she knows about the target customers. It is especially critical to determine the kind of atmosphere in which customers prefer to be exposed to specific kinds of merchandise. Customers buying expensive merchandise such as furs or jewelry, for example, usually expect an "expensive" atmosphere, such as that portrayed by Neiman Marcus. Next, the retailer should review the overall *desired store image* and design the atmosphere to be compatible with and to enhance that image and all of its components. Table 18.2 lists some components of store image.

To enhance the overall store image, the retailer must review the strategic plans for all of the other *retailing mix elements*. The store's atmosphere must be compatible with retailing mix elements; any conflicts reduce the likelihood of customer purchases.

Figure 18.2 highlights the relationship between atmosphere and the retailing mix. Consider a potential customer who develops positive expecta-

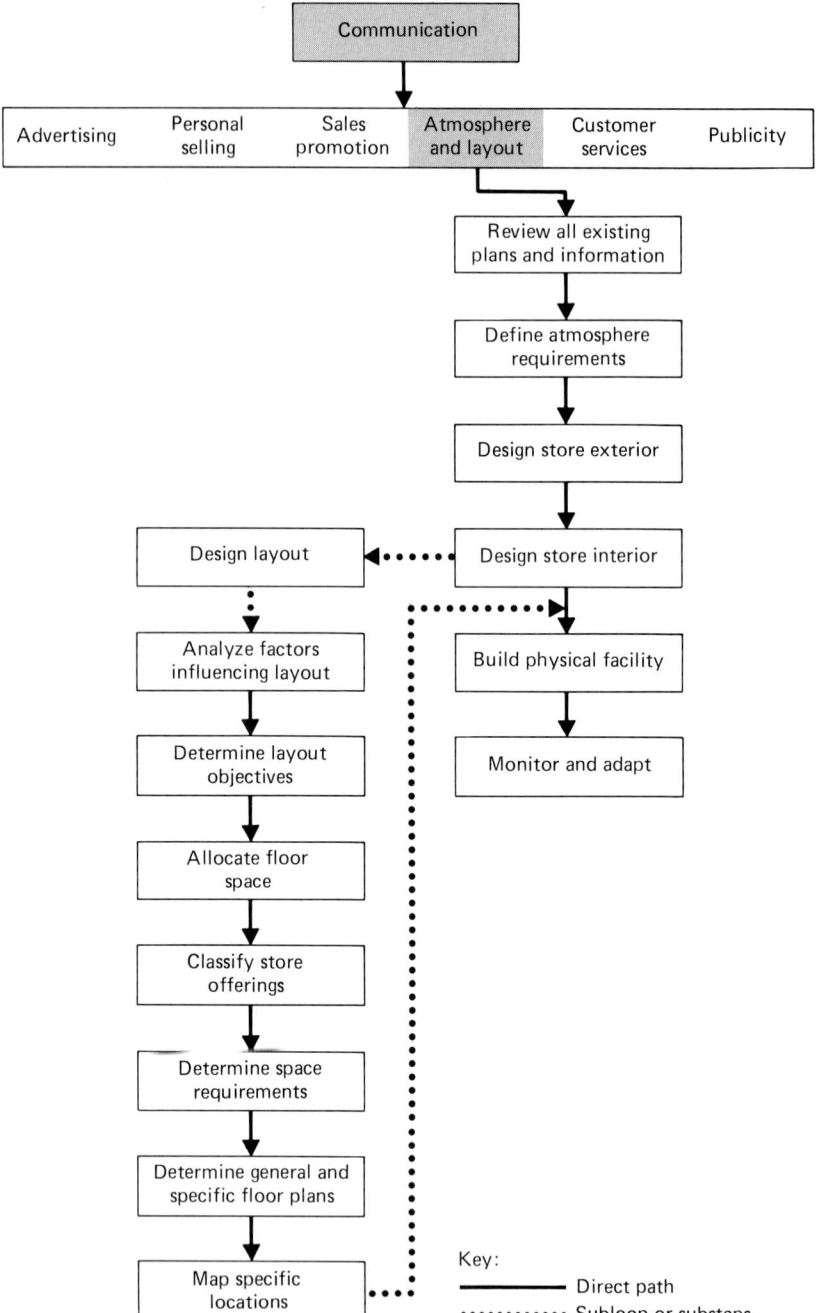

Figure 18.1
Atmosphere and layout decision model

Table 18.2
The dimensions and components of store image attributes

DIMENSION	COMPONENT	DIMENSION	COMPONENT
Merchandise	Quality	Physical facilities	Cleanliness
	Selection		Store layout
	Style		Shopping ease
	Price		Attractiveness
Service	Lay-away plan	Convenience	Location
	Sales personnel		Parking
	Easy return	Promotion	Advertising
	Credit	Store atmosphere	Congeniality
	Delivery	Institutional	Store reputation
Clientele	Customers	Post-transaction	Satisfaction

Source: R. Hansen and T. Deutscher, "An Empirical Investigation of Attribute Importance in Retail Store Selection." Reprinted with permission from *Journal of Retailing* Vol. 53, no. 4, Winter 1977–78, pp. 59–73.

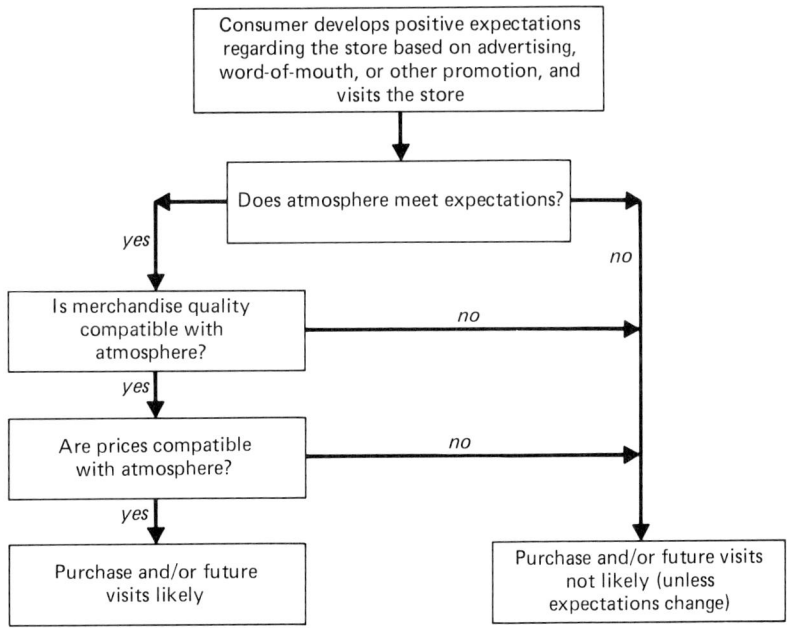

Figure 18.2
The interaction of atmosphere and the retailing mix elements

tions regarding a retail store (primarily because of advertising and word-of-mouth influence) and decides to visit the store. Upon arriving at the store the customer first makes a conscious or subconscious evaluation of whether the store's atmosphere is consistent with his or her expectations. If the expectations and atmosphere are inconsistent (the customer expects a modern, high-prestige, high-quality store but finds a drab, run-down, poorly lit outlet), the customer is unlikely to purchase merchandise or return again. If expectations and atmosphere are consistent, the customer might make a second evaluation, such as between atmosphere and merchandise quality. Inconsistencies between atmosphere and merchandise quality are likely to lead to no purchases and no return visits. If atmosphere and merchandise quality are consistent, however, the customer may make a third evaluation, comparing atmosphere and prices. Again, any inconsistencies are likely to lead to no purchases. The possibility of purchases and/or repeat visits will exist only if the atmosphere is consistent and compatible with all retailing mix elements. From this perspective, atmosphere is an integral part of overall strategic planning.

DEFINE ATMOSPHERE REQUIREMENTS

The retailer must decide exactly what is needed from the atmosphere to create the desired image and competitive position. Since the store image created by atmosphere is the total stimulus inputs to customers, the retailer must consider each of the five sensory reactions.[5]

Scent Considerations

Odor can have a strong influence on store image. Many retailers can benefit from introducing and emphasizing specific smells. Many specialty eating establishments, such as bakeries, coffee houses, and stores specializing in fresh-roasted nuts, benefit from careful placement of fans and blowers, especially when targeting pedestrian traffic. Although no store should smell "bad," retailers must also be careful to avoid contradictory scents. A prestigious clothing store, for example, should avoid odors such as of popcorn and grease.

Sound Considerations

Sound can either enhance or detract from a store's image. Most exclusive shops try to eliminate almost all extraneous sound by using devices such as heavy carpeting, multiple partitions, low ceilings, and a low-key, hushed tone from salespeople. Other retailers, such as teen shops, normally desire a much greater noise level, perhaps including recordings of current popular music. Still other retailers can benefit from extraneous sounds; for example, freight salvage stores might benefit from sounds such as switching trains and semi-trailer trucks.

**Touch
Considerations**

Many types of merchandise can be sold best after they have been touched and handled. Touch is especially important for selling products when their use involves touch, such as clothing, automobiles, toys, and tools. Some retailers discourage handling with signs like "Touch at your own risk." Unfortunately, these signs do not discourage the primary danger—young children—and often do discourage the primary target—adults.

**Sight
Considerations**

Sight considerations can be viewed as **visual merchandising,** which is a combination of every factor that can affect the consumer's visual perception of the store. Retailers should use every square inch of space (both inside and outside the store) to sell the company and its merchandise to the consumer; customers should be exposed to visual merchandising every moment they are in the store. Retailers too often overlook opportunities for visual merchandising in traditional nonselling areas, such as elevators, credit departments, personnel departments, and restrooms. The retailer might consider putting samples of carpet, wallpaper, fabrics, or other products in elevators, or toiletry and cosmetic samples in restrooms.

Colors and lighting are of paramount importance for sight considerations. Each can be used to help create specific moods and atmospheres and can be used to create the effect of separating departments.

Colors vary in their symbolic communication value. Cool colors such as lighter greens and pastels suggest relaxation, gold and silver can suggest luxury, warm colors such as red and yellows tend to be more stimulating, and darker colors suggest richness. Studies have indicated that higher socioeconomic groups prefer delicate hues, whereas lower socioeconomic groups prefer bright, pure hues.[6]

For many years, retailers emphasized equal lighting distribution throughout the store. Many retailers are now highlighting aisles, departments, shelves, displays, and specific products by carefully selecting and blending lighting types, intensity, and arrangements.

Another critical sight consideration is cleanliness. Few retail stores, especially supermarkets, can survive without being clean.[7] In fact, many supermarkets attempt to emphasize cleanliness—for instance, by devoting special attention to the produce department—to help maintain an image of freshness, newness, and health.

**Taste
Considerations**

Perhaps the best example of utilizing taste is in ice cream parlors, where customers are often permitted small samples of various flavors before selecting their purchase. Supermarkets and other retailers can focus on taste with cooking demonstrations and free samples.

A retailer must consider each of the stimulus factors we discussed. He or she should avoid the negative possibilities of each and make the most of the positive aspects. One retailer specializing in western clothing stated in his strategy plans the general requirement that the overall atmosphere must be "western" and appeal to all five senses. Tactics were designed as follows:

- *Scent:* the smells of leather and new blue jeans
- *Sound:* country-and-western music piped in
- *Touch:* all merchandise available for customer handling, including boots; salespeople trained to encourage customers to handle merchandise
- *Sight:* leather products arranged throughout the store to help achieve the scent, touch, and sight objectives; many western pictures and products (such as branding irons) displayed; displays constructed of rough, unfinished wood; partitions arranged to create simulated corrals; salespeople wearing store's products
- *Taste:* licorice twists, one cent each

Note that this retailer's atmosphere was successful from both an atmospheric and a functional standpoint.

STRATEGY IN ACTION 18.1

Supermarket Atmospherics

Sunshine beaming through a skylight-like construction in a lowered ceiling appears to illuminate the produce bins.

A trellis hung with potted houseplants and stocked with colorful cut flowers frames the dairy aisle, prompting produce shoppers to pause and cast an admiring look, if not head their carts, that way.

Next to a display of seafood on ice, lobsters squirm in a tank eye level to a small child.

There's a lot to see and enjoy in the Grand Union on Barnum Road in Stratford, Connecticut. The store is the latest version in the chain's continuous design program and "not a permanent model," stresses Milton Glaser, the designer.

"We're approaching the supermarket as if it had no history," Glaser says. After redesigning *L'Express,* the French newsmagazine, he was asked if he knew anything about supermarkets by its owner, Sir James Goldsmith, also CEO of Cavenham Holdings, Grand Union's British parent company. The co-author of *The Underground Gourmet* and designer of the Windows on the World restaurant at New York's World Trade Center accepted Sir James' challenge. "We want to make food shopping more entertaining and less oppressive," Glaser says, referring to the traditional arrangement of the supermarket corridors.

The Stratford store isn't just a replica of Glaser's first effort at the Wyckoff, N.J., Grand Union, particularly in layout. A wide center aisle features foreign foods near the front of the store and a kitchen shop in the back, breaking up the usual arrangement of evenly spaced aisles. In one corner, near the dairy section, is an "island" where fresh cheeses are cut to order and crackers logically merchandised overhead.

"We've treated space organically," Glaser explains, pointing out that "compression and expansion create areas of kinetic opportunity" as opposed to the "oppression" of unvarying corridors.

He says he drew on remembrances of the "kinetic excitement" he experienced as a youth growing up in Bologna, Italy, where the winding streets date back to the Middle Ages.

Asked about marketing studies, the food maven and social observer responded with a blank look. Then he spoke eloquently from his own experience of the "explosion of interest in food in the last decade" and how "obsessed" people have become with "all aspects of food" including gourmet home cooking, cooking classes and shopping.

The Grand Union redo, which involves advertising and packaging as well as promotion, merchandising and display, now involves 15 to 20 people. In line with Glaser's latest thinking, they may well soon be considering the supermarket as "a gathering place for social interaction," possibly incorporating community bulletin boards and cooking classes.

Although Grand Union officials are apparently pleased with the design, they declined to comment on the performance of the remodeled stores. One customer, however, is struck by its "beautiful fruit and vegetables" which are "cared for differently now" by its produce staff. "They're so proud of their new produce department that they walk around like little roosters," she says.

So far, the most prominent aspects of the Glaser design are the interior decor and the customer service departments—baker, butcher, deli, fish, and cheese—with a bonus in the Stratford store of pockets of spatial excitement such as a plant arbor between the produce area and the dairy aisle.

Blond butcher block paneling warms up the produce department, tile walls hung with wire baskets give atmosphere to the fish market, and in the ceiling over the checkout counters, spelled out in old-fashioned script, are the words, "clean, fresh, and good."

Since the Stratford Grand Union was unveiled, the Dobbs Ferry, New York, store and one in New York City have received some aspects of the Glaser makeover.

DESIGN STORE EXTERIOR

The importance of the store exterior is captured in the following:

> The first thing the public sees when approaching a store is its exterior facade; this is the store's permanent advertisement. A properly designed store exterior is informative; it conveys to the customer an impression about the store. Just by looking at the facade, he not only recognizes that this is a retail store, but he can also interpret from the design the caliber and type of merchandise sold within. The entire building concept should communicate whether it is a drug store, a supermarket, a furniture outlet, a couturier shop, or a full-line department store. And it should do so without requiring any intricate thought process on the part of passers-by.[8]

The major exterior features were listed in Table 18.1. Because of the infinite variety of exterior possibilities, retailers without proven expertise in this area should consider obtaining the services of an experienced architect.

There is, however, something only the retailer can do: Decide what the exterior should contribute to the desired store image and atmosphere. Perhaps the most fundamental contribution of the store exterior is to *facilitate*

Table 18.3
Potential benefits of a store's exterior

1. *Visible:* Is the exterior readily visible to vehicular or pedestrian traffic, whichever is the target?

2. *Unique:* Does the exterior need to be different from all other retail stores?

3. *Distinctive:* Does the exterior need to stand out from the surrounding stores or blend in?

4. *Consistent:* For multiunit retailers, does each unit need to be consistent or identical to all other units?

5. *Identity:* Does the exterior identify the type of merchandise inside?

6. *Stability:* Does the exterior give the impression of stability and permanence?

7. *Protection:* Does the exterior protect the interior from natural elements, especially sun damage?

8. *Cost:* Will the exterior design have reasonable construction *and* maintenance costs?

9. *Modern versus traditional:* Does the exterior need to portray a modern, progressive image or a traditional, conservative image?

10. *Excitement versus relaxation:* Does the exterior (especially colors) create a feeling of excitement and movement or one of relaxation, quiet, and serenity?

Figure 18.3
Examples of store exteriors

identification. In addition, the retailer should decide which of the benefits shown in Table 18.3 should be supplied by the exterior design and see that the architect's rendering is appropriate. Look at the store fronts shown in Fig. 18.3 to see how many of the benefits each store front possesses.

DESIGN STORE INTERIOR

The exterior and the interior of a retail store must be complementary and present a sense of oneness. The interior must deliver what the exterior has promised. The interior must reinforce customers' impressions about the type and characteristics of the store. Further, all design elements, both inside and out, should reflect the merchandise being offered.

General Considerations

Many interior design elements such as floors, walls, ceilings, and colors are readily apparent. As mentioned earlier, the retailer must see that these elements are designed to complement the merchandise. Other interior elements are described briefly below.

Fixtures and Equipment. These terms are often used interchangeably by retailers. However, a **fixture** is "any durable good that the retailer uses to display, store, protect, or sell merchandise."[9] Examples are shelves, counters, gondolas, cases, cabinets, racks, tables, and freezers (see Fig. 18.4). On the other hand, **equipment** is "any durable good used in or outside the store to facilitate both retail selling and non-selling activities."[10] Examples of equipment are cash registers, delivery trucks, elevators, escalators, and air-conditioning units (see Fig. 18.5). Factors to consider in selecting fixtures and equipment include consistency with customer expectations, degree of self-service, merchandise protection, display effectiveness, initial cost, maintenance cost, and flexibility.

Lighting. Lighting should achieve a twofold objective for the retailer: present merchandise effectively and provide the desired atmosphere. These objectives can be attained by appealing to both the physical and the psychological properties of human vision. The three basic functions of lighting that can be used as tools are *illumination, color rendition,* and *provision of contrasts* through intentional variation of intensities.[11] Table 18.4 presents several lighting tips for specific merchandise.

Aisle Width. Aisle width can have a large impact on atmosphere, especially as it pertains to crowding.[12] Wide, uncrowded aisles tend to foster a more prestigious and/or relaxed atmosphere. They are generally more appropriate when the retailer offers shopping goods and extensive service from the sales force. Conversely, relatively narrow and crowded aisles tend to foster a busy atmosphere and can be more interesting to consumers. Narrow aisles are generally more appropriate for discount-oriented retailers who emphasize self-service.

Dressing Rooms. Although not seen directly from the sales floor, dressing room facilities can have a large impact on a store's atmosphere. The decor used in the dressing rooms must be an extension of the store's decor, both physically and psychologically. The retailer should avoid drab, coffinlike boxes with faded mirrors and no place to hang clothing.

Vertical Transportation. Vertical transportation must be provided in multistory stores. The basic options are stairs, elevators, and escalators. Many larger retailers offer a combination of all three. Whatever the mode,

Figure 18.4
Examples of store fixtures
Photos courtesy of Sears, Roebuck and Co.

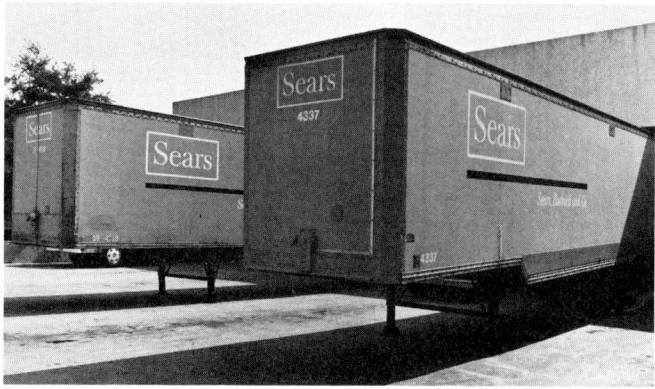

Figure 18.5
Examples of store equipment
Photos courtesy of Sears, Roebuck and Co.

Table 18.4
Lighting tips for specific merchandise

1. Use large area lighting fixtures plus incandescent downlighting to avoid heavy shadows when displaying major appliances and furniture.

2. Use general diffuse lighting accented with point-type spotlights to emphasize the beauty of china, glass, home accessories, and giftware.

3. Bring out the sparkle and luster of hardware, toys, auto accessories, highly polished silver, and other metalware by using a blend of general light and concentrated light sources (spotlights).

4. Use concentrated beams of high-brightness incandescent sources to add brilliant highlights to jewelry, gold and silver, or cut glass.

5. Highlight the colors, patterns, and textures of rugs, carpets, upholstery, heavy drapes, and bedspreads by using oblique directional lighting plus general low-intensity overhead lighting.

6. Heighten the appeal of men's wear by using a cool blend of fluorescent and incandescent, with fluorescent predominating.

7. Highlight women's wear — especially the bright, cheerful colors and patterns — by using natural white fluorescents blended with tungsten-halogen.

8. Bring out the tempting colors of meats, fruits, and vegetables by using fluorescent lamps rich in red energy, including the deluxe cool white type. Cool reflector incandescent lamps may also be used for direct lighting.

Source: Charles B. Elliot, "Pointers on Display Lighting," Small Marketers Aids No. 125 (Washington, D.C.: Small Business Administration, November 1972), p. 5.

vertical transportation should (1) be functional in moving the necessary number of customers; (2) be esthetically pleasing; and (3) perform a selling function such as advertising.

Dead Areas. Dead areas created by beams, corners, restrooms, dressing facilities, and vertical transportation should be investigated for improvement. These areas often can be used for advertising displays, catalogs, vending machines, lounge areas for the elderly, mirrors, and so on.

Store Personnel. Store personnel also affect atmosphere by their appearance, manner, and number. In addition to the relatively obvious factors contributing to a positive atmosphere (politeness, good grooming, knowledge, and unique attire, as shown in Fig. 18.6), several other factors can be important. Since customers tend to respond better to similar individuals, store personnel should closely match the target market. Although salespeople should be similar to customers, salespeople generally should dress the part and have the appearance of store personnel. Another important factor is the relationship between the number of employees and the store's image. It is usually very difficult to create a prestigious image in a self-service atmosphere and, conversely, to create a discount image with a large sales force.

Figure 18.6
Example of store personnel and atmosphere
Photo courtesy of The Equestrian Shop, N. Andover, Massachusetts

Design Layout

A major consideration in designing a store's interior is the layout. The **layout** of a retail store refers to the physical arrangement and specific location of equipment, fixtures, merchandise, aisles, checkout facilities, and sales-supporting area.[13] The *strategic layout process* is organized below in a series of seven basic steps.

1. Analyze factors influencing layout. The retailer should investigate those factors that can influence the layout of the store. Among the more important factors are (1) the size and shape of the available space; (2) location and amount of space needed for permanent installations such as receiving department, elevators, escalators, and the like; (3) amount and characteristics of merchandise to be handled; (4) the type of operation (self-service versus full service); (5) buying habits and other characteristics of target market; (6) nature and number of fixtures and equipment; and (7) retailer's personal preferences.[14]

2. Determine layout objectives. There are three general layout objectives: (1) to provide customer convenience, (2) to utilize space effectively and efficiently, and (3) to expose the customer to the maximum amount of merchandise. Note that there is a basic layout conflict between customer convenience and maximum exposure to merchandise. Each retailer must determine the best compromise.

3. Allocate floor space. Floor space must be allocated among three main functional areas—building functions, nonselling services, and the sales area—and miscellaneous services and departments must also be included. See Table 18.5 for a checklist of these functions.

Building functions are fulfilled by items such as stairs, elevators, escalators, plumbing, electrical conduits, air ducts, and equipment rooms. Usually the building function requirements for space are fairly constant, between 7 percent and 10 percent of the gross area for single-story stores. It may go as high as 20 percent or more for multistory stores.[15]

After building function areas are subtracted, the retailer must strike a proper balance between space allocated to nonselling and selling areas. The retailer wants to obtain the maximum **selling area** without limiting nonselling service areas to a point where they create bottlenecks or handicap the sales function. **Nonselling service areas** can vary from 8 percent to 15 percent of the gross space, depending on the support facilities needed. Most stores average between 70 percent and 85 percent for selling area.[16]

4. Classify the store's offerings. Before the retailer can determine the space requirements and location of various merchandise groups or departments, he or she must decide which products fit into which groups. Table 18.6 summarizes four possible product groupings: functional, purchase motivation, market segment, and storability. Many retail stores actually use a combination of the four types of groupings. To determine the best groupings, the retailer must balance three key considerations: customers' preferences and responses, the retailer's needs, and merchandise characteristics.

Table 18.5
Checklist of functions for retail store space considerations

BUILDING FUNCTIONS

Stairways	Ejector pit
Escalators	Simulated building walls (outdoor shop)
Freight elevator	Vestibules
Passenger elevator	Janitor closets
Building walls	Flues
Switchgear room	Sliding door closet (enclosed mall)
Toilets	Public telephones
Meter room	Refrigerated can storage
Passageways	Telephone equipment and switchboard
Electric closets	Mechanical equipment rooms
Sprinkler shut-off room	Engineer's office
Baler room	

NONSELLING FUNCTIONS

Packing	Dishwashing room
Receiving and marking	Protection, timekeeper, and advertising
Fixture storage	Time-card station
Carpentry, paint, and display shops	Checkroom
Canteen area	Paymaster and vault
Housekeeping	Hospital
Credit office	Office area
Show windows	Female customer lounge
Loading platform and truck dock	Floor receiving and truck storage
Male employees' locker room	Sign shop
Female employees' locker room	General stock room
Employees' cafeteria	Workshop and lamp storage
Employees' cafeteria kitchen	

SALES DEPARTMENT

Dress fabrics and patterns	Fine jewelry and watches
Sewing machines and sewing notions (laces, trimmings, and ribbons)	Silverware and clocks
	Art needle
Linens	Stationery, greeting cards, and religious articles
Domestics and bedding	
Notions and closet accessories	Books
Cosmetics and drug sundries	Umbrellas
Costume jewelry	Neckwear and accessories

SALES DEPARTMENT *(Cont.)*

Handkerchiefs	Pianos and musical instruments
Gifts and flowers	Gift shop
Handbags and small leather goods	Furniture and bedding
Millinery (better and budget)	Unpainted furniture
Gloves (women and children)	Lamps and shades
Intimate apparel	Floor coverings
Pantyhose-hosiery	Curtains, draperies, bedspreads, upholstery fabrics
Women's and children's shoes	
Coats and suits (women, misses, and juniors)	Pillows and hassocks
Dresses (women and misses) (better and budget)	China and glassware
	Housewares
Women's	Major appliances
Juniors	Small electric appliances
Bridal	Radios, TV, records
Maternity shop	Pictures and mirrors
Blouses and sportswear	Curtains, hardware, and accessories
Layette, infants, and toddlers	Wallpaper and paint
Infants' furniture	Sporting goods and adult games
Children's accessories	Cameras
Girls' and boys' wear	Toys and games
Preteen	Candy and food
Furs	Luggage
Men's furnishings	Optical and hearing aids
Men's clothing	Smoke shop
Men's sportswear and casual wear	Beauty salon–barber shop
Boy's clothing and furnishings	Auto accessories and tires
Men's and boy's shoes	Outdoor shop
Men's hats	Restaurant

MISCELLANEOUS SERVICES AND DEPARTMENTS

Community room	Travel bureau
Prescription department	Post office
Lending (circulating) library	Theater tickets
Fur storage and repairs	Handbag and shoe repair
Jewelry repair	Gift-wrapping service
Contract department	

Source: Reprinted with permission of Chain Store Publishing Corp. *Store Planning & Design,* by Adolph Novak (New York: Lebhar-Friedman, 1977), pp. 20–21.

Table 18.6
Types of product groupings

GROUPING	DESCRIPTION	EXAMPLE
Functional	Classification according to consumer and uses.	Shoes, laces, polish versus shirts, ties, cufflinks, tiepins.
Purchase motivation	Classification according to the consumer's way of shopping and the amount of time consumer is willing to devote to shopping.	Impulse and other goods usually purchased quickly are often located near entrances; goods that are stronger draws or require more thought are normally away from entrances, perhaps on third floor.
Market segments	Products appealing to a specific target market are grouped together.	A record store separating merchandise into rock, jazz, classical, rhythm and blues, country and western, and popular music selections.
Storability	Products requiring special handling.	A supermarket has a freezer, refrigerator, and room-temperature sections.

Source: Drawn from Berman and Evans, *Retail Management,* pp. 408–409. Reprinted with permission of Macmillan Publishing Co., Inc. from *Retail Management* by Barry Berman and Joel R. Evans. Copyright © 1979 by Macmillan Publishing Co., Inc.

5. *Determine space requirements.* Now that the store's merchandise is grouped into the desired classifications, the retailer can determine how much space is needed for each merchandise group. Note that there is usually a direct relationship between sales volume of a merchandise group and the space allocated to that group.[17]

There are four basic approaches to determining space requirements. First, the *model stock approach* calls for tabulating the amount of floor space necessary to carry a proper assortment of merchandise for each merchandise group (see Chapter 11 for a discussion of model stock). Suppose a department store retailer calculates the model stock for the dress department to be 6,000 units. Further analysis of proposed display fixtures and aisle requirements shows that ten dresses will require 6 square feet of sales area. The entire model stock will therefore require 3,600 square feet of space (6,000/10 × 6). If the fitting room, adjacent stock area, wrapping, and point-of-purchase display requirements are a total of 800 square feet, the total space required for the dress department would be 4,400 square feet (3,600 + 800).

Second, the *sales productivity approach* calls for assigning floor space on the basis of sales per square foot. Suppose the retailer in the previous example anticipated sales of $6,000,000 for the entire store and has total floor space of 80,000 square feet. The average sales per square foot *for the entire store* is $75. Therefore, if the sales volume for dresses is anticipated at $300,000, the dress department would be allocated 4,000 square feet of floor space ($300,000/$75). In effect, the department is assigned the same percentage of floor space (in this case, 5 percent) as it contributes to sales. Note that this approach results in 400 fewer square feet being allocated to the dress department than in the model stock approach.

Third, the *profit productivity approach* calls for assigning floor space on the basis of gross profit per square foot. In effect, those departments that contribute more to gross profit are allocated proportionally more floor space. If the dress department contributes 5 percent of total gross profit, it would be allocated 5 percent of the floor space, or 4,000 square feet. If it contributes 6 percent of the total gross profit, it would be allocated 6 percent of the floor space, or 4,800 square feet.

Fourth, the retailer can rely on the *experience of the trade*. If dress departments of other stores in similar markets produced average sales of $72 per square foot and sales were forecast at $300,000, the retailer would allocate 4,167 square feet ($300,000/$72) to the dress department.

Regardless of the approach used, the retailer must remember that product groups differ drastically in the amount of space required to produce a given dollar volume of sales. Compact merchandise with a high unit value will deliver far above the store average per square foot; other classifications simply require more space for stocking and display and deliver less sales volume per square foot. In department stores with sales of five to ten million dollars, the median sales per square foot for jewelery is $276.40 but only $45.30 for home furnishings.[18] Table 18.7 presents a typical breakdown of space allocation for a store consisting of 110,000 square feet.

6. *Determine general and specific floor plans.* The **general floor plan** concerns the overall layout of the store; the **specific floor plan** concerns the layout alternatives within the general floor plan.

There are three basic general floor plans.[19] First, the **open plan** specifies a completely open sales space surrounded by perimeter walls (see Fig. 18.7). All fixtures and dividers are kept below eye level for good visibility. Although beneficial for security, staff coverage, and merchandise exposure, it reduces the opportunity for a complete separation of merchandise groupings.

The **enclosed plan** (sometimes called boutique or shop plan) calls for the grouping of merchandise so that each group has its own "shop" within the store (see Fig. 18.8). Additional wall separations allow each shop to have its own identity, style, colors, and atmosphere. The enclosed plan has so far been limited to higher-priced items that have margins large enough to cover the higher construction and security costs.

The **zone and cluster plan** incorporates the best features of the open and enclosed plans. The sales floor is zoned into large areas of associated merchandise groups, rather than into small, individual merchandise bou-

Table 18.7
Typical breakdown of space allocation for a store of 110,000 square feet*

FIRST FLOOR	
Gross area of floor	55,000 S/F (100%)
Building functions	4,225 S/F (8%)
Nonselling areas	5,175 S/F (9%)
Available selling area	45,600 S/F (83%)

BUILDING FUNCTIONS		NONSELLING	
Exterior walls	1100 S/F	Truck dock	1115 S/F
Stairs	1160	Floor receiving	385
Escalators	280	Security	115
Passenger elevator	65	Parcel check	220
Freight elevator	125	Alteration room	635
Elevator machine room	210	Show windows	195
Electric closets	100	Circulation	810
Electric service room	330	Trucking corridor	1050
Incinerator room	455	Vestibule	350
Water, gas, and meter room	260	Service desk	300
Janitor closet	60		
Pump room	80		
	4225 S/F		5175 S/F

SELLING AREA (PLANNED)

DEPARTMENTS	AREA	FITTING ROOMS	STOCK	TOTAL
Foundations	1700	170	300	2,170 S/F
Daytime dresses	2775	210	225	3,210
Lingerie (intimate)	2275		400	2,675
Dresses	4100	610	220	4,930
Coats and suits	2855			2,855
Sportswear	3920	420	340	4,680
Candy	340		325	665
Promotion	750			750
Millinery and wigs	550			550
Hosiery	1075			1,075
Handbag, small leather goods	1800			1,800
Neckwear, handkerchiefs	1045			1,045
Jewelry	650			650
Juniors	4160	365	250	4,775
Women's shoes	1750		1740	3,490
Cosmetics	2600		60	2,660
Men's furnishings	2800			2,800
Men's clothing	2650	175	900	3,725
Men's shoes	220		200	420
Accessories			245	245
Stationery	430			430
				45,600 S/F

*This example presents a typical breakdown developed for a store of 110,000 square feet, a conventional store whose operation provides for receiving of partial shipments from manufacturers with credit and general office functions performed from a remote central flagship or present store.

SECOND FLOOR

Gross area of floor	55,000 S/F (100%)
Building functions	7,125 S/F (13%)
Nonselling areas	11,940 S/F (22%)
Available selling area	35,935 S/F (65%)

BUILDING FUNCTIONS

Exterior walls	1100 S/F
Stairs	990
Escalators	360
Passenger elevator	65
Freight elevator	125
Electrical closet	225
Boiler room	1460
H.V.A.C. room (1)	1440
H.V.A.C. room (2)	1360
	7125 S/F

NONSELLING

Key rec.	300 S/F
Display and sign writer	640
Gift wrap — shipping	525
Employees' facilities	1,900
Employees' canteen	900
Maintenance shop	235
Circulation	100
Receiving and marking	4,650
Public toilets and offices	2,690
	11,940 S/F

SELLING AREA (PLANNED)

DEPARTMENTS	AREA	FITTING ROOMS	STOCK	TOTAL
Housewares	5000		1800	6,800 S/F
Bath shop	600			600
Domestics and pillows	4700		590	5,290
Curtains and draperies	4520		1500	6,020
China and glassware	2600		1000	3,600
Girls 7–14	1830)	)	)	
	)	)	)	
Girls 3–6	1115)	125)	520)	4,500
	)	)	)	
Teens	910)	)	)	
Children's shoes	420		280	700
Infant's and layette	1705		670	2,375
Toddlers	915			915
Accessories and underwear	700			700
Boys 8–20	2170)	)	)	
	)	50)	600)	3,650
Boys 4–7	830)	)	)	
Luggage	785			785
				35,935 S/F

RECAP OF AREAS

LEVELS	BUILDING FUNCTIONS	NONSELLING AREAS	SELLING AREAS	TOTAL
First floor	4,225 S/F	5,175 S/F	45,600 S/F	55,00 S/F
Second floor	7,125 S/F	11,940 S/F	35,935 S/F	55,000 S/F
Totals	11,350 S/F	17,115 S/F	81,535 S/F	110,000 S/F
	(10.32%)	(15.56%)	(74.12%)	(100%)

Source: Reprinted with permission of Chain Store Publishing Corp. *Store Planning & Design,* by Adolph Novak (New York: Lebhar-Friedman, 1977), pp. 74–75.

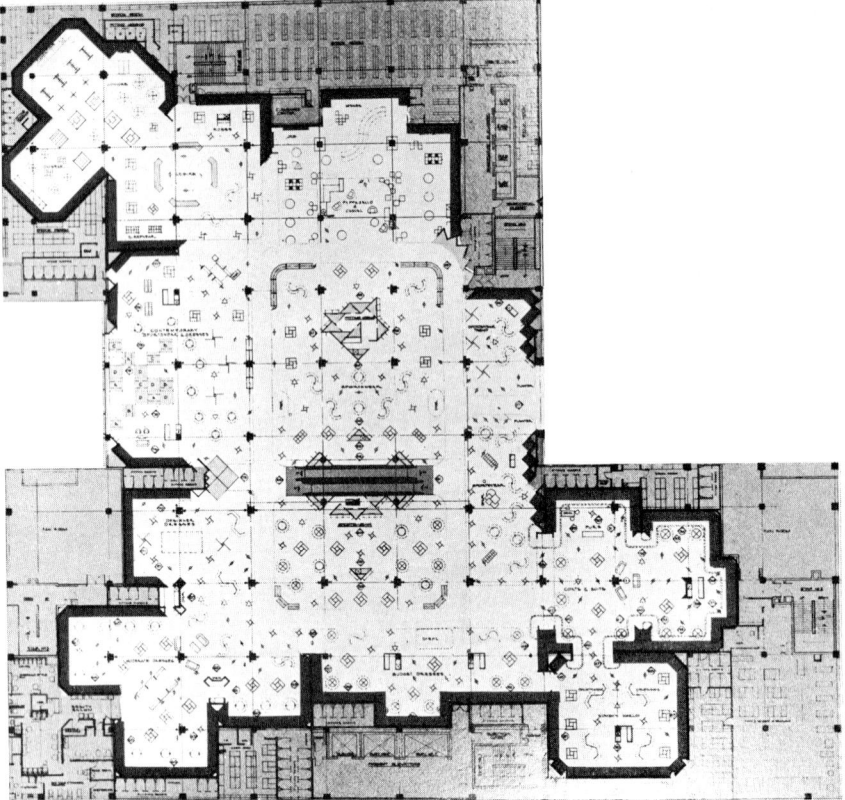

Figure 18.7
Example of the open plan
This open concept plan has a few shops that are enclosed around the perimeter. The central area and surrounding merchandise groupings have no high wall obstructions or partitions. Generally, the partitions encompass only a section of a department and are used mostly as background. This arrangement provides an unobstructed view of the floor's sales area.

Source: Reprinted with permission of Chain Store Publishing Corp. *Store Planning & Design,* by Adolph Novak (1977).

tiques (see Fig. 18.9). High wall dividers or fixtures separate the zones. Mobile fixtures are used inside the zones to cluster merchandise in the desired pattern. Proponents of this plan point to its advantages of keeping costs down, providing flexibility, maintaining security, and providing some definition between merchandise departments and groups.

The specific floor plan generally specifies the layout within the areas designated by the open, closed, or zone and cluster plans. The specific floor plan for a men's department, for example, must be decided after the open, closed, or zone and cluster general plan is chosen. The two basic specific floor plans are the grid plan and the free-flow plan.

The **grid plan** is constructed in a regular rectangular pattern (see Fig. 18.10). Since the aisles direct the flow of traffic, the grid plan is designed to enhance retailing efficiency.

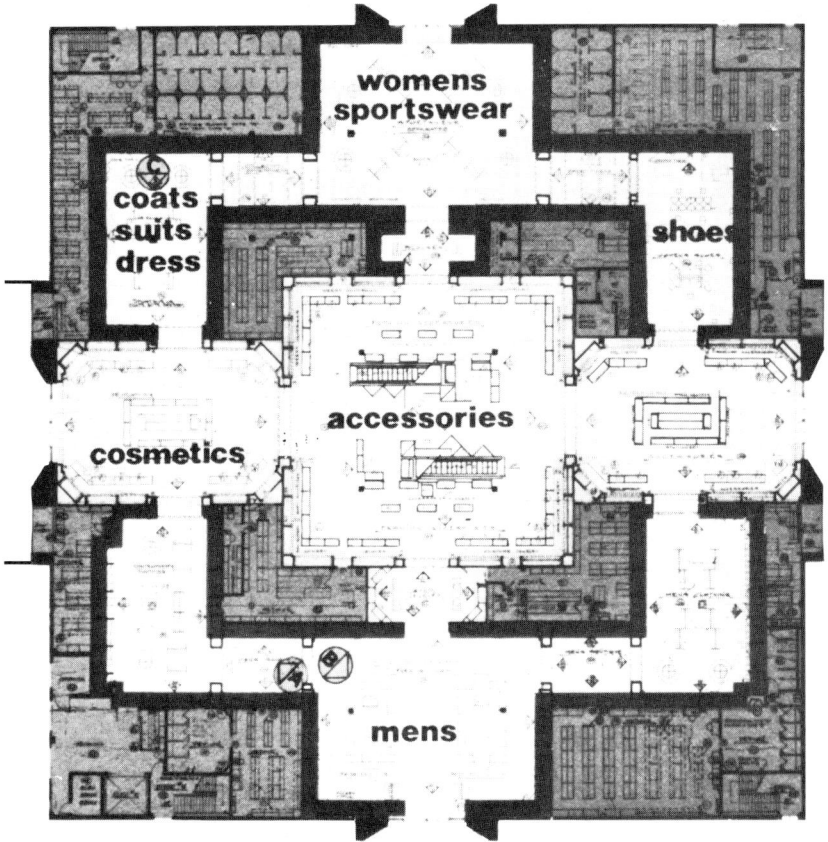

Figure 18.8
Example of enclosed plan
This layout shows an enclosed concept plan. Each merchandise classification is located within an enclosed area that is surrounded by high walls. All shops are interconnected through walkways that surround the central area and provide access to it.

Source: Reprinted with permission of Chain Store Publishing Corp. *Store Planning & Design,* by Adolph Novak (1977).

The **free-flow plan** (sometimes called a curving traffic flow) has displays and aisles arranged in a freely flowing pattern, as shown in Fig. 18.11. The primary advantage of this plan is that it encourages customers to browse and, therefore, to be exposed to some merchandise more than once.

An important point is that a store must be relatively large to incorporate both general and specific floor plans. Many smaller retailers need to consider only the specific plans: grid or some variant of free-flow. Some larger retailers use the grid or free-flow plan for their general floor plan. Supermarkets, discount stores, hardware stores, and convenience stores often use the grid pattern because it enhances self-service, simplifies inventory control and security, maximizes use of floor space, and helps regular customers develop routinized shopping patterns.[20] Many "shopping" stores, such as clothing stores and boutiques, use the free-flow plan.

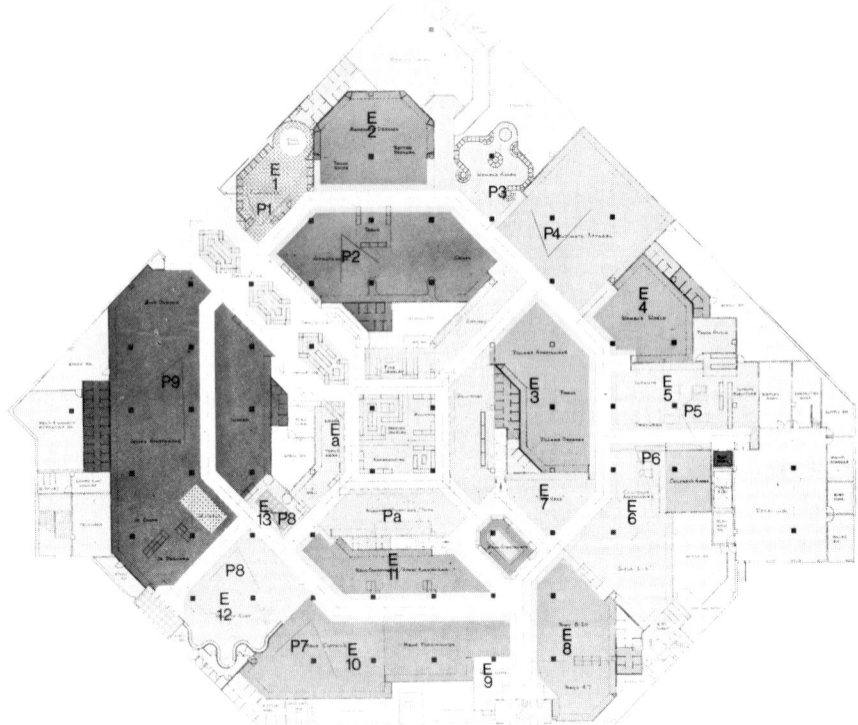

Figure 18.9
Example of zone and cluster plan
This plan shows the floor concept of a store using the zone and cluster plan. Each department that specializes in a category of merchandise is zoned around a central area. Within each zone the related classifications of merchandise are clustered to create a particular merchandise world.

Source: Reprinted with permission of Chain Store Publishing Corp. *Store Planning & Design*, by Adolph Novak (1977).

7. Map specific locations. The retailer can now determine and map specific locations for the departments. The following questions must be considered:

1. Which products should be placed in the basement and on the first floor, the second floor, and so on?

2. On a given floor, how should the groupings be placed in relation to doors, vertical transportation and so on?

3. Where should impulse or unplanned product categories be located in relation to categories that consumers preplan to buy?

4. Where should convenience products be situated?

5. How should associated product categories be aligned?

6. Where should seasonal and off-season products be placed?

7. Where should space-consuming categories like furniture be located?

8. How close should product displays and stored inventory be to each other?

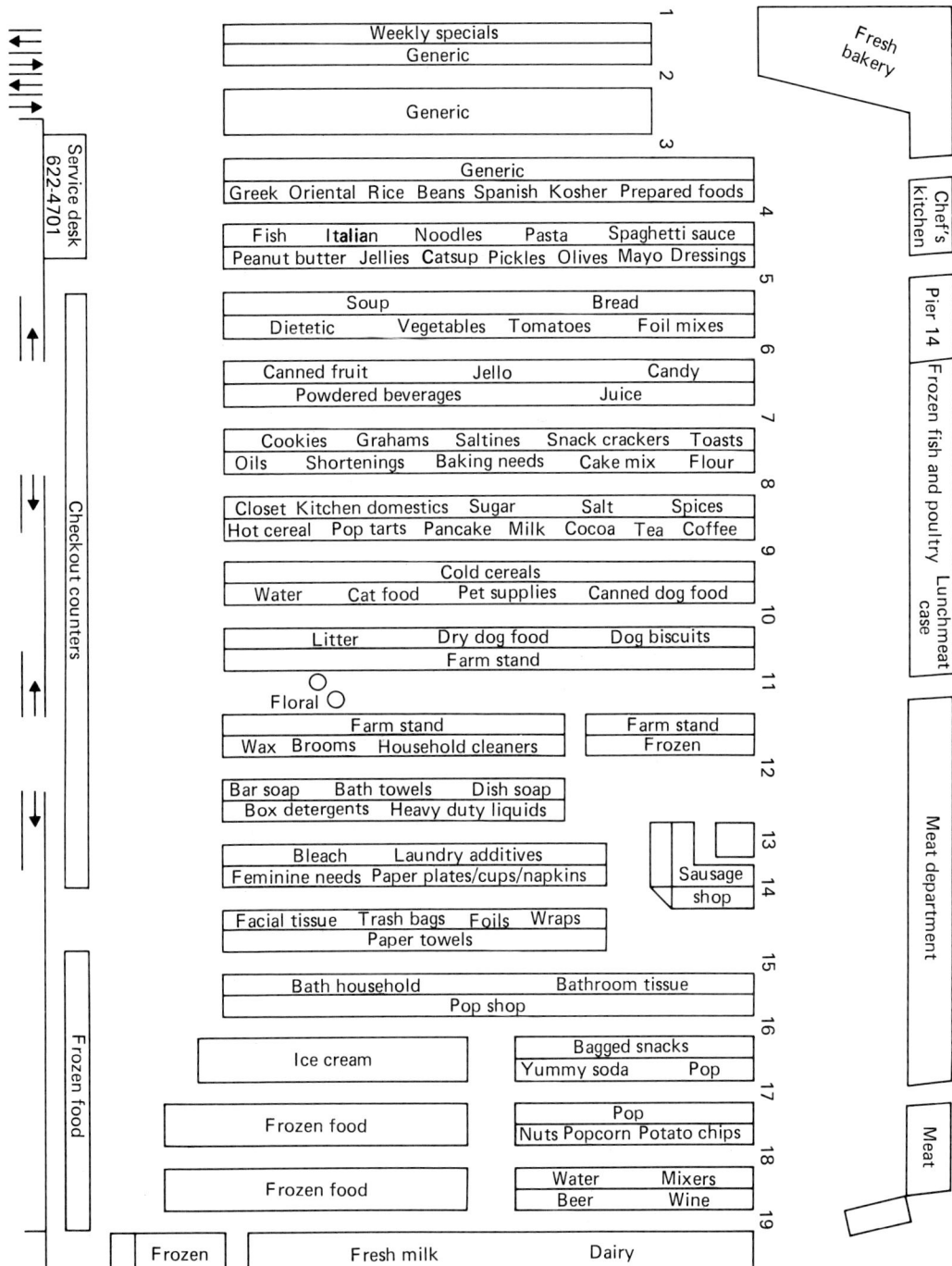

Figure 18.10
Example of the grid plan
Source: Progressive Grocer, September 1977.

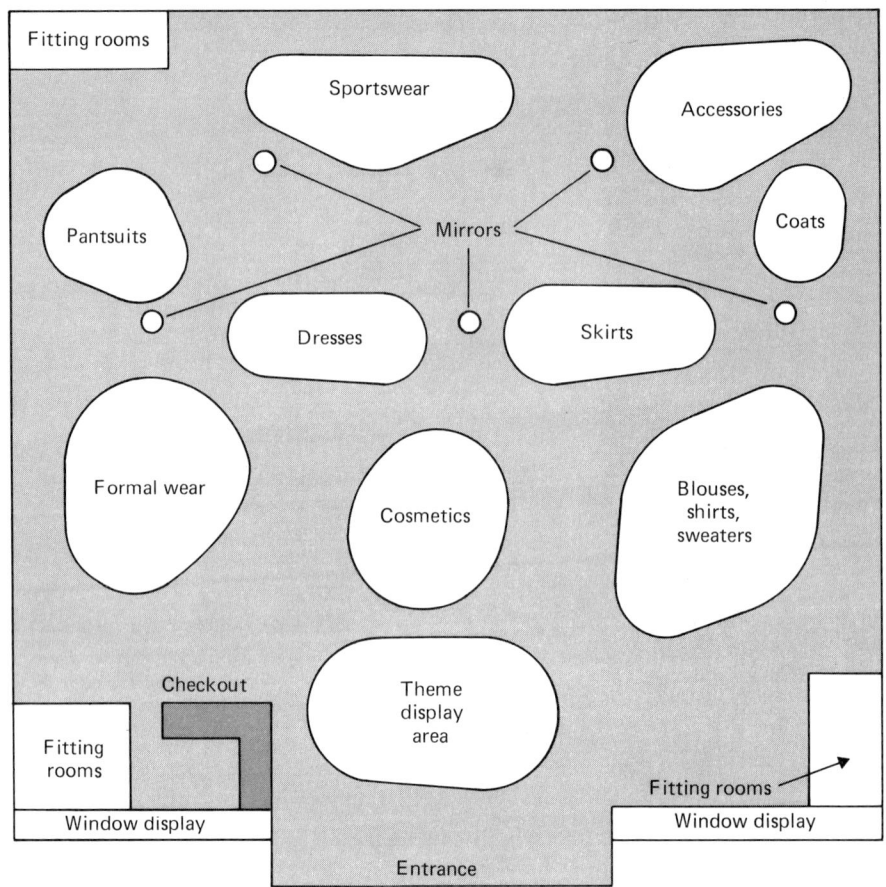

Figure 18.11
Example of a free-flow plan

9.   What travel patterns do consumers follow once they enter the store?

10.   How can lines be avoided near the cash register, and how can the overall appearance of store crowding be averted?[21]

Several generalizations can be made about specific locations. First, *plan the layout with customers in mind.* The layout and specific locations should be designed to serve the target market (in addition to facilitating store operations).

Second, *plan definite themes.* The sum of all departmental themes equals the overall store theme. The departments' layout and decor should blend together to form a consistent theme.

Third, *avoid natural shoplifting areas.* Minimize secluded areas that do not lend themselves to observation.

Fourth, *direct the flow of traffic* while maintaining customer convenience. Both grid and free-flow plans can be designed to funnel traffic.

Fifth, *plan store perimeters and aisle intersections efficiently*. These locations should be reserved for impulse, high-margin goods, and specials.

Sixth, *plan midstore sales appeal*. Although high-margin goods should be given choice locations, midstore locations are often poor merchandising areas, especially when they are not visible from perimeters and main aisles. As a result, these areas should be carefully designed to contain merchandise that serves as strong customer attractors. Coffee has good midstore appeal for supermarkets, for example, because about two-thirds of the customers are attracted to it.[22]

Seventh, *eye-level space should be devoted to the retailer's "bread-and-butter" lines*. An exception can be made when an item is so popular that customers will look for it no matter where it is.

Eighth, *try to maximize return per unit of selling space*. The retailer should consider space in terms of square feet, linear feet (of shelf space), and cubic feet of store space. The cubic feet consideration is often overlooked, but is important because it focuses attention on the potential for placing merchandise higher, thus increasing usable space.

DEVISE INTERIOR DISPLAY

Display refers to the manner in which merchandise is exhibited to the customer (see Fig. 18.12). It can play an important role in a store's atmosphere strategy and in its communications strategy by providing information to customers. Both **display hardware** and **display strategy** are based on merchandise characteristics such as perishability, value, bulk, risk of breakage,

Figure 18.12
Display in a Sears sporting goods department
Photo courtesy of Sears, Roebuck and Co.

risk of theft, packaging, danger to customers, attractiveness, seasonable nature, and fashion.

Display hardware is limited only by the retailer's imagination. Examples are shelves, tables, racks, cases, baskets, and so on. Display strategy refers to how the display hardware is arranged. Five basic display strategies are described below.

Assortment Display

An **assortment display** contains a wide assortment of a particular merchandise variety. The merchandise variety "magazines" typically must have a wide assortment or choice. An **open assortment** encourages the customers to handle the merchandise; this might be used for magazines and greeting cards. A **closed assortment** encourages the customer to look but not to touch the merchandise; such a display would be appropriate for records and games.

Theme Display

A **theme display** is a setting designed to create a specific atmosphere or mood. All or part of a store can be part of the theme, as demonstrated in Fig. 18.6. Some retailers actually program a series of year-round special themes. An Independence Day theme may be used for a month preceding July Fourth, and on July fifth, a new theme will begin.

Ensemble Display

An **ensemble display** consists of visually coordinated related merchandise. Examples are mannequins displaying clothing (see Fig. 18.13) and a complete room setting for furniture.

Aisle Tables

Aisle tables are tables placed in main aisles to form merchandise islands. Although used for either regular or special merchandise, aisle tables are most often used to display currently advertised specials.

Counter Displays

Counter displays are those on and around checkout counters. These are often supplied by manufacturers and often used for impulse items.

MONITOR AND ADAPT

Once the store is built and furnished, the retailer must continually monitor and adapt atmosphere features. There are also some long-run considerations the retailer should monitor.

Retail physical facilities can lose their punch either from simply wearing out or from visual or functional obsolescence. Retailers must continually monitor the condition of the facility and its impact on marketing strategy and anticipate future requirements. Short-run adaptations normally involve altering displays or layouts; longer-run adaptations include the following:

1. *Face-lift:* Is the clean up, freshen up of the overall environment without getting into costly physical and investment expense. Examples are: new floor coverings, painting, and wall coverings, and general housekeeping maintenance from cleaning light fixtures and replacing lamps to cleaning

Figure 18.13
Ensemble display at Sears
Photo courtesy of Sears, Roebuck and Co.

furniture. The impact of these limited activities gives the impression that something has changed for the better. All done with minimum disruption.

2. *Update:* Adds activities necessary for the environment and function to appear current. Examples are: rearrangement of loose functional items, replacement of limited number of fixtures (say 20%) and furniture, recovering of existing units, and new signing and/or graphic programs. The results, through strategic placement of new and redone items and a well thought out face-lift program, signal that everything is new and that a major investment has been made.

3. *Remodel:* Adds to the project a new level through the introduction of physical changes and changes in space allocation. Examples are: relocating activities, departments and functions within the existing physical shell. This is in response to demands for reallocating space for better balance of production. Such changes introduce the need for electrical, circulation modifications, and limited construction. Also the percent of new furniture, fixtures, and accessories would increase. As extensive as this level can get, it may not respond to the overall long-term demands on the space because a conscious decision was made to go into the next level and over the threshold that exposes the project to a multitude of new and different expenses. The effect both visually and functionally can be most effective.

STRATEGY IN ACTION 18.2

Woolco's Layout Strategy

In September of 1981, F. W. Woolworth Company's Woolco division opened its first Woolco "Store of the Future" in Ocean Springs, Mississippi. The new store is an "upscale" discount store with a new merchandise mix and floor layout. One-fifth of the Woolco stores will be revamped to look like the prototype during the first half of 1982 and all Woolco stores will have the new format by 1985, according to company officials.

The new Woolco stores will range in size from 70,000 to 90,000 square feet, whereas the existing stores average around 115,000 square feet. Despite this smaller size, Woolco officials say they can fit just as much merchandise into the smaller stores by using taller, narrower counters. Seven-foot counters will replace the existing 4- and 5-foot counters. In addition, counter width is being reduced from 4 or 5 feet to only 26 inches.

A "racetrack" floor plan will be used in lieu of conventional central aisles. This plan involves shorter aisles running perpendicular to two long aisles. The new layout, with wider aisles, is intended to expose customers to more departments.

Source: Marjorie Leedy, "Sparring Starts for Scarcer Retail Dollars," *The Clarion Ledger* (Jackson, Miss.), 20 September 1981, p. C-1.

4. *Renovation:* Brings a whole array of additional activities and costs. This level responds to management's decision to do it all, making a major financial investment. The need for demolition appears for the first time and brings with it a chain reaction from business disruption to need for heating, ventilating, air conditioning, lighting, and sprinkler changes. Examples include: relocation of departments and/or activities from one area of floor to another, conversion of stock and support space to selling office, or other customer/client activity. Also changes to wall configurations, ceiling layouts, material handling systems, and office functions. Items such as totally new furniture, fixtures, and accessories also might be a part of the program. The results can be significant from a new look, a new image, to providing projected space requirements, and arrangements for function improvements well into the future.[23]

If none of these four possibilities fits the retailer's requirements, the fifth possibility is to *build a new store.*

Because of the potentially large impact of the adaptation decision, the retailer must conduct some sort of cost-benefit analysis. Each alternative must be analyzed to determine its cost and anticipated contribution to the firm's strategy (benefit).

Generally, the "redo cost" increases as the retailer moves from face-lift to update to remodel to renovate to new store. If each of these five options is considered feasible, specific cost figures for each should be gathered. Similarly, each succeeding level should deliver a greater impact on store performance. A critical point, however, is that *increases in cost and impact are not in direct proportion.* It is quite likely that each succeeding level will deliver proportionately less impact. A situation could arise, for example, in which a face-lift would cost $5,000 and deliver 25 percent of the impact of a new store. An update would cost $10,000 and deliver 40 percent of the impact of a new store. If budget constraints limit redo options to those costing $10,000 or less, only face-lift and update could be considered. In this situation, the retailer's essential choice is between the greater impact of the update (40 percent versus 25 percent) and the greater impact per dollar of the face-lift. If conditions warrant, the retailer might choose to do a face-lift now and another face-lift in the future.

A last point is especially critical for larger, multiunit retailers who employ many managers in various positions. These managers often remain in a given position a relatively short period of time (maybe three to five years) and they typically are evaluated on short-run, bottom-line performance. Although this type of evaluation program has merits, *it encourages the managers to ignore long-term maintenance and repair burdens.* Ignoring these burdens tends to shorten the redo cycle, thereby greatly increasing the costs associated with the physical plant.

KEY CONCEPTS

Atmosphere	Specific floor plans
Atmospherics	Open plan
Scent considerations	Enclosed plan
Sound considerations	Zone and cluster plan
Touch considerations	Grid plan
Sight considerations	Free-flow plan
Visual merchandising	Display
Taste considerations	Display hardware
Store fixtures	Assortment display
Store equipment	Open assortment
Layout	Closed assortment
Building functions	Theme display
Selling area	Ensemble display
Nonselling service areas	Aisle table displays
General floor plans	Counter displays

REVIEW QUESTIONS

1. Why are store design and atmosphere important to retailers?
2. Develop the strategic atmosphere and layout planning process.
3. Discuss the relationship between store exterior and atmosphere.
4. Distinguish between store fixtures and store equipment.

5. Develop the strategic layout planning process.

6. Discuss the key factors that influence layout.

7. What is the basic layout conflict?

8. Discuss four approaches to determining space requirements for a merchandise group.

9. Discuss five basic display strategies.

10. Discuss the long-run adaptation alternatives for a retail facility.

LEARNING EXERCISES

1. Analyze a local retailer's use of atmosphere components. Analyze how these components appeal to the various senses.

2. Analyze two or three local retailers' use and breakdown of available square footage. (Suggestion: Consider three restaurants.)

DECISION SITUATION 18.1: **ATHLETIC OUTFITTERS IV**

A group of marketing students from the local university recently conducted a study for Athletic Outfitters. One key problem was discovered during the study. Many respondents indicated that the atmosphere at Athletic Outfitters was incongruent with the overall image of the store. Most said the store had high-quality products, high prices, and was, in general, a high-quality store. However, they indicated that the store's appearance was not "high quality."

In looking around, the owner began to realize that there was some truth in this finding. The store was not well decorated. The walls above the fixtures were blank. The sales racks did look a little jumbled. Also, the table of sales merchandise near the door was not tidy and it contained some less desirable merchandise.

QUESTIONS

1. How important do you think atmosphere is to Athletic Outfitters?

2. What changes in atmosphere would you recommend?

3. What image changes would you expect as a result of the changes you recommend? Why?

DECISION SITUATION 18.2: **QUICK MART**

Kathy Johnson is the owner of a convenience store in a small university town. The store has not been earning Kathy the income she thought it should. She is not sure why, but a customer who teaches marketing at the university has mentioned that she should change the store layout.

Kathy likes the layout as it is now, but she is willing to change it if necessary. The present layout philosophy is simple; high sales items (milk, bread, beer) are placed near the cash register at the front doors. Kathy thinks this is good because it makes buying those items convenient for customers. Slower-moving items are placed farther back in the store. Items with low sales are displayed on the worst aisles and in the worst locations.

QUESTIONS

1. Do you agree with Kathy's layout philosophy?

2. Assuming that the store's sales area is 35 feet wide and 60 feet long, what layout would you recommend? Specify the type of merchandise to put in each area.

NOTES

1. Philip Kotler, "Atmospherics as a Marketing Tool," *Journal of Retailing* (Winter 1974), p. 50.

2. *Ibid.*, p. 53.

3. *Ibid.*

4. *Ibid.*, p. 61.

5. Raymond A. Marquardt, James C. Makens, and Robert G. Roe, *Retail Management* (Hinsdale, Ill.: Dryden Press, 1979), pp. 183–186.

6. Watson S. Dunn and Arnold M. Barban, *Advertising* (Hinsdale, Ill.: Dryden Press, 1979), p. 432.

7. R. Hansen and T. Deutscher, "An Empirical Investigation of Attribute Importance in Retail Store Selection," *Journal of Retailing* (Winter 1977/78), pp. 59–73.

8. Adolph Novak, *Store Planning and Design* (New York: Lebhar-Friedman Books, 1977), p. 51.

9. Marquardt, Makens, Roe, *op. cit.*, p. 189.

10. *Ibid.*

11. Novak, *op. cit.*, pp. 132–133.

12. See, for example, Gilbert D. Harrell and Michael D. Hutt, "Crowding in Retail Stores," *MSU Business Topics*, Winter 1976, pp. 33–39.

13. Marquardt, Makens, Roe, *op. cit.*, p. 192. See also Delbert J. Duncan and Stanley C. Hollander, *Modern Retailing Management* (Homewood, Ill.: Richard D. Irwin, 1977), p. 147.

14. Duncan and Hollander, *op. cit.*, pp. 148–149.

15. Novak, *op. cit.*, p. 72.

16. *Ibid.*, pp. 75–76.

17. Novak, *op. cit.*, p. 77.

18. *Merchandising and Operating Results of 1979* (New York: Financial Executives Division, National Retail Merchants Association, 1980), pp. 81–93.

19. Novak, *op. cit.*, pp. 79–82.

20. Barry Berman and Joel R. Evans, *Retail Management* (New York: Macmillan, 1979), pp. 409–410.

21. *Ibid.*, pp. 412.

22. Marquardt, Makens, Roe, *op. cit.*, p. 202.

23. From Jim Ruess (1980), "In 1980's, Redoing Retail Facilities Requires Analytical Framework, Options, Master Plan," *Marketing News* (March 7), published by the American Marketing Association.

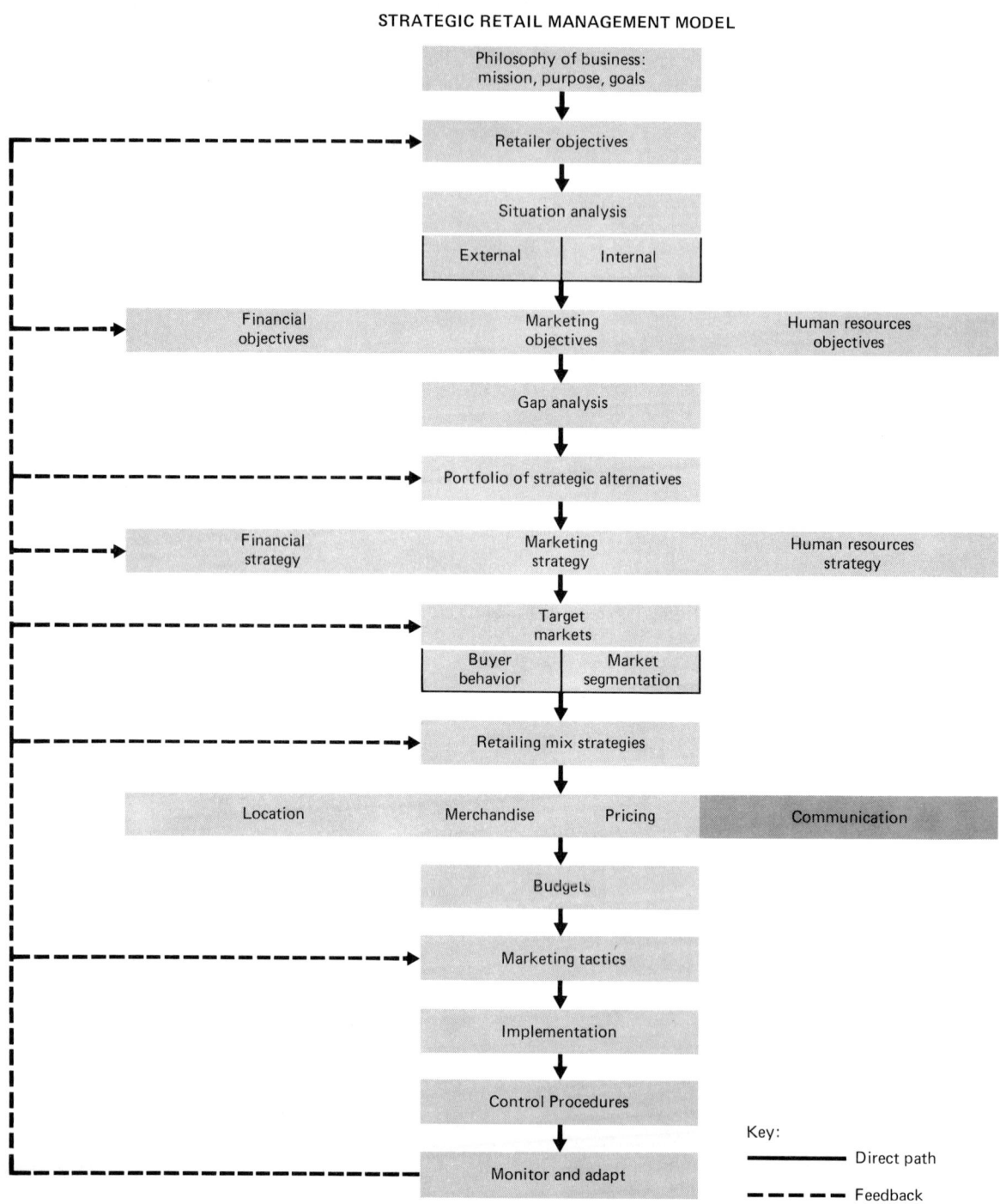

STRATEGIC RETAIL MANAGEMENT MODEL

Philosophy of business:
mission, purpose, goals

Retailer objectives

Situation analysis

| External | Internal |

Financial objectives | Marketing objectives | Human resources objectives

Gap analysis

Portfolio of strategic alternatives

Financial strategy | Marketing strategy | Human resources strategy

Target markets

| Buyer behavior | Market segmentation |

Retailing mix strategies

Location | Merchandise | Pricing | Communication

Budgets

Marketing tactics

Implementation

Control Procedures

Monitor and adapt

Key:

———— Direct path

- - - - Feedback

Chapter 19
Customer Service Decisions

LEARNING OBJECTIVES

1. To understand the role and importance of customer service decisions.

2. To understand the strategic customer service planning process.

INTRODUCTION

The field of retailing involves the delivery of goods and/or services to ultimate consumers. The retail offering can range from pure goods to pure services, including any combination in between. Because most retailers incorporate a service component in their offering, however, the discussion in this chapter concentrates on those retailers who offer a core good along with ancillary (or supplementary) services. Ancillary services may be highly desired by customers, but they are usually desired in conjunction with something else, such as a core product or shopping for a core product.

The strategic decision model for customer service is shown in Fig. 19.1. It consists of the following steps:

1. Review all existing plans and information.

2. Define customer service objectives.

3. Analyze service alternatives.

4. Determine services to be offered.

5. Determine level of each service.

6. Determine form of services.

7. Evaluate cost efficiency of services.

8. Plan and organize customer service department.

9. Monitor and adapt.

REVIEW ALL EXISTING PLANS AND INFORMATION

The service component is often a major factor in the retailer's marketing strategy. As with all other strategic factors, the service strategy must be anchored to existing strategic objectives, plans, and information.

The demands and expectations of the *target market* should have a major influence on the retailer's service strategy. It is not necessarily correct to assume that customers want more and more services, however, especially if they are accompanied by higher prices (this is discussed in more detail below).

All components of retailing strategy, including the service strategy, must be consistent with the retailer's *desired store image*. If the desired store image involves high prestige and quality, a full range of services is usually necessary. Conversely, a low-price, economy-oriented image calls for only a few selected services.

Certain merchandise almost requires offering certain types of services. The characteristics of large appliances (bulk and cost) lead most appliance retailers to offer delivery and credit services, for example.

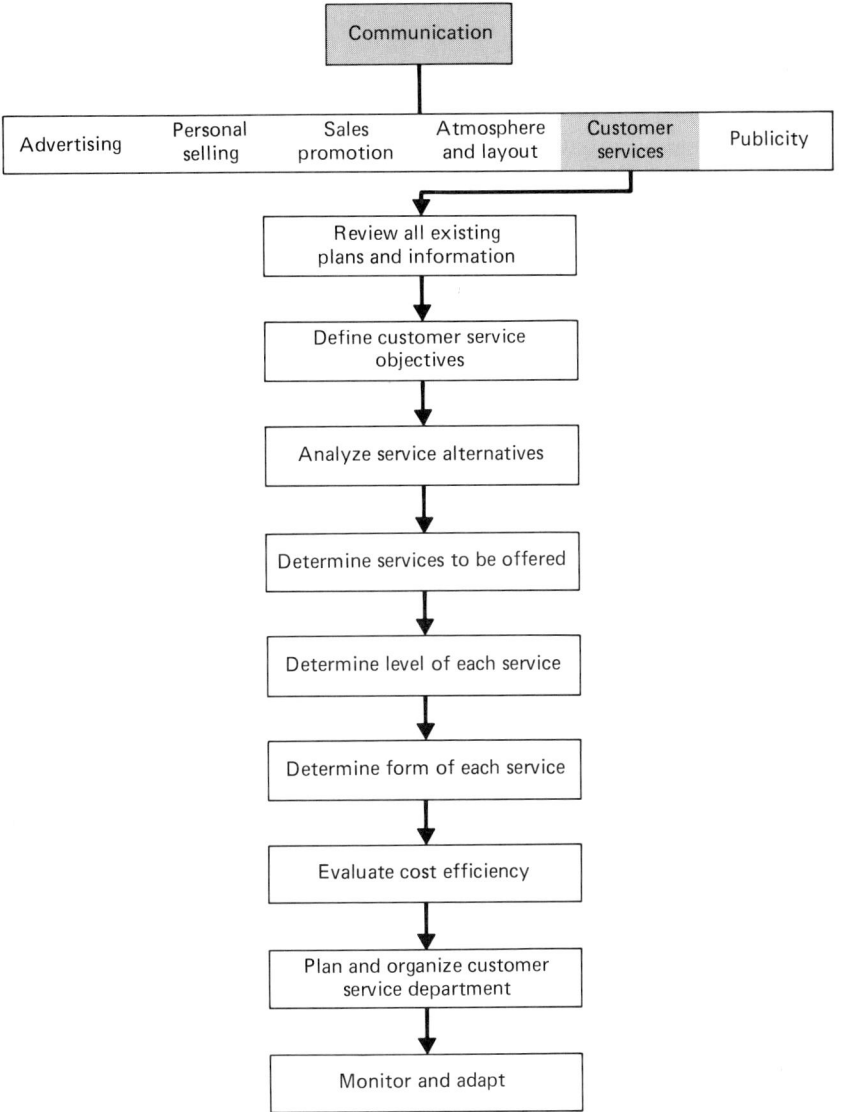

Figure 19.1
Customer service decision model

The service package offered by a retailer can be an excellent vehicle for securing a competitive advantage. The proper mixture of services can help the retailer develop a store image that is difficult to duplicate. Conversely, retailers must not allow competitors' service offerings to put them at a competitive disadvantage. In considering competititve service offerings, *the retailer must not forget the customer.* What services do the customers want? What services will they respond to?

DEFINE CUSTOMER SERVICE OBJECTIVES

The customer service program is a *competitive tool* and thus can be used in a defensive or offensive fashion. As a **defensive tool,** the retailer would offer only those services that are absolutely necessary, such as fitting rooms and alterations for a men's apparel store. On the offensive side, the retailer aggressively seeks to obtain a competitive advantage from the service program. A men's apparel retailer using **offensive tools** might offer credit, delivery, professional wardrobe consulting, and similar services.

Bearing in mind that all services must be compatible with the desired store image, each service should have a more specific objective, such as the following:[1]

- *Increase the Form Utility of Merchandise.*   Examples: clothing alterations, engraving, carpet installations.

- *Expand Target Market for Merchandise.*   Examples: sewing classes, fashion advisory services, golf instructions.

- *Provide Comfort and Convenience for Customers.*   Examples: restrooms, meeting places, drinking fountains.

- *Generate Additional Traffic.*   Examples: post office branches, dental clinic branches, community exhibits.

ANALYZE SERVICE ALTERNATIVES

The range of service alternatives is perhaps limited only by the retailer's imagination. New service alternatives are continually evolving. The retailer must review and analyze the pros and cons of these alternatives to see if they can achieve the stated objectives. Table 19.1 contains a listing of forty frequently offered services. We discuss several additional services below.

Customers with Special Needs

Since services should be designed to fullfill the needs and desires of customers, retailers should consider designing special services for customers with *special needs*. Handicapped customers have special needs to which certain retailers have responded.[2] Sears installed an experimental teletype catalog ordering system for deaf customers in Los Angeles. Selected McDonald's units have Braille menus built into the counters.

Other customers with special needs to which some retailers have responded are the elderly and U.S. residents and tourists who do not speak or read English. One group of customers with special needs that the authors feel are usually ignored is parents who must shop with their children. Younger children often create problems for their parents and sometimes for the retailer. Retailers who provide play areas and other devices (such as cartoons) to occupy children while parents shop often find that the parents are then much better customers.

Table 19.1
Examples of retail services

Free (or reduced-rate) parking	Home economists
Free (or reduced-rate) bus services	Public restrooms
Product delivery	Birthday (anniversary) reminders
Telephone shopping	Extended product warranties
Mail-order (catalog) shopping	Use of *Consumer Reports* or other consumer journals
Lay-away	
COD payment	Special orders for items not stocked
Bridal registry	Free coffee (or champagne) while shopping
Fashion shows	Information desks
Gift wrapping	Party counseling
Alterations	Baby strollers
Liberal returned goods policies	Gift certificates
Check cashing	Trade-ins
On-sight product usage (such as pools for testing fly-casting equipment)	Children's playrooms
	Product locator (checking with other stores on product availability)
Demonstration models (for at-home use)	
Parcel-pickup service	Product repair
Baggage/parcel lockers	In-store banking
After-hours shopping (for preferred customers)	Free telephone calls
	Personal shopping
Stag nights (male shopping only)	Lost-and-found
Shopping consultants	Bill payment (in-store)

Source: From Albert D. Bates, *Retailing and Its Environment* (New York: D. Van Nostrand Company, 1979), p. 290. © 1979 by Litton Educational Publishing, Inc. Reprinted by permission of Kent Publishing Company, a Division of Wadsworth, Inc., 20 Providence Street, Boston, MA 02116.

Shopping Services

Increases in transportation costs and the increasing number of working women have caused the demand for an increase in shopping services, primarily some form of catalog or telephone shopping. Sears, for example, offers a combination of both catalog and telephone shopping in many locations. Customers can select merchandise that is not available locally from the catalog, order by telephone, and either pick up the merchandise when it arrives or have it delivered. In the future, it is conceivable that retailers will be able to sponsor "shopping shows" on cable television systems.[3] These programs would present a variety of merchandise in realistic settings and the audience could then call to order specific products.

Revenue Services

More retailers are beginning to offer services that generate supplemental revenue. Examples are repair services, installation, carpet cleaning, landscaping (by nurseries), and service contracts. Renting and leasing various kinds of equipment can also generate supplemental revenue.

STRATEGY IN ACTION 19.1

Service Strategy At Bonwit Teller

Bonwit Teller, a 12-store "fashion-forward" clothier, has for years stressed quality merchandise. It is also committed to service. Helen Galland, president, says that "service is almost more important than the merchandise we carry." She believes service is what colors a consumer's perception of Bonwit Teller.

Service, politeness, and good manners are a part of the offering to consumers. Coming to a Bonwit Teller store should be like an "extension of coming into your home."

Gallard stated Bonwit's merchandise-service philosophy as "very high standards for the merchandise we bring in, for the way we conduct business, for the style in which we present what we sell, and provide a touch of class." This atmosphere for retailing appeals to the busy, involved, affluent women whom Bonwit Teller attempts to attract.

Source: "Bonwit Teller's Chief Editor." Reprinted from *Retail Week,* 15 June 1981, pp. 22–24.

Credit

Most retailers include some form of credit in their customer service program. Even the last major holdouts, supermarkets and discount houses, have begun to accept credit cards. Because of increasing costs and legal constraints, typically only the larger retailers can maintain a viable in-house credit operation. Smaller retailers have begun to rely on various bank and club cards such as Visa and American Express.

The decision regarding whether to offer credit should be anchored to the retailer's customer service objectives and strategy. The key credit decisions are to determine the type of credit, amount of credit, and collection procedures.

Before making any decisions the retailer should review any information and plans that could influence the design or implementation of the credit system. Examples of factors to review include customers' expectations, desired store image, and cost or profitability of various credit systems.

Type of Credit. The first major decision that a store has to make after deciding on whether to offer credit is the type of credit to give. Three general or basic types of credit are (1) in-house open charge accounts, (2) in-house credit cards, and (3) bank credit cards. Each type offers certain advantages and disadvantages and each type has its own role in a credit system. The following paragraphs present a thumbnail sketch of each type of credit. For a more complete discussion of each type we recommend consulting a credit management text.

Until recently, the major type of retail credit was **in-house open accounts.** They have lost some of their popularity and are now used primarily by larger, prestigious retailers and small mom 'n' pop general stores. The main reason for their decline in popularity is the increased use of credit cards.

In-house open accounts are still frequently used for big-ticket items such as furniture. The customer is not given a line of credit (as may happen with a credit card) but is simply allowed to purchase one item on credit. If the customer pays the bill in a reasonable manner, additional items may be bought on the open account.

A problem with open accounts, and one reason for their decreasing use, is that a good credit check (one that can really indicate whether a customer is a good potential risk) is difficult to perform as quickly as necessary. That is, when a customer comes in to buy an item, that customer wants to know immediately whether he or she can charge the item. The retailer can ask for information such as age, income, home ownership, and credit cards held to help establish credit worthiness, but the retailer often does not have time to verify much of the information. Therefore, there is a large risk to the retailer in this type of account. After customers have become good customers and have paid other accounts, the risk to the retailer is obviously much lower. Another problem involves denying someone credit. Sometimes individuals who are credit worthy may be turned down because the decision must be made quickly. The retailer must be diplomatic when anyone, worthy of credit or not, is turned down. An individual who is judged not to be a good credit risk now may become one later.

Closely related to the open accounts are **in-house** or **company-owned credit cards.** These cards are essentially *formalized* open accounts. That is, the retailer gives the credit card only to customers whose credit background has been examined closely. Customers are allowed to charge up to a stated limit, which is normally specified in the credit agreement. Customers get automatic credit by presenting the credit card to the retailer. Large chain and department stores usually offer these credit cards.

For the large store, it reduces the amount of time spent and the number of credit decisions that have to be made for each customer. Once a customer's credit background has been checked and determined to be good, additional evaluation is accomplished simply by monitoring the customer's account.

Interest is normally charged on credit card accounts, which is not always the case with open accounts. In fact, some retailers can make more money from their credit operations than they can from selling merchandise. This is especially true in times when the prime rate of interest is well below the rate charged on most credit cards. The retailer has to be careful to abide by the truth-in-lending laws (by telling customers the true annual percentage rate, among other disclosures) and the state's usury laws.

In-house credit cards can be a promotional aid in that the retailer guarantees individual customers that credit is available. Customers may then come to that retailer simply because of the convenience of established credit.

The principal advantages of the in-house credit card over the open account are that better credit checks can be performed before issuing the credit card and time is saved when the customer comes in to buy and charge an item. The retailer does bear the risk of the customer's not paying or delaying payment, particularly in an uncertain economy.

With both the open accounts and credit cards, the retailer will have to set up some type of credit office. The responsibilities of the credit office include investigating the credit background of applicants and collecting on the credit cards or open accounts. The overhead of this office may force the retailer to charge a little bit more for merchandise. Another problem occurs when the interest a retailer must pay is higher than the interest rate the retailer charges customers. Under those conditions the cost of offering credit is high.

To diminish the risk associated with in-house credit, many retailers have begun to accept **third-party credit cards** such as Visa and Mastercard. With these cards the risk of nonpayment is borne by the issuing party. The retailer must pay a set fee, usually about 3 to 5 percent of the value of the charge sales, as a handling fee. The retailer also has no chance of earning any interest.

The principal operating advantage of using third-party credit cards is that the retailer does not have to establish a credit department. The retailer does not have to do credit checks and does not have to worry about collection. All the retailer has to do is submit the receipts to the clearinghouse for the credit card and receive the payment, less the handling fee. For a small retailer, the bank credit cards have real potential. The retailer has sure and relatively quick payment (normally within about a month or so from the time the item was sold).

Large department stores that once offered only in-house cards now often accept one or more bank credit cards. Table 19.2 shows the top one hundred department stores and the outside credit cards they accept, if any, as of July 1981 (seventy-six stores do accept them). In July 1979, only fifty-seven of the top one hundred accepted third-party cards.[4] Larger stores previously used their own credit and shunned third-party cards because they felt the use of the third-party cards would result in decreased use of their own card. Some retailers now think, however, that third-party cards allow people who are not regular customers to purchase. American Express research indicates that 39 percent of the domestic charges of their cardholders are made by customers who live outside the retailer's trade area.[5]

Today, the use of third-party credit cards is so extensive that a retailer may not gain a competitive advantage by accepting them but may in fact be at a competitive disadvantage by *not* accepting them. The acceptance of cards may be a defensive strategy rather than one to increase market share. If the retailer chooses to use only third-party credit cards, few other credit-related decisions are necessary. Retailers who use either of the in-house credit types have to decide on the amount of credit that a customer can get and on how to collect the receivables.

Amount of Credit. The amount of credit or the **credit limit** to allow a customer is one of the more important questions in setting credit policies. The overriding factor in determining the credit limit for a specific customer is the ability of that customer to repay the credit. Also, the retailer must consider the likelihood of the customer's simply *not* paying, even if he or she has the ability to pay. For many retailers, these factors are difficult to evaluate.

If in-house credit is to be used to any extent, the retailer should hire someone capable of making judgments about the ability of customers to pay and the probability that individual customers will in fact pay the bill. There are several factors that can help determine the likelihood of repayment. Other credit, home ownership, possession of a telephone, and income are some of the factors that should be considered. Various texts devoted specifically to credit management give a more complete list of factors to examine and their importance.

When credit is granted, the retailer should be sure that the customer understands the total amount of credit that will be extended. For many retailers the credit limit for customers may be relatively small, on the order of a few hundred dollars. For retailers who sell expensive or big-ticket items such as furniture, the amount will usually have to be quite a bit larger, maybe a thousand dollars or more. Once the retailer has set a credit limit for a customer, that customer should not be allowed to go over the credit limit except in extenuating circumstances or when an extension of the limit has been requested by the customer. Keeping the limits at a relatively low level is one way to reduce the risk associated with nonpayment of the bill. The retailer should keep the credit limit relatively low until the customer has established a history of paying the debt.

Collection Methods. Any retailer who grants in-house credit will have customers who do not pay their bills on time. More liberal credit policies result in more collection problems. The retailer must develop collection procedures that are effective in collecting overdue accounts, while not causing a customer to discontinue buying from the retailer. This is not an easy task.

The retailer must understand *why customers do not pay* their bills before he or she can design an effective collection procedure. There are many reasons customers do not pay bills on time. The customer may have not received (or forgot receiving) a bill. The customer may not be able to pay because of extenuating economic or other circumstances. Also, the customer may be a deadbeat who simply does not pay bills.

Obviously, the reason a customer is not paying the bill should affect the collection procedure. Using the same procedure to collect from a normally good customer who missed a payment and a customer who is trying to steal the goods by not paying is a serious mistake. Even if the procedure works in collecting the debt, the good customer is likely to become an ex-good customer who happened to miss a payment. If this happens often, the retailer may have more ex-customers than customers.

Table 19.2
The top 100: Who is accepting third-party credit cards

COMPANY/DIVISION	AFFIL.	VOLUME (MILLIONS)	COMPANY/DIVISION	AFFIL.	VOLUME (MILLIONS)
1. Macy's New York A	(RHM)	$775	29. Sanger-Harris, Dallas	(Fed)	262.1
2. Bamberger's New Jersey	(RHM)	725	30. Carson, Pirie, Scott, AV Chicago	(Ind)	255
3. May Co. California A*	(May)	650	31. Gimbels New York AMV	(BAT)	240
4. Hudson's, Detroit	(D-H)	641.5	32. Strawbridge & Clothier, MV Philadelphia	(Ind.)	225
5. Broadway — So. California A*	(CHH)	625	Maas Bros., Tampa AD	(All)	225
6. Macy's California A	(RHM)	600	34. Shillito's, Cincinnati MV	(Fed)	215.1
7. Bloomingdale's, New York A	(Fed)	566.8	35. May Co., Cleveland	(May)	215
8. Marshall Field, Chicago A	(MF)	550	Kaufmann's, Pittsburgh	(May)	215
9. Abraham & Straus, M* V* Brooklyn	(Fed)	547.6	Jordan Marsh, Miami AD	(All)	215
10. Burdine's Florida DMV	(Fed)	498.8	38. B. Altman & Co., New York AD	(Ind)	210
11. Dillard's, Little Rock ADMV	(Ind)	470.7	39. H.C. Prange Co., MV Sheboygan	(Ind)	209.7
12. Lord & Taylor, New York A	(ADG)	460	40. D.H. Holmes, New Orleans MV	(Ind)	197.3
13. Foley's, Houston A* M* V*	(Fed)	453.0	41. L.S. Ayres, Indianapolis	(ADG)	190
14. Bullock's, Los Angeles A* M* V*	(Fed)	447.4	Higbee's Cleveland AMV	(Ind)	190
15. Emporium-Capwell, No. A* California	(CHH)	415	43. Hess, Allentown AMV (Ending 4/30/81)	(CAC)	189.9
16. Dayton's, Minneapolis M* V*	(D-H)	382.1	44. Frederick & Nelson, Seattle AMV	(M-F)	185
17. Hecht's, Balt.-Washington AMV	(May)	365	45. Elder-Beerman, Dayton A* MV	(Ind)	180
18. Jordan Marsh, New England AD	(All)	360	46. Davison's, Atlanta A	(RHM)	175
19. Rich's Atlanta AMV	(Fed)	351.7	Thalhimer's, Richmond AMV	(CHH)	175
20. Wanamaker's, Philadelphia AMV	(CHH)	335	Macy's-Midwest A (in. LaSalle's)	(RHM)	175
21. Lazarus, Columbus	(Fed)	332.8	49. Gimbels-Philadelphia AMV	(BAT)	170
22. Joske's, Texas AD	(All)	315	50. P.A. Bergner, Peoria AMV	(Ind)	165
Famous-Barr, St. Louis	(May)	315	G. Fox, Hartford	(May)	165
24. The Bon, Northwest A	(All)	310	J.B. Ivey, Charlotte AMV	(M-F)	165
25. Woodward & Lothrop, AMV Washington	(Ind)	308.4	53. Wieboldt's, Chicago AMV	(Ind)	164.9
26. Robinson's, Los Angeles A	(ADG)	295			
27. Filene's, Boston	(Fed)	288.7			
28. Goldblatt's, Chicago MF	(Ind)	265.9			

Smaller retailers can sometimes easily determine why a customer has not paid by simply asking why the bill is overdue. Larger retailers, who normally have less direct contact with customers, can get a similar effect by using a collection procedure that progresses from reminders (for the good customer) to legal remedies (for the deadbeat).

COMPANY/DIVISION	AFFIL.	VOLUME (MILLIONS)	COMPANY/DIVISION	AFFIL.	VOLUME (MILLIONS)
54. Gimbels-Midwest, Milwaukee	(BAT)	160	77. McAlpin's, Cincinnati AMV	(MS)	100
55. Younker's, Des Moines, MV	(EI)	152.1	M. O'Neil, Akron	(May)	100
56. Stern's, Paramus A	(All)	150	Denver Dry Goods	(ADG)	100
Liberty House, California AMV	(Amfac)	150	Boscov's, Reading MV	(Ind)	100
58. Joseph Horne, Pittsburgh	(ADG)	145	81. Donaldson's, Minneapolis A	(All)	95
59. Meier & Frank, Portland	(May)	135	82. Jones Store, Kansas City AMV	(MS)	90
Weinstock's, Sacramento A*	(CHH)	135	Hahne & Co., Newark	(ADG)	90
Stix, Baer, Fuller, St. Louis	(ADG)	135	J.L. Brandeis, Omaha AMV	(Ind)	90
Gimbels-Pittsburgh A	(BAT)	135	85. Gertz, Long Island A	(All)	85
Howland-Steinbach, White Plains A* MV	(SG)	135	Goudchaux, Baton Rouge MV	(Ind)	85
64. Broadway-Southwest A	(CHH)	130	Gottschalk's, Fresno AMV	(Ind)	85
Miller & Rhoads, Richmond AMV	(GBB)	130	88. Block's, Indianapolis A	(All)	80
66. ZCMI, Salt Lake City AMV	(Ind)	127.0	Strouss, Youngstown	(May)	80
67. Gayfer's Mobile, AMV	(MS)	125	McCurdy's, Rochester MV	(Ind)	80
68. Diamond's Phoenix, AMV	(D-H)	123.1	91. Bullock's-No. California	(Fed)	75.7
69. Rike's, Dayton	(Fed)	115.5	92. Hutzler's, Baltimore MV	(Ind)	75
70. Pomeroy's Pennsylvania A	(All)	115	93. Goldwater's, Phoenix A	(ADG)	70
May-D&F, Denver MV	(May)	115	94. Adam, Meldrum, Anderson, Buffalo MV	(Ind)	65
72. Goldsmith's, Memphis	(Fed)	110.9	H&S Pogue, Cincinnati	(ADG)	65
73. Sibley, Lindsay, Curr, Rochester	(ADG)	110	Read's, Bridgeport, A	(All)	65
74. Halle's, Cleveland AMV	(M-F)	105	Pizitz, Birmingham MV	(Ind)	65
75. McRae's, Jackson MV	(Ind.)	104	Robinson's, Florida	(ADG)	65
76. Boston Store, Milwaukee	(Fed)	101.3	Joslin's, Denver AMV	(MS)	65
			Miller's, Tennessee AMV	(GBB)	65

Note: Figures ending in "5" or "0" are estimates; others are exact sales as reported. Affiliation Code: All, Allied; ADG, Associated Dry Goods; BAT (BATUS, Inc. Retail Division); CHH, Carter Hawley Hale; CS, City Stores; DH, Dayton-Hudson; EI, Equitable of Iowa; Fed, Federated; GBB, Garfinckel, Brooks Bros.; Ind, Independent; MF, Marshall Field; MS, Mercantile Stores; RHM, R.H. Macy; SG, Supermarkets General.

(Note: Gottschalk's, Fresno has been moved into a tie for 85th place, with 1980 sales of $85 million, to correct an error in the July 1981 STORES' chart.)
A = American Express; D = Diners Club; M = Mastercard; V = Visa. *Card accepted at select branches only.

A **general collection procedure** to help collect overdue accounts is shown in Table 19.3. Each retailer should adapt the timing of communication to the specific customers. Adjustments can be made for unusual circumstances. If a customer explains after the first letter than an accident has caused a loss of income and that an insurance payment is forthcoming, the

Table 19.3
General collection procedure

TIME OVERDUE	TONE OF COMMUNICATION
30–60 days	Gentle reminder; nonthreatening; questioning reasons for oversight in not paying
60–90 days	Nonthreatening; direct question as to why bill unpaid; request for immediate attention (possibly requesting a meeting or letter)
90–120 days	Slightly threatening; direct request for immediate payment; point to need for good credit standing
120–150 days	Threatening; demand immediate payment; indicate consequences of nonpayment
150–180 days	Direct threat of legal actions or turning account over to collection agency
181 days and over	Notice of legal action or turning over to collection agency

retailer can stop sending reminders until the insurance settlement is scheduled. In fact, at any point in the procedure the process can be accelerated or slowed down.

One way to generate quicker cash flow from accounts receivable is **factoring,** which involves selling the accounts receivable to a third party such as a bank. The buyer pays the retailer less than the face value of the accounts; the discount is the factoring agent's fee to cover costs, risk, and profit.

A retailer who uses credit, especially in-house credit, must continually examine credit activities to see that they pay for themselves. They may pay for themselves by either increasing sales or by generating interest income. When the cost of giving credit exceeds the benefits, adjustments must be made. Adjustments may range from simply fine-tuning credit-granting and collection procedures to discontinuing credit operations.

Check Acceptance   Almost all retailers accept checks in payment for merchandise. In fact, **check acceptance** is almost mandatory for many retailers. The focus of this section is on controlling **bad checks** without alienating customers.

As the volume of checks continues to increase, so do the losses to retailers from bad checks. The determination of whether a check will be accepted should be considered part of the strategic planning process.

The principal emphasis from a strategic standpoint is how much customer identification and evaluation will occur before a customer's check is accepted. Some retailers will accept checks only when a great deal of identification is provided, sometimes including the customer's fingerprints. Obviously, fingerprinting and other highly involved identification procedures may aggravate some customers. Consequently, the retailer must also consider the impact of such rigid procedures on the store image. Sometimes, however, stores that require a great deal of identification may foster the image that they are trying everything possible to keep the prices down, including weeding out bad customers. Thus, a generalization as to what type of check acceptance procedures a store should use is very difficult to make. As with other elements in the retailer's strategic planning, a careful check of all the other plans and procedures will aid a retailer in determining the procedures to be used in accepting a check.

One way of trying to limit the number of bad checks is to use a check-acceptance service company. Basically, such companies will guarantee a check to be good if the retailer calls a number and gives certain information about the customer, such as a driver's license number. The fee for these services is usually about 2 to 4 percent of the dollar amount of the checks.[6] The use of one of these services transfers the risk of a bad check to the service company.

Another possible control is some type of photo surveillance system that takes pictures of people who are writing checks. These can be placed in a store in an inconspicuous manner so that the customer does not have great apprehension. The photos can then be used to help locate people who have given checks that are not accepted by the bank.

If losses from bad checks mount for a retailer, the fingerprinting services can also be bought. These services generally cost about two to three cents per check.[7]

The retailer should constantly monitor the losses occurring because of bad checks. Since retailers cash more checks than banks, bad-check losses can have quite an impact on the financial position of the company.[8] Retailers should understand that losing a check because of insufficient funds or other reasons requires that a large amount of merchandise be sold to make up that loss.

When bad checks become enough of a loss, the retailer should use whatever means are necessary to control those losses. Although customer reaction may be negative, many customers will probably begin to realize that the retailer must control losses owing to bad checks. Even if more stringent forms of identification and verification of checks are necessary, the retailer should try to diminish the negative impact they will have for most of the customers by attempting to give the impression of trying to keep losses and prices as low as possible rather than of just being suspicious.

Handling Returned Merchandise

A special type of consumer complaint is one that results in the return of merchandise of the consumer has purchased. Retailers should make a decision very early in the store's life as to what the procedures will be for **returned merchandise.** The establishment of these procedures should also follow the strategic planning process.

The retailer who plans to provide full customer service will normally need a relatively liberal return policy. Retailers who choose not to compete

STRATEGY IN ACTION 19.2

Bouncing Checks

Christmas shoppers had more than long lines to contend with this holiday season. They also faced problems paying for their purchases with personal checks. In the wake of a surge in so-called rubber checks, retail businesses across the U.S. are severely curtailing or eliminating check-cashing privileges. "When economic conditions worsen, people look to other means to solve their problems, including fraudulent checks," says Timothy K. Healy, a vice-president of Harris Trust and Savings Bank in Chicago. Harris' bad-check losses this year are running 97% above last year's.

At one discount drug chain in New York, customers can no longer use checks to pay for anything but prescriptions. "In the five years since we've been accepting checks, I don't think we had more than 25 or 30 checks bounce in a year, and of those, we collected money back on all but five or six," says Ralph Funt, co-owner of Raemart Drugs, Inc. This year the number of bounced checks in each of Raemart's three stores has been averaging 100 to 120 and half of those have been uncollectible.

The Illinois Retail Merchants Association estimates that 2% to 3% of all retail sales are now written off because the checks used to pay for goods are not collectible. Frank Abagnale of Houston, a consultant on bad checks to banks and retailers, contends that of the checks the Federal Reserve processed from January to September, 400,000 a day were "worthless"—drawn against insufficient or closed accounts. Abagnale says that two years ago, merchants could recover their money within 90 days on 72% of all worthless checks. "Today," he adds, "61% of those checks are not collected ever." He figures that retailers are losing $12 million a day.

Cash Crunch

People started using more checks to pay for purchases when banks and credit-card companies began tightening up on consumer debt, following Fed restrictions on bank loans in March, 1980. Great Atlantic and Pacific Tea Company saw an 18% rise in the use of checks by its East Coast customers after the credit restrictions took effect, according to Patrick A. Gilligan, A & P's director of check-cashing systems. The current recession has exacerbated the problem. From March to May of this year, he says, A & P's write-off on bad checks rose by a record 12% from the same period last year.

"We've looked at our experience in the 1974–75 recession, and we saw the same swing, the same pattern of fraud loss," says Harris Bank's Healy. "That period was the top of a bell curve, and we are seeing another top now." In June the bank raised its charge for bounced checks to $15 from $5, and it has started tightening its procedures for opening accounts and approving checks. Philadelphia's Girard Bank recently doubled—to $30—its charge on consumer and commercial accounts for each rubber check written or deposited, and First National Bank of Chicago closes new accounts after the third bounced check.

But higher fees alone do not seem to be the answer to the bad-check problem. King Sooper, Inc., the largest grocery chain in the Denver area, found that even charging customers a $10 penalty has not stopped bad checks. According to King Sooper's president, Jim D. Baldwin, customers view the $10 as a loan fee. "They're willing to have that $10 charge to buy groceries," he says.

New Laws

Fraud experts such as Houston's Abagnale are advising retailers that most bad checks come from people who have checking accounts less than six months old. To help identify these people, Abagnale successfully counseled retailers in six states—Minnesota, Utah, Colorado, Wisconsin, Illinois, and Virginia—to get their legislatures to force banks to put the date on which a new account is opened on all checks and to start new customers off with checks numbered 101.

A & P's Gilligan says that the next step is to ensure that people are who they say they are and to verify their banking relations. A & P has already reduced its bad-check write-off by $400,000 this year by verifying the credit and bank records of most of the 50,000 people who request check-cashing cards annually. As a result, A & P's denial of checking privileges has risen from 0.5%—the grocery industry average—to 2.5%.

At California's Broadway department stores, antifraud efforts have cut bad-check losses by 75% this year. The chain is using an on-line check authorization system that tracks how many checks a customer tries to write on any day and that rings a bell when a customer writes checks at more than one Broadway store. And for checks of more than $150, the clerk must ask the bank if the customer's account has sufficient funds. "We used to require just a Broadway charge plate and a California driver's license," says Winston H. Bowman, Jr., vice-president of credit.

Source: "Trying to Halt a Flood of Rubber Checks," p. 53. Reprinted from the 28 December 1981 issue of *Business Week* by special permission, © 1981 by McGraw-Hill, Inc., New York, NY 10020. All rights reserved.

on the basis of service may be able to have more stringent procedures about returning of merchandise. Although these generalizations will not be true to every case, they can help form the basic idea or the basic way that a retailer will handle returned merchandise.

Almost all retailers have to accept some returns to stay in business. This is especially true for damaged and broken merchandise. A customer who has just bought something, taken it home, and discovered that it does not work is probably not in the mood to be told that it can be shipped to the manufacturer and the manufacturer's warranty will take care of it.

The retailer's formal procedures for returned merchandise should be adequately displayed and made known to the customers. Rules such as the necessity of having cash register receipts or special procedures for sale merchandise certainly must be made known. The retailer should also not let rules overcome common sense on returns. How can a customer have a receipt for an item received as a gift, for instance? The retailer who demands receipts before allowing returns may have to make some concessions to common sense.

Returned merchandise creates inventory control problems, especially when the merchandise is still in condition to sell. It is often relatively difficult to return the merchandise to inventory and inform those responsible for inventory control records. The retailer must establish policies and procedures that clearly explain how to get merchandise back into inventory and how to process the necessary paperwork.

Policies and procedures relative to returned merchandise should be monitored regularly. If a significant amount of similar merchandise is being returned, something is wrong. The problem may be with return policies or it may be with some other facet of the store. The retailer should make an attempt to find out what is causing the problems. The retailer should also be alert for an abnormally small quantity of merchandise being returned.

There usually will be some merchandise that must be returned to any store because of improper fit, damage, or some other reason. If this is not occurring, it is possible that the return policies are too stringent. In this case, the retailer is likely losing some frustrated customers. The retailer should use the monitoring process as input for adapting the policies and procedures for handling returned merchandise.

Merchandise Delivery

Merchandise **delivery service** can be either an offensive or a defensive tool. Some retailers offer free delivery and emphasize this in their promotion (an offensive tool). Other retailers offer free delivery, but do not use it in their promotion (a defensive tool). Still others offer a delivery service but charge the customer for it (usually a defensive tool). Whatever the retailer decides regarding delivery, it should be consistent with overall retail objectives and strategy.

Once management decides to offer delivery service, store operations personnel must control the expense and handle deliveries. The operations decisions usually involve minimizing the cost of delivery while maintaining the desired delivery level. As gasoline and related costs continue to rise, delivery expense will also rise, but proper management can help control these increasing costs. Better scheduling, for instance, can help control delivery costs. Most customers who need delivery service are willing to wait a reasonable period of time before getting delivery. Keeping this in mind, the retailer may make deliveries on only a certain day during the week or in different market areas on different days of each week. This allows for better routing of the delivery trucks, thereby reducing expenses. A key to more efficient scheduling is to determine what defines a reasonable delivery time. If someone is replacing a broken refrigerator, the retailer would probably have to offer fast delivery service. If, however, the product being bought was new dining room furniture, the retailer could probably afford to wait several days before delivering. Since it is possible that the same retailer could encounter both of the above situations, some difference in the timing of deliveries may be necessary because of differences in the products.

As with other strategic decisions, the retailer must monitor delivery services to see that the costs are kept under control and that the benefits derived are greater than the costs. If the benefits and costs of delivery do not compare favorably, the retailer must reconsider the decision to offer the service. Some retailers may find it beneficial to charge a fee for delivery service, particularly if delivery is demanded by customers on short notice. The fee can be minimal and cover only the variable cost of offering the deliveries. Charging for delivery may irritate some customers, particularly if they bought quality merchandise from a quality-image retailer; therefore, it may be advantageous for the retailer to simply include the cost of delivery in the original price of the merchandise.

Setup Service

The retailer may choose to offer **set-up or installation service** for several reasons, not the least of which is to ensure that the product is installed correctly. Many complaints from customers are related not to the product but to the way the product was installed. The retailer can partially control this problem by offering set-up service either free or for a fee. The retailer should keep in mind that the service has a cost associated with it and that operations personnel must control these costs.

The retailer should also be careful that the employees who deliver and set up the merchandise act as salespeople for the store and do not detract from the image of the store. They should portray the image that the store is trying to maintain. If the store has a high-quality image, the employees setting up and/or delivering the merchandise must foster that image with clean uniforms, courteous manners, and so on.

As with delivery service, the set-up services should be monitored continuously to see that the benefits outweigh the costs. If set-up service costs more than the store benefits from the service, then the retailer may have to discontinue that service or increase the price of the service or of the merchandise.

Training Service

Another service that may be offered by the retailer is training consumers to use or operate products. The primary benefit may simply be fewer complaints about products. The offer to train customers may be used as a strong selling point for some products, such as microwave ovens.

Training programs should be conducted in a manner that achieves the desired results of helping to sell merchandise and helping the consumer use the products. As with delivery and set-up, the benefits derived from the service and the costs of the service are the keys to determining whether the retailer can offer the service on a continuing basis.

Hours of Operation

Another element of store operations that should be considered from the perspective of services is the **hours of operation.** Since the hours of operation must blend with the overall strategy, they should be considered a stategic decision area. Information and plans that should be reviewed before setting the store hours include the target market, the desired store image, and the types of merchandise carried.

Perhaps the most dominant element in selecting store hours is the target market. The hours a store is open should be based on the needs and shopping patterns of the retailer's target market. If a retailer is catering to young adults or two-income couples, the store will likely have to be open in the late afternoons and early evenings to give the working people a chance to shop. A store selling building materials to both contractors and ultimate consumers will also have to consider both target markets in setting the hours of operation. Many of these supply houses have historically served a commercial market, with minimal retail emphasis. In recent years, however, there has been a widespread shift toward the retail market. Unfortunately, many of those who have increased their emphasis on retailing still maintain operating hours designed for contractors, which are basically early in the morning, usually 6 or 7 A.M., until 5 P.M. Further, to serve contractors, the store only need to be open until noon on Saturday, if at all. These hours frequently do not fit the needs of consumers who tend to perform do-it-yourself activities at night or on weekends when many suppliers are closed. Probably the hours of 6 P.M. to 8 P.M. and weekends would be major selling periods to these consumers.

Sometimes store hours will depend more on the season or special sales events. Most people are familiar with stores maintaining longer hours just before Christmas or other major selling periods. These periods should be planned carefully and should be coordinated with the overall operations of the store because extended hours effect the personnel planning, merchandise availability, utility expenses, and so on.

DETERMINE SERVICES TO BE OFFERED

The retailer should offer services that are important to target customers. Therefore, the retailer's basic task is to identify the **primary service components** in the trade and their relative importance to target customers.

A relatively simple but effective approach is to ask a selected group of customers to name the services they consider important and then to rank or rate the degree of relative importance of each. Table 19.4 presents an example of such ratings for an automobile dealer's service department.

In determining the services to be offered, the retailer should review the pricing objectives. If the store is to compete on the basis of price, the retailer can consider a service strategy that involves emphasizing no services. Customers will often accept a reduction or elimination or certain services, if there is a corresponding decrease in price. Many supermarkets, for example, now have customers bag their own groceries and carry them to their cars. Some warehouse furniture and appliance outlets do not provide free delivery.

DETERMINE LEVEL OF EACH SERVICE

Part of the determination about the level of each service can result from an extension of the previous step. Along with ascertaining the importance of each service, the retailer needs to find out which are qualifying services and which are determining services.

A **qualifying service** is a service that a retailer must offer to even qualify for the customer's consideration. A service may become a qualifying service because it is extremely important to customers or because most competitors are perceived to be equal in this attribute. A prestige apparel store

Table 19.4
Importance and performance ratings for
an automobile dealer's service department

ATTRIBUTE NUMBER	ATTRIBUTE DESCRIPTION	MEAN IMPORTANCE RATING[a]	MEAN PERFORMANCE RATING[b]
1	Job done right the first time	3.83	2.63
2	Fast action on complaints	3.63	2.73
3	Prompt warranty work	3.60	3.15
4	Able to do any job needed	3.56	3.00
5	Service available when needed	3.41	3.05
6	Courteous and friendly service	3.41	3.29
7	Car ready when promised	3.38	3.03
8	Perform only necessary work	3.37	3.11
9	Low prices on service	3.29	2.00
10	Clean up after service work	3.27	3.02
11	Convenient to home	2.52	2.25
12	Convenient to work	2.43	2.49
13	Courtesy buses and rental cars	2.37	2.35
14	Send out maintenance notices	2.05	3.33

[a] Ratings obtained from a four-point scale of "extremely important," "important," "slightly important," and "not important."

[b] Ratings obtained from a four-point scale of "excellent," "good," "fair," and "poor." A "no judgment" category was also provided.

Source: John A. Martilla and John C. James, "Importance-Performance Analysis," *Journal of Marketing,* January 1977, p. 78. Reprinted with permission from *Journal of Marketing* (published by the American Marketing Association).

that does not offer alterations would not normally be considered by many customers; alterations would therefore be a qualifying service. Retailers are usually forced to offer these services but can seldom develop them into a competitive advantage.

A **determining service** is a service that actually determines the customer's store preference and choice. Retailers often find it difficult to attract customers by trying to outdo the competition on basic qualifying services. The service attribute that helps attract certain groups (the determining service) may seem relatively unimportant. A small hardware retailer, for example, realized that he was receiving more and more requests for relatively short lengths of wire fencing (50 feet). His standard policy was not to sell anything but complete rolls (100 feet and up). Contemplating this situation, the retailer pinpointed three key causal factors: (1) a new leash law for dogs was to take effect in a few months, (2) more and more people were gardening, and (3) no other hardware retailers would sell fencing in less than full rolls, such as for dog yards and small gardens. As a result, the retailer began a new service policy of offering to cut wire fencing to any desired length. Although a minor service, the policy turned out to be a *determining service* for a surprising number of new customers and helped the retailer establish a distinct competitive advantage.

In general, higher levels of customer service enhance customer satisfaction, store image, and sales. There is a limit, however, to the benefits of any service. Some services, no matter how much improved or well provided, have little impact on sales. A supermarket could substantially improve its unit pricing scheme and not increase sales at all, for example. The retailer's task in determining service levels is to balance the expected benefit and the expected cost.

DETERMINE THE FORM OF SERVICES

The form of services involves two elements: *pricing* and *how to provide*. A retailer like Sears, for example, has three basic pricing options for repair service on its consumer durables: (1) free repair service for a specific time (such as one year), (2) service contracts, and (3) no repair, thereby leaving it to independent specialists. Similarly, three how-to options are available for repair service: (1) hire and train service personnel and locate them throughout the country, (2) make contract arrangements with independent specialists to become authorized service centers, and (3) let each retail unit make its own decision. The specific form chosen must be compatible with all other strategies.

EVALUATE COST EFFICIENCY OF SERVICES

All services offered by the retailer have a corresponding cost, which should be relatively easy to determine. Most services have both direct and indirect cost components. The direct cost for delivery service is the sum of vehicle cost, employee costs, and maintenance, repair, and operating costs. The primary indirect cost is managerial time.

The benefits are often much more difficult to quantify than the costs. Each retail trade typically has basic services that individual retailers are almost forced to view as competitive necessities or defensive services. Most furniture dealers, for example, feel they must offer delivery, usually free. Rather than trying to quantify the benefits of services such as these, the retailer should try to provide the service effectively and at minimum cost.

Some other services call for the retailer to make a qualitative judgment of the service benefit. Usually services can be judged in light of their contribution to the desired store image. Examples of this type of service include children's playrooms, information desks, free coffee, and public restrooms.

Still other services can yield their benefit by their impact on the sales of specific product lines. Examples include providing demonstration models, facilities for on-site product usage, extended warranties, and bridal registry.

Service Charges

The retailer faces a decision about whether to charge the customer a fee for rendering some services. For traditional services, such as listening to complaints, the retailer simply cannot charge. Customers usually expect to pay a fee for services such as product repair, credit, and snack bars.

A key point to remember is that the customer eventually pays for the service, either in the form of a direct service charge or indirectly through higher prices for merchandise. The retailer's fundamental service strategy must be based on how he or she wants to compete with other retailers. Retailers who want to compete on the basis of price should lean toward "unbundling" services, which means reducing the base price of the merchandise and charging separately for each service. Some furniture retailers, such as Levitz, have adopted this procedure. Retailers who want to compete on the basis of services must price the merchandise high enough to include all service costs.

Third-Party Service

Sometimes customers may need services that the retailer cannot or does not want to offer, perhaps because of lack of skill, high start-up costs, or not enough demand. In such situations, the retailer might consider utilizing a third party to provide the service. An appliance store might not maintain a repair shop but simply contract with or recommend a shop that specializes in appliance repair to customers.

PLAN AND ORGANIZE CUSTOMER SERVICE DEPARTMENT

Although many larger retailers maintain customer service departments, their scope and authority vary widely. At minimum, this department should be charged with the responsibility of helping to coordinate and integrate customer services. Depending on a firm's organizational structure, the customer service department can be made responsible for (1) complaints and adjustments, (2) credit operations, (3) repair and parts, and (4) technical assistance for customers.

Complaint Handling[9]

Complaint handling deserves special attention because of its tremendous potential for both positive and negative impact on retailers. A major recent survey of consumer complaint handling in the United States turned up some interesting findings:

1. 41.1% of surveyed households that initiated complaints reported *totally unsatisfactory results.*

2. Nearly 70% of reported complaints were not satisfactorily remedied.

3.   31% of households who experienced problems did not complain.

4.   Of those who did not complain, 55.6% felt it was not worth the effort, 13.5% did not know where to go or what to do, 21.1% felt that no one would be interested in their problem, and 63.2% *did not intend to re-purchase from the store [emphasis added]*.[10]

The following is excerpted from a discussion of those and other findings:

> Complaining consumers give business a chance to retain their patronage. Responsive companies were rewarded by the greatest degree of continued brand loyalty. Noncomplaining dissatisfied consumers may not have been angry enough to complain but were more often unhappy enough to switch brands . . . Given the high costs of marketing, it may be less expensive to resolve the problem of an old customer than to win new customers . . . it may be to businesses's self-interest to solicit complaints. . . . Complaints whose problems were satisfactorily resolved exhibited much stronger brand loyalty than households whose complaints were not solved. Businesses that did not satisfy their complaining customer lost much of the marketing advantage resulting from complaint handling.[11]

Table 19.5 lists the most common customer complaints. As you can see, most of these complaints are related directly to retailers. The overall implication for retailers is that complaint handling can be an effective retailing strategy. Attaining the potential benefits, however, requires that retailers make a serious commitment to upgrading complaint-handling capabilities *and* resolving customer problems.

Complaint-handling activities are part of the routine store operations and should be approached from a strategic planning perspective. As with other areas of the strategic planning process, the retailer should begin with a review of other plans and information. Complaint-handling procedures can have a major impact on store image, for example.

A key factor in handling complaints effectively is to develop standard procedures to follow. Information about these procedures should be made readily available to both customers and employees. All employees and customers should understand that when a customer desires to make an official complaint, there is a specific place for that customer to take the complaint.

The complaint-handling procedure should not be so complex that it makes customers forget the complaint and decide to shop at another store. At the same time, it has to be difficult enough to deter insignificant complaints. Unfortunately, some customers simply like to complain and, if allowed the opportunity, will complain about everything the store does. A tiered approach designed to have lower-level employees handle minor complaints and higher-level employees handle major complaints can be effective. A problem with this approach, of course, is that what seems like a relatively inconsequential complaint may be major enough for a particular customer to decide to shop elsewhere.

Table 19.5
Most common consumer complaints

TYPE OF CONSUMER PROBLEM	HOUSEHOLDS HAVING THIS TYPE PROBLEM		TYPE OF CONSUMER PROBLEM	HOUSEHOLDS HAVING THIS TYPE PROBLEM	
	NO.	%*		NO.	%*
1. Store did not have product advertised for sale	203	24.9	12. Goods received in damaged condition	65	8.0
2. Unsatisfactory performances/ quality of product (workmanship/ingredients)	182	22.4	13. Manufacturer/dealer didn't live up to gurantee/warranty	58	7.1
3. Unsatisfactory repair	165	20.3	14. Dealer/salesperson misrepresented product/service	53	6.5
4. Unsatisfactory service (unrelated to repair)	127	15.6	15. Failure to receive refund	43	5.3
5. Long wait for delivery	84	10.3	16. Product unsafe	30	3.7
6. Failure to receive delivery	83	10.2	17. Item received different than one bought	27	3.3
7. Overcharge or excessive price	78	9.6	18. Product harmful to environment	26	3.2
8. Distasteful or offensive advertising	75	9.2	19. No return from repair or service	19	2.3
9. Product/service not as ordered/agreed on	72	8.8	20. Instructions for use/care unclear/incomplete	19	2.3
10. Incorrect/deceptive or fradulent billing	70	8.6	21. Credit terms misrepresented	14	1.7
11. Deceptive advertising/ packaging/pricing	66	8.1	22. Unauthorized repair or service	13	1.6
			23. Other	10	1.2

*N = 814 households that experienced consumer problem(s); 1,528 incidences of problems.

Source: John Goodman and Marc Grainer, Technical Assistance Research Programs (TARP), Inc., 1979, Washington, D.C.

Another major problem with complaint handling is determining whether complaints were handled effectively. One way of doing this is to send letters or short questionnaires to customers who have made official complaints and, if possible, to those who have simply indicated dissatisfaction with the store. This procedure only allows the retailer to find out how well complaints the retailer knew about have been handled. Another dissatisfied group may be customers who do not complain but who have legitimate complaints about the business. A way of handling these customers is to have some type of periodic check to see if there were any complaints that customers did not bring to the attention of the store. These checks, in the form of questionnaires sent out periodically or random in-store surveys, may give customers the idea that the retailer does have them foremost in mind and may help to convince the customer of the desirability of shopping in that particular store. Thus, the handling of complaints can become a type of promotional activity to aid the retailer as well as a defensive activity to keep the retailer from being hurt.

The investigation of complaints should have two objectives. First, the retailer should try to be sure that the problem has been rectified as well as possible in the mind of the consumer. Second, the retailer should determine why the complaint occurred. If complaints are occurring for the same reason on a regular basis, that reason should be corrected. That is, the retailer might find that changing the procedures within the store or training employees a little differently or even terminating some employees will help to keep the complaint level down.

MONITOR AND ADAPT

Customer service programs are not static; they tend to be dynamic because customer needs and preferences change over time. From the retailer's standpoint, services can be viewed as having a **service life cycle,** which can be divided into five stages:

1. *Introduction.*   A service is first introduced in an area by a retailer seeking a differential advantage. The retailer may be the first in the trading area to open on Sunday or at night or to offer trading stamps. A service in this stage is used as an offensive tool.

2. *Duplication.*   Competitors add the same or a similar service to neutralize its drawing power.

3. *Stalemate.*   All retailers offer the service, but it is not a differential advantage for any retailer. If the service is popular with consumers, none of the retailers will want to drop it because they would then be at a competitive disadvantage. A service in this stage is a defensive tool.

4. *Institutionalization.*   If the stalemate remains unchanged for some time, the service will become institutionalized as a basic part of the trade's offering.

5. *Replacement or Abandonment.*   Some institutionalized services seem to never disappear completely, but some retailers may abandon a service when it loses its attractiveness to consumers. Some of these retailers may promote the abandonment as leading to lower prices. Other retailers may simply replace the service with another one. Eventually, an abandoned service may be reintroduced by a retailer, beginning the cycle again, as in the case of trading stamps.[12]

A major implication of the service life cycle is that retailers should add services cautiously. Once a service is added, it is difficult to eliminate when the benefits to the retailer dwindle.

Retailers should continuously monitor their own and their competitors' service programs in relation to customers' attitudes and expectations. This monitoring can take the form of comparison shopping, periodic customer surveys, suggestion boxes, and input from an established complaint-handling system.

The periodic customer survey can be especially useful. Table 19.4 presents importance ratings for various service attributes. In addition, it presents in the right-hand column the retailer's *performance rating* for each service attribute. The retailer could also obtain performance ratings for key competitors. These data can tell the retailer how important various services are to customers and how well the store is performing the service relative to customer expectations and, perhaps, to the competition. The dealer in Table 19.4, for example, probably needs to concentrate efforts on improving performance on attributes 1, 3, and 9. Conversely, the dealer is performing well on factor 14, but that service is not particularly important to customers; perhaps the expense of this service is not justified.

KEY CONCEPTS

Defensive tool (services)

Offensive tool (services)

In-house open accounts

In-house credit cards

Third-party credit cards

Credit limit

Collection procedure

Factoring

Bad checks

Check acceptance service

Returned merchandise

Delivery service

Set-up or installation service

Training service

Hours of operation

Qualifying service

Determining service

Complaint handling

Service life cycle

REVIEW QUESTIONS

1. Develop the strategic customer service planning process.
2. Discuss the key factors to review for customer service planning.
3. Discuss the ramifications of a no-service strategy.
4. Discuss the problems of determining the cost efficiency of a service.
5. Discuss the idea of using complaint handling as an offensive retail strategy.
6. Discuss how the target market might affect hours of operation.
7. Why are dissatisfied customers who do not complain more of a potential problem than those who do complain?
8. Discuss the advantages and disadvantages of the three types of credit.

LEARNING EXERCISES

1. Analyze three retailers competing in the same trade to find out how they use services as a part of their overall strategies. In each case, do you think the service strategy fits the overall strategy?

2. Check the hours of operation of five competing stores. Explain any differences (such as in terms of strategy and target market).

3. Ask the manager of a large retail store how complaints are handled. Ask three employees the same question. Are there any differences in their answers? Why or why not?

DECISION SITUATION 19.1: **ATHLETIC OUTFITTERS V**

Athletic Outfitters realized that offering customer services could help the store remain profitable. One service dealt with uniforms for the city's recreation activities. When the city had tryouts for youth soccer and baseball leagues, Athletic Outfitters sent a representative to take orders for the shirts participants had to buy. After participants were assigned to teams, Athletic Outfitters ordered the correct sizes and put names and numbers on the shirts. The profit margins on these shirts were not as large as on regular merchandise, but there were no inventory costs and the goodwill developed was very positive.

QUESTIONS

1. Do you think the service described above is appropriate? Why or why not?

2. What other services could be offered for organized sports?

3. What impact would late arrival of shirts have on Athletic Outfitters' image? Can this risk be avoided?

4. What services could Athletic Outfitters offer to other customers?

DECISION SITUATION 19.2: **TERESA'S PHARMACY**

Teresa is the owner of a pharmacy in a town of 30,000 people. The store is located in the busiest shopping center in town. Teresa opened the store last week and is still trying to decide exactly what she wants to do with the store. She is sure she does not want to compete on price. She wants to give good service to the customers and become their only drugstore.

QUESTIONS

1. What customer services do you think Teresa will have to offer as a defensive strategy? Why?

2. What additional services could Teresa offer to attract customers?

3. How would your answers change if Teresa wanted a low-priced image?

NOTES

1. William R. Davidson, Alton F. Doody, and Daniel J. Sweeney, *Retailing Management* (New York: Ronald Press, 1975), p. 459.

2. Marian Burk Rothman, "The Customer with Special Needs," *Stores*, October 1979, p. 54.

3. John E. Conney, "With Video Shopping Services, Goods You See on the Screen Can Be Delivered to Your Door," *Wall Street Journal*, 14 July 1981, p. 48.

4. Marian Burk Rothman, "Third Party," *Stores*, September 1981, p. 41.

5. *Ibid.*

6. Brian McNamara, "Checking Out Your Customers' Checks," *Chain Store Age Executive*, July 1980, p. 31.

7. *Ibid.*

8. *Ibid.*

9. The *Journal of Retailing* published a special issue, Fall 1981, on consumer satisfaction, dissatisfaction, and complaints.

10. "Consumer Complaint Handling in America: Final Report," Technical Assistance Research Programs, Study for United States Office of Consumer Affairs, Washington, D.C., 1979, pp. 10–13.

11. *Ibid.*, p. 15.

12. Don L. James, Bruce J. Walker, and Michael J. Etzel, *Retailing Today* (New York: Harcourt, Brace, Jovanovich, 1981), pp. 367–368.

PART IV

RETAILING CONTROL

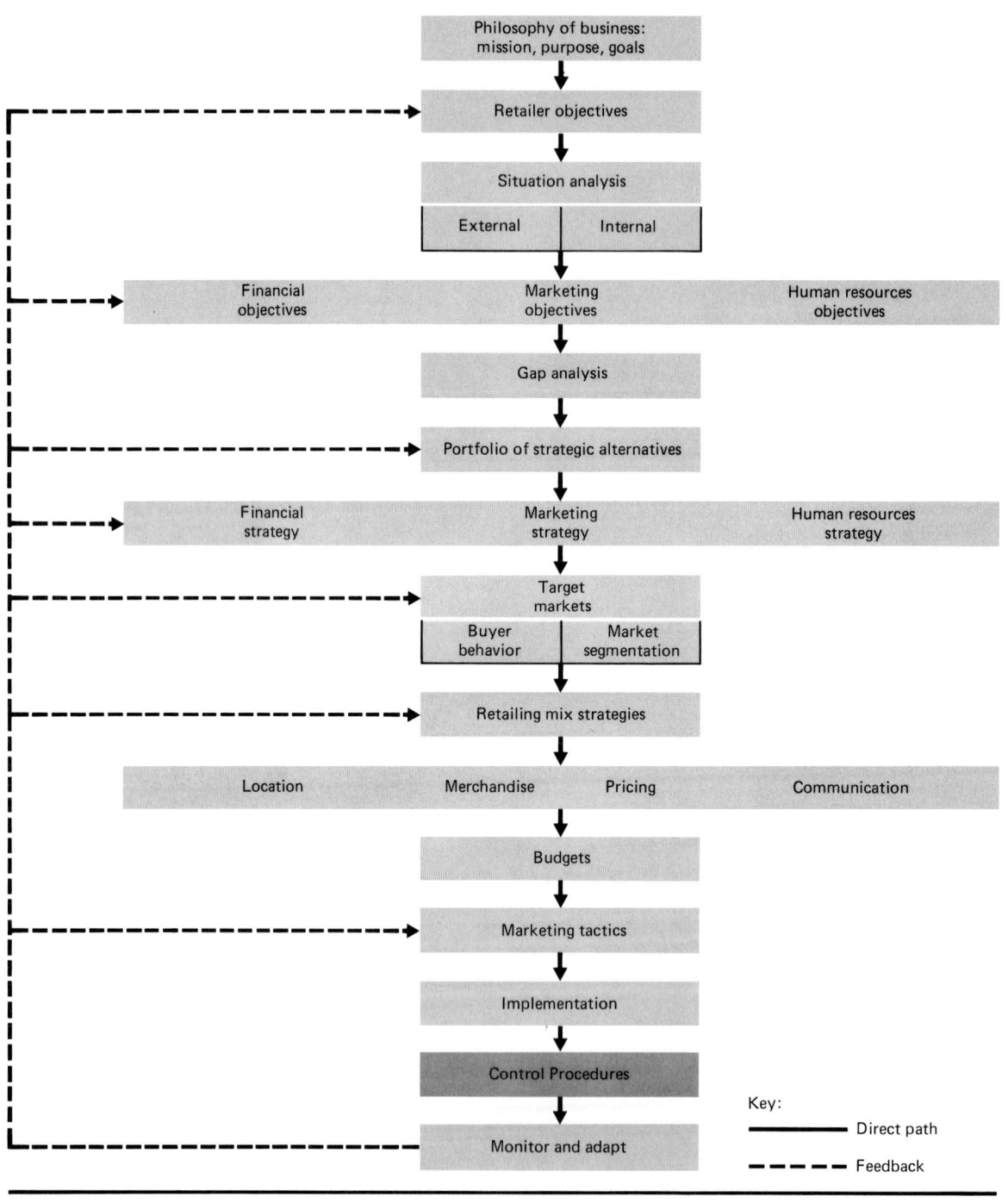

STRATEGIC RETAIL MANAGEMENT MODEL

Philosophy of business:
mission, purpose, goals

Retailer objectives

Situation analysis

| External | Internal |

Financial objectives   Marketing objectives   Human resources objectives

Gap analysis

Portfolio of strategic alternatives

Financial strategy   Marketing strategy   Human resources strategy

Target markets

| Buyer behavior | Market segmentation |

Retailing mix strategies

Location   Merchandise   Pricing   Communication

Budgets

Marketing tactics

Implementation

Control Procedures

Monitor and adapt

Key:
———— Direct path
– – – – Feedback

Chapter 20
The Retail Control Process

LEARNING OBJECTIVES

1. To understand how the control process relates to retailing strategy.

2. To understand the actions necessary to construct and use an effective retail control process.

INTRODUCTION

Strategic retail management provides a framework for developing both overall and functional strategies. We have emphasized that the overall retail strategy and each of the functional strategies must be integrated to form a consistent and cohesive whole. The effectiveness of these strategies is predicated on the proper implementation and operation, as envisioned by the retail planners. However, since there are no perfect plans, deviations will occur. These deviations from planned strategy must be detected so that any necessary adjustments can be made. Consequently, the latter segments of the strategic retail management model depicted at the beginning of the chapter deal specifically with the **strategic retail control process.** If the control function is handled properly, any deviations from the strategic plans generated and implemented by the retailer will be indicated so that adjustments can be implemented.

Recall that the decision model for each of the functional chapters of this text concludes with "monitor and adapt." Essentially, these monitor and adapt steps represent the control element for each specific functional area. The basic process underlying functional control and overall control is the same. In fact, the various functional control processes form the foundation of the overall control process.

THE CONTROL PROCESS

Effective control exists when (1) measurable standards exist, (2) actual performance and desired performance are compared, and (3) corrective action is taken when necessary. Figure 20.1 presents a model of the strategic control process that is designed to fulfill these three conditions. Note that Fig. 20.1 begins with objectives and strategies. These two elements were discussed in detail in Chapter 2 and briefly in each of the functional chapters. Most of the other elements depicted in the model have also been discussed. The setting of performance standards, for example, is part of planning the control procedures and was discussed extensively in Chapters 3 and 13 and more briefly in each functional chapter, and contingency planning was alluded to in Chapters 2 and 4.

The components of the control model can be viewed as a four-step control process:

1. Plan control procedures.

2. Implement control procedures.

3. Monitor performance measures.

4. Determine and implement necessary adaptations.

Plan Control Procedures

Planning **control procedures** involves a variety of actions, including making plans for the remaining three steps of the control process. The key

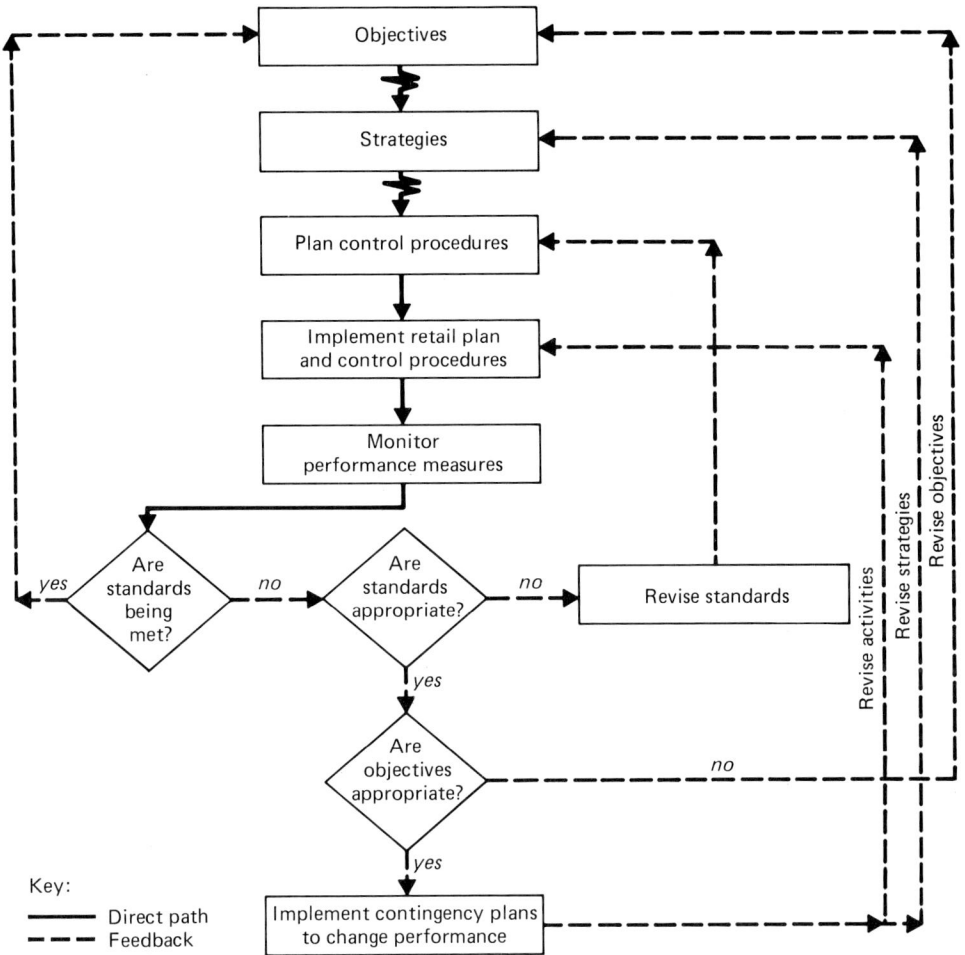

Figure 20.1
A model of the strategic control process

elements discussed here are determining what to control, establishing performance standards, and choosing specific measurement techniques.

What to Control. Although a seemingly easy task, determining what to control can be surprisingly difficult. The retailer should consider developing control procedures to account for any performance or result that is important. Consider the importance of the various functional areas, such as location, human resources, the organizational structure, merchandise, pricing, advertising, and financial matters. The results generated by these and other functional areas mentioned below and discussed throughout this text can have a major impact on the retailer's ability to achieve overall objectives.

Specific performance standards should be established for each factor chosen for control.

Performance Standards.   Specific **performance standards** must be derived from the objectives stated earlier in the strategic planning process. Each objective should have a corresponding standard. The standards must meet three criteria. First, each standard must be *quantifiable*. It is impossible to establish satisfactory levels of performance without some quantitative direction. A standard stated as "improve merchandise turnover," for example, does not help those responsible for merchandise planning; to meet this criterion, the standard might be stated as "improve merchandise turnover from 5 to 7 during the next year."

Second, standards must be *measurable*. Some objectives can be couched in such general terms that developing measurable standards is next to impossible. Objectives involving the retailer's social responsibility or employee courtesy are desirable but difficult to measure. For standards such as these, specific control is impossible unless the retailer can formulate a "surrogate" measure or divide the objective into measurable subobjectives. Measurable standards for social responsibility could involve the number of recyclable merchandise items carried, the amount of money donated to charities, the number of memberships in civic organizations, and the like.

Third, standards must be *congruent* with each other and with all other facets of the strategic plan. Incongruent standards only lead to confusion. Standards involving relatively high profit margins and relatively large market share can be in conflict; sometimes large market share can be obtained only by accepting lower prices and lower profit margins. Another example of an incongruent standard is an advertising objective such as "increase awareness from 50 percent to 70 percent" that has a standard of "dollar sales generated."

The retailer should also specify **tolerance limits** for each standard, although they are not a criterion for standards. These tolerance limits consist of an *upper control limit* and a *lower control limit* (which were depicted graphically in Fig. 13.2). Ideally, the retailer desires to achieve exactly the stated standard. Many times, however, other levels of performance are acceptable in that they do not cause adaptations or adjustments. Note also that the stated objectives may be too optimistic or pessimistic, which would result in over- or understated performance standards. Corrective actions when actual performance deviates from an unrealistic performance standard might lead to even greater problems.

The retailer should carefully select those performance levels at which performance is no longer acceptable; these levels form the tolerance limits. The retailer could choose a standard for market share as 10 percent and set tolerance limits of 9 percent and 11 percent. As long as market share remained between these figures and no sharp trends were evident, no action would be taken. However, a dip below 9 percent would alert the retailer that corrective action is necessary. A share greater than 11 percent could be an indication that a competitor is weakening and becoming vulnerable to more aggressive marketing activity (which is also a corrective action).

Measurement Techniques.[1]   Specific measurement techniques or yardsticks must be selected for each performance standard. These yardsticks can be divided into growth and profitability measures and efficiency measures.

Growth and profitability measures are designed to examine whether planned results are being achieved. Key measures include sales, market share, and contribution. **Sales measures** can be devised relatively easily for the entire store, for specific departments, and perhaps for specific merchandise lines. **Market share or penetration measures** for a store can be devised for the direct competitive market (such as grocery stores versus grocery stores) and for the total competitive market, including indirect competitors (grocery stores versus convenience stores and restaurants). Additional market share yardsticks can be devised for specific product classifications (share of total shoe sales in local market, regardless of store classification). **Measures of contribution** (in terms of net profit and gross profit) can be generated for each department or other merchandise control unit (MCU), as discussed in Chapters 11 and 13. Multiunit organizations can also measure the contribution of each separate unit. Note that there are numerous other measurement techniques such as financial measures (ROI, ROA), consumer attitude measures, and merchandise control measures (turnover, GMROI). These measures were discussed in detail in Chapters 3, 8, and 13, respectively.

Efficiency measures are used to evaluate the efficiency of retailing expenditures. These measures are normally designed for the performance standards set in each functional area. Inventory turnover (Chapter 13), for example, is a control mechanism for inventory control. Although no ideal turnover rate can be suggested for all retailers, certain ranges are appropriate for specific types of merchandise and stores. A lower than acceptable turnover rate indicates too much inventory relative to sales, or possibly the wrong inventory is being stocked. The latter explanation can be verified by applying another control measure such as inventory aging. Combining inventory age with turnover would provide a clearer indication of the actual problem and, thus, which corrective actions should be taken.

Other efficiency control measures discussed earlier include merchandise budgeting and open-to-buy (Chapter 11), advertising effectiveness measures (Chapter 16), and salesperson performance measures (Chapter 17). Although a complete list of efficiency measures would be quite lengthy, a fairly comprehensive list is presented in Table 20.1.

Implement Control Procedures   Once the control procedures are planned, the retailer must implement them. As shown in Fig. 20.1, the initial implementation of the control procedures (including the measuring techniques) should occur at the same time

STRATEGY IN ACTION 20.1

Operating Control in Supermarkets

Retailer control over operations can mean the difference between a profit and loss. Those retailers that are able to identify and use control measures through strategic management and follow-up control will be more successful than other retailers. The retail food industry, as much as any retailer group, has had to keep tight control over operations to maintain their small net profit margins. The following illustrates some of the operation control measures in use and the 1979 national figures for these measures.

	SALES SIZE*				
	$1–2	$2–4	$4–6	$6–8	$8+
$ Sales/week	$27,600	$52,100	$90,000	$127,500	$214,300
No. checkouts	3.0	4.4	6.0	7.3	9.5
Full-time employees	8.9	14.5	22.4	31.7	46.6
Part-time employees	7.6	13.9	24.5	33.4	49.2
Sq. ft. of selling space	6,280	9,770	14,140	17,670	23,150
Weekly sales/sq. ft.	$4.39	$5.33	$6.36	$7.21	$9.26
Weekly sales/checkout	$9,200	$11,840	$15,000	$17,460	$22,550

*In millions

Selected operating results for a typical supermarket are:

- Sales trend vs. a year ago (%)   +12.4
- Store labor expenses/sales (excluding fringes)   8.3
- Store labor expenses/sales (fringes)   1.8
- Store rent & real estate/sales   1.2
- Utilities/sales   1.0
- Sales per employee-hour $68.56
- Average hourly labor cost $5.92
- Grocery inventory turnover rate — Stores   18.7
- Grocery inventory turnover rate — Warehouse   15.5
- Gross profit %, with own central warehouse   22.3
- Gross profit %, without own central warehouse   20.5
- Sales transaction per customer $12.00

While these are national figures, the point to be made is that this is the type of data the individual retailer should be gathering and analyzing to maintain control over store operations. Goals should be established and deviations, when they occur, should indicate the need for management decision making. For a food retailer, figures such as these might provide rough estimates for developing an operating control base.

Source: "Retail Operating Performance" and "Labor and Productivity," *Progressive Grocer,* April 1981, pp. 127, 130, 131. Reprinted with permission.

the retailing plans are implemented. Additional control procedures can be designed and implemented as needed. Examples of control procedures include merchandise budgeting, financial analysis and budgeting, employee evaluations, and consumer attitude surveys. Note that the overall procedure should specify the person responsible for monitoring the performance measure to use, the timing of the performance analysis, and the person who should receive the results.

Table 20.1
Examples of efficiency measures

Location

Traffic generated per day or week

Number of new customers per time period

Merchandise

Merchandise turnover per store, department, or product

Percent merchandise returned

Percent sales on promotion (reduce price)

Number of out-of-stocks recorded

Number of rainchecks issued

Average inventory age

Percent of inventory shrinkage

Cost per order placed

Number of inquiries for nonstocked merchandise

Percent of converted customers (those who visit store and actually buy)

Sales per square foot of floor space

Percent of sales accounted for by new products

Price

Profit margin per store, department, or product

Average dollars per transaction

Promotion

Advertising cost per thousand viewers reached, for each time period and for each medium

Percentage of advertising audience who noted, saw, or recalled message

Attitude tracking of target market (image and position)

Number of inquiries per advertising campaign or time period

Advertising cost per sales dollar

Number or percent of coupons redeemed

Display costs per sales dollar

Personnel

Sales-force turnover

Managerial turnover

Average sales-force cost per sale

Average number of sales per salesperson

Average revenue per salesperson

Number of customer complaints about sales force

Once control procedures are on-line, data should be generated for the next step, monitoring. The data needed for monitoring and comparing standards with performance were defined in the discussion about measurement techniques.

It is important to note that the control process relies heavily on the retail information system (Chapter 8) for appropriate data. In fact, providing data for the control process may be the most important function of the internal component of the information system.

Monitor Performance Measures

The specific purposes of monitoring are to (1) compare the retailer's actual performance with the performance standards and (2) analyze any deviations of performance from the standards. The control procedures developed and implemented in steps 1 and 2 are used to monitor the retailer's performance. Any deviations beyond the tolerance limits must be analyzed by the retailer.

An important question at this point (and for the overall control process) is who does the monitoring. Ideally, the manager responsible for monitoring (and analyzing deviations) will also have the authority to initiate corrective action in the following steps. If these tasks are separate, the retailer must ensure that effective communication channels exist between the two individuals. The purpose of analyzing performance deviations is to find out why the deviation occurred so that corrective actions can be taken.

Determine and Implement Necessary Adaptations

Making the necessary adaptations involves taking corrective action to alleviate or eliminate the deviations discovered in Step 3. The type of corrective actions needed depends on the nature of the performance deviations. The two basic forms corrective actions can take are to *change the standard* or *change the performance*.

Despite good planning, the objectives and corresponding performance standards may be improper because of mistakes or unforeseen environmental changes. The performance standard for sales, for example, would probably need to be reduced if a major new competitor moved into the market. Conversely, if a major competitor left the market, perhaps the performance standard for sales should be raised.

If the retailer determines that the performance standards are appropriate, the remaining alternative for correcting the deviations is to change the performance. Adjusting the retail performance can involve a wide variety of actions. First, the strategy developed to achieve the stated objectives may be inappropriate. If dollar sales objectives are not being achieved using a strategy of price reductions, the retailer's efforts to improve the sales performance could involve price maintenance, price increases, more advertising, and so on.

Second, if the strategies are appropriate, the retailer may have to adjust the manner in which the strategies are being implemented (change the way specific activities are performed, for instance). Assume that a retailer's store traffic (a performance measure) falls below standard tolerance limits. Since

STRATEGY IN ACTION 20.2

Getting Strategies under Control

The Limited, a clothing chain appealing to fashion-conscious sixteen-to thirty-five-year-old women, began to have problems in the late 1970s. Often admired for its success and sound strategic decisions, The Limited found itself on hard times.

After analyzing the situation, Leslie Wexner, founder and chairman of the chain, decided that they were engaging in too many long-range projects at one time. Problems became evident in the conditions of huge inventories, high interest expenses, and a computerized storage system that failed to improve inventory control.

The Limited needed to pare its strategies to a more manageable level. To institute this control, weekly reports were established and the objectives the company could not accomplish were eliminated. Store growth was curtailed, expenses were reduced, fewer markdowns were taken, and the distribution system was improved as a result of Wexner's control methods. Earnings have increased, sales per square foot are the highest in their store product category, returned merchandise is below industry average, and return on equity is above average.

Retailers must not only select the appropriate strategy, but must also perform within their capabilities. The Limited apparently did not engage in selecting poor strategies; they were simply exceeding their capacities. Controlling growth and expectations is necessary for long-term orderly growth.

Source: "The Limited: A Dramatic Turnaround," pp. 39–41. Reprinted by permission from *Chain Store Age/Executive* © September 1981. Copyright Lebhar-Friedman, Inc. 425 Park Avenue, New York, NY 10022.

diminished store traffic is likely to have negative repercussions on sales and profits, the retailer needs to take corrective action to improve store traffic. Examples of corrective actions that might improve store traffic include changing the advertising theme, increasing the advertising appropriation, having a special sale, and enlarging the sign for the store front.

Conclusion

The retailer must have an effective control system to find (1) whether the retail organization is performing satisfactorily and (2) why some strategies are effective while others are not. In addition, the control process provides a mechanism for adjusting the retailer's strategy and activities and, therefore, performance.

Although most retail control systems suffer from an indequate scope or breadth, it is also possible to have a system that is too costly. Retailers must perform a cost-benefit analysis on the overall control process and on each element (including the retail audit, discussed below). Potential benefits must be greater than the costs of the system in time and resources.

A related problem is trying to use too much control information and simply being overwhelmed with data. Specific performance measures should be examined as needed. Some measures should be examined daily, while others may need only weekly, monthly, or quarterly examination. The key is to examine the information whenever necessary rather than every day.

The control process discussed in this section is designed to permit *continuous* monitoring and to indicate the need for *periodic* evaluations. These larger, more in-depth evaluations are called retailing audits.

THE RETAILING AUDIT

The **retailing audit** is a systematic examination of the components of the strategic retail management process and of their interrelationships. The task of the retailing audit is to pinpoint present weaknesses, potential problems, and potential opportunities. Thus the retailing audit serves as a control device and provides input for the planning function. Unfortunately, very few retailers have been willing and able to conduct retailing audits.

The thesis of the strategic retail management approach is that the retailer analyzes the environmental situation and then attempts to deploy available resources in a manner that achieves the desired objectives. Effective deployment or utilization of the resources is the result of developing and staffing the right organization, developing, integrating, and implementing the right strategies, and acquiring the right information for planning and control purposes. If everything has gone well, the individual components and the overall operations will be productive and, therefore, the desired objectives will be attained. Effective control of these elements is accomplished with the *continuous* control process discussed above and with *periodic* retailing audits. Strategic components specifically addressed in the retailing audit include philosophies, environment, objectives, organization, functional strategies and procedures, personnel, and control procedures.

In addition to the strategic components themselves, the interrelationships between the components must be examined. The purpose of this examination is to determine whether each component is congruent with or matches properly with other components. This is identified as strategic fit. Each component should strategically fit with the other components. The retailer's *objectives* should match or fit *environmental conditions;* the *strategies* should match the *objectives;* the *organizational structure* should match the *strategies,* and so on. It is helpful to view these components and interrelationships in relation to the strategic retail management model presented at the beginning of this chapter. Essentially, the retailing audit should be focused on each box (component) and each line (interrelationship).

To be effective, the retailing audit must be well planned. Several steps are necessary to prepare for and conduct an effective retailing audit. Eight sequential steps are suggested:

1. Determine timing and duration.

2. Determine who conducts the audit.

3. Determine the scope of the audit.

4. Develop audit measuring instrument.

5. Establish audit communication procedures.

6. Conduct the audit.

7. Prepare and disseminate audit report.

8. Implement recommendations.

Determine Timing and Duration

The retailer must decide when the audit will begin, how long it will last, and how often to conduct an audit. Since the audit should provide input for the planning function, the retailer should allow ample time for completion. In addition to considering time estimates for collecting and analyzing data, time for preparing and disseminating reports must also be permitted.

Because audits are so extensive and time-consuming, it is difficult to conduct a total audit more than once a year, but a *total retailing audit* should be conducted at least every two or three years. *Partial retailing audits,* depending on how extensive they are, may be conducted more often, perhaps annually or semiannually.

Determine Who Conducts the Audit

Audits can be conducted by internal or external sources. *Internal sources* include company executives, middle managers, internal auditing staffs, and special task forces. The primary advantages of internal sources are that they are more familiar with the retailer's organization and quicker implementation of audit recommendations is usually possible. Disadvantages are that internal sources have a narrow retailing perspective (because of limited audit experience and history), restricted independence, lack of training, reduced attention to normal responsibilities during the audit, and personal relationships with co-workers.

External sources can usually provide the retailer with less biased views, broad-based experience, thoroughness, and a history of previous audits. Disadvantages include a lack of familiarity with the retailer's organization, difficulties in locating information, lack of employee cooperation, and higher expense. Despite these potential disadvantages, which can largely be eliminated by recurring use of one outside source, outside sources are generally thought to provide better results.

Determine the Scope of the Audit

The scope of a retailing audit can range from very broad to very narrow. The broad-based audit is generally referred to as a *total retailing audit* or a **horizontal audit,** and it entails an evaluation of the entire retailing operation. The focus is often on problem definition, or determining which functional area should be investigated in more depth.

A **vertical audit,** or partial audit, involves a more in-depth analysis than the horizontal audit, but is much more narrow in scope. It focuses on one specific component or interrelationship, such as promotion, pricing, or organizational structure. The vertical audit is usually the result of poor performance indicated by the control process or by a horizontal audit that pinpointed specific problem areas.

A vertical audit of the pricing area may identify whether the retailer is using price in a strategically effective manner. Issues such as pricing objectives and how they are determined, price strategies, maintained markup, price match with store image, price line relationship with merchandise assortment, price line relationship to target market, identification of price-sensitive merchandise, mechanisms for increasing and decreasing prices, uses of temporary markdowns, and how prices compare with competing retailers would be examined. The vertical audit should establish the effectiveness of the variable being audited (price in this example) and how well it interrelates with the other retailing strategies.

Develop Audit Measuring Instrument

A key to the success of any retailing audit is asking the right questions. Poorly selected questions or poorly constructed questionnaires will result in less than adequate information for control and strategic planning purposes. The time devoted to planning the questionnaire will help ensure higher-quality information. Appendixes A and B to this chapter present some examples of questions for a retailing audit. These two sets of questions are by no means all-inclusive, but they do offer some ideas on the types of questions and areas that should be examined in an audit.

Appendix A focuses on obtaining an overall perspective of the effectiveness of the retailing effort. A low score (below 14) suggests that improvements can be made in how the strategic planning process is conducted in the retail organization. This or a similar measuring instrument should be completed by the owner-manager or top management of the retail organization.

Other measuring instruments in the retailing audit should concern the effective use of the retailer's resources in the retailing environment. As you can see in Appendix B, the areas examined are the components and interrelationships discussed earlier, such as the retailing environment, retailing strategy, retailing organization, retailing systems, retailing productivity, and retailing function audits. Although the checklist format may appear to make the audit a simple task, each question can require a significant amount of information and time to answer in a definitive manner. Thus, even a narrow vertical audit can demand large quantities of time and effort.

Establish Audit Communication Procedures

A research study found that one of the pivotal aspects for the success of a retailing audit is to keep open the lines of communication before, during, and after the audit.[2] An audit should be announced to the employees in advance, stating its purpose and how it is to be conducted. Specific sources of information should be defined to accomodate any questions that arise during the audit. After the audit has been completed, information relevant to specific individuals should be disseminated. Failure to communicate the purposes, mechanics, and results of retailing audits is generally detrimental to the success of current and future audits.

Conduct the Audit

Once all the details have been arranged, the retailing audit must be formally conducted. Some data can be gathered during the store's operating hours, while other types of information are easier to gather during nonoperating hours. Sales-force behavior and customer traffic analysis can be obtained only during operating hours. On the other hand, analysis of the retail environment and productivity measures might be better obtained during nonoperating hours.

Prepare and Disseminate Audit Report

A well-written, well-organized, and well-presented audit report provides the retailer with valuable input for control and planning purposes. An inadequate report (even of a "good" audit) reflects poorly on the auditors, whether they are internal or external, and possibly reduces the likelihood of management's using the results for decision making. Audit reports usually contain an executive summary, which highlights the major findings and recommendations. The entire report presents the research methods, findings, and recommendations in detail. While it is not necessary that all employees have access to the final audit report, each employee involved ought to have access to sections pertaining to his or her position.

Implement Recommendations

If a retailing audit is to be of any value, the results and recommendations should bring about some changes in retail decision making and/or operations. Failure to implement recommended changes negates the purpose of the retailing audit. Some changes may be difficult to implement, such as those for eliminating certain departments or jobs. If decisions of this type are necessary, the relevant audit results should be made clear to the employees responsible. After changes are made, follow-up via the regular control process must occur to determine how well the changes improve retailing effectiveness.

Retailing Audit Problems

Several problems faced by the retailer in conducting an audit have been alluded to during this discussion. First, a retailing audit requires a large amount of data. In many instances, especially during the first audit, some of the data may not be available, may not be in the right form, or may not be sufficiently detailed for auditing purposes. Fortunately, these problems are usually reduced in subsequent audits.

Second, as with any type of research, there is a danger of gathering more data than are necessary or the wrong data may be gathered. Having well-organized, concise measuring instruments can substantially reduce this problem.

Third, retailing audits, by their nature, are time-consuming. After several audits have been completed and the data are gathered and stored in a format conducive to retail auditing, the time factor can often be improved.

Finally, the dollar outlay, whether for internal or external auditors, may seem exorbitant. However, the long-term value in improved retailing productivity that a retailing audit can provide should reduce the concern for the cost of the audit. The benefits are likely to outweigh the costs.

SUMMARY

Control is a basic component of the strategic retail management process. A model of strategic retail management was introduced in Chapter 2 and has been referred to throughout this text. Figure 20.2 presents a simplified version of the larger model to demonstrate the continuous circular flow between the strategic retail management components and to highlight the notion that control closes the loop.

Let us begin with the *analysis component*. Recall the points at which you have been admonished to *analyze:* financial analysis in Chapter 3, macroenvironmental analysis in Chapter 4, competitive and channel analysis in Chapter 5, consumer analysis in Chapter 6, and review and analysis as the foundation for strategic planning in every other chapter of the text. The *output* of analysis serves as the *input* for planning.

The *planning component* has been the essential focus of the entire text. Recall that strategies are plans of action. Almost every chapter has

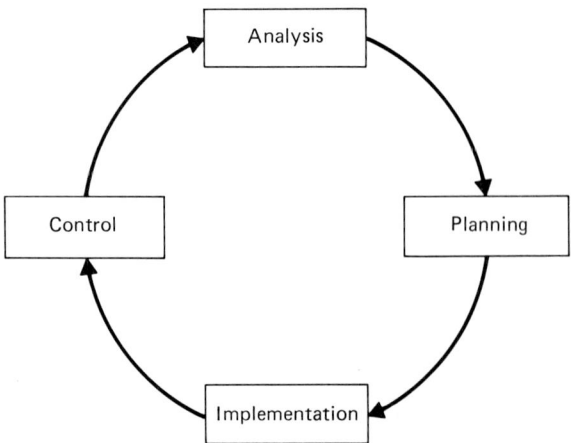

Figure 20.2
Simplified flow of strategic retail management

concentrated on planning or formulating strategy. The *output* of planning serves as *input* for implementation.

Although the *implementation component* has not been emphasized, it has been mentioned repeatedly in conjunction with strategies. Strategies are obviously useless unless they are implemented effectively. Implementation results, or *output*, create the *input* for control.

The *control component* has been discussed in most chapters in terms of monitor and adapt. Overall control has also been the focus of this chapter. Control is directly important to the implementation component in that ongoing control activities help ensure correct implementation. Control is also critically important in that the *output* of control "closes the loop" by serving as *input* for the analysis component.

Perhaps the key point to take from the preceding discussion and the entire book is that *all retailing plans and activities are interrelated and must therefore be integrated, coordinated, and controlled to achieve desired objectives.* We feel that the most effective means of achieving these objectives is *strategic retail management.*

KEY CONCEPTS

Retail control process	Market share measures
Control procedures	Contribution measures
Performance standards	Efficiency measures
Tolerance limits	Retailing audit
Growth and profitability measures	Horizontal audit
Sales measures	Vertical audit

REVIEW QUESTIONS

1. What is the purpose of the control function?
2. Why is it necessary to develop control measures at the same time objectives are established?
3. What is the purpose of performance measures?
4. What are efficiency measures?
5. What circumstances would necessitate changing performance standards?
6. What is the purpose of a retailing audit?
7. What is the process for conducting a retailing audit?
8. What areas are examined in a retailing audit?
9. Why is it important to develop a measuring instrument for an audit?
10. What are the problems a retailer might encounter in conducting an audit?

LEARNING EXERCISES

1. Interview three local retailers concerning their control procedures. Identify which procedures they use and why they use them. Determine how they selected the control procedures.

2. Interview several retailers to determine if they use the retailing audit for control purposes. Subtly determine if they are familiar with the retailing audit.

DECISION SITUATION 20.1: **PIZZA PALACE**

Robert has just purchased a chain of three pizza restaurants. The previous owner-manager was forced to sell the restaurants because of lack of profits. Robert intended to make as few major changes in operation as possible but soon discovered that many changes were in order.

The problems with Pizza Palace principally involved lack of effective cost control. Major areas where cost increases had occurred included labor, materials, delivery service, energy consumption, and maintenance. Robert realized that all these costs would need to be controlled to make a profit. He also wondered whether a price increase would be advisable.

QUESTIONS

1. What control procedures would you recommend for Pizza Palace?

2. How would you implement these procedures?

3. What problems would you expect to occur because of the control procedures?

DECISION SITUATION 20.2: **MEG'S FASHIONS**

Megan has just finished reading a retailing textbook that discussed a retailing audit. She wonders if an audit would help her manage her store more effectively.

Meg's Fashions has been a successful store for the ten years it has been in existence. Today it is one of the most successful women's clothing stores in a town of about 50,000. One reason for success has been Megan's hard work. She has always tried to stay abreast of fashions and of store management techniques in the up-scale store. The store enjoys a good location and is well designed. The reputation of the store is good, with most customers thinking that they get good value for their money. Megan knows of no major problems and firmly believes the store will continue to provide a good income for her and her two teenage children.

A professor at the local university has always been willing to help Meg when she needed assistance. In a casual conversation the professor told Meg that she would have a retailing class perform an audit if Meg desired. The professor did indicate that Meg would likely want to define the limits of the audit since she might not want students checking everything normally listed in a complete audit form. The professor has even stated that for a fee of about $1000 she would perform the audit.

QUESTIONS

1. Do you think Meg should have an audit performed? Why or why not?

2. Would you prefer the partial student audit for free or the more complete audit for a fee?

3. If Meg were to choose a partial audit, what items would you recommend be included? Why?

4. Design a partial audit for the task environment and for pricing. How would you get the needed information?

Appendix A
Retailing Effectiveness
Measure

(Check one answer to each question.)

CUSTOMER PHILOSOPHY

A. Does management recognize the importance of designing the company to serve the needs and wants of chosen markets?

Score

0 [ ] Management primarily thinks in terms of selling current and new products to whoever will buy them.

1 [ ] Management thinks in terms of serving a wide range of markets and needs with equal effectiveness.

2 [ ] Management thinks in terms of serving the needs and wants of well-defined markets chosen for their long-run growth and profit potential for the company.

B. Does management develop different offerings and plans for different segments of the market?

0 [ ]   No.

1 [ ]   Somewhat.

2 [ ]   To a good extent.

      C.   Does management take a whole marketing systems view (suppliers, channels, competitors, customers, environment) in planning its business?

0 [ ]   No. Management concentrates on selling and servicing its immediate customers.

1 [ ]   Somewhat. Management takes a long view of its channels although the bulk of its effort goes to selling and servicing the immediate customers.

2 [ ]   Yes. Management takes a whole marketing systems view, recognizing the threats and opportunities created for the company by changes in any part of the system.

INTEGRATED MARKETING ORGANIZATION

      D.   Is there high-level marketing integration and control of the major retailing functions?

0 [ ]   No. Sales and other retailing functions are not integrated at the top and there is some unproductive conflict.

1 [ ]   Somewhat. There is formal integration and control of the major retailing functions but less than satisfactory coordination and cooperation.

2 [ ]   Yes. The major retailing functions are effectively integrated.

      E.   Does marketing management work well with management and research, manufacturing, purchasing, physical distribution, and finance?

0 [ ]   No. There are complaints that marketing is unreasonable in the demands and costs it places on other departments.

1 [ ]   Somewhat. The relations are amicable although each department pretty much acts to serve its own power interests.

2 [ ]   Yes. The departments cooperate effectively and resolve issues in the best interest of the company as a whole.

      F.   How well organized is the new merchandise selection process?

0 [   ]   The system is ill defined and poorly handled.

1 [   ]   The system formally exists but lacks sophistication.

2 [   ]   The system is well structured and professionally staffed.

ADEQUATE MARKETING INFORMATION

      G.   When were the latest marketing research studies of customers, buying influences, channels, and competitors conducted?

0 [   ]   Several years ago.

1 [   ]   A few years ago.

2 [   ]   Recently.

      H.   How well does management know the sales potential and profitability of different market segments, customers, territories, and products?

0 [   ]   Not at all.

1 [   ]   Somewhat.

2 [   ]   Very well.

      I.   What effort is expended to measure the cost-effectiveness of different retailing expenditures?

0 [   ]   Little or no effort.

1 [   ]   Some effort.

2 [   ]   Substantial offort.

STRATEGIC ORIENTATION

      J.   What is the extent of formal retail planning?

0 [   ]   Management does little or no formal planning.

1 [   ]   Management develops an annual plan.

2 [   ]   Management develops a detailed annual plan and a careful long-range plan that is updated annually.

K. What is the quality of the current retailing strategy?

0 [ ] The current strategy is not clear.

1 [ ] The current strategy is clear and represents a continuation of traditional strategy.

2 [ ] The current strategy is clear, innovative, data-based, and well reasoned.

L. What is the extent of contingency thinking and planning?

0 [ ] Management does little or no contingency thinking.

1 [ ] Management does some contingency thinking although little formal contingency planning.

2 [ ] Management formally identifies the most important contingencies and develops contingency plans.

OPERATIONAL EFFICIENCY

M. How well is the marketing thinking at the top communicated and implemented down the line?

0 [ ] Poorly.

1 [ ] Fairly.

2 [ ] Successfully.

N. Is management doing an effective job with the retailing resources?

0 [ ] No. The resources are inadequate for the job to be done.

1 [ ] Somewhat. The resources are adequate but they are not employed optimally.

2 [ ] Yes. The resources are adequate and are deployed efficiently.

O. Does management show a good capacity to react quickly and effectively to on-the-spot developments?

0 [ ] No. Sales and market information is not very current and management reaction time is slow.

1 [ ] Somewhat. Management receives fairly up-to-date sales and market information; management reaction time varies.

2 [ ] Yes. Management has installed systems yielding highly current information and fast reaction time.

TOTAL SCORE

The instrument is used in the following way. The appropriate answer is checked for each question. The scores are added; the total will be somewhere between 0 and 28. The following scale shows the level of marketing effectiveness:

0–3 = None	14–18 = Good
4–8 = Poor	19–23 = Very good
9–13 = Fair	24–28 = Superior

Appendix B
Components of a Retailing Audit

PART I. THE RETAILING ENVIRONMENT AUDIT

Macroenvironment   *A.*   Economic-demographic

1) What does the company expect in the way of inflation, material shortages, unemployment, and credit availability in the short run, intermediate run, and long run?
2) What effect will forecasted trends in the size, age distribution, and regional distribution of population have on the business?

B.   Technology

1) What major changes are occurring in product technology? In process technology?
2) What are the major retail substitutes that might replace us?

C.   Political-legal

1) What laws are being proposed that may affect retailing strategy and tactics?
2) What federal, state, and local agency actions should be watched? What is happening in the areas of pollution control,

Source: Philip Kotler, *Marketing Management: Analysis, Planning, and Control*, 4th ed., © 1980, pp. 652–655. Adapted by permission of Prentice-Hall, Inc., Englewood Cliffs, N.J. Adapted from the original.

equal employment opportunity, product safety, advertising, price control, etc., that is relevant to retailing planning?

D.   Social-cultural

1)   What attitudes is the public taking toward business and toward products such as those sold by our company?
2)   What changes are occurring in consumer life styles and values that have a bearing on the company's target markets and retailing methods?

Task Environment   A.   Markets

1)   What is happening to market size, growth, geographical distribution, and profits?
2)   What are the major market segments? What are their expected rates of growth? Which are high opportunity and low opportunity segments?

B.   Customers

1)   How do current customers and prospects rate the company and its competitors, particularly with respect to reputation, product quality, service, sales force, and price?
2)   How do different classes of customers make their buying decisions?
3)   What are the evolving needs and satisfactions being sought by the buyers in this market?

C.   Competitors

1)   Who are the major competitors? What are the objectives and strategy of each major competitor? What are their strengths and weaknesses? What are the sizes and trends in market shares?
2)   What trends can be foreseen in future competition and substitutes for this product?

D.   Distribution and dealers

1)   What are the main trade channels bringing products to customers?
2)   What are the efficiency levels and growth potentials of the different trade channels?

E.   Suppliers

1)   What is the outlook for the availability of different key resources used in retailing?
2)   What trends are occurring among suppliers in their pattern of selling?

F.   Facilitators

1)   What is the outlook for the cost and availability of transportation services?

2)   What is the outlook for the cost and availability of warehousing facilities?

3)   What is the outlook for the cost and availability of financial resources?

4)   How effectively is the advertising agency performing? What trends are occurring in advertising agency services?

PART II. RETAILING STRATEGY AUDIT

A.   Retailing objectives

1)   Are the objectives clearly stated?

2)   Are the objectives stated in a clear form to guide planning and subsequent performance measurement?

3)   Are the objectives appropriate, given the company's competitive position, resources, and opportunities? Is the appropriate strategic objective to build, hold, harvest, or terminate this business?

B.   Strategy

1)   What is the core retailing strategy for achieving the objectives? Is it a sound strategy?

2)   Are enough resources (or too much resources) budgeted to accomplish the retailing objectives?

3)   Are the resources allocated optimally to prime market segments, territories, and products of the organization?

4)   Are the resources allocated optimally to the major elements of the marketing mix, i.e., product quality, service, sales force, advertising, promotion, and location?

PART III. RETAILING ORGANIZATION AUDIT

A.   Formal structure

1)   Is there a high level officer with adequate authority and responsibility over those company activities that affect the customer's satisfaction?

2)   Are the retailing responsibilities optimally structured along functional, product, end user, and territorial lines?

B.   Functional efficiency

1) Are there good communication and working relations in the organization?
2) Is the department-management system working effectively? Are the department managers able to plan profits or only sales volume?
3) Are there any groups that need more training, motivation, supervision, or evaluation?

C.   Interface efficiency

1) Are there any problems between functional areas that need attention?
2) What about research and other areas?
3) What about merchandising and financial management?
4) What about selling and purchasing?

PART IV. RETAILING SYSTEMS AUDIT

A.   Retailing information system

1) Is the intelligence system producing accurate, sufficient, and timely information about developments in the marketplace?
2) Is marketing research being adequately used by company decision makers?

B.   Retailing-planning system

1) Is the planning system well conceived and effective?
2) Is sales forecasting and market-potential measurement soundly carried out?
3) Are sales quotas set on a proper basis?

C.   Retailing control system

1) Are the control procedures (monthly, quarterly, etc.) adequate to insure that the annual-plan objectives are being achieved?
2) Is provision made to analyze periodically the profitability of different products, departments, markets, and territories?
3) Is provision made to examine and validate periodically various retailing costs?

D.   New merchandise selection

1) Is the company well organized to gather, generate, and screen new merchandise ideas?
2) Does the company do adequate concept research and business analysis before investing in a new product?
3) Does the company carry out adequate product and market testing?

PART V. RETAILING PRODUCTIVITY AUDIT

A. Profitability analysis

   1) What is the profitability of the company's different products, served markets, departments, and territories?
   2) Should the company enter, expand, contract, or withdraw from any business segments or departments and what would be the short- and long-run profit consequences?

B. Cost-effectiveness analysis

   1) Do any activities seem to have excessive costs? Are these costs valid? Can cost-reducing steps be taken?

PART VI. RETAILING FUNCTION AUDITS

A. Merchandise

   1) What are the merchandise objectives? Are these objectives sound? Is the current product line meeting these objectives?
   2) Are there particular products that should be phased out?
   3) Are there new products that are worth adding?
   4) Are any products able to benefit from quality, feature, or style improvements?

B. Price

   1) What are the pricing objectives, policies, strategies, and procedures? To what extent are prices set on sound cost, demand, and competitive criteria?
   2) Do the customers see the company's prices as being in line or out of line with the perceived value of its offer?
   3) Does the company use price promotions effectively?

C. Location

   1) What are the location objectives and strategies?
   2) Is there adequate market coverage and service?
   3) Should the company consider changing its degree of reliance on certain locations?

D. Sales force

   1) What are the organization's sales force objectives?
   2) Is the sales force large enough to accomplish the company's objectives?
   3) Is the sales force organized along the proper principle(s) of specialization (territory, market, product)?
   4) Does the sales force show high morale, ability, and effort? Are they sufficiently trained and are there sufficient incentives?

       5) Are the procedures adequate for setting quotas and evaluating performances?

       6) How is the company's sales force perceived in relation to competitors' sales forces?

E.   Advertising, sales promotion, and publicity

       1) What are the organization's advertising objectives? Are they sound?

       2) Is the right amount being spent on advertising? How is the budget determined?

       3) Are the ad themes and copy effective? What do customers and the public think about the advertising?

       4) Are the advertising media well chosen?

       5) Is sales promotion used effectively?

       6) Is there a well-conceived publicity program?

NOTES

1. For a more detailed discussion of these measurement techniques see Philip Kotler, *Marketing Management* (Englewood Cliffs, N.J.: Prentice-Hall, 1980), pp. 630–646

2. Louis M. Capella and William S. Sekely, "The Marketing Audit: Methods, Problems and Perspectives," *Akron Business and Economic Review*, Fall 1978, pp. 37–41.

Comprehensive Cases

CASE 1

Jodie's Ladies Wear

Yvonne and Craig Wakefield, proprietors, have enjoyed a considerable success during the two years in which they have owned and operated Jodie's Ladies Wear, a specialty shop that sells mainly ladies' outer wear.

The two young owners have been able to increase sales substantially by widening the lines and styles offered and by advertising effectively. During the same period they have learned and taught themselves much about the management of a retail store.

With sales volume now pressing the limits of the physical resources of their present operation, Yvonne and Craig are attempting to decide the future directions of Jodie's Ladies Wear. The choice of continued growth in the present and /or a new location is not easy or simple for it involves substantial financial and managerial problems.

BEGINNINGS

"Looking back, I think that it was a lapse in mental capacity that led us to buy out the previous owner and take over Jodie's Ladies Wear. It would have been more difficult to start a venture, but it might well have made more sense." So Craig

Source: William H. Newman and James P. Logan, *Strategy Policy and Central Management,* 8th edition (Cincinnati, Ohio, South-Western Publishing Co., 1981), pp. 697–715. Reproduced by special permission of South-Western Publishing Co. Cincinnati, Ohio.
Questions have been added at the end of the case.

623

Wakefield began his story about the acquisition and the early history of the store under his and his wife's (Yvonne Wakefield's) management.

"We took over a store that sold clothes in misses' and women's sizes to a 'mature clientele'—to use the previous owner's words.[1] They were mature enough. We literally watched them die off. The median age was 65 years. If we held a lay-away for three months and then sent a card as a reminder, the card was often returned with the notation that the buyer had died.

"We purchased $15,164 of inventory and retained two saleswomen (one full-time and one part-time) from the previous operation. The building had 950 square feet, of which 750 square feet made up the sales floor and the balance was the office, backroom, and bathroom. We negotiated a new, 3-year lease for a rent of about $240 per month plus $6.50 per month for maintenance plus $\frac{1}{2}$ of 1% of gross sales as dues to the Monterey Village Merchants' Association.[2]

"The previous owner had claimed $65,000 in gross sales for the past year, but our later reconstruction from her partial records indicated a gross of $43,000. The inventory, when valued at the lower of cost or market, turned out to be worth $9,000. Much of the merchandise was old.

"There was no customer file. The only sales records available were for 40 charge-account customers. The clientele did fit the clothes well—most were in the Misses' size cut.

"To finance the inventory we signed a note for $14,000 payable to the former owner at $200 per month for 5 years with a lump sum due at the end of the period. We borrowed $2,500 from a bank to provide working capital, and we put up the balance of the equity ourselves.

"What was a merchant not yet 30 years old with a wife just turned 21 doing in a deal like this? It certainly required a far stretch of the imagination."

Craig Wakefield had, over the previous ten years, been a policeman, a rancher, a manufacturer and wholesaler of women's jewelry, a computer programmer, and a business systems analyst. He was carrying on the ranching, the jewelry wholesaling, and the systems analysis work for small companies simultaneously just before the purchase of Jodie's Ladies Wear.

"I was tired of school, I had learned all that I thought I could at the University. We had made some money in the stock market and had to do something with it quickly. The ranching showed a net loss, but not for long enough, so that soon the cash would be taxable.

"Neither of us had any background in retailing women's wear. Yvonne's contribution was a knowledge of fabrics and clothing construction, skill as a seamstress, and no fear of work. I also knew how to sew and looked on the new venture as a challenge to master and a field to find out something about.

"Our first major decision was to increase the total inventory and the selection available. We used all the increased investment to stock a younger style of merchandise in an attempt to satisfy younger walk-ins—although they were few and far between at first. Over eighteen months we gradually added $15,000 to the inventory, bringing it to a total of $30,000.

"We tried to eliminate all the things we did not like about the stores we used to shop in. Commission payments to employees created a pushy atmosphere which we wish to avoid. So our employees are on straight salary. Refunds for cash create three problems: (1) banks charge us 5% for credit card use, which we lose if we give a full cash refund; (2) customers who pay by check get irate if they are asked to wait until the check clears, but a small percentage of them are known to get a cash refund and then stop payment on their checks; (3) a few persons will steal clothes and then ask for a cash refund while claiming they have lost the sales receipt. So no cash refunds and merchandise credits only.

"We want to allow the customers to browse and feel comfortable while having a chance to look around the store and find out what we carry. We also want to eliminate the feeling that, as a customer, you are always being watched and that the merchant does not trust you. There is a fine line between being ignored and being inspected that we want to walk.

"At first we hoped to alter and tailor clothes at no charge to the customer. We sell clothes in a medium-price range, but the clothes are not inexpensive to the customer. We soon found that many women wanted us to go beyond alterations that were necessary to fit the garment. They would say, 'Oh, it will only take you a minute to take the sleeves up ¼ of an inch here and to let out the upper back an inch while raising the hem.' Some expect a major remodeling for no charge.

"The inventory increase was designed not only to attract younger customers but also to offer a wider selection and a younger look to the original customers. We believed that they did not want to look as old as the clothes that were represented in the inventory that was originally in the store.

"Overall we wanted to make the store a pleasing place in which there was a soft atmosphere—not a hard or crass sell and not a place in which the customers felt that the merchandise was being pushed down their throats."

BUYING AND MERCHANDISING

The Wakefields purchased Jodie's Ladies Wear in early February. By that time orders had already been placed with manufacturers for the summer season to come. They cancelled no orders because they had no knowledge about where to buy nor experience in buying.

To buy for the fall season they decided to continue to purchase from the manufacturers whose lines were already represented in their store or from those whom the previous owner had recommended for a particular season. Some suppliers have especially good fall or holiday collections but not good selections for a Tucson summer. To show their fall lines, a group of salespersons set up displays in Del Webb's Town House in Phoenix. The Wakefields attended this so-called market, but they limited their buying to familiar lines and looked at new lines to learn rather than to purchase. Fall items are bought in May and delivered in July.

For the holiday season they looked for a market in which more complete collections were shown. For this they went to Los Angeles in July. There they concentrated their buying on younger sportswear, younger dresses, handbags (a new item for Jodie's), accessories such as scarves, gloves, shawls, and hosiery (also new items), and a change in the jewelry from big pins and brooches for the staid and proper country club set to less expensive jewelry in line with the time and what people were wearing (necklaces, bracelets, rings, and earrings). During the fall and holiday seasons, hosiery produced the maximum revenue per square foot of display space of any line in the store. Hosiery sales for these seasons amounted to $1,000 from a display area of 2 square feet. It should be noted that Jodie's is located next door to a lingerie and hosiery specialty shop. This experience proved to the Wakefields that they could do more with Jodie's than just sell ready-to-wear outer clothing.

A check of inventory just before the spring and summer buying season (November of the previous year for first orders and January for additional summer items and manufacturers' closeouts of spring items) showed that handbag and jewelry inventories were depleted as were the younger-styled items of clothing. The older styles still showed a substantial carryover. Craig Wakefield then decided to add shoes, all kinds of purses (casual and evening bags, cloth, good leather, and beaded bags), and a limited millinery selection.

"The question to date has not been how to decide what to purchase but who will sell to us. We can rely on suppliers who have been with the store for years, on hungry or brave new suppliers, and on those who are large enough to be willing to take a chance on a small order and give us credit. Credit is the problem. For example, the East Coast division of United Factors will deal with us, but the West Coast division will not.

"From manufacturers who will sell to us we look at style, fabrication, colors, price, and fabrics all together and attempt to judge what will interest our customers. For the first six months we had little choice. We had to buy from whomever came around. So we purchased the younger-looking items in the lines of our old suppliers. Buying in the first year was strictly good and bad luck. We are badly overstocked on sportswear by Koret of California. The salesman was experienced and we were not. Koret does not produce one line with coordinated items but 36 groups of sportswear per year. No two groups in any one year can be put together. Their items sell in great quantities, but, at the end of the season, we are stuck with lots of inventory. In a sense we are a warehouse for the manufacturer. It gets so that our customers, who are no dummies, wait for a sale. They come in often, check the racks, and then predict how long we can hold out before . . . a sale.

"We are, for some items, and hope to for all, changing to manufacturers whose entire line works together and who blend in one season's colors and fabrics with the next. It takes about three years to learn who does this successfully and then you have to be able to get to their salesman first so that he is not sold out and also hope that the firm will allow credit.

"We would like to carry Loubella Extendibles, for example. The entire line is blended. The separates (pants, blouses, sports tops, and sweaters) are all dyed to coordinate within their 8 or 9 combinations of body styles and fabrics. The line is carefully thought out so that one blouse can be worn with 5 or 6 different pairs of pants.

"Both Yvonne and I do the purchasing. We argue about the items and should argue more than we do. Then we would wind up with fewer markdowns. We work purchases down to those garments on which we both agree. If I like the print and she dislikes the style, the line or item is ruled out. We don't agree on very many things, and we find that if we do agree, there is a much better chance of selling those goods.

"Some days one of us feels incompetent, so we do no buying at all. Or one will screen the entire line to pick out favorites and the other will go through what has been picked. This is our way of buying only what we need.

"We look at the line of any manufacturer whose salesman comes around to the store. We do not pass up any chance to look at ladies' wear. It took us a while to learn how to say no, because there are some highly proficient sales people on the road.

"We now plan to attend markets in Denver, Phoenix, Los Angeles, and San Francisco (but not the two big ones–New York and Dallas) five times per year for the five seasons (spring, summer, transition, fall, and winter). At the markets we visit those manufacturers whom we definitely want to buy from and then use the rest of our time to look for a new resource to replace a line that is not performing well. Manufacturers change all the time. Bobbie Brooks and Gay Gibson are not now what they used to be.

"Purchasing takes constant attention. Anyone can buy, but few can know ahead how they are going to sell what they buy before they buy it. We now formulate ad ideas and promotions and combinations of wearing apparel and accessories before we buy. We look for bargains that will allow better than the full retail markup (customarily 50% of the selling price is markup). So we buy from an unknown manufacturer who sells at a relatively low price those items of a quality suitable for our customers. Before buying, you must know what your customers want. What are the fashion trends now or what are they going to be with our clientele? Should we take a chance on a new idea and possibly offend some of our existing clientele for the sake of bringing in new clients? For example, 18-to-25-year-olds buy 10% of the pants suits sold. To carry items for them makes the whole rack lean a bit toward being sexy and younger. Older clientele then get offended, although not outraged. Some will say directly, 'How could this be in my store? There must be some mistake.' We still carry what they want, as did the previous owner, but they are not happy to be in an atmosphere where the younger-looking things are."

PROMOTION

The first promotion of Jodie's Ladies Wear, with the Wakefields as owners, was entirely by word of mouth. Old customers told their friends about the change — if they so desired; the Wakefields told their friends and new employees told their friends. Craig Wakefield quickly realized that this was insufficient promotion. He turned for help to officers of the Monterey Village Merchants' Association. They suggested the use of radio and newspapers. After trying these media Craig concluded that the cost per thousand readers of newspapers was excessive. He also learned from experience that radio was best for an immediate reaction and for sale announcements. Newspaper trials for one year demonstrated that a small, obscure, or unknown retail store could never afford to pay enough for space to compete with chain stores, department stores, and the already known large specialty shops of the city. The cost per thousand readers was considerably higher than the cost per thousand female viewers available on daytime television.

With some help from friends in the advertising business, Craig purchased early morning spots on the Today show, late evening spots on the Johnny Carson show, and sporadic spots throughout the day. The friends chose stations and shows that had the largest female audiences. They also prepared ads that were fair-to-middling as to their ideas, in the Wakefields' opinion. But when asked the age distribution of the female audience, his friends did not have data available. Also they made no story boards so that the commercial could not be judged before it was presented.[3]

By asking questions at the television stations, Craig Wakefield found that he could develop precise information about audiences. His friends could recommend, with no research, shows with a high percentage of women viewers, but they could not distinguish between 16- to 30-year-old viewers and 65- to 85-year-old viewers. The distinction is important to Jodie's. Further questioning of persons at the television stations and a close review of the Audit Research Bureau's data let Craig dig out the audience characteristics. This way he found out what was the best buy— the optimal combination of his prime audience and the cost of spots. By extensive searching he found out what kinds of audiences watched television in Tucson at what times of the day and on what channel. With this research completed, he was in a better position to purchase time suitable for Jodie's Ladies Wear than was the agency.

To prepare commercials, Craig Wakefield took his own photographs and selected his own locations. His idea was to try to do something a little different—a little unorthodox. Both Wakefields worked hard at this until they were pleased with the results. One commercial showed evening gowns in a horse corral. Another had models in black, baby-doll nightwear posed on a patio at the Community Center during the day. This commercial was shot on a Sunday morning when few, if any, people were ordinarily around. But one father and his young son rode by on a bicycle. The boy said: "Daddy, look at the pretty ladies." The father turned his head to look, held the look, and rode into the pond below the small waterfall.

Yvonne and Craig drove to the Colorado Rockies to show swimsuits and shorts outfits in the snow-laced tundra above the timber line at 12,000 feet. The commercial went well when shown in Tucson in July. Another ad pictured a girl dressed in an elegant, crisp pants suit unloading garbage into a Dumpster.

"We strove for something a bit unusual to make viewers think—which most agencies believe people can't do. We are not trying to convince viewers that our stuff is better and cheaper than anyone else's. But we are trying to get their attention and then keep it with a visual style and with graphic effects. We do not talk a lot at the audience. We use little or no verbiage, because the more you talk, the more you and the audience forget the rest of the effects and the visual message.

"We began television advertising a year after we took over the store because no one seemed to be coming in as the result of the newspaper ads and, as far as we could tell, we could not get results from the radio advertisements. We dipped into our cash reserve and decided to allocate 25% of gross sales for advertising. We figured that the only way to get new people into the building was to let them know we existed and that we might have what they liked and that we were not too terrible to do business with.

"When I had studied advertising earlier, the best book that I read on influencing other persons' decisions convinced me that you cannot expect anyone to listen to your message unless you have their attention. This hit me over the head. In the world of advertising, where you are bombarded day after day with thousands of ad messages in all media every time you turn around, how many do you remember? Those that you dislike and those that are humorous and appeal to your sense of humor. Those that are out of place and those that are, esthetically, extremely pleasing. Analysis of various surveys convinced me that the most obnoxious soap commercial was the most effective because it stayed in the viewer's mind—consciously or unconsciously. But we did not want that kind of thing. The other route to getting attention was the hard sell. 'Mine is better and cheaper than anyone else's.' This is very old and very crass and very successful. But we did not like it and it did not fit with the idea of the kind of store we were trying to build.

"This still left the question of how to get the viewer's attention so that she would watch our message. The solution I developed for a 30-second spot was to have dead silence for the first twelve seconds — no audio at all; to show slides during those opening seconds. My reasoning was that if the viewer hears nothing at all when she knows it is the time for a commercial, she will look at the set to see what is wrong. Then we can say, 'Now we can talk with you, now that we have your attention.'

"Then we stated our copy theme: 'Jodie's has fashions that won't (pause) just hang in your closet.' How did we work out that theme? Well, there are two classes of women — married and single. Each class has two subclasses — happy and unhappy. Each group has associated with it a particular activity. The happy singles are playing the field, the unhappy singles are attempting to get married, the happily married are acting to keep their husbands happy, and the unhappily married are playing the field or trying to get their husbands reinterested in them. A good appearance is part, only a part, of the activities. That is why women buy new and stylish clothing — one of four reasons depending upon their situation. You can't say this in an ad because it is offensive. How then do you tell all four? We state that we have clothes that will not just be hanging in a closet. Then women can read any connotation they want into the statement and read the idea for themselves.

"For the first three months we spent 25% of gross sales on television advertising. After that we kept the dollar amount level. Our idea was and is that television advertising is in part a capital investment — getting our name and merchandising point of view embedded in the audience's long-term memory, and in part a period expense — showing our new fashions of the season.

"Some time later the station rates for spots were increased and I also decided to use less of the really off-hour times (1 A.M. and 7 A.M., for example). So we reduced the ads from 30 to 10 seconds. By then we had created a unique commercial — 10 seconds in length, little said verbally, and it did not demand attention over any long span of time. I learned indirectly through trade sources that advertising courses at the University of Southern California were using Jodie's commercials as prime examples of how to use TV effectively for advertising. We have been widely copied in Tucson. Wigglesworth Volvo, for example, did an almost exact copy of our style. It is a super-soft sell, a complete reverse from the hard, harsh sell. Because it is a dramatic change in style, it is a success for us. We certainly created the image we wanted. I think that the major reason why it worked was that it was a new way in Tucson. The ads are not displeasing. That is a big plus for them.

"Our surveys showed that we created customers more from husbands sending in their wives to buy than from decisions by the women themselves. The evening ads had more results than the morning ads.

"Jodie's slogan became known — not a household word, but definitely by the other business people in town. Yvonne could shop in Steinfeld's (a major, locally owned, department store) and all the salesclerks there would recognize who she was and what Jodie's advertised.

"A year's experience with television advertising showed us that it is not a promotional expense. It can be best used to sell or create an image. To sell a specific product or a price or to maintain an image, newspapers are the most effective.

Radio is used for fast results. If you do not get a response within 24 hours from a radio commercial, then change it.

"We have not really been successful in radio advertising. We have not found the key. The best that we have done with radio is to buy a cut-rate monthly package — X number of spots for the month — and then cram them all into one week to gain maximum exposure to that station's clientele. Then we either move to another station or try out a second idea at the first station to test any contrasts in response.

"In using television we expect and have found a 30- to 90-day delay before any results come from a particular idea. Since we are a small store we do not have lots of money to buy lots of space to sell a product now. The large department stores and chain stores (Levy's, Sears, Steinfeld's, Wards, Diamonds, Lerners, and Broadway) can do that.

"For our first fashion show, held at the Skyline Country Club, I wrote a letter to our manufacturers to explain this reason for the increase in the size of our order and to explain what had happened to our sales volume. Most of the manufacturers knew nothing about us and did not remember our history with them. Since I wanted our orders filled early on their first cutting, and also wanted dating on them since early shipments and early payments would not fit our cash-flow schedule, I wrote a detailed letter.[4] Somehow *Women's Wear Daily* picked up this letter and published an article based on it featuring Jodie's as "The Small Retailer of the Year."

"The show at the Skyline Country Club was shown on television news programs by the local stations — the first production of its kind. And at no expense to us.

"By now I do all the buying of time and space. I decide exactly what I want and when and where. I also control the production of the commercial and then have to sit at the television station to supervise the broadcast. Otherwise the station workers will inevitably foul up the commercial. I remember the panic one engineer went into when he got no audio — only video — on the first few seconds of an early commercial. He cut us right off the air.

"Tape has major advantages because it can be flowing and vivid and the station can't make errors with it. But we don't use video tape because it is too expensive. Instead, we use audio tape and slides. We have 200 slides so they can be changed readily. For each commercial I set a sequence: numbers 1, 11, 22, and 27 at 6 P.M. and numbers 8, 10, 23, and 27 at 9 P.M. Although the station has detailed information about the sequence, they cannot follow intricate scheduling. This takes my personal attention."

PERSONNEL

The two employees of the previous owner stayed with the Wakefields when they took over Jodie's. One lady who worked part-time is still with the store. Craig Wakefield characterized her as "a capable salesperson, a hard worker. She was once in business for herself so her outlook toward us differs from that of all our other employees." The other full-time employee, a woman aged 62 and an experienced seamstress, did not want to step onto the sales floor unless a customer whom she knew came in the door. "We eventually found that she would reluctantly do what I asked of her but would not take direction from Yvonne. She was determined not to let some young girl tell her how to work. It took us a while to recognize this and even more time to get up the determination to do something about it. We kept her 9 months—6 months longer than we should have.

"We tried to keep 2 employees in the store as well as Yvonne—who is there to manage. For the first 9 months we had a considerable amount of friction—a Donnybrook occasionally. There were disagreements over the day for pay, how often wages were to be paid, and how the business was going to be run.

"Our policy as to labor was to attempt to find reliable persons who could and would sell—persons who were looking for work, not just employment. So far we have found that we can only tell reliability and sales skills through experience—not through references or statements about past experience. Our initial employment practice was to hire people of various ethnic backgrounds. We took whoever walked in and applied for a job we happened to have open. We would hire them if they had the appearance and seemed to have the basic capability to do the work.

"In sequence we had a Mexican-American girl, a Jewish girl, another Chicano, and an Oriental. They all carried the idea of being a member of a minority group to an extreme. If we had any complaints, they each attributed this to racial prejudice on our part.

"Then we turned to friends. This also turned out to be wrong. The first friend of Yvonne's worked well for a short time and then wanted the summer off. Summer is a bit slow and we agreed. Then her husband stopped traveling overseas when he changed jobs in the fall. So we lost her shortly after she returned to work. She was a good woman. Then another friend won a battle over custody of her son with her ex-husband. Since she really could not take care of herself, let alone her son, she had to move to California to be with relatives. Then we brought in a personal friend of mine who had good experience and was highly recommended by her previous employer. She turned out not to justify the recommendation. Then we hired another friend—an out-of-work school teacher who could not find work in District One (the large, local school district) because she had a Master's degree. The district has to pay a relatively high wage to teachers with advanced degrees, so such teachers are not hired. She really felt that she was doing us a favor by working for us. There were several problems.

"Had we been willing to pay an average wage plus commission, we might have gotten better help. But we are not willing to pay top dollar nor commissions. Turnover of employees to date has not been as rapid as it should have been. Also I may not yet have quite learned that my function with employees is not to be a counselor.

"We have just changed the system for disseminating information to employees. We do not now bring them into decision-making, but we do take the posture that they should have full knowledge of what we plan and why we plan it and that we want their opinion. If they think an item or a line is going to bomb, we want to know why they think so.

"For some reason our employees seem to feel that they should have or that they want to have loyalty to the proprietors more than to the business. I want them to be attracted to the work—their tasks—rather than to us and what they may regard as a pseudo or substitute family. In most cases loyalty is not enough. Incompetence can thrive when loyalty is rewarded. What I want to do is to create a good atmosphere, but only with employees who really are an asset to the firm.

"If you make an employee into a friend, it becomes difficult to let her go. It is hazardous to turn a friend into an employee. We have hired friends with long and successful experience in the apparel field. But they then expected us to make allowances for their personal problems. They brought problems with parents, with husbands, and with finances to work. At first we tried to help them work out the problems because we thought that they would be better employees if they felt freer on the job. They talked with us freely. We thought this would help them ease their minds. But those who came in having been friends prior to their employment expected to be able to dump their problems and disrupt the work-flow. We were to understand why they took three days off without notice and that they would tell us about it later.

"A big advantage of a very small operation is rapport. But supposed rapport can turn into a big disadvantage if it becomes assumptions about being understood.

"Either Yvonne or I can manage the store. But one of us needs to be there."

CUSTOMERS AND SALES

Located as it is in a small shopping center (Monterey Village) on the southwest corner of Speedway and Wilmot Road (see Exhibit 1), Jodie's draws most of its customers from sections of the city north of Speedway Boulevard and east, northeast, or northwest of the corner of Speedway Boulevard and Wilmot Road (location A on the map). The people who live in these sections are generally in the middle-income or upper-middle-income groups.

Expansion of Tucson takes place on the fringes. New housing developments—tract houses, town houses, and condominiums—are particularly common toward the northeast, east, and southeast. New apartments are built just north of Ft. Lowell Road, and mobile home developments are most common toward the southwest. Some lower-priced tract developments are also found in the southern and southwestern parts of the urban area.

Monterey Village Shopping Center contains 28 stores in total. The largest are a Ben Franklin variety store and a Bayless Supermarket (one outlet of a local grocery chain). Other stores include a home furnishings shop, a franchised radio and phonograph equipment shop, a franchised ice cream parlor, another women's dress shop, a lingerie and hosiery specialty shop, and a hardware store. Services available include a movie theater, a real estate agent, a beauty salon, and a branch of one of the large commercial banks.

As stated before, Jodie's original group of customers was of an age range of 55 to 85 years. This range has been changed to 17 to 60 years. The store still carries clothes that the older clientele wear, but most of them do not seem to want to be in an atmosphere where contemporary clothes predominate. The customer list has increased from 40 to 8,000. Charge customers have been reduced from 40 to 28.

"Customers shop here for a mixture of reasons. All of the variables tend to apply to each shopper. They are attracted by our promotions, by the availability of goods in which they are interested, by the behavior of any one of our employees toward whom they may be attracted (some of those who work here have personal followings), and by our flexibility about alterations.

"We want our customers to get all the help they desire if they ask for it, but not to feel pushed. This feeling can be eliminated, but watching can't be. Shoplifting is always a possibility, and the salesperson has to be ready to give help and answer questions at the exact instant the customer wants aid or information.

"My experience as a policeman and in this dress selling business makes it necessary for me to assume that everyone who walks in our door is a thief. So we develop ways to achieve our objectives. We train our salespeople to continually straighten and re-size the clothes. The girls can be working and yet be within easy reach of a customer and alert to the customer. This awareness will tell them whether the customer wants help or information or needs to be watched.

"The salesgirls are doing small jobs to make sure that the store does not have a disheveled look. They are not bothering the browsers or the customers, but they are right there on the spot when they are needed.

"It is easy for a merchant to forget about goods on layaway. So we have a tickler file that warns us a month after the date of the layaway. If the customer makes no payment, we send her a postal card to let her know that the goods are still being held for her. After another 60 days, we remind her again. This friendly note asks her to pay within two weeks. We are making every effort to keep in contact.

"A very brief experience with free alterations and tailoring convinced us that such a policy is too generous. So we decided to limit alterations to those necessary to fit the garment and to charge a healthy fee for tailoring. We want from $2.50 for the simple hemming of a skirt to $15 to $20 to change the sleeves or do a major remodeling of a garment. These charges are substantial, so they are waived for a good, regular customer. Yvonne or I decide when to waive the charge.

"Some customers began to know the stock better than I did. They came in daily, looked at the sale rack and at the new merchandise we had brought in. They predicted how long we would keep a garment and waited for a sale to come along. So thus began musical garments.

"We moved racks from the right side of the store to the left side and from the back middle to the front middle. We then sold stuff that was five years old just because it was in a different place. Now we change the store randomly. We move items closer to the front window or farther away. We change the location of the fluorescent fixtures. We paint the walls a different color. We changed the sizing from right to left rather than left to right, but this became too confusing so we gave it up. Eventually we saw this practice recommended in trade journals after we began to read them, but we had had to stumble on it. A few trade journals have some very helpful display, layout, and merchandising ideas. We learned that Bonwit Teller, for example, constantly remodels its stores so that the interior decor, the coloration, the store design, the location of items, and the way they are displayed changes — but not on a predictable basis. One of our goals is to be able to spend $4,000 each year for remodeling the store. Doing so will easily increase annual sales by $16,000."

NEW LOCATIONS

"About six months ago we decided that we had to think about expansion because we cannot maintain an inventory of $35,000 and, over the long run, make sales of more than $12 per square foot per month in the present shop. The limiting factors are how fast we can buy, how fast we can process the stuff that is bought, and the disruption of deliveries through the front door since we do not have a back entrance into our 900 square feet of space.

"Ideally, provided that we could manage it, we should add a second location with 1,100 square feet minimum to 1,600 square feet maximum and with a rear entrance for delivery. This would allow us to check purchases and to price the garments efficiently. With two stores we would not need to double our inventory but would increase it at most by 50%. With two stores we would also have the advantage of being able to move merchandise from one location to the other either to increase sales or to take advantage of slight differences in the buying habits and decision patterns of the different clientele. A second store would also allow us to have more than three dressing rooms here. Sometimes three is not enough.

"The developer of a new shopping center, El Capri, at 7000 East Tanque Verde Road (see location B on Exhibit 1) wants us to lease space at $10 per square foot on a yearly lease. He is, however, only renting a shell in a major new shopping center. We would have to invest $20,000 in leasehold improvements before moving in.

"Another deal is available at the Park Mall at 5870 East Broadway (location C on Exhibit 1). This center is still under construction, but Broadway Stores, Diamond's, and Sears all are operating major department stores there. The traffic patterns on Broadway, near Wilmot, are such that people who drive there tend to come in from the southeast and the west rather than from the northeast or the north. The developer will lease either 2,000 or 2,500 square feet of space in either

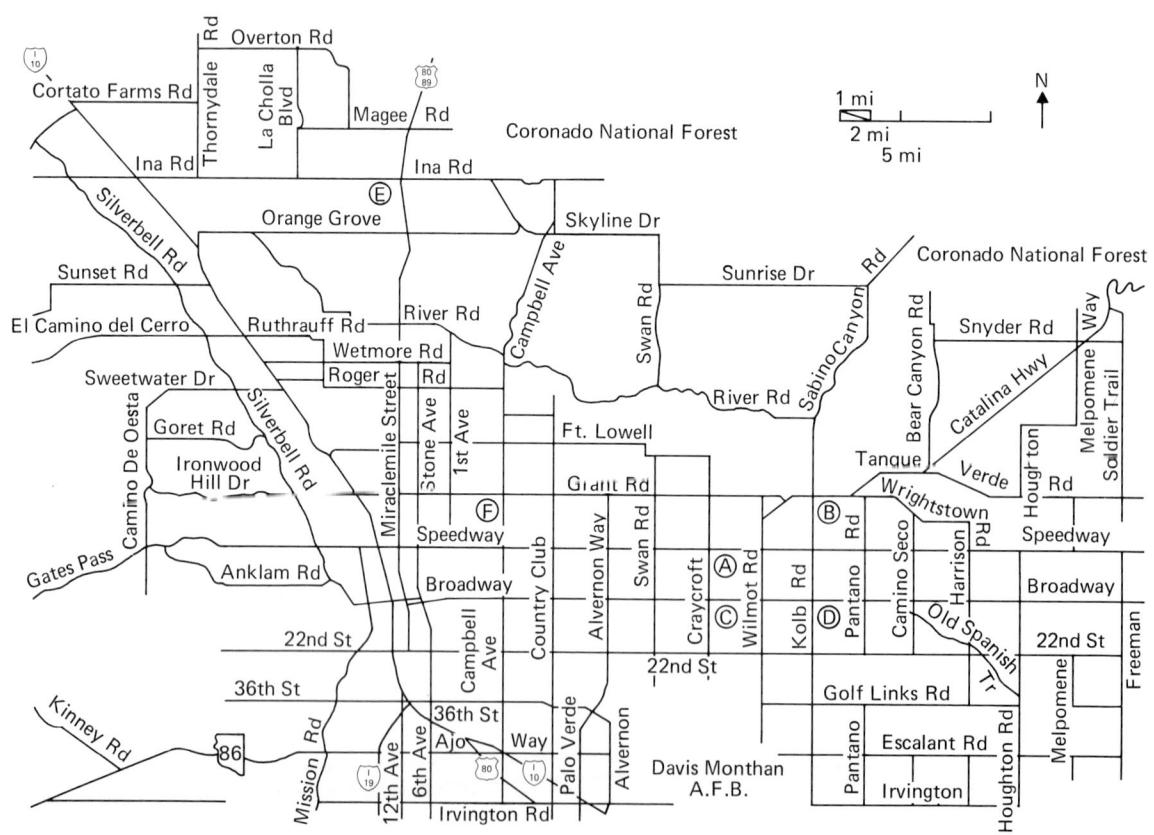

Exhibit 1

a rectangular or a square configuration. The size would be ideal for a single operation, but we would have to pay $10 per square foot and pay for leasehold improvements. Also, we would lose customers if we moved.

"We could look for space in a minor shopping area, but that would mean pioneering a new location. There are one or two way out east on Broadway that I have considered. Space costs would be about half as much as at El Capri shopping center on Tanque Verde Road. But we would have to have a free-standing unit because there are no vacancies in any shopping centers. Well to the east there is considerable population growth, and the population density is increasing. Census statistics show that young-marrieds to middle-aged persons (our target population) of middle-level incomes live there. About 5 miles from our present location would certainly differentiate the two buying groups geographically. Despite our advertising, however, I doubt that we are well enough known to support a separate building on our own. I really want a shopping center location for the traffic it brings. One developer who plans to put in a center beyond Kolb Road (see location D on Exhibit 1) has offered a lease of $4.50 to $6.00 per square foot, depending upon our location in the center. But we would need $15,000 for leasehold improvements and we would be pioneering a new location. The developer wants to sign us to a firm lease and then use our balance sheet to help him get financing to build the complex.

"My ultimate goal is to earn $1,000 net profit per year per store if we have 50 stores or $2,000 if we have 25 stores.

"There are other locations in town we can consider. Two spots in the southwestern part of the city have stores available at the right size for a second location. Both have lots of traffic. But neither Yvonne nor I speak Spanish, so there would be a language barrier to some extent. The lease conditions are very favorable. Since the socioeconomic pattern differs from the east side, we would be running essentially a completely new store. Our merchandising pattern would differ.

"On the northwest side, on Oracle Road near Ina (see location E on Exhibit 1), there is a shopping center with clientele and stores analogous to Monterey Village where we are now. The center has had three vacant buildings for over a year, but the landlord won't talk with us. I suspect that an existing store has threatened to move out if we move in. That store carries the same merchandise as we do, bought from the same manufacturers. But they put on their own labels and sell the clothes as exclusives.

"Our bank suggested a north central location on Campbell Avenue (see location F on Exhibit 1). Their branch in that area has the largest deposits per capita of all of its branches. We looked a bit further into who the depositors are. The bank figure is for savings deposits. Census tract data shows that the median age there is 20 years above the median for the city. The depositors are wealthy in bank cash holdings, but do they use the money for retirement funding or for consumer purchases? The one clothing store that has done well there in the 20 years of operation of the center is a budget store.

"The rental office here in Monterey Village has a location with 3,200 square feet available a few doors from where we are now (see Exhibit 2). It can be rented for $900 per month plus another $144 per month for taxes, maintenance, and dues to the Merchants' Association. It is L-shaped, with the main entrance at the top of the L and windows all along the side of the L paralleling a walkway that goes to a mall at the rear of the store. The shape provides limited wall space.

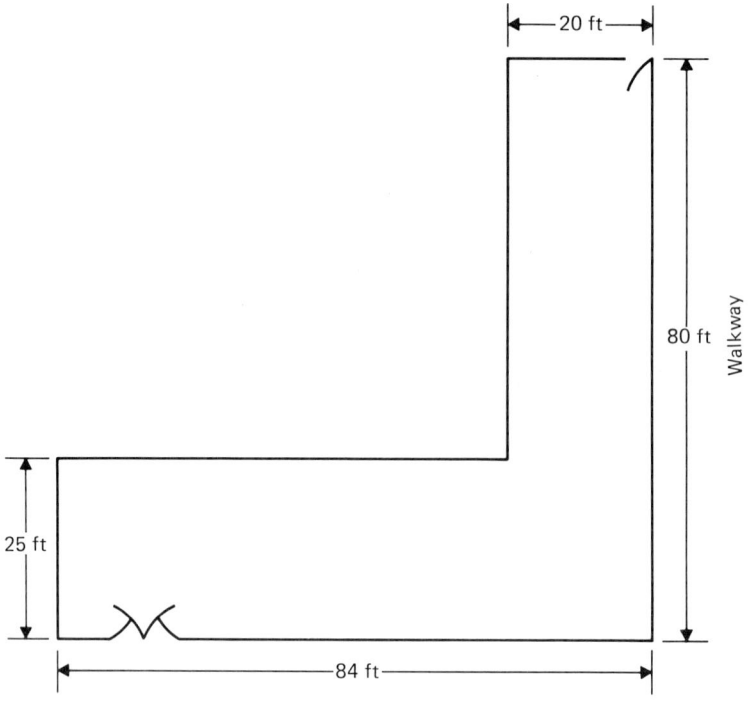

Exhibit 2

"A round rack for dresses usually has a diameter of 5 feet. Straight racks require a minimum total horizontal distance of 5 feet to allow for space to hang the garments and a walkway of a minimum size along one side so that the garments can be looked at.

"Dressing rooms (how many should we have?) would need an aisle of at least 39 inches, and the rooms themselves should have interior dimensions of no less than 4 feet by 4 feet. And how could they be built so that a salesclerk or store manager could check or control the flow in and out of the rooms? An easy way to lose merchandise is to have a customer walk out wearing two or three costumes in the layered look.

It would be a difficult store to force traffic through and the size calls for either a vast, open operation or for increasing the inventory to $65,000 to fill the space. An inventory of that size, even if turned 3 times per year at 50% markup, requires sales of $390,000 per year to support it.[5] I don't really have the expertise to lay out such a store to utilize its shape effectively.

FINANCES

Craig Wakefield stated that the first accountant used by Jodie's Ladies Wear was of no help. "She had a good reputation as a general accountant, but she did nothing for us other than to relist our checks. Then I turned to a CPA firm. They would prepare a balance sheet and income statement but wanted me to keep the journals, make ledger entries, reconcile the bank statement, and be available to answer a lot of questions about their trial balance. Even with 8 years of accounting study and practice behind me, I couldn't do everything. There were too many operating and merchandising decisions that had to be made on the spot for me to spend time with bank reconciliations and ledger entries.

"So I let the CPA firm go and hired 2 part-time accountants—both students at the University. One of them also worked as an auditor for the city. He turned out to be an inept accountant and compounded our troubles by leaving town with 20% of our accounting records. He never returned.

"The other fellow has worked out well. His eagerness to learn and his common sense have made up for his lack of professional experience. He takes a low wage to get training in retail accounting. We have had to work our balance sheets backward from what we have now to reconstruct the past balance sheets. We have had to estimate and improvise. I would not call it the usual accounting practice.

"I do the tax work (both payroll and income) myself. There have been some complications with the farm and ranching business and with the wholesale jewelry operation in the past that made this necessary. Now we depend upon the store for our living.

"You can see from looking at the statements what our financial problems are."

(Exhibits 3, 4, and 5 are the financial statements for Jodie's Ladies Wear. Exhibits 6 and 7 give data about retail sales activity and competition in the Tucson area.)

Exhibit 3
Gross sales by month, Jodie's Ladies Wear

MONTH	YEAR 1	YEAR 2	YEAR 3
January	—	$ 3,992	$12,962
February	$ 1,630	9,559	12,762
March	4,044	6,828	
April	3,961	9,874	
May	4,041	10,317	
June	3,382	10,148	
July	4,607	10,021	
August	3,288	6,657	
September	3,055	6,313	
October	4,832	9,746	
November	4,969	12,127	
December	8,165	18,537	
Year's Total	$45,974	$114,119	

Exhibit 4
Balance sheets, Jodie's Ladies Wear

	OPENING	END OF YEAR 1	END OF YEAR 2
Cash	$ 4,526	$ 4,870	$ 3,333
Accounts receivable	—	289	1,477
Inventory	15,164	26,351	35,000
Leasehold improvements (net)	16,934	13,934	10,934
Total assets	$36,624	$45,444	$50,744
Accounts payable	—	$ 5,514	$10,985
Note payable, bank	$ 2,500	5,375	3,355
Note payable (see Note A)	16,934	12,751	9,600
Proprietor's equity	17,190	21,804	26,804
Total liabilities and net worth	$36,624	$45,444	$50,744

Note A: Note payable to former proprietor to be paid at a minimum rate of $200 per month for 5 years. There is no penalty for prepayment. The balance is then to be paid in one lump sum.

Exhibit 5
Income statements, Jodie's Ladies Wear

	YEAR 1 (11 MONTHS)	YEAR 2
Sales	$45,975	$114,119
Cost of goods sold	24,969	73,671
Gross profit	$21,006	$ 40,448
Wages—employees	$ 6,770	$ 7,015
Advertising	1,159	12,401
Rent	2,598	2,940
Utility expense	1,106	944
Maintenance	73	78
Depreciation and amortization of leasehold improvements	3,000	3,000
Dues—merchant's association	230	570
Total expenses	$14,846	$ 26,948
Net income before taxes	$ 6,160	$ 13,500

Exhibit 6
Index of retail sales, Tucson standard metropolitan statistical area

MONTH	PREVIOUS YEAR	YEAR 1	YEAR 2	YEAR 3
January	120	145	173	195
February	131	144	173	185
March	123	147	168	
April	129	145	171	
May	139	159	171	
June	139	153	185	
July	127	151	176	
August	127	145	167	
September	126	147	185	
October	145	157	174	
November	135	171	176	
December	149	182	233	

Note: Tucson, like almost all cities in the United States, undergoes changes in its general economic activity. The effect of the depressions of the 1960's and 1970's was somewhat lessened in Tucson because of the predominance of government as the major sector of the economy of the Tucson Standard Metropolitan Statistical Area.

Exhibit 7
Number of competitive shops, City of Tucson

	YEAR 1	YEAR 2	YEAR 3
Department stores	10	11	13
Ladies wear specialty shops	68	70	80

NOTES

1. Ladies dresses are made in six cuts or size ranges: (a) Junior Petite—sizes, 1, 3, 4, 7, 9, 11, and 13; (b) Junior—sizes 5, 7, 9, 11, 13, and 15; (c) Junior Misses—sizes 4, 6, 8, 10, 12, and 14; (d) Misses—sizes 8, 10, 12, 14, 16, 18, and 20; (e) Half-sizes—12½, 14½, 16½, 18½, 20½, and 22½, (these are roughly Misses' sizes cut somewhat more fully); and (f) Women's—sizes 20, 22, 24, 26, etc. to 40. These are definitely for the larger women. Dresses are sold generally in two styles: (a) Contemporary (short dresses or "swinging" dresses) and (b) Mature, that is, more conservatively styled. No two manufacturers have identical cuts—even for a given size and size range. Each manufacturer has its own idea of the shape of a woman's body.

2. Monterey Village is a small shopping center in the northeast sector of Tucson. It is located on the southwest corner of Speedway Boulevard and Wilmot Road. (See location A on Exhibit 1.)

3. A story board is a sequence of still photographs—each with a caption—pasted upon one piece of Bristol board (a stiff cardboard) to show the key action elements, the development of the story of the commercial, and the expression of the copy theme. It is made up before the commercial is filmed. Often several story boards are developed to allow the advertising manager a choice.

4. "Dating" means shipping the goods but dating the invoices to be paid several months (usually up to six) after the shipment. The manufacturer gives credit to the retailer in this way.

5. Average inventory turnover for the industry is 2.7 times per year.

QUESTIONS

1. What is the outlook for womenswear shops in Tucson in terms of sales, profits, crucial factors for success, and the future of singly managed shops?

2. What strengths and weaknesses does Jodie's Ladies Wear have with its present ownership, relative to competition? How do these strengths and weaknesses match the crucial factors for success (question 1)?

3. What strategy do you recommend the Wakefields adopt for Jodie's Ladies Wear in regards to: (a) product/market scope, (b) sources of competitive advantage, (c) location, (d) sequence of major steps, and (e) key results to be sought in the next two, five, and ten years?

4. What recommended changes would you make in: (a) sales promotion, (b) purchasing, (c) personnel practices, (d) administrative organization, and (e) controlling operations?

CASE 2

Colonial Drug*

"I've still got a lot to learn about the business end," observed Mr. Paul Prather, sole owner and proprietor of Colonial Drug. "I've priced lower than the independents, tried to give better service than the chains or discounters, and experimented with several kinds of advertising to draw customers, but starting in business is really a hassle."

After two years as a pharmacist, and three years as manager of a discount chain's pharmacy department, Mr. Prather, aged thirty-one and a registered pharmacist, had decided to open his own drug store in Woodlake, a growing city of 25,000 in the southeastern U.S. His store, which began operations in April 1977, occupied leased quarters in a recently completed shopping center, close to the hospital, but several blocks from the downtown business district (see exhibit 1).

Mr. Prather had planned his venture for some time. He perused various trade publications and Small Business Administration pamphlets for information about location, physical layout, product mix, pricing, and promotion policies before he opened his doors and, in late 1977, he was still engaged in trying to complete a management-course which Eli Lilly and Company, a large drug manufacturer, offered by correspondence.

*This case was prepared by Professor Leete A. Thompson, California State University, Sacramento.

From *Marketing Management: Cases and Readings* edited by Dennis H. Tootelian, Ralph M. Gaedeke and Leete A. Thompson. Copyright © 1980 Scott, Foresman and Company. Reprinted by permission. Questions have been added at the end of the case.

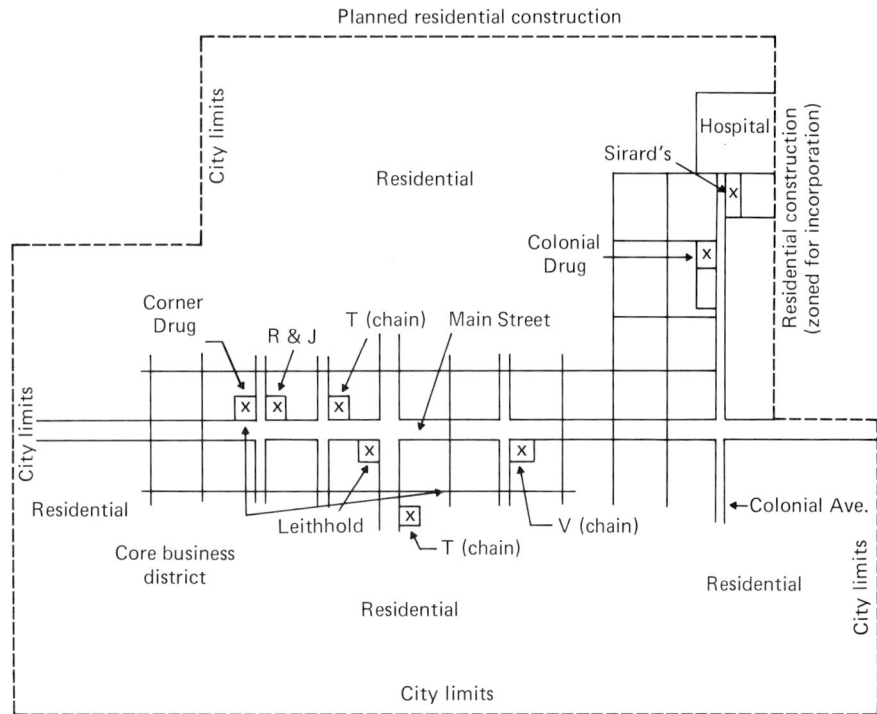

Planned residential construction

City limits

Residential

Hospital

Sirard's

Residential construction
(zoned for incorporation)

Colonial
Drug

Corner
Drug

R & J

T (chain)   Main Street

City limits

Residential

Leithhold

T (chain)

V (chain)

←Colonial Ave.

Core business
district

Residential

City limits

Residential

City limits

Exhibit 1
Map of Woodlake: Location of drug stores (stubs of streets only)

Approximately 1,000 of the 4,200 square feet of floor space was devoted to pharmacy and inventory storage. The remainder of the space was sectioned into functional groupings of health aids, cards, cosmetics, hair care, photography, and small appliances. Various toys, ceramics, and other gift items were distributed throughout the well-lit sales area.

Mr. Prather was uncertain as to how he might best gain rapid acceptance in the community. Although recent U.S. Supreme Court decisions had made it legal to advertise prescription drugs by price, druggists generally seemed to see no real benefit in the practice. One survey of 299 pharmacists showed that nine of ten would not advertise such drugs, and two-thirds felt that prices had little effect on customers' decisions to patronize a prescription drug store.[1] Nevertheless, Mr. Prather was convinced that some promotion and salesmanship were crucial. He hoped to quickly establish goodwill, trust, confidence, and a reputation for both reasonable prices and superior service.

In the first six months of operation, Colonial had spent from $180 to $1,170 per month for advertising and promotion. Occasional quarter-page advertisements in the local daily newspaper cost $180 each and featured eight or ten specials. Flyers designed at a cost of $16 per design hour and printed at $26 per 1,000, were distributed by third-class mail on occasion. In November, the merchants in his shopping center were starting a cooperative advertising program, and Mr. Prather expected to participate. In the near future, he planned to place a prominent advertisement in the 1978 telephone directory, at a cost of $40 per month. He also was considering placing ads in each of three out-of-town newspapers (from two nearby cities) which enjoyed significant circulation in Woodlake.

His promotional efforts had included distributing the free samples from various drug suppliers to retirement and convalescent homes in Woodlake. He also subscribed to the "Baby Showers" program of the local Welcome Wagon organization, wherein expectant or post-delivery mothers were given boxes containing Colonial Drug's card and some appropriate gifts. Forty and fifty boxes had been distributed in the last two months, at a cost of $1.30 per box.

Employees, too, had been encouraged to greet and assist customers with great courtesy. Two part-time clerks were hired in the early months, but a full-time clerk, four part-time clerks and a part-time delivery boy were on the September payroll. Mr. Prather and one of his employees each had been featured in the *Woodlake Daily Democrat*'s "Profiles," complete with pictures, backgrounds, and personal philosophies.

Colonial had not yet employed contests, demonstrations, coupons, or money-refund offers, but Mr. Prather was considering such promotional efforts.

FINANCES

Originally, Mr. Prather had invested $40,000 in Colonial Drug in the hopes that it would be profitable enough to provide him a moderate income and a satisfying occupation. Sales in the first six months had been disappointing. Furthermore, he had lost money, even without allowing himself a salary (see exhibits 2 and 3).

Fortunately, October sales appeared to be about twice those of September and, with cold and influenza season approaching, and with the expected patronage of Christmas shoppers ahead, Mr. Prather's goal of $175,000 sales probably would be attained by the end of the fiscal year, March 31, 1978: but he could only hope that Colonial would show a small profit for the first twelve months. His personal funds were not yet exhausted; moreover, two local banks had expressed their willingness to consider loans up to $25,000.

THE MARKET

According to one national study, the number of retail drug stores in the U.S. had remained relatively stable in recent years at just under 50,000, while the number of chain stores had increased markedly. Independent stores constituted about 75 percent of all drug stores in 1972, but they were only 68 percent of the total in 1975 — their sales representing 48.9 percent of total market share. Both chain and independent prescription sales continued to grow with inflation. However, the number of prescriptions filled by chain stores declined in 1974 and 1975 (in part, because of the increasing tendency of hospitals and other institutions to dispense outpatient prescriptions), while independent drug stores filled slowly growing numbers of prescriptions in both 1974 and 1975. Evidently, chain stores expanded their up front sales enough to overcome any drop in the numbers of prescriptions they filled, while independents' increase in prescription sales were offset by declines in other than drug sales. In any event, drug store sales failed to keep up with retail sales of all goods in the 1970s.[2]

Exhibit 2
Colonial Drug income statement April 1–September 30, 1977

	6-MONTH TOTAL	APRIL	MAY	JUNE	JULY	AUGUST	SEPT.
Sales:							
Prescription drugs	$37,125						
Other sales	41,080						
Total sales	$78,205	$6,540	$9,344	$11,337	$13,772	$16,591	$20,621
Cost of goods sold:	52,727						
Gross margin	$25,478						
Expenses:							
Wages	$ 8,185	$ 965	$ 965	$ 1,215	$ 1,560	$ 1,700	$ 1,780
Rent	12,280						
Utilities	3,180						
Insurance	717	317			400		
Licenses	1,165						
Advertising	4,052	728	335	180	546	1,093	1,170
Misc.	1,546						
Total expenses	$31,125						
Loss	($ 5,647)						

Exhibit 3
Colonial Drug balance sheet September 30, 1977

Assets:			Liabilities:	
Current assets			Accounts payable	
Cash	$ 307			
Accounts receivable	1,450			
Inventories	40,260			
Total current		$42,017	Capital investments:	$34,353
Fixed assets:				
Automobile	$ 4,770			
Leasehold Improvements	6,416			
Total fixed		11,186		
Total assets		$53,203	Total liabilities and net worth	$53,203

Of course, national market trends do not necessarily apply to market conditions for a drug store in a particular community. This is especially true when sales of prescription drugs, rather than up front goods are considered, and Mr. Prather considered Colonial to be primarily a prescription drug outlet.

THE WOODLAKE MARKET

In 1976, Woodlake's Chamber of Commerce estimated the city population to be 25,486, 8,387 of whom were under eighteen, and 2,561 of whom were over age sixty-five. No accurate estimates of income were available, but Mr. Prather believed that family incomes were "slightly above average."

Although druggists in a larger city some forty miles from Woodlake had found that people over age sixty-five spent two and one-half times as much per prescription as those under age sixty-five, Mr. Prather preferred "middle-upper-income people," most of whom he judged to be under age sixty-five. He indicated that he hoped to attract middle-aged people and "grow with them."

The city of Woodlake had been growing at a rate of about $4\frac{1}{2}$ percent per year, and Mr. Prather was anxious to attract people relatively new to the communicty—customers without loyalty to other local drug stores. Woodlake's 1976 ratio of 1,120 families per pharmacy would soon surpass the 1,200 familes per store experts had recommended to him. In fact, city officials estimated a population of about 45,000 in twelve years.

In justifying his views, Mr. Prather pulled a trade publication from his desk and pointed to a survey which reported that:[3]

1. The most important reason for patronizing a preferred pharmacy is: it is close to home or work (46.1 percent); price (21.8 percent); and various services in considerably smaller percentages.

2. Prescriptions are filled at: one pharmacy (75 percent); two pharmacies (20 percent); three (4 percent) and four or more (1 percent).

3. Have used the same pharmacy: more than 1 year (86 percent); more than 2 years (73 percent); more than 5 years (38 percent); and more than 10 years (21 percent).

Mr. Prather arranged for a local college student to conduct a small survey of Colonial Drug's market in September, 1977. The student polled a sample of thirty, selected at random from Polk's city directory. Responses to six questions were tabulated as follows:

1. Have you heard of Colonial Drug Stores? 21 yes; 9 no.

2. Do you know where it is located? 17 yes; 4 no.

3. Have you been in the store? 7 yes; 14 no.

4. How did you learn about the store? 6 ads; 15 other.

5. Do you feel that you can trust Colonial Drug (about same as), (more than), or (less than) other drug stores? 7 about same; 0 more; 0 less.

6. Do you feel that Colonial Drug provides (average), (above average), (below average) service compared with other stores? 7 average; 0 above; 0 below.

Although Mr. Prather questioned the validity of results based upon such a small sample, he was pleased that about 70 percent of those polled had heard of his store, and he opined that his advertisements had been at least partially effective. He was inclined to be disappointed by Colonial's neutral image, although he recognized that reputations were not likely to be built in a mere five months.

COMPETITION

Seven drug stores, three of them branches of two large chains, operated in Woodlake before Colonial opened its doors. Their reported taxable sales during the second and third quarters totalled $1,002,000 in 1976 and $1,050,000 in 1977. Supermarkets, gift shops, dime stores, notion shops, and other nonpharmaceutical retailers also carried many of the same items Colonial offered for sale.

State law required all pharmacies to post prices of the 100 most-often prescribed drugs and to indicate which of eight standard services were provided. The results of a September, 1977 study conducted by Woodlake druggists showed that Colonial's prices on seven listed drugs were considerably lower than those of other

Exhibit 4
Drug price survey—Woodlake Drug Store Association

STORE	DRUG							AVERAGE
	(1)	(2)	(3)	(4)	(5)	(6)	(7)	
Colonial	$ 4.65	$5.65	$19.65	$3.25	$ 8.85	$ 6.50	$ 8.60	$ 8.16
Corner	8.95	8.94	18.95	4.50	12.50	10.95	14.50	11.33
R & J	8.70	6.40	17.20	3.55	8.95	8.05	10.75	9.09
Leithhold	10.00	7.85	24.00	5.00	10.70	9.70	13.35	11.51
Sirard's	9.70	7.40	21.95	4.85	12.85	9.05	10.55	10.91
T (chain)	6.44	6.29	13.63	2.79	6.39	6.13	7.78	7.06
V (chain)	6.10	5.93	13.13	2.69	6.09	5.79	7.58	6.76

Note: Drugs included in September 1977 survey: (1) Ampicillin; (2) Darvon; (3) Diabinese; (4) Donnatal; (5) Erythrocin; (6) Lasix; and (7) Valium.

Exhibit 5
Survey of drug services offered—Woodlake Drug Store Association

STORE	SERVICE OFFERED							
	(1)	(2)	(3)	(4)	(5)	(6)	(7)	(8)
Colonial	X	X	X	X	X	X	X	X
Corner	X	X	X	X	X	X	X	X
R & J		X	X	X	X	X	X	X
Leithhold	X	X	X	X	X	X	X	X
Sirard's	X	X	X	X	X	X	X	X
T (chain)		X		X	X			X
V (chain)		X		X	X	X		X

Note: Services included in September 1977 survey: (1) Personal medication record—family's drug usage and cost; drug allergies recorded; (2) Professional consultation—insure consumer understanding proper use of a drug; (3) Emergency prescription—emergency telephone number and willingness to fill prescription after hours; (4) Compounded prescription service—will mix ingredients when prescribed; (5) Health service information—provide information about appropriate community agencies and services; (6) Charge account service—major credit cards or personal charge accounts accepted; (7) Prescription delivery—delivery service within stated area and above minimum purchase price; (8) Medi-State prescription service—fill Medi-State prescriptions at uniform prices.

independents, but they were somewhat higher than those of the chain outlets (see exhibit 4). The results also showed that Colonial and other independent drug stores offered a wider range of services than did the chain outlets (see exhibit 5).

Mr. Prather was reasonably certain that some of his competitors obtained merchandise at lower prices than he. He utilized jobbers to maintain Colonial's stock of such merchandise as stationery and hair goods. Drug related products were ordered through wholesalers, but Mr. Prather was not always able to order in large enough quantities to obtain discounts. He noted, however, that customers seldom consulted the drug prices he posted, so he was not at all certain that his attempt to maintain low prices was appreciated. He was reasonably confident that most of his gift items were profitable, for he attended gift shows periodically and ordered most gift items directly from manufacturers.

Most of Colonial's product prices were "cost plus." Nondrug items were marked up by from 30 to 50 percent, while prescription drug prices were based upon a price list Mr. Prather secured from his former employer (a chain discount store). He arbitrarily added 85¢ to each item on the price list.

THE FUTURE

Mr. Prather was still uncertain about Colonial's proper direction. No profit had been earned, despite his seven-day-a-week work schedule, aggressive promotion, and consultation with people he considered to be knowledgeable. He looked forward to experiments with contests and coupon promotions, cooperative advertising with local merchants, advertising in out-of-town newspapers, and even advertising over the local radio station. The station operated around the clock and provided interviews, news, public affairs announcements, and music. Thirty-second ads ranged from $7 to $18, depending upon the time of day and day of the week, but eighteen to thirty-four year-olds predominated in the audience.

Mr. Prather confided that he sometimes considered the possibility of returning to work for a drug chain, but he was at least encouraged by the recent growth in sales, and he felt that Colonial had potential if only he could find the proper combination of price, promotion, and service policies.

NOTES

1. J. H. Goldbert, "Why Rx Price Advertising Is Doomed," *Drug Topics*, April 1976, pp. 39ff.

2. B. S. Garcha, J. H. Goldberg, and P. Grayson, "Big Surge in Total Sales Is Marred by Fewer Scripts," *Drug Topics*, March 1976, pp. 41–47.

3. "1305 People Tell What They Seek in a Pharmacy," *American Druggist*, Sept. 1976, pp. 28–36.

QUESTIONS

1. What are some current trends in the drug store trade?

2. How are these trends affecting Colonial Drug?

3. What changes in location, product line, services, price, and/or promotion should Prather make?

4. Should Prather sell Colonial Drug and return to the drug chain as an employee? Why?

CASE 3
_____

American Park Golf Center*

In June 1979, Mr. Jeffrey Robbins, president of American Park Golf Center, was evaluating the past operations of his golf course and trying to determine what future actions he should take. Mr. Robbins opened his golf center on December 26, 1976, after approximately six years of planning, developing, and legal battles with the city. Although the course was privately owned, it was open to the public and, in Mr. Robbin's opinion, had been reasonably successful.

THE GOLF CENTER

Located in a large metropolitan area in northern California, the American Park Golf Center (APGC) was an executive style nine-hole golf course, with two par four holes and seven par three holes. While the course was only 1,635 yards long, the golfer could use woods on occasion and was faced with a multitude of water hazards, trees, and sand traps. Providing further obstacles, and enhancing the beauty of the course, was a large river bordering the west side of the course. During the summer months (May through September), the course was open for twelve hours per day, and during the winter for ten hours per day (hours open are equivalent to hours available for starting times, which are at five minute intervals).

In addition to the course itself there was a practice putting green, a practice chipping area, and a temporary clubhouse. The clubhouse was actually a converted mobile home which contained vending machines for snacks and beverages, and a small pro shop operated independently by the course pro, Mr. James Kilgore.

To staff this golf center, Mr. Robbins hired one full-time employee and one part-time employee to work in the clubhouse. In addition, one full-time and two part-time employees were hired to maintain the course. Mr. Robbins prided himself in keeping the course as well maintained and litter free as was physically possible.

BACKGROUND

Although Mr. Robbins, 46, enjoyed golf, he was not an avid golfer himself. His previous work experience included merchandising and site location studies for a large retail chain, ownership of a doughnut shop, and the development of a similar type of golf center in southern California. He principally enjoyed the challenge of starting new ventures and tried to maintain more of a business rather than a golfing orientation in this operation.

After deciding to pursue this venture, Mr. Robbins took one year in looking for a suitable location for a golf center. He wanted to locate in a high traffic area close

_____

*This case was prepared by Professor Dennis H. Tootelian, California State University, Sacramento.

From *Marketing Management: Cases and Readings* edited by Dennis H. Tootelian, Ralph M. Gaedeke and Leete A. Thompson. Copyright © 1980 Scott, Foresman and Company. Reprinted by permission.

Questions have been added at the end of the case.

to the center of the city so as to appeal to the afternoon businessperson. As he stated: "I travelled up and down many streets around the city until I found this site. It was worth it, however, since I found just what I wanted, despite the legal troubles I ran into."

After purchasing the land (twenty-five acres) in 1967, Mr. Robbins began planning for the construction of the course itself. In 1974, however, the city filed a condemnation suit which it won in 1975. Because the land bordered a river and was adjacent to a public bikeway, the city wanted to obtain ownership of the land for "public use for the public good." As a result, the land was resold to the city and Mr. Robbins was given a forty-year lease on it. When the lease expires, the golf center will be operated by the city. The terms of the lease were such that Mr. Robbins paid $6,000 per year rent and the taxes on the land (currently $6,500 per year).

According to Mr. Robbins, his troubles with the city did not end with the disposition of the condemnation suit.

> They have fought me on virtually everything I have tried to do. The taxes should be roughly 8 percent of expenses instead of the current 13 percent. I am fighting this now. I have made every effort possible to make this course a beautiful one which fits into its surroundings. I have no intention of altering the landscape in any significant way. You would think the city would help me build up business since it will be theirs someday, but for some reason they give me a bad time.

APGC was incorporated in 1974. With respect to the disposition of the common stock, Mr. Robbins held 65 percent, his son 20 percent, and the other 15 percent was held by individuals who had assisted in starting the business.

THE COMPETITION

Within the city and surrounding area (twenty-five miles), there were thirteen major golf courses open to the public, and five private ones. Of those open to the public, six were responsible for approximately 75 percent of the golf starts in the area (see exhibit 1).

Although there was one publicly owned nine-hole golf course within the city, it did not compare favorably to APGC in terms of beauty or difficulty of play. Mr. Robbins felt that the course most similar to American Park in terms of being relatively short and well maintained was located about twenty-five miles away, and was an eighteen-hole course (course F). The other major courses in the area (courses A through E) were of standard length, requiring four and one-half to five hours to play eighteen holes. The average player at APGC could play nine holes in approximately one and one-half hours.

Mr. Robbins felt that APGC had several advantages relative to the competition in the area. First, the course was close to highly populated areas and numerous business offices. With respect to housing, there were fifteen apartment complexes within a two-mile radius of the golf center, and two of these bordered the center itself (230 units). Within this area, therefore, there were well over 1500 apartment units. Accounting for a large part of this concentration of apartment units was a university with some 18,000 students located approximately one mile from the APGC. In addition to the apartment complexes, there were twelve relatively small

Exhibit 1
Golf courses in relevant market

	NUMBER OF HOLES	PAR	OWNERSHIP	DISTANCE FROM CENTRAL CITY
Course— High Volume				
A	18	72	County	8 miles
B	18	72	City*	20 miles
C	36	72 (per 18 holes)	City	5 miles
D	18	72	City*	25 miles
E	18	72	City*	25 miles
F	18	61	Private	25 miles
Course— Mid Volume				
G	18	72	City*	25 miles
H	18	72	City*	15 miles
I	18	71	City*	25 miles
J	18	70	City	9 miles
K	9	27	City	7 miles
L	18	72	Private	15 miles
APGC	9	29	Private	5 miles

*Not the same city in which American Park is located.

centers (business offices) within this area also. The average professional center contained approximately twenty-five individual business offices. Because of this concentration, Mr Robbins thought that this site was good for a golf center.

A second advantage of the APGC was its outstanding reputation. Because the course had been professionally designed and was so well maintained, it received excellent word of mouth advertising. In 1977, Mr. Robbins commissioned some university students to do a small market survey of golfers at his course and at two of the public courses (courses A and C). While the survey was not professional in nature, it did offer insights into the attitudes of the various golfers (see exhibits 2 and 3).

The third advantage Mr. Robbins felt he had was that while the course was busy (some 44,000 starts in 1977 and 47,000 starts in 1978), it was relatively easy to get a convenient starting time. Many of the high volume courses averaged anywhere from 175,000 to 250,000 starts per year, and golfers without advance reservations often waited one to two hours, whereas at APGC the golfer normally did not have to wait for more than fifteen to twenty minutes even during relatively busy times.

Exhibit 2
Market study—most desirable characteristics

WHAT THEY LIKED ABOUT THE COURSE	APGC	COURSE A	COURSE C
Challenging course	22%	12%	19%
Long course	0	20	15
Short course	9	0	0
Beauty of course surroundings	21	10	16
Well kept landscape (general)	11	5	3
Location	3	10	16
Well maintained greens	9	5	6
Course well laid out	12	8	10
Other	13	30	16
	100%	100%	100%

Exhibit 3
Market study—least desirable characteristics

WHAT THEY DISLIKED ABOUT THE COURSE	APGC	COURSE A	COURSE C
No rakes in traps	16%	0%	2%
Lack of sufficient ball washers	19	0	0
Debris on course	0	10	10
Price	14	3	0
Poorly maintained greens	5	21	14
Overcrowded	0	32	24
Lack of organization in teeing off	28	0	7
Too many children playing course	0	26	5
Other	18	8	38
	100%	100%	100%

Consequently, for golfers who wanted to play with no advance starting time, the APGC was very appealing. Coupled with the fact that the course was close to the center of the city and challenging golf could be played in a shorter time period, Mr. Robbins thought that the course was ideally suited for businessmen and students.

Despite these advantages, however, there were several disadvantages. First, while the golf course was in a high traffic area, it could not be seen directly from the main cross streets. Golfers had to turn onto a relatively obscure side street in order to reach the clubhouse. Although there was a small sign stating "Golf" on one of the main cross streets, the clubhouse was not readily visible.

The second disadvantage was the fact that the green fees were somewhat higher for APGC than for the publicly owned golf courses (see exhibit 4). In assessing his pricing structure, Mr. Robbins did not believe his market to be overly price sensitive except perhaps for the university students. To compensate for this a $.50 discount was given to students with valid university identification cards for weekday afternoon play. Publicly owned courses, however, gave $.70 reductions to players under eighteen and allowed those over seventy years of age to play free on weekday afternoons.

The final disadvantage recognized by Mr. Robbins was that the course was a short, nine-hole course. Because of the nature of the course, the "true" golfer normally preferred a regulation eighteen-hole course. Consequently, Mr. Robbins felt that his course had somewhat limited appeal. Even though some golfers played the course twice, most only played nine holes.

MARKETING ACTIVITIES

Mr. Robbins engaged in few marketing activities since he believed that location and word of mouth advertising sold the course itself. Other than the "Golf" sign, membership in a "Let's Dine Out" type of group, and an advertisement in the yellow pages of the telephone directory, no efforts were made to promote the golf center. Furthermore, knowing that most of the city- and county-owned golf courses operated

Exhibit 4
Comparative prices

GREEN FEES	APGC	CITY-COUNTY OWNED	PRIVATE COURSE
Weekdays			
9 holes	$ 2.50	$1.75 to $2.00	$3.00 to $10.00
18 holes	$ 4.50	$3.25 to $4.00	$5.00 to $15.00
Weekends			
9 holes	$ 3.00	$2.50 to $3.00	$5.00 to $15.00
18 holes	$ 5.50	$4.00 to $5.00	$7.50 to $20.00
Special prices			
Monthly card	$20.00	$15.00	—
All day play			
Weekdays	$ 5.00	$4.00 to $4.50	—
Weekends	$ 6.00	—	—
Junior players (under 18)			
9 holes (weekdays only)	$ 2.00	$1.50 to $2.00	—
18 holes (weekdays only)	$ 3.00	$2.00 to $2.75	—
All day (weekdays only)	$ 3.50	$3.00 to $3.50	—
Senior players (70 or over)			
Weekdays only	—	Free	—
Students (weekdays only)	$ .50 discount	$ .70 discount	—

at a loss, Mr. Robbins made no effort to compete with them on a price basis. He did, however, give free rounds of golf to some of his regular customers, but this was very sporadic. In addition, he made some price concessions to lure in local tournaments by giving $.25 off for nine holes of play.

FINANCIAL STATUS

The financial statements for APGC are presented in exhibits 5 and 6. Although the golf center had always been profitable, Mr. Robbins recognized that his costs could be lower. The care and maintenance of the course were of prime importance to him, and he was very reluctant to trim these costs.

Exhibit 5
APGC income statement

	1978		1977	
Golf starts (sales)	$64,884	(90.1)	$60,742	(95.4)
Merchandise sales (net)	7,136	(9.9)	2,956	(4.6)
Total sales	$72,020	(100.0)	$63,698	(100.0)
Variable costs				
Labor	$14,685	(20.4)	$13,884	(21.8)
Fertilizer	3,500	(4.9)	3,750	(5.9)
Equipment repair	1,200	(1.7)	750	(1.2)
Misc. (sand, etc.)	400	(0.5)	650	(1.0)
Total	$19,785	(27.5)	$19,034	(29.9)
Fixed costs				
Utilities				
Water	$ 4,000	(5.6)	$ 3,700	(5.8)
Electricity	800	(1.1)	775	(1.2)
Telephone	360	(0.5)	360	(0.6)
Misc. (garbage, etc.)	180	(0.3)	180	(0.3)
Advertising	3,750	(5.2)	3,540	(5.5)
Supplies (scorecards, etc.)	450	(0.6)	840	(1.3)
Loan payments	3,992	(5.5)	3,992	(6.3)
Lease payments	6,000	(8.3)	6,000	(9.4)
Property taxes	6,500	(9.0)	6,500	(10.2)
Administrative salaries	15,315	(21.3)	14,250	(22.4)
Depreciation	3,700	(5.1)	3,700	(5.8)
Total	$45,047	(62.5)	$43,837	(68.8)
Total variable and fixed costs	$64,832	(90.0)	$62,871	(98.7)
Income before taxes	$ 7,188	(10.0)	$ 827	(1.3)

Exhibit 6
APGC balance sheet

	1978	1977
Current assets		
Cash	$ 2,300	$ 1,100
Net accounts receivable	3,415	595
Prepaid expenses	2,875	268
Total	$ 8,590	$ 1,963
Net fixed assets		
Portable clubhouse	$14,275	$15,050
Equipment for course	2,800	2,410
Features for course	750	300
Office equipment	475	324
Golf accessories	635	290
(carts, clubs, etc.)		
Leasehold improvements	44,000	44,000
Total	$62,935	$62,374
Total assets	$71,525	$64,337
Current liabilities		
Accounts payable	$ 3,725	$ 3,160
Wages payable	1,285	350
Total	$ 5,010	$ 3,510
Long-term liabilities		
Bank loan	$38,500	$40,000
Total	$38,500	$40,000
Common stock	$20,000	$20,000
Equity	$ 8,015	$ 827
Total liabilities and equity	$71,525	$64,337

I know that I go a little overboard on some things. For example, I use only the best fertilizer on the course, and I make sure the course is mown three times per week compared to city and county courses which are mown two times per week. In the winter when most courses close due to the excess moisture on the greens, I use highly absorbent sand so that the course can stay open and be playable. I believe, nevertheless, that these things are important for the reputation of the course. Over time these activities will pay off.

The lengthy delay and high legal costs involved in starting operations, furthermore, made it difficult for Mr. Robbins to put more of his personal wealth into the business. Although he was not opposed to bringing in outside investors, he did not want to lose control of the corporation.

FUTURE OPERATIONS

In reviewing his operations, Mr. Robbins wanted to increase the utilization of the course and maximize his profit position. Since the costs of operation did not vary significantly with the number of players, Mr. Robbins felt that by increasing the number of starts, profits would increase appreciably. In his deliberations, he had identified several possible courses of action.

While it was impossible to acquire enough additional land to add nine more holes to the course, Mr. Robbins had thought about putting lights on the existing nine holes to allow for night play. This would allow the APGC to stay open for three more hours in the summer and five more hours in the winter. No other course in the area had lights. He had approached the city with this idea about one year earlier, but met with strong resistance from a group of ecologists. Given his past experience with the city, he was somewhat skeptical about carrying this effort further. He anticipated the costs of installing the lighting to be approximately $36,000. The other costs are presented in exhibit 7.

Mr. Robbins was also considering the feasibility of putting a driving range near the clubhouse. A church adjacent to the land had excess parking facilities, and Mr. Robbins thought they would lease some of this space to him at a yearly fee of $2,500. Although the costs of a driving range were relatively low (see exhibit 8), he was unsure of its profit potential. The one main limitation was that there was not enough space to allow the use of woods unless specially designed plastic golf balls were used. These were very expensive, but would travel only about one-third

Exhibit 7
Costs of nightlights

Installation of nightlights		$36,000
Additional annual costs:		
Labor	$5,648	
Electricity	6,000	
Misc. costs	2,000	
Interest on loan	2,400	

Exhibit 8
Driving range costs

Initial outlay	
Machine to pick up golf balls (5-year life)	$2,500
Baskets—50 at $4 per basket (5-year life)	200
Golf balls—75 per basket at $.20 per ball (3-year life)	750
Protective screens around range	6,000
Labor costs	2,190
General maintenance	200
Insurance	300
Anticipated loss of golf balls—20% per year	

the distance of regular golf balls. If plastic golf balls were not used, Mr. Robbins would have to limit the range to irons only.

A third idea Mr. Robbins had was to build a modern clubhouse to replace the temporary mobile home. He felt that this would provide for a better image and enhance the sales of merchandise. While all merchandise sales and lessons were handled by Mr. Kilgore, Mr. Robbins received a commission of 5 percent on gross sales (including lessons). He estimated the cost to build a clubhouse was approximately $22,000.

One other idea was to convert APGC to a private club and membership. Although Mr. Robbins was certain the city would object since his contract states the course will be open to the public, he felt that he could try to fight that battle. The anticipated miscellaneous costs of making such a switch were considered to be approximately $3,000 and would necessitate the building of a modern clubhouse with some added features like showers, lockers, etc. The costs of this clubhouse were thought to be about $60,000.

In his evaluations, Mr. Robbins could not decide whether to take one of these, or other alternatives, or whether he should stick with or improve his present operations.

QUESTIONS

1. What is the environmental situation facing American Park?

2. What can be determined from the financial ratios?

3. What is American Park's main problem? Secondary problems?

4. What alternatives exist to solve these problems?

5. Which alternative solution would you recommend? Why?

CASE 4

The Silver Goblet*

Mary Matlock was quite excited about the potential of improving the sales volume of The Silver Goblet if only she could move to the location on the corner. She had recently been approached by the attorney of the present tenant with the idea that

---

*The research and written case information were presented at a Case Research Symposium and were evaluated by the Case Research Association's Editorial Board. This case was prepared by C. Kendrick Gibson of Henderson State University as a basis for class discussion.

Distributed by the Case Research Association. All rights reserved to the authors and the Case Research Association. Permission to use the case should be obtained from the Case Research Association. Questions have been added at the end of the case.

she purchase their inventory so that she could move. The proposed location was on the corner of a main street in the busy downtown shopping district and was exposed to high levels of foot traffic. Mary knew that she wanted to make an offer to buy the inventory, but had been urged by a friend to seek help in the evaluation of the opportunity. She had done very little evaluation but believed strongly that the location would help her business.

BACKGROUND

The Silver Goblet is located in a medium-sized mid-western community of approximately 30,000 population. The store is primarily a gift shop selling ceramics, brass items, a few paperback and hard cover books, and various types of specialty retail items. Mary and her partners have targeted themselves at the middle to upper income retail shopper through store image and pricing. The Silver Goblet has a unique layout using contemporary and up-beat furnishings and advertising to gain a competitive advantage in the local area.

There are four partners involved in the business. Mary and her husband (a lawyer), and another couple each have a 25% interest in the ownership. Mary, along with the wife of the other couple and part-time employees provide most of the active supervision of the firm. The group began operating in December 1978 and through the end of December 1979, expected to have received $80,000 in sales. Sales for the year have been as follows:

December 2 (opening day)–December 31, 1978	$13,368
January 1–March 31, 1979	8,899
April, 1979	4,371
May 1–May 12, 1979 (Present date)	1,954
	$28,592

Even though the store has only been operating for a few months, all the partners are pleased with the results. The gift shop business, however, is quite volatile. Turnover of firms on the average is very high.

Mary recently read a report in the local newspaper which reviewed the risks of this particular type of business and the failure rate in their town. In addition, a *Business Week* article concerning small businesses gave the following information (*Business Week,* August 6, 1979, pp. 94–97) concerning gift shops:

Investment Required	$20–30,000
Estimated Return	7–10%
Failure/10,000 Businesses	25

Mary and her partners were therefore encouraged and cautious at the same time. These feelings of enthusiasm and fear were characteristic of new small business owner/managers she was sure. She recognized the risks and the fact that she needed more business knowledge to handle these pressures.

To help offset the risks of failure, Mary and the wife of the other couple enrolled in a Small Business Management seminar conducted in March of 1979. One of the factors she remembered being emphasized was the importance of locations. The seminar also emphasized financial management, but Mary always found numbers hard to deal with and confusing. She considered herself a good salesperson but not an accountant!

THE PRESENT OPPORTUNITY

In spite of the problems of the business, Mary was ready to make an offer to buy the inventory of the business on the corner so that she could move there. She knew that the other family would go along with her but was concerned about her husband's feelings since he was not available to discuss it.

The attorney for the other business stated that his client will only accept an offer of $30,000 for the business. He emphasizes the good foot traffic and visibility The Silver Goblet would have in that location as opposed to their present location and that the purchase price could be quickly recovered.

Mary has asked for copies of the businesses' tax returns or financial statements for the most recent two or three years, but the attorney had been unwilling to forward them. In addition, Mary has suggested a formal inventory, but the owners have not provided her with that either.

In spite of these drawbacks, Mary is prepared to offer the $30,000 for the inventory and fixtures. If they move, the lease for the space would decrease from the present $800/month (on a month to month cancellable basis) to $650/month. The new lease rate would include all utilities whereas the present lease does not. She believes that sales would increase to approximately $150,000 per year in that location at the most optimistic levels.

To satisfy the questions she knows her husband will ask, Mary has decided to ask a business consultant to evaluate the alternative for her and to make his recommendations for her consideration. Mary has prepared some information for him that he has requested. Exhibits 1–3 are what she plans to give him. She worked most of the previous evenings preparing these for him. She needs his conclusions by Friday morning even though it is Wednesday. Mary is pretty sure that she will make the offer anyway.

The consultant has told her he will prepare the following for her to review:

1. Projected sales figures per month for the present location for 1979.

2. Projected operating expenses for the new location during the first year's operations.

3. Projected income statement for the first year @ $80,000; the second year @ $98,000 and $150,000.

4. A cash flow projection reflecting the profitability, debt service and remaining cash inflow or outflow.

Exhibit 1
Basic operating assumptions

Break-even profit objective for first year.

Gross profit objective = 40% of sales.

Average turnover = 4.5 times per year.

Average turnover value = $11,400 based on present levels.

Borrow $30,000 purchase price as well as $10,000 additional working capital.

Plan to increase average inventory to $17,000 per inventory turnover.

Estimated sales volume—present location $ 80,000
                      New location (conservative)   98,000
                      New location (optimistic)   150,000

Increased advertising expenses—$2,000/year.

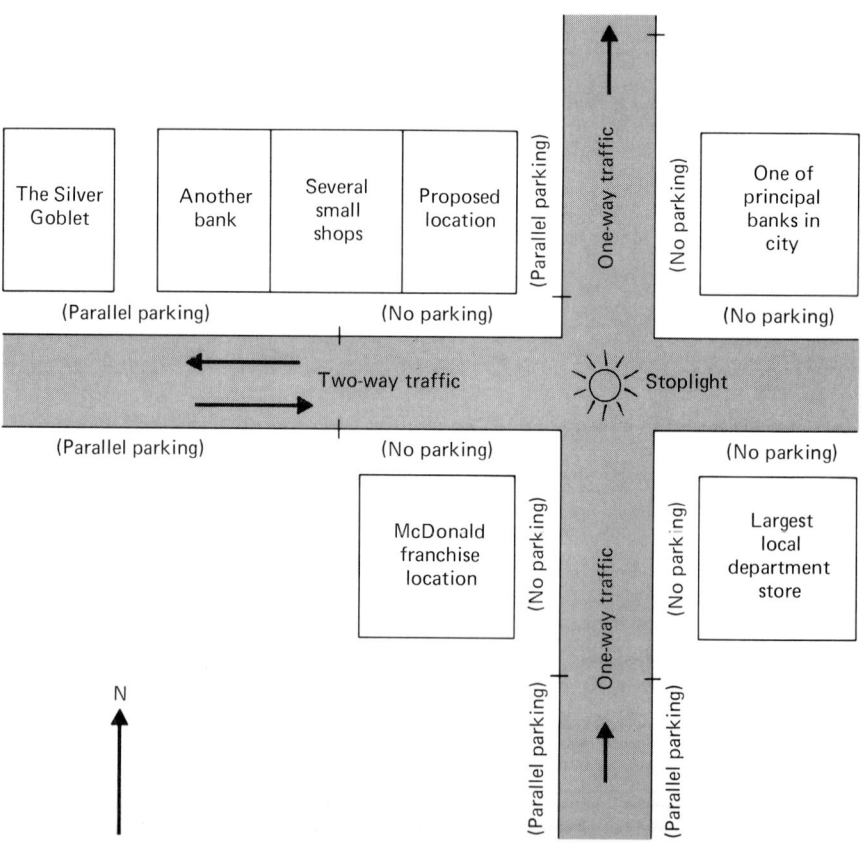

Exhibit 2
Map of present and proposed locations

Exhibit 3
Financial statements

THE SILVER GOBLET BALANCE SHEET DECEMBER 31, 1978

Assets

Cash		$ 2,610.23
Inventory		11,400.63
Supplies		204.05
Prepaid insurance		379.50
Furniture and equipment	$1,896.66	
Less: accumulated depreciation	31.61	1,865.05
Total assets			$16,459.46

Liabilities

Accounts payable		$ 611.90
Loan payable		5,000.00
Accrued interest payable		45.83
Sales tax payable		497.80
FICA tax payable		40.80
Total liabilities			$ 6,196.33

Owner's equity

Capital, Mary Jo Williams		$ 2,515.78
Capital, Clarence Williams		2,515.78
Capital, Mary Mattlock		2,615.78
Capital, Bob Mattlock		2,615.79
Total owner's equity			$10,263.13
Total liabilities and owner's equity			$16,459.46

THE SILVER GOBLET STATEMENT OF OWNER'S CAPITAL DECEMBER 31, 1978

	Mr. Williams	Ms. Williams	Mr. Mattlock	Ms. Mattlock
Beginning balance	$2,500.00	$2,500.00	$2,500.00	$2,500.00
Add: net income	115.78	115.78	115.78	115.79
Total	$2,615.78	$2,615.78	$2,615.78	$2,615.79
Less: withdrawals	100.00	100.00		
Ending capital balance	$2,515.78	$2,515.78	$2,615.78	$2,615.78

Exhibit 3 *(Cont.)*

THE SILVER GOBLET PROFIT & LOSS STATEMENT FOR PERIOD ENDED DECEMBER 31, 1978

Revenues:			
Sales			$ 13,367.67
Cost of goods sold:			
Beginning inventory		$ 5,000.00	
Purchases	$ 15,237.51		
Transportation in	262.52		
cost of purchases	$ 15,500.03		
Less: purchases discounts	696.86		
Net purchases		14,803.17	
Cost of goods available for sale		$19,803.17	
Less: ending inventory		11,400.63	
Cost of goods sold			8,402.54
Operating income			$ 4,965.13
Expenses:			
Interest expense		$ 45.83	
Sales tax expense		497.80	
Travel expense		241.29	
Telephone expense		62.17	
Insurance expense		34.50	
Supplies expense		116.06	
Miscellaneous expense		162.71	
Rent expense		1,858.44	
Cash register expense		151.08	
Payroll expense		20.40	
Wage expense		337.23	
Depreciation expense		31.61	
Advertising expense		942.88	
Total expenses			4,502.00
Net income			$463.13

Exhibit 3 *(Cont.)*

THE SILVER GOBLET BALANCE SHEET (3 MONTHS ENDING) MARCH 31, 1979

Assets		
Cash		$ 511.86
Inventory		
Supplies		121.91
Prepaid insurance		276.00
Furniture and equipment	$2,366.88	
Less: accumulated depreciation	148.44	2,218.44
Total assets		
Liabilities		
Accounts payable		39.90
Loan payable		9,000.00
Accrued interest payable		265.83
Wages payable		550.00
FICA payable		43.04
Sales tax payable		144.36
Equipment payable		33.95
Total liabilities		$10,077.78
Owner's equity		
Capital, Mary Jo Williams		$ 2,515.78
Capital, Clarence Williams		2,515.78
Capital, Mary Mattlock		2,615.79
Capital, Bob Mattlock		2,615.78
Total owner's equity		$10,263.13
		$20,340.91

Exhibit 3 *(Cont.)*

THE SILVER GOBLET INCOME STATEMENT (3 MONTHS ENDING) MARCH 31, 1979

Revenues:			
Sales		$ 8,898.63	
Less: sales returns & allowances		42.27	
Net sales			$8,856.36
Cost of goods sold:			
Beginning inventory (adjusted)		11,400.63	
Purchases	$5,267.84		
Transportation in	458.95		
Cost of purchases	$5,726.79		
Net purchases		5,726.79	
Cost of goods available for sale		$17,127.42	
Less: ending inventory		15,273.00	
Cost of goods sold			1,854.42
Operating income (loss)			$7,001.94
Expenses:			
Cash register expense	$ 75.54		
Advertising expense	1,428.05		
Rent expense	1,603.32		
Telephone expense	111.48		
Miscellaneous expense	151.85		
Travel expense	212.00		
FICA expense	43.04		
Wage expense	2,186.65		
Sales tax expense	195.48		
Supplies expense	289.95		
Depreciation expense	106.83		
Interest expense	220.00		
Insurance expense	103.50		
Utilities expense	225.43		
Total expenses			$6,953.12
			$ 48.82

QUESTIONS

1. What is the projected balance sheet and income statement for the firm in the new location?

2. What is the ability of the business to provide debt service and meet the needs of the owners?

3. What recommendations would you make to the owners?

CASE 5

The Kneadery*

In January, Mr. John MacHenry, owner of the Kneadery, was preparing his annual assessment of the operations of his health food bakery. Although sales increased over the last two years, he had expected a faster rate of growth in both sales and profits. He was also concerned about possible expansions in his product lines since they had not progressed as he had hoped. Finally, Mr. MacHenry was worried about the competition he faced. The health food market was expanding rapidly and thereby bringing in much stronger competition. Local bakeries were introducing more natural foods; nationally franchised bakers were starting to make significant penetrations; and retail grocery stores were opening bake shops and coming out with health food products of their own.

HISTORY OF THE COMPANY

The Kneadery was established in a medium-size city in the southwest in early 1972 by Mr. William Kraus for the purpose of supplying whole grain breads to health food stores in the area. First year sales increased nearly month-to-month, and at a rate that even surprised Mr. Kraus. However, as the typical business day grew longer due to increased demand, cleanliness and quality control began to suffer. Customers became dissatisfied and sales began to decline. By August 1973, Mr. Kraus became disillusioned with the baking business and decided to sell out.

The purchasers of the Kneadery were a commune of nine people in the immediate area. After the first month of operation, this group dwindled to three members who took active charge of the operation of the business. Not only did they continue to sell to health food stores, but they also began to sell bread and made-to-order sandwiches on the premises. Business lost by the previous owner was regained and sales began to increase again at a rapid pace. Once the novelty wore off, however, and the workload increased, two of the remaining group dropped out. By May 1974, Mr. John Marsh became the sole proprietor of the business.

For the next eight months, Mr. Marsh continued to run the bakery. Over the course of this time, he too became tired of handling all facets by himself. His primary interest was in baking and all else was done on a time-available basis. Records were not kept, management became that of instinct, and the breakdown of two key pieces of equipment convinced him to sell the business.

In December 1974, Mr. MacHenry purchased the Kneadery and began operations in January 1975. Having no experience in baking or in running a business, he was faced with a number of problems. The main ones were the complete absence of records upon which to base operations and the lingering ill-will created by the past owners. Although Mr. MacHenry discussed the various aspects of the operations with Mr. Marsh, he was essentially starting the business anew.

---

*This case was prepared by Professor Dennis H. Tootelian, California State University, Sacramento.

From *Marketing Management: Cases and Readings* edited by Dennis H. Tootelian, Ralph M. Gaedeke and Leete A. Thompson. Copyright © 1980 Scott, Foresman and Company. Reprinted by permission. Questions have been added at the end of the case.

PRODUCTS

The Kneadery produced whole grain breads for health food stores in the area and for its own retail sales. Completely organic whole wheat bread was the backbone of its product mix. This product outsold all other products combined. Other breads included: Russian rye, vegetable seed, cinnamon, carrot-raisin, herb, and sour rye. In addition, the product mix included buns made in the same varieties as the breads, date bars, cookies of various kinds, and banana-nut cake.

The retail operation of the Kneadery included the sale of all bakery products produced as well as other assorted natural food items. A refrigeration unit was stocked with a variety of cheeses, yogurts, and cold drinks. Mr. MacHenry also continued to make and sell made-to-order sandwiches which were composed entirely of natural ingredients.

Product characteristics focused mainly on the special organically grown ingredients used. No sugar or preservatives were added to any of the breads, cakes, or cookies. Honey and molasses were substituted as sweeteners. Although the recipes were obtained from Mr. Marsh, Mr. MacHenry had been experimenting with some existing and new product lines.

Main expansion efforts centered on producing health food cakes and pastries. Although pastries were still in the concept and testing stages, a banana-nut cake was the only cake success so far. Most of the problems encountered in product development centered on the baking process. With health food cakes, for example, the exterior tended to burn before the interior was fully cooked. Despite these problems, Mr. MacHenry wanted to continue in these two particular areas (cakes and pastries) since they tended to have higher markups than the other product lines.

PRODUCTION

Planning and control of daily operations were carried out through the use of production forms which also doubled as order forms. Orders were received from customers over the telephone or by Mr. MacHenry during his normal deliveries. Orders were taken over the telephone on Monday, Wednesday, Friday, and Saturday. Rush orders were also accepted the morning of a baking day if received early enough. Baking days at the Kneadery were Tuesday, Thursday, and Sunday.

Baking days usually began around 10:30 a.m., depending on when Mr. MacHenry completed the day's deliveries and any other work needing attention. The baking process, for a single batch of bread, usually took a total of three and one-half hours to complete. The baking process centered around the mixing, panning, baking, and slicing operations. Between mixing and panning, a one-half hour waiting period was required to allow the bread to rise. This slack time was used to complete or begin additional operations in the process.

Normally, it took seven hours to produce all of the scheduled loaves. Mr. MacHenry only did the mixing and panning processes and used a part-time employee to do the baking, slicing, and wrapping. Each loaf was individually wrapped and labeled with the Kneadery's specially designed label. Two female employees prepared and baked all of the cookies and date bars scheduled. Everybody helped in the preparation of the banana-nut cake.

Quality control over the product centered mainly around the quality of ingredients used. Baking times and recipes acquired from the previous owner were based on trial and error, but not subject to much variation. Occasionally, a bad batch of bread was made and sold, but was immediately replaced when discovered. The only reason for the occasional bad batch was that for some reason the bread did not rise enough before baking. Mr. MacHenry had yet to discover why this occurred. Regarding the returned loaves, the Kneadery gave away this bread as "ducky bread" to be used by people to feed the ducks in the park across the street. The Kneadery had developed increasing goodwill with the children and senior citizens in the neighborhood through this policy.

Purchases of supplies were established by the independent distributors who serviced the Kneadery. Small order sizes make it impossible to take advantage of bulk discounts, and cash discounts for early payment were not given by the independent distributors. Because of this, Mr. MacHenry was negotiating with the local co-op over the use of the Kneadery's flour mill. Since the Kneadery had no room available to operate the mill, Mr. MacHenry was willing to lend it to the co-op in return for which it would purchase freshly ground flour at cost. This was especially favorable to Mr. MacHenry since he was presently buying flour from one of the Kneadery's major competitors. In addition to these efforts, Mr. MacHenry also completed negotiations to rent out the Kneadery's baking facilities several nights a week to a local restaurant so that it could bake pies and pastries for its own use.

COMPETITION

Although competition in the local market was fragmented, it was becoming increasingly keen due to greater public interest in natural foods and the "return to nature" movement. While health foods enjoyed popularity with members of various cults for years, the newer interest in whole grain breads had a much broader base. Mr. MacHenry thought that although all age groups were possible buyers, the primary purchasers of these products were young adults and senior citizens.

Within the city, there were only two major bakers of health food products, one of which was the Kneadery. Two other competitors worked the area, however, with one being thirty-five miles away and the other more than one hundred miles away. None of the four could really claim a hold on the market, and all were about equal in terms of size and quality of output. In addition to these independent bakeries, large nationally franchised bakers began to enter the whole grain bread market. These breads could not be sold in health food stores because of their inferior ingredients, but they were able to capture the purchasers who wanted the convenience of buying these products in their grocery stores.

Mr. MacHenry thought that one of the more serious threats was from the increasing number of bakeries being placed in larger supermarkets. Not only did they produce a wide range of traditional products, but they also extended into health foods since many of the stores maintained distinct health food sections. Pushing the freshness and convenience, many of the would-be buyers from health food stores were finding it advantageous to buy at the same time they were doing their normal shopping. Prices at the supermarkets, furthermore, tended to be lower due to bulk buying and the ability to spread costs over the entire bakery operations.

PRICING

Mr. MacHenry used the same wholesale and retail price schedules for baked goods as the previous owner. As the Kneadery's products were competitively priced with

Exhibit 1
Kneadery price list

	WHOLESALE			RETAIL		
	1 LB.	1½ LB.	2¼ LB.	1 LB.	1½ LB.	2¼ LB.
Whole wheat	$ .52	$ .65	$ .90	$ .62	$ .78	$1.13
Sour rye	.80	.96	—	.96	1.08	—
Specialties:	.60	.75	—	.72	.89	—
Herb, vegetable seed,						
Russian rye, cinnamon						
Whole wheat buns	—	.75	—	—	.89	—
Specialty buns	—	.85	—	—	.99	—
Rolled loaves	—	.96	—	—	.1.08	—
Date bars	.20 each			.25 each		
Cookies	.10 each			.12 each		
Cakes (banana-nut)	$2.75			$3.25		

other suppliers of similar products, he was somewhat leery of changing them. A price list is presented in exhibit 1.

Most owners of health food stores carried bread only as a convenience to their customers, due to the low markup of ten cents to twelve cents per loaf and their high perishability. Brand loyalty was not thought to be overly strong, although people look for quality products with healthful ingredients, and not necessarily for lower prices. Therefore, Mr. MacHenry felt that reducing the wholesale price of the bread would do little to increase the sales of the Kneadery's products.

DISTRIBUTION

Bread and other baked goods were either delivered by Mr. MacHenry the day following baking, or picked up by the wholesale customer at the store. Even though there were only five deliveries, the time involved typically ranged from two to three hours, depending on traffic conditions. The same wholesale prices were charged regardless of the distribution method. Indirectly, the Kneadery also reached some of the outlying regions by selling its products to the co-op, which in turn sold to health food stores in these areas. The breakdown in sales on a delivered versus nondelivered basis is presented in exhibit 2.

In April, 1975, a restaurant owner asked that bread be delivered on a regular basis to his restaurant some thirty miles from the Kneadery. The sale was lost because Mr. MacHenry felt it was too much trouble to deliver bread beyond a ten-mile radius and because his time was at a premium. Of the twenty-two health food stores located in the area, all carried breads of the whole grain health food variety. Only five, however, carried bread from the Kneadery. The stores not carrying Kneadery products were divided about equally among the competition. The primary reason for the small number of outlets carrying its products was the delivery policy

Exhibit 2
List of wholesale customers' weekly sales

Delivered bread

American Food Company	$109
General Food Co-op	96
Leonard's	82
Nutritional Products	56
Williamson's	24
Total	$367

Non-delivered bread

Mandy's (70 miles away)	$ 81
Health Food City (70 miles away)	61
King's Health Foods (96 miles away)	48
Back to Nature (25 miles away)	24
Nature's Delite (95 miles away)	21
Total	$235

of the bakery. Since most wholesale deliveries were for relatively small orders and delivered three times a week, Mr. MacHenry felt that the distribution costs would be prohibitive and would consume too much of his time. See exhibit 3 for a schematic of the location of health food stores and the anticipated costs of distribution.

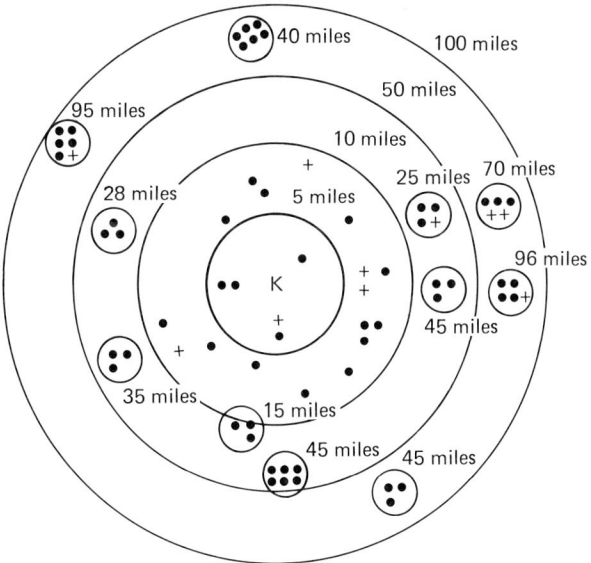

Exhibit 3
Location of buyers

PROMOTION

The Kneadery had no advertising budget nor did Mr. MacHenry expect to allocate much, if any, money for advertising in the future. Most of the promotional effort centered on word-of-mouth advertising and the distinctive labels placed inside each loaf of bread. Because the retail operations had become quite successful, some attention was directed at product placement and the overall appearance of the facilities. A few point-of-purchase displays were used, but were not considered especially important.

FINANCE

Financial aspects of the Kneadery were somewhat encouraging. No debt was incurred in the purchase of the company nor has any been needed since. It was anticipated that cash would be used to cover all future expenses or capital investments. The major liabilities were accounts payable and salary taxes payable. Financial statements are presented in exhibits 4 and 5.

Exhibit 4
Kneadery income statement

	LAST YEAR	THIS YEAR
Sales		
Wholesale	$34,267	$31,304
Retail	35,666	41,246
Facilities rental	—	250
Total	$69,933	$72,800
Cost of goods sold	35,176	37,856
Gross profit	$34,757	$34,944
Controlled expenses		
Salaries	$ 8,675	$ 9,352
Store gas	250	291
Transportation	2,037	1,919
Labels, molds, baking utensils, etc.	2,997	2,012
Total	$13,959	$13,574
Fixed expenses		
Rent	$ 3,100	$ 3,540
Electricity	250	291
Telephone	981	728
Insurance	270	291
Employer tax	631	655
Total	$ 5,232	$ 5,505
Net profit before taxes	$15,666	$15,865

Exhibit 5
Kneadery balance sheet

	LAST YEAR	THIS YEAR
Current assets		
Cash in bank	$ 2,198	$ 4,759
Petty cash	250	222
Accounts receivable	319	809
Prepaid insurance	200	238
Inventory	831	2,078
Paper supplies	450	476
Total	$ 4,248	$ 8,582
Fixed assets		
Office equipment	143	130
Baking equipment	6,996	6,663
Refrigeration and		
display equipment	1,378	1,253
Bread racks and utensils	2,189	1,824
Stone mill	1,100	1,000
Misc. equipment	972	1,602
Total	$12,778	$12,472
Total assets	$17,026	$21,054
Current liabilities		
Accounts payable	$ 3,173	$ 3,753
Salary taxes payable	78	95
Misc. taxes payable	37	48
Advances from customers	781	535
Total	$ 4,069	$ 4,431
Capital account	12,957	16,623
Total liabilities and capital	$17,026	$21,054

FUTURE OUTLOOK

In making his assessment, Mr. MacHenry noted that the retail section of the store was growing at a much faster rate than the wholesale bakery operation. The retail part had increased from about 51 percent to 57 percent of total sales. Mr. MacHenry attributed most of the increase to his made-to-order sandwich business. This market was composed largely of staff members of a hospital located two blocks away and to visitors to the park across the street.

Despite the success of the retail section, he was somewhat disappointed with overall sales and profits and was unsure of a course of action to pursue. Of added concern was the exterior appearance of his store. While the yearly lease had become more and more expensive, normal maintenance by the owner had all but ceased. Mr. MacHenry was worried about the possible effect of this on retail sales. He knew, however, that no other facilities were available within a reasonable distance and price range.

QUESTIONS

1. How can a retail business be "too large"?

2. What do the financial ratios tell us?

3. Should Mr. MacHenry concentrate on retail operations? Sales to health food stores?

4. What type of distribution structure would you recommend?

5. What products should be offered in the health food area?

CASE 6

La Quinta Motor Inns, Inc.: National Advertising Campaign*

In early 1979, Joyce Wilson, Vice-President of Marketing for La Quinta Motor Inns, Inc., was composing her thoughts prior to preparing an important memo. The memo was an assignment given to all upper level executives who had attended a management conference conducted for the company by a team of professors from well-known business schools. The memo, directed to President and Chief Executive Officer Sam Barshop, was to address the continued growth rate that top management recommended for the company over the next five years. Also, managers were to discuss the impact that growth would have on their department and the role of their department in achieving growth objectives.

Ms. Wilson knew the 22 percent compound annual growth rate in revenues and profits achieved by La Quinta during its first ten years would be a challenge to sustain. The next few years would see the chain's expansion into "frontier" areas where it lacked the recognition achieved in the Southwest. She knew some top managers occasionally questioned the efficacy of the company's recent commit-

---

*The following case was made possible through the cooperation of La Quinta Motor Inns, Inc. This case was prepared by Roger A. Kerin and M. Edgar Barrett and appears in Roger Kerin and Robert Peterson, *Strategic Marketing Problems: Cases and Comments* (Boston: Allyn and Bacon 1981). It has been adapted. Reprinted with permission.

The case was prepared as a basis for class discussion and is not designed to illustrate effective or ineffective handling of administrative situations. The assistance of Ms. Phyllis B. Riggins, graduate student, in the preparation of this case is gratefully acknowledged. Issues raised at the end of the case are introduced solely for discussion purposes. They do not necessarily represent the opinions of La Quinta management.

Questions have been added at the end of the case.

ment to a national advertising campaign and the narrow market segment sought out by La Quinta. The national campaign was just entering its second year, and Ms. Wilson knew her comments on the campaign and target market would have implications for the role of both the campaign and market orientation in La Quinta's future.

NOTE ON THE LODGING INDUSTRY

According to the October 1978 *Wall Street Transcript* "Roundtable Discussion" on the lodging industry, "the historic growth rate of the industry is something near two percent or a little less." Motels and motor hotels combined, however, have shown a larger growth rate than hotels.

Occupancy rates were as high as 80 percent in the early 1960s. High occupancy rates made the industry attractive for investment and supply began to seriously outstrip demand in the late 1960s and early 1970s. The recession of 1974 and the energy crisis that preceded it caused a slowdown in travel and many financial institutions were forced to foreclose on lodging properties. By 1970, average industry occupancy rates approached 60 percent. The recovery proceeded slowly and only in 1979 did industry occupancy rates approach 70 percent. Reluctance of financial institutions and investors to re-create the oversupply situation of the early 1970s served as a check during the recovery. Capacity actually declined in 1976. There were about 2.25 million lodging rooms in the United States in 1979. More than 60 percent of these rooms were over ten years old. Holiday Inns accounted for approximately 12 to 15 percent of available rooms in 1974.

Four general motel classifications have emerged in the last twenty-five years: (1) small, individually owned tourist courts; (2) budget motels, such as Days Inn and Motel 6; (3) medium-priced chains, such as La Quinta and Rodeway; and (4) large, full-service chains such as Holiday Inn. The trend is away from small, independently owned units toward largely franchised, absentee owned motels. With regard to the second classification, "One Howard Johnson executive predicted the budget motel would be to the motel industry what the Volkswagen was to autos . . . . How did the word 'budget,' perfectly respectable when applied to cars, airline flights, and department stores, fall into such disgrace in motels? Because many a budget motel was cheap as well as less expensive . . . . In a country where a clean, well-maintained room is the bare minimum the traveler requires, anything less is an insult."

LA QUINTA MOTOR INNS

The first La Quinta Motor Inn was built by the Barshop family in San Antonio, Texas, in 1968. Sam Barshop, referred to by *Forbes* in a June 1978 article as "the reluctant motelier," was heavily involved in the family real estate business and initially considered the lodging industry a sideline. The family built its first motel in 1961 after Ramada Inns had expressed interest in a piece of family property in San Antonio. When it was announced that the 1968 World's Fair would be held in San Antonio, Sam and his brother, Phil Barshop, who had by then built other inns as franchises of Ramada and Rodeway, decided that "the occasion warranted a hotel with a different flavor." The first La Quinta Motor Inn was located across the street from Hemisfair '68. The name and architecture recalled San Antonio's Spanish Colonial heritage. Both characteristics have been retained in subsequent inns. La

Exhibit 1
La Quinta Motor Inns, Inc.—Number of motor inns and rooms (fiscal 1974–79)*

	1979	1978	1977	1976	1975	1974
Motor inns						
Company owned (50% or more)	64	55	49	49	45	36
Licensed	14	13	14	11	10	4
Total	78	68	63	60	55	40
Rooms						
Company owned (50% or more)	7,288	6,161	5,355	5,183	4,633	3,544
Licensed	1,770	1,638	1,776	1,388	1,267	596
Total	9,058	7,799	7,131	6,571	5,900	4,140

Source: Company records.
*Fiscal year ends May 31.

Exhibit 2
La Quinta Motor Inns, Inc.—Income statements (fiscal 1975–79)*

	1979	1978	1977	1976	1975
Revenues (000's)					
Motor inn	$44,682	35,580	27,256	22,173	16,272
Restaurant rental	1,881	1,545	1,127	990	790
Restaurant and club	1,094	1,029	960	1,084	1,097
Other	1,267	1,039	780	593	389
Total revenues	48,924	39,193	30,123	24,840	18,548
Operating costs and expenses (000's)					
Motor inn direct	22,958	18,410	15,139	12,762	9,602
Restaurant and club direct	1,038	988	1,013	1,113	1,166
Selling, general and administrative	4,512	3,450	2,292	1,836	1,410
Depreciation and amortization	4,438	3,743	2,964	2,554	1,997
Total operating costs and expenses	32,946	26,591	21,408	18,265	14,175
Operating income	15,978	12,602	8,715	6,575	4,373
Other income (deductions) (000's)					
Interest, net of capitalization	(6,172)	(4,946)	(3,922)	(3,499)	(2,803)
Gain on sale of assets, principally motor inns	1,477	553	501	215	289
Partners' equity in earnings and losses: Operations	(2,437)	(1,719)	(897)	(385)	(45)
Sales of motor inns	(589)	—	—	—	—
Total other income (deductions)	(7,721)	(6,112)	(4,318)	(3,669)	(2,559)
Earnings before income taxes	8,257	6,490	4,397	2,906	1,814
Income taxes	3,385	2,759	1,939	1,205	707
Net earnings (000's)	$ 4,872	3,731	2,458	1,701	1,107

Source: 1979 Annual Report.
*Fiscal year ends May 31.

Quinta Motor Inns, Inc., was formed when Barshop Motel Enterprises offered stock for public sale in 1973.

Exhibit 1 summarizes the growth in the number of inns and rooms from fiscal years 1974 through 1979. Exhibit 2 shows La Quinta's income statements from 1975 through 1979.

LA QUINTA SERVICE CONCEPT

La Quinta's service concept is described in its 1978 annual report: "Because we define our primary market as the individual business traveler, we design and manage our inns to serve his or her needs: clean, quiet accommodations at a reasonable price." Every aspect of La Quinta's service is based on the company's perception of the business traveler's needs. Research conducted in early 1978 indicated that this service concept had worked effectively in attracting and satisfying these needs (see Appendix A).

The average La Quinta Motor Inn has about 120 rooms. There is a pool, color television, direct dial telephone, a twenty-four-hour switchboard, and one-day laundry service. La Quinta leases free-standing restaurant facilities, contiguous to the inns, to national restaurant chains, such as Denny's or Jojos, who operate them. These restaurants typically provide food service twenty-four hours a day. The inns are located on premium sites on major highways close to major industrial and office complexes, large retail shopping centers, and universities. Site selection is considered a key part of La Quinta's marketing strategy. According to Sam Barshop: "Part of our company's marketing monies go toward purchasing a top notch site because all the advertising and publicity in the world can't change a bad site." As of 1979, Sam or Phil Barshop had personally selected every La Quinta Motor Inn site.

The majority of inns are managed by older married couples. Their duties include filing timely reports with the home office, keeping their inns clean and in good repair, and being friendly and courteous to customers. An article on "Husband/Wife Management Teams" in *Southwest Hotel-Motel Review* describes the advantage of these teams: "A husband and wife team gets to know their guest. . . . It's sort of a personal touch . . . . It builds a very great repeat business, which is important." La Quinta managers carry this personal touch to the point of calling each regular customer by name. *Innput,* the company newspaper, is filled with letters that reflect the success of unit managers in creating this friendly feeling.

La Quinta has prospered using this service concept. Exhibit 3 shows the occupancy rate data for new and existing La Quinta Motor Inns over the last five years. The company has consistently experienced some of the highest occupancy rates in the lodging industry.

Exhibit 3
La Quinta Motor Inns, Inc.—Percentage of occupancy (fiscal 1974–78)

	1979	1978	1977	1976	1975	1974
Motor inns open one year or more	90.6%	89.1%	86.6%	82.1%	80.3%	81.4%
Overall	88.1	88.6	85.8	80.5	74.0	79.7

Source: Company records.

INN LOCATION AND SITE SELECTION

Exhibit 4 shows the location of La Quinta Motor Inns completed or under development as of late 1979. The company has expanded geographically by means of a three-part strategy. *Adjacency,* the first of these three, involves expansion to new cities of over 100,000 population within a 300-mile radius of an existing La Quinta

Exhibit 4
La Quinta Motor Inn locations as of late 1979

ALABAMA	KANSAS	TENNESSEE
Mobile	Kansas City	Memphis
ARIZONA	Wichita	Nashville
+ Flagstaff	KENTUCKY	TEXAS
+ Kingman	Louisville	Abilene
Phoenix	LOUISIANA	Austin (3)
Tucson	New Orleans (2)	Beaumont
ARKANSAS	MISSISSIPPI	Brazosport
Little Rock (2)*	Jackson	Bryan/College Station*
CALIFORNIA	MISSOURI	+ Corpus Christi (2)
Costa Mesa*	St. Louis	+ Dallas/Fort Worth (14)*****
COLORADO	NEBRASKA	Denton
Denver (3)*	Omaha*	El Paso (2)*
FLORIDA	NEVADA	+ Galveston
Jacksonville*	Las Vegas	Houston (7)*
+ + Orlando	Reno*	Killeen
Tallahassee	NEW MEXICO	Laredo
+ Tampa	Albuquerque	Lubbock
GEORGIA	OHIO	+ McAllen
Atlanta	+ Cincinnati	Odessa*
Columbus*	Columbus*	+ San Angelo
ILLINOIS	+ + Dayton	San Antonio (7)
Champaign*	OKLAHOMA	Texas City
+ Moline	Oklahoma City	Waco
INDIANA	Tulsa	Wichita Falls
Indianapolis (2)**	SOUTH	UTAH
Merrillville	CAROLINA	Salt Lake City
	Charleston*	WYOMING
	Columbia*	Casper*
	Greenville*	Cheyenne*

*Inns under development

+ Licensed property

( ) Number of inns located in each city

Motor Inn property. This strategy can be observed in the existence of the various "frontier" properties, such as Casper, Wyoming, and Salt Lake City, Utah. *Clustering,* the second part of the plan, consists of the construction of several inns in one city. Dallas and Houston are both examples of cluster cities. The third part, *filling in,* is the construction of inns in other, usually smaller, cities within an established market area. Seventy-eight company owned or licensed inns in the La Quinta Motor Inns chain would be operating in twenty states by the end of fiscal 1979. There were twenty-five inns under development in an additional four states at the time.

PRICE AND COST STRUCTURE

La Quinta's no frills approach has enabled the company to minimize capital and operating costs and remain very reasonably priced. According to Sam Barshop, "La Quinta sells rooms, period . . . . no atriums or meeting rooms to swell construction costs." La Quinta's price per room is typically 20 to 25 percent below comparable rooms at motor inns with more elaborate facilities. The average daily rate per occupied room in 1979 was $20.21.

In discussing the company's cost structure, Walter Biegler, La Quinta's Vice-President of Finance and Chief Financial Officer, mentioned the difficulty of performing a strict cost-profit analysis of their operations. He felt that some of the costs were actually semi-variable with occupancy. Thus, he noted the variable cost component was not easy to isolate precisely. In general, however, he estimated the industry ratio of variable costs to revenue of 55 percent to be representative of La Quinta's situation.

SALES FORCE

La Quinta employs a small, but effective sales force under the direction of two divisional sales directors. The sales force is divided into eastern and western divisions.

The company employs eight sales representatives. These representatives made over 7,000 sales calls in 1979. Sales call activity is heaviest during the period preceding and during new La Quinta Motor Inn openings. Sales representatives are responsible for calling on large corporations whose employees are potential customers of the entire network of La Quinta Motor Inns. Another function of the sales group is to assist unit managers in increasing occupancy rates of existing inns. Unit managers are also expected to make sales calls. The total number of prospective customers reached by all these efforts exceeded 25,000 in 1979.

MARKETING AND ADVERTISING

Joyce Wilson joined La Quinta in 1975 to manage the newly formed marketing department. Her primary responsibilities at that time included assistance in formulating strategy, advertising, sales and promotion programs, and marketing research. In 1977, Ms. Sue Moore joined La Quinta as Director of Advertising to manage the company's in-house advertising agency. Creation of a marketing department and subsequent formation of an in-house advertising agency contributed to a more systematic approach to marketing and communications at La Quinta. Prior to that time, responsibility for advertising was dispersed among a variety of executives and often handled on an inn-by-inn basis.

The first formal advertising campaign was launched at the beginning of the 1977 fiscal year. The campaign's objectives were to enhance local or regional awareness (markets with existing inns), communicate the broader geographical scope of the chain, and further establish La Quinta's identity, or positioning, within the industry. Space in *Media Networks,* a mix of major weekly magazines with regional editions such as *Time, Newsweek, U.S. News and World Report,* and *Sports Illustrated,* was purchased for fifteen La Quinta markets. (Markets relate to major cities and immediate environs.) Three to four full page advertisements (depending on the market) were placed in the southwest edition of both the *Wall Street Journal* (twenty ads scheduled throughout the year) and *Business Week* (four ads scheduled throughout the year). The rationale for this selection and schedule was that these publications reached present and potential customers and they would convey a "national image" for La Quinta even though their distribution was on a regional basis. Their readership also represented an "investor" audience. Two general audience monthly magazines, *Southern Living* and *Texas Monthly,* carried three advertisements each that were scheduled for placement throughout the year. Three advertisements were placed throughout the year in in-flight magazines published by Southwest, Ozark, and Texas International Airlines since these airlines service the majority of La Quinta markets. Finally, an advertisement was placed in each of several hotel and motel reference books used by independent and corporate travel agencies and two advertisements were placed in *Discovery,* a quarterly magazine for Allstate Insurance Company policy-holders, with a circulation of one million. The total media budget for this campaign was $135,000 with an estimated cost of one cent per reader per year. La Quinta executives believed that this effort achieved its objective.

The objective of the fiscal 1978 campaign was to retain the regional orientation, but take a step toward national recognition of La Quinta Motor Inns as inn locations expanded beyond states in the Southwest. This step was twofold: (1) to reach "feeder" markets for La Quinta cities, and (2) to create a higher level of awareness in new markets where La Quinta was building new inns. This national effort was reflected in the selection of *Time* magazine (B edition). This edition has a selective nationwide circulation focusing on subscribers classified as manager-professionals in addition to distribution to airlines and business offices. Four two-thirds-page advertisements were scheduled for placement throughout the year. The *Media Networks* purchase was timed to coincide with inn openings and included one advertisement each in five new markets. The number of insertions throughout the year in each of the remaining magazines is summarized below:

Business Week (southwest edition):   5 insertions

Wall Street Journal (southwest edition):   6 insertions

Southern Living: 2 insertions

Discovery: 1 insertion

Airline Magazines: 3 insertions in Southwest, Ozark, and Texas International Airlines

Total funds invested in advertising in fiscal year 1978 declined from the previous year due to a reallocation of marketing expenditures within the company. Nevertheless, the $95,000 allocated to advertising space was viewed as getting "more bang for the bucks" by Sue Moore. The reach of the 1978 plan was 17 percent

Exhibit 5
La Quinta Motor Inns, Inc.—Allocation of media expenditures

	FISCAL 1977 JUNE 1976– MAY 1977	FISCAL 1978 JUNE 1977– MAY 1978	FISCAL 1979 JUNE 1978– MAY 1979
Wall Street Journal (southwest edition)	$ 18,000	$ 3,000	$ 8,000
Time		56,000	77,000
Business Week (southwest edition)	5,000	7,000	
Media Networks	85,000	12,000	
Business Week (national edition)			50,000
Hotel and motel reference books	6,100		
Southern Living	5,000	9,700	
Texas Monthly	5,000		
Discovery	4,600	3,000	
Airline Magazines	6,400	4,300	—
	$135,000	$95,000	$135,000

Note: These figures do not include outdoor (billboard) advertising or miscellaneous promotional efforts of individual inns in La Quinta markets. Costs associated with these efforts are assumed by individual inns.

higher than the previous year and the estimated cost per subscriber per year had been reduced to slightly over six-tenths of a cent. The expanded coverage was showing increased inquiries about La Quinta Motor Inns from interested companies and individuals throughout the country.

The 1979 fiscal year advertising objectives were to accelerate the momentum begun in the 1978 campaign and further direct La Quinta's advertising toward a national audience. Two-thirds-page advertisements were placed throughout the year in *Business Week* (national edition) and *Time* (B edition). Each magazine carried five insertions. Sixteen insertions were scheduled throughout the year in the *Wall Street Journal* (southwest edition), again with the investor community in mind. Examples of fiscal 1979 advertisements are shown in Appendix B. Total funds spent for advertising was $134,000. The cost per reader per year was approximately one cent. Although the company subscribed to no readership survey service, Sue Moore noted that the amount of qualified responses in terms of sales leads was very encouraging. Typical response letters reflected several key advertising goals: company letterhead, content of letters, titles of signees, city or state origin, and oftentimes, size of company sales force. A summary of the media allocations by year is shown in Exhibit 5.

MANAGEMENT MEMO

Thinking back over the growth La Quinta Motor Inns had achieved in the last decade and the crucial question of her department's role in sustaining that growth,

Joyce Wilson began to list issues she would address in her memo to Mr. Sam Barshop.

One issue was the size of the advertising budget itself. Since 1975, La Quinta subscribed to the policy of budgeting marketing and advertising expenditures on a per room per day basis. This was a standard reporting procedure in the lodging industry. Each individual inn contributed a set amount for the marketing department, including the advertising budget. In 1975, the figure was 10 cents per room per day which has since been raised to 12 cents per room per day for La Quinta. As a percentage of revenue, however, Ms. Wilson believed that other chains of similar or slightly larger size budgeted as much as $100,000 to $200,000 per year more for advertising than La Quinta. She knew that if she raised this issue, a sound economic justification would be necessary, since such additional funds would most likely need to be obtained from corporate funds rather than from individual inns.

A second issue was the national versus regional thrust of La Quinta advertising campaigns. Preliminary discussions with Ms. Moore indicated that national coverage would be proposed for the 1980 fiscal year campaign. However, company executives occasionally questioned this orientation on the grounds that La Quinta operated in forty-seven cities in twenty states. In reviewing a *Media Networks* local trade area audience plan, similar to the 1977 program, Ms. Moore determined that *Media Networks* offered their magazine combination in only thirty-two of the current La Quinta Inn cities and that one insertion for that geographical coverage would cost $87,000. Two insertions in each magazine would cost in the neighborhood of $150,000, with a volume discount, and so forth. These cities contained all but fifteen La Quinta Motor Inns currently in operation. In the past, some company executives expressed the opinion that the regional advertising approach would be more effective due to the regional aspects of the company's operations. Ms. Wilson felt that the memo provided a unique opportunity to address this issue, as well as the decision to insert advertisements throughout the year rather than focusing only on inn opening periods.

A third advertising related issue was the number of vehicles La Quinta used to communicate its message. Since 1977, La Quinta had systematically reduced the number of vehicles so that in 1979, only *Business Week, Time,* and the southwest edition of the *Wall Street Journal* were used. This focused effort was not only an advertising strategy related to the target audience, but also a result of the customer profile as portrayed by the company's 1978 market research. Other lodging chains around the country spread their advertising funds across many vehicles including magazines, hotel and motel reference books, newspapers, direct mail, airline magazines, and occasionally spot and network radio and television, but their budgets were also larger. Expense was an important issue in this regard and supported the reduction of vehicles. However, Ms. Wilson felt that other arguments should be made as well.

A broader issue was the topic of market targeting. Ms. Wilson was aware that some top level managers had considered broadening the target market beyond the individual business traveler to include the entire family or pleasure traveler. Advocates of this strategy were concerned that La Quinta was losing these travelers by ignoring them in a direct advertising appeal. Arguments made in favor of expanding the target market were:

1. Room occupancy on weekends was lower than during the week. Friday, Saturday, and Sunday night occupancy rates were about 75 percent. If weekend occupancy were increased, overall occupancy rates would rise.

2. Broadening the target market might increase the trial of La Quinta Inns in frontier areas such as Casper, Wyoming.

Proponents of this strategy proposed that "weekend specials" of 25 percent off the average room rate be provided on Saturday and Sunday since other chains had done so. Furthermore, one-fourth of the media funds might be spent promoting the weekend business.

Such an approach was contrary to La Quinta's existing concept, but the idea was raised often enough that Ms. Wilson knew her memo must deal with it. Both she and Ms. Moore maintained that the "business travelers" appeal attracts pleasure travelers as well.

An issue related to the target market question was the creative strategy. La Quinta had rested its advertising message on four pillars: service, price, location, and no frills. If the target market were expanded, other messages would have to be communicated.

As Joyce Wilson sat back in her chair, she wondered aloud about what positions she should take on these and other issues. She was fully aware that Mr. Sam Barshop expected a thoughtful and thorough appraisal of the issues listed on her scratch pad.

APPENDIX

Selected Results of March 1978 Customer Mail Survey*

1. *Average number of different occasions a traveler stayed at La Quinta during the past twelve months*   10.2 times

2. *Average number of nights stayed on most recent visit*   2.6 nights

3. *Purpose of trip* (percentages exceed 100% due to multiple answers)
   Personal   9.5%
   Business   79.8
   Pleasure   12.2
   Convention   3.5
   Vacation   2.0

4. *Frequency of staying at motels or hotels*
   Once a week or more   39.0%
   Once every few weeks   21.7
   About once a month   16.4
   Less often than every few months   21.2

5. *Type of trip and payment on most recent visit*
   Business trip paid for by the company   65.7%
   Business trip paid for by self   16.4
   Pleasure trip paid for by self   18.0

*(Number of Respondents = 5,600 of 10,000)

6. *Rented a car on most recent trip*
    Yes   23.1%
    No   75.9

7. *Mode of travel on most recent trip*
    Airline   34.0%
    Car   64.8

8. *Reason for choice of a particular La Quinta Motor Inn on most recent visit*
    (percentages exceed 100% due to multiple responses)
    Close to next day's activities   47.5%
    Saw it when ready to stop   5.7
    Recommended by friend, relative, etc.   15.4
    Specified by the company   7.3
    Personal preference based on previous experience   48.1
    Price   36.6
    Stayed here before   40.9
    Friendly and courteous personnel   27.9
    Other motels full   3.1

9. *Source of reservations*
    Self   55.4%
    Secretary   13.3
    Company   10.4
    Travel agency   2.7
    Association or convention   2.2
    Relative, friend, etc.   4.7
    No reservations   10.4

10. *Person(s) sharing room on most recent visit*
    (percentages exceed 100% due to multiple responses)
    Spouse   21.6%
    Children   5.2
    Friends   3.4
    Business associates   4.1
    None, stayed alone   68.9

11. *Likelihood of staying at a La Quinta Motor Inn on return visit to the city*
    Extremely likely   54.2%
    Very likely   30.3
    Somewhat likely   11.0
    Not very likely   2.6
    Not at all likely   1.0

12. *Likelihood of staying at a La Quinta Motor Inn*
    if one were available in another city visited
    Extremely likely   45.5%
    Very likely   35.4
    Somewhat likely   15.3
    Not very likely   2.3
    Not at all likely   .7

13.   *First stay in a La Quinta Motor Inn*
      Yes   27.0%
      No   70.1

QUESTIONS

1.   How would you describe the lodging industry and La Quinta's market niche?

2.   What is La Quinta's existing marketing strategy? Has it been successful?

3.   What are La Quinta's objectives?

4.   What are the pros and cons of a national and/or regional advertising campaign?

5.   How would you evaluate increasing media, the "Weekend Special" idea, and increasing advertising expenditures?

CASE 7

Southgate Shopping Center*

In April 1976, Mr. Dale Schlesinger, manager of Southgate Shopping Center in southeast suburban Cleveland, Ohio, pondered a formidable new competitor destined to open a bare eight-tenths of a mile away by the following August. The new competitor was a gigantic shopping mall, Randall Park Mall, billed as the largest in the world. It had been under construction for well over a year. In April, one of the department store sites had been finished, and the Penney store at Southgate closed its doors and moved to the new shopping center. In so doing, the J. C. Penney Co. enlarged its store from 65,000 square feet to 200,000 square feet. The new mall when completely opened in August would have five other major department stores in addition to hundreds of smaller stores.

SOUTHGATE

Origin and Facilities
The center is located on major traffic interceptors near an interstate highway. Southgate is presently the largest shopping center in Ohio and one of the largest in the United States. However, it is nothing like the behemoth soon to open. It con-

---

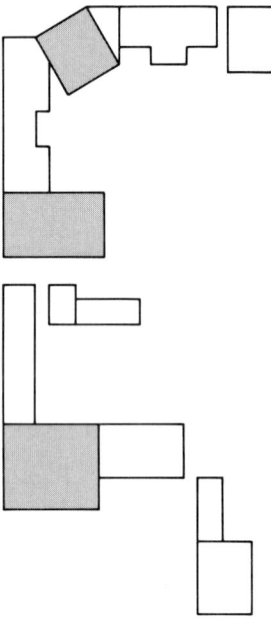

Exhibit 1
Physical layout of Southgate

sists of 135 stores and 1,350,000 square feet of building area; parking is available for 9,000 cars. However, it is old. It was opened in 1955 with 36 stores. Penney's was the first department store to come into Southgate, doing so in 1956 with the same 65,000 square foot store that it was leaving in 1976. Over the next several decades, Southgate experienced several expansions that brought it to its present sales of $150 million a year.

Southgate is not an enclosed mall for the all-weather comfort that is the mark of most new shopping centers constructed in the last decade. Furthermore, Southgate is not even a mall. (A mall center is the prototype for virtually all large centers today. Two or more department stores typically are placed at either end, with smaller specialty stores between. The major feature of a mall is a pedestrian walkway in the center. The entire complex can be enclosed or roofed to create all-weather shopping. Benches, trees, fountains, and "outdoor" restaurants are often placed in the mall. Parking typically is on all sides. The larger malls may have several floors of stores, each opening to the mall.) Rather, Southgate is a strip center that has grown in separate phases to accommodate the increase in consumer demand. Exhibit 1 shows the layout of Southgate.

The Stores
There were three department stores: the Penney store of 65,000 square feet, and the May Company and Sears Roebuck stores, each having approximately 200,000 square feet. These stores are known as generator stores. That is, they pull people to them, sometimes from a considerable distance, and thereby contribute greatly to the traffic flow in their vicinity. Typically, in most shopping centers

Exhibit 2
Southgate store directory

Department Stores, General Merchandise, and Variety Stores

F. W. Woolworth
J. C. Penney
May Company
Sears, Roebuck

Apparel Stores (Men's)

Bond Clothes
Calvin's Specialty Shop
Cleveland Tux Shop
Diamond's Men's Shop
Harry's Clothing
Jerry Mills Clothes
Lyon Tailors
Parker's
Richman Brothers
Southgate Custom Tailor
Tie Rack

Apparel Stores (Women's)

Bride & Formal
Klothes Line
Lane Bryant
Lerner Shop
Life Uniform
Motherhood Maternity Shop
Parklane Hosiery
Red Robin
Town & Country Shop
Ups & Downs
Winkelman's

Shoe Stores

Dr. Scholl's Foot Comfort Shoes
Faflik Shoes
Flagg Shoes

Hahn Shoes
Miles Shoes
Nobil Shoes
Thom McAn Shoes
The In Step

Food Stores and Restaurants

A&P
Arby's Beef House
American Harvest Health Food
Blue Grass Restaurant
Butcher Shop, The
Euclid Fish
Famous Recipe Restaurant
Fanny Farmer Candies
Fisher Fazio-Costa
Hough Bakery
International House of Pancakes
Lombardo's Pizza & Spaghetti
Maxson's Restaurant
New York Bakery
Oriental Terrace Restaurant
Pick-N-Pay
Teddi's Restaurant
York Steak House

Service Establishments

Allied Wigs
Andre Duval
Central National Bank
Cleveland Automobile Club
Cleveland Trust Company
Continental Bank
Cuyahoga Savings
D. O. Summers
Midland Guardian Loans

Mr. Angelo Wigs
National City Bank
Southgate Key & Shoe Repair
Southgate Laundromat
Southgate Patio Barbers
Southgate Village Barber Shop
Southgate Village Beauty Salon
Sun Finance
The Hair Dresser
Third Federal Savings & Loan Association
Travel Agent Tours
Union Commerce Bank
Union Savings & Loan
Universal CIT Credit Corporation
U.S. Life Credit
United States Post Office

Miscellaneous

Agency Rent-A-Car
Alexander Flowers
A. M. Rose Tile
Bandstand Records
Bedrooms Unlimited
Big Auto Center
Blonder's
Burrow's
Candle Barn
Cleveland Typewriter
Fun City
Goodyear Service Center
Great Phone Company
Immerman's Craft Center
Industrial Electric
J. B. Robinson Jewelers
Jo Ann Fabrics

Kronheim's
Laurel Camera
Leader Personnel
Lemon Tree Cards & Gifts
Marlen Jewelers
Mr. Magic Car Wash
Olan Mills Studios
One-Hour Martinizing
Owl Optical
Pearl Carpet
Pet Kingdom
Pompelli Organs
Putt-Putt Golf Course
Radio Shack
Rayco Seat Covers
Regal Carpeting
R.H.P. Auto Centers
Sample House
Sherwin Williams Paint Store
Singer Sewing Center
Southgate Beverages
Southgate Cinema
Southgate Jewelry
Southgate Lanes
Southgate Music Center
State Liquor Store
Sun Optical
Uniroyal Home & Tire Center
Furniture Land
Vision Center
Weight Watchers

Drug Stores

Cunningham Drug
Gray Drug
Southgate Medical Pharmacy

the greatest customer traffic is near the major department stores; these then become vital to the overall success of a shopping center. With the imminent opening of Randall Park Mall, Southgate is facing an erosion of its generator stores. As noted before, Penney's has already left, and as of June 1976, the 65,000 square foot former Penney store was standing vacant. Sears will be leaving Southgate in March; the May Company store intends to remain there, but May Company and Sears are both opening new units in the new mall, only eight-tenths of a mile away. Exhibit 2 [on p. 683] shows the directory of stores in the Southgate Center prior to development of the Randall Park Mall.

Draw of Southgate

The major newspaper of Cleveland, *The Plain Dealer,* has for many years served its advertisers by conducting research as to the "draw" of the major shopping centers in the Cleveland metropolitan area. In this research, license plates of cars in the parking lots of their respective shopping centers are recorded and then traced to their home address. In 1975, a study was made about the Southgate shopping center: 6,631 cars were thus observed and their home locations geographically plotted. This study was done long before Randall Park Mall had opened, although it was under construction at the time.

It was found that 42.9 percent of the cars in attendance at Southgate came from more than five miles away. The survey also found that 48.9 percent of the cars were from the suburban communities of Maple Heights, Garfield Heights, and Bedford—these being located either contiguous to Southgate or south and southwest of it. The next highest percentage of cars was from east Cleveland, with 21.5 percent. An analysis of traffic by economic areas showed that 77.1 percent of the cars were from census tracts with median incomes of more than $11,000.[1]

RANDALL PARK MALL

Randall Park Mall is located almost straight north of Southgate. It will have six major department stores for generators, and 260 other stores, altogether some 2.2 million square feet all under one roof. Exhibit 3 shows a physical diagram of the complex. Sales have been estimated "conservatively" at $200 million for the first year.

In typical mall fashion, parking in profusion will be on all sides of the complex. The enclosed mall will permit an array of amenities upon which one can only speculate before the grand opening. Two interstate highways are in close proximity to the new center.

TRENDS IN SHOPPING CENTER DEVELOPMENT

Mr. Dale Schlesinger, manager of Southgate, indicated that the trend in shopping centers is toward giantism. But as shopping centers become larger, it seems reasonable to expect that there must be an ultimate limit to size. How far is the average customer willing to walk? How many levels of stores can be piled up without confusing the customer? How many cars can be accommodated in a parking lot before the logistics of parking, finding one's car, and hiking to it will become too burdensome? And how about traffic congestion near a huge shopping center?

Despite these nagging worries, developers are building ever-bigger shopping complexes, and seemingly doing so successfully:

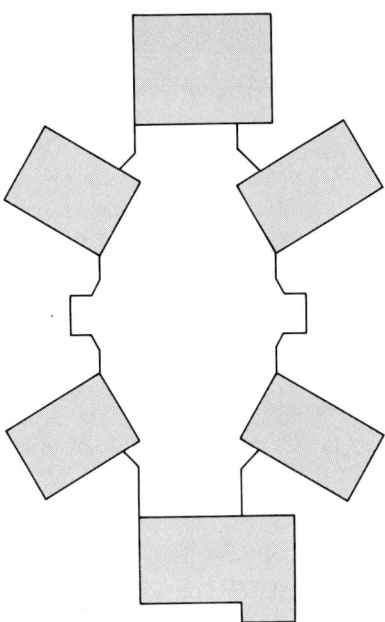

Exhibit 3
Physical layout of Randall Park Mall

Billed at the time as the world's largest enclosed multilevel shopping center, Woodfield opened 25 miles northwest of Chicago. It cost $90 million to construct, has 2 million square feet of space, 215 shops and services, and three major department stores, including the largest stores Sears and Penney have ever built and the largest suburban store that Marshall Field has ever put up.[2]

Along with these huge retail centers, often other commercial, recreational, and cultural facilities are developed nearby, such as hotels, apartment houses, office buildings, cultural centers, churches, and theaters. The result is that more and more the newer giant shopping centers are becoming miniature downtowns. A. Alfred Taubman, developer of Woodfield, says: "We are not competing against other centers or suburban business districts. We are competing against downtown Chicago. So we must come as close as we can to the strength and depth of selection you find in Chicago's core area. And if that kind of philosophy means building gigantic centers, then that's what we'll build."[3]

Edward J. DeBartolo, the nation's largest shopping center developer (who is building the Randall Park Mall), has built over 30 large ones in ten years. He has never had a failure and he knows of few. DeBartolo says, " . . . the national failure rate [of large shopping centers] over 25 years has been a fraction of 1 percent."[4]

What kind of a drawing power can a large center generate? Gene A. Robens, general manager of a southern California 1.2 million square foot mall, says: "When you talk about a shopping center as large as ours, you have to be sure you can draw from a 10- to 15-mile radius."[5] For the 2.2 million square foot facility of Randall Park Mall, conjecture is that it will draw from Akron, 30 miles to the south, from Youngstown, 50 miles to the southeast, and even from western Pennsylvania, 70 miles to the east.

REACTIONS OF SOUTHGATE

Mall Manager
Despite the looming threat of unknown magnitude, and the actual or imminent departure of two of his major tenants, Penney's and Sears, Dale Schlesinger was not unduly worried. While he expected to lose some business initially, he thought this would be soon regained. He admitted that for the first three months of the Randall Park opening, it would be impossible to compete. The sheer volume of grand opening advertising — both on the part of the mall itself, and that of individual tenants — and the natural curiosity that the general public would have to visit this huge agglomeration of stores, would defeat any defensive efforts Southgate might take at this time. Schlesinger conceded that he was projecting a 10 percent loss of sales the first year after the Randall opening. He expected sales to be back to normal in the second year. "We think Southgate will remain viable, and will even have long-term growth," Schlesinger stated.

While the loss of two of his major traffic generators might seem like a major blow to the center, Schlesinger was negotiating with both K mart and Wards to replace Penney's and Sears. In the spring of 1976, there was still a waiting list of prospective tenants for the smaller stores and shops.

Strengths of Southgate Relative to Randall Park Mall
In defense of his optimistic attitude regarding the new competition, Schlesinger noted a number of natural advantages that should accrue to Southgate.

First, he thought Southgate would benefit from a "spillover effect." By this, he expected that the sheer size and resulting volume of traffic drawn to the Randall Park Mall would result in such congestion, confusion, and shopping inconvenience that a goodly portion of shoppers would look around for a nearby and more convenient center to fill at least some of their shopping needs. Because Southgate was less than a mile away, it would be the primary beneficiary of this spillover business.

Southgate presents its tenants with a definite rent advantage over the new mall. The range of rents per square foot are $2 to $8 at Southgate, versus $8 to $18 at Randall Park Mall. The difference in rents — which reflects the older center constructed at a time of much lower costs — could provide a major deterrent for any Southgate tenant contemplating a move to the new mall. More profit could be achieved at considerably less sales volume than would be the case at Randall. The lower cost structure also means that most tenants should be able to ride out the several lean months associated with the grand opening at the competing mall.

Southgate presumably offers its customers more ease and convenience of shopping. Being smaller and an attenuated strip type of center, customers can park close to the doors of those stores they want to visit; and they can get in and out faster than would be possible in a large mall. Furthermore, Southgate has three large supermarkets and these are big generators of customer traffic on a continuous basis. It is not expected that Randall Park Mall will have any supermarkets, and indeed an enclosed mall is not the ideal setting for such a store due to the inconvenience of handling bulky purchases. Therefore, Southgate is assured of considerable customer traffic regardless of Randall Park Mall.

Schlesinger also cited the probability that customer loyalty built up over 20 years with the "friendly merchants" of Southgate would not be quickly lost. "While customers may initially go to Randall Park Mall out of curiosity, many of them will come back here to buy, back to where they're known and appreciated."

Perhaps Southgate has another potential advantage vis-à-vis Randall. A major part of its customers come from the south. And the new Randall Mall is north of Southgate. This puts Southgate in the position of being an "interceptor." It is sited between a major source of customers and the new shopping mall. Many people may evince reluctance to pass by a shopping center—such as Southgate—to get exactly the same product at a greater distance. Of course, Randall Park Mall will act as an interceptor for customers coming from the north, and Southgate may get few of these customers. But according to the shopping center study of customer attendance conducted by the Cleveland *Plain Dealer,* Southgate was not getting much of this business before the opening of the Randall Park Mall.

Southgate Merchant Attitudes

The attitudes of the mall management at Southgate are optimistic. But how about the attitudes of the individual store operators? Are they as optimistic, or are they running scared? In a research study conducted by students at Cleveland State University, 30 merchants at Southgage were interviewed. While part of the interviews are unstructured, one aspect was completely structured. The merchants were asked to check their attitudes and intentions to react on a series of scales numbered from 1 to 7, as shown in Exhibit 4.

While the range of responses, particularly to questions 1 and 2, was wide, reflecting those who thought the new mall would affect Southgate and their business severely to those who thought the effect would be favorable, the median and the concentration of attitudes was that there would be no more than a slight effect. And the planned reactions to the new mall were generally "do nothing different." Thus the general optimism of Dale Schlesinger regarding the impact of Randall Park Mall on Southgate was supported by a majority of the merchants.

PLANNED CENTERWIDE PROMOTIONS AND MARKETING STRATEGY

The management of Southgate Center conceded that nothing could be done to combat or defend against the expected massive promotional thrust of the grand opening of Randall Park Mall. "Any advertising or other promoting we do for the first three months of the grand opening push of Randall would be simply money down the drain." But promotional efforts are being expanded, both for the period before this grand opening and for the time after the initial excitement of a grand opening has ebbed.

Starting April 12, 1976, more than three months before the scheduled opening of Randall, TV commercials (which are new for the shopping center industry in Cleveland) are planned for the three major TV channels. These will be narrated by Ted Knight of the "Mary Tyler Moore Show" and will stress the convenience and

Exhibit 4

1. What do you think will be the effect of Randall Park Mall on your shopping center?

Will affect severely		Will affect slightly		Will not affect		Will affect favorably
1	2	3	4	5	6	7

Results: median of 30 responses, 3.5.

2. What do you think will be the effect of Randall Park Mall on your store here?

Will affect severely		Will affect slightly		Will not affect		Will affect favorably
1	2	3	4	5	6	7

Results: median of 30 responses, 3.9.

3. What changes, if any, do you think you will make due to Randall Park Mall?

(a) Much more advertising		Somewhat more advertising			No change in advertising	
1	2	3	4	5	6	7

Results: median of 30 responses, 5.3.

(b) Much lower prices		Somewhat lower prices			No change in prices	
1	2	3	4	5	6	7

Results: median of 30 responses, 6.0.

(c) Much more merchandise assortment		Somewhat more merchandise assortment			No change in merchandise assortment	
1	2	3	4	5	6	7

Results: median of 30 responses, 6.1.

(d) Substantial remodeling		Some remodeling			No change in facilities	
1	2	3	4	5	6	7

Results: median of 30 responses, 6.5.

variety of stores and services available at Southgate. These TV commercials will be run over a two-year period, but with time out during the three months of the Randall grand opening.

Radio has been used regularly in the past 20 years to promote the entire shopping center, informing about special events, and in particular playing up the convenience of shopping at Southgate. It will continue to be used with newspapers, the traditional medium for retail advertising.

Southgate has had annual major shopping center promotions that have always attracted large crowds. A Christmas Parade and a Sidewalk Fair have been two of the most successful. It should be recognized, however, that an extended strip center such as Southgate has more difficulty in running overall shopping center promotions than mall-type shopping centers. Malls are more compact, less strung out, and the new enclosed center malls are adaptable to a variety of promotions. Auto shows, art exhibits, mini-circuses, special exhibits of all kinds, and many types of entertainers such as rock 'n' roll bands and magician acts can readily be accommodated in the mall. These pull considerable customer traffic which benefits all tenants.

The Southgate management does not plan to permit the center to run down or deteriorate. Mr. Schlesinger responded that external repairs will be made as needed: "We certainly are not running scared." At the same time, there is no need to do extensive remodeling to make Southgate "more competitive." Eventually there may be some remodeling, especially in the area of lighting, but not until after Randall opens and the initial impact becomes more muted.

Admittedly the huge new mall cannot be entirely countered by Southgate. There is no way for it to remake itself into another colossal mall to match Randall. Its physical structure does not permit some of the "extra touches" that developers can throw into a mall, such as fountains and waterfalls; two- and three-story sculptures; trees, shrubs, and flowers; and colorful birds in huge cages. Nor can Southgate match the greatest amenity of all: an enclosed, climate-controlled mall for comfortable all-weather shopping, impervious to rain, sleet, snow, and summer heat.

But Dale Schlesinger is betting that Randall Park Mall is too big for its own good. "After all, a customer needs only so much variety of goods; after that, the additional variety simply becomes redundant." Southgate stands ready and conveniently nearby to catch the spillover of customers satiated with the sheer size of Randall.

NOTES

1. *Analysis of Customer Attendance, Southgate, 1975,* Marketing and Research Department, *The Plain Dealer,* Cleveland, Ohio.
2. "Shopping Centers Grow into Shopping Cities," *Business Week,* September 4, 1971, p. 34.
3. *Ibid.,* p. 38.
4. As quoted in *Forbes,* "Why Shopping Centers Rode out the Storm," June 1, 1976, p. 35.
5. "Shopping Centers Grow into Shopping Cities," p. 38.

QUESTIONS

1. What are the attitudes of the management and merchants of Southgate regarding the effect of the new shopping mall? Are these attitudes justified?

2. Is the planned reaction of Southgate to the new mall adequate?

3. Are there other promotional and merchandising ideas and/or overall strategies that might reduce the impact of Randall Park Mall?

4. Are the sales projections of Southgate for the next several years realistic?

5. Is the current blend and combination of stores at Southgate ideal? If not, how should it be changed?

CASE 8

Holiday Inns, Inc.*

COMPANY HISTORY

Holiday Inns, the namesake of the old Bing Crosby movie *Holiday Inn,* is the world's largest hotel and motel chain. Headquartered in Memphis, Tennessee, the firm was founded by Kemmons Wilson in 1953. Kemmons Wilson was a Memphis developer who came up with the Holiday Inn concept after taking his family on a vacation during which the motels they stayed in were poor in quality and high in price.

Under the leadership of Kemmons Wilson, Holiday Inns expanded rapidly and by the end of the sixties construction was beginning on a new Holiday Inn every two and one half days. This tremendous growth continued until 1973 when the Arab oil embargo cast a dark shadow over the hotel and motel industry. This marked a major turning point for Holiday Inns. The energy issue continued as a major influence throughout the 1970s. Management realized that the days of their entrepreneurial management and expansionist strategies were over and that new operations and efficiency-minded management was needed to ensure continued growth and stability for the company.

The long-term objective of Holiday Inns is to be the world's foremost hospitality company. Holiday Inns has over 300,000 rooms worldwide in over 1,700 inns, 1,515 of which are franchised and 240 which are either owned or operated by Holiday Inns.

Holiday Inns is not trying to be a hospitality company by just merely furnishing lodging. The firm is also involved in the gambling industry, the restaurant business, and shipping. Holiday Inns purchased Harrah's, a large gambling company in February 1980 and now owns the largest U.S. gambling operation. Facilities are located in the four main gambling markets: Atlantic City, Reno, Lake Tahoe, and Las Vegas. Gambling operations contributed 13% of the operating revenue of Holiday Inns in 1980.

Recently, Holiday Inns acquired Perkins Cake and Steak, Inc., which has 375 family restaurant locations. Perkins has not yet proved to be a profitable business.

Although management admits that it is not a particularly good fit with their concept of a hospitality company, Delta Steamship is owed by Holiday Inns. The company says it retains Delta Steamship to provide cash for the development of other segments of Holiday Inns.

Holiday Inns is the self-professed leader in innovation in the hotel industry. They were first to have a swimming pool at each inn and the first to have a color television in each room. Hotels are increasingly trying to design their rooms and services to provide hotel guests with all the conveniences of home. Holiday Inns has led the way by providing free in-room movies via their network of satellite television receiving stations. Many units are introducing indoor recreation centers to pro-

---

*The information for this case was obtained from those sources listed at the end of the case. Our thanks go to Frank E. Puryear, Jr., for his assistance in preparing this case.

vide guests exercise opportunities year round. Holiday Inns has also started adding small extras such as larger towels, larger bars of soap, and toiletries.

MANAGEMENT

Holiday Inns management group is marketing oriented. The top management of Holiday Inns is committed to helping Holiday Inns grow and retain its number-one position in the industry. Roy E. Winegardner is Chairman of the Board of Holiday Inns and Chief Excutive Officer. He was brought in by Kemmons Wilson during the troubled times of 1973–74. Mr. Winegardner was a long-time owner of many franchises and is very marketing oriented. Mr. Winegardner replaced many of the older top management with younger executives, many from Harvard. One of these is Michael D. Rose, who is now President of Holiday Inns. Holiday Inns has also added two highly respected individuals to its board. These are Walter J. Solmon (a Harvard professor) and Frederick W. Smith (chairman and chief executive officer of Federal Express).

TRENDS IN THE LODGING INDUSTRY

A key trend in the lodging industry involves changes in the locations of hotels. Many consumers now have more leisure time. Therefore, construction of hotels in resort areas is on the rise. With the high cost of travel, travelers do not want to travel long distances, which has caused most hotel resort development to be near major metropolitan areas. The decrease of travel by car has also caused a rise in the occupancy rate of rooms in metropolitan areas, as more people are traveling by bus, plane, and train. However, business is also beginning to pick back up for hotels located on major highways.

The entrance of Holiday Inns into gambling will probably signal the entrance of other hotel chains into the gaming industry, as it is one of the fastest-growing markets in the hotel industry. Hilton, Hyatt, Sheraton, and Ramada Inn also own some gaming interests and many other chains might be forced into the gambling market if they want to continue to grow.

THE ENVIRONMENTAL SITUATION

Legal
Holiday Inns has few legal constraints placed on it, except concerning its gambling operations. The gaming boards of Nevada and New Jersey are very strict and the gambling industry is heavily regulated. Holiday Inns recently decided against building a new hotel casino on the Boardwalk in Atlantic City because of the New Jersey regulatory environment.

Economic
The financial well-being of Holiday Inns is closely tied to the economic conditions of the United States. When economic conditions are depressed, business travel often decreases as firms attempt to cut back on expenses. Further, consumer leisure activities are expected to be reduced as the overall financial situation becomes tighter, meaning a reduction in the number of vacationing couples and families.

The price and availability of energy is probably the largest economic con-straint being placed on Holiday Inns at the moment. The high cost of gasoline was expected to keep many Americans off the highways and also force cutbacks in other modes of travel. The cost of energy used in inns is a large expense, as guests are typically not as conservative with their use of lights, heat and air conditioning, and hot water as they would be in their own home.

COMPETITION

Although there are many firms competing with Holiday Inns in the lodging industry, Holiday Inns retains the number-one position in the market. Holiday Inns is the un-disputed market leader, verified by the fact that every night they are the choice for one of six guests that stay in a hotel. The only chain in the mid-price segment of lodging that could be considered a market "challenger" is Best Western Interna-tional. However, Best Western has only half as many rooms as Holiday Inns. Market followers include Ramada Inn (with only 603 units compared to Holiday Inns 1,700), Quality Inn, and Howard Johnson. The market "nichers" consist of two different types of hotels, budget and luxury hotels. The competitors in the budget line are Days Inns, Motel Six, La Quinta, and Vagabond. Competitors in the luxury area are Hilton, Sheraton, Hyatt, Marriott, and the traditional old established hotels in larger cities.

Since it has ventured into gambling, Holiday Inns is now competing directly with the luxury hotels in Nevada and Atlantic City. Holiday Inns is also competing with the luxury hotels to try to regain some of the business travelers that the luxury hotels lured from Holiday Inns in the seventies.

Although Holiday Inns operates inns worldwide, it has very little foreign com-petition here in the United States. Foreign companies are just now beginning to in-vest in hotels in the United States. For instance, Howard Johnson was recently purchased by a British group.

TARGET MARKETS

Holiday Inns has been considered a family institution in the past and the family has long been its traditional target market. The inns are primarily designed for the traveling family. Most of the rooms contain two double beds, a pool is provided at each inn, and many inns provide a kennel for the family pet. At some locations, chil-dren can stay free in a room with their parents.

Today Holiday Inns views the market as having two segments, those traveling for leisure and those traveling for business. Holiday Inns is devoting much more at-tention to the business traveler. The firm has already renovated 40,000 of its tradi-tional two-double-bed rooms to "King Leisure" rooms. These rooms are designed specifically for the business traveler with a king-size bed, large chairs, and a work space, AM-FM clock radios, and massaging shower heads. Twenty thousand King Leisure rooms are slated to be added annually.

The leisure segment of the market has also seen some change. With the increasing average age of the population and with less marriages resulting in chil-dren, more of the leisure travelers are couples rather than families.

In both the leisure segment and the business segments, Holiday Inns is try-ing to satisfy the wants of the middle-class travelers who desire quality lodging at moderate prices.

The most profitable market segments are business travelers and vacationing couples and singles. Business travelers are usually traveling at a company's expense and therefore are more liberal in their spending. A business traveler usually stays more than one night and requires less attention than a family. As a matter of convenience, business travelers will dine in the hotel restaurant or use room service. Also, many business travelers are repeat customers.

Vacationing couples and singles are more apt to rent one of the nicer rooms available in the hotels and often stay more days than a family if the hotel is in a metropolitan or resort area.

MARKET EVALUATION

Analysts predict that the demand for hotel rooms will be greater than the supply over the coming years. According to Holiday Inns, demand is growing at twice the rate of supply because of the increased number of business travelers and foreign travelers. As the rate for rooms increases, travelers are demanding more than just a place to sleep. Travelers want the assurance of quality and all of the extra items that make a hotel stay more pleasurable. Hotels are scrambling to develop innovative ideas for their customers to enjoy.

THE TRAVELING AUDIT

The main thing that Holiday Inns wants to know is *who* their customer is. They determine this by conducting a "travel audit," which determines whether the customer is staying in an inn because it is his or her destination or if it is just a stopover. They then determine whether it is business or leisure travel. The final part of the audit determines the use of chains in each category and the reasons why chains are or aren't used. Almost all of the information they seek is quantitative instead of qualitative. The firm spends about one million dollars annually on marketing research.

DISTRIBUTION STRATEGY

Franchises

Of the more than 1,700 Holiday Inns worldwide, 1,515 are franchised. This allows Holiday Inns to continue to grow and expand without having to invest capital in the construction of inns. Once a franchise is granted, Holiday Inns helps in every step of development. They help select the building site, assist with supervising construction, and help set up operating policies for the inns. A franchisee can also contract with Holiday Inns for the daily management of the hotel.

The franchise system has worked very well for Holiday Inns. Holiday Inns has much to offer to franchisees. Their most valuable asset is the vast amount of experience they have in hotel management. They also offer an excellent reputation, Holidex II, Holiday Inn University, and HI-NET (satellite receiving stations).

Holiday Inns owns or operates more than 200 inns itself. These inns are used extensively to test new management procedures and for new product development.

Relationship Between Franchisor and Franchisee

The relationship between Holiday Inns and their franchisees is an excellent one, evidenced by the fact that 70% of all new franchises are purchased by current franchise owners. Holiday Inns offers a lot to their franchisees, and in return they expect a lot from their franchisees. As in any franchise system, quality control can be a problem. Holiday Inns demands that their franchisees maintain the consistent quality specified by Holiday Inns. Holiday Inns inspectors check into inns periodically, unannounced, and check more than 1,000 items for quality and control. Inns must set up and follow room refurbishing and building renovation schedules in order to maintain attractive, comfortable rooms.

Franchise district directors work with each inn to develop proper operational procedures. Also, innkeepers are required to attend Holiday Inn University annually for training sessions.

Holiday Inn University
Holiday Inns owns and operates its own training facility in Olive Branch, Mississippi. Executives, innkeepers, and food and beverage managers are all trained in this modern facility. Innkeepers come to the University for an initial training course and then return each year for seminars. By training their own employees here, Holiday Inns has more control over the quality of its product, as each inn manager is taught to do things consistently with other inns.

Hotel Location
One weakness, although not a real problem, is the fact that many Holiday Inns are located on highways and not in heavily populated areas. The cutback in traveling has somewhat hurt these inns, but not to a point of putting them in a financial bind.

PRODUCT STRATEGY

Holiday Inns views itself as selling much more than just a room. According to James Schorr, executive vice-president for marketing, they are selling a hotel experience. "I'm selling the room, the way they treat you at the front desk, the way the bellman treats you, the way the waitress treats you" says Schorr. Holiday Inns is trying to sell the customers comfort and relaxation. This is why they have color televisions and free movies, food, stationery, free ice, a swimming pool, and other recreational facilities. They have meeting rooms available, easy check-in with Holidex II reservations, and transportation to the airport. Holiday Inns' product is to give you quality lodging at a moderate price.

PRICE STRATEGY

The price objective of Holiday Inns is to provide a quality room at a moderate price. They want the traveler to feel that he or she is getting excellent service at a low price. The room prices are aimed at attracting middle-class business travelers and vacationing couples, singles, and families. Children are allowed to stay free in their parents' room.

Room rates are determined by the payback period desired by the inn owner, cost of operations, locations, demand, extra services offered, and recreational facilities available. Prices are not uniform throughout the system.

COMMUNICATION STRATEGY

Campaign and Basic Theme

Holiday Inns' current campaign, "No. 1 in people pleasin'" is about two years old and, according to Holiday Inns, is the most successful campaign in the hotel industry. Holiday Inns recently extended the theme with a "We want to make you smile" campaign. According to marketing vice-president James Schorr, "Our selling message revolves around location and standards and is likely to remain the same over the years because that is what the consumer is looking for from a moderately priced hotel."

Advertising

Holiday Inns' advertising budget for 1980 was $18 million, $10.5 million of which was on television advertisement promoting its "people pleasin'" theme. The hotel chain industry as a whole only spent $21.4 million on television advertising, so Holiday Inns was the leader in this area. Holiday Inns was also the leader in magazine advertising, spending $3.6 million. Only $2.6 million of Holiday Inns' advertising budget was for newspapers, ranking it second in newspaper advertisement. Holiday Inns was also first in outdoor advertising, spending $1.2 million dollars.

Sales Promotion

One of Holiday Inns' newest sales promotions is the "Holiday Inn Preferred Corporate Traveler Card," which is being issued to companies and their employees. Over 100,000 cards have already been issued. It can be used to pay for food, entertainment, and lodging. The card is designed to help the cash flow of companies with travel expenses.

The company recently started publishing a sports directory that lists its 600 hotels that are considered sports hotels. The inns have golf, tennis, racquetball courts, saunas, exercise rooms, and handball courts either at the hotel or within a ten-minute drive.

The Holiday Inns directory is distributed free and contains a listing of all of the Holiday Inns worldwide. The directory gives the location of the inn, facilities and services available, and the room rates.

CUSTOMER SERVICES

Holidex II is Holiday Inns' new computerized reservation system. Each Holiday Inn has a Holidex II and therefore contact can be made with any Holiday Inn in the world for quick, dependable reservations. Holidex II usually fills one-third of the rooms in each inn each night. Also, administrative messages can be sent on the Holidex II to any of the inns.

The installation of their satellite television receiving stations at more inns offers a tremendous opportunity for the teleconferencing market. Instead of tremendous expense of having national meetings, companies can have regional points where employees can go for a meeting. The teleconferencing capabilities allow one-way video and two-way audio communication between the person conducting the meeting and points across the nation simultaneously.

SOURCES

Forsten, Michele. "Record Occupancy Profit Pace '80s Industry Growth." *Hotel and Motel Management,* January 1980, pp. 1, 18.

Getschow, George. "New Deal: Holiday Inns Discards Family Image for Stake in Gambling Industry." *Wall Street Journal,* 11 January 1980, pp. 1, 31.

"Holiday Inns: A Good Idea. And a Good Investment." Insert in *Hotel and Motel Management,* December 1980, pp. 25–28.

Holiday Inns Annual Report, 1980.

"Holiday Inn Postpones Decision to Build New Casino." *Wall Street Journal,* 20 January 1981, p. 7.

"Holiday Inns Preferred Corporate Traveler Cards Issued." *Hotel and Motel Management,* May 1981, p. 3.

"Holiday Inns Publishes New Sports Directory." *Hotel and Motel Management,* March 1981, p. 27.

"Holiday Inns: Refining Its Focus to Food, Lodging—and More Casinos." *Business Week,* 21 July 1980, p. 100.

"Holiday Inns Schultz Forecasts High Industry Demand." *Hotel and Motel Management,* December 1979, p. 27.

"Holiday Inns: Starting to Flirt with the Restaurant Business." *Business Week,* 18 September 1978, pp. 160–161.

"Holiday Inn University: More Than a Training Facility." *Training and Development Journal,* October 1978, pp. 36–37.

"Hotel Chains Spend 21 Million on TV Ads." *Hotel and Motel Management,* December 1981, p. 30.

"Innkeeper to Stay No. 1 with Datacom Network." *Infosystems,* July 1980, pp. 15–16.

Kinsely, Gary. "Greater Emphasis by Holiday Inns Breaks Mold." *Advertising Age,* 13 October 1980, p. 36.

Kreisman, Richard. "Holiday Inns Market Decor: Upgrade Moderate." *Advertising Age,* 13 October 1980, p. 36.

"Reservation from Outer Space." *Hotel and Motel Management,* January 1979, pp. 25–26.

QUESTIONS

1. What are the principal environmental opportunities and threats for Holiday Inns?

2. Do you think the ownership of gambling interests will hurt Holiday Inns' reputation?

3. What do customers desire most in a motel?

4. What strategic changes do you think Holiday Inns should make?

CASE 9

K Mart Corporation*

In mid-1980, Mr. Bernard Fauber, chief executive officer of K mart Corporation, was considering the position and performance of his company. Mr. Fauber was concerned that K mart was losing momentum after pursuing a "blitzkrieg" expansion strategy during the last several years. During this expansion phase, K mart has become the nation's second largest retailer (behind Sears, Roebuck and Company) and was expected to become the largest by 1985.

Current environmental conditions were expected to prevent K mart from maintaining its 20+ percent annual growth rate. Key environmental constraints involved the recession, increasingly fierce competition, saturation of major markets, and soaring operating costs. In fact, K mart was forecasting only a 12 percent annual growth rate for the next three years. This growth rate depended heavily on the continued construction of new store units.

K mart's management faced a number of strategic alternatives. Key alternatives were (1) continue to strive to become the number-one retailer, (2) accept slower growth and concentrate on internal productivity gains, and (3) diversify and acquire other businesses that offer higher growth potential.

COMPANY HISTORY

K mart traces its origin to 1899 when its founder, Sebastian S. Kresge, opened a variety store in Detroit, Michigan. By the early 1960s, the S. S. Kresge Company had more than 800 Kresge stores (specializing in a limited line of low-priced merchandise) and Jupiter stores (a limited-line discounter).

The first K mart unit was opened in March 1962 and soon became a chain of discount department stores. The present company name of K mart Corporation was adopted in May 1977. The name change seemed appropriate since the K mart units were contributing about 96 percent of the corporate sales and earnings. The corporate headquarters are now in Troy, Michigan. As shown in Table 1 and Fig. 1, the company operated K mart, Kresge, and Jupiter stores in the United States, Canada, and Puerto Rico.

K mart Corporation also possesses two wholly owned subsidiaries, both of which operate departments (analogous to leased departments) in all domestic K mart stores: the K mart Apparel Corporation operates the women's ready-to-wear departments and K mart Enterprises, Inc., operates the firm's sporting goods and automotive departments. The corporation also has a 49 percent equity in substantially all of the K mart footwear departments in the United States, which are operated by the Meldisco Division of Melville Corporation. K mart is also engaged in the life, accident, and health insurance field through its ownership of Planned Marketing Associates, Inc.

---

*The information for this case was obtained from those sources listed at the end of the case. Our thanks go to Mitzi Green for her assistance in preparing this case.

Table 1
K mart's 1979 expansion program

	K MART	KRESGE	JUPITER	TOTAL
Stores in operation January 31, 1979	1,496	313	82	1,891
Stores opened	193			193
Stores closed	(1)	(13)	(4)	(18)
Stores converted		(4)	7	3
Stores in operation January 30, 1980	1,688	296	85	2,069

     K mart Limited was established in 1967 to operate K mart stores in Australia; K mart Corporation retained 51 percent interest while G. J. Coles and Coy Limited (Coles) obtained 49 percent interest. By December 1978, there were 39 K mart stores in Australia. At this time, however, K mart Corporation transferred their 51 percent interest in K mart Limited to Coles in exchange for stock representing 20 percent of Coles' outstanding shares. K mart Canada Limited, wholly owned subsidiary, operated over 170 K mart, Kresge, and Jupiter stores throughout Canada.

     Since 1961 (one year before K mart units were established), the estimated compound annual growth rate for sales and net income has been 21 percent and 24 percent, respectively. This booming growth rate has allowed K mart to surpass

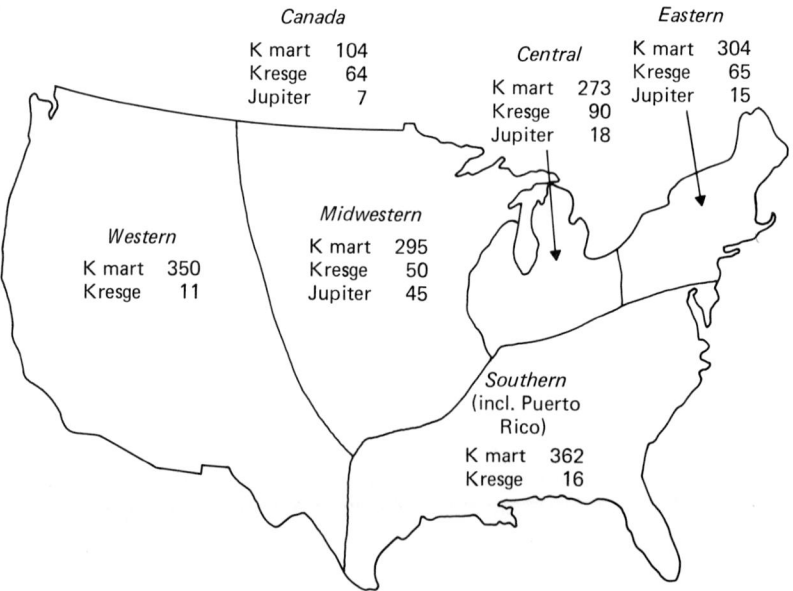

Figure 1
K mart Corporation store units on January 30, 1980

J. C. Penney Company to become the second largest mass-merchandising chain in the United States (behind Sears). Sears' sales were $17.5 billion in 1979 while K mart's were $12.7 billion. K mart's 1979 earnings were $358 million.

COMPETITION

K mart's primary competitors in the department store group are Sears and Penney's. Much of K mart's growth occurred during the 1970s after Sears attempted to upgrade its merchandise offerings; many Sears customers became confused and turned to other retailers, including K mart. As a result, from 1974 to 1978, K mart's revenues grew 21 percent, while Penney's and Sears' growth rates were 12.6 and 11 percent, respectively. K mart's share of the total general merchandise, apparel, and furniture market was about 6.1 percent.

In 1977, Sears attempted to win back its former market share by slashing prices, which triggered a price war among the nation's 28 leading retailers. By 1980, these 28 retailers accounted for 41 percent of general merchandise, apparel, and furniture sales. Further, many competitors were wiped out and additional market share gains became more difficult and costly to achieve.

As of 1980, most of the major markets (SMSAs) were saturated by the retail chains. For example, at least 5 of the 28 leading retailers had outlets in 276 of the country's major metropolitan areas.

Since the metropolitan areas had been saturated, more and more of the leading retailers (including K mart) began to explore the smaller markets, such as suburban areas and small towns. However, the leading retailers found a new group of competitors entrenched in these smaller market areas. These "small market specialists" had been dominating the smaller markets while the larger retail chains had been slugging it out in the major market areas. Most of these competitors were discounters such as Wal-Mart, Caldor, and Fed-Mart. The real gains from 1974 to 1978 for the following firms (with inflation and store expansion factored out) indicate their strength in smaller markets: Wal-Mart, 47.5%; Caldor, 30%; Fed-Mart, 37%; Penney, 6.9%; and Sears, 0.5% decline.

TARGET CUSTOMERS

The primary customers attracted to K mart tended to be between 25 and 44 years old with household incomes ranging from $15,000 to $35,000. K mart officials felt that the group of shoppers were becoming polarized between low-margin and high-margin stores; they also expected that this trend would accelerate as the economy worsened and middle-class households "traded down" for merchandise. K mart expected to gain even more customers as the recession continued and consumers' discretionary income dwindled; those consumers who normally shopped conventional department stores were expected to turn to lower-priced stores such as K mart.

RETAILING STRATEGY

Overview

K mart's traditional retailing strategy has focused on offering low prices to achieve high turnover rates; value and service have also been an important part of their strategy.

In the late 1970s, K mart decided to change their promotional emphasis from price to quality and value for their private-label items. However, this decision called for upgrading the quality of merchandise, which caused an image problem. Many of K mart's shoppers were blue-collar, lower-income consumers who were hard hit by inflation. These and other shoppers were becoming more concerned with price while K mart was beginning to emphasize quality. As a result, K mart encountered resistance to their attempts to increase margins. K mart also attempted to improve their appeal by adding 14-karat gold jewelry, higher-quality house paints, optical departments, and Book Korners (offering best-sellers at 25% off list price).

Pricing

K mart has attempted to decrease its emphasis on low-priced merchandise so that certain higher-priced merchandise would be more readily accepted by shoppers. However, K mart still wanted to offer the lowest price possible on a wide variety of merchandise to attract customers to the store; hopefully, the customers would then be attracted to other departments where more discretionary, higher-margin goods were offered.

K mart has traditionally pursued a low-margin, high-turnover philosophy. This approach has been successful and has previously resulted in record sales volume. However, the new pricing strategy has led to declining volume.

Merchandise

K mart's traditional merchandise strategy has been to offer a variety of low-priced merchandise that appealed to a wide consumer base. Although prices were stressed almost to the exclusion of fashion, quality and value were implied with the motto "Satisfaction Always." K mart's merchandise, which included both national and private brands, offered bargain buys. K mart stores have offered a line of merchandise comparable to that found in department stores, but at a lower price. Key merchandise lines include apparel, furniture, appliances, paints, sporting goods, cosmetics and toiletries, and building supplies.

Executives felt that softgoods, particularly apparel, offered the best potential for improving profit margins. However, K mart had not previously demonstrated good merchandising skills for higher-priced, discretionary items. For example, the apparel department had only recently been converted from bargain tables to racks. Although executives felt this change was an improvement, apparel sales declined from 12.7 percent of total revenues in 1978 to 11.8 percent in 1979.

For the fall of 1980, the executive vice-president of merchandising planned to invest half of the men's sweater merchandising dollars in more than 70,000 acrylic loop sweaters. These sweaters cost $12 and would sell for $18 to $20 (K mart's usual price was around $11) and would allow a margin three to five points higher than usual on a lower-priced sweater.

Inventory turnover was 3.6 in 1979 as compared to 8.0 during the 1960s. On the average, other retailers managed a 4.7 turnover rate and discounters around 4.0.

Store Size

K mart stores are generally single-story, free-standing units ranging in size from 96,000 square feet to 40,000 square feet. Four basic prototypes have been designed to serve various demographic and geographic segments:

1. 84,000-square-foot unit (standard unit): for heavily populated urban and sub-
    urban areas

2. 68,000-square-foot unit: for medium-sized cities and less densely populated
    areas

3. 55,000-square-foot unit: for smaller markets often found on outer fringes of
    metropolitan areas

4. 40,000-square-foot unit: for smaller rural markets

Location

K mart was well equipped to enter both the urban and small-town markets. The
primary thrust has been in the major metropolitan areas, especially in the higher-
growth-potential suburban sections. K marts have also been built in older areas of
some cities to take advantage of high population density. Figure 2 indicates the
growth in the number of K mart stores.

K mart's basic strategy has been to cluster stores in new and existing markets. The "old" location strategy placed the optimum distance between K mart
stores at 10 miles. A newer location strategy reduced the distance between stores
to 3 miles. Under the new strategy, K mart claimed that only 60 percent of its
urban market potential has been reached as of 1980.

The smaller prototype units have been utilized to enter the smaller industrial
and agriculture-based cities throughout the United States. Despite the stiff competition, K mart enjoys a strong competitive position in most of these areas. Plans
call for nearly half of the company's new stores to be the smaller prototype units.

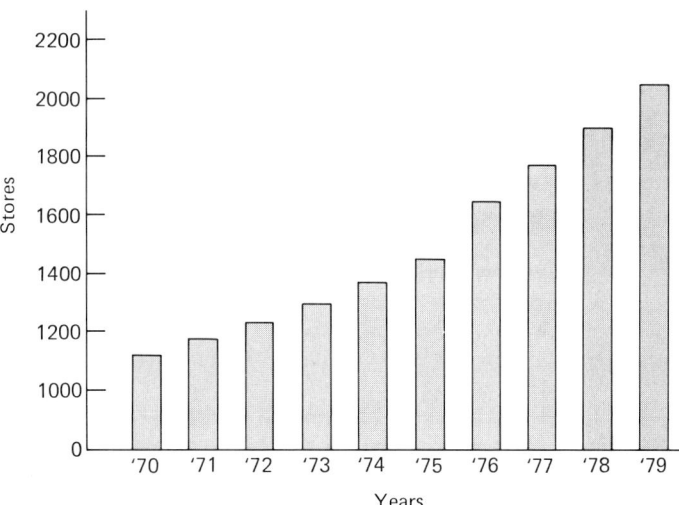

Figure 2
Number of stores, K mart Corporation, 1970–1979

Since the early 1960s, K marts have spread to all regions of the United States. K mart's ability to quickly expand the number of stores while maintaining managerial control is one of the company's most significant skills.

Distribution

In the 1970s, K mart operated six major distribution centers. By 1981, five additional distribution centers were to be on-line to meet increased demand generated by the new stores. This expansion will provide a total of over 14 million square feet of space in the distribution centers, which are to incorporate the latest technology in materials handling and computerized operations.

Information System

A major addition in the late 1970s was K mart Information Network (KIN), a computer-based information processing system. K mart needed more efficient and accurate processing of the vast amount of information generated and analyzed at each store and reported to headquarters. Basic procedures were not changed by KIN; rather, its aim was to improve the speed and quality of existing procedures. KIN has also been adapted to link the distribution centers to suppliers and store units to facilitate order filling. All stores will probably not be plugged into the system until 1984. As of 1980, approximately 300 stores were utilizing KIN.

Training for Customer Relations

To promote store relations, the Management Group Development Program was initiated in 1976. To launch this program, case studies were developed from actual problems sent in by store managers. These cases aimed at getting store management teams in the habit of communicating and solving problems positively and provided management personnel with simulations to better cope with "people" problems.

All stores were required to have a minimum of one class a week for all full-time and part-time employees. A training film prepared by the corporate training staff is presented periodically. Topics for other classes were chosen by the store management team. The objective of these classes was to emphasize the importance of upward and downward communication. Employees were encouraged to give input in the sessions. Additional classes were held for specific groups such as sales personnel or checkout operators.

DIVERSIFICATION STRATEGY

K mart had made two attempts to diversify its operations. First, the firm tried to enter the grocery market by opening a box store in Detroit. (Box stores sell groceries from cartons at cut-rate prices and had become popular in the Sunbelt and elsewhere.) However, with sales 30 percent below plan, the store closed after less than one month. One K mart officer called it simply an experiment.

Second, K mart acquired Furr's Cafeterias, Inc., a 76-unit chain located in the Southwest, in early 1980. Executives described this purchase as a logical outgrowth of the already existing K mart store cafeterias. Unfortunately, the cafeterias were vulnerable to consumer cutbacks in spending. As a result, Furr's added less than one percent to K mart's sales.

THE MID-1980 SITUATION

K mart executives were recognizing clear signs of weakening by mid-1980. Inventory turnover had fallen to 3.6 (compared to a 4.7 average for all other retailers) and earnings growth was only 4.2 percent (compared to a 12.8 percent average for all other retailers). Further, profit margin (on sales) had fallen from 2.9 percent in 1978 to 2.8 percent in 1979; the target profit margin was 3.0 percent. This drop in profits was largely due to excessive markdowns taken during the fourth quarter of 1979. The fourth-quarter drop in profits was the first in K mart's history.

Although K mart executives felt strongly that diversification offered one of the best alternatives for achieving growth, they still insisted that the firm's future depended on improving merchandising skills in their existing operations. These gains from internal productivity were also seen as offering potential for growth, but at a slower rate than from diversification. As a result, executives felt it necessary to continue to expand the firm by adding additional stores. Plans called for 2,400 K mart stores by 1984 and 3,000 by 1989, or expansion at the rate of 180 new stores per year.

Another important consideration in deciding which of the two growth strategies to pursue was that K mart had accumulated a large amount of cash. With $300 million in cash and short-term investments on its 1979 balance sheet, K mart had a definite financial advantage for pursuing high-growth opportunities.

SOURCES

K Mart Annual Reports, 1977, 1978, 1979, 1980 (Troy, Michigan).

"K Mart Expands Outlets, Bucks — So Far — Retail Slowdown." *Barrons,* 25 June 1979, pp. 29ff.

"K Mart's Fast Track." *Forbes.* 30 April 1979, p. 97.

"K Mart Grapples with Cash Glut." *Chain Store Age Executive,* August 1979, pp. 93–94.

"K Mart to Invade Smaller Markets." *Chain Store Age Executive,* September 1979, p. 46.

Moody's Industrial, 27 May 1980.

"Where K Mart Goes Next Now That It's No. 2." *Business Week,* 2 June 1980, pp. 109–114.

"Will K Mart Retreat?" *Financial World,* 1 March 1979, pp. 32–33.

QUESTIONS

1. Evaluate K mart's past strategy.

2. Do you think the new strategies being planned will be effective?

3. What retailing mix strategies would you recommend for K mart? Why?

Index